Unwinnable

Britain's War in Afghanistan, 2001–2014

Unwinnable

Britain's War in Afghanistan,

2001–2014

THEO FARRELL

THE BODLEY HEAD
LONDON

1 3 5 7 9 10 8 6 4 2

The Bodley Head, an imprint of Vintage,
20 Vauxhall Bridge Road,
London SW1V 2SA

The Bodley Head is part of the Penguin Random House group of companies whose
addresses can be found at global.penguinrandomhouse.com.

Penguin
Random House
UK

First published by The Bodley Head in 2017

www.penguin.co.uk/vintage

A CIP catalogue record for this book is available from the British Library

ISBN 9781847923462

Printed and bound by Clays Ltd, St Ives plc

Penguin Random House is committed to a sustainable future
for our business, our readers and our planet. This book is
made from Forest Stewardship Council® certified paper.

MIX
Paper from
responsible sources
FSC® C018179

For my old friend, John Murnane

Contents

Maps   ix

List of Acronyms   xvi

Introduction   1

 1 *Atta in America*   11

 2 *Shoulder to Shoulder*   38

 3 *Original Sin*   65

 4 *Road to Helmand*   117

 5 *Bad Beginning*   143

 6 *Mission Impossible*   192

 7 *The Campaign Flounders*   229

 8 *American Surge*   274

 9 *Showdown*   292

10 *Undefeated*   325

11 *Time Runs Out*   370

    Acknowledgements   427

    Notes   429

    Select Bibliography   511

    Index   521

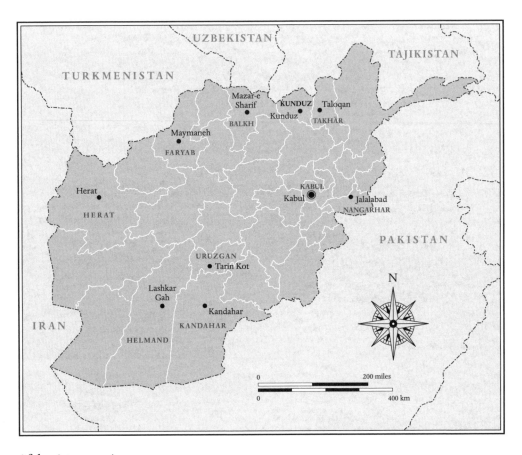

Afghanistan provinces

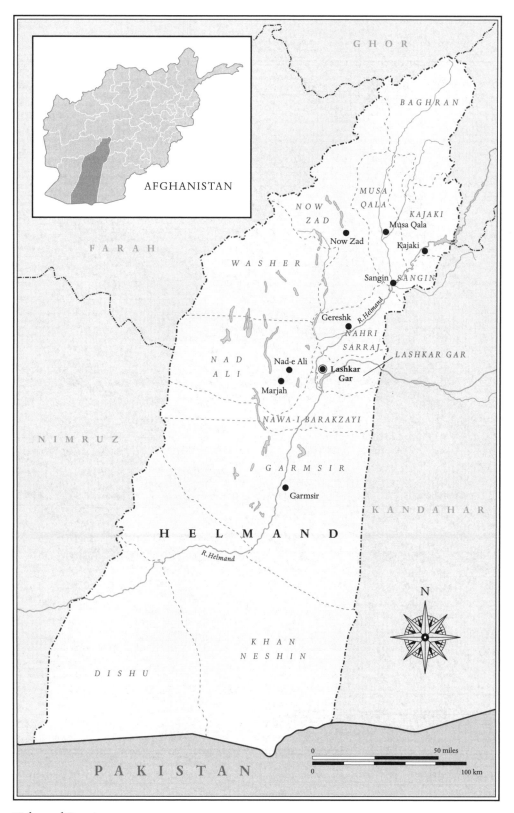

Helmand Province

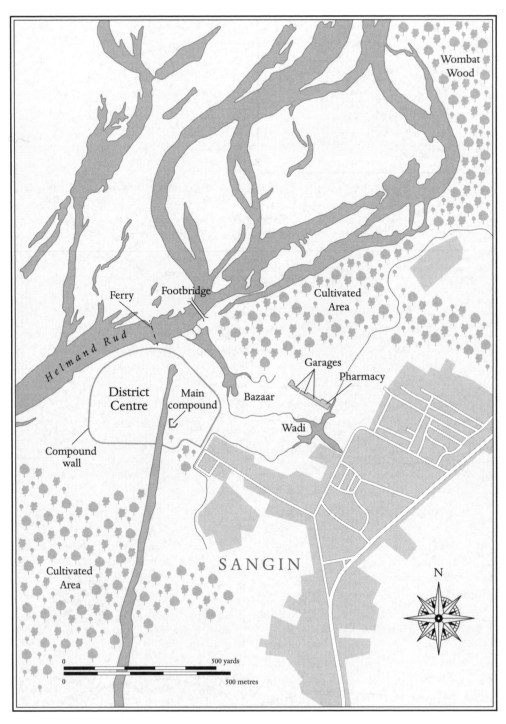

Sangin District

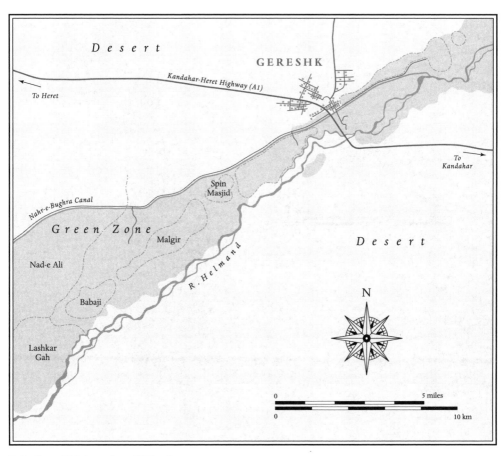

Babaji and Nahr-e Seraj District

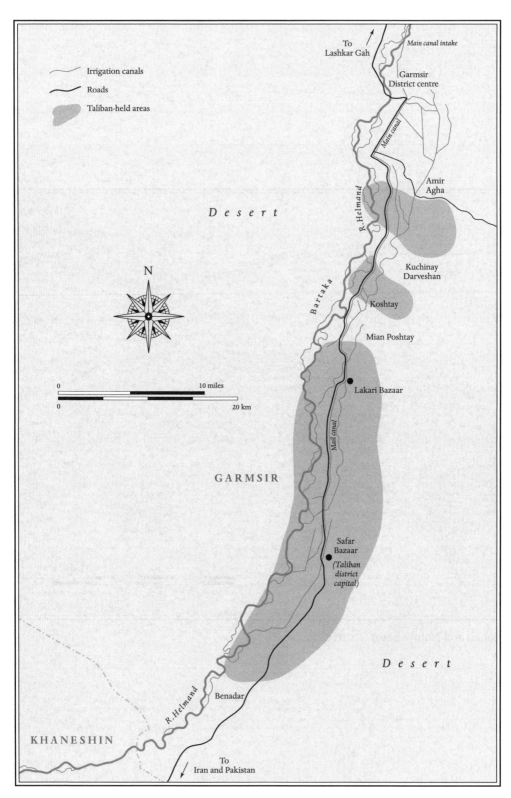

Garmsir District

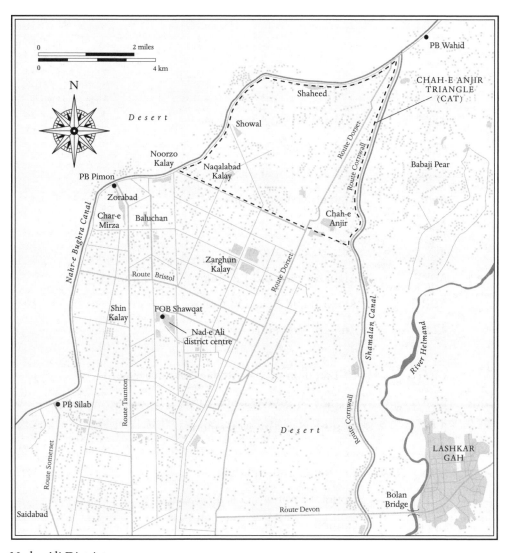

Nad-e Ali District

List of Acronyms

ADZ	Afghan Development Zone
ALP	Afghan Local Police
ANA	Afghan National Army
ANP	Afghan National Police
ANSF	Afghan National Security Forces
AO	Area of operations
APRP	Afghan Peace and Reintegration Programme
ARRC	Allied Rapid Reaction Corps
ATF	Afghan Task Force
1 BANG	1st Battalion of the Afghan National Guard
BRF	Brigade Reconnaissance Force
BSA	Bilateral Security Agreement
CENTCOM	Central Command (US)
C-IED	Counter-improvised explosive device
CJTF	Combined Joint Task Force
CJSOTF	Combined Joint Special Operations Task Force (US)
COBRA	Cabinet Office Briefing Room A (group of senior cabinet ministers and officials convened in times of national crisis)

COIN	Counter-insurgency
CPA	Coalition Provisional Authority (Iraq)
CSG	Counterterrorism Security Group (US)
CSTC-A	Combined Security Transition Command-Afghanistan (US)
DDR	Disarmament, Demobilisation and Reintegration programme
DFID	Department for International Development (UK)
DOD	Department of Defense (US)
EUPOL	European Union Police
FAA	Federal Aviation Administration (US)
FATA	Federally Administered Tribal Areas
FCO	Foreign and Commonwealth Office
FOB	Forward operating base
GCHQ	Government Communications Headquarters (UK)
GIRoA	Government of the Islamic Republic of Afghanistan
GMLRS	Guided Multiple Launch Rocket System
HESCO	Blast- and bulletproof defensive barriers
IED	Improvised explosive device
IJC	ISAF Joint Command
ISAF	International Security Assistance Force
ISI	Inter-Services Intelligence agency (Pakistan)

ISTAR	Intelligence, surveillance, targeting and reconnaissance
IX	Information exploitation
JPEL	Joint Prioritized Effects List
K2	Karshi Khanabad airfield (Uzbekistan)
LZ	Landing zone
MAGTAF	Marine Air-Ground Task Force (US)
MEU	Marine Expeditionary Unit (US)
MoD	Ministry of Defence
MERT	Medical emergency response team
MOG	Mobile Operations Group
MRAP	Mine Resistant Ambush Protected (armoured vehicles)
NEADS	Northeast Air Defense Sector (US)
N-KET	Non-Kinetic Effect Team
NMCC	National Military Command Center (US)
NORAD	North American Aerospace Defense Command (US)
NSID	National Security, International Relations and Development Subcommittee of the UK Cabinet
OMLT	Operating, Mentoring and Liaison Team
PAG	Policy Action Group (high-level policy coordinating committee of Afghan and international officials)

PB	Patrol base
PCRU	Post-Conflict Reconstruction Unit (UK)
PEOC	Presidential Emergency Operations Center (US)
PJHQ	Permanent Joint Headquarters (UK)
POR	Post-operation report
PRT	Provincial Reconstruction Team
RAW	Indian Intelligence Service
RC	Regional Command (ISAF)
ROE	Rules of engagement
RPG	Rocket-propelled grenade
RUSI	Royal United Services Institute
SAD	Special Activities Division (CIA)
SAS	Special Air Service (UK)
SBS	Special Boat Service (UK)
SIGACTS	Significant Activities (involving insurgents)
SIS	Secret Intelligence Service (UK)
SOF	Special operations forces (US)
TCAF	Tactical Conflict Assessment Framework
TFH	Task Force Helmand
TTP	Tehrik-i-Taliban Pakistan
UNAMA	United Nations Assistance Missions to Afghanistan
USAID	United States Agency for International Development
WMIK	Weapon Mounted Installation Kit

GOODBYE

Allow me to go and to say goodbye to you,
Dear mother! I won't stay anymore, goodbye.
Englishmen have occupied my home,
By no means, I cannot stay anymore.
They play with our dignity and chastity,
I shy with my conscience.
It would be better at this moment to go to fight.

Alam Gul Naseri
25 July 2007

From Alex Strick van Linschoten and Felix Kuehn (eds),
Poetry of the Taliban (London: Hurst, 2012), p. 138

Introduction

In retrospect, Britain probably should have quit while it was ahead. Following 9/11, Britain supported the US invasion of Afghanistan in order to stop al-Qaeda from launching further catastrophic attacks against Western cities. By mid 2002, al-Qaeda terrorists, and the leaders of the Taliban regime that had played host to them, had been killed or captured, or had fled to Pakistan. British Royal Marines roaming eastern Afghanistan found nobody left to fight. At that point, with the job done, the British could have left Afghanistan. Instead, they stayed on and later sent yet more forces as part of an enlarged international effort to stabilise the country. Thirteen years later, British and Western troops departed having failed to stop a Taliban resurgence in the country.

Britain has paid dearly for attempting to secure Afghanistan. Four hundred and fifty-six British troops were killed during the campaign, and over six hundred sustained life-changing injuries; in total, more than 2,000 British troops were wounded in action. Britain spent £37 billion on the campaign and aid to Afghanistan.[1] These are the official figures, and it would be reasonable to assume that there may be many billions more in hidden expenditure, including long-term medical care for veterans and the cost of recovering and retrofitting the British Army from Afghanistan.[2] These costs pale in comparison to those of Britain's close ally in Afghanistan. The United States had over five times more fatalities than Britain, with 2,352 US service personnel dying in Afghanistan between 2001 and 2014.[3] At $686 billion, the financial cost was a staggering eighteen times higher for the United States than for Britain.[4] This is a conservative estimate, only including direct military expenditure. When medical and other costs for returning veterans are added, the total bill runs into the trillions.[5] Of course, the highest price has been paid by Afghans. The United Nations estimates that 25,000 civilians have perished in the war. These official figures capture only verified and recorded civilian deaths since 2007; nobody knows the actual death toll.[6]

Hindsight suggests that Britain and the United States should not have fought the Afghanistan War. However, hindsight is the super-power of historians, enabling them to rerun the past and through counterfactual reasoning pass judgement on what has gone before. It is utterly beyond the reach of political leaders, policymakers, military commanders, and others living in the moment. Knowing this, the historian must exercise hindsight responsibly, and seek to understand and record the perspectives of those caught up in events and those trying to chart a way forward. This is the approach taken in this book.

Drawing on hundreds of interviews with British officers, Western officials and Afghan Taliban, this book offers a contemporary historical account of Britain's war in Afghanistan from 2001 to 2014. Of course, this was primarily America's war, with Britain as a major partner. British forces also operated within the framework of the International Security Assistance Force (ISAF), led from 2003 by NATO. Thus coalition politics and pressures, played out between London and Washington, and within NATO headquarters in Brussels and ISAF headquarters in Kabul, shaped the course and conduct of Britain's war.

Our story starts with the terrible events of 11 September 2001. It is essential that we understand the full horror of what unfolded in New York, and the chaotic conditions in which momentous decisions were taken in Washington DC and London that would commit US and British forces to war in Afghanistan. The necessity for war needs to be seen in the context of the scale of the attack suffered by the United States (which was also the worst terrorist attack against British citizens), and the legitimate fear of future such attacks against the United States and Britain. Add the Taliban refusal to surrender those responsible for 9/11, and the understandable political and public outrage in America at what had happened, and war was inevitable. The American story looms large in the early chapters of this book for the simple reason that Britain played a relatively minor role initially to what was a mostly US war against al-Qaeda and the Taliban. In contrast, the British government and armed forces played a central role thereafter in developing the ISAF mission to secure and stabilise Afghanistan.

Britain ended up being drawn into a lengthy military campaign against a fierce insurgency in Helmand province, a remote backwater in southern Afghanistan. It is not uncommon for militaries to go to war without the right plans, tactics and equipment. For reasons such as these, mistakes and setbacks in the early phases of war are not at all unusual. This was certainly the case for the British in southern Afghanistan. They underestimated the extent of the Taliban return to Afghanistan, and had no understanding of local conflict dynamics in Helmand. Early British tactics, focused on using firepower to militarily defeat the Taliban, made matters worse by driving locals into the arms of insurgents. Moreover, British forces lacked the personnel and materiel (especially helicopters and armoured vehicles) for the job. Military success depends on the ability and willingness of states to commit more resources to turn around a struggling campaign, and on the ability and willingness of militaries to learn and adapt in the field. This book examines how British plans and tactics evolved in Helmand, and how the political machinery in Whitehall responded to the pull from field commands for more troops and better equipment.

I show how, over time, Britain and its NATO allies got better at waging this counter-insurgency war. By 2010, British forces had achieved significant results in Helmand, creating the security for governance and development to flourish in many parts of the province. This reflected a more general trend across Afghanistan, as the United States poured more resources into the country and took a grip of a meandering war effort. However, the British and Americans were unable to convert these tactical gains into strategic success due to the sheer scale of Afghan government corruption, which gave the Taliban righteous cause and support from those oppressed by venal government officials. In addition, Pakistani support to the Taliban gave the insurgency secure rear bases in Pakistan from which to regroup and direct their campaign. Finally, time ran out, as Western publics tired of the war and NATO politicians responded in late 2010 by setting a four-year deadline to end ISAF. For these reasons, Britain's war was unwinnable.

Much has been written about Britain's latest war in Afghanistan. There is a deluge of books by former military officers and embedded journalists about the tours of particular brigades and battalions in Helmand province. These first-hand accounts furnish plenty of tales of derring-do, and give us much valuable insight into the tactical conduct of the war by British forces.[7] Of course, there is the ever-present risk of bias in these accounts, especially in books by former British officers. Such accounts are also limited by perspective, in that they provide a 'worm's-eye view' of Britain's campaign. Few lift their gaze to consider the wider strategic and political context of the war.[8]

In contrast, this book explores the origins, conduct and outcome of the war from multiple perspectives, including policymakers in Whitehall and Washington, and NATO generals and Afghan leaders in Kabul, as well as British forces in Helmand and their Taliban opponents. Critics of the war dismiss the British campaign as both strategically misguided and tactically incompetent.[9] The historian William Dalrymple is among these, finding 'substantive' parallels between the First Anglo-Afghan War and Britain's latest war in Afghanistan. 'In both cases, the invaders thought they could walk in, perform regime change, and be out in a couple of years. In both cases they were unable to prevent themselves getting sucked into a much wider conflict.'[10] In broad outlines, he is right. However, when viewed up close and from multiple perspectives a far more complex story emerges.

Britain entered this war with clear strategic purpose – a purpose defined by the events of 9/11. Strategic direction in this war was lost following the defeat of the Taliban and al-Qaeda, when American attention turned towards Iraq, and the other Western states signed up for a hugely ambitious project to rebuild Afghanistan anew. In this way, NATO allowed itself to be pulled into a drawn-out counter-insurgency war and alliance politics dragged the mission aimlessly along. It took US re-engagement with Afghanistan in 2009, following the election of President Barack Obama, for a strategy to be formu-lated for the war.

However, Afghan and regional politics remained the major stum-bling blocks to the success of this strategy. The conventional wisdom on counter-insurgency is that it is mostly about politics.[11] The key to success is not to defeat the insurgents militarily but to persuade ordinary people to side with the government.[12] The problem for British and American policymakers and ISAF generals was that while they could change the way that Western forces operated, to focus more on winning local 'hearts and minds', there was little they could do about Afghan government corruption and Pakistani support to the insurgency. In addition, ISAF headquarters in Afghanistan had to contend with politics back home, most importantly in Washington but also in London.

Drawing on extensive interviews in Kabul, London and Washington, and on ISAF war plans and internal campaign assessments, this book charts the strategic fits and starts of the war. I reveal how efforts by ISAF commanders to create a military strategy for success were undermined by political realities in Kabul and back home. The US government in Washington and US commanders in Kabul dominated the development of ISAF strategy from 2009 to 2014. However, this book also shows the extent of British influence over the ISAF mission. Indeed, the British military led the formation and early command of ISAF in 2001–2. After the Americans, British officers held the most senior positions in ISAF headquarters, and hence British fingerprints are all over successive strategic initiatives.

The main effort for the British military campaign from 2006 to 2014 was in Helmand province. The British arrived just in time to blunt a major offensive by the Taliban across southern Afghanistan. From 2006 on, a succession of brigade-sized task forces rotated through Helmand on six-month tours. Each came with a different concept of operations, and accordingly each focused on different objectives and fought in different ways. Broadly speaking, in early tours British task forces attempted to defeat the Taliban insurgency in battle, while in later tours the British concentrated more on winning over the local population and supporting the aid and development efforts of British civilian advisers in the province. Drawing on military plans and post-operation reports, over two hundred interviews with British military officers and civilian advisers, and field research in Helmand, this book provides a detailed history of the tactical conduct of the campaign. Academics studying the Helmand campaign have been highly critical of British military over-reliance on firepower, the failure to adapt, and lack of continuity across the task force tours.[13] I consider early tactical errors by British commanders and the reliance on firepower in the context of the immense pressures they faced, and I explore how, in fact, British forces did adapt over time. I also show how the British campaign in

Helmand gained more continuity of effort from late 2009 on, as a consequence of clearer direction from a strengthened ISAF Command. However, success has proven ephemeral.

While this is a history of Britain's war in Afghanistan, I have sought to bring Afghan voices into the narrative, and in particular those of the Taliban. This is important to explaining the roots and resilience of the insurgency. Here I am conscious of the criticism, recently articulated by Thomas Barfield in his compelling cultural and political history of Afghanistan, that in most Western accounts, 'Afghanistan itself remains just the vague backdrop in a long-running international drama where others hold the speaking parts. It often appears that the Afghans only provide an unchanging, turbaned chorus in this play.'[14] As it happens, there are a number of note-worthy exceptions where Afghan voices are given prominence, including important books on the Taliban by Antonio Giustozzi, Ahmed Rashid, Rob Johnson, Alex Strick van Linschoten and Felix Kuehn, and Peter Bergen, and two recent Afghan oral histories of the conflict in Helmand by Mike Martin and Carter Malkasian.[15] This book draws on all these studies in seeking to present Afghan perspectives of the conflict. In addition, I commissioned Afghan field researchers, working under the supervision of Antonio Giustozzi, to interview sixty-seven Taliban field commanders and fifty-nine locals in Helmand about the insurgency. Using this rich trove of interview transcripts, Antonio and I were able to reconstruct the Taliban campaign in Helmand.[16] The resulting study, published in 2013, was soon assigned as compulsory reading for all British officers deploying to Afghanistan.[17] I have woven the research findings from this earlier study, along with much additional textual material from the transcripts, into the fabric of this book. For insight into strategic thinking in the Taliban, I draw on lengthy face-to-face talks with Taliban figures in Dubai in 2012 and 2013, original inter-views with senior Taliban officials undertaken in 2014, and a final set of talks with Taliban leaders outside of Afghanistan in late 2016, all of which I undertook with Michael Semple, a leading expert on reconciliation in Afghanistan.[18] The Dubai talks provided remarkable insight into the tantalising possibilities for a negotiated end to the conflict, provided the conditions were right. Unfortunately, they were not.

THE ANGLO-AFGHAN WARS

British forces had been in Afghanistan before. Indeed, this was Britain's fourth foray into a country with a fearful reputation as 'the graveyard of empires'.[19] In his recent and deservedly acclaimed history of the First Anglo-Afghan War (1839–42), Dalrymple places the blame squarely on British shoulders for the disaster that unfolded. Ill-informed scheming within the British East India Company led to a quite unnecessary war on behalf of the disposed Afghan king, Shah Shuja ul-Mulk; war was uncalled for because the incumbent ruler in Kabul, Dos Mohammad Khan, was already seeking closer ties to the British authorities in India. Having returned Shah Shuja to his throne, the British left behind an embassy and garrison to protect company interests. Crass insensitivity to local customs fuelled growing Afghan hostility to the British occupiers. British commanders in Kabul demonstrated staggering incompetence, in not taking immediate action to stop the massacre of the British embassy by an enraged mob, failing to secure the British encampment and supplies, and then abandoning Kabul in the harshness of the Afghan winter. The British retreat to Peshawar was equally incompetent, leading to wholesale slaughter of the 4,500-strong Kabul garrison (and their 12,000 camp followers) at the hands of gleeful Afghan tribesmen. For the government in Whitehall, this stain on British honour could not go unanswered. An 'Army of Retribution' was sent in from British India to exact revenge and this it did with terrifying efficiency. By the time it was over this war had cost £50 billion in today's money, emptying the coffers of the East India Company. Furthermore, the company ended up back at square one, when it returned Dos Mohammad to power in 1844.[20]

The Second Anglo-Afghan War of 1879–82 went little better for the British. It too was caused by incompetent British diplomacy, which this time gave Russia an opening to interfere in Afghanistan and triggered a British invasion to prevent further Russian encroachment. As before, the British installed a new ruler and left behind a diplomatic mission that was duly massacred by the locals. Britain suffered further humiliation when its army was thoroughly defeated by a larger Pashtun force at the Battle of Maiwand in 1880. Overall, however, the British military acquitted itself better this time, especially in the relief of its besieged garrison in Kandahar by a British force from Kabul. All the same, this was yet another unnecessary and very costly war.[21]

At least the Third Anglo-Afghan War was not started by the British. Rather it began with Afghan forces seizing a number of border posts and towns along the North-West Frontier in May 1919. The background to the war was growing Afghan agitation for full independence from Britain, and a power struggle in Kabul following the assassination of the incumbent amir. In order to win popular support for his rule, and to take advantage of widespread unrest in British India following the Amritsar Massacre of 1919, the new amir decided to invade. The British were taken by surprise, but this was always going to be a one-sided fight. As one historian notes:

> British forces in India were depleted, war weary, and unprepared yet they remained inherently superior to those of Afghanistan in training and equipment, and given that there was not the slightest possibility that His Majesty's government would stand by while the borders of British India were altered by force, the course of the subsequent fighting was a foregone conclusion.[22]

It took just a month for British forces to mobilise and drive the Afghans back across the border. In a military innovation, the British were able to use air power to disrupt tribal forces from massing, and to bomb Kabul – albeit using a single plane, causing limited damage but demoralising Kabulis nonetheless. By August, both sides had reached an equitable agreement: the British recognised Afghanistan as having full sovereign rights, and the Afghans recognised the (till then disputed) Durand Line as demarking the border between Afghanistan and British India.[23]

Already by the end of the Second Anglo-Afghan War the British were pretty fed up with Afghanistan and its unruly tribes. The Third Anglo-Afghan War did nothing to change this view. Thus, the British were happy to leave Afghans to their own devices. It would be the better part of a century before British troops would return to Afghanistan. This book tells the story of what then happened.

NOTE ON SOURCES AND ACRONYMS

Many of the interviews for this book were conducted anonymously. This includes a very large number of interviews with military officers and civilian stabilisation advisers in Helmand, Kandahar, Kabul, the United Kingdom and the United States. In referencing these interviews, I have noted the role and seniority of the individual, and the location and date of the interview. A handful of interviews were so sensitive that they are simply referenced 'Confidential interview'. Interviews with Taliban field commanders, non-Taliban local elders and officials in Helmand simply note the category of interviewee, a number code, location and year. Interviews with members of the Taliban military command and Political Commission note the category of interviewee, a number code and year, as revealing the location might compromise the identity of the interviewee.

This book also draws on a substantial number of internal documents, including military plans, intelligence assessments, post-operation reports and campaign assessments (four of which I undertook: one for the British Army, and three for ISAF Command). I cite a number of these documents in previously published academic papers[24] that were cleared for publication by British military or ISAF authorities, and so I have been able to cite them in this book. However, most of these documents cannot be cited as they are classified, yet they inform my historical analysis nonetheless.

The military do love acronyms, and so it is nigh on impossible to avoid them in a book of this kind. However, I have tried to employ them as sparsely as possible and compiled the list above for the reader's convenience.

I

Atta in America

By the time he reached the age of thirty-three, Mohamed Atta was fastidious and fanatical in equal measure. Born and educated in Egypt, he spent the 1990s undertaking postgraduate studies in Hamburg, Germany, where he came to be radicalised in the al-Quds Mosque. The mosque preached a harsh and uncompromising form of Sunni Wahhabi Islam, common in Saudi Arabia. Atta's will, signed on the day Israel invaded Lebanon in April 1996, gives insight into his puritanical Islamic beliefs. It specified how his body should be prepared for burial, and decreed that no women or unclean persons should attend his funeral.[1] As things turned out, there would be no body to bury.

In many ways, Atta was a young man at odds with his time, and out of place in the West. His postgraduate thesis focused on how Western imported modernist architecture had ruined the traditional Arab city and way of life. The German host family with whom he stayed initially in Hamburg had to ask him to leave after six months because his strict religious beliefs and habits had become intolerable.[2] Views differ in Hamburg on Atta's character. To teachers and fellow students he appeared diligent and 'quite normal'.[3] Staff at the design company where he worked part-time described him as 'earnest and awkward'. But room-mates at the student accommodation where he lived until 1998 found Atta to be 'difficult, overbearing and anti-social'.[4]

In late 1999, Atta and three friends from the al-Quds Mosque – Ramzi Omar, Marwan al-Shehhi and Ziad Jarrah – travelled to Afghanistan to receive jihadi training at an al-Qaeda camp. Over a number of months they were indoctrinated in the al-Qaeda ideology of war on the 'enemies of Islam' and 'attaining martyrdom in the cause of God'.

They swore loyalty in person to Osama bin Laden, the Saudi-born leader of al-Qaeda. The four were then dispatched to the United States to learn how to fly aircraft, and prepare for al-Qaeda's most audacious attack to date.

Atta proved to be a difficult aviation student. Training on small planes is a messy business yet he turned up for lessons 'always immaculately dressed, with $200 Gucci shoes, silk shirts, double-hemmed pants'. He often ignored instruction, almost crashing his Cessna on at least one occasion. Staff and students in the flight school recall that Atta was 'arrogant' and 'very rude to the female employees'.[5] All the same, by December 2000, he had attained his pilot's licence. Nine months later, on 11 September 2001, Atta calmly boarded American Airlines Flight 11 from Boston to Los Angeles. At 8.15 a.m., just quarter of an hour into the flight, he and four accomplices overpowered the flight crew and took control of the plane. Thirty-one minutes later, Atta flew the Boeing 767 into the North Tower of the World Trade Center in New York. Within three minutes, CNN had broken the news. Showing live footage of smoke billowing from a huge gaping hole in the North Tower, CNN declared that 'we have unconfirmed reports this morning that a plane has crashed into one of the Towers of the World Trade Center'.[6] With no debris on the ground, to reporters and witnesses at the scene the plane appeared to be buried inside the building. In fact, the plane and everyone on it had been instantly incinerated on impact.

APOCALYPSE

Four aeroplanes were hijacked by al-Qaeda that day. All were domestic flights from the east coast to the west: United Airlines 175 along with American Airlines (AA) 11 departing from Boston; American Airlines 77 departing from Washington DC; and United Airlines 93 departing from Newark. By mid morning, all four planes ceased to exist. AA 11 hit the North Tower of the World Trade Center at 8.46 a.m., United 175 slammed into the South Tower at 9.03 a.m., and AA 77 hit the Pentagon at 9.37 a.m. United 93 crashed onto a field in Shanksville, Pennsylvania, just minutes after 10 a.m.; it had departed forty-five minutes late and never reached its intended target, which was either the Capitol or the White House. On 11 September, the terrorists killed 2,977 people – 2,606 in New York, 125 in the Pentagon, and 246 on the four flights. A decade later, the *New York Times* estimated the financial cost of these terrorist attacks to be $55 billion in damage, and a further $123 billion in lost business.[7]

When they were opened in 1973, the Twin Towers were the tallest buildings in the world at 110 floors high. They had been designed to survive the worst possible disasters, including a Boeing 707 airliner smashing into one. The Empire State Building was hit by a B-25 bomber in 1945, so such a scenario was far from inconceivable.[8] The Boeing 767, the plane used for United 175 and AA 11, is close in size to the Boeing 707. However, an accidental crash might reasonably be expected to involve a plane at the end of its journey crossing lower Manhattan, en route to Newark Airport for international flights or LaGuardia for domestic flights. That is to say, such a plane would be travelling at reduced speed and with little fuel. AA 11 and United 175 were travelling at top speed and with almost full fuel tanks when they hit the North and South Towers respectively.

Everybody above the ninety-second floor of the North Tower and the seventy-seventh floor of the South Tower were trapped by the raging inferno caused by the two plane crashes. With no escape from the flames and smoke, some two hundred people leapt to their deaths. It took ten long seconds for these people to fall to earth. To firefighters on the ground it 'looked like it was raining bodies'. Those who jumped exploded on impact a thousand feet below; body parts flew in all directions, injuring rescuers.[9] Onlookers broke down in uncontrollable tears. One police officer was heard to mutter helplessly: 'People don't even see this kind of shit in wars.' Another officer screamed at people to 'Get the fuck out of here. How do you know it's over? Go home, go home.'[10] The South Tower was still being evacuated when it suddenly collapsed at 9.59 a.m. The whole building came down in less than twenty seconds, scattering debris and dust all around. The North Tower followed at 10.28 a.m., much like its twin, all of sudden, and creating utter devastation and chaos in its wake. The Twin Towers were known to hold 50,000 workers. The Mayor of New York, Rudy Giuliani, told reporters 'the number of casualties will be more than any of us can bear'.[11]

The Pentagon was built during World War II to provide space for the bureaucracy that would be needed to service a military force that eventually grew to over 8 million. The five-sided building has five concentric rings (from the inner A Ring to most outer E Ring), each five storeys high, totalling 6.5 million square feet. AA 77 struck the west side of the Pentagon travelling at 530 miles per hour and carrying 5,300 gallons of fuel. In his memoir, Defense Secretary Donald Rumsfeld describes what happened next: 'With forty-four thousand pounds of thrust from engines at full throttle, the nose of the aircraft disintegrated as the rest of the plane continued to punch through the walls of the building – the E Ring, the D Ring, and the C Ring – at over seven hundred feet per second.'[12] The crash caused a massive fireball and demolished a section of the building. Viewed afterwards from the air, the Pentagon looked 'like a giant cake with a slice taken out'.[13] Nothing was left of the plane; 'it simply melt[ed] into the building'.[14] Rumsfeld was glued to the television in his office, watching the scenes in New York, when the plane struck the Pentagon. He recalls that '[t]he tremor lasted no longer than a few seconds, but I knew that only something truly massive could have made hundreds of thousands of tons of concrete shudder'.[15]

As luck would have it, the plane hit the one section of the Pentagon that had been rebuilt under a programme to strengthen key federal buildings following the Oklahoma City bombing of 1995. The improvements included 'a web of steel columns and bars to withstand bomb blasts' and two-inch-thick blast-proof windows. Moreover, because the reconstruction work had not been completed, only 800 instead of the usual 4,500 people were working in the section hit by the plane. The reinforced structure held for a crucial thirty minutes before collapsing, allowing hundreds to escape the fire.[16] All the same, many survivors in the Pentagon suffered horrendous burns, losing facial features and fingers; everybody on the plane died instantly. The Department of Defense (DoD) went to Defense Condition (DEFCON) 3, putting America's military on global readiness for action. The last time the DoD went to DEFCON 3 was in 1973, during the Yom Kippur War between US-backed Israel and its Soviet-backed Arab neighbours. With the Cold War over, the US State Department rushed to warn the Russians, who were about to start a major exercise of their strategic nuclear forces.[17]

The fourth plane, United 93, was hijacked around 9.30 a.m. Minutes later, Jarrah, who was now piloting, told terrified passengers, 'We would like you all to remain seated. There is a bomb on board, and [we] are going back to the airport, and to have our demands [met]. Please remain quiet.' By this stage, the terrible events unfolding in New York had been broadcast around the world. Using the plane's airphones and cell phones, flight crew and passengers learned that two airliners had hit the Twin Towers. They quickly put two and two together, and understood the imperative to wrest back control of the flight. At 9.57 a.m., a group of passengers charged the hijackers. As they gained entry to the cockpit, Jarrah rolled the aircraft sharply from left to right, and pitched it up and down, in an attempt to stop the assault. Six minutes later Jarrah plunged the Boeing 757 into the ground. In the final moments, the terrorists shouted, 'Allah is the greatest!' Thanks to the brave actions of desperate passengers, United 93 hit the ground 103 miles off target.

CHAOS AND CONFUSION

Ten minutes after the first attack, the US National Security Advisor, Condoleezza Rice, was told that a plane had crashed into the World Trade Center. She assumed that it was 'a small plane that had probably gone off course'.[18] Rice was then informed it was a commercial airliner. She immediately called the US president, George W. Bush, who was visiting an elementary school in Florida that day. The president was 'stunned'. In his memoir, he recalled thinking: 'That plane must have had the worst pilot in the world. How could he possibly have flown into a skyscraper on a clear day?'[19] Minutes later, the second plane hit the South Tower. The moment was captured live on CNN. However, because of the camera angle with the North Tower obscuring the South, it was initially misreported as a secondary explosion in the North Tower, caused by what was believed to be embedded plane fuselage. The CNN correspondents missed the second airliner, clearly visible on the live footage as it hurtled towards the South Tower. One minute later, CNN corrected their reporting: 'perhaps a second plane was involved' and 'the second Twin Tower is now on fire'.[20]

CNN correspondents continued to speculate for twenty-five minutes on how such an 'accident' could occur, that is until they were told by US officials that it was no accident. When the second plane struck, senior officials in the administration immediately knew that it was a terrorist attack. At that moment, the president was joining schoolchildren in a reading exercise when the White House Chief of Staff, Andy Card, leaned in and whispered, 'America is under attack.'[21]

Back in Washington DC, confusion reigned. The Counterterrorism Security Group (CSG) in the White House was immediately activated. Led by the White House counterterrorism coordinator, Richard Clarke, and located in the Situation Room in the West Wing, the CSG was the inter-agency team responsible for coordinating America's response to terrorist attacks. The Pentagon also activated an inter-agency network to manage the crisis in the National Military Command Center (NMCC). This set-up, with the two inter-agency groups, resulted in parallel processes for executing the national chain of command, notionally running from president to principal decision-makers, and on to crisis managers. In reality there was considerable confusion between and across these two national command channels. Further adding to the confusion were separate military and civilian agencies – respectively, the North American Aerospace Defense Command (NORAD) and the Federal Aviation Administration (FAA) – each with responsibilities for security of the sky over America. The 9/11 Commission, appointed by the president and Congress to investigate the events of that tragic day and the effectiveness of the US government response, concluded that NORAD and the FAA failed to coordinate their efforts 'to improve awareness and organize a common response'.[22] This is a polite way of saying that the US government response was utterly chaotic.

Following the New York attacks, the top two priorities were securing American government and securing America's skies. At 9.33 a.m., Reagan National Airport advised the US Secret Service that 'an aircraft [is] coming at you, and it is not talking to us'. This was AA 77, which was circling before heading for the Pentagon. Fearful that the White House was about to be attacked, the Secret Service decided to evacuate Vice President Dick Cheney to the hardened bunker deep below the East Wing of the White House, formally designated the Presidential Emergency Operations Center (PEOC). Four minutes later the vice president was underground, soon to be joined by Rice and other key officials.[23] Guarding them on both sides of the vault doors were Secret Service agents in body armour, packing shotguns and automatic weapons.[24]

Naturally, the Secret Service was taking no chances with the president either. A heated argument broke out in Emma E. Booker Elementary School between the president and his Secret Service detail.[25] Bush wanted to get straight back to Washington DC. The Secret Service was dead set against this, wanting him in the air 'as fast and as high as possible' and out of harm's way.[26] The Secret Service won the argument. The presidential motorcade left the school at 9.35 a.m. and 'charged down Florida Route 41' for the airport. Bush arrived to see Secret Service agents 'carrying assault rifles surrounding Air Force One'. Less than twenty minutes after leaving the school, the president was airborne.[27] The plane took off 'like a rocket', recalled one passenger, climbing rapidly to 45,000 feet. An officer on board later noted that 'there was so much torque that they actually tore the [runway] concrete'.[28] Around the same time, the Continuity of Government programme was implemented. A Cold War creation, it was designed to ensure government would survive a major attack on the United States. The Speaker of the House, third in line after the president and vice president, was whisked off by helicopter from Capitol Hill to a secure location.

With al-Qaeda turning airliners into missiles, the sky above America had to be emptied. There were around 4,400 planes in US airspace that morning. At 9.30 a.m., the CSG asked the FAA to halt all take-offs, and ground or divert all flights already in the air. Shortly after midday, this had been achieved.[29] The DoD was also asked to provide Combat Air Patrols to protect Washington DC and New York. Fifteen minutes later, three F-16 fighter jets from the 1st Fighter Wing out of Langley Air Force Base were screeching over the Capitol. Fighter jets from the Michigan National Guard were also dispatched to intercept a suspected hijacked plane over Pennsylvania (probably United 93), and six jets from Tyndall and Ellington air force bases were sent to escort Air Force One.[30]

Shortly before 10 a.m., Cheney called Bush from the PEOC. The president gave authorisation for US fighter jets to shoot down hijacked aircraft that refused orders to divert to nearby airports. By this stage, the FAA was tracking United 93. The hijackers had made it difficult for the FAA by turning off plane transponders, or changing codes; these provide a beacon system to triangulate with the ground-based radar system and thereby produce a very accurate picture of which planes are where in the sky. Without the beacons, the FAA was having to rely on radar alone. About fifteen minutes later, the FAA warned that United 93 was only eighty miles away. With communications to Air Force One patchy (the line kept going down, leading Bush to snap at his Chief of Staff: 'what the hell is going on?'[31]), the vice president was asked to confirm the shoot-down order. He did so without batting an eyelid. Five minutes later, a military aide advised Cheney that United 93 was only sixty miles out, and again he was asked to confirm authorisation to shoot it down, which he did. In fact, United 93 had been brought down by passenger action twenty minutes before. In the absence of sufficient radar signal, the FAA had been projecting its flight path and passing on warnings based on these projections to the Secret Service. At 10.30 a.m., the PEOC received urgent warning of another inbound low-flying plane, this time only five miles out. Cheney ordered that it be shot down. Luckily it was not, as it turned out to be a medical evacuation helicopter.[32]

In the end, the US Air Force did not shoot down any aircraft that day. As it happens, the fighter jets over Washington DC and New York would not have been able to do so in time. Indeed, nothing would have stopped United 93 hitting the White House or the Capitol (the actual target remains unclear) if passengers had not stormed the cockpit. The Combat Air Patrol arrived over Washington DC at around 9.45 a.m. However, the order to shoot down unresponsive airliners was not passed down the military chain of command until 10.30 a.m., that is ten minutes *after* United 93 would have hit its intended target. It took fifteen minutes for the shoot-down order to go from the White House to the NMCC, on to NORAD, and from there on to the headquarters of the Northeast Air Defense Sector (NEADS), which covers Washington DC and New York. Incredibly, the 9/11 Commission discovered that NEADS 'did not pass on this order to the fighters circling Washington and New York because they were unsure how the pilots would, or should, proceed with this guidance'. Instead, the fighter pilots were instructed simply to 'ID type and tail' suspicious planes.

An hour after the original Combat Air Patrol took up station, there was a second set of fighter jets flying over Washington DC from the Columbia District National Air Guard. These had been launched out of Andrews Air Force Base on the initiative of the commander of 113th Wing, General David Wherley, who had directly contacted the US Secret Service. The shoot-down order from the vice president was forwarded to Wherley outside of the formal military chain of command; it was relayed from Cheney's security detail in the White House to the Secret Service headquarters, and from there to the headquarters of the 113th Wing. Wherley authorised his fighters to shoot down any planes that threatened the White House or the Capitol.[33] The first two F-16 fighters that were scrambled were unarmed. It was going to take an hour to load missiles and ammunition onto the planes, and so the pilots took off with the plan of ramming their jet fighters into United 93, not realising that the civilian airliner had already crashed.[34]

The US Navy also swung into action. The Commander in Chief of the Atlantic Fleet, Admiral Robert Natter, was attending a NATO conference at Norfolk naval base when he was informed by an aide about the second plane hitting the World Trade Center. Natter immediately got up and excused himself, announcing to the stunned audience of senior NATO officers: 'America is at war ... I must take the fleet to sea.'[35] One report suggests that Natter received a call from the Deputy Mayor of New York City, Rudy Washington, who was responsible for coordinating NYC's emergency services on 9/11. Washington asked for air cover from the Atlantic Fleet's F-14 Tomcat and F-18 Hornet fighters. Natter conferred with the Chief of Naval Operations (the head of the US Navy), Admiral Vern Clark. It was decided to load up the fleet's Aegis guided-missile cruisers with surface-to-air missiles, recall the aircraft carrier USS *George Washington* from sea trials to recover its fighter wings, and call up the aircraft carrier USS *John F. Kennedy* from Mayport, Florida. Thus by mid afternoon, the Atlantic Fleet had two large-deck carriers and five Aegis cruisers, fully armed and on station off the east coast, guarding the aerial approaches to New York and Washington DC.[36] With US borders and skies closed, America was in lockdown.

THE ORIGINS OF AL-QAEDA

With so much death, destruction and chaos, one might be tempted to think that 9/11 was the work of lunatics. But nothing could be further from the truth. The men who masterminded and carried out these terrorist attacks were deeply committed to their cause. From their world view, these terrible acts made perfect sense.

Al-Qaeda was formed in 1988 in the city of Peshawar, on the western frontier of Pakistan, by a small group of Arabs who had fought in Afghanistan. The catalyst was the Soviet withdrawal from Afghanistan, which was completed a year later. These men shared a common bond through their experiences of the mujahedin war. Returning to a normal life at home in the Middle East was not possible, nor did it appeal to them. Having 'defeated' the Soviet Union, they were also enormously self-confident about taking on the world. In its origins, al-Qaeda was ill-defined and barely organised. As one authoritative study notes: 'Al-Qaeda was little more than a number of trained individuals who were sure that they wanted to continue the armed struggle and had access to financial resources, but were neither consolidated at the time and nor had they achieved any unity of purpose.'[37]

Al-Qaeda is a common term in Arabic with several meanings. It can denote principle, method, pattern, and foundation, home or base. It is likely that the term was adopted in the latter sense, to mean literally 'camp'.[38] Indeed, there were numerous jihadi groups in Afghanistan at the time that used the term in that way. Between 1996 and 2001 al-Qaeda 'matured' as a movement. However, it did not evolve into a formally structured organisation along the lines of established terrorist groups such as the Provisional IRA in Ireland, ETA in Spain and FARC in Colombia. Rather it comprised a core group (a few dozen men clustered around bin Laden), a global network of affiliated terrorist groups, and a unifying ideology.

That ideology can be traced back to two Egyptian scholars, Sayyed Qutb (1906–66) and Mohammad Abd al-Salam Faraj (1952–82), who most influenced the rise of militant Islam in the 1970s. Qutb returned to Egypt in 1950, from a two-year stay in the United States, disgusted by the moral degeneration of Western society. Americans who met Qutb recall him as unfailingly polite and not especially religious. Clearly, he kept his criticisms to himself. But writing to a friend, he concluded that '[t]he soul has no value to Americans'.[39] He found things little better at home. Egypt was ruled by the openly corrupt King Farouk, and the decadence of Cairo was manifest in the Westerners frequenting the city's bars, restaurants and nightclubs. Nationalist and Islamic discontent was growing in Egypt following the defeat of Arab armies by seemingly weaker Jewish forces in the 1948 Arab–Israeli War.[40]

Qutb took up his pen and preached Islamic revolution. He was to spend a decade in prison in Egypt, and was eventually executed in 1966 for his trouble. In his writings Qutb developed two concepts that were essential to the ideological landscape of al-Qaeda: the militant vanguard and *takfir*. For Qutb, westernisation had caused the Muslim world to descend into a state of 'ignorance of the divine guidance' (*jahiliyyah*). In his most famous work, *Milestones*, written in prison and published in 1964, Qutb called for the creation of a 'movement of Islamic revival in some Muslim country' that would 'eventually attain the status of world leadership'. He argued that this would require a 'vanguard which sets out with this determination and then keeps walking on the path, marching through the vast ocean of *Jahiliyyah* which has encompassed the entire world'.[41] This vanguard would wage a jihad to lead the people back on the true path of Islam. Jihad is a religious duty for all Muslims, involving the inner struggle against temptation and it may also include a physical struggle against non-believers. But Qutb proposed a far more militant form of jihad involving a violent struggle to remove those rulers who were responsible for keeping Muslims in a state of ignorance. Here Qutb also applied a new meaning to *takfir*, describing someone who has been excommunicated from Islam. Where traditionally this term was applied only to individuals, Qutb employed it for governments and whole societies, starting with Egypt. This move was significant because while Islam prohibits violence against fellow Muslims, heretics are fair game, as are infidels.

Faraj likewise emphasised militant jihad as the prime duty of Muslims. He also directed his fire at the 'apostate' rulers of Egypt. 'In the Islamic countries, the enemy is at home ... He is represented by those governments that have seized power over the Muslims, and that is why *jihad* is an imperative for every individual.'[42] He led the Cairo branch of the Islamic group al-Jihad, which sought to overthrow the secular government in Egypt and replace it with an Islamic regime. Faraj was arrested by the Egyptian authorities and executed in April 1982 for his central role in the assassination of President Anwar Sadat six months before. The importance of jihad led by a militant vanguard was echoed by Adballah Azzam, the leading ideologue of Arab militants in Afghanistan and a close associate of bin Laden. Writing in 1987, he declared: 'There is no ideology, neither earthly nor heavenly, that does not require … a vanguard that gives everything it possesses in order to achieve victory.'[43]

Qutb and Faraj, and later Azzam, provided the foundation for al-Qaeda's ideology. To this, bin Laden added a key twist. Where militant Islamists in Egypt were focused on jihad against the 'near enemy', that is, apostate rulers, bin Laden was focused on the 'far enemy', namely the United States. He reasoned that US support for the regime in Egypt and other Arab states in the Middle East prevented jihad against the near enemy from succeeding. The United States was also in the firing line for creating and sustaining the state of Israel. This was a deeply emotive issue for many Arab militants, both for the plight of Palestinians and also for the ignominious defeats inflicted on Arab states by Israel in successive wars. In the late 1990s, Ayman al-Zawahiri joined bin Laden, bringing an Egyptian terrorist faction into al-Qaeda. Al-Zawahiri was an associate of Faraj and had played a minor role in the plot to assassinate Sadat: the president was especially hated by Egyptian militants for making peace with Israel after the 1973 Yom Kippur War. Al-Zawahiri had previously declared that 'the road to Jerusalem passes through Cairo'.[44] In allying himself with bin Laden, and becoming his second in command, al-Zawahiri now recognised that the 'far enemy' had to be tackled first.

TARGETING AMERICA

On 7 August 1998, al-Qaeda drove a massive truck bomb into the car park of the US embassy in Kenya. When the bomb exploded it blew the whole front off the embassy building. The next-door building, which housed a secretarial college, collapsed entirely. The result was carnage: 213 people were killed, including 12 US citizens, and some 4,500 people were injured. Almost simultaneously, al-Qaeda detonated another truck bomb in the car park of the US embassy in Tanzania. This time, the damage and death toll was less: eleven dead, and eighty-five wounded, all of whom were African. Unlike other terrorist organisations, al-Qaeda did not make any demands before launching such terrible attacks. Afterwards bin Laden suggested that the attacks were revenge for the US 'invasion' of Somalia in 1992 and, bizarrely, the genocide in Rwanda in 1994. Mostly, al-Qaeda seemed intent on simply killing lots of people, and as many Americans as possible.[45]

Terrorism had already pushed up the national security agenda for US policymakers following major bombings of US-leased facilities in Saudi Arabia in 1995 and 1996.[46] However, the 1998 embassy attacks put al-Qaeda squarely on America's radar. It is not entirely clear how much attention was given to the organisation before these attacks. Insider accounts, published some time after 9/11, claim that US intelligence was on to bin Laden well before 1998. In 1996, the CIA set up a special team, called 'Alec Station', to develop actionable intelligence on terrorist financing. Alec Station decided to concentrate on bin Laden. According to the former head of the CIA, George Tenet, 'By 1996, we knew that Bin Laden was more than a financier.'[47] There was sufficient interest in al-Qaeda that, according to Richard Clarke, 'by 1996 and 1997 the CSG was developing plans to snatch Bin Laden from Afghanistan'.[48] However, it appears that US intelligence probably still under-appreciated the scale of the threat presented by al-Qaeda, and certainly failed to communicate this threat to senior US officials. On this, the 9/11 Commission concluded:

> Despite the availability of information that al Qaeda was a global network, in 1998 policymakers knew little about the organization. The reams of new information that the CIA's Bin Laden unit had been developing since 1996 had not been pulled together and synthesized for the rest of government.[49]

Senior policymakers knew about bin Laden, and plans to grab him had been discussed in the White House, but this was with a view to removing a key source of terrorism finance. Tenet claims that by 1996 the CIA knew that bin Laden was 'the head of a worldwide terrorist organization'.[50] But the 9/11 Commission questions this assertion, noting that '[a]s late as 1997, the CIA's Counterterrorism Center continued to describe him as an "extremist financier"' and that a 'National Intelligence Estimate on terrorism in 1997 had only briefly mentioned Bin Laden'.[51] To be sure, there was growing attention within the White House on the problem of international terrorism. In May 1998, Bill Clinton signed Presidential Decision Directive 622 on 'Protection Against Unconventional Threats to the Homeland and Americans Overseas', leading to the creation of a counterterrorism coordinator in the White House, and the appointment of Clarke in this post. However, it took the embassy bombings three months later to galvanise the US government to go after al-Qaeda.

Seven days after the attacks, the CIA and FBI had assembled enough evidence to conclude that al-Qaeda was responsible. George Tenet told Clinton, 'this one is a slam dunk Mr. President. There is no doubt that this was an al-Qaeda operation.'[52] The US response was measured. A general punitive bombing campaign against al-Qaeda camps in Afghanistan was ruled out due to the risk of collateral damage. President Clinton was scarred by what had happened when the United States launched cruise missile strikes against the Iraq intelligence headquarters in 1993, in retaliation for a plot to assassinate former President George H. W. Bush. A missile missed its target by a few hundred yards and killed one of the most famous female artists in the Arab world. Thus in late 1998, on one of the few occasions when the CIA was able to predict where bin Laden would spend the night, as a guest of the Taliban governor of Kandahar in southern Afghanistan, Clinton refused to approve a cruise missile strike because the governor's residence was next to a mosque.[53] Some senior US officials were also worried about America's reputation in the world. Clarke, who was an advocate of bombing, noted that the Deputy Secretary of State, Strobe Talbott, 'was adamantly opposed to making the terrorist camps in Afghanistan a free-fire zone for routine American bombing. Talbott thought it was bad enough that we had made southern Iraq such a "bomb anytime" area.' Officials like Talbott were also anticipating the possibility of having to bomb Serbia back into line (which indeed happened a year later over the Kosovo crisis), and were concerned that to European and Islamic eyes America was increasingly viewed as 'the Mad Bomber'.[54]

So instead mechanisms were put in place to take out the al-Qaeda leadership through covert means. The CIA was given explicit legal authorisation to use lethal force against bin Laden and other leading figures in al-Qaeda. The wording was careful to avoid presidential approval for an assassination campaign. Rather the purpose was to give CIA field agents legal cover to kill al-Qaeda leaders should capture prove impossible. The US Navy was also ordered to move ships and submarines into the Arabian Sea in preparation for possible cruise missile attacks against al-Qaeda targets in Afghanistan.[55] Bin Laden was constantly on the move and so he evaded the CIA. On 20 August, al-Qaeda issued a press statement denying 'any involvement in the Nairobi and Dar es Salaam bombings'.[56] This denial may have had something to do with al-Qaeda's attempts to placate their Taliban hosts in Afghanistan. Regardless, by coincidence an hour later the US Navy launched Operation Infinite Reach, firing some sixty-six cruise missiles at four al-Qaeda training camps in Afghanistan and a further eleven cruise missiles at a chemical plant in Sudan. As a retaliatory measure, these cruise missile strikes were a failure. Some buildings, tents and around thirty terrorists were killed in Afghanistan, no al-Qaeda leaders among them. One man was killed in Sudan. More to the point, while US offi-cials claimed at the time that the Al-Shifa plant in Sudan was manufac-turing nerve agents for al-Qaeda, this was never conclusively proven.

Al-Qaeda's strategy was to goad the United States into a dispropor-tionate military response. The logic is pretty clear: the objective of the weaker side (i.e. al-Qaeda) is to 'sting the stronger side into intemperate retaliatory action', and thereby mobilise wider support for the terrorist cause.[57] In this way, al-Qaeda was acting as the vanguard to shake Muslims the world over out of their complacency and state of ignor-ance.[58] The US cruise missile strikes did put bin Laden on the map for Muslims the world over. The editor of the London-based *Al Quds Al Arabi* newspaper recalls that bin Laden's 'profile increased a lot. He's the underdog and he's attacked by the mighty Americans. So this actu-ally elevated him to a higher prestigious position in the eyes and minds of those frustrated people in the Arab and in the Muslim world.'[59]

Al-Qaeda also wanted to draw the United States into a 'bleeding war' in Afghanistan, where it would suffer the same fate as the Soviet Union.[60] The Soviet invasion of Afghanistan in 1979 had mobilised a highly effective mujahedin resistance. By the time the Soviet Union withdrew in 1989, its military had suffered over 50,000 casualties and some 14,500 dead. The collapse of the Soviet Union two years later appeared to seal Afghanistan's reputation as 'the graveyard of empires'.[61] To provoke the United States, bigger and bolder terrorist attacks would be needed.

The mastermind behind 9/11 was Khalid Sheikh Mohammed, commonly known to Americans as KSM. His eventual capture and interrogation (including the use of 'enhanced interrogation techniques') enabled Western intelligence to piece together a detailed picture of how the 9/11 attacks came about. Planning mass terrorist attacks was something of a family business for KSM. His nephew, Ramzi Yousef, had masterminded the 1993 attack on the World Trade Center, when a truck bomb damaged the base of the North Tower, killing six and injuring over a thousand people. In 1994, KSM and Yousef travelled to the Philippines, where they hatched a complex plot to assassinate the Pope, blow up eleven American passenger jets over the Pacific, and crash a twelfth airliner into the CIA headquarters at Langley, Virginia. Funded by al-Qaeda, 'OPLAN Bojinka' was in advanced preparation when it was discovered by the Philippine police and had to be abandoned. Eventually, KSM joined up with bin Laden in Afghanistan in 1996; the two had fought together in 1987 in the mujahedin war against the Soviets. At that meeting, KSM proposed that passenger jets be hijacked and used to destroy strategic targets in the United States. Two years later, bin Laden gave the go-ahead to work up an operational plan.[62]

KSM came up with a scheme to hijack ten airliners, nine of which would be crashed into targets on both coasts of the United States. He would land the tenth plane at a US airport, execute all males on board, and make a speech denouncing American support to Israel and repressive regimes in the Arab world. This plot was rejected by the al-Qaeda leadership as overly ambitious, and KSM was instructed to concentrate on a smaller number of planes and targets. After some toing and froing, a plan was agreed involving four planes and four key targets in the United States.[63]

It took two years for al-Qaeda to plan, prepare for and execute the 9/11 attacks. Bin Laden and KSM agreed on the targets in early 1999. From late 1999, two teams were being trained for the mission. One team of veteran mujahedin hand-picked by bin Laden had the commitment and combat abilities but poor English. By chance, four post-graduate students from Hamburg turned up in Afghanistan seeking jihadi training; these were Atta, Omar, al-Shehhi and Jarrah. Well educated, with excellent English and used to living in the West, these offered a far better prospect. By the summer of 2000, all four would be receiving flight training in the United States.

THE RISE OF THE TALIBAN

Over this whole period, the Clinton administration redoubled its efforts to get bin Laden. Afghanistan was the most difficult terrain imaginable from which to root out al-Qaeda. It was a country that had been shattered by twenty years of war – starting with rural resistance to Kabul in 1978, then the mujahedin war against the Soviet Army from 1979 to 1989 and the Soviet puppet regime from 1989 to 1992, followed by a brutal civil war from 1994 to 1998 that led to the rise of the Taliban.[64]

The Taliban originated from Kandahar province, in southern Afghanistan, and had grown out of the Soviet War of the 1980s. The Afghan mujahedin in this war comprised hundreds of armed groups of between twenty and a hundred men, raised locally by a tribal or clan leader. Many mujahedin came from massive refugee camps across the border in Pakistan; the Soviet War had created a tide of refugees, with 3 million Afghans fleeing to Pakistan. By the mid 1980s, with material support from the United States and Saudi Arabia, the Pakistan Army was training up to 20,000 mujahedin drawn from the Afghan refugee population and sending them back across the border to liberate their country.[65] The mujahedin were generally effective guerrilla fighters but ill-disciplined when it came to field craft; they tended to be very poor at digging trenches, conserving ammunition and saving their wounded. The groups relied heavily on local communities for food and shelter. They also formed into larger networks, or 'fronts', each led by a great leader who was able to disburse military supplies from foreign donors across his front to field commanders.[66]

Taliban fronts differed in that they were mostly formed of young men, fresh out of religious schools (or madrasas) in Pakistan, and motivated by Islamic jihad to wage war on the Soviet infidel. 'Talib' is Arabic for 'student', and so the name 'Taliban' reflects the importance of Islamic teachings to the self-identity of this fighting community. As one major study on the Taliban notes: 'In greater Kandahar, there were literally hundreds of Taliban commanders and dozens of Taliban fronts ... The Taliban sought to distinguish them-selves from other mujahedeen groups by offering a more ostentatiously religious *jihad* to those who fought with them.'[67] The Taliban ascribed to the strict Deobandi school of Sunni Islam which had emerged in British colonial India in the mid nineteenth century as an Islamic revivalism movement. Thousands of Deobandi madrasas flourished in Pakistan during the 1980s thanks to Pakistani state patronage and Saudi money, and it was these that gave birth to the Taliban.[68]

Following the end of the Soviet War, most Taliban returned to their studies, while Afghanistan was fought over by warlords. Large warlord fiefdoms emerged under Ismail Khan in the west, Abdul Rashid Dostum in the north-west, and Ahmad Shah Massoud in the north-east, where non-Pashtun tribes – Tajik, Uzbek and Hazara – predom-inated. In effect, these were mini-states, possessing centralised political and military organisations and able to provide a range of public services.[69] The situation in the Pashtun heartlands of eastern and southern Afghanistan was more complicated, with many smaller warlords aligned to different Pashtun mujahedin parties, the most powerful of which was Hizb-i Islami led by Gulbuddin Hekmatyar. Predation on the local population was rife and often brutal in the south; the kidnapping and raping of girls and boys by ill-disciplined mujahedin was common. The rural economy collapsed as banditry and roadblocks by different armed groups prevented farmers from bringing their produce to market and goods from reaching villages.

In this context, the Taliban returned to impose law and order in 1994. Mullah Mohammed Omar emerged as a key figure in rallying Taliban fighters to inflict harsh punishment on local warlords for abusing the population. In a place and moment of immense symbolic importance to the Taliban, Mullah Omar visited the shrine of the Cloak of the Prophet Muhammad, next to the main mosque in Kandahar, in April 1996. Taking out this holiest of Islamic relics, he showed the cloak to a large crowd of Taliban who declared him to be the 'Commander of the Faithful' and the Amir of Afghanistan. Omar's success in leading the Taliban owed more to aesthetics than his intellect; with his simple tastes and lifestyle, he encapsulated the

Taliban ideal of the spartan leader. One Taliban close to Omar later described him as 'a low-level scholar and a very poor public speaker'.[70] Nonetheless, under Mullah Omar, the Taliban were able to raise large forces and moving out from Kandahar rapidly gained territory. They were very successful in rallying some former mujahedin commanders under their banner and terrifying others into submission, and within three months they were at the outskirts of Ismail Khan's stronghold in the western city of Herat, as well as outside the capital Kabul, which was being fought over by Massoud, Dostum and Hekmatyar.[71]

Bin Laden arrived with his family and some associates in eastern Afghanistan in May 1996. He did not do so at the invitation of the Taliban, but rather his move from Sudan was facilitated by other mujahedin leaders, most notably Abdul Rasoul Sayyaf. Indeed, the Taliban were unaware of his presence until they took control of Nangarhar province, where bin Laden was based in the city of Jalalabad. The Taliban were well disposed towards bin Laden, given his service to the mujahedin in the Soviet War, and also the promise of Arab riches. Some accounts have suggested that bin Laden donated £3 million from his own funds to support the Taliban war effort, which had then stalled outside of Kabul. In fact, bin Laden had arrived with far more limited funds, but he was able to act as a conduit for donations from wealthy Arab sympathisers. He also played a key role in brokering the deal that led the major eastern mujahedin commander, Jalauddin Haqqani, to join forces with the Taliban. In short, bin Laden made himself indispensable to the movement, and indeed ended up acting as the leader of Arab jihadis that had flocked to Afghanistan to fight for the Taliban. Arab fighters entering from Pakistan were directed to al-Qaeda training camps outside Jalalabad and Kandahar; many went on to man the Taliban's elite Brigade 055, which was heavily involved in the toughest fighting on the northern front.[72]

By October 1996, the Taliban had taken Kabul and were in control of 90 per cent of the country. Herat had also fallen and Ismail Khan had taken refuge in Iran. Likewise, the Taliban had overrun Dostum's Uzbek fiefdom, and he too had fled the country. Only Massoud's Tajik forces held out, in a small enclave centred on the Panjshir Valley. On seizing power, the Taliban imposed their strict interpretation of Islamic living on the Afghan people, including the more cosmopolitan populations of Herat and Kabul. All forms of entertainment – cards,

music, singing, dancing, television, kite-flying and fighting birds –
were banned on the grounds that they encouraged gambling and
distracted people from their religious duties. For some reason, toothpaste was also prohibited. All men were required to grow beards to
a specified length. Women were banned from the workplace, and
were required to wear the burka to cover themselves entirely when
out of their homes. Girls were not allowed to attend school.[73] Religious
police patrolled the streets of Kabul and other cities meting out harsh
punishments to any caught not observing the ever-growing list of
Taliban regulations.

US POLICY TOWARDS THE TALIBAN

Initially, the US government kept silent about the seemingly bizarre
and increasingly repressive manner of Taliban rule. A classified State
Department cable sent to all embassies declared that the United States
sought to engage with the 'Taliban interim government at an early
stage'. US diplomats were instructed to 'demonstrate [US] willingness
to deal with [the Taliban] as the new authorities in Kabul', to find out
what the Taliban intended to do, and to communicate the US government's position on human rights, narcotics and terrorism. The first
formal encounter between the two governments occurred in early
November 1996 at a meeting in Islamabad between the US ambassador
to Pakistan, Tom Simons, and the Taliban foreign minister, Mullah
Ghaus. Simons urged the Taliban to show more religious tolerance
and to be prepared to negotiate an end to the conflict with the northern
warlords. Ghaus's response was uncompromising: Massoud and
Dostum would have 'to submit to the will of God and the will of the
people, which are manifested in the Taliban'. A month later, Ghaus
returned with a formal request for the United States to recognise the
Taliban government, and to help the Taliban take the Afghan seat in
the United Nations. To encourage Washington to support this request,
the Taliban proposed to appoint a non-Taliban Pashtun leader, Hamid
Karzai, as their UN representative. However, American diplomats
refused to provide this support, declaring that 'the US government is
not in the position to recognize any group as the formal government
of Afghanistan, including the Taliban'.[74]

In follow-up meetings in Washington, Karzai told US officials that the Taliban were 'intrinsically Afghan, and ... a force that cannot be assumed will go away'. At the same time, he said they were 'very simple, unsophisticated people', and he urged Washington to become more 'actively and directly' involved in Afghanistan to encourage the Taliban to moderate their policies.[75] By 1997 there was growing international unease at the Taliban treatment of women, as well as with public executions in football stadiums in Kabul and elsewhere. Some of the executions were especially savage – murderers had their heads hacked off, and the punishment for sodomy was to have a wall collapsed on those convicted. Calls by the United Nations Secretary General and the heads of several UN agencies for the Taliban to moderate their policies all fell on deaf ears.[76]

As the Taliban regime became ever more repressive, so they became increasingly isolated. Only Pakistan remained stalwart in its support. Throughout the 1990s, when Pakistan had five civilian governments under Nawaz Sharif and Benazir Bhutto (as well as four caretaker administrations), policy on Afghanistan was controlled by the Pakistan Army and, in particular, its Inter-Services Intelligence (ISI) agency. Pakistan had two key objectives during this period. The first was to prevent the non-Pashtun northerners from seizing power, and thereby providing a possible opening for India to gain influence in Afghanistan. The second was to end the brutal civil war, which was causing immense disruption to the Pakistani trucking mafia that moved goods through Afghanistan to Iran and central Asia.[77] Pakistan was also facing an energy crisis, and Turkmenistan had huge energy reserves – 159 trillion cubic feet of gas and 32 billion barrels of oil – that it was keen to pipe to Pakistan. However, this required a new pipeline to be built through Afghanistan, which was not possible while the country was at war.[78] Following the collapse of the Soviet client regime in Kabul in 1992, Pakistan sought to negotiate a power-sharing agreement between the various mujahedin warlords, the fruit of which was the 1992 Peshawar Accord. This offered the last and best hope for peace but it failed as the major warlords fought for control of Kabul and for their own areas of the country.[79] The rise of the Taliban offered the ISI an alternative way to achieve their objectives.

In 1995, Prime Minister Bhutto claimed that Pakistan was not taking sides in the Afghan civil war, when in fact it had decided to switch support from Gulbuddin Hekmatyar – who had proven to be uncompromising in his dealings with the other mujahedin warlords and managed to alienate the United States and Saudis with his zealotry – to the Taliban, who had already reopened the road network in southern Afghanistan. According to one account based on interviews with key participants, a senior ISI adviser, Brigadier Sultan Amir, was on the ground from the beginning helping the Taliban to re-establish themselves in Kandahar; he was known to the Taliban as 'Colonel Imam'.[80] The ISI helped to recruit, train and arm foreign fighters – Pakistanis, Arabs and Uzbeks – many of whom were studying in Taliban madrasas in Balochistan and the North-West Frontier Province, and transported them across the border to Afghanistan. Pakistan was determined to see the Taliban win, and accordingly sent hundreds of military trainers and advisers into Afghanistan to help the Taliban in its war against the northern warlords. When the Taliban offensive against Ismail Khan's forces stalled, Pakistani special forces directly intervened to help the Taliban seize the city of Herat in September 1995.[81] In 1997, Pakistan, along with Saudi Arabia and the United Arab Emirates, formally recognised the Taliban government and provided it with $30 million dollars in much needed aid, as well as wheat, fuel and heavy weapons.[82] A classified US national security assessment from that year concluded that Pakistan played an 'overbearing role in planning and even executing Taliban political and diplomatic initiatives'.[83] Thus Pakistan stood by the Taliban when the United Nations Security Council slapped sanctions on the regime in October 1999 for failing to hand over bin Laden.

Pakistan's line was that the Taliban would become more reasonable in time as they settled into government, and that international engagement with the movement would help to speed up this process.[84] Yet Pakistani influence waned as Taliban confidence grew. Pakistan proved unable to encourage the Taliban to moderate their behaviour, even to protect its own citizens from abuse at Taliban hands. A Pakistani football team visiting Kandahar was beaten up and deported by Taliban religious police in 2000 because they wore shorts at a soccer match.[85] In early 2001, Pakistan tried to reason with the Taliban to stop them from destroying the Buddhas of Bamiyan, two gigantic statues carved in the fourth century into a standstone cliff face. President Musharraf sent his interior minister to appeal to Mullah Omar not to order an act of such staggering cultural vandalism, if only to avoid the universal international condemnation that was sure to follow.[86] The former Pakistan Army Chief of Staff General Jehangir Karamat noted: 'we reached out to them and they told us to get lost'.[87] It took ten days for the Taliban to destroy the Buddhas; when the ancient statues withstood tank shells and rockets, they used piles of explosives.[88]

Looking back at their time in government, Taliban leaders today are proud of what they achieved. Before they seized power, governance and security had completely collapsed in southern and eastern Afghanistan, and Kabul had turned into a battleground between rival warlords; the situation was better in the west under Ismail Khan, and the northern areas controlled by Dostum and Massoud. The Taliban brought law and order to the conflict affecting south and east, and also restored basic public services and repaired major roads. However, they were woefully unqualified to govern; few had the faintest idea of what to do. Over time, the Taliban government split between the hardline leadership in Kandahar and a civil administration in Kabul. It fell to a small handful of capable administrators in the capital to keep the country ticking over.[89] Added to this the Taliban government was very poor, with an annual budget of around $80 million, most of which was spent on its war effort. At least Taliban leaders were not corrupt – according to one Taliban deputy minister, the annual salary bill for the entire cabinet was only $5,000 – and hence little was wasted in this respect.[90] As one (admittedly sympathetic) account notes, 'Considering this dire lack of resources, the Kabul government's achievements were actually remarkable.'[91]

The Taliban world view had been shaped by an austere way of life, fundamentalist religious instruction and the rigours of war. Indeed, many Taliban leaders carried physical disabilities from the conflict: like Mullah Omar, the foreign minister and the justice minister had each lost an eye, and the Taliban mayor of Kabul and the governor of Kandahar had both lost a leg. Given that it was led by hardened men with fervent religious views, the extremist character of Taliban government is hardly surprising in retrospect. Thus, for one Taliban leader, life in Kabul 'was returning to normal' as the Taliban 'started to implement *shari'a* law: women were no longer working in government and men throughout the city had started to grow beards'.[92] Some Taliban leaders claim that they sought advice and assistance from the United States but were snubbed: 'At various [international] conferences in the late 1990s, we tried to talk to the Americans, but whenever we sat down next to Americans, they kept moving table.'[93]

It seems that the Taliban were more than a bit bemused by Western complaints about their treatment of women. Far from oppressing them, they believed they were protecting women from violence and dishonour. In fairness, many of the discriminatory practices – such as purdah, the practice of secluding women from public view – long pre-dated the Taliban and remain common in rural Pashtun areas. Such practices became more widespread when the mujahedin parties seized power from the Communist-supported regime of Dr Mohammed Najibullah in 1992. Thus, in the early 1990s, the *non-Taliban* mujahedin supreme court demanded that girls stop going to school because 'schools are whorehouses and centres of adultery', and decreed that 'women are not to leave their homes at all, unless absolutely necessary, in which case they are to cover themselves completely'.[94] That said, by some accounts things got even worse for women under Taliban rule. One woman activist recalls of that time: 'Afghan women lost almost everything under the Taliban government. They were just alive but they were not living like a human. They were watching outside from behind their windows. They were pretty hopeless.'[95] The Taliban did ban the Pashtun custom of settling tribal feuds by trading and sometimes even executing women. Thus, from their perspective, the Taliban were 'well ahead of the world in terms of protecting women's rights'.[96]

Not surprisingly, the world saw things differently. Aid donations for Afghanistan were drying up from Western states weary with the war and increasingly concerned about funding 'gender apartheid' in Afghanistan. The UN High Commissioner for Refugees and Save the Children both halted operations in Afghanistan in protest at restrictions on female staff and clients. Particularly damaging for the Taliban was the arrest, manhandling and detention of the European Union's Commissioner for Humanitarian Affairs, Emma Bonino, and several international reporters on a visit to a women's hospital in Kabul in late September 1997. On leaving the country, Bonino described the Taliban as a 'repressive, grotesquely misogynistic regime'. The Taliban later apologised but the damage had been done.[97] Three weeks later, on a visit to Islamabad, the US Secretary of State, Madeleine Albright, indicated a clear shift in American policy. 'We are opposed to the

Taliban because of … their despicable treatment of women and children, and their general lack of respect for human dignity.'[98]

REFUSING TO HAND OVER BIN LADEN

Days after the US cruise missile strikes in 1998, Mullah Omar phoned an official in the US State Department in Washington DC to complain. For a head of state to phone a mid-level diplomat in this manner was an unusual way of going about things, and it was indicative of the Taliban's ignorance of normal diplomatic practice. Mullah Omar declared the US retaliatory action to have been unhelpful and he called on President Clinton to resign. The US State Department official suggested a dialogue between the United States and the Taliban over bin Laden. This led to a number of meetings over a two-year period between the new US ambassador to Pakistan, William Milam, and the Taliban ambassador to Pakistan, Mullah Abdul Salam Zaeef. The United States made Taliban surrender of bin Laden a precondition of improved relations between the two countries. In his memoirs, Zaeef outlines 'three possible solutions' offered by the Taliban to the bin Laden problem: the United States could hand over evidence of bin Laden's responsibility for the 1998 bombings to the Supreme Court of Afghanistan and he would be punished according to sharia law if found guilty; a court could be formed, chaired by the attorney generals of three Islamic countries, and held in a fourth Islamic country to try bin Laden; or alternatively, in the absence of an agreed framework to try the al-Qaeda leader, the Taliban could 'offer to curb any and all activities of Osama'. However, the Americans insisted that bin Laden be surrendered unconditionally to US authorities. The Taliban countered that Afghanistan did not have an extradition treaty with the United States.[99] Throughout, US diplomats showed scant regard for Islamic doctrine and Pashtun customs, especially the practice of *nana-watai*, which created an obligation on hosts to provide refuge to guests and protect them from their enemies. The view from Washington DC was that the Taliban were stalling. In her memoirs, Albright recounts: 'The Taliban leaders didn't say no; instead they offered a menu of lame excuses. They argued that it would violate cultural etiquette to mistreat a beneficiary of their hospitality and that Bin Laden was a hero to Afghans because of his 1980s anti-Soviet role.'[100] US intransigence arguably proved counterproductive, as it closed down debate within the Taliban – between the more moderate civil administration in Kabul and the more hardline core leadership in Kandahar – over whether to cut ties with bin Laden, and reinforced their determination not to accede to US demands.[101]

The Clinton administration also worked through its allies to put pressure on the Taliban to give up bin Laden. In mid September 2000, the head of Saudi intelligence, Prince Turki Al Faisal, flew to Kandahar to meet with Mullah Omar. On a previous visit, Omar had promised to surrender bin Laden to the Saudis, but now he refused, saying 'Why are you persecuting and harassing this courageous, valiant Muslim?' Omar went off on a rant to insult the Saudis. A furious Turki stormed out of the meeting. Days later, the Saudi government broke off relations with the Taliban and attempted to cut off private Saudi sources of finance for the movement, with mixed success.[102] US policymakers had not expected diplomacy to work, and so in the meantime the CIA developed plans working with anti-Taliban tribal groups to snatch bin Laden, and the US Navy worked up new options for cruise missile strikes.

In October 2000, al-Qaeda attacked again. A small boat packed with explosives was allowed to approach a US Navy destroyer, the USS *Cole*, while it was moored in the port of Aden. Seventeen US sailors were killed, and over forty injured, in the explosion that blew a massive hole in the ship. The FBI sent a large team to Yemen to investigate, and the CIA pursued all its leads, but this time neither agency was able to conclude that al-Qaeda was responsible.[103]

The effort to bring bin Laden to justice lost momentum in January 2001, when President George W. Bush came into office. His administration had a very different set of national security priorities, including the Middle East peace process, relations with Russia and ballistic missile defence, and a crisis in April when a Chinese fighter jet collided with a US spy plane, forcing the US aircraft to land in China. The Bush administration kept on Clarke and his entire team in the CSG. Clarke tried to get senior leadership in the new administration to focus on the threat from al-Qaeda, sending successive memoranda to report findings collated from US and foreign intelligence sources, all pointing to the continued and growing threat from the organisation. Particular attention post-9/11 has been paid to a memorandum submitted by Clarke on 6 August 2001 entitled 'Bin Laden Determined To Strike in US', which was briefed to President Bush at his ranch in Texas, where he was enjoying a four-week vacation. The memo notes that 'Bin Laden since 1997 has wanted to conduct terrorist attacks in the US' and that 'After US missile strikes on his base in Afghanistan in 1998, Bin Laden told his followers he wanted to retaliate in Washington'. It also noted that 'FBI information since that time indicates patterns of suspicious activity in this country consistent with preparations for hijackings [of aircraft] or other types of attacks, including recent surveillance of federal buildings in New York'.[104]

This is not to suggest that the Bush administration did not take the threat from terrorism seriously; indeed, they requested substantial increases in counterterrorism funding for the CIA, FBI and other agencies. It is just that terrorism was not top of their list of national security priorities. Hence, rivalry between the FBI and CIA was allowed to fester and led to the jealous guarding of intelligence; better intelligence coordination could well have led to the discovery and tracking of al-Qaeda operatives as they entered the United States.[105] Equally, no action was taken to improve airport security. Thus six of the hijackers on 9/11, including Atta, were identified under a computer pre-screening system as requiring additional security measures prior to boarding. But the only real consequence of this was that their bags were not loaded into the hold until they had boarded their respective planes. The hijackers were still able to bring knives and mace spray in their carry-on bags, and use these to murder flight crew and passengers and gain entry to flight decks.[106]

On 25 January 2001, Clarke had called for an urgent 'Principals level review on the al-Qaeda network' involving the president, vice president, Secretaries of State and Defense, and other senior national security advisers. But with so many other national security priorities, a Principals meeting focused on al-Qaeda did not occur until 4 September 2001.[107] One week later, the urgency of dealing with al-Qaeda was evident for all to see.

2

Shoulder to Shoulder

The British prime minister knew that 11 September was going to be difficult. His office had been preparing for days. Tony Blair was going to address the Trades Union Congress annual conference in Brighton, and he was expecting a rough reception. Traditionally, the Labour Party and the unions enjoyed warm and close relations, as might be expected. But things were different under Blair. He came into office in 1997 proposing a 'third way' between the small-government ethos of the Conservative Party, and the tax-and-spend ways of old Labour. His New Labour government set out to reform British public services, in particular by creating partnerships with the private sector to build schools, hospitals and transport infrastructure. The unions saw this as a direct threat to their members, and to the Labour tradition.[1] 'The unions were really cranking things up in advance of tomorrow' was how Blair's inner circle saw things on the eve of his speech.[2] No one imagined the horrific events that were about to unfold across the Atlantic – events that would sweep aside the mundane concerns of everyday politics and lead Britain down the path to war.

Blair arrived at the seaside town around lunchtime on 11 September and went straight to the Grand Brighton to make final preparations for his speech. Somewhat ironically, this seafront hotel was the site of one of the worse terrorist attacks on British soil, when the IRA blew it up in 1984 in an attempt to assassinate the then prime minister, Margaret Thatcher, and her Cabinet who were staying in the hotel for the Conservative Party Conference; Thatcher escaped uninjured but five people were killed. Terrorism was far from Blair's mind as he paced in his suite, gathering his thoughts. Blair's advisers knew better than to disturb him before a major speech, so he realised that something really serious was up when Alastair Campbell, his director of communications, walked in just after 2 p.m. and turned on the television. 'You'd better see this,' he told the prime minister. Blair recalls seeing 'pictures of the World Trade Center like someone had punched a huge hole in it, fire and smoke belching forth'.[3] A few minutes later he saw the South Tower also being struck by an airliner and knew straight away that it was some kind of attack. Blair was leaving for the conference venue when the Twin Towers collapsed. To the prime minister's team, 'the scale of the horror and the damage was increasing all the time'. It was decided to call off the speech and have Blair make a short statement to the conference instead. The prime minister told delegates: 'I am afraid that we can only imagine the terror and carnage there and the many, many innocent people who have lost their lives. This mass terrorism is the new evil in our world today.' He declared that 'the democracies of the world, are going to have to come together to fight it together, and eradicate this evil completely from our world'. He received a standing ovation, his first and only from the Trades Union Congress.[4]

For all anybody knew, London was in imminent danger from similar terrorist attacks. But there was no question of keeping the prime minister at a safe distance. Unlike the US Secret Service who prevented President Bush from immediately returning to the capital, the Special Branch detail guarding Blair sought to get him back to Downing Street by the fastest and safest route. To this end, they caught the next train. So while President Bush was in Air Force One, thousands of feet in the air, and Vice President Cheney was tucked away underground in the White House bunker, Blair was barrelling along on the 15.49 to London Victoria, albeit with remarkably calm Special Branch officers guarding either end of his private carriage.[5]

COBRA

Blair's Chief of Staff, Jonathan Powell, was looking forward to a 'dull day', having stayed behind at 10 Downing Street when his boss went to Brighton. He was about to start a meeting on decommissioning weapons in Northern Ireland, when he was told that a plane had crashed into the Twin Towers. A few minutes later the Number 10 duty clerk interrupted the meeting to say that a second plane had struck the towers. At first, Powell assumed that the clerk had got it wrong, that 'it was just the TV running the film again'.[6] A block away, the new Foreign Secretary, Jack Straw, initially thought that 'some ghastly accident' had occurred until the second plane hit the World Trade Center, at which point 'it was obvious that this was the most monstrous terrorist act ever seen'.[7] Initially there was chaos in Downing Street: 'nobody seemed to be in charge or giving orders' was how one official remembered it. Powell and other senior staff were manning the phones. The Cabinet Secretary, Richard Wilson, wanted to activate the newly formed 'Civil Contingencies Unit', only to discover that it was on a team-building exercise in Yorkshire. Incredibly, defence and security officials from the Cabinet Office had also left by coach that morning for an exercise outside London. To top it all off, the prime minister's foreign policy adviser, David Manning, was stuck in New York, returning from a visit to his US opposite, Condoleezza Rice.[8]

Still, the British government quickly swung into crisis mode. Across Whitehall, officials rushed back from lunch. The Defence Secretary, Geoff Hoon, returned from an exhibition in London's Docklands to find that the Ministry of Defence (MoD) 'was already gearing up' to defend the country. He recalls that 'there was a strong sense that we were next' and that early discussions focused on measures to take against any hijacked airliners heading for London.[9] The Home Secretary, David Blunkett, also recollects that 'it was expected there would be a second phase of attacks on London', with a strong presumption that these would be 'targeted on the financial sector', based in Canary Wharf and the City of London, where the tallest buildings in the capital are concentrated. The Department of Transport closed London City Airport next to Canary Wharf, and two RAF fighter jets were scrambled to enforce a no-fly zone over the capital. The Metropolitan Police stepped up security at the London Stock Exchange, Canary Wharf and other key sites. Blunkett notes that while government officials debated what advice to give workers in Canary Wharf and the City, 'people took action for themselves' and abandoned their tall and vulnerable buildings. Reminiscent of a disaster movie, the financial heart of London emptied with endless lines of workers streaming home all afternoon. As Chancellor of the Exchequer, Gordon Brown's main concern 'was to get them back [to work] the following day', to limit damage to the UK economy.[10]

Powell was not concerned about the safety of Downing Street, as he considered it too difficult a target for any airliner to hit. Few shared this view in Number 10. One official recalls that 'there was a stronger fear in the building than most people later realised'.[11] It is easy to see why those in Downing Street were so nervous. The roof of Number 10 had been reinforced following an audacious attack by the IRA, when it launched three mortar shells against Downing Street in 1991. However, this would have provided little protection from an airliner smashing into the building at over 500 miles per hour; the force of such an impact would be equivalent to over 8,000 tonnes.[12] One senior security official later noted: 'Number 10 is an eighteenth-century building; if a plane hit it, the whole thing would fall down.'[13]

The prime minister was collected by police convoy at Victoria Station and, with sirens blaring and motorcycle outriders blocking off traffic, was rushed back to Downing Street. Staff recall Blair striding into Number 10, head held high with purpose. He went straight into a meeting with John Scarlett, the chairman of the Joint Intelligence Committee, and Stephen Lander, the director of MI5. Richard Dearlove, the director of MI6, was en route back from Stockholm, and so Lander was also covering his portfolio.[14] The first thing Blair wanted to know was who was responsible for the terrorist attacks on New York and Washington DC. Scarlett thought there was an 'outside chance' it was some far-right American group, along the lines of the 1995 Oklahoma bombing. But he said it was far more likely to be Osama bin Laden. Lander agreed, reminding the prime minister of al-Qaeda's attacks against the US embassies in Kenya and Tanzania in 1998, and on the USS *Cole* in 2000. Both felt it unlikely that a foreign state was involved, simply because al-Qaeda had already shown that it was perfectly able to carry out large complex terrorist attacks by itself.[15]

British security officials had begun to track Osama bin Laden in 1996, around the same time as the CIA. Bin Laden was identified as a significant terrorist financer and so MI6 was monitoring his communications. However, as one senior British security official recollects, 'We did not see him as a direct threat to the United Kingdom or the

United States.' This view changed following the 1998 attacks in Kenya and Tanzania. By then, MI5 were having weekly meetings with the Home Secretary about terrorist financing through bogus charities based in Britain, and the recruitment of British nationals for overseas terrorist operations. Ministers were frustrated at how little MI5 could do to tackle these problems: 'all these people were followed but we could find no evidence of any laws being broken'.[16] The authorised history of MI5 notes that from the summer of 2001, 'the Security Service received mounting intelligence which pointed to a major Al Qaida attack on US targets, but gave no indication of the attack plan'. MI5 concluded in early July that al-Qaeda was 'well advanced in operational planning for a number of major attacks on Western interests'. As the history goes on to note, the intelligence received by MI5 'did not point either to a major attack in the United States, or to an operation based on hijacked aircraft'.[17]

At 5.30 p.m., the prime minister chaired his first formal meeting of COBRA. This was the group of senior Cabinet ministers and officials convened in times of national crisis, so named because they met in Cabinet Office Briefing Room A. Even well-informed observers imagined COBRA to be a secure bunker that 'lay deep under the Cabinet Office'.[18] In fact, as one senior security official put it, COBRA was more of 'a basement rather than a bunker', and a pretty dingy one at that.[19] David Blunkett remembers it as a 'horrible unpleasant place with no air conditioning'.[20] COBRA comprises a central room, with a large conference table at which sit ministers and the heads of MI6, MI5, the Metropolitan Police and the armed forces, and around which are a series of connected cubicles with support staff from the foreign, intelligence, security and police services and the military. Ministers were then, and still are, regularly trained in how to use the COBRA facility. Blair walked down the steps into a packed room; one official remembers everyone being 'crammed in … without enough seats'.[21] The walls were covered with maps of Sierra Leone, as COBRA was then being used to coordinate ongoing British civil–military operations in that country. Blunkett describes Blair as 'always good in a crisis' and so he was that afternoon, quickly taking charge. Ministers and senior officials in turn gave succinct briefs to the prime minister, updating him on measures taken to secure Britain. There was some discussion on the rules of engagement for the RAF fighters enforcing the no-fly zone over London. It was agreed that any shoot-down order would be given by the Chief of the Defence Staff, and only after prime ministerial approval.[22] It would be a fortnight before precise criteria and protocols for shooting down civilian aircraft in such scenarios were developed.[23] Discussion finally turned to the grim business of estimating how many Britons had died in New York. While some public reports were suggesting that the British death toll was as high as 2,000, officials in Downing Street estimated it to be closer to two hundred; eventually it was confirmed that sixty-seven British citizens had been killed.[24]

The COBRA meeting ended promptly so the prime minister could make a press statement in time for the six o'clock news. Reading from notes he had drafted on the train up from Brighton, and echoing what he had said to the Trades Union Congress, Blair told the British people: 'This is not a battle between the United States of America and terrorism, but between the free and democratic world and terrorism. We, therefore, here in Britain stand shoulder to shoulder with our American friends in this hour of tragedy, and we, like them, will not rest until this evil is driven from our world.'[25] Blair later reflected in his memoir that 'shoulder to shoulder came to be something of a defining phrase'. He understood that he was making a 'big commitment that would come to be measured not in words but in actions'.[26] Straw echoes this in his own memoir: Blair 'meant "shoulder to shoulder" when he said it, not just as a metaphor, but literally'.[27] The then Home Secretary, David Blunkett, later reflected that standing 'shoulder to shoulder with the Americans was not questioned post 9/11', adding that 'the whole emotion of it demanded that people go along'.[28]

President Bush made his broadcast to the nation on the evening of 11 September. It was 2 a.m. on 12 September in Britain, and Campbell thought Bush 'looked a bit shaky', perhaps understandably so.[29] In a stilted address, he told the American people: 'The search is underway for those who are behind these evil acts. I've directed the full resources for our intelligence and law enforcement communities to find those responsible and bring them to justice.' Crucially, the president added: 'We will make no distinction between the terrorists who committed these acts and those who harbour them.'[30] This spelt trouble for the Taliban.

THE GLOBAL WAR ON TERROR

Britons woke up on 12 September 2001 to a changed world. The newspapers made for a harrowing read. The New York correspondent for *The Times* described the scene, almost too awful for words:

> At first, we thought it was burning debris falling from the upper floors of the 110-storey World Trade Center. Then we noticed that the debris had arms and legs. Soon, the horrible truth became clear: the bankers and lawyers who inhabited the most-prestigious floors of the WTC had decided to take the quarter-of-a-mile plunge to the street below rather than be incinerated by aircraft wreckage.

The entire front and back pages of *The Times* were taken up with the image of Manhattan island, enveloped in gigantic clouds of dust and debris, in the immediate aftermath of the collapse of the towers. The headline simply noted: '10.02 AM, SEPTEMBER 11 2001'. The *Daily Mail* front page followed suit, showing a similar image of Manhattan devastated under the headline 'APOCALYPSE. NEW YORK. SEPTEMBER 11, 2001'. The *Daily Telegraph* front page showed the massive fireball that erupted the moment United Airlines 175 ploughed into the second tower of the World Trade Center; the headline boldly declared 'WAR ON AMERICA'. The *Guardian* front page showed the same dramatic image under the headline 'A DECLARATION OF WAR'. Most of the newspapers in Britain and around the world led on this theme of the terrorist attacks constituting an act of war.[31] The British and American newspapers identified Osama bin Laden as the most likely culprit. Under the banner 'TERROR FOR ALL', the *Times* editorial noted, 'Very few events, however dramatic, change the political landscape. This will.'[32]

This much Blair knew already. He received an update on British security at an early-morning meeting of COBRA. It was decided to keep City Airport closed and maintain the air exclusion zone over London. It would be another day before these security measures were relaxed. The Metropolitan Police Commissioner reported that a thousand extra officers were guarding key sites around London. Blair spent the rest of the morning in the Cabinet Office receiving briefings on al-Qaeda and the Taliban given by intelligence officials and experts from the Foreign Office and MoD.[33] From the beginning, Blair 'was pretty clear that we would end up going for the Taliban'.[34] By the end of the meeting, which was scheduled to last forty-five minutes but had stretched on for two hours, he was sure of it.

After midday, the White House contacted Downing Street to set up a call between the president and the prime minister. Blair was relieved finally to be speaking with Bush; British officials were equally pleased that Blair was the first foreign leader Bush had called. One official later recounted how 'Blair had woven everything that he had picked up that morning into his advice to Bush'.[35] It is clear that Blair sought to exert a moderating influence on the president, and to help the United States harvest the immense goodwill from around the world, as foreign leaders and their peoples expressed heartfelt solidarity with the United States. Indeed, reporting on the 9/11 attacks, *Le Monde* had declared '*nous sommes touts Americains*'. The two leaders agreed to mobilise support in the United Nations and NATO. Both organisations had already issued supportive statements; Bush told Blair that these would provide 'useful cover for the work that we have to do'.[36] Later that same day, NATO invoked, for the first time in its history, Article 5 of the Washington Treaty, whereby an attack against one member state is considered an attack against the whole alliance.[37] A senior British defence official recalls that 'the Americans were taken by surprise by NATO's Article 5 declaration' – and not pleasantly so: 'the Americans didn't want to have endless NATO meetings banging on' and slowing things down.[38] In the days that followed, America received offers of help from around the world. Almost all were politely rebuffed, and many were just ignored. The Under Secretary of State for Political Affairs, Marc Grossman, would later admit to the *Washington Times* that the United States 'blew off' its allies.[39] One senior NATO official noted that 'an immense reservoir of solidarity was wasted'.[40]

Across the Atlantic, things were moving quickly. The 12th of September began for the president with a 6 a.m. meeting at the Pentagon. Bush put the assembled military chiefs and senior defence officials on notice: 'we believe that we are at war and we'll fight it as such. I want us to have the mindset of fighting and winning a war.' The president wanted military options and not just symbolic ones. 'I don't want a photo-op war.' Referring to the ineffectual responses that followed the 1998 terrorist attacks, Bush declared, 'we won't just pound sand'. So war it was to be, but what kind of war and waged against whom? At a meeting of the war cabinet later that day, the National Security Advisor, Condoleezza Rice, presented 'the concept', which was for 'a broad war, not a single event'.[41] Shortly thereafter Bush began to use the terms 'war on terrorism' and 'war on terror', which were adopted by his administration as the official terms for the war; usage of the former gradually gave way to the latter, with the addition of 'global', thus making 'the global war on terror'.

European experts on strategy found much to criticise in the concept of a global war on terror. The British doyen of strategic studies Sir Michael Howard took issue with the very idea of declaring war, which he argued simply conferred legitimacy on al-Qaeda and served the ends of those that sought to radicalise young Muslims to attack the West. Howard suggested that instead a criminal justice approach ought to be taken, and that al-Qaeda leaders should be apprehended and brought to trial.[42] However sensible this suggestion, it ignored the raw politics of the situation. It would have been extraordinary for the United States not to go to war after suffering such a catastrophic attack. As Bush noted in his diary on 11 September: 'The Pearl Harbor of the 21st Century took place today.'[43] Just as the Japanese ill-advisedly awoke a sleeping giant in December 1941, so did al-Qaeda sixty years later. Failing to retaliate was not a realistic political option. For Hew Strachan, then Chichele Professor of the History of War at Oxford University, the global war on terror was 'astrategic', in that 'Its declared objective was to eliminate a means of fighting, not to achieve a political goal'.[44] As it happens, Donald Rumsfeld recognised that 'saying we were in a war on terrorism was like saying we were in a war against bombers or we were waging war on tanks, as opposed to a war against the people using those weapons'. However, his alternative – 'the struggle against violent extremists' – lacked the mobilising force of the president's war rhetoric.[45] Similarly, the Under Secretary of Defense for Policy, Douglas Feith, recalls that senior US officials 'fully understood ... that you can't declare war on a tactic' but they 'struggled with how to describe the war'.[46] In particular, the administration was 'very sensitive to avoiding use of the "Islamist" label for fear that people would hear "Muslim"'. Strachan was also critical of the lack of 'geographical focus' in the global war on terror: 'the notion that it embraced the whole world was not particularly helpful. It created a field of operations too big even for the world's only superpower.'[47] Yet what Strachan saw as a flaw, US officials considered a major advantage. Framing it as a global war on terror gave the Bush administration flexibility while it figured out who to go after. Al-Qaeda and the Taliban were definitely in the firing line, but what about the myriad other terrorism organisations, especially violent Islamist extremist groups? And how about other state sponsors of terrorism like Iran, Iraq and North Korea? As Feith later noted in his memoir, the term global war on terror 'allowed the Administration to defer naming the enemy while it considered these perplexing questions'.[48]

From the beginning, Iraq was also in America's gunsights. At the war cabinet on 12 September, Bush wanted to know about possible Iraqi involvement in the terrorist attacks. The CIA director, George Tenet, said that his agency was still looking into this. The chairman of the Joint Chiefs of Staff, General Hugh Shelton, told the president that the problem with Afghanistan was that there were few targets for US bombers to hit; in a country already torn apart by war, there was little infrastructure left to destroy. Here Rumsfeld chimed in, with the observation that Iraq presented a far better target for US air power. Whereas Afghanistan had descended back to medieval times under Taliban rule, Iraq was still a modern state and, as such, vulnerable to air attack. For some in the room, most notably Vice President Dick Cheney and Deputy Defense Secretary Paul Wolfowitz, there were deeper ideological reasons for going after Iraq. For them and other 'neoconservatives' scattered in senior positions across the Bush administration, Iraq was 'unfinished business' from the 1991 Gulf War, and effecting regime change there was believed to offer the opportunity to transform Middle Eastern politics and America's fortunes in the region for the better.[49] This prevalent thinking may explain why nobody in the meeting questioned the absurdity of attacking Iraq simply because it was militarily convenient to do so. Instead, arguments were piled on to justify this option. Rumsfeld noted that in Iraq 'we can inflict the kind of costly damage that would cause terrorist-supporting regimes around the world to rethink their policies'. Moreover, the US military already had pre-packaged strike options for Iraq. The chairman of the Joint Chiefs of Staff also assured the president that US forces would be able to take on Afghanistan and Iraq at the same time. The meeting ended with the president instructing senior officials to move things along to 'get something of consequence done soon'. Then, turning to the Secretary of State, Colin Powell, he said, 'It may be time to give the Taliban a heads up.'[50]

The British were still largely in the dark when it came to what was going on inside the Bush administration. The chiefs of MI5, MI6 and GCHQ (the British signals intelligence agency) flew to Washington DC on 13 September, on a plane that had been specially cleared for entry to America's otherwise closed skies. As one official later noted, 'The Americans were too busy to talk to us (on the phone), so we had to get in to see them.'[51] One senior British official recalls that the discussions at the CIA headquarters in Langley 'on who was responsible went well into the night', but at the same time 'there was no doubt it was al-Qaeda'.[52] The British spy chiefs flew back to London the following day, taking with them David Manning as well as former Prime Minister John Major and an assortment of other British politicians who had been stranded in the United States. An official with the party recalls the view of devastation, flying over New York City: 'It looked like there was a missing tooth.'[53]

PARLIAMENTARY SUPPORT

The British were far from pleased with the idea of widening the war to encompass Iraq. In a call to the prime minister on 14 September, Bush indicated that this war would be like a pebble dropped in a pond. 'We focus on the first circle' – that was Afghanistan – 'and then expand to the next circle' – that was Iraq.[54] Blair could foresee a roller-coaster ride ahead. Afterwards, he told his advisers, 'my god, fasten your seatbelts'. Campbell later noted Blair's view that 'we had to persuade Bush that we had to go for OBL [Osama bin Laden] and the Taliban but if he went for Iraq the Russians and the French would peel off'.[55]

Earlier that morning, Parliament had been recalled to debate the terrorist attacks and how Britain should respond. Labour whips warned the prime minister that the Parliamentary Labour Party 'may be a bit dodgy' on the notion of going to war. The party had always had a pacifist streak but all the same Blair found this incredulous. 'Are they mad?' he responded. 'Do we just let these people get away with killing thousands of people?'[56] The prime minister need not have worried. MPs were as shocked and outraged as the government by the attacks on New York and Washington. Watching in horror from her constituency in Birmingham as the terrible events unfolded on 11 September, the Labour MP Gisela Stuart wondered, 'Is it going to stop?' Stuart later recognised that the 9/11 attacks befuddled the left of the Labour Party, which was antipathetic towards the United States. Complicating matters, many Labour MPs represented largely Muslim constituencies. But none of this changed the overwhelming sense of abhorrence at what al-Qaeda had done.[57] On the Conservative bench, which was more pro-American by inclination, there was even less equivocation. One senior Tory MP recalls, 'I don't remember a great discussion in the Conservative Parliamentary Party on the response to Afghanistan.'[58] It was obvious to the Tories that the United States would need to respond with military force, and equally obvious that the United Kingdom should join in that endeavour.

The mood in the House of Commons was 'serious and sombre' for the debate.[59] In his address to the house, Blair reiterated his view that these were not only attacks on America. 'By their acts, these terrorists and those behind them have made themselves enemies of the entire civilized world.'[60] Predictably, the Conservative opposition backed the government in its strong support to the United States. The new Tory leader, Iain Duncan Smith, agreed that al-Qaeda's attacks constituted 'an act of war', and declared: 'The message needs to go out loud and clear: those Governments who harbour terrorists will have to learn to live with the consequences of their actions.'[61] Only two members of the House of Commons spoke out against the government. Donald Anderson, the long-standing Labour MP from Swansea, warned of the lessons from history when it came to Afghanistan: 'We know about the history of the United Kingdom's 19th century involvement and the bleeding wound of the Soviet Union in the 1980s ... Bin Laden and his like will not be crushed by missiles or invasion.'[62] Dennis Skinner, another long-standing Labour MP from the socialist wing of the party, and former chairman of the Parliamentary Labour Party, angered the House with his intervention. 'Does the Prime Minister agree that there is a world of difference between standing shoulder to shoulder with the American people in their fight for justice and hanging on to the coat tails of an American

President whose first act when firefighters stood ten feet tall in the rubble of the World Trade Center was to scurry off to his bunker?' He was shouted down to cries of 'shame' from MPs on both sides of the House.[63] The will of the House was clear: Blair had the support of Parliament for military action against al-Qaeda and the Taliban.

That same day, the US Congress passed a joint resolution authorising the use of military force against 'nations, organizations, or persons' responsible for the 9/11 attacks. Crucially, in this resolution, Congress also recognised the president's right to use force to prevent 'any future acts of terrorism' against the United States, and in so doing provided the authority for the administration to prosecute its wider war on terrorism. Four days later, Joint Resolution 23 was signed into law by President Bush.[64]

Blair saw his main role as keeping the Americans focused on Afghanistan, and rallying international support for the coming war against al-Qaeda and the Taliban. In the end, the Bush administration did decide to concentrate military action on Afghanistan and put Iraq aside for later, but Blair had little influence over this decision, which was taken by the president when the war cabinet met at Camp David the weekend after 9/11.[65] The meeting began with the CIA and the military presenting their respective war plans. The CIA's plan involved the agency sending paramilitary teams into Afghanistan to provide assistance to the Northern Alliance, and to 'accelerate contacts' with southern Pashtun leaders, 'including six senior Taliban leaders' in order to split the Taliban.[66] General Shelton briefed three military options for Afghanistan – none were particularly promising. The first option involved cruise missile strikes. The US Navy had two hundred sea-launched cruise missiles 'in the shoot basket' for Afghanistan. However, Bush had already said that he wanted more than cruise missile attacks. The second option was for a more extensive bombing campaign lasting up to ten days, using the US Air Force's 'Global Power' capability based on twenty B-2 stealth bombers.[67] With its distinctive bat-shape frame, the B-2 was the most expensive warplane ever built, costing the American taxpayer $2 billion apiece. Practically invisible to radar, each B-2 can carry up to eighty 500-pound GPS-guided bombs. But again, the problem was that there were few targets to bomb in Afghanistan. The third option was for bombing and 'boots on the ground', with the deployment of special forces and possibly regular infantry and marines. General Shelton later noted that 'nothing was decided [in the meeting], although it was obvious that nobody would be backing options one or two'.[68] The war cabinet discussed the challenges of a ground war in Afghanistan, leading Rumsfeld and Wolfowitz to once again argue for the virtue of attacking Iraq at the same time. Iraq was more vulnerable to attack, they said, and victory in Iraq would maintain momentum in the war on terror should the US military get bogged down in Afghanistan. Colin Powell countered by warning that the United States risked losing international goodwill and support if it went to war against Iraq in the absence of clear evidence of Iraqi involvement in the 9/11 attacks. The president did not seem too bothered by this, having earlier said that 'At some point, we may be the only ones left [in the war on terror]. That's okay with me. We are America.' All the same, he was not convinced of the case for attacking Iraq, especially when the military should be focusing on Afghanistan.[69]

WHIRLWIND DIPLOMACY

Downing Street spent the weekend worrying about what the Americans were up to. The Foreign Office had got wind that Rumsfeld and Wolfowitz were pushing the case for war in Iraq. Campbell noted in his diary: 'There was real unease among our side now, that the Americans would do something to fracture the coalition that was being built up.'[70] It would be some days yet before the British were brought up to speed on the evolving US strategy. Meanwhile, Blair threw himself into whirlwind diplomacy to build support for the war. In the days that followed he met in turn with the Italian prime minister, the French president and the German chancellor. He also spoke with the Russian, Pakistani and Iranian presidents, and the Chinese premier. To one reporter, travelling with the prime minister on his 'non-stop, sleep-defying, time-zone hopping diplomacy', Blair had 'the wide-eyed, somewhat startled look of someone running on adrenaline'.[71]

On Thursday, 20 September, Blair flew directly from France to the United States. The prime minister had been invited to attend the president's address to Congress the following day. Some of Blair's advisers were worried it would 'play into the whole poodle thing' and 'that the whole thing would become an orgy of US patriotism, with [Blair] in a kind of nod-along role'.[72] But it was a great privilege to be invited, and gave Blair the opportunity for a face-to-face meeting with Bush. By this stage, British intelligence and military chiefs had been briefed by their opposite numbers on US planning and so were able, in turn, to brief the prime minister.

Blair's party landed in New York to attend a memorial service for British citizens killed on 9/11. The sombre mood was matched by miserable weather, strong winds blowing great sheets of rain in from the Atlantic. Inside St Thomas's Church, 'it is clammy and packed and unutterably sad'.[73] Before giving a reading at the service, Blair told the congregation that 'Amid the enormity of what has happened to America, nobody will forget that this was the worst terrorist attack on British citizens in my country's history'. The British ambassador, Christopher Meyer, read out a message from the Queen that ended with the poignant line 'Grief is the price we pay for love'. Blair was visibly moved as he passed through the crowd of grieving relatives alongside former President Bill Clinton. Inevitably, the prime minister spent longer at the church than scheduled. This, combined with awful traffic jams in New York and heightened airport security, meant that he was very late flying into Washington DC for his meeting with Bush. Blair's party arrived just in time for pre-dinner drinks. Over the meal, Bush made his view clear: Afghanistan was run by 'a bunch of nuts' that had to be replaced.[74]

Blair was shown many honours on the visit. He rode to Capitol Hill in the president's armoured limousine. In the chamber, he was seated next to the first lady in the 'Heroes Gallery', and Bush singled out Britain and Blair for thanks in his address. 'America has no truer friend than Great Britain. Once again, we are joined together in a great cause. I'm so honored the British prime minister has crossed an ocean to show his unity with America.' Going off script, the president added, 'Thank you for coming, friend.' In this speech, Bush formally issued the ultimatum to the Taliban regime. The US government demanded that the Taliban hand over the leaders of al-Qaeda, released foreign nationals in Taliban detention, permanently close all the terrorist training camps, and give the United States access to confirm the closure of these facilities. 'These demands are not open to nego- tiation or discussion. The Taliban must act and act immediately. They will hand over the terrorists or they will share in their fate.'[75] Blair was understandably impressed by the occasion, later reflecting, 'As the President spoke, you could feel the representatives come together around love of the nation.'[76] Campbell took a more jaundiced view. 'It was all a bit Politburo, standing ovations constantly interrupting the speech, rapturous applause for good lines, off the radar if they were really good.'[77] For the British ambassador 'two things jumped out of the speech: the Manichean division of the world into states that were with America and states that were against' and 'the challenge not simply to terrorists but to regimes that harboured them'.[78] The message to the Taliban could hardly have been more clear.

WHO WILL FACE THEIR ANGER?

Osama bin Laden was desperate to watch American television on 11 September. Early that morning he headed east out of Kabul into the hills of neighbouring Logar province, having travelled up from his camp in Kandahar the day before. In his convoy was a mobile media centre – a minibus kitted out with a personal computer, a video camera and video player, and a satellite receiver. Bin Laden told his 'personal media technician', Ali al-Bahlul, that 'it is very important to see the news today'. We know what happened because al-Bahlul was later captured and sent to the US detention facility at Guantánamo Bay. Al-Bahlul was unable to tune into the US television networks: mountainous terrain prevented him from obtaining a satellite signal. A shortwave radio was dug up instead and bin Laden heard the news from the BBC Arabic Service: normal broadcasting had been interrupted to report a major plane crash in New York. It was 8.48 a.m. in New York and 5.18 p.m. in Afghanistan. Thirty minutes later came news of the second plane hitting the World Trade Center. Bin Laden's entourage was ecstatic; some wept with joy. Bin Laden hushed his followers, telling them to listen for news of further strikes. The attack on the Pentagon was reported by the BBC one hour later. Then bin Laden held up four fingers to indicate that there was one more to come, but there was no news of the final plane.[79]

Many Taliban rank and file were also jubilant, feeling the attacks were just payback for the US missile strikes on Afghanistan in 1998 and for the harsh economic sanctions imposed on their country for refusing to hand over bin Laden. Some Taliban leaders were not so delighted, however, realising the danger they now faced. The Afghan ambassador to Pakistan, Mullah Zaeef, watched the television with tears in his eyes, but he was not weeping with joy. Rather, he was horrified at the unfolding scene in New York, and more than that, he was deeply worried about the likely repercussions. Turning to those with him who were celebrating, Zaeef asked, 'who do you think the United States and the world will blame for what has just happened? Who will face their anger?'[80] The Taliban foreign minister in Kabul, Mullah Mutawakil, contacted Mullah Omar in Kandahar to ask what he should do. He was told to 'Condemn this action as harshly and strongly as you can'. Mullah Zaeef was told to do likewise, and he released a press statement from the Taliban government declaring: 'All those responsible must be brought to justice.'[81]

This did not mean that the Taliban were about to give up bin Laden. On 16 September, President Musharraf sent the chief of the ISI, Lieutenant General Mahmud Ahmed, to Kandahar to try and persuade Omar to hand over bin Laden. Accounts differ on how far and hard Ahmed pressed Omar, if indeed at all. According to Pakistan's former Foreign Secretary, Riaz Mohammad Khan, 'those from the ISI, were often impressed and overawed by the certitude of conviction and faith the Taliban demonstrated'.[82] Either way, Ahmed came back empty-handed and would pay the cost for his mission: three weeks later he was replaced as chief of the ISI by President Musharraf, who was looking to stay on the good side of the Bush administration.

The CIA also tried to exert pressure through direct meetings with senior Taliban figures, but without success. The CIA station chief in Islamabad, Robert Grenier, twice met Mullah Akhtar Mohammad Osmani, the overall commander of Taliban forces in southern Afghanistan and probably number two in the movement. The first meeting took place on 15 September, in a 'quiet hotel' in Quetta. Grenier outlined a number of options whereby the Taliban could cooperate in bringing bin Laden to American justice and avoid a war. None were agreeable to Osmani and after five exhausting hours of 'mostly circular conversation', the meeting ended inconclusively. A second meeting on 2 October, also in Quetta, was facilitated by the ISI. When Grenier again pushed Osmani, the Afghan responded that the Taliban were in a jam. 'Bin Laden has become synonymous in Afghanistan with Islam. The Taliban can't hand him over publicly any more than they can publicly reject Islam.' He further complained that public threats from the United States had made matters worse by 'arousing the people' and hardening public support for bin Laden. An exasperated Grenier even tried to encourage Osmani to stage a coup to overthrow Mullah Omar and save the Taliban Emirate; that was a forlorn hope.[83] A CIA team also met with Mullah Abdul Haq Wasiq, deputy director of intelligence of the Taliban, outside Kabul; on proving uncooperative, Wasiq was simply grabbed by the CIA team and taken away for interrogation.[84]

Many Taliban leaders also travelled to Kandahar to implore Mullah Omar to expel bin Laden. One recalled: 'We pleaded with him for hours but it was as if he covered his ears.'[85] Under pressure, Omar agreed to convene a conference of *ulema*, respected religious clerics, on 19 September to deliberate on the matter. About a thousand clerics attended from around Afghanistan and Pakistan. It took the *ulema* just one day to determine that bin Laden should be asked to leave Afghanistan 'whenever possible', in order 'to avoid the current tumult and also to allay future suspicions'. However, Omar ignored this decision. He also refused to give in to pressure from his civil government in Kabul, accusing his ministers of only caring about their posts and declaring: 'I am not prepared to give up my brother-in-religion to non-Muslims.' Instead, Omar denied that bin Laden was responsible for the attacks on America. In an interview with an Egyptian journalist on 14 October 2001, he claimed: 'Neither Osama nor the Taliban has the resources to implement the recent incidents against the United States.' Omar went on to suggest that 'the perpetrators were from inside the United States itself', and hinted at a Jewish plot: 'the investigation has not taken into account the absence on the same day of the incident of 4,000 Jews who worked in the World Trade Center'.[86]

It is entirely possible that Omar actually believed all of this. According to Mullah Zaeef, Omar had summoned bin Laden to explain himself, and bin Laden swore that he had nothing to do with the 9/11 attacks. With the US government refusing to provide proof, Omar was inclined to believe him. This story is credible given that Omar was largely cut off from the outside world. He had become a highly reclusive leader who rarely left his compound; hence a 'special office' had been established so he could govern the country from Kandahar. Yet Omar's special office was so badly networked that it did not even have the bandwidth to send audio files via the Internet.[87] Following the US missile strikes in 1998, Omar's compound was reinforced to withstand air attack, creating something of a 'bunker mentality'. Omar became increasingly paranoid and by 1999 'was convinced of an international Judeo-Christian conspiracy against his "Emirate"'. This was reflected in the tone of Taliban communications following the 9/11 attacks. The initial Taliban communiqués condemning what had happened were soon followed by more defensive statements. On 19 September, Omar accused the United States of 'trying to finish us on various pretexts. One of their pretexts is Osama bin Laden's presence in Afghanistan.' A week later he declared: 'What they want in Afghanistan is that they want to end [the] Islamic system in Afghanistan, create chaos and install a pro-American government here.'[88]

Actually the US government had a good appreciation of the relationship between the wider Taliban movement and al-Qaeda. On 23 September, Cheney, Rumsfeld, Powell, Tenet and Shelton met to discuss a top-secret assessment from the CIA station chief in Islamabad, which correctly identified the growing tensions within the Taliban between Afghan nationalists and the hardline Islamists gravitating around Mullah Omar. Omar's unstinting support for bin Laden, in particular, had become a major source of disagreement. The key recommendation was for the United States to use the threat of military action to create fissures within the Taliban. This was taken to Bush when the whole war cabinet convened the following morning. Speaking for the group, Cheney said that the first priority was to go after al-Qaeda's facilities in Afghanistan. With regard to the Taliban, he told the president, 'we're going to focus on Omar, to encourage the current Taliban leadership to replace him with someone more amenable to what we need done with respect to al-Qaeda'. There was still the considerable problem of how to do this in practice. Conscious of Bush's determination to do more than 'pound sand', Rumsfeld worried that 'there is not a lot of al-Qaeda to hit'. Inevitably, and early on in the campaign, US air power would have to be unleashed on the Taliban. Aside from targeting the hardline Brigade 055, it was not clear how an air campaign could be designed to encourage the Taliban to replace Mullah Omar.[89]

While in private the war cabinet debated how to exploit differences between moderate and hardline elements within the Taliban leadership, in public, the message was uncompromising. Two days after Bush's address to Congress, Rice gave a television interview in which she suggested the Taliban's days were numbered regardless of whether or not they complied with US demands. 'It's a terrible and repressive regime,' Rice noted. 'The Afghan people would be far better off without it. We will see what means are at our disposal to do that.'[90]

WAR PLANNING

The military on both sides of the Atlantic were struggling to come up with good options for Afghanistan. Not only was there little to bomb but there was no clear route in for Western armies. Afghanistan shares borders on the west with Iran, south and east with Pakistan, and north with Turkmenistan, Uzbekistan and Tajikistan. Not withstanding tense relations between Iran and the Taliban regime, relations with 'the Great Satan' were far worse: it was unimaginable that Iran would permit any American soldiers on its soil. Under immense pressure from senior US officials, Pakistan agreed to back America in the war against the Taliban. President Musharraf told the US ambassador on 12 September that 'we'll support you unstintingly'. Musharraf gave the US military use of several airfields for helicopter flights to move special forces and rescue any downed US pilots. However, he refused to allow the United States to launch attacks from Pakistani soil.[91] This left the three 'stans', each presenting a combination of formidable political, geographical and logistical challenges.

In his first meeting with the prime minister on 17 September to discuss the prospective military campaign against al-Qaeda and the Taliban, the British Chief of the Defence Staff, Admiral Michael Boyce, was so downbeat that Alastair Campbell wondered if 'he wasn't something of a fellow depressive'. He told Blair that the campaign would require an invasion force some 250,000 strong, and Britain would need to deploy two aircraft carriers and the Royal Marines. Number 10 officials were somewhat bemused: wasn't Afghanistan a landlocked country? Two days later, Admiral Boyce returned 'looking grave', to report to the prime minister on what he had picked up through unofficial channels about evolving US military plans, which centred on a massive bombing campaign. Boyce was 'very sceptical' that this would succeed. A week on, little had improved. Of a meeting between Blair and British defence and intelligence chiefs on 27 September, Campbell noted in his diary: 'It was pretty clear that the US remain undecided, could not find that many good targets, and didn't have the bases in the region.'[92]

Over this period, British intelligence was busy reactivating old contacts in Afghanistan. During the Soviet War, MI6 had developed especially strong links with Ahmad Shah Massoud's group in the north. However, following the withdrawal of Soviet forces in 1988 and the collapse of the Soviet-backed regime in 1992, the British Foreign Office lost interest in Afghanistan. As one former senior official noted, Britain 'aggressively disinvested' in the country; 'our intelligence effort had been in support of Massoud and the message was this stuff is ending'. But 'a small cell of British officials' remained involved in Afghanistan to track the problem of massive drug convoys that formed up and streamed across into Iran, and thereon into Turkey. British intelligence monitored the pitched battles on the border as the Iranians tried, unsuccessfully, to stop the drug convoys: 'the Iranians often came off second best' was how one senior official put it. Around 90 per cent of the heroin that ended up on Britain's streets came via this route. Accordingly, 'when 9/11 happened, there was a core of thirty people in the [British] intelligence service working on Afghanistan'. This, in turn, provided a 'caucus of people who could be deployed immediately, knew many of the [Northern Alliance] commanders, and spoke the language'.[93]

Writing in the *New York Times* in late September, Rumsfeld declared America would engage in 'a new kind of war' in its global fight against terror, a war in which military force would be 'one of many tools' to stop terrorism. '"Battles" will be fought by customs officers stopping suspicious persons at our borders and diplomats securing cooperation against money laundering.'[94] However, the war against al-Qaeda and the Taliban in Afghanistan would mostly involve military force. But here, too, Rumsfeld had a new way of war in mind. Indeed, on becoming Secretary of Defense in January 2001, Rumsfeld championed a broad effort to transform America's military, to better harness the promise of information technology so as to create more agile, networked military forces that required less logistical support. He now sought to put this vision of 'military transformation' into practice. He rejected as outdated the principle that the United States had to mass its land, air and naval forces in order to be able to numerically overwhelm opponents, as it had done against Iraq in the 1991 Gulf War. (This was called the 'Powell Doctrine', so named after Colin Powell, who had been chairman of the US Joint Chiefs of Staff in the early 1990s.) New strike technologies offered the possibility of creating devastating effects with precision-guided bombs and missiles, and thereby enabling a smaller ground force to defeat the enemy.[95] The Soviet experience in Afghanistan, where a large army was sucked in and mauled by Afghan irregulars, reinforced the logic of minimising the US footprint in Afghanistan.

Afghanistan fell within the theatre of operations of the US military's Central Command (CENTCOM), which stretched from the Arabian Peninsula to central Asia. While General Tommy Franks, as commander of Central Command, was formally in charge of producing the war plan, there was something of a tussle between the Department of Defense and the CIA over control of the war. The CIA knew far more about Afghanistan than the US military, and it was not shy in telling the president what needed to be done. However, this was more about institutional politics than differences over how the war ought to be fought; Rumsfeld's vision of precision air power and light US ground forces neatly fitted the CIA's concept for victory in Afghanistan. In the war cabinet meeting on 13 September, Tenet proposed what ended up being the US war plan: America would pour resources into supporting factions opposed to the Taliban, principally the Northern Alliance, and this effort would be led by CIA paramilitary teams inserted into Afghanistan to link up with the Northern Alliance and crucially direct US air power against Taliban front lines. Accompanying Tenet to the meeting was the head of the CIA's Counterterrorism Center, Cofer Black, who claimed that al-Qaeda and the Taliban would be defeated in a matter of weeks. He told the president: 'When we are through with them, they will have flies walking on their eyeballs.'[96]

Once US policymakers had settled on an Afghan-led strategy for the war, debate opened on which Afghans to back. The Department of Defense became strong advocates of supporting the 20,000-strong Northern Alliance just as the CIA began to change their tune, and raise questions about this strategy. Based in the Panjshir Valley in north-eastern Afghanistan, and a couple of other enclaves in the north of the country, the Alliance was a loose coalition of over twenty Tajik, Uzbek and Hazara tribal groups opposed to the mostly Pashtun Taliban. These groups were of varying military competence and reliability; moreover, many had fought each other during the civil war of the 1990s. Taliban forces were twice the size and far better equipped, with many more tanks, artillery and armoured vehicles. And fighting alongside the Taliban were thousands of fanatical Arab jihadis, most directly under the command of Osama bin Laden. To make matters worse, the Northern Alliance was in disarray following the assassination of its charismatic leader Ahmad Shah Massoud by two al-Qaeda operatives on 9 September 2001; his successor, the dour Marshal Mohammed Fahim, instilled the CIA with little confidence.

Some in the CIA were also concerned that the 'northern strategy' risked backfiring, in that it could unify Pashtuns behind the Taliban in resistance to the Tajik and Uzbek northerners. Accordingly, it was argued that the United States should instead focus on fomenting opposition to the Taliban among Pahstun tribes in the south and east. It so happened that the CIA had developed stronger contacts with Pashtun mujahedin in the south and east during the Soviet War than with Tajik and Uzbek fighters in the north. This option was also promoted by the Pakistanis, who were alarmed at the prospect of what they saw as the pro-Indian Northern Alliance sweeping into power at American hands.[97] In the end, the US strategy combined both elements: CIA paramilitary teams and US special forces would go in to provide direct assistance to the Northern Alliance, and the CIA would in addition seek out and support Pashtun opponents of the Taliban. One such anti-Taliban Pashtun leader, Hamid Karzai, would end up president of Afghanistan.

The United States did not need its NATO allies to fight this war. More to the point, it did not want its allies involved. The Bush administration sought to avoid a repetition of the 1999 Kosovo War, when the prosecution of NATO's air strikes against Serbia was severely hampered by the political and legal concerns of alliance partners in Europe; many of the bombing targets required prior vetting by the governments of all nineteen NATO members.[98] This largely accounts for the ready dismissal of NATO assistance by the United States. Britain was an exception. By sending military forces, Britain would deliver on the symbolism of standing alongside the United States – something that was as important to the Americans as to the British. Britain had world-class special forces: the much famed Special Air Service (SAS), and the less well-known but no less proficient Special Boat Service (SBS). Special forces were going to play a central role in this war. And while the CIA had good contacts with Pashtun groups in southern Afghanistan, British intelligence had far better links with the Northern Alliance.[99] So the British were welcome, but on the expectation that they would simply follow the US war plan.

Unfortunately, US planning was a mess. Hence, Boyce had good reason to be downbeat. On 20 September, Franks presented his operational concept (in effect, the outline plan) to Rumsfeld and the Joint Chiefs of Staff in Washington. The meeting did not go well. The service chiefs each made critical suggestions, basically arguing from their own service perspective: the army chief argued for more ground troops, the air force chief for more bombers, and so forth. As the chiefs poked holes in the outline plan, suggesting it was bound to fail, Franks snapped. 'Bullshit! It's my plan. I'm responsible for its execution,' he declared, after which the Defense Secretary drew the discussion to an abrupt close.[100] Franks had originally told Rumsfeld that CENTCOM would need two months to produce a fully worked-up war plan. In the end, his command had eight days (from 20 to 28 September) to turn the approved war concept into an operational plan.[101] Adding to the confusion, the CIA was preparing to conduct its own war on al-Qaeda and the Taliban following presidential approval on 14 September; just four days later, Tenet told Bush: 'we are launching our plan'.[102] Amazingly, Franks and the chief of CIA Special Operations did not meet until 3 October to coordinate the CIA's and the military's respective war planning.[103]

Even more troublesome was the failure to clarify the war goals. CENTCOM and the CIA proceeded in their planning without formal presidential guidance on war objectives. The closest Franks got was when he presented his operational concept to the president and the war cabinet on 21 September, at the end of which Bush declared: 'We are going into Afghanistan to destroy the Taliban and al-Qaeda.' Franks later noted that 'this was one of the most direct and decisive statements of policy I have ever heard'.[104] Be that as it may, it was a poor substitute for a formal statement of war objectives. For a start, it did not provide an ordering of objectives. Logically, removing the threat from al-Qaeda should take priority, and there was still debate within the administration over the need to overthrow the Taliban to achieve this end. At the time, senior policymakers still held out hope that the Taliban could be pressured into playing ball.

By the end of September, the president's patience was wearing thin as CENTCOM had yet to produce the campaign plan. However, the bombing and basing problems continued to dog military planners. By 18 September, the US military had identified seven hundred targets but none were of high value to al-Qaeda or the Taliban. US Air Force General Richard Myers, incoming chairman of the Joint Chiefs, readily admitted: 'You're not going to topple a regime with this target list.' The US military was also struggling to find nearby bases from which to provide aviation support to special forces and CIA teams in Afghanistan. As Franks noted, 'The MH-53 Pave Lows and MH-60 Direct Action Penetrators of the 106th Special Operations Aviation Regiment needed a relatively large base, with room for big choppers as well as adequate maintenance and ordnance facilities.' This was also crucial to the air campaign, as these bases would be used for flying missions to rescue any US pilots shot down in Afghanistan. It was decided to use a large-deck aircraft carrier to provide air cover for southern Afghanistan. The nearest carrier was the USS *Kitty Hawk*, then based in Japan; it arrived off the coast of Pakistan two weeks later, on 13 October.[105]

This still left the north, and the lack of an airbase there had become a major stumbling block to starting the war. Uzbekistan had been identified as the best prospect, and diplomatic efforts had focused on persuading the Uzbeks to give the United States use of Karshi Khanabad airfield (known as K2), a former Soviet base in the south-east of the country. From the beginning, CENTCOM recognised that Uzbek cooperation would be crucial to the campaign.[106] However, it would be late September before US negotiators could get the Uzbeks to agree even to the possibility of the United States flying search-and-rescue missions out of K2. CENTCOM had yet to send in a team to assess if the runways at K2 were long enough to take US transport planes; if they were not, then the US would have to seek Uzbek permission to use the national airport – an even more remote possibility.[107] When Bush asked about the backup plan should Uzbekistan not pan out, Rumsfeld replied, 'If we have no CSAR [combined search and rescue] in the north you can't have air operations in the north. Just in the South.' Rumsfeld added that 'the Uzbeks have not okayed special forces' to operate from the base either. This situation threatened to undermine the whole US plan.[108]

Meanwhile, as Geoff Hoon recalls, the British Ministry of Defence looked at 'what we could do to help the Americans'.[109] Following Blair's visit to Washington in September, Britain's military (in Boyce's words) 'geared up for the offensive'. Initially, Britain's main contribution was to come from its nuclear-powered Trafalgar-class submarines armed with cruise missiles. Boyce noted that 'I had to switch some of our subs from the Atlantic to south of Pakistan. We moved pretty quickly – within two or three weeks.'[110] It was also fairly obvious from the beginning that Britain would be deploying her formidable special forces. Indeed, immediately following 9/11, Hoon told the director of special forces, Brigadier Graeme Lamb, 'if we will do anything, you people will be involved'. On Hoon's instruction, Lamb had flown to the United States on a commandeered Royal Air Force VC10 (getting special permission to enter closed US airspace), stopping at Tampa in Florida to meet with Franks, then on to Fort Bragg in North Carolina to meet with US Army Special Operations Command, and finally to Washington for meetings at the Pentagon and at CIA headquarters in Langley. On his return on 17 September, he began to prepare Britain's special forces for action.[111]

Then, at the end of September, things came together. The Russians and the Tajiks both offered to provide airbases for the US campaign. While welcome, neither option was ideal; the US military really wanted use of the K2 airfield. On 5 October, Rumsfeld flew to Tashkent to negotiate directly with the Uzbek president, Islam Karimov. Clearly, Rumsfeld was persuasive: the following day, Uzbekistan gave permission for the US military to operate from K2.[112] On 3 October, Blair was back in Brighton, this time speaking at the Labour Party Conference. In a bullish speech he declared: 'I say to the Taliban: surrender the terrorists or surrender power.'[113] The following day, the British government released a dossier that basically made the case for war. Entitled 'Responsibility for the Terrorist Atrocities in the United States', the document presented evidence to prove that al-Qaeda carried out the 9/11 attacks; by this stage, few in the West thought otherwise. It further asserted, not unreasonably, that al-Qaeda 'retain[ed] the will and resources to carry out further atrocities', and that the United Kingdom and its citizens were 'potential targets' for such future attacks. The dossier concluded that '[t]he attack could not have occurred without the alliance between the Taleban and Osama Bin Laden, which allowed Bin Laden to operate freely in Afghanistan, promoting, planning and executing terrorist activity'.[114] As it happens, both Blair's speech and the dossier had been toned down by the Americans: the White House worried that the speech was 'too forward' and gave away too many details about the military campaign; and US intelligence agencies requested that key pieces of information be removed from the dossier before publication.[115] Blair continued his whirlwind diplomacy, flying in turn to Russia, Pakistan and India from 4 to 6 October, in order to win over Russian and Pakistani support for the campaign, and to make an attempt at diffusing a simmering crisis between India and Pakistan. It is not clear what difference this made as, by this stage, President Putin of Russia and President Musharraf of Pakistan had already pledged to support the US-led military campaign.

Blair returned exhausted but elated from his trip. Whether true or not, he felt that he had drawn the Russians and Pakistanis further into the wider coalition supporting America's global war on terrorism. The following day, 7 October, he received a call from Bush to warn him that the first air attacks would be launched that evening. At 7 p.m., flanked by the deputy prime minister, the Foreign Secretary and the Secretary of State for Defence, the prime minister gave a press statement announcing that 'military action against targets inside Afghanistan has begun'. Blair revealed that British 'missile-firing submarines are in use tonight. The air assets will be available for use in the coming days.' In defence of military action he noted that 'It is more than two weeks since an ultimatum was delivered to the Taleban to yield up the terrorists or face the consequences. It is clear beyond doubt that the Taleban will not do this.' He concluded with the thought that 'sometimes to safeguard peace, we have to fight'.[116] Little did he know that for British forces, this fight would drag on for thirteen years.

3

Original Sin

A mighty US Air Force armada was unleashed on Afghanistan on Sunday, 7 October. Giant B-52 strategic bombers flew from the British airbase at Diego Garcia, B-1B supersonic bombers took off from Oman in the Gulf and B-2 stealth bombers from Whiteman Air Force Base in Missouri. US Navy F-14 and F/A-18 fighter-bombers flew from the carriers USS *Carl Vinson* and USS *Enterprise*, on station in the Indian Ocean. Despite this assembled air power, the opening salvo of Operation Enduring Freedom was remarkably cautious. Only thirty-one targets were struck, mostly in or around the major cities of Kabul, Kandahar, Herat and Mazar-e-Sharif. As the US Army's official history of the war observes, 'The first night of bombing was far from over-whelming in either scope or effect.'[1] The British contribution to this initial attack was similarly modest: a total of three Tomahawk cruise missiles were fired from the Royal Navy submarines HMS *Trafalgar* and HMS *Triumph*, roaming underwater some 1,300 miles away in the Arabian Sea.[2] Downing Street had expected things to go with more of a bang. 'There was a pretty clear impression the operation had not been as effective as had been hoped,' Alastair Campbell noted in his diary.[3] Assessment of the bomb damage the following day revealed that many targets had been missed.[4]

Downing Street and the White House liaised in advance to ensure that the prime minister and the president were sending out similar public messages in announcing the onset of military action; in particular, that the Taliban had been given the opportunity, as Blair put it, to side with justice or side with terror. The final draft of Blair's public statement had to be 'cobble[d] together' as Bush gave his earlier than expected.[5] For all that, Blair provided a clearer articulation of the war objectives than Bush. The prime minister declared that 'we have

set the objective to pursue those responsible for the attacks, to eradicate Bin Laden's network of terrorism and to take action against the
Taleban regime that is sponsoring him.' In contrast, the president said
that US military operations were 'designed to disrupt the use of
Afghanistan as a terrorist base of operations, and to attack the military
capability of the Taliban regime'.[6]

This pointed to a more general problem, which was that the goals
of the military campaign were never agreed upon by the US and
British governments. The British government did have clearly defined
'immediate objectives' for Operation Veritas (the official code name
for Britain's war against al-Qaeda and international terrorism more
broadly). These were identified as bringing al-Qaeda leaders to justice,
preventing al-Qaeda from continuing to pose a threat, ensuring that
Afghanistan ceases to harbour terrorists and, in order to achieve all
of the above, effecting regime change as required.[7] Unfortunately,
British campaign objectives, however well defined, were of limited
relevance as British forces were expected simply to roll under the US
plan. As we have seen, things were pretty shambolic on the American
side, with CENTCOM failing to produce a credible plan to the timescale required by the president, and the CIA rushing ahead with its
own rough-and-ready campaign plan. Even as the war got under way,
different parts of the US government had varying understandings of
the war objectives. The president and senior national security officials,
including Defense Secretary Donald Rumsfeld and National Security
Advisor Condoleezza Rice, were focused on the need to deny al-Qaeda
the ability to operate from Afghanistan and on defeating the Taliban
regime that had given them refuge. Curiously, destroying al-Qaeda
was not emphasised as a war goal by US civilian leaders. The US
military saw things differently. According to the new chairman of the
US Joint Chiefs of Staff, General Richard Meyers, the primary objective
was 'to capture or kill as many al-Qaeda as we could'. Similarly, the
deputy commander of CENTCOM, Lieutenant General Michael
Delong, listed the primary objective of the campaign as to 'wipe out
al-Qaeda in Afghanistan'.[8]

In short, America went to war, and Britain along with it, without
a common strategic vision for the military campaign. This had
two profound consequences. The first was that for all the talk of
'wiping out' terrorists, military operations were actually focused on

overthrowing the Taliban and ejecting al-Qaeda from their camps in Afghanistan. Thus, incredibly, al-Qaeda leaders and many hundreds of trained terrorists were allowed to escape to Pakistan. The second was that a merciless war was waged on the Taliban, and waged to the bitter end. Thus an attempt by Mullah Omar to negotiate the Taliban's surrender was rebuffed. The Taliban were also excluded from international peace talks held in Bonn in December 2001, which were aimed at constructing a stable post-conflict order in Afghanistan. In this way the seeds of continued war were sown. The United Nations special representative to Afghanistan, Lakhdar Brahimi, would later lament that '[t]he Taliban should have been at Bonn'. Of the failure to invite them, he admitted: 'this was our original sin'.[9]

SPOOKS AND SPECIAL FORCES

American and British spies and special forces deployed into Afghanistan in advance of the bombing. Everything surrounding MI6, the SAS and the SBS is highly secretive; the identities of MI6 agents are never revealed, and the government refuses to comment on special forces operations. Hence, very little is known publicly about this aspect of Britain's contribution to the war effort. In contrast, we know a lot about what the CIA and US special forces got up to mainly because the first two leaders of CIA paramilitary operations in Afghanistan – Gary Schroen and Gary Berntsen, also known as 'Gary 1' and 'Gary 2' – published detailed accounts of their experiences.[10]

The first CIA paramilitary team arrived in Afghanistan on 26 September, flying in on an old Soviet helicopter ten days before the bombing started. Code-named Jawbreaker, the team comprised seven highly experienced operatives from the CIA's legendary Special Activities Division; SAD officers are recruited from America's elite special forces with decades of field experience and a range of specialist military skills. The team was led by a very senior CIA operative, 59-year-old Gary Schroen, who held the rank of a three-star general within the CIA and had twice met Ahmad Shah Massoud in the late 1990s in Afghanistan. Jawbreaker received marching orders from the chief of the CIA's Counterterrorism Center, Cofer Black. The team's immediate task was to re-establish links with the Northern Alliance, in order to persuade them to work with US military forces. Black told the team that 'beyond that, your mission is to exert all efforts to find Usama bin Ladin and his senior lieutenants and to kill them'. He underlined this point in somewhat colourful language: 'I don't want bin Ladin and his thugs captured, I want them dead ... I want bin Ladin's head shipped back in a box filled with dry ice.'[11]

Schroen arrived in the Panjshir Valley with $3 million in cash to buy influence with anti-Taliban forces. In his first meeting with Marshal Fahim, Massoud's successor as head of the Northern Alliance, Schroen handed over $1 million in order to express the seriousness of American intent. Schroen's initial requests to Fahim were to allow his team to conduct GPS mapping of Northern Alliance front lines so American air strikes would not hit friendly forces, and to establish a joint intelligence cell so the CIA could harvest Northern Alliance intercepts of Taliban radio transmissions, as well as human intelligence from Afghans who travelled across Taliban lines. The first request was easy as Northern Alliance commanders were keen to see Taliban front lines pummelled by US air power. Fahim readily agreed to the second request also, even though this intelligence gathering would be focused on targeting key al-Qaeda leaders and on locating eight Western aid workers (including two Americans) being held hostage by the Taliban, as well as on assessing the disposition of Taliban forces. In the first month alone, the joint intelligence cell produced over four hundred reports.[12]

Once Uzbekistan gave permission on 5 October for US forces to operate from its soil, US transport planes from airbases across Europe descended on the former Soviet airfield at Karshi Khanabad. With its dilapidated buildings and runways, K2 was soon overwhelmed by the sheer volume of air traffic, with cargo planes arriving every two hours. One of the first units to arrive was the 160th Special Operations Aviation Regiment, who managed to offload and assemble their Chinook and Blackhawk helicopters (specially kitted out for covert operations) and achieve operational readiness inside forty-eight hours – just in time to provide search and rescue for US aircrew in northern Afghanistan as the bombing campaign got under way. On 10 October, the US Army's 5th Special Operations Group led by Colonel John Mulholland arrived to take charge of all US special operations in Afghanistan. Initially, the focus was on getting the search-and-rescue capability up and running, but thereafter it was on getting special forces A-teams into Afghanistan to support the Northern Alliance.[13]

While the Alliance and America now had a common enemy in the Taliban, military cooperation was far from assured. For a start, Fahim was unhappy to discover that the United States would be establishing direct links with a number of Northern Alliance commanders – including General Dostum in the north-west and Ismail Khan in the west, both of whom had previously competed with Massoud – and would be doing likewise with Pashtun leaders in the east and south. Fahim's request that all dealings with the Northern Alliance go through him was firmly rejected, and sensibly so given that the United States wanted to directly influence events on the ground so far as possible.

In a country that, given Afghanistan's history, was understandably hostile to the presence of armed outsiders, hosting US forces also carried reputational risks for the Northern Alliance leadership. When CENTCOM tried to deploy the first twelve-man A-team to the Panjshir Valley in mid October, Fahim insisted that only two soldiers be sent and that they dress in civilian clothing. He agreed to the whole team deploying when it was explained that they would bring the ability to guide US bombs onto Taliban positions with highly accurate laser targeting. He still insisted that they arrive in civilian attire, which caused some consternation in K2. Schroen recalls that Mulholland 'exploded in anger'.[14] The concern for Pentagon lawyers was that US special forces captured by the enemy while fighting out of uniform would not be entitled to treatment as prisoners of war, and could be shot as spies. On the other hand, as General Tommy Franks observed, 'any captured Green Beret would likely be executed regardless of what he wore'. Moreover, there was a counterbalancing tactical consideration: Americans in uniform among Northern Alliance troops in their Afghan dress would stick out nicely for Taliban and al-Qaeda snipers. A compromise was worked out whereby US special forces would wear at least 'one prominent item' of regulation uniform, such as shirt, jacket or trousers.[15]

In the end, Mulholland deployed six A-teams to support the Northern Alliance over a two-week period. Rather than work to an overall CENTCOM plan, American special forces made things up as they went along. Mulholland later explained that 'basically, we wrote our own plan'. A-teams deploying into Afghanistan were simply given a 'handful of powerpoint slides' telling them to conduct unconventional warfare, defeat al-Qaeda and overthrow the Taliban. One A-team leader wistfully recalled that 'we were given an extraordinarily wonderful amount of authority to make decisions'.[16]

THE NORTHERN FRONT

The bulk of Northern Alliance forces were arrayed in an L-shape protecting the north-east corner of Afghanistan. The 'Takhar front' stretched south from the Tajik border for around 150 miles, at which point the 'Kabul front' swung east for a hundred miles to the Pakistani border. In addition, General Dostum held a small Northern Alliance enclave south of Mazar-e-Sharif with his Uzbek militia, and Ismail Khan commanded Tajik forces scattered to the west in Herat and Gor provinces. On their first visit to the Kabul front, the CIA team was impressed by the organisation and discipline of Northern Alliance forces and their charismatic commanding general, Bismullah Khan. The troops occupied the high ground in a series of foxholes and bunkers with dug-in heavy weapons. A number of villages dotting the Shomali Plain below were occupied by Taliban forces, and Arab jihadi units held key positions in buildings reinforced with concrete and sandbags. With only eight hundred yards separating the front lines, the Northern Alliance and Taliban traded rifle and artillery fire on a daily basis. The Takhar front was actually three separate defensive lines, with the main one being just south of the Tajik border; here Northern Alliance forces again held the high ground along a line of hills for about ten miles facing Taliban forces in reinforced positions on lower ground below. Forces thinned out on both sides going south as the mountainous terrain became too rugged for combat operations, except at two points where river valleys extended westwards; the mouths of the valleys were blocked by Northern Alliance defences. On both the Kabul and Takhar fronts the Taliban held forces in reserve beyond the range of Northern Alliance artillery, making it impossible for the Alliance to break through Taliban lines.[17] This was where American air power came in.

In a last-ditch attempt to avoid war, the Taliban offered to free a British hostage, Yvonne Ridley, and negotiate the release of the eight

aid workers they were holding on suspicion of being Christian mission-
aries. Ridley was a journalist who had entered eastern Afghanistan
without Taliban permission in Afghan dress on 26 September, and was
apprehended as she attempted to return to Pakistan two days later.
A spokesman at the Taliban embassy in Islamabad confirmed that she
was under investigation for being a spy.[18] Perhaps understandably, given
news reports of US and British special forces infiltrating Afghanistan,
the Taliban were disinclined to believe reassurances from the British
government and Ridley's employer, the *Sunday Express*. The Taliban's
information minister declared in early October that 'Surely her crime
is high', suggesting that 'She could be one of those special forces'.[19]
It later transpired that Ridley was a captain in the British Territorial
Army. While British diplomats sought her release behind the scenes,
publicly London and Washington refused to be diverted from military
action.[20] Remarkably, on the day after the US and Britain started
bombing the Taliban, Ridley was released and formally 'deported' to
Pakistan.[21] Of her Taliban captors, Ridley said, 'They treated me with
respect and courtesy.'[22]

When the bombing started, Northern Alliance commanders were
unimpressed as so few targets were hit and, from their perspective, all
were of 'low value'. Actually the purpose of the first evening had been
to cripple the Taliban's crude air defences and so these targets were
critical to the US Air Force. Still no front-line Taliban positions
were hit on the Kabul or Takhar fronts. Schroen recalls that 'the disappointment within the Northern Alliance senior ranks to the first night's
bombing was palpable'.[23] Concern over minimising the risk of civilian
casualties was a significant constraint on the early stages of the bombing
campaign. Potential targets required approval by military lawyers in
CENTCOM and back in the Pentagon; where there was a risk of
considerable collateral damage, target approval went up to Rumsfeld
and even the president.[24] Some targets also required British approval,
which was not always forthcoming as British forces operated to stricter
rules of engagement with regard to avoiding civilian casualties. On 19
October, the Chief of the Defence Staff, Admiral Boyce, reported to
the prime minister that 'the Americans were getting a bit fed up with
us for not agreeing to all the targets'.[25]

The air campaign did ramp up such that by the end of the first
week US warplanes had dropped over 1,500 bombs and munitions on

Taliban targets. Initially, there had been some speculation in the British press that twelve Tornado GR4 fighter-bombers, which happened to be in Oman on a military exercise, might join the air campaign. But in the end the Royal Air Force played an entirely supporting role, deploying four ageing Canberra PR9 reconnaissance planes, and six tanker aircraft (four VC10s and two TriStars) to provide in-flight refuelling for US planes. Meanwhile, the US Air Force committed ever more air power to Afghanistan, including formidable AC-130 gunships. These came in two varieties: AC-130H 'Spectre' gunships armed with a 40mm Bofors cannon (capable of firing 120 rounds per minute) and a 105mm howitzer; and AC-130U 'Spooky' gunships armed with a 25mm Gatling gun (capable of firing 1,800 rounds per minute). AC-130s are designed to loiter and lay down withering gunfire on ground targets; Northern Alliance commanders called them the 'death ray'. By week two, everything on CENTCOM's target list had been destroyed and so attention was turned to 'targets of opportunity'.[26]

On 20 October, US special forces made their most audacious raid of the war, sending a large force way behind enemy lines in an attempt to capture Mullah Omar. Operation Rhino proceeded in two phases. First, two hundred army rangers parachuted onto a small desert airfield fifty miles south-west of Kandahar, following suppressive bombing by the US Air Force. The airfield was held for five hours while a ninety-strong force of elite Delta commandos arrived in heli-copters, refuelled, and then flew on to assault Mullah Omar's compound in Kandahar. AC-130 Spectre and helicopter gunships kept the Taliban at bay while the commandos went in. Mullah Omar had long since fled. The US Army's official history claims that the Delta force did not come away entirely empty-handed, in that they were able to recover 'valuable intelligence' from the compound, although there is no way to judge its true value. The following day the raid was made public by the chairman of the US Joint Chiefs of Staff, General Richard Myers, who said that it showed that US forces were able to operate at will anywhere inside Afghanistan 'without significant interference from Taliban forces'.[27]

Even so, by late October, US bombers had yet to start pounding Taliban front-line forces. Schroen noted that on 23 October, 'The daily target deck for planned CENTCOM air strikes still focused on Taliban targets in deep rear areas, with supply and warehouse facilities being high on the list.'[28] The Northern Alliance grew ever more frustrated. Some in Washington were worried about the atrocities that might be committed against Pashtun civilians by the Tajik troops of the Northern Alliance when they conquered Kabul. Pakistan, Russia and Iran were all publicly warning of a likely 'bloodbath'. This, more than anything, was behind the delay in supporting a Northern Alliance offensive, but it was not without military consequences. The start of America's war on the Taliban and al-Qaeda became a rallying call for jihadists in Pakistan and further afield. US intelligence showed thousands of fighters flooding into Afghanistan and swelling Taliban ranks; Taliban forces on the Kabul and Takhar fronts were estimated to have risen by 50 per cent in just two weeks. This alarmed senior policymakers in Washington, who ironically blamed the Northern Alliance for inaction.[29]

Downing Street was equally unhappy about the slow progress of the war. The Chief of the Defence Staff did not shy away from outlining the difficulties facing British and American forces. Alastair Campbell, Blair's communications director, noted in his diary on 22 October that Admiral Boyce 'gave his usual very downbeat assessment, focusing mainly on the problems'. The following day, Boyce was no more inspiring, basically telling the prime minister (in Campbell's words): 'we couldn't take Mazar, the [Northern Alliance] were impossible to deal with, and the Americans were not being totally open'. Little had improved when the war cabinet met on 25 October. Campbell observed that it was 'all a bit grim', with the war 'not really going anywhere', and that Boyce had not changed his tune: 'as ever telling us what we couldn't do rather than what we could'.[30] The following day Boyce told reporters that British forces faced the most challenging campaign 'in my lifetime', and that it would be 'extraordinarily difficult' to achieve the campaign objectives unless the Taliban 'folded'.[31] Campbell was far from pleased, noting that 'Boyce's interview and the gloomy photos of him played to the idea, gathering too much pace, that the war was "going nowhere"'.[32]

At the end of October, Fahim and Franks met in Tajikistan to review progress in the war; the meeting was held in a huge US Air Force C-17 Globemaster cargo plane, fitted out as Franks's mobile headquarters, which had flown into Dushanbe International Airport that morning. To Franks, Fahim 'looked like a Mafia enforcer' rather than a general. Fahim told Franks that of the 15,000 troops he commanded, many were poorly equipped, and they faced three times that number of Taliban. He said that he needed supplies, weapons and, crucially, American air power. Franks outlined his war plan, which was for the Northern Alliance to first seize the northern city of Mazar-e-Sharif, then the city of Talaqan on the Takhar front, and then, before Christmas, to rally forces for an assault on Kabul. Mazar-e-Sharif would give the Americans a secure airport inside Afghanistan only forty miles away from K2, and thereby provide a major logistics hub for operations against Kabul. Fahim tried to argue for an immediate offensive on Kabul but Franks refused to budge. The US commander had presented a military logic for his plan, but unstated was another major reason: Washington was still trying to figure out what to do about securing Kabul once the Taliban had been pushed out. There was also bartering over how much financial assistance the Americans would give the Northern Alliance. Fahim asked for $7 million a month; Franks got him down to $5 million for the whole campaign. Franks recalled, 'As Fahim and his finance minister left the plane, I could picture duffle bags filled with millions of dollars being loaded into his Mercedes.'[33]

The offensive in the north unfolded as Franks had planned, only far more quickly than he or anybody else had expected. The Taliban had flooded forces into the north once the war began, sending up to 5,000 extra fighters to Mazar-e-Sharif. The Northern Alliance closed in on the city, with Dostum leading the main force from the south, and Atta Mohammad Noor leading a second force from the south-west. On 19 October, Dostum led his 3,000 militia on horseback (the terrain being too mountainous for vehicles) on a two-week approach to Mazar-e-Sharif, moving northwards up through the main river valley in Balkh province, and overcoming a series of Taliban defences along the way. Initially, the Taliban were ignorant of the effectiveness of US air power. On one early engagement, the A-team with Dostum were having difficulty pinpointing Taliban bunkers five miles distant. Dostum got on his radio to the Taliban. 'This is General Dostum. I am here with the Americans, and they have come to kill you … Tell me, what is your position?' Incredibly, the Taliban proceeded to confirm their location. On this occasion, US bombers still missed these bunkers. But as they got closer to enemy positions, the A-team were able to call down highly accurate and devastating air attacks to soften Taliban defences just ahead of cavalry charges by Dostum's militia.[34] Radio intercepts revealed growing panic on the part of Taliban commanders as they came to realise the extent of their losses, which were in the many hundreds. The Taliban urgently tried to rush yet more fighters to Mazar-e-Sharif as well as sending more military supplies from nearby Kunduz.[35] All this would be in vain.

Dostum and Atta joined forces on 5 November, to push through the last twenty-five miles of Taliban defences along the Balkh river valley. This was when the US Air Force dropped two 15,000-pound BLU-82 'Daisy Cutter' bombs. Each was the size of car, and shoved out the back of a C-130 transport plane on a pallet, whereupon a drag chute was deployed to gently lower the bomb to the ground. On detonation, each BLU-82 went off like a small nuclear device, obliterating anything within a 600-yard radius and leaving behind a giant mushroom cloud. Two A-team members observing from a mile away were blown to the ground by the first Daisy Cutter; one was knocked unconscious, the other commented that the Taliban were 'getting an early look at what hell is like'.[36] This was followed by four days of pummelling by B-52 strategic bombers as well as targeted air strikes by US Navy fighter-bombers. It enabled Dostum and Atta to move their forces up the river valley with few losses on the final approach to Mazar-e-Sharif.

The Taliban's final line of defence was at a narrowing in the valley called the Tangi Gap. Northern Alliance forces entering the canyon were met with 'dozens of Taliban rockets' and 'sheets of bullets from Taliban small-arms fire'. CENTCOM committed all of that day's air strikes (some 120 sorties) to supporting the Northern Alliance assault.[37] The following day, Dostum's troops rode into Mazar-e-Sharif with the Taliban reportedly ahead of them 'fleeing the city in droves'.[38] Several hundred hard-core Taliban and foreign jihadists who had made a last-ditch stand at a girls' school in the city were killed when the compound was flattened by US bombers. In explaining why Mazar-e-Sharif had fallen to the Northern Alliance, a Taliban spokesman told a regional news agency on 10 November, 'For seven days continuously they have been bombing Taliban positions. They used very large bombs.'[39]

It was around this time that the British intelligence team arrived in the Panjshir Valley to link up with the Northern Alliance and the CIA's field headquarters. According to one former intelligence officer, 'SIS [Secret Intelligence Service] operates in penny packages – one or two people instead of dozens. We had some people with Dari language and so were able to deploy a handful.' Foremost among these was Paul Bergne, who arrived with the intelligence team. A former SIS agent, as well as a former UK ambassador to Uzbekistan and Tajikistan, and widely considered the 'most talented linguist of his generation' in the service, Bergne was comfortably ensconced at St Antony's College in Oxford when he was brought out of retirement following 9/11 to act as the prime minister's special representative to the Northern Alliance.[40]

The British SIS team did not arrive to help with the fight. As the former intelligence officer explained, 'Unlike the CIA, SIS does not have paramilitaries – if it needs rough stuff done, it relies on special forces to do it.'[41] Rather, Bergne was to 'open a channel with the Panjshiri gang' while the rest of the SIS team gathered intelligence for MI6 headquarters, then situated in a drab office block near Waterloo Station in London.[42] SIS offered far less to the Northern Alliance than the CIA: they did not bring suitcases of money or guide air attacks against the Taliban. Thus, it is not clear that the British government was able to exercise any significant influence through Bergne. Indeed, he appears to have mostly tried to get the government to appreciate Northern Alliance concerns. Some in Whitehall would later complain that Bergne had 'gone native'.[43]

OPERATION EVIL AIRLIFT

Northern Alliance forces wasted no time closing in on the remaining Taliban-held cities of Taloqan and Kunduz in the north, Bamiyan in central Afghanistan, and the main prize, Kabul. According to one press report, the Northern Alliance offensive benefitted from the delivery of fifty main battle tanks from Tajikistan. These were older model T-55s and T-62s, but hugely welcomed all the same as the Northern Alliance had only thirty T-55 tanks, with little ammunition and fuel. The new tanks reportedly arrived with sixty shells each and a thousand litres of fuel, all paid for by the Americans.[44] Radio intercepts revealed that the Taliban believed the defence of Taloqan to be hopeless, and had decided to retreat west to Kunduz, which served as the main garrison of Taliban forces in northern Afghanistan. Thus, Taloqan was captured with little resistance on 11 November. Northern Alliance forces then converged on Kunduz from three different directions. Dostum moved in from the west, General Daoud Khan advanced from the east, and General Bariullah Khan led a force from the north that had broken through on the Takhar front. On 13 November, a Taliban counter-attack against Daoud's troops was obliterated by US air power. Northern Alliance forces adopted a very methodological way to overcome a series of Taliban defensive positions on the approach to Kunduz, described thus by one A-team leader: 'bomb the mountain, then hit it with artillery, then take the mountain. The next day … on to the next mountain.' After ten days of fighting, in which up to 2,000 Taliban had been killed or wounded, the Northern Alliance was at the outskirts of Kunduz and had encircled the city.[45]

What happened next, the only formal surrender of Taliban forces in the war, was witnessed by the *New York Times* reporter Carlotta Gall. Following several days of talks via radio, and some additional 'encouragement' from the US Air Force, the Taliban leaders agreed to meet with Dostum at the old fort of Qala-i-Jangh to the south-west of Mazar-e-Sharif.[46] On 23 November, a heavily armed convoy from Kunduz drove at speed bringing the commander of Taliban forces in the north, Mullah Fazel Mazloom, and the governor of Balkh province, Mullah Norrullah Noori. A straightforward deal was offered and readily accepted by the Taliban: they would be allowed to retreat south once they laid down their weapons. The talks got stuck on what to do with the hundreds of foreign jihadists, a mix of Pakistanis, Saudis, Qataris, Yemenis, Iraqis, Uzbeks and Chechens, many of whom were members of al-Qaeda. It was eventually agreed that they too would lay down their weapons and be taken into Northern Alliance custody. At midnight, reporters travelling with Northern Alliance forces were called in to hear Mazloom announce the Taliban surrender, and to witness him and Dostum shake hands on the deal.[47]

On 24 November, hundreds of foreign jihadi fighters turned up outside Mazar-e-Sharif, taking Northern Alliance guards by surprise. Over the day, they were disarmed in groups and taken in trucks to Qala-i-Jangh fort, which was hurriedly turned into a makeshift prison. Here things rapidly got out of hand. Many foreign fighters had been told they would be sent home, and were surprised to be taken into custody. Further confusing matters, Uzbek fighters feared deportation to their home country as this would have meant certain torture and death. One prisoner killed the Northern Alliance officer supervising the operation, letting off a hand grenade in a suicide attack. Another group of jihadis blew themselves up elsewhere in the fort. The following day the foreign fighters were searched more thoroughly and questioned by two CIA agents. Some of the jihadis now over-powered their guards, seizing their weapons and killing several, including one of the CIA agents. Thus began a battle that was to leave hundreds dead.

The jihadis quickly gained control of the inside of the fort, while the Northern Alliance held the outer battlements. One Western aid worker saw two minibuses pull up outside and US special forces pile out, followed by two Land Rovers with British special forces. The jihadis began firing mortars and rockets out of the fort, while Northern Alliance troops and Western special forces poured in machine-gun fire. When US special forces tried to call in an air strike it hit their own side by accident. On the fifth day, Dostum's forces drove a tank into the fort and blasted the buildings where jihadi fighters were held up at point-blank range. That all but ended the battle. The final few dozen jihadis were forced to surrender when freezing water from a nearby irrigation channel was diverted into the basement of the building where they were making a last stand. As Gall recalls, 'we watched them emerge from the basement like cave men, soaking wet, with blacked faces and matted hair'. Many had serious injuries and had to be taken out by stretcher. Many hundreds of foreign fighters had been killed. Those that survived were bound and packed into trucks for transportation to Shiberghan prison ten hours to the west; many were put into airtight shipping containers and died en route.[48]

Another extraordinary aspect of the Kunduz story was a massive airlift by the Pakistan Army of a large number of its own personnel, and possibly many Taliban and al-Qaeda leaders, out of the besieged city and back to Pakistan. It was well known that Pakistan had sent intelligence agents and military specialists to bolster the Taliban northern front. All had pulled back to Kunduz and so needed to be brought home. According to one US official, President Musharraf had made a direct request to President Bush to let the Pakistan Army recover its people. The official confirmed that two Pakistani transport planes then 'made several sorties a night over several nights' into Kunduz airport and that 'certainly hundreds and perhaps as many as one thousand people escaped'. Since CENTCOM controlled the skies over Afghanistan, this could only have taken place if an air corridor had been opened for the Pakistani flights. Arguably, Bush had little choice as Pakistan was permitting CENTCOM to operate across its airspace as well as discreetly from several Pakistani airbases. Nonetheless, the Northern Alliance was incensed. The head of the CIA in Afghanistan, Gary Berntsen, recalled his Northern Alliance liaison officer screaming at him, 'Why are you Americans trying to save the Taliban?' Frustrated US special forces observing Pakistani planes flying in and out of Kunduz over several days dubbed it 'Operation Evil Airlift'.[49]

THE DASH TO KABUL

While the drama in Kunduz was unfolding, the Northern Alliance seized Kabul, taking London and Washington completely by surprise. It all started as planned. On 11 November, US bombers conducted twenty-five air strikes against Taliban positions on the Kabul front, reportedly killing 2,000 fighters and destroying twenty-nine tanks. The following day Bismullah Khan's forces broke through the Kabul front and advanced across the Shomali Plain in two columns, each about 10,000 men strong and led by dozens of tanks. Northern Alliance forces faced a succession of Taliban defensive lines.[50] They assaulted the first of these following a solid pounding from US bombers, and broke through after five hours of intense fighting, some of it hand-to-hand. Overnight, the remaining Taliban lines crumbled. On 13 November, Northern Alliance intelligence realised that the Taliban had evacuated Kabul and the city was theirs for the taking. The White House remained concerned about what would happen to the mostly Pashtun population should its ally occupy Kabul. The CIA field team reminded Northern Alliance leaders of their promise to stop five miles short of Kabul, and allow time for some kind of international peacekeeping force to be assembled to take charge. It was unrealistic to expect the Northern Alliance not to take Kabul if they could; and now the opportunity presented itself. Bismullah Khan reassured the CIA that there would be no abuses of the Kabul population by Northern Alliance troops: 'I have given strict orders that no killings, no brutality will take place – on pain of death.' His forces easily overcame pockets of stubborn resistance as they advanced the final ten miles to Kabul. By the evening of 14 November, the city was in Northern Alliance hands.

Reporting for BBC Radio 4, John Simpson witnessed the 'wild dash' over the final miles. He told stunned listeners that 'it was only BBC people who liberated this city. We got in ahead of Northern Alliance troops.' He was widely and rightly ridiculed for this slip of the tongue, and indeed later apologised for getting carried away. Other journalists also ventured into Kabul on the day it fell, including one ITN news reporter who was offered a lift on a Northern Alliance tank; much to his alarm, he discovered that it was being driven by an eleven-year-old boy.[51] On entering Kabul, Simpson found rejoicing crowds chanting 'kill the Taliban', and lynch mobs hunting down remaining Taliban stragglers.[52] There was little evidence of the Kabul population being worried about the arrival of the Northern Alliance.

London and Washington debated what to do next. The default among the European states, learned from the Western interventions in the ethnic wars in the Balkans in the 1990s, was to send in peacekeepers to protect the delivery of humanitarian assistance and prevent atrocities against civilians. At a specially convened meeting of the UN Security Council in New York, Lakhdar Brahimi outlined the scale of the challenge. He estimated that the United Nations would need to ship in and distribute '52,000 tonnes of food per month over the next few months', and provide health care for 7.5 million people and shelter for over 1 million displaced persons. He also emphasised the urgent need for a peacekeeping force to secure Kabul, in order to avoid rival factions once again fighting over the capital, as had happened during the Afghan civil war. Brahimi's preference was for an 'all-Afghan force' but he recognised that this would take time to recruit and train. In the interim, he called for the rapid deployment of an international security presence.[53]

US policymakers were prepared to send in one thousand soldiers with the 10th Mountain Division based in K2, as well as one thousand US Marines based on the USS *Kitty Hawk* in the Indian Ocean. However,

Bush told his National Security Council on 13 November that 'US forces will not stay', adding: 'we will not do police work'. He directed that the United States should 'pass these tasks onto others'.[54] In contrast, Blair believed strongly that the coalition should take up the burden of providing humanitarian assistance and security for Afghanistan. Indeed, one senior official recalls 'long discussions about the humanitarian fallout' in Downing Street, with everyone reflecting on the experience of Bosnia and Kosovo.[55] Blair's foreign policy adviser, David Manning, noted that the prime minister 'felt it was very important to send a signal of continued involvement after Kabul had fallen'.[56] Accordingly, the British government announced that 4,000 Royal Marines and paratroops were on standby for rapid deployment into Afghanistan.[57] As *The Times* noted, these elite forces were capable of far more than humanitarian operations: 'the choice of 45 Commando Royal Marines and the 2nd Battalion the Parachute Regiment suggested that the force would have a strong offensive capability'.[58] The plan was to deploy via Bagram airfield. Nobody had stopped to think how the Northern Alliance might feel about the arrival of a powerful British force just thirty miles north of Kabul.

On 16 November, an advance group of two hundred British troops, including members of the SBS and Pathfinders from the Parachute Regiment, flew into Bagram, arriving at night in two C-130 aircraft.[59] The British government had not given any forewarning of this, let alone sought permission from the Northern Alliance. The contrast could not have been more stark with the carefully negotiated deployment of far fewer US special forces early on in the campaign. The Northern Alliance foreign minister, Abdullah Abdullah, was apoplectic. He considered the uninvited arrival of British troops to be a 'violation of our sovereignty'. He complained bitterly to the head of the CIA field office: 'you have communicated every detail of your deployments and operations with our people. Why have [the British] not done the same?'[60] As it happened, the British government did alert the United Nations that they were flying in troops to Bagram, albeit at extremely short notice. On the day of the flight, the deputy head of the UN mission to Afghanistan, Francesc Vendrell, received a call from a British official who told him that 'you are going to see British forces land near Kabul tonight'. Vendrell asked if the British had consulted in advance with the Northern Alliance. The official confirmed, rather sheepishly, that they had not. Hours later, an agitated Abdullah called Vendrell to say that 'the British are invading!'[61]

London quickly realised that a diplomatic crisis was unfolding. The Foreign Secretary, Jack Straw, remembers that 'all hell broke loose'.[62] One senior official recalls that the Northern Alliance was 'seriously furious' and threatening to open fire on British planes.[63] Abdullah declared, somewhat implausibly, that he would resign if the British did not withdraw. Arriving on the first flight was Brigadier Graeme Lamb. The special forces director simply ignored Abdullah's bluster and drove straight off to the Panjshir Valley, to pay his respects at Massoud's grave and hold talks with Northern Alliance leaders. He told his people meanwhile to find out what was happening in Kabul.[64] British intelligence agents also entered the city. According to one senior official, 'once Kabul fell, SIS presence was immediately established'.[65]

The Foreign Secretary tried to reassure the Northern Alliance that this was not the vanguard of a British peacekeeping army: 'our forces are there to … bring Osama bin Laden and his senior associates to justice'.[66] But Northern Alliance leaders did not buy this story. Not helping matters was the Ministry of Defence announcing that the British force was to be increased in size to 6,000 strong.[67] In the face of such strong resistance from the Northern Alliance, and the threat of irate mujahedin taking potshots at incoming Royal Air Force troop transports, the British deployment was quietly put on hold.[68] Paul Bergne thought this was no bad thing. He told journalists that 'the whole idea of us sending masses of troops in uninvited is not acceptable'.[69] One month later, the British would lead the deployment of a large UN-sponsored force into Kabul. But crucially, this would be at the invitation of the new interim Afghan government. Before then, there was still the small matter of defeating the Taliban in their Pashtun heartland of southern Afghanistan.

THE SOUTHERN FRONT

The United States asked Britain to send all of its special forces to Afghanistan, or so the press reported. These comprised four squadrons of fifty men each from both the SAS and the SBS. In late October, the *Daily Telegraph* wrote that 'British generals have said that they will meet the Pentagon's unprecedented request for the SAS to be deployed in full, with the exception of one of the regiment's four squadrons' which was to be kept back for 'any potential emergency on British soil'. However, the *Telegraph* also sounded a note of caution by British defence officials. The special forces were waiting to agree a plan with the Americans before deploying. 'It is a huge country and the SAS believes they will be able to get their man in time, but they don't want to go bumbling around the Afghan hills in the hope they might stumble across Osama bin Laden.'[70]

British special forces are treated as a 'strategic asset', much like the nuclear deterrent, and accordingly report directly to the Chief of the Defence Staff in London; all other British forces on overseas deployment are controlled by the UK's Permanent Joint Headquarters (PJHQ), located in the leafy suburbs of north London. This gives the special forces far more independence of action than regular military formations. Lamb intended to use this operational freedom to achieve strategic effect in the campaign. He was conscious of the fact that 'the Northern Alliance were a bloody long way away' from the seat of Taliban power in Kandahar. Accordingly his plan was to launch a second front in the war, using two squadrons of SAS flying in over Pakistan to attack the Taliban from the south, where 'their back was absolutely exposed'. The purpose was to 'stress the Taliban leadership' and thereby contribute to the collapse of the regime. This was no mean feat logistically. The special forces found that while they could fly themselves and their vehicles into remote areas of southern Afghanistan on C-130 transport planes, the planes would be unable to take off again 'due to inverse ingestion of dust'. This necessitated a 'creative solution' to get the troops in and the planes out (this new technique remains classified). According to one senior source directly involved in these operations, the SAS did hit a large number of Taliban targets in the south, and anecdotal evidence suggests that the operation shook Taliban morale. At one point, an SAS team stumbled across 'twelve beards in a row' discarded on the ground; in a sure sign of defection, a party of Taliban had hastily shaved off their beards.[71]

American special forces pursued a different strategy in the south, focusing instead on identifying and supporting leaders that could rally Pashtun tribesmen against the Taliban. More by luck than design, they stumbled across the head of the Popalzai tribe, Hamid Karzai. Urbane, with a postgraduate degree in political science and international relations from India, and a former deputy foreign minister of Afghanistan, within a matter of months Karzai would become president of Afghanistan, a position he would hold for thirteen years. Karzai had been an early supporter of the Taliban who turned into one of the movement's staunchest critics following the assassination of his father, almost certainly by the Taliban, in the southern Pakistani city of Quetta in July 1999. The terrorist atrocities of 9/11 gave Karzai the opportunity to make his move. In late September, he called a number of fellow Popalzai tribal leaders from Uruzgan province to visit him in Quetta. He intended to foment rebellion against the Taliban in their homeland in southern Afghanistan. To each, Karzai gave a satellite phone to keep in touch, and up to 20,000 rupees (US$350) in cash to buy support from their followers.[72]

A couple of days after the Americans and British began to bombard the Taliban, Karzai decided to leave Quetta and return to Afghanistan. His brother Ahmed Wali 'thought he was mad'. He later recalled: 'It was a suicide mission and we begged him not to go.'[73] But Karzai had made up his mind. He snuck across the border into Kandahar with his nephew and just two bodyguards, riding on a couple of old motorcycles.[74] They headed for the area around Tarin Kot, the provincial capital of Uruzgan, where the Popalzai had influence. This was also where many of the Taliban's top leaders originated; Mullah Omar himself was from a town just west of Tarin Kot. Karzai hoped that by seizing control of the city, he would achieve a 'psychological victory' over the Taliban and rally support from across Uruzgan.[75] He spent two weeks in the area slowly building support among the Popalzai and other Pashtun tribes. Pashtun villagers had grown resentful of the Taliban's repressive rule, and especially the conscription of their sons in the late 1990s to fight the Taliban's war against the Northern Alliance. Karzai also found support from among the Hazaras, who as non-Pashtuns had suffered under Taliban rule.

In late October Karzai received some news that shocked him deeply. 'The Lion of Kabul' (so-called because he was the only mujahedin commander during the Soviet War to attack Russian forces in the capital) and fellow anti-Taliban Pashtun leader, Abdul Haq, was captured and brutally executed on 25 October, just twenty-four hours after he had entered eastern Afghanistan in an attempt to rally opposition to the Taliban.[76] Karzai knew that it was only a matter of time before the Taliban came after him. He instructed his followers to recruit more fighters. He also called his CIA contact in the US embassy in Islamabad requesting urgent assistance. On 1 November, US planes dropped food, supplies and weapons, including around three hundred Kalashnikov automatic rifles.[77] According to eyewitnesses this initial American attempt to help Karzai was 'chaotic': US helicopters arrived later than expected, some missed the drop site, and 'when the weapons and equipment were airdropped, hundreds of Afghans appeared from the mountains and stole everything'.[78]

The next day Karzai heard that a large force was being sent from Kandahar to capture him. Many of the men who had rallied to Karzai fled at this news, but enough held their ground to fight off the Taliban force.[79] Karzai realised that the Taliban would be back with more troops. He ordered his followers to return to their homes, and headed off to the hills with a small band of men. On 4 November, he called the Americans once again for help. He was told to mark a landing site and wait to be collected. Karzai later recalled: 'We lit fires and they just came – very easy, exactly on the minute that they told [us] they would be there, on the very minute. Our people couldn't believe it.'[80]

Karzai was evacuated to an airbase in Jacobabad in Pakistan, which was being used by the CIA and US special forces. He was quick to realise that it would do his image no good if news got out that he had escaped with US help. It was agreed that the story would be buried.[81] Unfortunately, somebody forgot to tell Rumsfeld, who announced to the world's media that 'we have airlifted [Karzai] and taken him to Pakistan for consultation'. Karzai's family hurriedly put out a counter-story, insisting that the Defense Secretary had been misinformed.[82] It was now that Western policymakers looking for a Pashtun figure they could promote as a future leader of the country began to consider Karzai. The Americans were searching for a compromise candidate, somebody the Northern Alliance and Pakistan could accept. Abdul Haq had been top of everyone's list; when he was killed, attention turned to Karzai.[83]

On 14 November, Karzai returned to Uruzgan, this time with an A-team and CIA agents in support. By now his fellow tribesmen had risen up in Tarin Kot, driven the Taliban from the provincial capital and hanged the Taliban town mayor for good measure. Thus Karzai was able to take the city without a fight. But holding it was a different matter. Once again, the Taliban dispatched a large force from Kandahar: a pair of American F/A-18 planes observed a convoy of pickup trucks speeding towards Tarin Kot. Only twelve strong, and with Karzai's men on the verge of fleeing, the A-team had to rely on air power to stop the Taliban attack. CENTCOM was alerted to the seriousness of the unfolding situation, and every available warplane across theatre was diverted to stop the Taliban attack in its tracks. The first bomb missed its target but the others did not. The A-team guided US bombs onto approaching Taliban vehicles with utterly devastating effect. Only two pickup trucks got through with twenty or so Taliban; armed tribesmen easily dealt with them, and the US Air Force finished off what was left of the Taliban convoy as it tried to retreat to Kandahar.[84] For *New York Times* reporter Carlotta Gall, the Battle for Tarin Kot was 'a turning point in the south'. People in the south finally saw what those in the north had already witnessed: the Taliban could not withstand US air power and were in disarray. As Gall notes: 'tribal elders, mujahideen commanders, and opposition groups rush forward to join the winning side'.[85]

By late November, the Americans and their Afghan allies turned their attention to isolating Kandahar city. On 18 November another A-team was sent into southern Afghanistan, to link up with Gul Agha Sherzai, a powerful Pashtun warlord from Kandahar province. Sherzai had around eight hundred armed men under his command, though to the arriving American special forces they 'looked more like a mob than a military organization'. Four days later this ragtag force had managed to take a key town and valley south of Kandahar city, cutting off Taliban supply lines from Pakistan. By this time, Karzai had worked his way south from Uruzgan in a massive and disorderly convoy of vehicles, and was headed towards the Arghendab Bridge in order to cut off the Taliban route north out of Kandahar. The Americans had strengthened their support to Karzai by sending in an additional team of special forces officers. When the Taliban counter-attacked at the Arghendab Bridge, Karzai and his men fled, leaving the special forces to hold off the Taliban with repeated air strikes. The following day, Karzai returned and his troops were able to rout the shaken Taliban forces.[86] Kandahar city was now cut off from the north as well as the south.

THE BONN CONFERENCE

On 27 November, an international conference was convened in Königswinter, a small town in western Germany near Bonn, to decide on the future of Afghanistan. A luxurious hotel in the town had been selected as the site for the conference, away from the prying eyes of the world's media. The objective was to manage the transition to a post-Taliban government that represented all the main groups in Afghanistan, and thereby avoid a return to civil war. The victorious Northern Alliance could not seize power for the simple reason that it was comprised of Tajik and Uzbek groups, whereas most people in Afghanistan were Pashtun. The conference was sponsored by the United Nations and formally led by Brahimi, with the United States, Britain, France, Italy, Germany, Russia, Iran, India and Pakistan all sending delegations. Obviously, the United States was to have a big say on the conference outcome. Britain's role was modest. As Robert Cooper, the head of the British delegation, later put it: 'the Brits were supporting cast in the Bonn conference'.[87] There were four main Afghan groups represented: the Northern Alliance and three Pashtun factions – the so-called 'Rome group', comprised of supporters of the disposed king of Afghanistan; the 'Cyprus group' of émigré intellectuals connected to Iran; and the 'Peshawar group', largely put together by Brahimi and intended to represent the southern Pashtun voice.

The head of the US delegation, James Dobbins, visited CENTCOM ahead of the Bonn conference, where he heard about Karzai for the first time. Dobbins then travelled to Islamabad, where the new head of the ISI suggested Karzai as the best candidate to lead Afghanistan, and to Kabul, where Abdullah did likewise. At Bonn, Dobbins found that the Russians, Indians and Iranians too were all supportive of Karzai's candidacy. Dobbins recalls that 'there was a clear consensus among international observers that he was the most broadly acceptable'.[88] Brahimi arranged for Karzai to speak via satellite phone to the opening meeting of the conference. The Rome group, who saw Karzai as a rival, were furious at this stunt. They doubted that Karzai was calling from Uruzgan, as he claimed.[89] But that is exactly where he was, surrounded by his men in an unheated room, ad-libbing a short speech about the need for the various parties to unite to tackle the challenges ahead.[90]

In the end it took just nine days for the different Afghan groups to settle on an interim constitution and interim administration. It was agreed that after six months, a Loya Jirga (a traditional meeting of elders) would be convened to form a transitional government that would take over from the interim administration for a further eighteen months, during which time a new constitution would be drafted and national elections organised. The two people most responsible for this remarkable outcome were Brahimi and Dobbins. The basic formula of an international conference leading to an interim administration, and in turn to a Loya Jirga to decide on a transitional government, had been outlined by Brahimi to the UN Security Council some weeks before.[91] Through patient diplomacy, he got the various parties to buy into it. The final stumbling block was on the question of who would lead the interim administration. Dobbins persuaded Brahimi to suggest Karzai as the only Pashtun leader who would be acceptable to all parties and the regional powers. The problem was the Rome group wanted the king of Afghanistan, Zahir Shah, to be appointed as the head of state and given the right to select the chairman of the interim administration – a position that several individuals within the Rome group were vying to fill. The Northern Alliance and Iran were vehemently opposed to this idea. On the final day, Dobbins came up with a breakthrough proposal. He suggested that Zahir be given the privilege of nominating the chairman of the interim administration, provided that nominee was Karzai, and of opening the Loya Jirga in six months' time.[92] Under the final agreement, the Northern Alliance picked up the other key posts in the interim administration: Mohammed Fahim became vice chair and defence minister; Mohammed Yunus Qanouni, who had led the Northern Alliance delegation at the Bonn conference, was appointed interior minister; and Abdullah Abdullah took the office of foreign affairs minister.

Incredibly, Karzai was almost killed by an American bomb on the very day that agreement was reached at Königswinter. On 5 December, as Karzai's militia advanced on Kandahar city, they received intelligence of a Taliban force held up in a nearby cave. Given his political importance, the Americans were taking no chances around Karzai, and so to remove this threat a loitering B-52 bomber was tasked to drop a laser-guided bomb on the Taliban position. The bomb was being guided onto the target by a US tactical air controller with Karzai's group, when the batteries on the laser designator failed. Tragically, nobody realised in time that when the batteries were replaced, the laser designator transmitted its own GPS coordinates as part of a self-test cycle. The 2,000-pound bomb killed eight (including three US special operators) and injured over seventy US and Afghan troops. It was a very close call for Karzai, who suffered only minor injuries. Just minutes after the blast, he received a call from the BBC asking how it felt to be appointed chairman of the interim administration.[93] The US team wanted to evacuate Karzai but he refused, as he sensed the Taliban were close to surrendering Kandahar. He was right.[94]

THE FALL OF KANDAHAR

During this time, Sherzai's militia continued to advance on Kandahar from the south. The Taliban attempted to attack his force from behind as it moved up Highway 4. It was to prove a fatal mistake. The gaze of the Americans with their laser designator turned to Sherzai's southern flank, where they found a 'target-rich environment'. The head of the A-team later noted that US bombers left 'a lot of burning vehicles' on Highway 4.[95] The Taliban were also under growing pressure from the powerful Alikozai tribe in Kandahar led by the legendary mujahedin commander Mullah Naqibullah, who was credited with chasing the Soviets out of Kandahar. When the Taliban originally rose to power in 1994, Naqibullah had let them take control of the province. Now he warned Mullah Omar that the Taliban had to go or the Alikozai 'will take up arms against you'.[96]

The Taliban leadership decided that it was time to open talks with Karzai. By this stage, Omar was beginning to lose his grip on things. He was understandably shocked by the rapid collapse of the Taliban Emirate, and was 'distraught ... at times on the verge of weeping'. According to one account, his 'final appeal to fighters to "completely obey your commanders and not to go hither and thither" and to "regroup, resist and fight" ... was apparently received ambivalently among members of the movement still fighting'.[97] Omar instructed the Taliban minister of defence, Mullah Obaidullah, to meet with Karzai to discuss surrender terms. A meeting was agreed in a small town a hundred miles north of Kandahar for 5 December. Karzai

received the Taliban delegation only hours after the friendly-fire incident. The Taliban party, led by Obaidullah, recognised Karzai's leadership, referring to him as 'Chairman': that is, the title he had just been
given by the Bonn conference. They offered to hand Kandahar city
over to Mullah Naqibullah. According to one account, Karzai in turn
offered to let Omar and other senior Taliban remain in Kandahar
under the supervision of Naqibullah, and he even discussed state
pensions, bodyguards and cars for Taliban leaders. In a custom that
might appear extraordinary to Western eyes, Obaidullah then offered
hospitality to Karzai and both sides sat down for a meal together;
breaking bread with someone is a customary way of sealing a deal
in Afghanistan.[98]

After the Taliban delegation had left, Karzai discussed the proposed
deal with the senior US special forces officer accompanying him,
Lieutenant Colonel David Fox, who in turn pushed it up to CENTCOM.
Meanwhile Karzai confirmed to the *New York Times* that the Taliban
had agreed to surrender across the south – in Kandahar, Helmand,
Uruzgan and Zabul – and that under the deal 'Taliban militants would
turn over their arms and ammunition to a council of tribal elders and
would be allowed safe passage to their homes'. This was confirmed
by the Taliban ambassador to Pakistan, Mullah Zaeef, who announced
on 6 December that 'tomorrow, the Taliban will start surrendering
their weapons to Mullah Naqibullah'.[99] Deal-making of this kind is
integral to the Afghan way of war, which seeks to avoid bloody fights
to the finish. In effect, the Taliban were 'recognizing the new dominant
power'. And the custom in such situations was for the losing side to
'surrender their weapons and vehicles in the expectation that some
of these weapons and vehicles would be handed back'.[100] In contrast,
the American way of war, as practised in the American Civil War and
World War II, has a proclivity towards unlimited war aims and the
utter defeat of opponents.[101] Not surprisingly, therefore, the US government sought to bring Omar to justice, and accordingly Rumsfeld ruled
out the possibility of allowing him 'to live in dignity' in Kandahar.[102]
Under instruction from CENTCOM, Fox told Karzai that America
would not make deals with the Taliban.[103]

The Taliban delegation returned on 6 December with a letter from
Omar outlining what was agreed. The leading Taliban expert Michael
Semple describes the letter as a 'formal instrument of surrender'. It

is not entirely clear what happened at this second meeting. One account suggests that Karzai refused to accept the surrender letter, but Semple disputes this based on his discussions with Taliban eyewitnesses.[104] Regardless, sometime between 5 and 7 December, the Taliban quietly abandoned Kandahar city. Fox's view was that the Taliban had been using the surrender talks as a ruse to delay the advance on the city in order to buy time to escape.[105] Given Afghan culture, and subsequent Taliban attempts at peace talks, it is more likely that this was a genuine effort to negotiate an end of the conflict by the Taliban leadership. In any event, there was no reason for Taliban fighters to hang around to see if the talks would be successful.

Even with the Taliban gone, the capture of Kandahar did not go entirely smoothly. Karzai had promised the governorship of Kandahar to Mullah Naqibullah. However, Sherzai's militia entered the city first and promptly occupied the main buildings including the governor's palace. Karzai was furious. He considered evicting Sherzai's militia by force but Fox persuaded him against this by warning: 'you are on the verge of starting a civil war'.[106] This was a real risk as commanders loyal to Sherzai were preparing for a showdown by bringing in extra fighters from Pakistan. One source from Quetta reported that 'They are actively recruiting and moving men across the border'.[107] At the same time, it seems quite likely that US special forces had an agenda of their own. Sherzai had managed to convince them that Mullah Naqibullah was 'the Taliban governor of Kandahar', and so they wanted to see control of Kandahar go to Sherzai. Naqibullah's right-hand man would later complain that 'The Americans were such amateurs … They were honest to the point of simplemindedness. Anyone Sherzai or his interpreter told them was a Talib, they would take it on faith.'[108] Undoubtedly, this view is biased given the man held a grudge against the Americans. However, there is plenty of evidence that US forces were stumbling about in complete ignorance of the subtleties of Afghan tribal politics, and so were easily misled and misdirected by warlords looking to remove rivals.[109] Karzai was left with a fait accompli. Under American pressure, he ordered Naqibullah to rein in his Alikozai militia. Naqibullah was allowed to occupy Kandahar airport and the shabby compound that Mullah Omar had evacuated; ironically this reinforced the US mistaken belief that he was really Taliban.

It is not entirely clear when Mullah Omar fled Kandahar city or where he went. Some reports suggest that he was in hiding some thirty miles north-west in Maiwand district while the negotiations for the Taliban surrender continued.[110] However, what is clear is that with the fall of Kandahar, the Taliban Emirate was finally defeated.

THE BIRTH OF ISAF

While the US military focused on hunting down the remnants of al-Qaeda and the Taliban following the fall of Kandahar, the international community began to concentrate on the implementation of the Bonn Agreement, which had been concluded on 5 December and was endorsed the following day by the UN Security Council.[111] Providing security for the new government in Kabul was widely considered to be crucial at this stage. Here, at last, Britain played a major role. Noting that it would take some time to establish the new Afghan security forces, Annex I of the agreement requested the early deployment of a UN-mandated force to 'assist in the maintenance of security for Kabul and its surrounding areas'.[112] In fact, Brahimi had been calling on members of the UN Security Council to provide such a force ever since Kabul had fallen in mid November. British diplomats in New York had been strong supporters of this position and, as we have seen, Britain had attempted unilaterally to deploy a robust force to secure Kabul.

Initially, however, it was reported that Britain would not be contributing a contingent to the proposed international security force. CENTCOM was opposed to the introduction of a peacekeeping force that might get in the way of ongoing counterterrorist operations. Rumsfeld also warned that peacekeepers might become terrorist targets.[113] This view was echoed by the Chief of the Defence Staff, Admiral Boyce, who told the prime minister that he was concerned about sending in British peacekeepers to Kabul while British special forces were helping the Americans hunt down what remained of the Taliban and al-Qaeda elsewhere in Afghanistan.[114] Boyce's concerns fell on deaf ears. Blair was keen on Britain being involved in, and possibly leading, the international security force. On 11 December, Boyce went public with his concerns at a speech to the Royal United Services

Institute (RUSI), declaring that Britain had to choose between joining the UN security force or continuing to take part in the US-led war on terror. Boyce was unaware that the prime minister had already decided on the matter and tipped off the Americans before informing his own defence chief. Just as Boyce was telling his RUSI audience that Britain had yet to decide on whether or not to contribute to the international security force, the US Secretary of State, Colin Powell, told a reporter in Paris how pleased he was that Britain had volunteered to lead the force.[115]

Thereafter, things began to move rather quickly. Major General John McColl, General Officer Commanding UK 3 Division, was selected to command the international security force. McColl went to PJHQ in Northwood to receive his mission orders from the Chief of Joint Operations, which were initially to 'see if it can be done, and if not to say so'.[116] McColl dispatched a reconnaissance and liaison team led by Brigadier Barney White-Spunner, the commander of 16 Air Assault Brigade, and Brigadier Peter Wall from PJHQ. White-Spunner's job was to assess logistical challenges and advise on the composition of the security force. Wall's job was to negotiate with the Northern Alliance, who were deeply ambivalent about a foreign force arriving in Kabul. The advance team arrived at Bagram airfield in mid December for their quick four-day visit, and were escorted into Kabul by the SAS. They found few people and no cars on the city streets. Their first port of call was the British embassy, which had been abandoned in 1989. The main embassy building had been burned down by a mob in 1995, with only some outbuildings surviving intact. The newly appointed British ambassador, Stephen Evans, had only arrived a couple of weeks before to reopen the embassy.[117] In a scene from a bygone era, White-Spunner and Wall were offered tea served in fine bone china amid the wreckage of the building. White-Spunner, who as a young hitchhiker had taken tea at the Kabul embassy in the early 1970s, was amazed to find waiting at the door 'the same old guy, and same tray, and same teacups'.[118]

Back in London, McColl chaired a 'force generation' conference on 14 and 15 December, with some fifteen troop-contributing nations represented. He recalls that 'we got pretty much what we wanted'. 3 Division would provide the command headquarters and focus on strategic matters, in particular supporting the new interim administration and liaising with the Northern Alliance. 16 Air Assault Brigade would provide the tactical headquarters and be in charge of operations on the ground. The security force was not finalised by the end of the conference, but it was expected to be between 3,000 and 5,000 strong, with contributions from seven countries. Some in Whitehall argued that it was enough for Britain to provide the headquarters and there was no need for any British infantry. McColl 'put a red card down on the table' at this suggestion. He insisted that since the situation was so unstable, it was essential he have 'a reliable force' at his disposal, and accordingly he was given the 2nd Battalion the Parachute Regiment, drawn from 16 Air Assault Brigade.[119]

While the international security force was being assembled in London, Karzai flew from Kandahar to Bagram on a US Air Force C-130 transport plane, arriving under cover of darkness. Waiting for him on the runway was Marshal Fahim with a couple of hundred of his fighters, turned out in their best uniforms. Fahim was stunned to see Karzai get off the plane without a large militia escort of his own. 'Where are your men?' he asked. In a brilliant statesmanlike gesture, Karzai simply responded: 'You are my men.'[120] By this stage, Fahim's excited militiamen began crowding around to get a look at Karzai. Gary Berntsen, the senior CIA agent in Afghanistan, did not like the unfolding scene. 'It was clear that the man who embodied the future of Afghanistan had no security detail. I didn't want him shot or trampled before he reached Kabul.'[121] He whisked Karzai into a car and off to the capital. One American journalist in the city at the time observed that 'Karzai arrived here not as the triumphant hero but almost as a discreet envoy seeking to avoid antagonizing jealous rivals already eager to undercut him'. Karzai went straight to meet with Burhanuddin Rabbani at the presidential palace. A Northern Alliance leader and former president of Afghanistan, Rabbani had been cut out of the interim administration, and was not at all happy about it.[122] Berntsen observed that 'two guards with rifles provide the only external security' at the presidential palace, and inside 'stood another Afghan soldier with a revolver'.[123] Security was going to have to be beefed up if Karzai was to survive. A week later Britain rushed a contingent of fifty Royal Marines to Kabul to help protect the new Afghan leader and other senior officials.[124]

Karzai also met with other prominent Afghan warlords who stood to lose out under the Bonn Agreement, as well as with Northern Alliance leaders that had been appointed to senior positions in the administration, especially Fahim and Qanouni. Karzai knew that he was reliant on the Northern Alliance to keep the peace in Kabul. This is why a neutral security force provided by the international community was so urgently needed.

McColl flew with White-Spunner and Wall to Kabul to get the international force up and running. The first order of business was to get the Northern Alliance, who controlled the capital, to agree to the deployment. Marshal Fahim grudgingly accepted that an international force was coming but he wanted to keep it to no more than one thousand strong, and to have it confined to guarding key government buildings; he did not want to see British or other foreign troops patrolling in Kabul.[125] McColl was not having any of it. He simply explained that 'under those conditions the force would not deploy and [Western] aid would not follow'. At that point, McColl recalls, the 'Tajaki Three' – Fahim, Qanouni and Abdullah – 'disappeared for a powwow and came back saying okay'.[126]

On 19 December, the Secretary of State for Defence was able to inform the House of Commons that 'the United Kingdom is formally prepared to take on the leadership of an international security assistance force for a limited period of three months'. The word 'assistance' had been added to delimit the role of the force to assisting Afghan troops in maintaining the security of Kabul and its surrounding area; hence, Hoon told the House, 'ultimate responsibility for security will remain with the [Afghan] Interim Authority'. Responding to Hoon's statement, the Conservative Shadow Defence Secretary, Bernard Jenkin, raised a number of concerns including whether the US military was 'fully committed to supporting and sustaining, and if necessary to protecting, multinational forces in Afghanistan'.[127] Behind the scenes, this was also a worry for the British government. Rumsfeld considered the International Security Assistance Force mission to be a distraction from the main counterterrorism mission, and so he had refused to guarantee US military support to ISAF troops should they get into trouble. As Hoon later recalled, 'That led to difficult discussions between the Prime Minister and the President.' It is not clear that Britain got the assurances it required. Hoon suggests Britain did:

that Blair 'prevailed eventually' in his discussions with Bush. Rumsfeld remembers it differently, recalling that 'we did not have a written commitment to drop everything else we may have been doing anywhere in the world to solve an ISAF problem'.[128]

The British had originally suggested that ISAF fall under CENTCOM command; this would have improved coordination between ISAF and the US military's Operation Enduring Freedom. This suggestion was welcomed by US military chiefs as it would have given them some control over the new international force entering their area of operations. However, it was roundly rejected by the French and Germans; as Campbell notes in his diary, it was opposed 'by the French because they are French, the Germans because their parliament would only support peacekeeping forces'. In contrast, the British were keen on putting the force under CENTCOM because 'it meant that [the Americans] would have to stay involved and make sure our troops got out if things got really tricky'.[129] The prime minister was able to work directly with President Jacques Chirac to overcome French objections. But Germany, which was due to assume command of ISAF after the British, would not budge on the issue. The German defence minister insisted on a strict separation of the ISAF stabilisation and US counterterrorism missions. Given the constitutional and political restrictions on deploying its military overseas, Germany was prepared to send peacekeepers but not combat forces.[130] This division between states and militaries prepared to undertake peacekeeping and those willing to do war-fighting was to become a significant debilitating feature of the ISAF campaign.

The Shadow Defence Secretary was also little reassured by Hoon's statement that this would be a time-limited deployment. He noted the view expressed by Field Marshal Peter Inge, the former Chief of the General Staff, that this 'operational commitment has ... "mission creep" written all over it'. Jenkin further observed that 'Bosnia was meant to be a short-term deployment, and years later we still have thousands of troops there. Sierra Leone was meant to be "over in a month", according to the then Foreign Secretary. Yesterday we learned in a written answer that British troops will be there beyond two years.'[131] Jenkin was right to be sceptical, as time would tell.

On 20 December, the UN Security Council formally authorised the deployment of ISAF under Chapter VII of the United Nations Charter, thus giving it authority under international law to use force to protect its mandate.[132] Understandably, there was still quite a bit of toing and froing over the Military Technical Agreement, which was the legal agreement between ISAF and the Afghan interim administration. The negotiations, led by Wall, continued into the early new year. McColl recalls that just before Christmas, the Ministry of Defence told him that the draft agreement was 'excellent' and that he should sign it, only to get a message from the Foreign Office on Boxing Day saying it was 'no good, don't sign'.[133] The final agreement gave ISAF remarkable latitude, including 'complete and unimpeded freedom of movement throughout the territory and airspace of Afghanistan' and 'use of any areas or facilities' it required. Of particular note is Article 4.2, which effectively gave the ISAF commander carte blanche: 'The Interim Administration understands and agrees that the ISAF Commander will have the authority, without interference or permission, to do all that the Commander judges necessary and proper, including the use of military force, to protect ISAF and its mission.'[134] In short, ISAF could pretty much do what it wanted without any further approval from the interim administration or indeed future Afghan governments. It would be nine years before an ISAF commander bothered to seek permission from the Afghan president before launching a major military offensive on Afghan soil.

The immediate challenge was to deploy ISAF, and to set up the headquarters. McColl's team was temporarily camped out in the British embassy, and had to find an alternative site for ISAF headquarters. White-Spunner's driver, Corporal Jamey Simon, stumbled across an old Afghan army sports club that was in a derelict state; it later turned out to be the site of the British East India Company's cantonment from the First Anglo-Afghan War.[135] British Army engineers were convinced that the building was impossible to renovate but McColl found some local tradespeople who cleaned and patched it up.[136] The end result was far from the Ritz. One official visiting from London recalls that it was 'austere extreme', and that there was plastic sheeting covering the windows 'to keep the wind and snow out'.[137] Nonetheless, it was still preferable to remaining in tents in the freezing temperatures of an Afghan winter.

It took some time for ISAF as a whole to take shape. Hoon recalls that he 'spent most of Boxing Day fielding offers for contributions for

ISAF', mostly for infantry that was not needed, as opposed to logistics and engineering, which was.[138] Helicopters were also in desperately short supply; this was to become a persistent theme in Britain's war in Afghanistan. The British produced 'a plan for staged deployments, reflecting the ability of partners to deploy'; thus, British and French troops would be sent first, followed by the Germans and then the Turks.[139] An advanced guard of three hundred Royal Marines duly arrived, flown in before Christmas from the amphibious ship HMS *Fearless* in the Arabian Sea. In the weeks to come, they would be joined by a further 1,500 British troops from the Parachute Regiment.[140] ISAF equipment was flown in on Russian military transport, leading some Kabulis to think that the Russians were coming back. It was the end of January before the whole of ISAF was deployed.[141]

'Security came very quickly' to Kabul, recalls White-Spunner; there was 'some gunfire exchanged with criminal gangs', but the two main security threats to ISAF – namely a Taliban attack or armed action by rival militia groups – never materialised. From the beginning, ISAF conducted joint patrols with the Northern Alliance. To facilitate this military cooperation, ISAF 'ended up dealing with Bismullah Khan', and not the more difficult Marshal Fahim.[142] Khan, who would later become chief of the Afghan army and eventually minister of defence, developed a reputation with successive ISAF commanders for being competent and reliable – qualities that were often in short supply among the Afghan partners.

In his operational orders to ISAF, McColl defined the mission objective as 'to create a secure environment within Kabul within which the developing Afghan government can gain traction'. It was clear to him that he had to do all he could to support the interim administration. Thus, he made himself 'always available to Karzai', and tried to follow through on any requests from the new Afghan leader, however unusual. When it was discovered that the new aviation minister had stolen the funds to fly Afghan pilgrims to Mecca for the hajj – he was caught attempting to fly out of Kabul and shot on the spot – McColl arranged for a Royal Air Force C-130 transport plane to be made available.

McColl's command faced two major challenges. The first was capacity building in the new Afghan ministries. This was actually the responsibility of the United Nations, working with major donors such as the British Department for International Development (DFID) and the United States Agency for International Development (USAID). However, development assistance was very slow to arrive in Kabul. In this sense, Bonn was a 'big disappointment' for the Afghans. ISAF tried to help out where it could. Thus it provided a rudimentary ambulance service for Kabul using six field ambulances; interestingly, most call-outs were for childbirth.[143] Reflecting the British Army's experience of three decades of operating under civil leadership in Northern Ireland, McColl treated Brahimi as 'the head of the international community in theatre' and accordingly 'deferred to him and followed his lead'.[144]

The second challenge was to help create the new Afghan army. The aim was to have the 1st Battalion of the Afghan National Guard (the '1 BANG') trained up in time to formally take the lead in providing security for the Loya Jirga in June 2002 that would decide on the transitional government. The 1 BANG was meant 'to be fully representative of the Afghan people'. Bismullah Khan produced the five hundred troops and actually did a good job of ensuring its multi-ethnic composition. The Turks supplied the uniforms and the British provided the instructors. The battalion formed up at the end of February and undertook eight weeks of basic training. The recruits were far worse than expected in terms of competence but made up for this by the sheer pride of being in the first unit of the new Afghan army.[145] By June, the 1 BANG was able to provide the perimeter security for the Loya Jirga. In stark contrast to British success in training the new army was Germany's lacklustre performance in training the new national police force. According to one senior official, the 'pace of German training of police was glacial', and it included sending Afghan recruits off on three-year training courses.[146] ISAF compensated by stepping up its joint patrols in areas of Kabul most affected by criminality.

Many Afghans, Karzai included, wanted ISAF to expand beyond the capital. McColl recalled that 'every week [tribal] delegations were coming to Karzai to request that ISAF deploy outside of Kabul'. McColl had developed a plan for this to happen which would require ISAF to be grown fourfold to 20,000 troops. He managed to persuade Dobbins to present the plan to Rumsfeld when he visited Kabul on 16 December. The US Defense Secretary was firmly against the idea: once again he argued that peacekeeping was a distraction from the primary counterterrorism mission. Already McColl had gone further than Rumsfeld would have liked, signing a memorandum of understanding with President Karzai that, for many in the Bush administration, 'gave ISAF more responsibility than we wanted'.[147]

The idea of expanding ISAF beyond Kabul was raised again by Secretary of State Colin Powell at a US National Security Council meeting in February 2002, only to be shot down for good. In advance of the meeting, National Security Council staff circulated a paper claiming that peacekeeping was 'a failed concept'. Dobbins later noted with disgust that this 'ludicrously misleading paper went unchallenged'.[148] Without American buy-in the plan was dead. London told McColl to stop pushing it, not least because Britain was due to give up command of ISAF and there was concern that talk of expansion might scare off other nations from taking over.[149] The Turkish Army was scheduled to take command of ISAF in March but when their advanced party saw the state of ISAF headquarters, they were shocked at the very basic living conditions. They refused to deploy until the departing British engineers had built them three new buildings and a cookhouse.[150] Finally, on 20 June 2002, McColl handed over command of ISAF to Turkish General Zorlu, and the 1st Battalion the Royal Anglian Regiment (which had taken over from 2 Para) handed over their duties to a Turkish infantry battalion. This was the very day on which the Loya Jirga ended, having elected Karzai head of the Transitional Government of Afghanistan.[151] Against all the odds, this first ISAF mission had been a success. McColl's command conducted well over 2,000 joint patrols, disarmed over 3 million munitions (mostly anti-personnel mines), and got the new Afghan army off to a pretty good start.

THE BATTLE OF TORA BORA

The top priority for the CIA was to track down Osama bin Laden. On 8 November, bin Laden left Kabul for the city of Jalalabad, a hotbed of militancy about five hours' drive to the east of the capital. Defeat hung in the air, with the streets full of surly foreign jihadists, sullen Taliban, and civilians displaced by the fighting to the north. On 11 November, bin Laden gave a rallying speech, calling on local elders and Taliban commanders to resist the Americans, and reportedly handing out $100,000 for good measure. The following day, he fled to the hills. Thirty-five miles south-west lay the snowy peaks of the White Mountains. In one wooded area, some 14,000 feet up in the mountain range, known to locals as Tora Bora, lay hundreds of caves that had been occupied by mujahedin in the Soviet War. During the 1990s, bin Laden had made some improvements to this cave complex and used it as an al-Qaeda base. Some news media would later imagine a fantastical underground fortress befitting a James Bond villain; in fact, the improvements were more modest, such as installing generators to provide ventilation, lighting and heating. All the same, this was enough to enable al-Qaeda to occupy the deeper caves up to a thousand feet underground. It is to here that bin Laden headed in a convoy of two hundred Toyotas and Land Cruisers.[152]

Within days, the CIA had found him. On 17 November, Berntsen told Mulholland that he was going to insert an eight-strong CIA team outside Jalalabad to hunt down bin Laden, and he asked for an A-team to accompany them. Mulholland was not prepared to risk it. 'Send your team in,' he told Berntsen. 'If in a week they're still alive and operating, I'll send a team to work with them.'[153] That is exactly what happened. Within a couple of days, four members of the CIA team climbed high up the Milawa Valley that led towards Tora Bora, bringing with them a laser designator. Much to their astonishment, local guides took them to a ridge overlooking a major al-Qaeda camp with 'trucks, houses, command posts, checkpoints, machine-gun nests, an obstacle course and hundreds of bin Laden's men'.[154] In less than an hour, American bombs and missiles rained down on the camp. For four days straight, the CIA team called in air strikes; thereafter they were joined by an A-team with two more combat air controllers. By this stage, the surviving jihadists had fled the camp, many heading up into the Tora Bora complex. With 90 per cent of available US air power committed to the battle, a seemingly endless stream of B-52s and B-1Bs kept up an unrelenting bombardment of al-Qaeda positions over the following days, while six AC-130 Spectre gunships ensured that the jihadists had no rest at night. A BLU-82 Daisy Cutter bomb and an AGM-142 Have Nap missile with a special rock-penetrating warhead were used against parts of the cave complex believed to be housing al-Qaeda leaders.[155] By the end of the battle, the US Air Force had dropped a staggering 1,650 bombs on an area measuring eighteen square miles.[156] Doubtless for some al-Qaeda fighters the bombing was harrowing. However, for those in the deeper caves, it was tolerable. One later recalled that 'We got used to the bombing even when it was near us'.[157] With al-Qaeda so well entrenched in the cave complex, ground forces had to be sent in to flush them out. This is where things ran into trouble.

The ground assault on Tora Bora was launched on 8 December. With only around ninety US special forces troops on the scene, the operation depended on the forces of the so-called 'Eastern Alliance', comprising militia provided by two rival commanders, Hazarat Ali and Haji Zaman Ghamsharik. A report by the Senate Foreign Relations Committee into the events at Tora Bora would later describe this pair in less than inspiring terms: Ali had 'a fourth-grade education and a reputation as a bully' and had previously fought for the Taliban; and Zaman 'was a wealthy drug smuggler who had been persuaded by the United States to return from France'.[158] These were the men entrusted with getting bin Laden. In a classic block-and-sweep operation, groups of militia were to push up north through the Milawa Valley into the mouth of Tora Bora, while other Afghan militia groups blocked al-Qaeda escape routes to the west, north and east in the mountains above. A-team and CIA combat air controllers remained in place overlooking Tora Bora to call in supporting air strikes.

The Eastern Alliance forces numbered around 2,000, although with Afghan militiamen coming and going the numbers fluctuated considerably over the course of the battle. Against this, US intelligence estimated that there were anywhere between 300 and 3,000 enemy forces in the Tora Bora area, and that these were a mix of Taliban and al-Qaeda.[159] In fact this appears to have been al-Qaeda's fight. When the Taliban tried to send a convoy before the battle to check out what was happening at Tora Bora, they were told to clear off by al-Qaeda fighters fearful of infiltration by Afghans working for the Eastern Alliance.[160] Studying accounts by Arab survivors (in US captivity in Guantánamo) and American participants, academic experts would later conclude that 'there was no significant Taliban or Afghan presence at this battle. This was al-Qaeda's moment.'[161]

The operation was disorganised from the beginning. Indeed it was delayed by almost a week due to a disagreement between Ali and

Mulholland over the role to be played by US special operations forces. Ali expected the A-teams to be in the fight, while Mulholland stuck to the doctrinal view that their role was to advise and assist local Afghan forces. Eventually Ali conceded because the Americans were paying him handsomely for the operation. Complicating matters was poor coordination and even downright rivalry between the different militia groups, which on several occasions spilled over into exchanges of gunfire between Ali's Pashtun militia (which was the largest group) and Zaman's Pashay force; it did not help that Ali's militia were supported by US special forces while Zaman's received help from a British special forces team. Much to the Americans' frustration, the Afghans were not very aggressive in assaulting al-Qaeda positions. The commander of US special forces at Tora Bora later complained that all their Afghan allies would do was 'go up, get into a skirmish, lose a guy or two, maybe kill an al-Qaeda guy or two and then leave'.[162] Another problem was that the Afghans would return to their camps each night for dinner, thus enabling the enemy to retake any ground lost during the day. The Afghan militias also lacked the logistical support to bring forward freshly prepared food; as British military advisers would discover in the years to come, Afghans refuse to eat pre-prepared military rations. Dinner was especially important as it was Ramadan, so Afghan fighters were not eating or drinking during the day. Still, special forces and CIA snipers and AC-130 gunships made it uncomfortable for al-Qaeda to move around at night.[163]

By 11 December, al-Qaeda leaders had had enough and attempted to negotiate the terms of a ceasefire that would have allowed them to lay down their weapons and walk away. This was completely unacceptable to the Americans who demanded unconditional surre-nder (as they had done with the Taliban the week before). The fighting therefore resumed for almost another week, with al-Qaeda diehards effectively providing a rearguard while their leaders fled. On 17 December the fighting ended and Ali declared victory. Three days later US and British special forces began to sweep the cave complex.

British special forces would later describe Tora Bora as 'one of the most daring engagements that the 22 SAS Regiment has undertaken in 30 years'.[164] The US Army's official history put the final number of enemy killed, wounded and captured at around 1,100. In his published account of the battle, the commander of US special operations forces provides a far lower estimate of 220 killed and 52 captured.[165] Either way, it is clear that most of the jihadists at Tora Bora had got away: according to the US Army official history, 'as many as 1,500 fighters may have escaped to fight another day'.[166] Crucially, this included bin Laden and other key al-Qaeda leaders.

Both Rumsfeld and Franks would later suggest that bin Laden may not have been at Tora Bora. In an op-ed in the *New York Times* in December 2004, Franks stated: 'We don't know to this day if Mr. bin Laden was in Tora Bora.'[167] Little credence can be given to this self-serving claim. As noted in the official history of US Special Operations Command: 'All sources reporting corroborated his presence on several days from 9–14 December.'[168] Indeed, in his own memoir, the deputy commander of CENTCOM, Lieutenant General Michael DeLong, wrote that bin Laden 'was definitely there when we hit the caves. Every day during the bombing, Rumsfeld asked me "did we get him?"'[169] So why was more not done to prevent him escaping?

The Pakistani border; is only fifteen miles from Tora Bora, and early on in the battle Berntsen had sent a request to CENTCOM for eight hundred US Army rangers to be rushed to the battlefield to help seal off al-Qaeda's escape routes.[170] This was rejected by Franks who, following instruction from Rumsfeld, was determined to minimise the US military footprint in Afghanistan. The US Army official history of Operation Enduring Freedom further suggests that 'Franks simply appeared not to have any ground forces inside CENTCOM's area of responsibility to assist the [Eastern Alliance]'. This is plain nonsense. Over one thousand soldiers with 10th Mountain Division were deployed to K2 at the start of the war, and many hundreds had subsequently been redeployed to Bagram airfield. There was also a 1,200-strong US Marine task force at Camp Rhino near Kandahar airfield under the command of Brigadier General James 'Mad Dog' Mattis. The official history claims that these units were 'busy with security tasks' – that is, guarding these airfields.[171] In fact, the soldiers at K2 were hanging around 'cleaning latrines and functioning as military police', and understandably itching to get into the fight in Afghanistan. Mattis was also keen: according to the US Senate report, he 'told a journalist that his troops could seal off Tora Bora, but his superiors rejected the plan'.[172] If necessary, CENTCOM could also have drawn on 75th Ranger Regiment stationed in Oman, or the Deployment

Readiness Brigade of the 82nd Airborne Division, which was able to deploy anywhere in the world within five days.[173] In short, lack of will and not lack of resources prevented Franks from deploying US ground troops to support the assault on Tora Bora.

Instead, the Pakistan Army was asked to intercept jihadists as they fled across the border. When President Bush asked if the Pakistan Army was up to the job, the deputy head of the CIA's Counterterrorism Center, Hank Crumpton, told him that it was not, but he added that 'with such a long border, rough terrain, high elevation, no army on earth can seal this'.[174] This assessment missed the fact that the Pakistan Army would not have had to seal the whole 1,500-mile border, but rather only the area around Tora Bora. And not helping matters was the lack of coordination between US special forces and the Pakistan Army, who learned about the start of the ground assault from CNN. The deployment of Pakistani forces was also delayed by the need to negotiate access to the high valleys behind Tora Bora with tribal elders, in order to avoid starting a battle on the Pakistani side of the border. In the final weeks of 2001, tens of thousands of Taliban and foreign jihadists were crossing over into Pakistan with the paid help of local smugglers. Those fleeing Tora Bora joined this deluge. The Pakistan Army did apprehend between six hundred and seven hundred foreign militants, handing many over to the Americans.[175] Bin Laden was not among them.

Tora Bora was a complete fiasco. The best that can be said is that Britain played little part in it. There was a sixty-strong team of British planners in CENTCOM led by Air Marshal Jock Stirrup as the UK National Contingent Commander for Afghanistan. Reporting on the preparations for Tora Bora, *The Times* noted that Stirrup 'has a reputation as an influential member of the coalition planning team'.[176] This may be so but it is doubtful that he was involved in the decision over whether or not to deploy US troops to support the battle. Nor was Britain likely to provide the necessary forces itself (not that it was asked to). Four thousand troops from 45 Commando and 2 Para were on standby for rapid deployment to Afghanistan. However, given the palaver around the aborted attempt to deploy this force outside Kabul just a few weeks before, there would have been little appetite in Whitehall to try to do so again. These concerns would not have applied to the deployment of a large US force, and there is no indication that any of the Eastern Alliance commanders would have objected to this. Indeed, quite the opposite; the commander of the largest militia force, Hazarat Ali, later expressed some bewilderment at the US failure to send reinforcements. 'A nose-picking semi-illiterate' he may have been,[177] but even Ali could see that something was not quite right: 'Why weren't there more Americans in Tora Bora?'[178]

OPERATION JACANA

Tora Bora had appeared to signal the end of major combat operations. Al-Qaeda and the Taliban seemed to have been defeated and fled the field. As US 10th Mountain Division took charge of US operations in Afghanistan in early 2002, its commander, Major General Franklin Hagenbeck, recalled that 'it was the general consensus from everyone that the war, the fight, in Afghanistan was done'. But a large number of al-Qaeda and Taliban fighters – estimates range from just under six hundred fighters to as many as a thousand – were found in the Shah-i Kowt Valley in Paktia province close to Pakistan.[179] Some of these were escapees from Tora Bora. Hagenbeck assembled a task force over 2,000 strong, initially comprising two battalions of US infantry and various special forces groups, which were later joined by a battalion of Canadian light infantry. German, French, Norwegian, Danish and Australian special forces also participated in the operation.[180] As in Tora Bora, it was expected that Taliban and al-Qaeda fighters would attempt to flee and so several hundred Afghan militia were brought in to block likely escape routes.

Lasting eighteen days from late February to mid March 2002, Operation Anaconda proved to be a very tough fight. Dug into well-prepared defensive positions, al-Qaeda and the Taliban put up stiff resistance and the initial assault into the valley got bogged down from day one. US forces frequently found themselves outnumbered and outgunned by the defenders, who were 'brave to a fault' but fortunately not very good shots. Heavy use was made of air strikes and helicopter gunships, often just to keep the assault forces alive. By now al-Qaeda and Taliban fighters had learned to hide in caves when warplanes appeared so as to avoid American bombs. Then, on 12 March, the battle began to peter out, with US and Canadian soldiers only facing sporadic fire. 10th Mountain Division estimated that it had killed over eight hundred al-Qaeda and Taliban fighters but other accounts suggest only two hundred enemy killed. It is likely that, once again, most had escaped.[181]

Throughout the war, Britain kept an Amphibious Readiness Group, comprising two companies of Royal Marines, in the Indian Ocean, as a rescue force should any British special forces get into trouble in Afghanistan.[182] CENTCOM had been pushing for some time for these to be deployed to support counterterrorist operations; as one senior British defence planner noted, given that they were specialists in mountain warfare, this mission 'had Royal Marines written all over it'.[183] A Royal Marine colonel sent on reconnaissance to Bagram airfield in late January found 'the US engaged in Operation Anaconda and not having too great a time of it'. Understandably, the 'Americans were interested in what we could bring to the party', especially by way of 'combat power'.[184] There was also internal pressure for this deployment. With the British Army and the Parachute Regiment taking the ISAF mission, the Royal Navy and Royal Marines wanted their slice of the action; the competition between the Parachute Regiment and Royal Marines is famously intense. Admiral Boyce, as Chief of the Defence Staff, was sympathetic to the Royal Navy's position and so pushed for Britain to agree to CENTCOM's request.[185]

In late March, the Secretary of State for Defence announced the deployment of 'our largest military deployment for combat operations since the Gulf Conflict' in 1991. Britain was sending 1,700 Royal Marines, committing the Amphibious Readiness Group already in theatre, and flying in the remaining troops of 45 Commando battlegroup, along with supporting artillery, engineers and combat logistics. Hoon told MPs that under Operation Jacana, the Royal Marines would be 'ready to commence offensive operations by mid-April'.[186] The following day, CENTCOM announced the formal conclusion of Operation Anaconda. However, Franks reportedly expected that more 'battles lay ahead as militants try to regroup'. Hagenbeck similarly thought that there were 'thousands of enemies [still] out there'. This view was shared by British defence officials, who told journalists that there were 'pockets of Taliban and al-Qaeda bubbling up over Afghanistan'.[187] All these views were wrong. Anaconda proved to be the final major battle until the Taliban swept back into southern

Afghanistan four years later. By the time the British force arrived on
the scene the enemy had long gone, leaving many disgruntled Royal
Marines to complain that they had been deployed 'a month too late'.[188]

Operation Jacana got off to a bad start. The task force was delayed
getting into theatre by Pakistan's refusal to give Britain use of Karachi
airfield, which the Royal Air Force had previously used for the ISAF
deployment.[189] In the end, some marines flew directly from the deck
of HMS *Ocean* into Kandahar on Chinook helicopters, and some
arrived from Oman and from England on C-130s along with their
heavy equipment; in all, it took one hundred C-130 flights to transport
the whole task force. There was also a problem with basing facilities
for 45 Commando in Bagram. The British were supposed to be housed
in old Russian barracks but these ended up being allocated to the new
Afghan army. So instead the Royal Engineers had to clear a large area
of mines, and construct temporary accommodation with power and
essential utilities, causing further delays.[190] The facilities in Bagram
proved challenging for the Royal Marines in other ways. Early on in
the tour, British personnel suddenly began to fall ill with vomiting
and diarrhoea at an alarming rate. Back in London, the defence officials
'wondered if this was a biological weapons attack'. The MoD's chief
nurse was sent out to investigate, and reported back that the cause
was a virulent stomach bug.[191]

Leading the British task force was Brigadier Roger Lane (who
was also the overall commander of 3 Commando Brigade), with
Colonel Tim Chicken under him as the commanding officer of 45
Commando battlegroup. Formally, the British task force was placed
under the operational control of 10th Mountain Division. Informally,
Lane was instructed by PJHQ 'not to let UK troops come under
direct US command'. The British did not trust 10th Mountain
Division after it had left a Canadian infantry battalion without
support during Operation Anaconda.[192] This injunction from PJHQ
was just as well, for when they arrived Lane and Chicken were less
than impressed with the way Hagenbeck was running things. Even
though they were supposed to fall under the major general's
command, the Royal Marines were never given a copy of 10th
Mountain Division's operational plan because it was classified
'NOFORN' (No Foreigners).[193] Chicken recalls that he 'wasn't filled
with a whole lot of confidence' in Hagenbeck.[194] As it happens, Lane

and Hagenbeck fundamentally disagreed on the approach to operations. 10th Mountain Division was conducting intelligence-led
operations, which meant that infantry units would deploy once
enemy forces had been found. Since foreign jihadists had fled to
Pakistan, and the Taliban had done likewise or gone to ground in
Afghanistan, 'sizeable elements of the US force was hanging around
waiting for the call'. This was also the case for the Canadian infantry
battalion under Hagenbeck's command. Chicken remembers that
the Canadians spent only 5 days out of 120 out and about. Lane
refused to follow this approach, instead sending his men out to find
the enemy. In consequence, Chicken recalls, 'we spent 75 per cent
of our time out' on operations.[195]

Under the umbrella of Operation Jacana, 45 Commando ended up
conducting four major operations – code-named Ptarmigan, Condor,
Snipe and Buzzard. The first of these, Operation Ptarmigan, was
launched in mid April, by which time only half of the British task
force had arrived in Bagram. The objective was to sweep through the
Shah-i Kowt Valley to check for any lingering jihadists, and to uncover
any arms caches hidden in caves. The Royal Marines were not
expecting much of a fight, and accordingly expectations were downplayed in the press. It was reported that this was 'a dress rehearsal
for future operations and was intended "to get the men into an
operational mindset" and accustom them to fighting in the Afghan
highlands'.[196] Two companies of Royal Marines swept the area thoroughly over five days, one moving along the valley floor and the other
along ridgelines above, and found nothing but abandoned fighting
positions 'and a whole lot of corpses'.[197] For Lane, Operation Ptarmigan
was a 'proving exercise, that we could project and sustain force'. It
was logistically and physically challenging for the marines to operate
at such extreme altitude. Chinook helicopters are only cleared to
operate up to 10,000 feet, but they had to ferry the marines to landing
zones over 14,000 feet up in the mountains. It was equally difficult
for the men themselves to move at such high altitude carrying weapons
and packs weighing over 130 pounds.[198] One marine described how
'you have to move very slowly, maybe taking a break every 200 metres
to catch your breath. One minute you are fine, the next your heart
rate is as high as it can get. So you rest, then start all over again.'[199]
Overcoming the elements was not enough for the marines, who

returned disappointed from their operation. By the end of April, 45 Commando had reached 'full operational capability'. However, frustration was growing among British as well as American troops; the *Observer* reported that 'a sense of aimlessness has settled over Bagram airbase'. One UK defence source summed up the situation perfectly: 'We have got a big, highly-trained, well equipped hammer and currently we can't find a decent sized nail to hit.'[200]

Royal Marine prayers appeared to have been answered when hundreds of enemy fighters were detected in the Mezai Mountains, in an area 13,000 feet up and covering over 120 square miles in the south of Gardez province.[201] The mountain terrain was preventing US signals intelligence from intercepting enemy communications, but Predator drones clearly showed what appeared to be a series of fortified positions and people moving about them.[202] The Royal Marines were given a large part of the area to sweep; US forces took the rest. All four marine companies were committed to Operation Snipe. As they stepped onto their Chinook helicopters, Royal Marines were eagerly anticipating 'a massive firefight' at the other end.[203]

Once again, the marines were to be sorely disappointed. Chicken recalls that the enemy 'bunkers' identified by US intelligence 'were in fact hovels used by locals'.[204] For X-Ray Company, which was given the task of assaulting an 'enemy compound', frustration quickly turned to farce. Following standard tactics, the company was dropped at some distance so it could walk onto the objective, which the company commander notes 'turned out to be a fucking wood'. The company was then advised 'that the area you are recceing is assessed to be a residual minefield'.[205] 45 Commando spent more than a week sweeping the area, eventually finding a massive arms stockpile located in four 'purpose-built caves', situated close to the main road running from Gardez to Khost. The Royal Marines spokesman in Bagram confirmed the discovery of '20 truckloads of ordnance' including artillery and mortar rounds, rockets and rocket-propelled grenades (RPGs). Probably desperate for a success story, the MoD claimed that this was 'an al-Qaeda munitions depot'. Lane told journalists that 'the operation had been successful in denying [al-Qaeda] a safe haven' and 'disrupting their logistic supplies'.[206] However, old Afghan hand Anthony Loyd of *The Times* was not convinced. Locals told him that the Taliban had abandoned the arms dump in January and that 'Afghan forces allied to the coalition had set up a base at the storage site', but they left as soon as the Royal Marines turned up.[207] Much of the ordnance was 'pretty unstable' and certainly too dangerous to move. So the marines attempted to seal the caves using explosives and inadvertently 'brought the mountain down'.[208] A *Sun* journalist was invited to push the detonator from over a mile away. The newspaper had heralded the start of Operation Snipe with the predictably jingoistic headline 'MARINES BLITZ ON BIN LADEN MEN'.[209] A rival tabloid captured the mood more aptly at the end of the operation: 'SHAM IN BAGRAM'.[210]

Thirty-six hours after getting back to Bagram, 45 Commando was stood up again to deploy urgently in support of an Australian SAS patrol that was taking heavy fire from Taliban groups near the town of Khost. The official record of what happened is recorded in the US Army's history: 'A 6-hour firefight ensued, during which the Australians had called in close air support from US AC-130 and helicopter gunships.'[211] Behind the scenes, Lane had informally promised to provide emergency support and extraction for the 150-strong Australian Special Forces Task Group at Bagram, should they get into trouble. Like the Canadians, the Australian experience of working with 10th Mountain Division had not been a happy one. The US Army had repeatedly failed to resupply Australian units in the field as it was supposed to, on one occasion leaving an Australian patrol without supplies for nine days. Hence, the Australians looked to the Royal Marines to guard their back. Lane now rushed to make good on his promise.[212]

45 Commando had to move fast as the Australians were two hundred miles away. Operation Condor was hastily planned and launched. Within hours, two companies of Royal Marines were dispatched in their Chinook helicopters, flying at night and 'nap-of-earth' for the final hour – down valleys and hugging the terrain in order to avoid detection. X-Ray Company was the first to arrive; as before, it was dropped a few miles away from the target and approached on foot. By this stage, the Australian SAS had disengaged and so the commander of X-Ray Company, Major Rich King, took a good hour to observe the enemy fighting positions. It soon became apparent that these were not al-Qaeda or Taliban but rather local Afghan militia. Without realising it, Australian special forces had been 'patrolling the boundary

between two rival Afghan factions and had got brassed up'.[213] As best as anyone could tell, the militia force mistook the Australians for their rivals and so opened fire; this actual story is not recorded in the US Army official history. By the time the rest of 45 Commando flew in, this muddle had been sorted out with the local militia. The battlegroup spent a week in the vicinity but had little to show for it. Once again, the Royal Marines returned to Bagram having not fired a shot in anger. The British press had a field day.[214]

Launched in late May, Operation Buzzard was Lane's last roll of the dice. The objective was to intercept enemy fighters and supplies moving across the border between Afghanistan and Pakistan in Khost province, a two-day drive from Bagram. The operation mainly involved setting up vehicle checkpoints along the main routes, many of which were just 'dusty tracks'; as Lane notes, 'This technique had been used extensively in Northern Ireland in border areas.'[215] One half of the battlegroup deployed in Chinooks, and the other half in a mix of Land Rovers, Pinzgauer all-terrain vehicles and quad bikes. 45 Commando spent a month on the Pakistani border. Chicken recalls that there was 'a lot of traffic and a lot of people to interact with', but none were al-Qaeda or Taliban, and that 'the more contact we had [with locals] the more it confirmed our suspicion that the American invasion had shattered the al-Qaeda/Taliban axis'. Towards the end, the Royal Marines found, in Chicken's words, 'a really, really impressive mujahedin tunnel complex, akin to the London Underground with lighting, water and concrete interior'. The smaller tunnels were being used by locals as shelter and so the marines left these intact; the rest of the complex they destroyed. On Operation Buzzard, the Royal Marines did finally get into a firefight of sorts, when X-Ray Company received heavy fire from a village. Chicken recalls that the US combat air controller attached to the company 'was desperate to drop high quantities of high explosives'.[216] But Major King refused to authorise this, and instead a patrol was sent into the village to talk to the elders. As had happened previously with Australian special forces, a local militia had mistaken the Royal Marines for a rival force and opened fire.[217]

Lane claims that Operation Buzzard had a major impact on the movement of people to and from Pakistan: 'We had intelligence reports that within twelve hours we had reduced trans-border activity by 70 per cent.'[218] What is not so clear is how much of this activity was al-Qaeda and the Taliban. King's view is that 'we weren't interdicting [enemy] supply-chains'. The area covered under Operation Buzzard was simply too large for the battlegroup to cover, especially when, as King puts it, for a marine on the ground 'my footprint is four hundred feet from my eyeball'.[219]

Things did not end well for Lane: he was relieved of his command following the conclusion of Operation Jacana. On 20 May, the MoD announced that Lane was being replaced a year early as commander of 3 Commando Brigade. Ironically this was just one day after Hoon went on breakfast television to defend him from press criticisms, declaring that he had 'every confidence in Brigadier Lane'. According to a defence spokesman, Lane's removal was a purely 'administrative arrangement within the Royal Marines' and had 'nothing to do with the operation or the way he has handled it'.[220] This claim was risible. Lane spoke his mind and this appears to have got him into trouble. When Hoon had announced to the House of Commons in October 2001 that the Royal Marines were ready to deploy immediately to Afghanistan, Lane had let it be known that the brigade was 'weeks away' from being prepared, adding: 'we will be ready when we are ready'. Following Operation Snipe, he had told journalists that the war was 'all but won', infuriating Rumsfeld, and earning him a private rebuke from London. At the start of Operation Condor, Lane had tried to conform to official spin by telling journalists that 45 Commando were going into battle against large numbers of heavily armed al-Qaeda and Taliban fighters, only to have senior officials in London describe his statement as 'overblown'.[221] In classic British understatement, the Chief of Joint Operations, Lieutenant General John Reith, said that Lane 'may not have got it right in the media handling side of things'.[222]

The simple fact is that by the time 45 Commando had turned up in eastern Afghanistan, al-Qaeda and the Taliban had gone. The Royal Marines had gone to Afghanistan looking for a fight, but all they had encountered were trigger-happy Afghan militia. They had been right, however, to blow up the military stores they found, even if these munitions belonged to Afghan militia, because soon the international effort would turn to disarming such groups and building up a new national Afghan army.

A FLAWED MASTERPIECE

Britain played a minor role in the fall of the Taliban, which were defeated on the battlefield by American air power. US warplanes dropped 18,000 bombs on enemy targets, including some 10,000 'precision munitions'.[223] Britain launched some cruise missile attacks but declined to commit any warplanes. On the northern and the southern fronts, the key function of US special operations forces was to guide American bombs onto targets. Taliban tactical incompetence made them especially vulnerable to aerial attack. As Stephen Biddle notes:

> [The Taliban] typically deployed on exposed ridgelines with little camouflage or concealment ... As a result, their positions could often be identified from even extraordinary distances. And once located, their poor entrenchment and exposed movement made them easy prey for precision weapons. The result was slaughter at standoff ranges, with little need for close combat.[224]

Later on, the Taliban would develop tactics to reduce their exposure to aerial attack, including using civilians as shields.[225] However, from October to December 2001 they provided rich pickings for US Air Force and Navy bombers.

To be at the receiving end of American bombing was utterly terrifying. Mullah Cable, a Taliban commander renowned for his brutality, recalled what happened early on in the war, when a convoy leaving his camp was bombed by a warplane: 'My teeth shook, my bones shook, everything inside me shook.' In the aftermath, he found 'severed limbs everywhere'. Lumps of 'melted steel and plastic' were all that remained of the vehicles. That night Taliban radio chatter reported that almost nine hundred fighters were missing, presumed dead, after a day of American bombardment. The following day, Mullah Cable gathered his men and told them to go home, before deserting himself.[226]

For defence analyst Michael O'Hanlon, however, Operation Enduring Freedom was a 'flawed masterpiece'. The speed with which al-Qaeda and the Taliban were defeated was indeed impressive, as was the manner with which the US conducted its military campaign, relying on a mix of CIA paramilitaries, special operations forces, local Afghan allies and American air power. Estimates put the number of Taliban killed at between 8,000 and 12,000, which was around 20 per cent of Taliban forces. When wounded in action are included, the Taliban probably lost half of their fighters in America's lightning war. Yet there was a crucial flaw: bin Laden and his lieutenants were allowed to get away when Rumsfeld and CENTCOM refused to deploy US ground forces to support the assault on Tora Bora. It was obvious that local Afghan militia and Pakistani frontier troops were not up to the task of interdicting al-Qaeda as they escaped the battle – indeed Bush was told as much by the CIA. O'Hanlon concludes that 'Putting several thousand U.S. forces in that mountainous, inland region would have been difficult and dangerous. Yet given the enormity of the stakes in this war, it would have been appropriate.' He places the blame on excessive caution on the part of the US Department of Defense, and this does indeed appear to have been a significant factor.[227] Equally, if not more, important was the failure to produce a coherent US strategy for Afghanistan, which clearly articulated agreed war aims and an appropriate tactical approach to the campaign. The CIA was focused on getting bin Laden but oddly the president never made this a central war aim; instead, civilian leaders talked about defeating the Taliban and denying al-Qaeda the use of Afghanistan. There was little Britain could do about this as it was expected simply to follow America's lead.

The absence of a coherent strategy meant that no thought had been given to what to do when al-Qaeda had been expelled from Afghanistan and the Taliban regime overthrown. Remarkably, US policymakers failed to anticipate that the Taliban might seek to surrender, and so Rumsfeld and CENTCOM were taken aback when Omar tried to do just this before the fall of Kandahar. Not helping matters was the tendency among US policymakers to conflate al-Qaeda and the Taliban, and thus to seek equal retribution from both. Hence, the United States was only prepared to accept the unconditional surrender of the Taliban. The poor human rights record and general eccentricities of the Taliban regime before 9/11 led US policymakers to underappreciate the legitimacy of the Taliban for a sizeable swathe of the Pashtun population in southern and eastern Afghanistan. For these reasons, it seemed only natural to US policymakers to exclude the Taliban from the post-war settlement of Afghanistan. This was the 'original sin' of the war.

The lack of strategy was also evident in the approach taken by the US and British representatives at Bonn. James Dobbins went to the talks without instructions from the White House on US objectives and how to proceed.[228] Robert Cooper, albeit playing a lesser role at Bonn, similarly recalls that 'there wasn't anybody in London who had thought more about Afghanistan than I had, so I made things up as I went along'.[229] Brahimi suggests that in hindsight the Taliban should have been invited to the Bonn negotiations. Bush's special envoy to Afghanistan, Zalmay Khalilzad, is not so sure. He notes that the Taliban 'was still putting up a determined fight' in the lead-up to the conference, and 'Kandahar had not yet fallen'. Thus, he concludes, 'I am skeptical that the international community could have lured the Taliban to the table at Bonn.'[230] Drawing in the Taliban would also have necessarily dragged out the talks, and there was immense pressure for a quick settlement that would stabilise the country and avoid a return to civil war. However, some process should have been put in place, ideally within the framework of the Bonn Agreement, for the interim administration to engage with the Taliban and draw them into the post-war political order.[231] The failure to do this would cost Britain, the United States and most of all Afghanistan dearly.

4

Road to Helmand

Blair fervently believed that the international community had a moral duty to help stabilise and rebuild Afghanistan. One senior official in Downing Street recalls that the prime minister spent December 2001 'drumming up international support for a nation-building effort'. Blair had initially wanted a large international peacekeeping force to maintain security across Afghanistan. The 5,000-strong ISAF confined to Kabul 'was a disappointment to Blair'.[1] In a clear sign of his commitment, the prime minister flew to Afghanistan on 7 January 2002, accompanied by his wife. It was a risky trip: Blair's party flew into Bagram airfield in total darkness. Waiting for him was an SAS close-protection team and, standing at the end of a red carpet, President Karzai with a hastily assembled Afghan honour guard. Blair remembers being 'warned not to step off [the red carpet] since large parts of the airfield were still mined'.[2] Karzai took the prime minister to a nearby building to meet his cabinet. Alastair Campbell recorded in his diaries that Karzai 'was clearly pleased that TB [Tony Blair] had come, particularly given the genuine security risks'. In front of Karzai and his ministers, Blair pledged that 'Britain would stay with them for the long term'.[3]

FORCE FOR GOOD

By 2001 Blair had a track record of committing Britain and its armed forces to saving strangers. Indeed, in this he was a bit of a trailblazer: Blair was the first world leader to articulate the general case for humanitarian intervention.[4] Using military force for humanitarian ends is a post-Cold War invention.[5] It was not accepted state practice before

1991 and has no basis in international law, as the United Nations Charter only permits use of force in self-defence or when authorised by the UN Security Council in order to uphold international peace and security.[6] Thus, in none of the four cases of credible humanitarian intervention during the Cold War – India's invasion of East Pakistan in 1971, Tanzanian intervention in Uganda in 1978, Vietnam's invasion of Cambodia the same year, and French intervention in the Central African Republic in 1979 – was use of force by the intervening state justified on humanitarian grounds; India, Tanzania and Vietnam all claimed to be acting in self-defence, and the French government did not bother to justify its action. Ironically, one year before its own intervention to remove the brutal dictator of the Central African Republic, France condemned Vietnam's invasion to overthrow the genocidal Khmer Rouge, telling the UN Security Council that 'the notion that because a regime is detestable foreign intervention is justified and forcible overthrow is legitimate is extremely dangerous'.[7]

Along with the rise of humanitarian intervention came a more robust approach to using force to keep peace. Peacekeeping had developed in an ad hoc way during the Cold War.[8] It involved neutral states deploying lightly armed troops, under a UN mandate and following cessation of armed conflict, to police a ceasefire or peace agreement between the rival states.[9] Contrary to the usual military practice of camouflage, peacekeepers wore bright blue helmets and drove white vehicles to highlight their presence. The end of the Cold War created the demand and opportunities for humanitarian intervention and peace operations. A series of regional peace agreements – in Angola, Namibia, Central America, Cambodia and elsewhere – required peacekeeping forces to oversee implementation. At the same time, cooperation between the East and West became possible in the UN Security Council (where previously they had blocked each other's resolutions), the surplus of military power no longer needed for the Cold War could be redirected towards humanitarian ends, and public pressure in the West increased for states to take action in the face of large-scale civilian suffering overseas. Between 1988 and 1993, twenty new peacekeeping missions were established, and the annual UN peacekeeping budget shot up from $230 million in 1988 to $1.6 billion by the end of the 1990s.[10] Not only was there a massive growth in the number of UN peace missions, but their size and complexity increased from simply policing ceasefires between two states, to supervising the demobilisation of various non-state armed groups and overseeing elections. Some of the more challenging peace missions also involved using force against 'peace spoilers' and the protection of aid workers and civilians.[11]

Initially, it was the United States under President Bill Clinton who was pushing for this more robust approach to peace operations. Clinton came into office in 1993 with a more idealistic foreign policy than his predecessor, the Cold War realist President George H. W. Bush. Clinton and his Secretary of State, Madeleine Albright, were true believers in multilateral interventionism.[12] At the time Britain, under the Conservative Prime Minister John Major, was more cautious. The British reluctantly sent troops into Bosnia along with the French and others in June 1992, at first to secure humanitarian aid convoys and then later on to protect civilian enclaves during an ongoing civil war. The end of 1992 saw a reluctant Bush deploy a 28,000-strong American force into Somalia, in order to ensure the distribution of humanitarian aid in the face of mass starvation.[13] Under Clinton, the mission expanded to brokering a peace deal and rebuilding the Somali state. It was a disaster: US troops and UN peacekeepers got drawn into a war against the dominant warlord and came off the worse for it. Indeed, America's involvement in the Somalia mission came to an abrupt end when eighteen US troops were killed in an ambush in October 1993.[14] Thereafter, the Clinton administration became more wary. It refused to land US peacekeepers in Haiti in 1995 when faced with resistance from a small mob. It publicly ruled out sending ground troops to stop ethnic cleansing by Serbian security forces in Kosovo in 1999, instead relying on air power to bomb the Serbs into submission.[15]

Things went the other way in Britain when Blair replaced Major as prime minister in 1997. Major had been decidedly uneasy about the Bosnia mission, and had resisted pressure from the Clinton administration for a more forceful approach to dealing with what the Americans considered naked Serb aggression.[16] In contrast, Blair brought an almost missionary zeal to British foreign policy. He and his Foreign Secretary, Robin Cook, declared that Britain would be 'a force for good in the world'.[17] This policy priority was reflected in the UK Strategic Defence Review conducted in 1998. Where previous defence reviews under the Conservatives had been little more than cost-cutting exercises, New Labour's election manifesto committed the new government to a proper foreign policy-led exercise. Involving an extensive process of consultation with a wide range of experts and interested parties inside and outside of government, the Strategic Defence Review did not disappoint.[18] It boldly declared that 'We do not want to stand idly by and watch humanitarian disasters or the aggression of dictators go unchecked. We want to give a lead, we want to be a force for good.' Moreover, the imperative was not simply ethical. With some prescience, it noted that Britain had a national interest in acting for the common good given that security threats often spring from zones of instability in the world and could reach British shores. The implication of this was clear: British forces 'must be prepared to go to the crisis, rather than have the crisis come to us'.[19] As one senior defence planner noted, the 'grand strategic guidance' that followed from this policy was to 'fight them over there not here'.[20] Thus, ethical concerns and strategic imperatives meshed in a simple and compelling logic: 'in a world that is fast becoming a global village', the British people could not afford to 'turn our backs on human suffering'.[21] Actions followed these words. In his first term in office, Blair committed British forces to fight for humanitarian causes in Kosovo (1999), East Timor (1999) and Sierra Leone (2000).[22] As Sir Nigel Sheinwald, a senior British diplomat and Blair's future foreign policy adviser, recalls, in 2001 there was 'a sense of success' among British officials when it came to the humanitarian interventions of the 1990s. Moreover, Blair in particular 'was in favour of a more muscular British foreign policy'.[23]

This, then, was the context in which the prime minister and his closest advisers viewed Afghanistan. The country had been destroyed by the mujahedin war against the Soviet invaders and their puppet regime from 1979 to 1992, and the bloody civil war that followed from 1992 to 2001. Life expectancy and living standards for ordinary Afghans had plummeted to medieval standards, and threats to life and property were endemic. These conditions had allowed the Taliban to sweep into power (the Afghan people were desperate for security, even if offered by religious zealots) and al-Qaeda to operate with impunity from the country. The United Nations was warning of a potential humanitarian catastrophe following the fall of the Taliban. Blair was determined to break the cycle of civilian suffering and violent extremism in Afghanistan. In fairness, most European countries thought likewise – though Britain under Blair was at the forefront of arguing for the deployment of an international security force.

In contrast, George W. Bush made in clear that he was not interested in nation-building. This view was shared by senior members of his national security team. Indeed, as National Security Advisor to the Bush election campaign, Condoleezza Rice criticised the idealistic humanitarian interventionism of the Clinton administration, and called on a future president to refocus US foreign policy on 'promoting the national interest'.[24] Similarly, Rumsfeld was determined to avoid US forces getting bogged down in Afghanistan, and for this reason was adamant that the US 'footprint' should remain light in Afghanistan. The Bush administration took firm action to contain US commitment to Afghanistan; hence Rumsfeld successfully killed the proposal to expand ISAF in size and geographical scope. The US special envoy to Afghanistan, James Dobbins, would later reflect that '[t]he fact that security was not extended beyond Kabul was largely driven by the disinclination of the U.S. administration to get involved in Afghan peacekeeping'.[25] Beyond providing basic support to the organisation of a donors' conference on rebuilding the country, the United States did not provide much by way of leadership in terms of what should be done with Afghanistan.[26] American attention had turned elsewhere.

DISTRACTED BY IRAQ

Well before the job was finished in Afghanistan, the Bush administration switched focus to a prospective war against Iraq. On 21 November 2001, General Tommy Franks was instructed by the chairman of the Joint Chiefs of Staff to begin revising CENTCOM's war plan for Iraq; this order came down from Rumsfeld. At that stage, the war in Afghanistan was in full swing, with Taliban forces retreating to Kandahar. Bob Woodward notes that CENTCOM 'was under immense pressure' and that 'the workload was staggering and round-the-clock because of the war in Afghanistan'. Franks was 'incredulous' that he was being tasked to plan for a second war while still prosecuting the first one. His response was suitably blunt: 'Goddamn, what the fuck are they talking about?' Ten days later, he received a formal order from Rumsfeld, again communicated via the Joint Chiefs, to come up with a new base plan for Iraq. Normally CENTCOM would be given a full month to produce a new base plan; Franks was given just three days.[27]

By early December, the Europeans picked up hints that the United States was looking with intent at Iraq. The US Deputy Secretary of State, Richard Armitage, noted that the United States was 'on a roll' in its military campaign in Afghanistan, and 'that President Bush intended to use the momentum to force Iraq to open its borders to United Nations inspectors looking for weapons of mass destruction'.

Quite how victory against the Taliban would generate usable momentum for Iraq was never explained. The German foreign minister, Joschka Fisher, was less than impressed: 'All European nations would view a broadening [of the war] to include Iraq highly skeptically – and that is putting it diplomatically.'[28]

Downing Street had worried about such a development from the start. In the days following the 9/11 attacks, the British learned that the US National Security Council was considering war against Iraq. But then, much to British relief, this option was dropped. British policymakers had no inkling that CENTCOM was told to spin up the Iraq war plan in November 2001. The British had a military team embedded in CENTCOM supporting the coalition campaign in Afghanistan. However, they were kept separate from the planners working on Iraq. Moreover, the Chief of the Defence Staff had ordered his officers at CENTCOM 'to tell the Americans that we were not interested in discussing Iraq'.[29] Thus, as late as March 2002, the British team was supposedly unaware that CENTCOM had developed a new war plan.[30] However, Number 10 could sense something was up. Blair's Chief of Staff, Jonathan Powell, later recalled that 'By the time you get to December, you have speeches being made in the Senate calling for action on Iraq, Senators Lieberman and McCain wrote to the President demanding action on Iraq'.[31]

It was Bush's State of the Union speech delivered on Capitol Hill on 29 January 2002 that caused alarm bells to ring in Whitehall. Honouring Karzai, 'the distinguished interim leader of a liberated Afghanistan', who was present for the speech, Bush declared that 'America and Afghanistan are now allies against terror. We will be partners in rebuilding that country.' So far so good – even if the last point was a little disingenuous, given the president's well-recorded dour view of nation-building. But then he went on to say that 'Our war on terror [has] only just begun'. He further identified Iraq, along with Iran and North Korea, as constituting 'an axis of evil' that 'pose a grave and growing danger' to the United States and the world. The president's message could hardly be more plain: 'I will not stand by, as peril draws closer and closer.'[32] Although it was perhaps not plain enough for some in Whitehall; according to Hoon, 'our first reaction in the Ministry of Defence was to think about precisely what the President was getting at in relation to his axis of evil speech'.[33] Number 10 tried to find out what was happening. David Manning, the prime minister's foreign policy adviser, recalls that in mid February 2002, Rice 'confirmed to me that the [US] administration was indeed looking at options but said there was absolutely no plan [for war] at this stage'.[34]

By early 2002, Blair had taken the decision to 'hug America close' as the best way to moderate the unilateralist tendencies of the Bush administration. As one Number 10 aide explained, 'what we wanted to do was influence American decisions, to be a player in Washington – as Churchill was with Roosevelt, or Macmillan with Kennedy, or Thatcher with Reagan'.[35] Accordingly, Blair began to align himself with Bush's increasingly belligerent position towards Iraq. In early March, *The Times* noted that 'Tony Blair began preparing Britain for the second phase of the war on terrorism', referring to comments the prime minister made about the dangers posed by Iraq. As if to underline the point, the *Daily Express* published an article by Blair with the title 'Why Saddam is still a threat to Britain'.[36]

Bush invited Blair to visit him at his private ranch in Crawford, Texas, over 5–6 April 2002. While the two leaders discussed a range of issues including the wider Middle East peace process, for many looking from afar this meeting was to all appearances an Anglo-American council of war. In advance, Britain's military chiefs met with Blair on 2 April at Chequers, the prime minister's country residence in Buckinghamshire, where they 'painted a gloomy picture of the military options for Iraq'.[37] Campbell recalls the senior British military representative at CENTCOM reporting that he thought the Americans were planning for war in late 2002 or early 2003.[38] Rumours about

CENTCOM planning had reached the British Chiefs of Staff in early March.[39] The problem was that the British military did not really know what was going on; they were out of the planning loop. The Ministry of Defence wanted the prime minister to push for British military planners to be brought into the CENTCOM team working on Iraq; this eventually happened in July.[40]

The Crawford summit was an eye-opener for the British. It quickly became clear that for Bush using military force to remove Saddam Hussein from power was the only option on the table for dealing with Iraq. 'It was when we first began to realise fully how serious they were about it,' remembers one Number 10 official. Blair confirmed that Britain would support US military action against Iraq provided certain conditions were met, including that every chance had been given for the UN inspectors to complete their work. In essence, Blair told the Americans 'we're with you' in order to maximise his chance of influencing US policy from inside the tent. However, in his own mind, he had not yet committed British forces. As one British official later put it, 'saying "we're with you" is different from saying "we're going to war with you"'. The problem was that this distinction was lost on the Bush administration, which ignored Blair's conditions. As Armitage later told the British ambassador, 'the problem with your "yes, but" is that it is too easy to hear the "yes" and forget the "but"'.[41] Blair returned from Crawford to face a wall of opposition. His Cabinet and Whitehall were deeply sceptical of the ethical, legal and prudential case for war on Iraq; and the British public, the Parliamentary Labour Party and fellow European leaders were openly hostile to the idea. Iraq was to dominate Blair's foreign policy agenda for the rest of his time in office.

As if Iraq wasn't enough, British and US governments had an even more serious crisis to deal with from December 2001 to June 2002: a military stand-off between India and Pakistan that carried the real risk of escalating to nuclear war. At issue was the disputed territory of Kashmir, which each country claimed (and still claims) for itself. Pakistan's support for militants in the Indian-governed part of Kashmir was a running sore in relations between the two countries. In 1998, Pakistan joined the club of nuclear-armed states when it test-detonated six nuclear devices. India, already a nuclear power, promptly followed suit with five nuclear tests of its own. In 1999, Pakistan triggered a small conventional war with India when it tried to seize some remote territory in the Kargil Mountains. Then on 13 December 2001, five Kashmiri terrorists armed with rifles, grenades and explosives attacked the Indian national parliament, killing nine people before being shot by security forces. The Indian government was understandably furious, and responded by moving its army to the border with Pakistan. It demanded that Pakistan close down the terrorist camps in its territory or the Indian Army would do so. Pakistan responded by mobilising its army, and soon around 1 million soldiers were facing off on the Indo-Pakistani border.[42] Campbell notes with some understatement that by New Year's Eve 'The tensions between Pakistan and India were dominating the serious news and getting very difficult'.[43] In his memoirs, Jack Straw recalls that this crisis, and not Afghanistan or Iraq, 'dominated' his time in early 2002: 'In public, we deliberately played down the risk so as not to create panic – one reason why so little is recalled of this potential nuclear conflagration today. However, the situation was very dangerous. We came very close to war.'[44]

REBUILDING AFGHANISTAN

With the United States and Britain temporarily distracted by the crisis on the Indian subcontinent and increasingly preoccupied with Iraq, the international effort to rebuild Afghanistan was allowed to drift. This was already evident at Bonn, when the head of the US delegation, James Dobbins, was given free rein to do as he pleased. On 21–22 January 2002, the international community gathered in Tokyo to pledge support for Afghanistan. Leading the US delegation again was Dobbins, who noted wearily that 'With forty to fifty countries represented, it meant several days of speechifying'. The World Bank, the Asian Development Bank and the United Nations Development Programme had produced a ten-year package of support for Afghanistan costing $14.6 billion. The Tokyo conference ended with states promising substantially less than this amount: $5.1 billion in aid over a five-year period. Indicative of its priorities, the United States provided only 5 per cent of the total aid pledged at Tokyo, some $290 million.[45]

The challenges facing Afghanistan were immense. The country had no manufacturing base and the licit economy was reduced to agriculture and small-scale trading. The roads were appalling and often impassable in wet weather; only part of the Kabul to Kandahar highway was tarmacked. Electricity supply to the main cities was erratic at best. The domestic telephone system had collapsed; international calls could only be made in the central post office in Kabul. Most of the population in Kabul had been surviving on food aid for the previous five years. The new Afghan government was completely broke. There was no system to collect tax, and the customs duties collected at the major border crossings were kept by local warlords.[46]

Compounding the pressure on the interim Afghan government, hundreds of thousands of refugees began to flood back from Pakistan and Iran under a voluntary repatriation programme administered by the United Nations; Pakistan had 3 million Afghan refugees and Iran had almost 1.5 million, and both countries were understandably eager to see these people return to Afghanistan. These returnees brought with them raised expectations as to what government should do and provide. They had received access to rudimentary health care and education facilities in the refugee camps. As Thomas Barfield notes: 'Poor as these [facilities] were by international standards, for Afghans who had come from villages with few schools, and no electricity, running water, or health care facilities of any type, the realization that government agencies or nongovernmental organizations could provide needed services on a large scale was a revelation.'[47]

Aid to Afghanistan from donor states was channelled through a number of international trust funds managed by the World Bank. These were used to pay the salary bill for Afghan civil servants, and to re-establish education and basic health-care services. A follow-on donor conference was held in Berlin on 31 March 2004. By then, as one observer noted, the earlier optimism of donors 'had given way to a growing realization that statebuilding and reconstruction would be a long, hard slog'. The new Afghan finance minister, Ashraf Ghani, presented a comprehensive seven-year development plan called 'Securing Afghanistan's Future'. Freshly returned from the United States, where he had taught at Johns Hopkins and at Berkeley and worked at the World Bank, Ghani was a trusted technocrat 'who spoke the language of donors'. He could also be blunt when required. He told the Berlin conference that the $5 billion pledged at Tokyo was 'peanuts'. He was asking for $28.5 billion for his seven-year plan. In the end, he walked away with another $5 billion.[48]

The paradox was that while Afghanistan needed all the aid it could get, it struggled to absorb the aid that it did receive. It simply lacked the administrative infrastructure to implement this level of expenditure. Life in Kabul had become so difficult for civil servants under the Taliban – who viewed educated urbanites with suspicion – that many had left government and even Afghanistan. Thus by 2001, many central ministries were effectively empty shells, with a minister and enough advisers to engage with the international community, but not to implement anything. Nor was there the time to develop sufficient administrative capacities given the volume and speed of international aid. In consequence, foreign consultants and aid organisations were contracted to manage the flow of funds into and around the country. Ironically, this served to further undermine the development of Afghan government in two ways. Firstly, many returning skilled Afghans took better-paid jobs with aid organisations rather than rejoining the civil service. Secondly, foreign consultants and hired Afghan advisers formed, in effect, a 'second civil service' that oversaw the development and delivery of internationally funded public services.[49]

The incompetence and corruption of Afghan bureaucracy made matters even worse. Excessive regulation made it difficult to get anything done; an electricity connection in Kabul, for example, required the signatures of twenty-three officials. Add to this the very poor pay of civil servants and you had a system that was designed to breed corruption. Officials had to demand bribes for access to public services just to provide for their families. The inflow of aid also created opportunities for large-scale corruption. International projects generated highly lucrative contracts for the leasing of land and buildings, and for construction, transport and security services. Afghan subcontractors had to pay handsome bribes to senior government officials for licences to bid for such contracts, and for introductions to the aid organisations that sought these services. As the inflow of aid increased in the second half of the decade, so the scale of government corruption grew.[50]

Afghanistan enjoyed a temporary respite from conflict in 2002. However, the effort to create a new security architecture for Afghanistan soon floundered under a British plan to parcel out key responsibility to five states, with each leading on a different element – the United States took the lead on raising the new Afghan army and creating the National Directorate of Security, Germany took the Afghan National Police (ANP), Italy justice reform, Japan the demobilisation, disarmament and reintegration of various militias, and Britain counter-narcotics. This 'lead nation' approach, proposed by the British, was adopted at a summit of the G8 states in April 2002. Without an overriding state or agency in charge, it almost guaranteed incoherence in the international effort to secure Afghanistan. Progress was also painfully slow.

The newly appointed Afghan minister of defence, the Northern Alliance warlord Marshal Fahim, had suggested merging the various militias into a new 250,000-strong national army. This notion found little favour with Western governments, who were less than keen on the idea of bankrolling a massive force whose loyalties to the state would be questionable. Britain and the United States proposed instead to raise a smaller, brand-new army, which would be more affordable and not have any prior links to any warlords. American special forces began in May 2002 to train up the 2nd and 3rd Battalions of the new Afghan National Guard, the 1st Battalion having been trained already by the British under ISAF. During this period the basic structure of Afghan field units was agreed: the new army would be organised into battalions (or *kandaks*), each with four infantry companies. The first *kandaks* were lightly armed and lacked motorised transport. Recruits were provided with ten weeks of training covering basic infantry skills. This US effort was modest: the aim was to train up 2,000–3,000 Afghan troops by November 2002. The new Afghan National Guard was far outnumbered and outgunned by the militias of the main warlords; Marshal Fahim's Jama't-e Islam militia alone numbered some 20,000 fighters. Compounding problems was a lack of morale among Afghan troops. Within a year, half had deserted.[51]

In late 2003, it had become apparent that the Afghan National Guard had fallen under the control of Fahim's Jama't-e Islam faction. The United States insisted that the entire Afghan MoD and National Guard be disbanded, and that everything start again from scratch. As one analyst notes, 'this paved the way for a new model Afghan National Army'. This one was much larger, eventually rising to 70,000, with a general staff and air corps, and supported by a more professional

MoD.[52] Leading this effort was the new US Combined Security Transition Command-Afghanistan (CSTC-A, pronounced 'see-sticka') based in Kabul, which was scheduled to produce 20,000 trained soldiers by 2006.[53]

The situation was even worse with the Afghan police. The Germans acknowledged the scale of the challenge. Their advance team reported that 'the police force is in a deplorable state', noting that 'there is a total lack of equipment and supplies. No systematic training has been provided for around 20 years.' However, as observed earlier, the German response was woefully inadequate: a training academy was set up in Kabul staffed by seventeen German police officers and requiring Afghans to complete a three-year course. This was hardly going to meet the need to produce tens of thousands of Afghan police. In 2003, the US State Department took over, reorganising the Kabul academy and setting up regional training centres in Kandahar, Mazar-e-Sharif, Gardez and Jalalabad. The State Department hired a private US contractor, DynCorp International, to do the actual training. Yet questions soon surfaced about the quality of the DynCorp trainers and training. The Afghan interior minister, Ali Ahmad Jalali, later complained that many DynCorp contractors 'had little or no useful background for training police in Afghanistan'. Eventually, in 2005, the US Department of Defense took over responsibility for ANP training and handed the mission over to CSTC-A. CSTC-A produced a damning report in 2006, finding that the ability of the ANP 'to carry out its internal security and conventional responsibilities is far from adequate'. This was an understatement. 'Illiterate recruits', 'pervasive corruption', poor leadership and lack of equipment were among the problems identified in the report; to these could be added high rates of drug use and desertion. Initially the commanding general of CSTC-A believed that he 'could change the police force in a few months'. However, he soon realised 'that it would take over a decade'.[54]

COUNTER-NARCOTICS

Blair had made staunching the flow of drugs from Afghanistan one of the grounds for British action against the Taliban. In justifying the start of the military campaign before a specially recalled House of

Commons on 8 October 2001, the prime minister noted: 'we know that the Taliban regime are largely funded by the drugs trade and that 90 percent of the heroin on British streets originates in Afghanistan.' He went on to conclude: 'so this military action we are undertaking is not for a just cause alone, though this cause is just. It is to protect our country, our people, our economy, our way of life. It is not a struggle remote from our everyday British concerns; it touches them intimately.'[55] The bulk of heroin in Britain did indeed originate from Afghanistan. Moreover, Blair had been elected on the promise, among other things, to tackle the problem of drugs. To this end, the incoming Labour government had appointed a 'drugs czar' to 'coordinate our battle against drugs across all government departments'.[56] However, this is not to say that the Taliban were behind the heroin trade. Notably, the push to include this issue in the reasons for military action did not come from the Home Office or Foreign Office (which had the lead on coordinating international efforts to combat drugs). Rather, the decision to portray the campaign as partly a war on drugs was taken from within Number 10 and probably by Blair himself. As one Whitehall official pointed out, 'The evidence on the claim regarding the Taliban involvement in drugs was limited and it shackled us to an unsolvable problem.'[57]

Afghanistan's emergence as a major drug-producing country was unrelated to the rise of the Taliban. Bans on growing opium poppy introduced in Iran in the late 1950s, and in Pakistan in the late 1970s, pushed drugs production into Afghanistan. Furthermore, in the 1980s Afghan agriculture was devastated by the Soviet War, and farmers turned to growing poppy as a resilient crop that was easy to store and sell. Money from the drugs trade also funded the mujahedin war on the Soviet invaders. According to the United Nations Office on Drugs and Crime, Afghanistan's share of world opium production shot up from 19 per cent in 1980 to 70 per cent in 2000. As it happened, the Taliban banned poppy cultivation in 2000, declaring drug use to be prohibited in Islam. Critics argued that they did so only to court international approval, and this explains why the Taliban only intro-duced the ban some years after seizing power. This argument is hardly persuasive, however, given that the Taliban showed scant regard for world opinion on other matters, such as women's rights or harbouring terrorists. A more convincing account is that the Taliban were slow to impose a ban because they knew it would be unpopular with farmers, and they wanted to ensure they would be able to enforce it. Whatever the reason, it was dramatically effective: opium production in Afghanistan plummeted from 3,276 metric tons in 2000 to only 185 metric tons in 2001. Western observers hailed the success of the Taliban ban as a 'rare triumph in the long and losing war on drugs'; one UN official described it as 'one of the most remarkable successes ever' in the fight against drugs. However, the Taliban did not ban the trade in drugs, probably because they derived taxation from it. Moreover, they were unconcerned about keeping heroin off European streets. Regardless, overthrowing the Taliban regime, and thereby removing the ban, made the drugs problem far worse for Europe as Afghan farmers went back to growing poppy in record quantities.[58]

The Foreign Office lead on counter-narcotics, Michael Ryder, had served on the UN team sent to verify the poppy ban under the Taliban and was familiar with the scale of the challenge. He realised that a ban in itself was unlikely to work without a programme to provide farmers with viable alternative livelihoods. Ryder proposed a ten-year plan to develop Afghanistan's licit agricultural economy by moving farmers over to growing wheat, and introducing high-earning crops like saffron. Following the Tokyo donors' conference in late January 2002, Ryder received £125 million to fund his counter-narcotics plan – a massive budget in Whitehall terms but, as one observer notes, 'it was minuscule compared to the $1 billion in revenue that Afghanistan's first poppy harvest since the Taliban was about to rake in'. In mid 2002, Ryder's budget was raided by MI6, who came up with their own plan to fund warlords to eradicate the poppy crop. Over £60 million was diverted to a scheme that was sure to fail since most warlords were heavily involved in opium production. Any eradication undertaken by warlords would be directed towards those farming communities not already under their control. It is more likely that the actual intent was simply to buy influence with those warlords favoured by British intelligence.[59]

Ryder's plan involved getting farmers to eradicate their own poppy crop by paying them $350 dollars for each *jerib* (unit of land). Of course this raised a host of challenges in terms of getting payment to farmers and verifying that they had in fact destroyed their crop, but the basic premise of directly engaging with farming communities was sound.

In time, more British officials would come to realise the importance of empowering local communities. All the same, the plan failed. There were simply too many incentives for farmers to grow poppy. Warlords and drug smugglers lent farmers the money to plant it, and collected the opium paste directly from them; thus, there was no need for farmers to bring their crop to market, with all the costs and risks that entailed. More importantly, a *jerib* of poppy would net a farmer seventeen times more income than a *jerib* of wheat. With the fall of the Taliban, opium production promptly increased to 3,400 metric tons in 2002, climbing up to 3,600 tons in 2003, and 4,200 tons in 2004.[60] Jack Straw would later reflect that 'we should have spotted that worrying about counter-narcotics was a hiding to nothing'.[61]

PROVINCIAL RECONSTRUCTION TEAMS

'The war in Afghanistan was over – we had won' was how one US official recalls the view in Washington DC in 2003.[62] According to another, 'Afghanistan was seen as like Bosnia, mostly a governance issue.'[63] In short, the Bush administration was done with Afghanistan. Indicative of this was the administration's aid budget request for Afghanistan in 2002 – a paltry $1 million. In the event, Congress ended up appropriating $250 million.[64]

However, for Western soldiers, diplomats and aid workers in Afghanistan, there was still much to do. In June 2002, 10th Mountain Division handed over command of Operation Enduring Freedom to Combined Joint Task Force (CJTF) 180, formed from the headquarters of 18th Airborne Division and led by Lieutenant General Dan McNeill. Britain sent three officers to join McNeill's command, one of whom was Nick Carter, an ambitious colonel from the Royal Green Jackets Regiment. In Carter's case, ambition was matched by abilities and achievements; he was to return to Afghanistan in 2009 as commander of ISAF forces in the south, and again in 2013 as deputy commander of ISAF, and would eventually rise to become Chief of the British General Staff. Carter was appointed Chief of Plans for CJTF-180 and in this role he designed the new Afghan National Guard, working with the capable Brigadier Sher Mohammad Karimi, then the National Guard's Chief of Operations (and future Chief of Staff of the Afghan National Army).

In a model of partnership, Carter travelled up to the Afghan Ministry of Defence 'every other day', in a soft-topped Land Rover with just a driver and a sidearm, to hammer out the new army design with Karimi. Curiously, Carter was never allowed on the top floor of the Ministry of Defence building. The running joke was that there were still Russians up there.[65]

Even more importantly, Carter was the original architect of the main platform for civil–military operations in Afghanistan, the Provincial Reconstruction Team (PRT). Carter recalls that 'McNeill did not want to put on a suit and get into the political space with Karzai', and yet the CJTF commander recognised that something had to be done to get the Afghan government up and running, especially in the provinces. Thus McNeill 'spent a lot of time in dusty tents on VTCs [video teleconferences] back to DC to persuade Rumsfeld and others on the need to develop government capacity'. The Bush administration was not interested in investing money or personnel in Afghanistan in 2002. So McNeill ordered Carter to find 'lateral ways' to meet the challenge.[66]

Carter needed to travel to the provinces to find out what was happening on the ground. He was only able to do so because on a visit to CJTF-180 headquarters, Brigadier Graeme Lamb ordered British special forces to 'resource this guy to get around the country'. Carter visited American special operations forces teams in Kunduz and Mazar-e-Sharif in the north, and Gardez in the east. In Gardez, he observed how the US team, who were all reservists and happened to include a doctor and a vet, were able to build strong links with surrounding communities; the vet, in particular, was very popular with locals. The Gardez team was 'the germ of the idea' for what Carter called the Joint Regional Team. The problem with the Bonn Agreement and with ISAF was that it was focused on Kabul. There was no mechanism to improve security and the rule of law out in the provinces and to extend the writ of government beyond Kabul. Joint Regional Teams were to act as 'hooks', to connect the regions to central government. Karzai liked the idea, although he objected to the name, so the Joint Regional Teams became PRTs. Karzai's view was that 'warlords do regions, the government does provinces'. The word 'reconstruction' was included even though initially, as the commander of the first British PRT recalls, 'we didn't do any reconstruction'.[67] In later years, reconstruction would become a major focus for PRTs.

McNeill pitched the PRT concept to Rumsfeld and got approval for three pilot American PRTs: one in Gardez in eastern Afghanistan, and the other two in Bamyan and Kunduz in central Afghanistan. Initially, the British considered establishing a PRT in Kandahar. However, because they wanted to 'stay small scale' for their first PRT, they decided to set it up in Mazar-e-Sharif, the capital of Balkh province. Both Dostum and Atta had militia in the region, and so Lieutenant General John Vines, who replaced McNeill as commander of coalition forces in Afghanistan in May 2003, and the British ambassador held a meeting with the two warlords to ensure that the British deployment had their support. The British PRT was established in Mazar-e-Sharif in July 2003 and staffed by around one hundred troops from the Royal Anglian Regiment, supported by a number of SAS reservists; a smaller, fifty-strong British PRT was set up in Maymaneh, the capital of Faryab province, in May 2004.[68]

The two British PRTs were supposed to cover five provinces in north and north-west Afghanistan, roughly an area the size of Scotland. Small and lightly armed 'mobile observation teams' were sent out to range across these provinces with the basic instruction to 'get out there and find out what is going on'. The British PRTs focused on building trust with local commanders, and demobilising and disarming militias. This was just as well, as they managed to stop a major row between Dostum and Atta escalating into an armed conflict. Dostum was muscling in on Atta's ground in Faryab, and had managed to buy off Atta's militia in the district: Atta was none too pleased. By the time the British had turned up both warlords had mobilised forces, 12,000 on Dostum's side against 8,000 on Atta's. The situation in Mazar-e-Sharif was especially tense, with each party accusing the other of breaking agreements. The commander of the British PRT, Colonel Dickie Davis, ended up getting Atta's and Dostum's respective chiefs of staff into his Land Rover, and drove around Mazar-e-Sharif to investigate these complaints. Davis recalls Atta as being reasonable and 'a bloke you could do business with'. Dostum was altogether more difficult. Davis had to threaten Dostum's prized 56th Division with aerial attack to get the warlord to climb down. With cautious support from the interim Afghan government, which was nervous about taking on such powerful warlords, the British got both sides to agree to surrender their heavy weapons, to be stored in cantonments outside of Mazar-e-Sharif. Atta honoured the agreement. To his amazement at the time, Davis recalls that all of Atta's armour suddenly emerged from the desert, about two battalions' worth. In contrast, Dostum did not play ball, only 'handing over crappy stuff and in dribs and drabs'. Atta was rewarded by being appointed governor of Balkh, whereas Dostum was increasingly shunned by the Kabul government. Davis recalls that there was a huge amount of optimism after Atta's demobilisation, and that 'the PRT had almost rock-star status' in Mazar-e-Sharif.[69]

Notwithstanding this early success, slow progress was made in disarming and demobilising the various militias across Afghanistan. In this respect, Atta was the exception and Dostum the rule. By the end of 2002, irregular militia still outnumbered the Afghan army. Formally, many of these militias came under the authority of the Afghan Ministry of Defence or Ministry of Interior. But in reality, they remained loyal to their respective warlords. In 2003, the Japanese launched a disarmament, demobilisation and reintegration (DDR) programme for these various irregular forces. The initial goal was to disarm, demobilise and integrate 100,000 militia. Official estimates put militia levels at over twice this amount, but there was considerable inflating of numbers in order to claim salaries for troops that did not exist. DDR had some success in getting militia to surrender heavy weapons. But the programme failed to break the link between warlords and militia that had entered the state security forces. DDR was replaced in 2005 by an Afghan-run programme called the Disbandment of Illegal Armed Groups, which fared little better. Of the 20,411 weapons surrendered in the first year of this new programme, only 13,500 were in usable condition.[70] In this, as in so many other Western-funded initiatives, Afghans found ways to fool foreigners in order to get rich quick.

PRTs were supposed to help extend government services outside Kabul. For those aid agencies in Afghanistan that had long operated to fill the gap left by the absence of effective government, this was most unwelcome. Ironically, aid agencies had been calling for some time for ISAF to expand beyond Kabul; a rainbow alliance of seventy-two aid agencies warned as early as June 2003 that 'unless security conditions improve, progress made to date in Afghanistan will be in jeopardy'.[71] What they wanted was security. They had not anticipated that ISAF would stray into their lane. In its report on PRTs, Save the Children complained that 'the engagement of these teams in relief activities … blurs the distinction between humanitarian and military actors'. In turn, this risked aid operators being viewed as working with the military 'and therefore being seen as legitimate targets in the ongoing conflict'.[72] Thus aid agencies grumbled when British PRT personnel drove around in unmarked white vehicles, making them indistinguishable from aid workers. The British PRT tried to develop a division of labour with the aid agencies so as to go some way to reduce this blurring of boundaries; thus, in response to protests from all aid agencies, the British PRT withdrew its mobile medical services for the local population in December 2003. Yet regardless of the concerns of aid agencies, PRTs became the primary vehicle for ISAF to expand beyond Kabul, and by June 2004 there were thirteen PRTs established across Afghanistan.[73]

EXPANDING ISAF

Initially, ISAF expansion was off the cards. Like the United States, Turkey was opposed to such a move. Turkey's views on this mattered because it took command of ISAF from the British in June 2002. The coalition government in Turkey was preoccupied with a financial crisis, and with the prospect of a US-led war on Iraq, which was expected to embolden the Kurdish separatists in Turkey. The collapse of the Turkish government in the autumn of 2002 resulted in the election of a brand-new administration for whom Afghanistan was even further down the list of priorities. Germany and the Netherlands jointly took over command of ISAF in February 2003. Both were more committed to Afghanistan than Turkey but they needed NATO's assistance to generate the forces they required; in particular, NATO agreed to deploy a multinational corps headquarters. This was the first step that led to the Atlantic Alliance assuming responsibility for the whole ISAF mission.

The background to this development was a crisis within NATO in early 2003 over the impending war in Iraq. On 22 January, at a joint press conference on the fortieth anniversary of the Elysée Treaty, the French president and German chancellor pledged to stand together against the war, leading Rumsfeld to dismiss France and Germany as 'old Europe'. This was not a transatlantic rift – seven European governments (including the British) published a joint letter of support for the Bush administration in the *Wall Street Journal* in late January – so much as a crisis within NATO. In February, France, Germany and Belgium blocked a request from Turkey for NATO to prepare to provide military assistance should Iraq retaliate in the war by attacking its neighbour. This led to 'angry exchanges and shouting matches' within the North Atlantic Council, NATO's governing body.[74] Writing in the *Washington Post*, Henry Kissinger observed that it was 'the gravest crisis in the Atlantic Alliance since its creation five decades ago'.[75] The US ambassador to NATO put it even more starkly, later describing it as a 'near-death experience' for the alliance.[76]

February was a pretty tough month also for the British government. As public opposition to a possible war with Iraq grew, Number 10 released a dossier providing evidence that Iraq was in breach of its obligations to disarm its chemical weapons, and that it presented a direct threat to the United Kingdom. Within days, it was discovered that much of this official dossier had in fact been plagiarised from the Internet. Mid February saw 1 million people come out against the war in a massive rally at Hyde Park. There was growing unease within British government, with the Development Secretary, Clare Short, openly criticising the prime minister for being 'reckless'. The French government declared that it would veto any UN Security Council resolution approving use of force against Iraq; in the end, the British government claimed that the legal grounds for war were already contained in previous Security Council resolutions. The crisis played out through to 18 March, when the House of Commons voted on British military action in Iraq. The vote was a close-run thing, with strenuous lobbying of MPs by Downing Street. The Leader of the House and former Foreign Secretary, Robin Cook, resigned in protest from the Cabinet on the eve of the vote.[77] Two days later, the Americans started the war without bothering to give their British allies advance warning.[78]

After the diplomatic disaster that was Iraq, the ISAF mission offered a way to mend the transatlantic alliance. As one study notes, 'Going to Afghanistan, from the perspective of mid-2003, offered a relatively pain-free way of regaining American favour and getting NATO politics back on course.'[79] It was also a good time to engage with the Americans about Afghanistan. In April 2002, Bush had made a major speech at the Virginia Military Institute in which he reaffirmed, 'in the best traditions of George Marshall', America's commitment to help rebuilding Afghanistan. With its reference to the Marshall Plan, the multibillion-dollar aid programme to rebuild the European economies following World War II, Bush's speech appeared to suggest a shift in US policy towards supporting nation-building in Afghanistan. As one analyst notes, 'that's how senior Afghan officials saw it'. However, within the US government, no major efforts were initiated 'to assess the requirements for a successful reconstruction effort or to generate the funding that would be necessary'.[80]

This changed in mid 2003. Condoleezza Rice directed an inter-agency group led by Zalmay Khalilzad to develop a Marshall Plan for Afghanistan. Called 'Accelerating Success in Afghanistan', it recom-mended that $1.2 billion be spent on Afghan reconstruction (Congress would end up providing $1.6 billion). When the plan was pitched to the president for his approval, it transpired that he was not interested in the details and more animated by the prospect of Khalilzad becoming America's first ambassador to Afghanistan since 1979. As Khalilzad recounts, 'Once [Bush] had decided that he wanted me in Kabul, it seemed that he was willing to go along with my proposed plan and provide the necessary resources.'[81]

For Rumsfeld, the Khalilzad plan was not about America making a long-time commitment to Afghanistan but rather the reverse. He had been won over to supporting the plan by the argument, proven erroneous in retrospect, that pouring more aid into Afghanistan would actually enable the US military to pull out more quickly. As one senior US defence official notes, 'the view inside the Rumsfeld camp was that Afghanistan had become a millstone around our neck and we needed somebody else to take over'. The solution for Rumsfeld's team was obvious: 'let's put NATO in charge'. Thus, the expansion of the ISAF mission can be traced to European eagerness to repair relations with the United States combined with a US eagerness to offload Afghanistan.[82] In mid August 2003 the NATO Secretary General quietly suggested to the Afghan government and UN Security Council that they might like to make a joint formal request to NATO for it to take charge of ISAF, which they duly did. NATO's first operational plan for ISAF (OPLAN 10149) was focused solely on Kabul. However, in a matter of months, NATO forces began to deploy beyond the capital.

In October 2003, Germany announced that it would send 250 troops to northern Afghanistan to set up a PRT in Kunduz. This would be the first deployment of German military forces on operations outside of Europe since 1945. The pro-American German minister of defence, Peter Struck, was looking for a way to mend relations with the United States, and for this reason sought to get his country more involved in Afghanistan. At the same time, Germany was keen to draw a clear distinction between the ISAF mission and the counterterrorism Operation Enduring Freedom mission, the latter being associated in German minds with the hugely unpopular US global war on terror. Being focused on governance and development, the PRTs offered an acceptable alternative. Within NATO, Germany pushed for the expansion of ISAF beyond Kabul using the PRTs as the platform to do so. This idea was vigorously debated within the North Atlantic Council. Some member states, France in particular, were sceptical both of expanding ISAF and of the PRT concept. All the same, agreement was quickly reached within NATO in support of the German proposal. It would mean that PRTs would be de-linked from Operation Enduring Freedom and instead attached to the ISAF mission (but importantly not placed under ISAF Command). The ISAF mandate and operational plan were revised accordingly; in mid October, the UN Security Council approved the revised mandate to provide security assistance beyond Kabul, and by January, ISAF had a new operational plan. Some NATO ambassadors would later complain in private that the Germans had 'steamrolled' the alliance into taking on the wider Afghanistan mission. Nonetheless, this set the way for further PRTs, with Germany and the Netherlands setting up PRTs in Feyzabad and Baghlan respectively in 2004.[83]

Yet the NATO counterclockwise strategy for expanding ISAF beyond Kabul quickly stalled in 2004. All thirteen previous PRTs had been established in northern and western Afghanistan. These were non-Pashtun areas where the Northern Alliance had a strong presence, and so the teams faced no serious security threats. ISAF was next due to expand into the Pashtun heartlands of southern Afghanistan. Here history revealed that Pashtun tribesmen disliked foreigners and were not shy about expressing this through armed violence.[84] Add to this the presence of large numbers of Taliban across the border in Pakistan, and the south looked less than inviting. Viewed from the MoD in London, 'there was no appetite that it was possible to discern anywhere in NATO for taking the campaign into the South'.[85] It was time for Britain to step up to the plate.

BRITAIN GOES SOUTH

At the time, the British had a few hundred troops in Afghanistan, with two companies manning the British PRTs in tranquil Mazar-e-Sharif and Maymaneh, and a company on patrol duty in Kabul. The view in the MoD was that Britain was punching below its weight in Afghanistan. As Hoon's successor as Defence Secretary, John Reid, put it: 'there was a feeling that British troops … were not doing the task that was up to the level that British troops were capable of doing'.[86] Besides, there was nobody else to lead the southern expansion of ISAF. As one senior British general noted, the Germans and Italians, who had contributed fairly large contingents to ISAF, 'would screw it up if they deployed south'.[87]

The years 2004 and 2005 were fateful for Britain's campaign in Afghanistan. At the NATO Summit in Istanbul on 29 June 2004, Blair announced that the British-led Allied Rapid Reaction Corps (ARRC, pronounced 'Ark') based in Germany would take command of ISAF. The prime minister's statement took the ARRC completely by surprise. General Richard Dannatt, then commander of the corps, recalls that 'it really did come out of nowhere'.[88] The United States had requested that the ARRC be sent to Iraq to take command of the southern provinces, and so the headquarters was focused on preparing for this deployment. One senior Cabinet Office official remembers that there was 'huge enthusiasm within the ARRC' for going to Iraq.[89] The Defence Staff in Whitehall took an altogether different view. The Iraq campaign lacked a driving strategic purpose; as one senior planner noted, 'By September 2003, we were perfectly aware that there were no weapons of mass destruction in Iraq.'[90] Afghanistan was seen as the more vital campaign; it was also viewed as 'a complete mess' and desperately in need of some 'unity of command'. Busy in Iraq, the Americans did not want to take command of ISAF, despite having the largest number of troops on the ground. This left the British as 'the only people other than the Americans that could take charge of Afghanistan and command US forces'. Optimism was running high in the Ministry of Defence: it was expected that the ARRC would 'achieve a transformative effect on the campaign'.[91] The idea of sending the ARRC to Afghanistan won support from within the British Cabinet, especially 'if it was not going to Iraq'.[92] Thus, at ARRC headquarters staff 'put away the Iraq maps and maps for Afghanistan came out'.[93]

This was followed in 2005 by British agreement to lead the ISAF expansion to the south. In January the Chiefs of Staff recommended to the Secretary of State for Defence that Britain agree to deploy forces to southern Afghanistan. Hoon in turn made this offer at the NATO ministerial meeting in Nice in February.[94] The question was then: to which province should British forces go? There were three to choose from: Uruzgan, Kandahar and Helmand. Canada and the Netherlands also offered to deploy forces to the south. Sitting above Kandahar, Uruzgan was the smallest and least important of the three, and as such suited the ambitions and capabilities of the Dutch Army. Kandahar was the most important, as the birthplace of the Taliban, with the second-largest city in Afghanistan (Kandahar city), and as the main gateway for vital trade routes crossing the country between Pakistan and Iran. Thus it was the most challenging province to secure. However, the Canadians and not the British ended up with Kandahar. General Rob Fry, who as Deputy Chief of the Defence Staff for Commitments had responsibility for producing the military strategy for Afghanistan, later revealed that the Canadians had insisted on taking Kandahar as 'their price' for agreeing to deploy south. The Canadians wanted a big role in Afghanistan. Fry observed that 'the Canadian military was in search of redemption, having had a long period of undistinguished activity'.[95] Put another way by one Canadian expert, 'taking on a serious combat role would do much to demythologize the Canadian forces as being just good for peacekeeping'.[96] Fry's account is confirmed by the former private secretary to the Defence Secretary, Nick Beadle: 'How did we end up going to Helmand rather than Kandahar? I can offer nothing more as a reason than a failure to persuade the US to support us, as against the preference of the Canadians to go to Kandahar. The US rightly guessed that we would go into southern Afghanistan anyway.'[97]

This then left Helmand for the British. Covering almost 10 per cent of the country, it was the largest province in Afghanistan and also a power base for the Taliban. But compared to Kandahar, it was a complete backwater. Richard Dannatt, who by 2005 had become Commander-in-Chief of Land Command, and would a year later become Chief of the General Staff, subsequently claimed that 'Helmand Province is the vital ground in southern Afghanistan. Control Helmand and you control Kandahar.' This assertion does not make any sense; controlling Kandahar province is the best way to secure Kandahar city. General David Richards, who would command ISAF in 2006 and thereafter succeed Dannatt as Chief of the General Staff, later expressed the doubts that many held at the time. On hearing that the British would take Helmand, Richards recalled thinking: 'Where's Helmand? That's not very important. Kandahar is what matters.' A rationale was found for Helmand by linking it to Britain's lead on counter-narcotics: some 46 per cent of the Afghanistan poppy crop was produced in the province in 2005. However, since counter-narcotics was not part of the ISAF mission, this was not a very good reason for sending the most capable force to Helmand. Certainly Richards was not convinced. He would later complain that 'I've never yet had a good reason given me why that decision was taken'.[98]

Once taken, this decision remained unchallenged. As Beadle notes, 'Ministers were advised not to try to reverse decisions that had been made in military circles some time previously.'[99] However, the fact is that British defence chiefs knew hardly anything about Helmand or Kandahar before acceding to Canadian demands. White-Spunner, who by then was commander of Joint Force Headquarters, visited Kandahar in October 2004. His Chief of Staff, Colonel Gordon Messenger, followed up with a visit to Helmand in February 2005. Both trips were very short, lasting just a few days, and neither afforded much real understanding of the socio-political and security landscape of these provinces.[100] The paper produced for the Chiefs of Staff when considering this decision stated bluntly that 'we didn't know much about either place'.[101] This was hardly an encouraging start to what was to become Britain's long war in Helmand.

5

Bad Beginning

For a while, things were good in Helmand. The province had been largely untouched by America's war on the Taliban and al-Qaeda. Some bombs were dropped on a Taliban camp in Gereshk and an old garrison in Bolan, close to Lashkar Gah, but otherwise American air power was focused on supporting the 'Eastern Alliance' offensive against the Taliban in next-door Kandahar province. All the same, the Taliban in Helmand knew their time was up. Insurgents from outside the province had fled to Pakistan in late November 2001, while most local Taliban simply had returned to their homes.[1]

In the months that followed the fall of the Taliban in December 2001, tribal leaders began to reassert themselves, and to mobilise local communities to take responsibility for their own villages and districts. Local power holders chased out of Helmand by the Taliban also began to return and reactivate their tribal networks. According to one elder from Nahr-e Seraj, 'In every district there were different local councils.'[2,3] The chief of Nad-e Ali council likewise noted that 'We set up a council to control the district. I was leading the council for six months … I was district chief and the police chief and we patrolled and we had guards at night to keep security. Everything was under the responsibility of this council.'[4]

In Garmsir district, a similar dynamic unfolded. Emboldened by the collapse of the Taliban Emirate, a delegation of tribal elders met with Mullah Naim Barech, the Taliban provincial governor, and other senior Taliban in December 2001. The tribal elders asked the Taliban to leave before the Americans began to bomb the district. Faced with united tribal opposition, the Taliban had no choice but to go. Only one Taliban leader, Abdul Majan, stayed, surrendering his weapons and vehicles and returning to his home village. A local shura of tribal leaders was convened to select a new district governor. Unsurprisingly, they chose the former governor Abdullah Jan, a noted mujahedin commander who had spent the previous seven years fighting against the Taliban in the west with Ismail Khan, and in the north with Massoud.[5]

According to Carter Malkasian, a historian and US diplomat who worked for two years in the district,[6] Abdullah Jan 'was Garmsir's benevolent warlord'. He imposed strict discipline on his band of fighters, to ensure that local people were not harassed or harmed. He set up a tribal council with representatives from every area of the district; tribal leaders were left alone to rule their areas, raising their own taxes and settling local disputes. Public services improved under Abdullah Jan. He set up a court in the district centre that was widely seen as fair. There were soon fifteen schools educating 1,500 children; fewer than under the Taliban as it happened, but the standard of education was far higher and extended to girls. Crucially, Abdullah Jan re-established the traditional militia. Ten communities contributed thirty fighters each, to be paid for by a general tax on wheat and poppy. Deployed at checkpoints dotted around the district, the tribal militia prevented the Taliban from returning. Malkasian notes: 'When five Taliban tried to infiltrate into Mian Poshtay [in central Garmsir], they could not get more than one AK-47 through Abdullah Jan's defensive belt.'[7]

By mid 2002, the big warlords had also returned to Helmand to occupy the main government positions, enriching themselves and their networks by stealing land and shaking down the local population. Among the most corrupt was Sher Mohammed Akhundzada, an Alizai warlord from Musa Qala, who returned to Lashkar Gah in mid December 2001 'with a militia comprised of ex-Taliban fighters' from his own tribal network.[8] He was shortly thereafter appointed provincial governor by Karzai. Malem Mir Wali, a Barakzai warlord from Gereshk, took his Hizb-i Islami militia into the newly designated Afghan Military Forces; Hizb-i Islami was one of the two most powerful mujahedin parties in Helmand, the other being Harakat-e Inqilab-e Islami, led in the 1980s by Mullah Nasim Akhundzada (the uncle of Sher Mohammed Akhundzada). With US weapons and backing, Mir Wali became commander of the re-established 93rd Division. Dad Mohammad Khan, an Alikozai warlord from Sangin, became the provincial chief of the National Directorate of Security, the Afghan security and intelligence service. Finally, Abdul Rahman Jan, a rising Noorzai warlord from Nad-e Ali, was appointed the provincial chief of police. Initially, Abdul Rahman's police force comprised various tribal militias from around the province but he gradually took control by appointing police commanders from extended and allied family networks within his Noorzai tribe.

In the months that followed, district and local leaders selected by tribal shuras were shoved aside and replaced by corrupt 'officials'. Abdul Rahman's police, and the other militia of pro-government warlords, increasingly abused and extorted the local population. US special forces made matters worse through their clumsy operations to hunt down Taliban in Helmand. Many locals mistaken for Taliban by American commandos were carted off to Guantánamo Bay for years of imprisonment; some of these unfortunates were handed over to the Americans by unscrupulous tribal and business rivals. By degrees, the common people began to turn against the government. This provided the perfect opportunity for the Taliban to re-establish themselves in Helmand, which they did gradually from 2004 onwards. In 2006, large numbers of Taliban swept into the province around the same time as the British deployed on an impossible mission to support a corrupt government that the people had lost faith in, and to work alongside Afghan police that were widely feared and despised.

THE PIVOT STRATEGY

For the British Army, Helmand offered the possibility of a 'good war'. The army was bogged down in a campaign in Iraq that had gone terribly wrong. Following the US-led invasion in March 2003, and prompt defeat of the Iraqi Army, the British military was given responsibility for the four southernmost provinces of Iraq, which included Basra, the second largest city in Iraq. British troop numbers rapidly declined from an initial invasion force of 46,000 down to 18,000 in May 2003, and then just 8,500 in May 2004. This coincided with Iraq's descent into chaos, and eventual civil war between the Sunni minority (who had held power under Saddam) and the Shia majority population.

The US mishandling of post-conflict security and reconstruction in Iraq is now common knowledge. Rumsfeld and other senior defence officials displayed staggering arrogance in assuming that US troops would be welcomed as liberators by ordinary Iraqis. CENTCOM under General Franks showed striking disinterest in 'phase IV' planning – that is, planning for what happened after America had won the war. Quite late in the day, the Bush administration appointed a Coalition Provisional Authority (CPA) to govern Iraq, staffed mostly by hopelessly ill-qualified but very eager Republican ideologues. The set-up would be comical were the results not so tragic. The head of the CPA, Paul Bremer, was given executive authority to rule by decree, which he did with aplomb. The effect was disastrous. Bremer's first decree banned any Iraqi who had been a member of the Ba'ath Party from holding public office. This applied to almost everybody in the public sector under Saddam. It was soon followed by his second decree disbanding the Iraqi Army. Overnight, Bremer swelled the numbers of those with reason and the means to violently oppose the US occupation. If Bremer had deliberately set out to create a Sunni insurgency, he could not have done a better job.[9]

The capture of Saddam Hussein in December 2003 brought a rare high point in a conflict that was going from bad to worse. Disillusioned by the failure to create jobs and security, the Shia majority also turned against the coalition in 2004. Growing violent sectarianism gripped Iraq, with Sunni and Shia death squads trading terrible atrocities on the streets of Baghdad. In March, the US Marines launched a major assault against Fallujah, a city forty miles west of Baghdad, in retribution for the brutal murder of four American private security contractors by Sunni insurgents. Around the same time, Bremer decided to put pressure on the main Shia militia, the Mahdi Army of Muqtada al-Sadr. This proved ill-timed. The Mahdi Army responded by overrunning cities and towns across southern Iraq. CPA compounds in the cities of Kut and Nasiriyah had to be hastily abandoned. The Mahdi Army laid siege to the main British base at Basra Palace and, from mid April to the end of June 2004, launched on average five attacks per day against British forces in the city. They had also raised their flag over the governor's offices at Basra. Bremer ordered the British commander in the south, Major General Andrew Stewart, to 'take back the building'. Stewart was not about to pour fuel on the fire, and so the British brigadier in charge of security for Basra was dispatched to persuade the Sadrists to leave the governor's offices. That brigadier was Nick Carter, fresh from his tour in Afghanistan. The Sadrists agreed to leave the building. In early August, however, the British ceasefire with the Mahdi Army broke down, and in that month alone six hundred mortar bombs and eighty-six assaults were launched against Basra Palace.[10]

Southern Iraq was increasingly a poisoned chalice for the British Army. The war was very unpopular back home. Hounded by the press over allegations that the country had been deliberately misled in going to war, the prime minister was forced in February 2004 to launch a public inquiry. The Americans were no happier. Following the Mahdi Army uprising in the spring of that year, a fuming Bremer formally requested that the British government replace Stewart as commander of British forces in Iraq.[11] This request was ignored, not least because Whitehall officials were annoyed at Bremer for stirring things up with the Sadrists. By this stage, the British government had completely lost confidence in the US handling of the war. Viewed from Whitehall, Lieutenant General Ricardo Sanchez, the US commander of coalition forces, appeared to have no grip on the military campaign. Equally worrying, relations had utterly broken down between him and Bremer, whom he blamed for provoking the insurgency.[12] The scandal over the abominable mistreatment of Iraqi detainees by US personnel at the Abu Ghraib prison, which went public in May 2004, underlined the sense that the American campaign had veered off course. Shortly thereafter the *Daily Mirror* published 'leaked pictures' of British soldiers beating up and urinating on detainees; the images proved to be fake but they nonetheless served to further stoke up opposition at home and in the Arab world to Britain's part in the conflict.[13] In June, Sanchez was replaced by a more senior commander, General George Casey, Vice Chief of Staff of the US Army, but by then the British Army was looking for an honourable way out.

Helmand was that way. According to Commodore Steven Jermy, former director of strategy at the British embassy in Kabul, 'it allowed us, in very senior military eyes, a "better go" at Afghanistan'.[14] Similarly, a senior officer on the British general staff recalled that the army's 'Ops [Operations] Directorate were extremely keen politically to move away from Iraq' and to the Afghanistan mission, 'that was doable and played to UK strengths'.[15] This view was confirmed by General Fry, who recollected that 'there was a sense in the British Army that Iraq had not been a success', that it was 'a scruffy indeterminate thing that was difficult to end'. In contrast, British Army leaders 'saw Afghanistan as this redemptive mission'.[16]

Hence, the British announcement at the NATO Summit in Istanbul on 28 June 2004, that the ARRC would take command of ISAF in 2006 (the French, Turks and Spanish were due to have command of ISAF for six months each, in the intervening eighteen-month period). Also announced at the summit was the formal end of the occupation of Iraq; shortly thereafter, the CPA handed authority over to a new interim Iraqi government. Earlier that month the United Nations Security Council had passed Resolution 1546, endorsing the interim government, and authorising coalition forces to remain in Iraq until January 2006.[17] The British intention, therefore, was to pivot its forces from Iraq to Afghanistan in 2006. Fry produced the strategy for this pivot, showing how the British Army would be able to take on the mission in southern Afghanistan as it withdrew from southern Iraq. The strategy made sense in 2004. Two years later, it was in tatters.

The pivot strategy depended on the British Army getting out of Iraq so it could go to Afghanistan instead. However, the army found itself stuck in Iraq as the situation there got steadily worse. The British Army had a full brigade with additional units deployed on operations in Iraq through to 2006. To maintain one brigade on continuous operations actually required five brigades – three cycling through various stages of pre-operation preparations, one on deployment, and one on post-operational recovery. The British Army had seven deployable brigades at the time; thus most of the field army was still committed to Iraq when it was supposed to be deploying to Helmand.

Land Command (the British Army's headquarters) viewed this situation with growing alarm. They would be responsible for generating the additional forces for the Helmand campaign. Throughout 2005, Land Command bombarded the MoD and PJHQ with memoranda warning of the problem with the pivot strategy. Under Defence Planning Assumptions set following the 1998 Strategic Defence Review, the British Army was supposed to be able to deliver one brigade for continuous operations on an overseas campaign, and one brigade for a time-limited operation of no more than six months. With the army's commitment to Iraq dragging on, General Richard Dannatt recalled that 'we were being asked to run two brigades plus on a campaign basis'.[18]

The Defence Secretary, Geoff Hoon, was also increasingly concerned about the prospects of the army having to wage two enduring campaigns at the same time. An impatient Chief of the Defence Staff, General Sir Michael Walker, in essence challenged Hoon to 'speak up' or shut up about the plan. Hoon chose not to raise his concerns with the prime minister.[19] In any case, there was no turning back. Blair had committed the British military to southern Afghanistan. In May 2005, the mild-mannered Hoon was replaced by the more forthright John Reid as Defence Secretary, 'in order to stiffen the MoD'. As one senior official put it, 'Reid was brought in to deliver the Afghanistan deployment.' Reid was no less pleased by the situation facing the British Army. However, he was advised by senior defence officials that Britain had to 'take the plunge'; in order to ensure that the Canadians, Dutch and Danish also sent forces to southern Afghanistan, Britain 'needed to start a snowball effect'.[20]

On 7 July 2005, Britain suffered one of its worst ever terrorist attacks (thereafter known as the 7/7 attacks). Shortly before 9 a.m., three British-born Islamic extremists detonated bombs on three different carriages on the London Underground, and an hour later, a fourth detonated his bomb on a bus in central London; all four terrorists were killed instantly, along with fifty-two commuters, and hundreds more were injured. The scene in London was one of carnage and total chaos. Blair flew straight back down to London from Perthshire in Scotland, where he had been due to start chairing a G8 Summit of world leaders. Since 9/11, the security services had long feared just such an attack on the British capital and had already foiled twelve terrorist plots. Moreover, British intelligence was increasingly highlighting the threat from home-grown Islamic terrorism.[21] There was a link of sorts with Afghanistan in that British Islamic extremists were travelling to the Pakistani border area to receive training in jihadi camps. Two of the 7/7 bombers visited Pakistan from November 2004 to early February 2005. The official report into the events on 7/7 concludes: 'It is possible that they went up to the border areas with Afghanistan or over the border for training but we do not have firm evidence of this.'[22]

Not one to shy away from controversy, the independent MP George Galloway was quick to blame Blair, declaring that the prime minister had 'paid the price' for Iraq. Galloway was not a lone voice in this. Expressing a similar criticism more carefully, the Liberal Democrat leader, Charles Kennedy, suggested that the invasion of Iraq had 'fuelled the conditions' for terrorism by Islamic extremists.[23] Of course, Downing Street utterly rejected this criticism. The prime minister vowed that Britain would take action against Islamic-inspired terrorism, to 'pull it up by its roots'.[24] At the time Blair highlighted the need to address the issues that fed Islamic extremism, including injustice and conflict in the Middle East. Yet he would clarify later that 'also you have got to have the means of combating these people and combating them on the ground'.[25] Thus, for Blair, 7/7 reinforced the case for sending British forces to southern Afghanistan.

Reid still wanted assurances that British forces would be sufficiently supported in the south. With help from his senior officials, he devised three conditions that had to be met before he would approve the deployment. First, the Treasury had to fully fund a task force of whatever size and configuration deemed necessary by the military chiefs. Second, there also had to be sufficient funding for DFID's reconstruction efforts in Helmand. Third, the Canadians had to deploy to Kandahar and the Dutch to Uruzgan around the same time as the British going into Helmand, to guard the eastern and northern flanks of the Helmand task force. The Canadians sent forces to Kandahar in November 2005 under the Operation Enduring Freedom counter-terrorism mission. However, the Dutch were slow to commit and only agreed in December to deploy a task force to Uruzgan. This, in turn, delayed the British military deployment, as Reid would not sign off on this until the Dutch had undertaken to go to Uruzgan. Reid recalls that at the time he was under 'immense pressure … from some people in the military' to let the army get on with the Helmand mission.[26]

For all the problems highlighted by Land Command, army leaders were desperately keen for the Helmand mission to go ahead. Ironically, the deteriorating security situation in Iraq served both to keep the British Army in Iraq and to increase the army's desire to pivot to Afghanistan instead. The British gradually ceded ground in 2005 to various Shia militias, including the Mahdi Army and their main rivals, the Iranian-backed Badr Brigade. Commanders took the view that the

British presence was the main cause of violence and so they began to limit their patrols.[27] When they did venture out on patrol, the British went in main battle tanks or convoys of a dozen Warrior armoured vehicles (basically mini-tanks) because it had become suicidal to patrol in Land Rovers. One officer told a *Sunday Times* journalist that 'we're in survival mode right now, we can't do anything at all'.[28]

The Iraq campaign would continue to go downhill in 2006. By the summer, as the task force arrived in Helmand, British forces in Basra had retreated to their bases and handed over control of the city to the militias. In his memoirs, Blair recalls that in 'late 2006, there was a pretty acute sense among the senior command in the army that we had done as much as we could in Basra'.[29] Small wonder, then, that army leaders in the Ministry of Defence were 'euphoric' when Reid finally gave the go-ahead for Helmand.[30] Everybody underestimated just how tough would be the fight ahead.

THE JOINT HELMAND PLAN

In mid 2005, Whitehall began planning for the Helmand mission. On the civilian side, the task was given to the Post-Conflict Reconstruction Unit (PCRU), a newly formed 'cross-government' agency that was formally 'owned' by the MoD, the FCO and DFID. In reality, the PCRU was something of an unloved bastard child, with none of the parent departments much interested in its success. According to one senior PCRU official, there 'was real antipathy towards this inter-loper' in Whitehall. Helmand offered the opportunity for the PCRU to have 'its first outing', to prove its worth.[31]

The PCRU team was first tasked with producing a desk-study of conflict dynamics in Helmand. One team member recalls that they 'interviewed every white person who had been in Helmand and spoke English', and they also reviewed the available intelligence from the MoD, such as it was. The former diplomat Rory Stewart, who walked across Afghanistan in 2002 and wrote a best-selling account of his journey,[32] told them that Helmand was 'the most dangerous province' in the country and 'you would be crazy to deploy there'.[33] The study's main conclusion was unsurprising: 'we know very little' about Helmand.[34]

Meantime, PJHQ tasked a preliminary operations team, led by Colonel Gordon Messenger, to begin the military planning for Helmand. The main task for prelim ops was to oversee plans for the creation of the main British base in Helmand, called Camp Bastion. This was to be sited in the middle of the desert, twenty-eight miles north-east of Lashkar Gah. According to Messenger, 'the location was chosen because of Afghan ownership issues'; in other words, it was available for rent to the British, and it was likely that a local power holder was financially benefitting from the deal. Messenger admitted that there was some concern at the time that the location was 'too far out and in the middle of nowhere'.[35] One British Army brigadier put it in more withering terms, telling a reporter: 'just when you think you've gone beyond the edge of nowhere, it's twenty minutes further, and that's flying!'[36] However, Messenger maintains that on balance the remote location turned out to be a major advantage because of how the camp expanded.

Unusually for a government project, Camp Bastion was completed ahead of schedule and within budget in early 2006, taking three months and costing £53 million. 39 Engineering Regiment ended up winning a prestigious architect award for this 'extraordinary feat … in the most inhospitable environment'. Not for nothing, a company of Royal Marines from 42 Commando provided security for the build. The original brief was for a camp able to accommodate 2,350 personnel, with a fifty-bed hospital, a helicopter base and a thousand-yard runway. Around 180 Afghan locals were hired for the construction, and over 1,200 containers had to be shipped to and trucked in via Pakistan.[37] From this modest beginning, Bastion grew over a number of years to the size of a small city, extending to some sixteen square miles, becoming home to around 20,000 personnel and the fifth-busiest UK-operated airport.[38]

In mid October 2005, the five-strong PCRU team was instructed to deploy to Kandahar airfield alongside the military prelim ops team. Led by Mark Etherington, an ex-paratrooper who had previously worked for the CPA as governor of the Iraq city of Kut, the PCRU team was instructed to produce a campaign assessment and report back to the Cabinet Office by mid December. Etherington and another senior team member, Minna Jarvenpaa, first flew to Kabul in early November for a hectic round of meetings with senior British, American and Afghan officials 'to gather information and present face'. They received a cold reception from the British embassy. Etherington found 'no appetite for new thinking' in Kabul; he felt like he had 'wandered into a gentlemen's club wearing white flares'. The British ambassador, Rosalind Marsden, claimed to be too busy to meet with him. The senior DFID representative 'didn't smile once' during the visit, and his parting comment to Etherington was 'always remember that you will be reported upon'.[39] After a few days, a fed-up Etherington flew on to Kandahar while Jarvenpaa stayed on to meet with Afghans in Kabul. Ashraf Ghani, the chancellor of Kabul University and former Afghan finance minister, left an especially strong impression on Jarvenpaa. He warned her that if the British arrive like occupiers and 'go in fighting … there will be a bloodbath'.[40]

This message was received loud and clear by the British planners at Kandahar airfield. The prelim ops team had arrived ahead of the PCRU team, and were well into their planning for the military deployment. Initially, prelim ops expected the civilians to act as advisers to support production of a military plan. However, by the time Jarvenpaa arrived in Kandahar a week after the rest of the team, Messenger had been persuaded of the need to produce a proper integrated civil–military plan. This was not going to be easy for Messenger's team, who were expert planners; in contrast, the civilians were rank amateurs. Etherington notes how Messenger 'slowed down the military planning to enable civilians to participate'.[41] PJHQ had expected Messenger to produce a military plan within a week. In the end, it took a month. Helping the integration of civilians into the planning process was Messenger's Chief of Staff, Lieutenant Colonel John Cole, who, as one civilian noted, 'just got it'. Equally helpful were 'really mundane things'. The PCRU team had arrived with a shipping container full of kit that they shared with prelim ops. Most appreciated was the PCRU boiler; the prelim ops boiler had broken down, severely curtailing the supply of much-needed cups of tea. According to one PCRU team member, 'this was the thing that probably made the biggest difference' to harmonious relations between the two teams.[42]

A few days after Jarvenpaa arrived in Kandahar, the PCRU team made their first visit to the American PRT in Lashkar Gah. Flying in a small plane, Jarvenpaa recalls the stunning view as 'the Helmand Valley opened up below us', before the plane 'did a corkscrew landing' in Lashkar Gah.[43] The American PRT was manned by a large US special forces team, numbering some two hundred. The overall threat picture was unclear. Etherington and Jarvenpaa both remember being told that Helmand was 'very quiet', and there was 'absolutely no fighting'. Moreover, Messenger's team were able to drive up through the Helmand River valley unhindered in unarmoured Land Rovers.[44] Against this, there had been increasing reports of attacks on Afghan police and on Western aid organisations since the spring of 2005.[45] Civil service security restrictions prevented the PCRU team from leaving the tiny PRT compound, and so they spent most of the time talking to the PRT commander. He was sceptical when it came to attributing the rising violence to the return of the Taliban. One PCRU member recalls the US commander saying that 'all the police are involved in drugs. So when the ANP say they are in a shoot-out with the Taliban, they are actually involved in a drug war.'[46] Similarly, Etherington remembers the PRT commander advising the British team, 'If you want to prepare for your time here, watch *The Sopranos*.'[47]

On 11 December, Messenger and Etherington presented 'The UK Joint Plan for Helmand: Final Report' to the Cabinet Office. Etherington notes that they had 'not been asked to produce a unified plan' but they had done so anyway. The UK strategic aim for the Afghanistan campaign was:

> An effective, representative government in Afghanistan, with security forces capable of providing an environment in which sustainable economic and social development can occur, without sustainable security support from the international community.

From this strategic aim, the Joint Plan articulated four strategic objectives for the campaign in Helmand, one for each of the four main lines of operations. For the Governance Line, the objective was 'to promote the development of effective and transparent provincial governance'; for the Security Line, it was 'to contribute to an environment which meets the security needs of the Afghan people [and] encourages adherence to the rule of law'; under Economic Development, the objective was to create 'greater economic opportunities ... and a sustainable improvement in the legal economy of Helmand'; and finally under Counter Narcotics, it was 'to make drug production and trafficking a high risk/low benefit endeavour in a sustainable manner'.[48]

The British ambition was staggering given the scale of the challenge. As two analysts wryly noted, 'it approximates the equivalent of the Enlightenment and the Marshall Plan in the context of Europe's one hundred years war'.[49] The Joint Plan itself pointed to a catalogue of profound problems. Seventy per cent of the population, including the provincial governor, was illiterate. Provincial government was 'dominated by patronage networks, tribal affiliation, and alleged links to the narcotics trade'. The security situation was deteriorating and 'illegally armed groups proliferate, particularly in inaccessible regions'. The police were 'widely thought to undermine the safety of the population rather than secure it'.[50] Added to this was the sheer size of the place; Helmand is a quarter of the size of Britain but with far more inhospitable people and weather, and terrain consisting mostly of desert and mountains. One American soldier told a British reporter in 2006: 'think of the worst place you can think of and times that by 50'.[51] Irrigated land, and therefore population and agricultural activity, is concentrated in a narrow strip along the course of the Helmand River, running north to south and covering only 3 per cent of the province. Called the 'Green Zone', this area provided plenty of lush cover for insurgents to operate.

The main thrust of the Joint Plan was actually to pour cold water on what was achievable in Helmand, especially within the planning constraints given to Etherington: £1 billion had been approved for a three-year mission, there would be a cap on the force of around 3,000 troops, and the mission had to include counter-narcotics. The Cabinet Office was told that the mission would take far longer – more likely a decade – and cost a lot more. Moreover, the deputy head of the PCRU, Gil Baldwin, had been warning the Cabinet Office and the MoD for some time 'that 3,000 troops was exactly the wrong number' for Helmand; it was too few to secure the province, but enough to be considered an occupying force by the local population. As for counter-narcotics, the recommendation was: 'Don't do much at first.'[52]

Thus the Joint Plan proposed a cautious approach. According to Jarvenpaa, 'the core idea was to provide security around Lashkar Gah and Gereshk, and create an incubator for building up government capacity'. Lashkar Gah is the provincial capital and, lying on the national Afghan ring road (Highway 1), Gereshk is the main economic hub of Helmand. The area surrounding Lashkar Gah and Gereshk was called the 'lozenge' by the PCRU and PRT teams. Jarvenpaa stressed that the Joint Plan was clear on one point, namely, 'Don't ever think British troops should be deployed out of these two centres.' Hence the Joint Plan called for British forces to stay within the lozenge, wherein, as one PCRU member noted, 'the raw material is located to build up public services' in Helmand. Overall, 'a very significant portion of the Joint Helmand Plan was "we don't know enough" [and] so the first tour should focus on building relationships [with Afghans] and developing knowledge'.[53]

The Joint Plan was received poorly in Whitehall. Etherington and Messenger presented it to a packed meeting in the Cabinet Office, with representatives from across government. The meeting was chaired by Margaret Aldred, who was deputy head of the Foreign and Defence Policy Secretariat in the Cabinet Office. Aldred was dismissive of the cautious tone of the Joint Plan. 'What do you mean we don't know anything?' she asked. 'We've been there since 2001!' It was clear to Etherington that 'the need to deploy into Helmand drove everything', and that he and Messenger had told Whitehall 'what they didn't want to hear'.[54]

THE BRITISH TASK FORCE

On 27 January 2006, the Defence Secretary announced to the House of Commons that a British task force would be deployed to Helmand comprising some 3,300 paratroops from 16 Air Assault Brigade, including an airborne infantry battlegroup from 3rd Battalion the Parachute Regiment (3 Para). It would be supported by eight Apache attack helicopters and four Lynx light utility helicopters from 9th Regiment Army Air Corps, and a detachment of six CH-47 Chinook transport helicopters from 27 Squadron Royal Air Force. Also included were Scimitar and Spartan light tanks from the Household Cavalry and a battery of 105mm light guns from 7 Para, Royal Horse Artillery, and elite troops of the Special Forces Support Group drawn from 1st Battalion the Parachute Regiment (1 Para). In his statement to the House, John Reid emphasised that the British task force was not being sent to hunt down terrorists or Taliban fighters in Helmand. Rather it was part of a 'fully integrated package' of development and security assistance to Afghanistan. The Defence Secretary told the House: 'Let me stress once more, we are deploying this potent force to protect and deter. The ISAF mission has not changed. It is focused on reconstruction.'[55]

The British task force was woefully undermanned and under-equipped for what followed. Within weeks of deploying, it was engaged in fierce combat as it struggled to stop the Taliban from overrunning Helmand. General David Richards, the incoming commander of ISAF, would later describe the fighting over the summer of 2006 as 'probably as intense as anything the British Army has seen since Korea'.[56] Given these events, the decision to 'cap' the original task force at around 3,000 soldiers was one of the most controversial of Britain's war in Afghanistan. So how was this decision taken?

When 16 Air Assault Brigade was notified in August in 2005 that it would deploy to Helmand in five months (as was then expected), they were told from the outset that their planning must assume that the task force would not exceed 3,150 and that the mission would last three years. Brigade staff officers worried that this force was too small and underequipped for the mission. One later noted that 'The feeling in the brigade was that, if everything went swimmingly and the enemy didn't have a vote, then it might just be achievable'.[57] Experienced officers knew to expect things to go wrong. 'Within a matter of weeks' brigade planners had identified 'significant shortfalls in core equipment areas such as helicopters'. According to the brigade commander, Brigadier Ed Butler, 'numerous requests' for additional equipment were rejected: 'the consistent line was that we had to make do'.[58] In desperation, the brigade even turned to Prince Charles. In February 2006, he visited the headquarters of 16 Air Assault Brigade in Colchester in his ceremonial role as Colonel-in-Chief of the Parachute Regiment. During the visit the commander of 3 Para, Lieutenant Colonel Stuart Tootal, told the Prince of Wales that the brigade had not been given enough Chinook transport helicopters. Prince Charles phoned Reid the following day. Reid did not take kindly to this royal intervention in government affairs, and was furious at 16 Air Assault Brigade for trying to circumvent the normal chain of command. Tootal recalls how 'the shit had hit the fan in the MoD'. Moreover, it was all for no good. 'The prince's intervention didn't lead to an increase in flying hours [i.e. helicopters], but plenty of people in the ministry were upset with me from the Secretary of State down.'[59]

The cost of the Helmand campaign did not come out of the Defence budget but instead was borne directly by the Treasury. Thus, it was widely assumed that the cap on the size of the task force, and length and hence cost of the mission – 3,300 troops for three years costing no more than £1 billion – came from Treasury officials. According to Matt Cavanagh, who at the time was special adviser to the Chief Secretary of the Treasury, this view was 'flatly incorrect'.[60] In fact the cap was driven by two considerations. The first was concern within the MoD, and especially from Land Command and PJHQ, about overextending British forces given that operations in Iraq were dragging on longer than expected. As the British Army was being asked to deploy to southern Afghanistan as well as maintain a brigade in southern Iraq, contrary to its own planning assumptions under the pivot strategy, it was essential to limit the scope of the Helmand deployment. *The Times* reported 'that service chiefs had also made it clear [to the Defence Secretary] that the Armed Forces could cope with running two significant operations at the same time … There was no need to draw down the forces in Iraq to cater for the expanded mission in Afghanistan.'[61] Reid had indeed received such an assurance from General Sir Mike Jackson, Chief of the General Staff, who told him that the army could just about handle this 'at a pinch, at a considerable pinch'.[62]

The second consideration was a political judgement, especially on the part of Blair and Reid, about what the wider Cabinet would accept. Reid's job was to deliver on Blair's commitment, made at the NATO Summit in 2004, to send British forces to southern Afghanistan. The prime minister was due to chair a major international conference on Afghanistan in London on 31 January 2006, and so the pressure was on to make a formal announcement on the deployment to Parliament before then. Reid convened and chaired a cross-Whitehall group, with senior representatives from the Cabinet Office, MoD, FCO, DFID, the Treasury and the military, to work out the details and push things forward. General Fry later observed that final agreement on the deployment 'probably would have happened without Reid's group but it would have happened more slowly and without the policy clarity that comes with ministerial leadership'.[63]

The Chief Secretary to the Treasury, Des Browne, was a member of the 'Reid group' and accordingly, as his special adviser, Cavanagh was privy to discussions within this group. (Browne subsequently succeeded Reid as Defence Secretary in May 2006.) Cavanagh notes that 'to the extent that the constraint came from ministers, it came from Blair's and Reid's sense of what they could get through Cabinet without a serious argument'. According to one insider, 'Blair and Reid were worried [in particular] that Gordon Brown would kick up a fuss.' Relations between the prime minister and the Chancellor of the Exchequer, Brown, grew increasingly strained under Blair's second term in office; Downing Street officials began using the term 'TB/GBs' to refer to the stormy relationship.[64] Cavanagh's impression was that '[t]he senior military [also] had their own sense of "what the market would bear": their guess as to the level of commitment politicians would be prepared to sign off without re-opening the whole question'. In particular, they knew that Blair would not stand up to Brown on this issue; in the lead-up to the 2003 Iraq War, the chancellor had refused to release additional resources, despite assurances by the prime minister to military chiefs on funding.[65] One senior government adviser close to the discussion thus notes how 'there was a convergence of interest between the military and those politicians in favour of deployment ... to make sure that it wouldn't look too massive and too kinetic'.[66]

According to Brigadier Ed Butler, Whitehall basically ignored the fact that 'during 2004 and 2005 detailed intelligence reports, produced in-country by special-forces operators, made it very clear that the Taliban were in a far stronger position than most of the government departments were basing their planning assumptions on'.[67] Without access to these intelligence reports, there is no way to verify how they presented the threat from a resurgent Taliban. One insider did note, however, that the Reid group 'only got a sample of the intelligence papers'.[68] Moreover, intelligence reports sent to a ministerial group would most likely come from Defence intelligence and MI6, and these may not have accurately captured or reported intelligence from special forces teams in the field. In any case, as we have seen, the Joint Plan for Helmand report presented a more ambiguous picture. There was rising armed violence in the province, but it was not clear if these 'illegally armed groups' were insurgents, local warlord militia, drug traders, or some mix of these groups. It is this view that appears to have prevailed in Whitehall in early 2006.

On 17 January, the Director General of Operational Policy at the MoD, Martin Howard, told the House of Commons Defence Committee that the armed violence in Helmand 'is still a series of relatively isolated incidents rather than a very wide spread campaign of the sort you are seeing in some areas of Iraq. There is a huge difference between those two.' Moreover, Howard told the committee, 'I have seen no evidence that the population is turning back to the Taliban.'[69] Two months later, the view in the MoD had not changed. In March, the armed forces minister, Adam Ingram, told the committee that 'while there are indicators of a Taliban presence on the ground, it is not an overwhelming presence'. Ingram further suggested that much of the armed activity was driven by opportunism, as opposed to an organised insurgency. Of those engaged in illegal armed activity, he said that 'when they get up in the morning they will put on a particular uniform. It depends who is paying them.'[70] In its report, the committee recorded Ingram's conclusion that 'the threat level on the ground can be over-stated'.[71]

THE RETURN OF THE TALIBAN

Ingram and Howard could not have been more wrong. By 2006, the Taliban had returned in force to Helmand, and this was greatly aided by the local population, once again, being driven into the arms of the Taliban by the predatory and abusive behaviour of local warlords and their militias.

As we have seen, by mid 2002 the major warlords that had been pushed out of Helmand under the Taliban Emirate returned to power in reincarnated form, as allies of Karzai and therefore in government office. Once back in power, these warlords returned to their bad old ways. Their militias soon clashed, first those of Sher Mohammed Akhundzada and Abdul Rahman Jan, then Rahman joining Akhundzada against Malem Mir Wali. Each attempted to fool US special operations forces into targeting their enemy as 'Taliban', with some success.[72] Of these warlords, Mir Wali formed the closest relationship with US special forces. Mir Wali was heavily involved in the drug trade in Helmand, as well as extorting money from road tolls and other means. The first US special forces A-team to arrive in Helmand operated out of Mir Wali's compound near Gereshk district centre, next to which they built a base in mid 2002, called Camp Price. Mir Wali's militia guarded Camp Price in return for a handsome fee. As Mike Martin notes in his oral history of the Helmand conflict, 'much more important than the money was the impression to the rest of the population that he, Mir Wali, was working with the foreigners and that he, alone, controlled access to their base'. Mir Wali also offered to have his militiamen accompany the US special operators, who were ignorant of local politics and personalities. This arrangement only reinforced the popular perception that he had American backing. Thus, in a pattern that was replicated across Afghanistan, US special forces unwittingly got drawn into and reinforced corrupt patronage politics in Helmand.[73]

Increasingly, the warlords turned their attention to violently exploiting those communities that did not form part of their patronage networks. One former member of the original provisional district council of Nad-e Ali recounted:

> In the first six months when we had the council, everything was going well. Everything was done by advising and in contact with the local villagers. When the official police chief and district chief arrived ... day by day the situation got worse. There was lots of extortion and stealing, and people were killed, and someone was even burned in their car by these government people, and day by day people got fed up with this Afghan government and welcomed the Taliban back into their districts.[74]

The Helmandi police under Abdul Rahman and his appointees were particularly notorious for robbing and abusing the local populace and carrying out extrajudicial murders.[75] On abusive governance as a major factor driving the villagers towards the Taliban, there is widespread consensus among local elders interviewed some years later.[76] It also meant that on their return to Helmand, the Taliban were able to present themselves as the sharia party – that is, the party of law and order.[77]

Pro-government warlords also harassed and targeted those former Taliban who had remained in Helmand, and were trying to stay away from trouble in their villages after the demoralising defeat of 2001. US special forces fuelled the problem by offering up to $2,000 for the capture of al-Qaeda terrorists or Taliban fighters. An early target was Mullah Baghrani, despite the fact that he had publicly reconciled with the government, causing him to go on the run. Some years later, a number of local elders and Taliban commanders from across the province attested that as a result, many former Taliban returned to the insurgency in self-defence.[78] Thus, according to local elders, when Karzai came to power, the former Taliban district chief of Nad-e Ali, Mullah Ehsanullah, 'surrendered all of his weapons and stayed at home, but once he saw that the situation was becoming worse and the Americans were looking for all of the former Taliban, he decided to escape, and he rejoined the Taliban and became a commander again'.[79] A similar dynamic unfolded in neighbouring Uruzgan and Kandahar provinces, where harassment drove former Taliban back to armed resistance.[80] A particularly important example was the former Taliban aviation and tourism minister, Mullah Akhtar Mohammad Mansour, who reportedly received amnesty from Karzai and returned to his home district of Maiwand in Kandahar province. On hearing about the harassment and arrests of so many former Taliban commanders in southern Afghanistan, Mansour fled across the border to Pakistan. He would later rise up the ranks of the movement to become leader of the Taliban.[81]

Many 'common people' – to use the Taliban term for non-Taliban locals – also got caught up in the net thrown by US special forces as they tried to catch terrorists and Taliban. As Martin notes, the Americans 'failed to understand how offering a bounty would cause people to denounce anyone they were having a feud with, or even innocent people, in order to collect the money'. Detainees 'sold' to the Americans often ended up in Guantánamo Bay. Martin uncovered records of a number of such people in the camp, including some accused of being members of a crack forty-man terrorist unit suppos-edly run by Mullah Baghrani; Martin could find no evidence of such a group having existed beyond confessions extracted under torture in Guantánamo. In another incident, a US special operations forces team was ambushed in Baghran in February 2003 as it hunted for Mullah

Baghrani. In response, the team rounded up ten locals – 'some of whom were most likely involved in some way in the incident, along with several who were not' – and sent them off to Guantánamo. Most were released between 2005 and 2007.[82] Afghan captives not sent to Guantánamo would end up instead at a US-run detention facility at Bagram airfield in eastern Afghanistan. The abuse and torture of prisoners at Bagram was as bad as anywhere else in the worldwide network of declared and secret detention facilities created by the United States for its global war on terror. The American journalist Carlotta Gall tracked down the family of one Afghan man who died while in US custody at Bagram, supposedly of a heart attack. The family showed her the death certificate issued by the US Army patholo-gist; as it was written in English, they could not understand it. Under cause of death it stated: 'Blunt force injuries to lower extremities complicating coronary artery disease.' Under mode of death was typed one word: 'homicide'.[83] Such injustice by US forces, and those they paid, increasingly infuriated many ordinary Helmandis, turning them against the foreigners and the government in Kabul that they were backing.

Lines of conflict formed and hardened between warlord-patronage networks that benefitted from government largesse, and disenfranchised and downtrodden tribal communities. The most noted example is the Ishaqzai community south of Sangin. The British journalist Christina Lamb notes how the Ishaqzai 'turned against the coalition early on', following a night-time raid in western Kandahar in which US special operations forces killed a prominent tribal elder and hauled off fifty tribesmen.[84] However, underlying Ishaqzai opposition in Sangin to ISAF and the Kabul government were longer-standing tribal rivalries. For generations, the Alizais and Alikozais to the north of Sangin had been in competition with the Ishaqzai. During the Taliban Emirate, Ishaqzais held a number of key Taliban government posts in Helmand, including that of the provincial governor. The tables were turned under Sher Mohammed Akhundzada, as the new Alizai provincial governor, and Dad Mohammad, the Alikozai head of the Afghan secret police, 'who used the cover of their government positions to tax, harass and steal from the Ishaqzai'.[85] As one Alikozai elder admitted in 2007, 'The Ishaqzai had no choice but to fight [back].'[86]

Divisions between pro- and anti-government groups also occurred at the sub-tribal level. For example, among the Alikozais, the Khotezais were excluded from power and provided many recruits to the Taliban, while their traditional rivals the Bostanzais were well placed within the government.[87] This problem of tribal and sub-tribal patronage politics persisted in Helmand and across Afghanistan more generally. As late as 2012 the tribal sections favoured by the government continued to feel entitled to control all government posts, exclude their local rivals, and push government and foreign troops for a more aggressive posture against those communities they portrayed as 'pro-Taliban'.[88] In this way, the Taliban resurgence in Helmand was greatly aided by inter-tribal rivalry and local resistance to predatory rule.

In late 2002, small groups of Taliban started to reorganise at the local level and engage in military activities. Over 2003, these various groups began to coalesce around a number of senior leaders from the emirate who had taken refuge in the Pakistani city of Quetta. In mid 2003, they announced the creation of a Taliban leadership council; calling itself the Rahbari Shura, it became better known as the Quetta Shura.[89] One year later, the Taliban started 'returning' to Helmand. The pattern and pace of this return varied in different areas of the province. In the southern districts, the Taliban began by sending in small infiltration teams from Pakistan. As Antonio Giustozzi notes, 'The strategic task of these "vanguard" teams was to prepare the ground for a later escalation of the insurgency.'[90] In the northern districts of Musa Qala, Sangin and Nahr-e Seraj, the vanguard teams arrived from the northern mountains of Helmand. In Musa Qala, the Taliban 'secretly entered the district and talked to some villagers and elders ... they told the people that they were coming back to the district to fight against the government'.[91] In 2005 they came back in force and 'within two to three months they had captured all the villages, although not the district centre'.[92] Similarly, in Sangin the Taliban 'reappeared' in 2004: 'there were one, two, three, four Taliban' and they tried to use the 'problems between the tribes' (i.e. Alikozai exploitation of Ishaqzais) to stir up resistance to the government.[93]

In contrast to Musa Qala, where most of the Taliban fighters came from neighbouring Baghran and Kajaki, in Sangin, Gereshk and Nad-e Ali most of them were locals who had gone to ground in 2002, while their commanders returned from Pakistan, where they had fled when the pro-Karzai warlords seized power.[94] They brought with them 'foreign fighters' from Pakistan and even further afield, including some Chechens. As one local elder from Nad-e Ali recalled: 'Taliban from the previous [Taliban] government started organising themselves again. They went to Pakistan and asked for help. That is when people from Pakistan started coming.'[95]

In most districts, the Taliban vanguard teams were cautious at first, and then became more bold as they removed opposition to their return and built support among the common people. Local elders described how this happened in Sangin: 'Taliban first appeared during the night, they came to Hyderabad village and killed those people who were working for the government. Day by day they started appearing during the day also and then they became more powerful.'[96]

Similarly, in Nad-e Ali, elders recall that 'when the villages began supporting the Taliban, they became more confident and powerful, and started to attack the district centre'.[97]

In the southern district of Garmsir, the precursor to the return of the Taliban was the removal of Abdullah Jan as district governor in December 2004, and the disbanding of his tribal militia guarding the district. Abdullah Jan had fallen foul of local Alizai chiefs over eradication of their poppy crops; they duly complained to the head of their tribe in Helmand, Sher Mohammed Akhundzada, who was already displeased with Abdullah Jan for stopping his pickups from transporting opium through Garmsir to Pakistan. Ironically, Abdullah Jan was removed for being involved in the drug trade. A succession of weak district governors followed Abdullah Jan; none could revive the tribal militia, or rein in the increasingly abusive behaviour of local police.[98] The district was ripe for Taliban takeover.

The former Taliban provincial governor, Mullah Naim, had fled in 2001 to a refugee camp in Baluchistan, just two hours across the Pakistani border. As one local elder notes, in 2005 'he started to send some of his men back in twos and threes'.[99] Among these were Taliban mullahs from Quetta and Peshawar who preached against the government and encouraged young men to join the Taliban. Moderate local mullahs were silenced through intimidation. Abdullah Jan tried to remobilise his old militia to stop the district falling into Taliban hands but it was too late. According to Carter Malkasian, 'By the end of

2005, sensing the shift in power, local village elders started working
with the Taliban.' In June 2006, Naim returned to Garmsir with
hundreds of fighters. Within three months, all but the district centre
had fallen into Taliban hands.[100]

Ironically the removal of the two most powerful warlords in
Helmand – Sher Mohammed Akhundzada and Malem Mir Wali –
made matters far worse. By late 2002, the Afghan Military Forces
formed from warlord militias had ballooned to 250,000 on paper; many
were non-existent 'ghost soldiers', the salaries for whom warlords still
claimed from Karzai's US backers. In 2003, the United Nations launched
a programme to disarm and demobilise 100,000 men from the Afghan
Military Forces. In their place, the US was recruiting and training a
new professional Afghan army.[101] Mir Wali's 93rd Division was scheduled to be demobilised in 2004 under this programme. The warlord
had no choice but to comply but he did so grudgingly. He lost his
artillery and handed over some of his small arms. More important
still, he lost his position as commander of the 93rd Division and,
through this, his ability to give patronage to his fighters and to use
the cloak of officialdom to protect his drug business.[102] In a final act
of humiliation, US special forces turned on Mir Wali, and with encouragement from Sher Mohammed Akhundzada twice raided his
compound searching for illegal weapons. As Gall notes, by degrees
he lost control of his militia: 'his men saw that he no longer had the
power to protect them or provide them with jobs and drifted away.'[103]
Having lost his patron, Mir Wali's most senior commander, Qari
Hazrat, formed an alliance with the Taliban, taking much of the
former 93rd Division with him. In this way, as one local elder put it,
the UN disarmament and demobilisation programme 'was what
started the Taliban in Nahr-e Seraj'.[104]

Sher Mohammed Akhundzada was to have his comeuppance, when
he was removed from the governor's post in December 2005 at the
insistence of the British. Once it was decided that the British would
take responsibility for securing and developing Helmand, Ambassador
Marsden was sent in May 2005 to meet with Akhundzada in Lashkar
Gah. She was less than impressed. The UK embassy had got the
measure of him. They knew that he was highly corrupt, had a private
militia that dealt violently with anyone who opposed him, and was
heavily involved in the drugs trade. They correctly surmised that much

of the local opposition to the Afghan government in Helmand was down to the predatory and abusive rule of Akhundzada and his fellow warlords. Marsden cabled London that he had to go. MI6 agreed.[105]

Minna Jarvenpaa recalls meeting Akhundzada when the PCRU team visited Lashkar Gah in October 2005. 'He was physically very short' and quite polite, but she 'felt deep steel and not in a benign way'. Her Afghan adviser 'saw him as a thug'. The PCRU team appreciated fully the need to replace Akhundzada with a more reliable partner for the British effort in Helmand. At the same time, they anticipated trouble when he was shoved from office. Thus, they strongly advised the embassy and the Cabinet Office that he should not be removed in advance of the deployment of the British task force. This advice was ignored.[106]

Karzai reluctantly replaced Sher Mohammed Akhundzada in December after the provincial governor's compound was raided and, as was expected, a very large quantity of drugs found. Akhundzada later claimed that 'we did keep opium in specially built basements nearby but we did that for the Interior Ministry either to burn it or send it to Kabul'.[107] Of course, nobody gave this credence. Former National Security Adviser Mohammad Daoud was appointed to succeed Akhundzada. Daoud was a competent, highly educated, English-speaking technocrat. Meeting him in early 2006, Jarvenpaa recalls that he was 'charming and very open-minded'.[108] While Daoud was born in Helmand, he had no tribal base in the province; he was also saddled with his predecessor's brother, Amir Mohammed Akhundzada, as the deputy provincial governor of Helmand. Thus, Daoud was reliant on British support to exert influence. He was none too pleased at how long it took British forces to arrive, which was some five months after he was appointed.

It was entirely predictable that Sher Mohammed Akhundzada would cause trouble. In his testimony to the House of Commons Defence Committee on 17 January 2006, Martin Howard noted approvingly the removal of Akhundzada by Karzai as 'a step in the right direction' in terms of the British mission to Helmand. This prompted one exasperated committee member to observe that 'the removal of somebody who is a governor from office when in the past he has been one of the warlords does not remove him from his ability to cause a lot of problems for the area and for British troops when they arrive'.[109] Sure enough, Akhundzada threw his weight behind the Taliban, financing their operations and, even more importantly, ordering his commanders to fight the British.[110]

In contrast to the prevailing view in Whitehall, which did not link the rising violence in Helmand to the return of the Taliban, the US embassy in Kabul concluded in March 2006 that 'Over the past year, as the insurgency has gained momentum in Helmand province, security has deteriorated'. US officials noted that the 'causes are varied, complicated, and intertwined', involving a 'nexus among drug traffickers, warlords, and Anti-Coalition Militia' (i.e. insurgents). But the US embassy accurately assessed the rising force of the insurgency, observing how in February anti-government forces had 'launched simultaneous attacks in Sangin, Mousa Qala, and Naw Zad districts'.[111] In fairness, the US ambassador, Ronald Neumann, was trying to alert Washington DC to the perilous situation in Afghanistan. But he was fighting an uphill battle as most US policymakers were 'ludicrously optimistic – to the point of delusion – about Afghanistan's progress and prospects in 2002–06'.[112] In December 2005, the Bush administration decided to reduce US forces in southern Afghanistan from three to two battalions. US officials in Kabul worried that 'the insurgents would see ISAF's expansion and the US contraction [in the south] as the moment to rekindle the war'. To punch home his message, Neumann gave a public talk at Georgetown University in March 2006 in which he warned that it would 'be an extremely bloody year'.[113] He was to be proven right: across Afghanistan, the number of reported attacks on Afghan security forces rose dramatically from 1,347 in 2005 to 3,824 in 2006.[114] Given the misplaced optimism in Washington, it is perhaps not so surprising that on a visit to British troops in Afghanistan in late April 2006, John Reid should tell reporters that 'we would be perfectly happy to leave in three years and without firing one shot because our job is to protect the reconstruction'.[115] This was a forlorn hope. 16 Air Assault Brigade ended up firing almost half a million rounds on their tour.[116]

THE PLATOON HOUSE STRATEGY

16 Air Assault Brigade was formed around the Paras, who prided themselves on being the toughest regiment of the regular army.[117] Ed

Butler, as brigade commander, notes that he had 'nothing to prove', having already done two tours in Afghanistan with the SAS.[118] However, 3 Para, which formed the infantry battlegroup for the first Helmand tour, had seen little action since the 1982 Falklands War, unlike much of the rest of the British Army, which had seen service in the 1991 Gulf War, or with the United Nations Protection Force in Bosnia from 1992 to 1995. Even within the Parachute Regiment, 3 Para were the poor cousins to 1 Para, who had been involved in intense fighting in Sierra Leone in 2000, and 2 Para, who provided the backbone for the first ISAF mission to Kabul in 2002. As the commanding officer of 3 Para, Lieutenant Colonel Stuart Tootal noted that, while 3 Para had taken part in the invasion of Iraq in 2003, the battalion 'had been disappointed by their experiences there … they saw relatively little of the action and felt that their combat talents had been wasted'.[119] Suffice to say, 3 Para was not going to shy away from a fight if the opportunity presented itself in Helmand.

Camp Bastion may have been built ahead of schedule but it still wasn't fast enough for 3 Para. After spending a few weeks in Kandahar airfield on in-theatre planning and preparations, the battlegroup head-quarters deployed to Helmand on 15 April, along with A Company and the Patrols Platoon. The advance troops arrived to find, in Tootal's words, 'a 2-square-kilometre building site'.[120] Even by Para standards, the living was rough. Each afternoon brought sandstorms covering everything and every person with a fine layer of dust. At night, the Paras baked in tents with no air conditioning. Given the unsuitable living conditions, PJHQ was delaying the deployment of the rest of the battlegroup. This was a major source of frustration for Tootal, who was already under pressure from an irate Daoud: the provincial governor had expected the British to arrive in January. In the end, B and C Companies did not arrive until mid May, and the artillery and light tanks did not turn up until July.[121]

16 Brigade had prepared for the deployment on the assumption that the UK task force would be led by Brigadier Butler. However, ISAF was due to take command of all international forces in the south in July 2006, and a Canadian brigadier, David Fraser, had been appointed commander of the new ISAF Regional Command South (RC-South).[122] The view in PJHQ and the MoD was that a British brigadier could not be under the command of a Canadian of the same rank. Hence,

at the last moment, Colonel Charlie Knaggs was brought in to take command of the UK task force. To make matters worse, Knaggs was an Irish Guardsman, not a Parachute Regiment officer. Butler was appointed the overall commander of British Forces in Afghanistan. This role, which basically involved liaising between the UK task force and the British embassy, and with PJHQ and the MoD back home, saw Butler travel back and forth between Kabul, Kandahar and Helmand. Tootal and Knaggs came under the ISAF chain of command and specifically Brigadier Fraser, and at the same time they answered to Butler, who did not. Thus, any orders that Knaggs received from Fraser had to be cleared with Butler. Since 3 Para was formally an ISAF battlegroup, Fraser also reserved the right to give orders directly to Tootal, which in turn had to be approved by Knaggs and Butler.[123] It would have been hard to design a more convoluted and dysfunctional command set-up for British forces.

The Joint Helmand Plan called for 3 Para to focus on creating security within the triangular area bounded by Lashkar Gah, Gereshk and Camp Bastion; this would later be called the Afghan Development Zone (ADZ). A Company established a forward operating base – which became know as FOB Price – on the north-west outskirts of Gereshk in mid April. Initially, foot patrols of the town went without incident. The locals seemed friendly enough. The main risk was from heat exhaustion as the Paras, loaded down with around 145 pounds of kit and body armour, had to endure temperatures of forty degrees in the midday sun; in July and August the average temperatures climbed to fifty degrees.[124] However, to the commander of A Company, beneath the surface 'there was a volatility to the situation'. He recalled that 'the patrolling we did there was not dissimilar to what I had done in Belfast. It might seem benign. But there was an edge there.'[125] As they walked through the narrow back alleys, the Paras noticed men observing them and speaking quietly into mobile phones. It did not take the Paras long to figure out that their movements were being tracked by Taliban sympathisers. Danger was never far away. On 30 April, an Afghan National Army (ANA) convoy travelling along Highway 1 on the outskirts of Gereshk was hit by an improvised explosive device (IED), killing four Afghan soldiers. When the casualties were brought into the local medical centre, Tootal recalls seeing '[t]he grisly residue of the body parts of the dead [as they were] lifted off the back of an ANA pick-up truck'.[126] Incidents such as these highlighted the challenges of creating a security bubble around the ADZ when the rest of the province was crawling with Taliban.

Ultimately this situation was to lead to the deployment of British forces into the northern districts of Sangin, Now Zad, Musa Qala and Kajaki, in what proved to be the most controversial command decision of 16 Brigade's tour. Under what became known as the 'Platoon House' strategy, small groups of infantry were sent to prevent these districts from being completely overrun by Taliban. This move was widely criticised for pulling British forces off the Joint Helmand Plan and leading to British troops 'fighting for their lives ... in a series of Alamos in the north of the province'.[127] As one defence expert later noted, it robbed the British task force of initiative and turned it into 'a thinned-out force locked into static defence'; moreover, it 'gave the Taliban, who were known to be concentrating on the British, a series of fixed targets to attack'.[128] Members of the Cabinet were left mystified; one minister was overheard asking: 'How the hell did we get ourselves into this position? How did we go charging up the valley without it ever being put to cabinet?'[129]

Actually it was easy for 16 Brigade to deviate from the Joint Helmand Plan because they had never taken ownership of it. The plan was produced by the PCRU and prelim ops with no real input from 16 Brigade. Butler and Tootal did visit the PCRU and prelim ops team in Kandahar airfield towards the end of their planning exercise. One PCRU member recalls 'a couple of meetings that were frankly disastrous', and that Butler and Tootal 'wanted to get development civilians out to the entire province'. At one point, 'Tootal seriously suggested tandem parachute jumps with civilians attached to Paras.'[130] To Etherington, 'it was clear that 16 Brigade wanted to go up north', and their basic plan was 'to mallet the Taliban'. He remembered Tootal 'getting out a white board and drawing pincer movements'.[131] When Jarvenpaa visited the British task force headquarters on a review visit in September 2006, she discovered that 16 Brigade planners had not bothered to read the Joint Helmand Plan.[132]

It is clear that once on the ground, Butler was quick to dismiss the plan. He felt that it was 'pretty thin on the military Line of Operation' and had been 'drawn up by people who did not properly understand the Brigade's skill sets and capabilities'.[133] Messenger later conceded that the Joint Helmand Plan was 'a top-level plan based on objectives and less on what was achievable with resources' and that it 'was diffi-cult to adapt tactically', and therefore that it was probably 'too big an ask to give the Joint Helmand Plan to 16 Brigade and ask them to implement [it]'.[134] For Butler, an equally serious shortcoming was that the Joint Helmand Plan failed to take account of the extent of the Taliban resurgence in Helmand. In this context, the problem with concentrating British forces in the ADZ triangle is that it gave insur-gents freedom to conduct attacks at will from the rest of the province. Butler was concerned that the Sangin Valley was 'likely to become a major highway for Taliban to launch attacks against the troops estab-lishing themselves in the ADZ'. Two IED attacks against the British PRT in Lashkar Gah on 7 and 14 April further highlighted this problem. Following these attacks, British commanders in Helmand asked for more troops and for the rules of engagement, which only allowed British forces to fire in self-defence, to be relaxed. Both requests were turned down. Butler observes how delivering the 'Sangin effect' – securing Sangin district centre with limited task force resources – dominated brigade discussions and planning in early April. Moreover, 'these discussions were not just taking place in theatre but were also raised with PJHQ, the MOD and other government departments'.[135]

Butler and Knaggs also came under increasing pressure from Daoud to deploy British troops into the northern districts in order to prevent them from falling to the Taliban. Since their arrival in Helmand in mid April, Daoud had been berating the Paras for turning up late and doing little. As Butler notes, Daoud 'was unsurprisingly frustrated and felt let down and exposed by the delayed arrival of 3,000 British troops, which he had been assured, by British officials, would occur in January'.[136] All the same, hopes had been riding high on the British. US embassy officials noted in March that notwithstanding the rising armed violence, there was 'widespread optimism [in the province] due to the upcoming UK deployment'.[137] British liaison officers attached to the US PRT in Helmand had been telling tribal elders in early 2006 that 'the deployment of over 2,000 UK troops, co-located with an ANA brigade, would bring better security to all parts of Helmand'.[138] This was not wholly accurate, for the Joint Helmand Plan did not envisage bringing security 'to all parts' of the province; moreover, out of 2,000 troops from the UK task force that were deployed in Helmand, only about half were infantry. This, then, was a major part of the problem: Daoud failed to appreciate just how few British troops there were to do the actual fighting.

At the same time, Butler felt that it was imperative for the British to support the provincial governor. The small Afghan army had no presence in Helmand at the time, and in most places the Afghan police were worse than useless. Thus, Daoud relied on the British 'to keep the Afghan flag flying' in the north of Helmand. The British were also entirely reliant on Afghan sources for information on what was happening on the ground. On multiple occasions in late May, British forces flew out on rescue missions to save government officials only to find no Taliban and little sign of trouble when they landed. Thus, Butler concluded that the UK task force 'needed a presence to develop situation awareness' in the north.[139] By the end of May, British platoon houses had been established in the district centres of Musa Qala and Now Zad. On both occasions, British forces went in to work alongside the local police, who 'were pretty much a joke really'.[140]

Late June was to see the task force finally deploy into Sangin, the most dangerous district in the most deadly province in Afghanistan. Once again, the Paras were sent in on a rescue mission and were only supposed to stay for a few days; by the time UK forces pulled out of Sangin in September 2010 – handing over to the US Marines – 106 British troops had been killed in action in the district.[141] Butler and Knaggs had been specifically warned against sending troops to Sangin by the PCRU; on a visit to Lashkar Gah in April 2006, Jarvenpaa had briefed them both on the struggle between the Alikozai and Ishaqzai tribes over land and drugs. The Alikozai were using their control of government positions to oppress the Ishaqzai, and hence the Ishaqzai had aligned with the Taliban. At that time, Butler was considering establishing a platoon house in the district centre in order to deliver the 'Sangin effect'. Jarvenpaa warned 16 Brigade against wandering into the middle of an inter-tribal fight. She also recalls looking at the satellite images of the district centre with Butler and Knaggs and, while no military expert, she was immediately struck by how in-defensible it was. The district centre comprised two buildings, a two-storey tower and a garden (which would serve as a helicopter landing site) surrounded by a crumbling mud wall. There were orchards on two sides and the bazaar was only a couple of hundred yards away;

these provided the insurgents with concealment and cover on three axes of attack.[142]

The plan to go into Sangin was temporarily shelved when it was decided to establish platoon houses in Now Zad and Musa Qala instead, in response to pressure from Daoud to stop the Taliban over-running these districts, and to send a force to protect the Kajaki Dam. Then on 17 June the Taliban ambushed and killed the former district governor of Sangin, Gul Mohammad Khan, who happened to be the brother of Dad Mohammad Khan, the former provincial head of the National Directorate of Security and powerful leader within the Alikozai tribe. When his family attempted to recover the body the following day, they too were attacked and over thirty were killed. Dad Mohammad demanded that his family be evacuated, and both Daoud and Karzai called on the British to do this. Tootal recalls the concerns in the UK task force headquarters about taking on this mission: 'there was a danger that the whole of 3 PARA would become fixed in holding static locations'.[143] On 19 June, Butler and Tootal received reports from Daoud that Sangin district centre was about to fall to the Taliban. Within an hour, four Chinooks full of Paras were en route. They arrived to discover no sign of the Taliban. Dad Mohammad's party was flown out by Chinook, and the ninety men of A Company were left behind to hold the fort along with twenty Afghan police. The fifty extra policemen whom Daoud promised would arrive in three days' time to relieve A Company never turned up.

The Paras were deeply ambivalent about their mission. They knew that Dad Mohammad's family were widely despised for their brutal rule of the district. They were also rescuing the district police chief, another senior member of the Alikozai tribe, whom locals wanted to lynch for abducting and raping children. One platoon commander noted that 'there was definitely a feeling among the blokes of "why the hell are we going to support this guy? We should go and kill him, then we would get the locals on our side straight away."'[144] Local elders pleaded with British commanders to leave in order to avoid a major battle. Two days later, Afghan police reported that families were leaving the town.

That evening, the insurgents opened up on the district centre with rocket-propelled grenades (RPGs), machine guns and rifle fire. The British returned fire, aiming at the muzzle flashes of insurgent weapons in the distance. The Taliban kept firing all night and there was little let-up in the days and nights that followed. On 1 July, the Taliban attempted to breach the district centre in a two-pronged assault. One group of twenty insurgents approached from the north, across a dry wadi, while another insurgent group approached from the east, down the straight road that led from the bazaar to the main gate of the district centre. The Paras had been tipped off by British intelligence in Camp Bastion and were lying in wait. In this instance, the Taliban assault was amateurish and easily repulsed; indeed, it was so badly executed that the Paras wondered if the insurgents were high on drugs. The attackers were mowed down by the Paras' heavy machine guns. As the Taliban attempted to withdraw they were raked with cannon fire from Apache gunships, and an A-10 arrived in time to drop a precision bomb on one group that had taken cover. The Taliban paid a heavy price with twelve insurgents dead including the commander.[145]

The Taliban learned the hard way that frontal assaults were suicidal. However, they continued to probe the British defences and to pour fire from machine guns, RPGs and 107mm rockets into the district centre each evening. A Company responded with their own machine guns, mortars and Javelin anti-tank missiles, which were proving very effective at destroying Taliban firing positions. The Paras also called on fire support from the 105mm guns of the Royal Horse Artillery in FOB Robinson, and from Apache gunships, A-10 tank-busters and AC-130 Spectre gunships hovering overhead. The sheer weight of British and American fire kept the Taliban at bay; it also caused enormous damage to the town and surrounding area.

By late June, the UK task force was under immense pressure across Helmand. The platoon houses in Sangin, Now Zad, Musa Qala and Kajaki were besieged by Taliban, making it impossible to resupply them by land. Supplies had to be flown in by Chinook. This created two problems. First, it put added pressure on the already overstretched UK Joint Helicopter Force (Afghanistan) based at Kandahar airfield; the force was joint because British Army pilots flew the Apache gunships and Lynx light helicopters, and Royal Air Force and Royal Marine pilots and crews manned the Chinook heavy-lift helicopters. Two Chinooks were forward deployed at Camp Bastion and kept on immediate readiness – one for emergency casualty evacuation and the other for a quick reaction force. Of the remaining four

Chinooks, at any time one or even two might be taken offline for mechanical servicing. Adding to the pressure on 'flying hours', the UK Joint Helicopter Force (Afghanistan) was tasked with supporting Regional Command South, which meant that British Chinooks could be tasked to support American, Canadian or Dutch forces, though most missions were flown in support of 3 Para. The second problem was that the frequency of flights into the platoon houses made it easier for the Taliban to detect British flying patterns. As much as possible the Chinooks flew at night but increasingly they were taking fire as they flew in to resupply beleaguered British troops. All five platoon houses in northern Helmand were designated 'amber landing zones' to indicate the extreme risk to helicopters flying into these bases.[146] The commander of Joint Helicopter Force (Afghanistan), Colonel Richard Felton, and Tootal both agreed that it was simply a matter of time before a Chinook was shot down.[147] The landing site for Musa Qala was particularly exposed; at 200 square yards it was also small (especially for the 100-foot-long Chinooks) and difficult to find.

A Royal Marine pilot, Major Mark Hammond, recalls flying fast and low into Musa Qala to collect a serious casualty: 'as we came over the edge of the town all hell broke loose'. The Taliban opened up with heavy machine guns and RPGs. One RPG missed the helicopter by three feet. The insurgents also began to fire mortar bombs onto the landing site. The Chinook crew expended over a thousand rounds returning fire with the helicopter's two M60 machine guns. The fire from insurgents was so intense that the mission had to be aborted. The Chinook returned a few hours later escorted by four Apache gunships armed with Hellfire missiles and 30mm cannon to suppress enemy fire. The Apaches did not stop firing throughout the time it took the Chinook to fly in and out of Musa Qala. Hammond says that 'All around the Apaches were pounding the shit out of the place'. Even more devastating was an American A-10 Warthog that arrived on station to help, with its fearsome 30mm Gatling gun able to fire 3,900 shells per minute: as one Chinook pilot later recalled, 'It was the Hog that ripped the place to pieces.'[148]

The Taliban kept British platoon houses under near constant attack from mortars, rockets and rifle fire, and the assaults were becoming ever more dangerous. British sniper teams fought duels with Taliban marksmen, who were a particular hazard. Claymore mines were rigged around the district centres to take care of any insurgent teams that attempted to infiltrate them. B Company, which had relieved A Company in Sangin in early July, relied heavily on fire support from the 105mm guns in FOB Robinson; supporting artillery fire often had to be called in at 'danger close' range to British defensive positions.

Sangin was especially under pressure. On 1 July, an insurgent 107mm rocket struck the tower in the district centre, which housed A Company's signals intelligence team and sniper section. Two para-troopers and an Afghan interpreter were killed, and five paratroopers were seriously injured. The injured had to wait for nightfall to be flown out to Bastion; it would have been suicidal to attempt to evacuate them during the day.[149] Even at night, it proved extremely difficult to fly into Sangin. Repeated attempts to bring in supplies and ammuni-tion had to be called off because the Chinooks came under heavy fire from insurgents. By mid July, B Company had almost run out of food and had to boil water from the canal. An attempt to parachute supplies in from a Hercules plane failed, with the bundles of rations over-shooting the mark and landing behind insurgent lines in Sangin town. Eventually, supplies were brought in using the light armoured vehicles of a Canadian infantry company. One Canadian officer later wrote home that 'When we arrived in Sangin, the locals began to throw rocks and anything they could at us – this was not a friendly place … during the last hundred meters we began receiving mortar fire'. Having to overnight in the British base, the Canadians got a taste of what the Paras had to endure. 'We were attacked with small arms, RPGs and mortars three times that night; I still can't believe that the Brits have spent over a month living there under those conditions.'[150]

The British public was oblivious to what was happening in Helmand until the *Sunday Times* published an article by Christina Lamb on 2 July, describing what happened when the British patrol she was accompanying was ambushed outside of Gereshk. Surrounded by determined Taliban attackers, for two hours the British platoon fought for their lives. It was touch and go. At one point the sergeant major asked Lamb if she had 'ever used a pistol', telling her, 'if it comes down to it, everyone's going to have to fight'. For Lamb, this incident called into question the whole British mission in Helmand.[151] The Ministry of Defence was horrified by the report. The ISAF spokesman (and former BBC journalist) Mark Laity later told Lamb that she was 'responsible for the single biggest media disaster since World War II'. He noted that after her report 'the MOD just shut down'. They made it far more difficult for journalists to visit Helmand, and all reports required prior approval by the MoD, which would only be given for reports that focused on reconstruction. The problem was that there was little reconstruction going on: as Lamb notes, the British Army appeared to be mostly engaged in the 'deconstruction' of population centres in Helmand.[152]

Around this time Whitehall woke up to the fact that Helmand was proving far more challenging than anticipated. On 7 July, the government decided to deploy another eight hundred troops, including two infantry companies from 1st Battalion the Royal Regiment of Fusiliers.[153] This rare good news aside, Tootal and Butler were becoming increasingly concerned about how overstretched and vulnerable their forces were. Something had to give. The Pathfinders Platoon had been sent to Musa Qala as a temporary deployment and they now wanted to pull them out. RC-South agreed to deploy a squadron of Danish reconnaissance troops; the column of Danish armoured vehicles fought their way into Musa Qala district centre on 26 July, but it proved impossible for the Pathfinders to fight their way out.[154]

RICHARDS GOES TO KABUL

On 4 May 2006, command of ISAF passed back to the British. NATO understood that the expansion of ISAF to the south and east of Afghanistan was going to be challenging. Hence, its most capable deployable headquarters, the ARRC, led by the British Army, was tasked to take over as ISAF headquarters. The plan was for CJTF 76 under Major General Ben Freakley to hand over responsibility for southern Afghanistan to ISAF headquarters under David Richards on 31 July, and for eastern Afghanistan in October 2006. However, Freakley was furious with the British, for what he saw as a lacklustre performance in Helmand. He was especially angry with Butler for being so reluctant to commit British forces to support US-led counterterrorism operations in the south. Given how stretched the British were in Helmand, such caution was prudent. On a visit to Lashkar Gah,

Freakley accused the British of sitting in their bases and failing to take the fight to the enemy. He shouted at British commanders to 'Get off your asses!'[155]

Richards had a year and a half to prepare for his role as commander of ISAF. He took command of the ARRC (based in Germany) in January 2005, just as it was announced that it would deploy as the next headquarters of ISAF. In the months leading up to this, Richards had been 'hoovering up information on Afghanistan' in his previous role as Assistant Chief of the General Staff. Earlier in his career he had been Chief of Staff of the ARRC and so he knew it well; the 350-strong headquarters, staffed by experienced brigadiers and colonels, was in Richards' view 'quite cocky and clearly very capable'. This had bred overconfidence. The previous ARRC commander, General Richard Dannatt, had agreed with NATO headquarters that the ARRC would not begin training for Afghanistan until October 2005. Richards thought this simply crazy. He instructed his new headquarters to begin immediately with preparing for the ISAF mission.[156]

Much like Butler, Richards became increasingly frustrated at the British government's failure to resource his mission. He discovered that 'my own country was not prepared to give me a helicopter or an aircraft to fly around a country that was half the size of Europe so I could properly exercise command'. Equally, the MoD was unwilling to give him a British reserve force that he could commit for major ISAF operations; he had to make do with 'a plucky Portuguese infantry company', which he was unable to use when things went wrong in Helmand 'because they would have been massacred'. Richards ended up having 'stand-up rows' which descended into 'literally shouting matches' with the Operations Directorate in the MoD. Richards was equally dismayed at Margaret Aldred's reaction when in a planning meeting he referred to NATO's OPLAN (operational plan) for Afghanistan, only to have her ask, 'What NATO plan?' Richards eventually raised his concerns with the Defence Secretary. This involved a 'clandestine breakfast meeting' in Berlin, because Reid did not want the Chief of the Defence Staff, General Walker, or the Deputy Chief of Staff for Commitments, General Fry, to know that he was talking directly to Richards. Among many other things, Richards was disturbed to discover that 16 Brigade were due to deploy without their artillery guns and Apache gunships, and he told Reid that the UK task force needed more firepower. Reid promised to 'sort it out', which true to his word he did.[157]

The centrepiece of Richards' campaign was an initiative to improve coordination of civilian and military efforts by the international community and the Afghan government. What was needed, in his view, was some kind of high-level policy coordinating committee of Afghan and international officials; Richards called this the Policy Action Group (PAG). After a concerted charm offensive, Richards won Karzai over to the idea. The PAG was chaired by Karzai or his national security adviser, Zalmai Rassoul. On one side of the table sat Richards, General Karl Eikenberry as commander of US forces in Afghanistan, the head of the UN mission, and the American, British and Canadian ambassadors; on the other side sat the key Afghan ministers. The PAG was a wholly British invention: Richards drove the agenda and British officers and officials provided the secretariat. This led some to speculate that the PAG was a device for the ISAF commander to exert control over the Afghan president. *The Economist* joked that PAG stood for 'Please Ask the General'.[158] Richards, understandably, takes a different line, arguing that the PAG was as much a mechanism to enable Karzai to better 'run his country' as it was a means to 'get things done' in Afghanistan.[159]

The other core idea in Richards' campaign was the ADZ, whereby military, diplomatic and development efforts would be focused in 'carefully defined areas ... no larger than could be properly secured by our limited numbers of troops'. The basic concept was that of an 'ink spot on a blotter' whereby the 'beneficial impact [would] spread out, psychologically as well as geographically'. In essence, Richards was dusting off and repackaging a well-worn concept of counter-insurgency, derived from the British experience in Malaya in the 1950s. Insofar as they involved coordination of international and Afghan efforts, the ADZs were supposed to be linked to the PAG. Richards met resistance from some NATO members to the idea, in particular from the Germans, who did not want their peacekeeping mission in northern Afghanistan associated with the counter-insurgency operations being conducted by others in the south and east. In advance of deploying, Richards and Tootal met over a pub lunch and agreed to trial the ADZ concept in Helmand; this was unproblematic as it was wholly consistent with the Joint Helmand Plan. Richards also met with the Canadian and Dutch ambassadors to get their support for establishing ADZs in Kandahar and Uruzgan respectively, and likewise with the provincial governors of the three southern provinces.[160]

The PAG and ADZ were ideas ahead of their time. Richards had correctly identified the lack of coordination between the international community and Afghan government, and between military and civilian efforts, as a key weakness in the NATO campaign.[161] Ronald Neumann, the US ambassador to Kabul, welcomed the PAG as giving structure to previous informal attempts at high-level coordination: 'it did not solve all our problems but it helped'.[162] However, the PAG would lose traction after Richards left Afghanistan. Britain and its coalition partners simply lacked the commitment to make the PAG work. The incoming British ambassador to Kabul in 2007, Sherard Cowper-Coles, felt that as the PAG grew in size, the 'meetings had degenerated into stock occasions, with no real debate, no serious decisions taken'. After a year or so, the PAG died out.[163] Coordinating the multitude of international civilian efforts and activities by foreign states, international bodies and aid agencies proved to be a nightmare throughout the war. Alongside the PAG was a larger Joint Co-ordination and Monitoring Board, established following the London conference on Afghanistan in February 2006, which periodically tried to bring together all the main international actors in Afghanistan. One European think-tank report in 2008 concluded that the PAG and the Joint Co-ordination and Monitoring Board failed to improve prioritisation and coordination of government action.[164]

The ADZ stuck as a concept but it too was problematic. The International Crisis Group was sceptical, noting that it came with no additional funding. It was basically an attempt to do more with little: the 'ADZ is supply driven by the international community, dividing up a small amount of resources to do something, rather than [a] needs-led approach to tackle the insurgency comprehensively'.[165] Afghan officials were also worried that if their citizens knew that development assistance was being concentrated in a few defined areas, those outside of ADZs would feel discriminated against and turn towards the insurgency. Neumann recalls that 'President Karzai was quite concerned about this point and gave explicit orders that while the ADZ approach was acceptable, it was absolutely not to be discussed in public'.[166] In any case, the ADZ concept proved impossible to implement properly in 2006–7 due to the deteriorating security in southern Afghanistan, and for this reason there was no public backlash.

RETREAT FROM MUSA QALA

August 2006 brought little respite for the UK task force in Helmand. In fact, things got worse. There was no let-up in the intensity of Taliban attacks against the northern platoon houses, and British troops were being steadily worn down – mentally and physically.

Royal Engineers had significantly improved defences in Sangin, installing HESCO defensive barriers around the British compound and helicopter landing zone. Originally designed for flood defences in Britain, HESCO are collapsible wire-mesh containers which when filled with rubble provided highly effective bullet- and blast-proof barriers for coalition bases in Iraq and Afghanistan. Comforting as it was, the Paras could not afford simply to hunker down behind the HESCO. Patrols had to be sent out to disrupt insurgent attacks, protect the Royal Engineers while they continued their work, and show the Taliban that British resolve was unbroken. In reality, as one junior officer noted, 'younger soldiers were shaking with fear, every time they went out'. Not helping matters, the thirty-strong Afghan army platoon in Sangin 'were going feral and threatening to shoot each other'. They were also abusing 'little boys off the street', behaviour which the Paras understandably found abhorrent.[167] Returning to Sangin in August for a second posting, A Company found that 'the inexperienced [Taliban] fighters [they] had encountered in June had been replaced by a core of battle-hardened guerrillas', whose 'ranks were also swollen by an increasing number of foreign fighters who brought their combat experience from other conflicts with them'.[168]

Given the dangers of venturing out of the base, the British had taken to sending out large patrols, often over forty strong. Still patrols would sometimes find themselves overmatched by swarms of insurgents, and have to make a fighting retreat to the district centre supported by liberal amounts of artillery fire and air power. Similarly, any overland logistics movement into the district centre required a huge security operation involving the whole battlegroup.

On 29 August, all three Para companies were required to move a portable bridge into Sangin, which would be used to span the Helmand River. The operation involved clearing insurgent positions in advance of the arrival of the logistics convoy. One such position, nicknamed 'Chinese Restaurant' by the Paras, was bombed from the air and pounded by Apache gunships and artillery rounds; much to Para amazement the Taliban 'were still firing'. The building was eventually cleared by two platoons of paratroopers.[169]

Throughout their tour, the Paras were heavily reliant on air power to defend their bases and for any ground operations. Joint Force Harrier – comprising No. 1 RAF Squadron, No. 4 RAF Squadron and 800 Naval Squadron – maintained six Harriers on rotational tour at Kandahar airfield throughout the campaign. One flight of two Harriers was kept on constant 24/7 alert, to provide 'emergency ground combat air support', on notice to scramble within thirty minutes of the bell. Usually, one Harrier would carry a couple of Paveway II laser-guided thousand-pound bombs, and the other would be armed with two CRV-7 rocket pods. Often the Paras had to call in air strikes at 'danger close' distance to friendly forces, and for this Harrier pilots revived the technique from the Falklands War for dropping bombs at ultra-low altitude.[170] Not everybody appreciated British air power. One Para company commander emailed a fellow officer in August about his frustration at the support he received from RAF Harriers, complaining that they were 'utterly, utterly useless'. The email went viral in the MoD. Tootal notes that the Paras 'generally preferred the air support of the American A-10s', which was a better ground-attack aircraft because 'it could fly slower than a Harrier and had better fuel endurance'. Tootal could not praise the US Air Force high enough: 'The support [the A-10s] gave us was awesome and they dug us out of the shit on numerous occasions.'[171]

In Musa Qala the Danes had had enough. On 12 August, they decided to pull out. The Danish contingent had only arrived in Musa Qala twenty days before. In capability terms, this was a major loss to the UK task force. The Danish reconnaissance squadron in Musa Qala was 140 soldiers strong with forty-six light armoured vehicles, and its own twelve-person medical team. They brought with them a lot of heavy machine guns, which came in handy for repulsing Taliban attacks. Arriving to relieve Pathfinders in early August, the aptly named

'Somme' Platoon of the Royal Irish Regiment had been warned that the Danish contingent was under daily attack and unable to venture out of the British compound; minor attacks were so frequent that the Danes had stopped recording them. The Royal Irish platoon commander had served in Iraq, and found the Taliban to be much tougher opponents than Iraqi insurgents. 'The Taliban kept on attacking and attacking and attacking. We were dropping one-thousand and two-thousand bombs on then, firing at them with Apaches and they came back again and again.'[172]

The Danes had suffered three casualties, including a serious head injury from a Taliban sniper on 2 August, and they were appalled at how difficult it was to evacuate their wounded. Ten days later the Danish government presented ISAF with a fait accompli: their contingent was withdrawing with only forty-eight hours' notice. Tootal had to pull together an ad hoc company of mostly Royal Irish infantry who flew in on 23 August to replace the Danish contingent; in all, 86 men were replacing 140 Danish troops, and the Royal Irish had no armoured vehicles. Thanks to pressure from Butler and Richards, the Afghan Ministry of Interior sent sixty Afghan Standby Police to Musa Qala; these were non-Pashtun northerners, which meant that they were not corrupted by local politics. This relief-in-place (the military term for when a unit changes over) required two companies of paratroopers to secure the ground around the district centre to enable the Danes to drive out and the Afghan Standby Police to drive in.[173]

By early September, Tootal and Butler had reached the conclusion that the British position in Musa Qala was no longer tenable. The intensity and audacity of Taliban attacks was extraordinary. Waves of insurgents would assault the platoon house from the narrow alleyways that abutted the compound walls, forcing British troops 'to lean out of their sangars to fire down on them and toss grenades on them'. One British corporal worried that 'some of the [compound] walls were six feet tall and easily jumpable'. US and British warplanes were regularly cued overhead to make continuous runs, strafing and dropping bombs at 'danger close' distances to keep the insurgents from overrunning the British base. For much of the time, the Royal Irish were dangerously low on ammunition. On 8 September, they had only thirty mortar rounds left, just enough to repulse one Taliban assault, and had run out of link ammunition for their light machine guns. The Royal Irish were unable to secure the surrounding area for helicopters bringing in supplies, and if a Chinook were shot down flying into Musa Qala, they would have been unable to send out a rescue force. They received fresh ammunition on only six occasions over their eleven-week deployment, each time when a Chinook was sent to evacuate wounded.[174]

On 6 September the British suffered multiple casualties in Sangin, Musa Qala and Kajaki. As Tootal had long feared, the UK task force was woefully ill-equipped to deal with this situation. The first casualties occurred in Kajaki, when a sniper team guarding the dam wandered into a Taliban minefield, and nine more troops followed them in to help the wounded. All were trapped. Tootal sent a Chinook, which hovered low over the minefield but the British troops were unable to move towards it; as it pulled away, the downdraught set off more mines, blasting two soldiers. In all, there were seven wounded, four of those with missing limbs. Eventually, over three hours later, a pair of US Blackhawk helicopters arrived with specialist teams and equipment to winch the British soldiers to safety.[175] That evening, the British compounds in Sangin and Musa Qala were hit by Taliban mortar fire, injuring six troops in Sangin and ten in Musa Qala. The UK task force had only one medical emergency response team (MERT); with a dedicated Chinook on standby, the MERT was a medical team able to stabilise the wounded in-flight to the field hospital at Camp Bastion. The MERT flew first to Sangin as one of the wounded had a very serious head injury. The insurgent fire was so heavy that it took two attempts for the Chinook to land. After dropping the wounded at Bastion, the MERT flew straight on to Musa Qala. Here, too, the Taliban poured fire at the Chinook, causing serious damage and forcing the pilot, Mark Hammond, to abandon his run and limp back to Bastion in a damaged helicopter. Hammond and the MERT returned three hours later in a different Chinook, this time with a lot more fire support. In addition to the standard protection provided by two Apaches, there were two A-10s, an AC-130 gunship, and an artillery battery in a desert location east of Musa Qala. Bombs, cannon fire and artillery shells rained down on the insurgent positions. 'Hammond dropped from the sky as an inferno raged in a circle around the LZ [landing zone]' to make a successful landing and evacuate the wounded.[176]

The nightmare scenario for Butler and Tootal was for a casualty evacuation helicopter flying into Musa Qala to be shot down, and then having to send in a second Chinook with a rescue team and to have that shot down too. Butler had been told in no uncertain terms by the new Chief of the Defence Staff, Air Marshal Sir Jock Stirrup, not to lose a Chinook, especially not one laden with troops. Stirrup's fear was that 'It will lose the war, potentially'. This view was reinforced when an RAF Nimrod reconnaissance aircraft suffered mechanical failure and crashed in Kandahar on 2 September, with the loss of all fourteen crew on board. Butler recalls being told afterwards by Stirrup that 'we cannot afford another strategic asset to be lost'.[177]

For Butler it was a matter of when and not if a Chinook would be lost in Musa Qala. He saw no choice: the British had to pull out. This put him on a collision course with Richards. Richards had been against the platoon house strategy in the first place. But now they were there, he did not want to see the British leave. He felt that a British withdrawal from Musa Qala would be viewed as a 'Maiwand Revisited'.[178] (The Battle of Maiwand in 1880 saw a 2,500-strong British brigade annihilated by an Afghan tribal force up to ten times in size, some thirty miles east of Sangin.[179]) Moreover, the timing was terrible. Richards had just launched Operation Medusa to clear a large number of insurgents out of Panjwai district, twenty miles south-west of Kandahar city; Panjwai was the birthplace of the Taliban as a movement. He later recalled that the 'Taliban had decided to occupy a totemic area and were psychologically challenging NATO in the south' as well as 'threatening the Afghan Development Zone in Kandahar'.[180] This was the first large-scale ground offensive in NATO's history, and Richards was determined that it would succeed. As he saw it, the British Army's presence in Sangin, Musa Qala and Kajaki was tying down Taliban forces in northern Helmand and thereby securing the western flank for Operation Medusa.[181]

Butler and Richards were both reaching back to London to argue their cases. Butler had briefed Dannatt, who as the incoming head of the British Army visited Helmand in early September, about how bad things had got and the dangers of losing a Chinook. Dannatt's view was clear: 'we can't take that risk, we must get out of Musa Qala'. Butler also alerted the Chief of Joint Operations, General Nick Houghton. It was Houghton who then phoned

Richards on 4 September to tell him of the decision to withdraw from Musa Qala and Now Zad. For his part, Richards got on to Sir Nigel Sheinwald, the prime minister's foreign policy adviser, to warn him that this would be viewed by Afghans as a British defeat. Similarly, he told Stirrup and Houghton that the British military were at risk of becoming 'ISAF's laughing stock'.[182]

On taking charge of ISAF in July 2006, Richards had tidied up the chain of command in Helmand. Butler took direct control of the UK task force and therefore came under Fraser as commander of RC-South, and Knaggs was moved sideways to become the military commander of the small British PRT in Lashkar Gah. This meant that formally Butler was answerable to Richards as the coalition commander. However, at the same time, Butler retained his role as the UK National Contingent Commander, and as such he was also answerable directly to the Ministry of Defence in London. Butler recalls Richards ordering him to 'stay put' in Musa Qala. Butler's response was: 'wearing my National Contingent Commander hat … I have received very clear political direction from the Chief of the Defence Staff on behalf of the government that we are not to lose a strategic asset and therefore … will pull out.'[183] Richards told Butler to go back and find some other way. At this point, fed up with the destruction of their district, a shura of local elders from Musa Qala came forward with a peace plan. Richards recalls that while 'we were nudging … to find another way', this plan 'sprang spontaneously from the elders'.[184]

Underlying the conflict in Musa Qala was a struggle between two branches of the Alizai tribe, the Hassanzai and Pirzai. The Akhundzada family (including Sher Mohammed Akhundzada and his brother, the deputy provincial governor, Amir Mohammed Akhundzada) who dominated district government came from the Hassanzai clan, and accordingly the disfranchised Pirzai clan supported the Taliban. The precise origins of the Musa Qala deal are murky, but it seems that Governor Daoud had been engaged in talks with a shura of elders headed by a Pirzai leader, Haji Shah Agha. With the British signalling their intent to withdraw, the Pirzai saw an opportunity to bring peace to their district and to wrest control from the Hassanzai. Echoing Richards' assertion, one Taliban leader from the area later recalled how 'the deal was sprung on the Taliban by Shah Agha and the local elders'.[185] By 12 September, a ceasefire had been agreed, which held aside from the odd potshot. The next day, Butler and Nicholas Kay, the civilian head of the British PRT in Helmand, flew to Musa Qala to meet with the elders. The shura took place in a desert location ten miles outside the district centre, secured by the Patrols Platoon and a troop from the Household Cavalry. A large party of elders turned up, and with them, sitting quietly at the back, were the Taliban. In the days that followed, agreement was reached on a fourteen-point plan that saw the Taliban pull back, and the British withdraw a month later in a convoy of locally provided jingle trucks with security guaranteed by the Pirzai. The Afghan government agreed to recognise a fifteen-man Loya Jirga led by Haji Shah Agha as the 'local authority', and the Jirga in turn undertook to reopen schools and collect government taxes. The Pirzai also agreed to provide sixty local men to be trained as Afghan auxiliary police; this local force would be responsible for ensuring that the Taliban stayed out of a three-mile exclusion zone around the district centre. It was an inglorious end of tour for the Royal Irish, with three dead and seventeen injured. But the accord did ensure that the Afghan flag was kept flying over Musa Qala.[186]

Still, the Americans were not pleased with the idea of a truce with the Taliban. Ronald Neumann took the view that 'if you have an area that is under the Afghan government flag but is not under the actual authority of the Afghan Government, then you are losing in a very big way'.[187] Similarly, while they recognised the short-term tactical benefits of the Musa Qala accord in terms of freeing up British forces, American military commanders worried that it also offered a respite for the Taliban that would enable them to regroup in northern Helmand. They took the view that 'the Alliance needs to pursue a [military] campaign that maintains pressure on the enemy'.[188] Thus on 23 October, Richards discovered that the US Combined Joint Special Operations Task Force (CJSOTF) was preparing an air strike against a group of suspect insurgents in Musa Qala. Richards' staff explained to the CJSOTF that 'they were there probably to parley with tribal elders and their deaths would cause a huge problem of strategic scale'.[189] Tracking implementation of the accord in the weeks that followed, the US embassy in Kabul noted that the 'shura appears to be keeping up its end' and that fighting across the North [of Helmand] generally has abated'. However, US officials were unsure if the decrease in armed violence was due to the agreement 'or to the onset of the poppy planting season', when local insurgents would have to tend to their farms. Even more worrying for the Americans was talk of the British reaching similar deals across northern Helmand. Karzai sought to reassure the US National Security Advisor, Stephen Hadley, that there were to be 'no more deals'.[190]

Against this, the British were keen to get out of their platoon houses, and saw the Musa Qala accord as a potential model to be applied elsewhere.[191] Daoud too felt that in the absence of additional international forces and more support from Kabul (especially more Afghan police), reaching local accommodations offered a second-best solution to keeping the Afghan government flag flying over district centres in Helmand. According to US embassy officials, 'Daoud was firm in his defense of the [Musa Qala] agreement and determined to move forward, with this and similar arrangements with leaders in other districts.'[192] Indeed, ceasefires were now agreed with shuras in Sangin and Now Zad, with the British remaining in these district centres but not patrolling; the Now Zad ceasefire broke down after three weeks, but peace lasted in Sangin until March 2007.[193]

In late November, a delegation from the Musa Qala Jirga visited Kabul to shore up Afghan government and international support for the accord. However, a rival delegation from the Hassanzai clan also travelled to Kabul claiming that the Taliban were in de facto control of the district centre.[194] The Hassanzai delegation included a female Helmandi Member of Parliament who complained that girls could no longer attend school. US officials uncritically accepted this as a 'worrying sign' of Taliban influence, not realising that the MP was a close associate of Sher Mohammed Akhundzada; they were also ignorant of the fact that girls had rarely gone to school in Musa Qala.[195] All too predictably, the Hassanzai delegation sought Akhundzada's reinstatement as provincial governor, claiming that 'Daud has given the Taleban Musa Qala as a sanctuary. We need an experienced fighter as a governor of Helmand. Daud is a weak man.'[196] As a political ally of Akhundzada, Karzai was increasingly vocal in his criticisms of the accord. He made no secret of the fact that but for British opposition, he would reinstate Akhundzada as governor.[197]

Critical voices in the Afghan national parliament also spoke out against the Musa Qala accord. One MP and former spokesman for the Northern Alliance, Sayed Mustafa Kazemi, rejected it as 'a model for the destruction of the country' because it allowed local shuras to appoint their own government officials and police. Kazemi added that 'it is just a defeat for NATO, just a defeat'.[198] Some official Afghan reports began to circulate in Kabul suggesting that Musa Qala had turned into a safe haven for the Taliban. Backing up this concern, US intelligence reported 'significant Taliban presence and influence in Musa Qala, and Musa Qala being used as a waypoint for movement of insurgents'.[199] Less visible in Kabul were attempts by Akhundzada supporters on the ground to scupper the deal, including armed activity around the exclusion zone.[200] Musa Qala was discussed several times by the PAG and it was eventually decided to test if the deal was still in place by having Afghan and ISAF forces transit through the district, as was permitted under the terms of the deal.[201] An intense firefight on 3 December between Danish troops and insurgents, albeit four miles outside the exclusion zone, poured further doubt on the deal.[202]

Five days later, Karzai sacked Daoud. This had wider repercussions for British ambitions in the province, but the immediate effect was to remove from Afghan government the strongest advocate of the Musa Qala deal.[203] The new governor, Asadullah Wafa, announced that he intended to renegotiate the accord to strengthen the hand of the Afghan government.[204] Thus the accord was already in serious trouble when, in late January, a Taliban leader in Musa Qala was targeted by a US air strike. He was outside the three-mile exclusion zone and so a fair target. However, this mattered little when the bomb missed him but killed his brother and most of his fighting group; the enraged commander entered the district centre to exact revenge but was arrested by the local militia. He escaped to Now Zad and returned with a larger Taliban force and overpowered the militia, arresting the Jirga and seizing control of the district centre. He was eventually killed by an air strike while travelling between Now Zad and Musa Qala on 4 February. But by then, the accord was dead, as was its original instigator, Haji Shah Agha.[205]

It is doubtful that peace in Musa Qala would have lasted anyway. Karzai was not seeking a wider agreement with the Taliban, telling US officials that if the Taliban attempted to resist the Afghan government in Musa Qala 'we will crush them'.[206] According to a senior Taliban commander from northern Helmand, it was precisely 'the failure to replicate it elsewhere that led to its collapse'; it confirmed the views of those within the Taliban leadership that 'the Karzai government were not serious'. This account is somewhat disingenuous in that the Musa Qala accord was replicated in Sangin. Moreover, as we have seen, a particular sequence of events led to the eventual collapse of the Musa Qala accord. But it is certainly fair to say that the accord was fatally undermined by 'a lack of trust on all sides'.[207]

After six months of fighting, everybody was worn out in Helmand. The Paras and Taliban alike had been tested to their limits, and locals were dismayed by the utter devastation that had been wrought on the district centres in northern Helmand. In addition to intense fighting in Sangin and Musa Qala, the British dropped 18,000 pounds of explosives on Now Zad, obliterating the town bazaar.[208] Many ordinary Helmandis were fed up with the predation of local officials and police but, even more, they had had enough of the fighting; most just wanted to be left in peace to grow their poppy. It was not to be. February 2007 saw US General Dan McNeill taking over from Richards as commander of ISAF. McNeill blamed the British for having 'made a mess of things in Helmand'. He was especially critical of the Musa Qala deal which, in his view, 'opened the door to narco-traffickers in the area', to the benefit of the Taliban.[209] A few days after they arrived in Kabul, McNeill and his command staff received a briefing from the outgoing ARRC team on the strategy Richards had been pursuing. Following the briefing, McNeill stood up and declared: 'That's all very well but we're going to change strategy. The bad guys are all up in the north-east, and we're going to kill them.'[210]

6

Mission Impossible

The last time the Royal Marines were in Afghanistan, they hardly covered themselves in glory. They spent six months chasing ghosts in eastern Afghanistan, and ended up leaving the country without firing a shot in anger – albeit through no fault of their own. The enemy had, quite literally, run away. Four years later, 3 Commando Brigade returned to take over from 16 Air Assault Brigade, and this time they had good reason to expect a fight.

Initially, however, 3 Commando Brigade were looking to reduce the armed violence in Helmand. They were unimpressed with the way that 16 Air Assault Brigade had handled the campaign so far. The marines believed that the Paras had adopted 'an overly-aggressive posture', and that they had drifted off the approved Helmand plan and got themselves bogged down in fixed positions in northern Helmand, allowing the insurgents freedom of movement across most of the province. Brigadier Jerry Thomas, the commander of 3 Commando Brigade and incoming commander of Task Force Helmand, was determined to tread more carefully. He warned his marines that 'we must gather the knowledge and, until then, beware acting precipitately. Misplaced actions could irrevocably turn swathes of the population against us.' He took a nuanced view of the insurgency, distinguishing between hard-core 'irreconcilable' Taliban, and locals that provided armed support to the Taliban but could be won over, including those who fought for money, often called 'ten-dollar-a-day Taliban'. This, in turn, suggested the need for a more calibrated approach: 'some elements [of the insurgency] will respond satisfactorily to information or influence; others may need persuasion or coercion; others may justify defeat or destruction'. The emphasis would be on getting to know locals rather than killing insurgents. Thomas told his troops, 'when in doubt, we will start with softer effects but be prepared to escalate as required'.[1]

This more gentle approach did not last long. On 19 October 2006, just ten days after 3 Commando Brigade formally took over as Task Force Helmand, the first British service member to be killed by a suicide bomber was blown up in Lashkar Gah. A two-vehicle patrol was driving through the provincial capital when it slowed at a junction. A young Afghan man, who had been chatting with some children on the roadside, walked up to the Snatch Land Rover and detonated his suicide vest. Marine Gareth Wright was killed instantly. According to the British journalist Sean Rayment, who later interviewed those who rushed to help, 'it was a scene of utter carnage, with body parts littering the streets'. Intelligence reports suggested that there were half a dozen more suicide bombers in Lashkar Gah waiting to attack the British. Rayment notes that following this attack 'The troops' attitude changed immediately and questions over the suitability of the initial "softly, softly" tactics were raised'. The Royal Marines wondered if the Taliban had not viewed their more cautious approach as a sign of weakness to be exploited. Within hours, the marines were back patrolling the streets of Lashkar Gah, only this time they threatened to shoot any locals who came too close.[2]

British brigades, each arriving for a six-month tour, struggled to contain a growing insurgency while also supporting civilian-led efforts to connect the people with the Afghan government through improved public services and local elections. Brigade plans show that successive commanders of Task Force Helmand understood the need to focus on reassuring locals that things would get better under the government. However, the scale of fighting in Helmand undermined this message. Under 3 Commando Brigade and 12 Mechanised Brigade which followed, the British spent another year trying to defeat the Taliban in battle. Once the Taliban had been beaten back, the thinking went, it would be possible to turn around and concentrate on what was supposed to be the main effort, namely, supporting the development of Afghan government in Helmand. Over this period, British forces were hopelessly overstretched and they depended on aerial bombardment to dislodge tenacious insurgents. British troops were too few in number to hold ground cleared of Taliban, and the Afghan police and army could not be relied upon to do it. Hence, the British ended up chasing the Taliban around Helmand. Afghan locals – those that did not join the Taliban – looked on helplessly. Only in late 2007 did a British brigade finally prioritise meeting the needs of the population above defeating the Taliban. By this stage, most district centres lay in ruins from the fighting, and most people simply wanted the British to leave.

ADVANCE TO AMBUSH

Brigadier Thomas set out to refocus British military efforts back on the original Joint Helmand Plan, co-produced by fellow Royal Marine Colonel Gordon Messenger. Thus, he wanted to 'unfix the north', to get British forces out of the platoon houses, and to provide security and support development in central Helmand. In the operational design for his campaign, Thomas stated that 'the military main effort' would be on supporting 'reconstruction in the Afghan Development Zone'. In so doing he would align the Task Force Helmand campaign with the overall ISAF campaign under General David Richards. In terms of dealing with insurgency, Thomas planned to withdraw British forces from the northern towns once Afghan forces were in place to take over, and then 'to threaten, disrupt, and interdict the enemy'. He declared that the Taliban would 'be targeted on ground of my choosing, at a time of my choosing'.[3] Things would not work out quite as he hoped.

In taking over as Task Force Helmand, 3 Commando Brigade deployed with more troops than 16 Air Assault Brigade. 3 Commando Brigade had two battlegroups (42 and 45 Commando) whereas 16 Air Assault had had only one, and thus the British task force grew from 3,500 to 4,500 troops. The Royal Marines also arrived with thirty-three new Viking armoured vehicles; from these, 3 Commando Brigade formed two troops of thirteen vehicles, keeping seven Vikings in reserve. Each Viking consists of two linked tracked units – a driver's cab and a second cab for carrying troops or supplies. Marines did not like the lack of visibility in the troop carrier, but it did afford protection from machine-gun, mortar and rocket fire. Unfortunately, the flat-bottomed Vikings were highly vulnerable to IEDs, as the British would soon find out.

At first, things were quieter in the north than the Royal Marines had anticipated. The commander of 42 Commando, Colonel Matt Holmes, sent Lima Company to Sangin because the company sergeant major was 'a hard fighting man, exactly the sort of company sergeant major I needed in a place like that'. In the event, there was no fighting due to the ceasefire agreed between the Taliban and Provincial Governor Daoud.[4] In mid October, Kilo Company was sent to cover the British withdrawal from Musa Qala. Local elders had guaranteed the security of the Royal Irish as they ignominiously pulled out in locally hired jingle trucks. Just in case, standing by in the desert a short distance away from the district centre was Kilo Company and the 105mm guns of 29 Commando Regiment, Royal Artillery. The British withdrawal went smoothly and so, here too, there was no fighting to be had.[5]

The lack of fighting in Musa Qala, Sangin and Now Zad, while disappointing for some marines, was helpful for Brigadier Thomas's ambition to refocus the military campaign on central Helmand. In this sense, he benefitted from his predecessor's 'overly-aggressive' approach. Butler maintained that he had had no choice but to go north, to support Daoud and also to keep the insurgents occupied elsewhere than Lashkar Gah and Gereshk. In his post-operation report, Butler argued that 'Had ejection of UK forces from the district centres not become the Taliban main effort, this season's campaign may well have been focused on the Afghan Development Zone rather than further north in Sangin, Musa Qala and Now Zad'.[6] There is some credibility to this claim, as the northern platoon houses were honey pots for insurgents. These northern towns were emptied of civilians as besieged British forces called in wave upon wave of air strikes and artillery fire to repulse successive Taliban assaults. Nobody knows for sure how many insurgents were killed and injured. 16 Air Assault Brigade put the number of Taliban dead at around a thousand.[7] What is clear is that after six months, the Taliban had had enough. Thus, they accepted ceasefire deals negotiated between local elders and Governor Daoud in Sangin and Musa Qala, and for a time in Now Zad.

The Sangin ceasefire was not without controversy. British officials on the ground were at pains to note that the agreement was between the local elders of Sangin and the provincial governor, and that Task Force Helmand and the PRT were not formally parties to the deal.

To underline the point, the head of the PRT informed Whitehall that 'we do not have a copy of the actual agreement between the two sides'.[8] In fact, British PRT and military officials were involved in the negotiations. The fourteen-point plan agreed between a shura of Sangin elders and Governor Daoud in mid September was almost identical to the Musa Qala agreement. It saw the shura take over responsibility for district governance, and promise to fly the Afghan government flag, collect taxes and ensure locals had access to public services. Crucially, freedom of movement for Afghan and international forces would be guaranteed and armed insurgents would be kept out of the district centre. Initially, the local elders also tried to get the British to agree to pull out of the district centre and relocate to FOB Robinson on the outskirts of Sangin, on the grounds that civilian buildings were being destroyed in the fighting between the Taliban and the Paras. PRT officials recognised that the British presence had wreaked havoc on the district centre but they also suspected that 'the interests of the druglords and the Taleban are driving the shura's maximalist demands'.[9] Besides, the platoon house in Sangin was less precarious than the one in Musa Qala, and so the British were in no hurry to move.

An unsteady peace held in Sangin while the negotiations were ongoing. The Sangin shura was under pressure to seal the deal, but the agreement had to wait for Karzai's approval; the president was overseas and not due to return to Afghanistan until the end of September. Meanwhile, with shuras in Now Zad and Garmsir looking to negotiate similar deals, anxious British officials fretted: 'we need to decide how far down the path of local autonomy we should go'. These peace deals were seen to offer the chance to separate hard-core Taliban from 'local and less doctrinaire Taleban'. But British officials were concerned that the ability of local shura to 'face down' Taliban, as would be needed to police the peace deal, 'is so far unproven'.[10] With regard to Sangin in particular, they worried that the district might turn into a 'safe haven for drug production'. Against this, peace in Sangin offered the possibility of secure access through Sangin to Kajaki to deliver a high-profile US hydro-electric project worth $127 million.[11] Contrary to what he had told the Americans about 'no more deals', Karzai did give his approval to the Sangin peace agreement. The US embassy was not happy, reporting back to Washington that 'Some

British officials feel that if an arrangement with the Sangin shura provides security for, and helps advance, a major US project like the one in Kajaki, the US may set aside possible reservations about these types of deals – they are wrong'.[12]

Under the terms of the Sangin deal, the UK agreed to a phased withdrawal. Initially, British troops would remain in the district centre but would not conduct any patrols. If the ceasefire held, then after thirty days they would withdraw to FOB Robinson.[13] The Royal Marines were less than impressed. For their entire time in Sangin, Lima Company were confined to their base in the district centre. Colonel Holmes recalls that 'it was very frustrating' for them. Throughout this time, the Taliban took potshots at them but the marines held their fire.[14]

Unlike Sangin and Musa Qala, the ceasefire in Now Zad did not last long. Kilo Company arrived at the end of October to find the town largely deserted. The local population had resettled at a new location about a mile north of the district centre. The marines found that they would take heavy fire whenever they ventured near Taliban positions to the east of the district centre.[15] Early on, Kilo Company had to call in air support to stop a determined Taliban attack. A British GR7 Harrier promptly showed up and quickly dispatched the Taliban insurgents with rocket fire. To the company commander, the British Harriers were 'fantastic': 'we were confident that once we had a GR7 overhead the pilot would be able to identify even the most difficult of targets and do precisely as asked'.[16] Accuracy was indeed one advantage of the Harriers, especially in comparison with the American B-1B bombers, which marines also relied on for air support. The B-1Bs were good for blanket bombing but not so good when it came to minimising collateral damage. As one Harrier pilot noted, 'the B-1 didn't have a targeting pod and often put down sticks of four or five bombs to obliterate a target. And in almost every case the job could have been done by a tactical jet like the Harrier, fitted with a targeting pod and able to place one bomb exactly where it was wanted.'[17]

About a week after Kilo Company arrived, the local elders concluded a ceasefire agreement with the Taliban. Importantly, under the agreement the Royal Marines were able to continue patrolling albeit with some limitations. On 8 December, however, the ceasefire collapsed, when a patrol of sixty-five marines approached a Taliban tunnel system

in the north-east of the district and triggered a predictably violent
response. It is not clear if the Royal Marines deliberately set out to
wreck the ceasefire. They were monitoring Taliban communications,
and as they approached the tunnel system they could overhear alarmed
insurgents saying that the British were attacking. The Royal Marine
patrol soon came under intense fire, and had to undertake a fighting
withdrawal. Apache gunships and Harriers were called in to bombard
the insurgent positions. To the commander of Kilo Company, 'the
Taliban had broken the ceasefire in a big way as the terms allowed
us to carry out these framework and familiarization patrols, which is
what we were doing when we were attacked'.[18] The local elders saw
things differently, and blamed the British for provoking the Taliban.

Juliet Company based in FOB Price, on the edge of Gereshk town,
was tasked with forming Mobile Operations Groups (MOGs) to
conduct long-distance combat patrols inside and outside of the Green
Zone to hunt down Taliban.[19] An MOG typically comprised 250 men
in forty or so vehicles, including a troop of Vikings and a number of
stripped-down Land Rovers festooned with heavy machine guns; these
were called WMIKs after the Weapon Mounted Installation Kit on
each Land Rover. The MOGs ranged over hundreds of miles with
patrols typically lasting up to three weeks. Often Juliet Company
would try to set up a temporary combat support base in an MOG
area of operations to provide cover by drones and artillery. The MOGs
were central to Thomas's operational design, and specifically his intent
to unfix the British task force and make it more manoeuvrable.

In his post-operation report, Thomas asserted that MOGs were
able to range 'across our AO [area of operations] in a fashion that
the enemy cannot anticipate' and that the '"dynamic unpredictability"
arising from being able to engage the enemy at times and places of
our choosing has disrupted him, undermined his will and shattered
his unity'. Thomas further noted that MOGs had 'created a fear of
encirclement' among insurgents, and 'had a considerable morale and
physical impact on the Taliban infrastructure in the Sangin valley'.[20]
There is reason to question these claims. The simple fact is that
insurgents had little difficulty tracking the movement of MOGs, and
so they were always aware of their arrival. As one Royal Marine
officer said, 'we were routinely on the back foot and subsequently
attempts to draw out the Taliban into killing areas of our choice were

often "fruitless"'.[21] The marines laughingly called what they were doing 'advance to ambush'. After a while, the joke began to wear thin.

Dislodging the Taliban from Garmsir became a major priority for 3 Commando Brigade. Large numbers had swept across the Pakistani border and into Garmsir along with the Taliban provincial governor, Mullah Naim. On 11 September 2006, an Afghan force of one hundred soldiers and seventy police, led by a seventeen-strong British advisory team from 1 Royal Irish, was dispatched to retake Garmsir. After a week of intense fighting, during which over fifty air strikes were called in, some four hundred Taliban were pushed out of the district centre. A company from 45 Commando then arrived to relieve 1 Royal Irish, who had established a base – FOB Delhi – in the grounds of an old agricultural college.[22]

The Royal Marines spent January and February conducting a series of major operations against Taliban strongholds in Garmsir. These relied heavily on aerial bombardment of Taliban targets by American B-1B bombers. One assault in mid January against the Taliban-held Jugroom Fort was preceded by B-1Bs dropping twenty 2,000-pound bombs. If the marines were hammering the Taliban in Garmsir, the shoe was on the other foot in Sangin. On 24 February 2007, Lima Company handed over Sangin to Mike Company. All hell broke loose the following day. The Taliban launched a coordinated assault on the district centre, firing salvos of mortar bombs and RPGs against the British compound. Intelligence indicated that the Taliban were massing in force in the district and planning to break the ceasefire, so the marines had some warning. Over the following fortnight, Taliban attacks grew in intensity and duration. For the final operation of his tour, Thomas planned a brigade-sized assault on Sangin town, to clear it entirely of Taliban. Operation Silver involved a classic pincer movement, with three infantry companies from 42 Commando dashing down Route 611 to approach the town from the north-east, and an American battalion from the 82nd Airborne Division, designated Task Force 1 Fury, flying in to attack the town from the south; support was provided by a company of Royal Fusiliers in the district centre. The battle started before dawn, with helicopter gunships blasting insurgent positions. The Taliban were taken completely off guard by the scale of the British and American assault. By noon, they began to retreat and British marines and American parachutists moved from compound to compound to mop up final pockets of insurgent resistance. Many Taliban moved on to Musa Qala, where the ceasefire had also recently broken down. By the time the operation was over, Sangin town was 'utterly devastated'. The plan was to hand over responsibility for Sangin town to the Afghan police and army, even though nobody believed that they would be able to stop the Taliban from coming back.[23]

For all the talk of 'treading softly', 3 Commando Brigade did the exact opposite. In Kajaki, Now Zad and Sangin in the north, and Garmsir in the south of Helmand, the brigade ended up fighting a series of pitched battles. 3 Commando Brigade initiated twice as many 'contacts' with insurgents as had 16 Air Assault Brigade. These were not exactly on British terms, though, as most involved foot patrols and MOGs 'advancing to ambush'. In his post-operation report, Thomas noted that there was a '45% drop in attacks on our bases' and he claimed this had been 'achieved by taking the fight to the enemy'.[24] The ceasefires in Sangin and Musa Qala for most of 3 Commando Brigade's tour would have contributed to this statistic. Nonetheless, it is likely that successive offensive operations by the marines kept the Taliban pretty occupied and limited their ability to launch attacks against Lashkar Gah and Gereshk – much as the Paras had done with their northern platoon houses. However, with all this fighting, there was scant development going on in Helmand, and little evidence for locals that life would be better under the Afghan government.

MOWING THE LAWN

Fierce fighting was to continue under 12 Mechanised Brigade when it took over from 3 Commando Brigade in April 2007. In fact, the new brigade arrived midway through Operation Silver and got to join in. The incoming commander of Task Force Helmand, Brigadier John Lorimer, considered this a good thing. '12 Mechanised Brigade derived considerable benefit from being pitched straight into an offensive battle from the outset.' In his view, 'this action gave the brigade forward momentum'.[25]

The brigade arrived ready for war. Having observed the Helmand campaign from afar, Lorimer knew what to expect. As he prepared for deployment, he recalls that 'people were talking up the [Taliban] spring offensive'. Lorimer was determined that 'any spring offensive was going to be an ISAF offensive rather than a Taliban offensive'. Thus, there was a heavy emphasis in brigade pre-deployment training on fitness, first aid and basic combat skills. There was added pressure because 12 Mechanised was the first regular army brigade to take on the Helmand mission; in contrast, 16 Air Assault and 3 Commando had been specialist brigades of elite troops. Lorimer remembers that there 'was a question about whether regular soldiers were up to the task'.[26]

Under 12 Mechanised Brigade, British forces in Helmand grew to 6,500 personnel. Originally the brigade was going to deploy with two battalions – 1st Battalion the Grenadier Guards and 1st Battalion the Royal Anglian Regiment. Then in January 2007 the government decided to add a third battalion from the Worcestershire and Sherwood Foresters Regiment, who were rebadged during their tour as 2nd Battalion the Mercian Regiment. The Royal Marine Armoured Support Company with their Viking vehicles remained in Helmand to support 12 Mechanised, as did a Danish reconnaissance squadron and an Estonian armoured infantry company.

Crucial additional capability also arrived over the summer of 2007 in the form of the GMLRS (Guided Multiple Launch Rocket System) and the Mastiff MRAP (Mine Resistant Ambush Protected) armoured vehicles. GMLRS is an armoured vehicle with two pods of six guided rockets. Introduced in the early 1980s to destroy Soviet armoured forces, GMLRS found a new role in southern Afghanistan. Dubbed 'the 70-kilometre sniper rifle', GMLRS was able to deliver a 200-pound warhead with pinpoint accuracy against Taliban targets at twice the range of any other artillery system in the British Army. Unlike field guns, insurgents could not hear incoming fire from GMLRS. As one Royal Marine commander noted, 'enemy forces are particularly unhinged by the lack of notice to take cover'.[27]

The Mastiff is a British variant on the American Cougar MRAP vehicle that was specifically designed to counter the threat from IEDs. While traditional armoured vehicles have a low profile, the MRAP is tall, with the armoured cab sitting high above its chassis and the distinctive V-shaped hull able to direct blast away from the crew and troops in the vehicle. In July 2007, the Defence Secretary, Des Browne, announced to Parliament that the Mastiff MRAP would be rapidly acquired under the MoD's Urgent Operational Requirement programme; by 2008 the Ministry of Defence had ordered almost six hundred MRAPs – including two variants on the Mastiff called Ridgeback and Wolfhound – at a cost of £1.3 billion.[28] Fully loaded, Mastiffs weighed twenty-eight tonnes, making them too heavy for most bridges in Helmand. They were also too large for many of the small tracks and back alleys in the province. Nonetheless, the Mastiff offered excellent protection against IEDs and for this it was highly prized. In his post-operation report, Lorimer notes that the Mastiff 'made an impact in Helmand worthy of its colossal size. It is now one of the most sought after assets in Helmand.'[29]

Lorimer was to take a new approach to the British campaign in Helmand – the third such change in eighteen months. True to their maritime mindset, the Royal Marines had focused on conducting raids by sweeping in from the desert to assault Taliban strongholds in the Green Zone. While this may have disrupted potential insurgent attacks, it did not provide security because towns were left unguarded by British forces. 'Persistent presence' therefore became the watchword for the new British approach. Lorimer recognised that Gereshk was especially important as the economic capital of Helmand and because it lay along the route of Highway 1. To Lorimer, if the concept of the ADZ was 'to be taken seriously', then Gereshk had to be secured. Thus, he designated the main effort of his campaign to be the 'provision of security in the Afghan Development Zone in order to support good governance and enable development'. In his 'Commander's Overview' to his brigade, Lorimer anticipated that 'Sangin and the Sangin Valley will remain a key focus for Enemy Forces activity throughout the Summer'. Accordingly, the campaign under 12 Mechanised Brigade concentrated on a series of large offensive operations to clear the insurgents from areas around Gereshk and Sangin and establish patrol bases in order to control the approaches to both towns. Meanwhile, British forces to the south in Garmsir and the north in Kajaki would simply hold the line.[30]

Over the summer of 2007 the Taliban took a beating from 12 Mechanised Brigade. The Royal Anglians alone recorded 350 major fights with the Taliban during their tour and over a thousand insurgents killed. Much of this killing was done at a distance. The Royal Anglians called in some 22,000 mortar and artillery rounds, and over 200,000 pounds of air-delivered ordnance.[31] However, some of the killing was up close and some even hand-to-hand, with British soldiers fixing bayonets for close-quarters combat. For Western militaries, bayonets had long fallen into disuse on the battlefield and were primarily used in basic training to inculcate aggression in soldiers.[32] In Helmand, the British Army rediscovered the utility of the bayonet.

Helmand also took its toll on 12 Mechanised Brigade, with thirty soldiers killed in action and many more wounded. Nine soldiers were killed and fifty-seven wounded from the Royal Anglians alone; when non-combat injuries were added, they had suffered 20 per cent attrition by the end of their gruelling tour.[33] It is all too understandable therefore that many British soldiers took delight when their enemy was pounded by bombs and artillery, and mowed down by Apache gunships. For others, though, it was harrowing. Midway through one battle with the Taliban, a heartbroken British Fijian soldier felt compelled to stop firing his general purpose machine gun, telling his section commander that he had 'killed too many today'.[34]

By the end of the summer, 12 Mechanised Brigade had established a network of patrol bases in the Green Zone to support a more 'persistent presence' by security forces. However, these offensive operations failed to achieve the larger goal of creating the underpinning security for the development of government, public services and infrastructure. One reason was that the ANA and provincial government proved to be poor partners. The high tempo of offensive operations by British forces meant that battlegroups and rifle companies moved around constantly. For example, the Royal Anglian battlegroup started their tour covering the area around Gereshk, but within a month it was moved to cover Sangin, Now Zad and Kajaki. Moreover, since Lorimer wanted to avoid British forces becoming fixed in bases, rifle companies spent much of their time out in the field conducting strike operations against insurgent targets. This meant that 12 Mechanised Brigade depended on the Afghan army to man the new network of patrol bases and provide the 'persistent presence' central to Lorimer's plan.

The ANA brigade based in Helmand, the 3rd Brigade of 205th Corps (3/205), was only able to field two *kandaks*. This was still pretty impressive given that it had been in existence for only a year. Mentoring 3/205 were the Grenadier Guards as the British Operating, Mentoring and Liaison Team (OMLT, pronounced 'omelette'), and to this end a Guards rifle company was paired with each *kandak*. 3/205 was an eclectic mix of ethnicities, abilities and backgrounds, including ex-mujahedin, former Northern Alliance fighters, Russian-trained soldiers and even former Taliban. The OMLT later noted that 'it was a small miracle that they were able to form cohesive fighting units at all'. The Grenadier Guards found Afghan soldiers to be eager if undisciplined fighters. The OMLT observed that 'They want to find, close with and defeat the Taliban at every opportunity'.[35] While the ANA was all too ready to fight, getting it to stay in the field was to prove more challenging. Afghan army commanders preferred to return to the relative comforts of their garrisons following operations instead of staying around afterwards in the austere conditions of small patrol bases. A major problem with staying in the field was the difficulty in supplying Afghan units with fresh hot food – mostly goat stew and baked flatbread – as Afghan soldiers simply refused to eat Western military rations; anybody who has had to survive on MREs (meal ready to eat) would sympathise with this view. In any case, the Afghan army considered that it was the job of the police to provide the 'persistent presence'. By this point, however, the British had realised that the highly corrupt Afghan police were a major source of insecurity.

On the upside, the British Provincial Reconstruction Team in Lashkar Gah grew from three to around thirty diplomats and civilian stabilisation advisers over the course of 2007.[36] Lorimer formed good working relations with the head of the PRT, David Slim. However, he was less than impressed with the provincial governor, Asadullah Wafa, whom he found to be a 'lovely old man but not that engaged'.[37] A more accurate portrayal of Wafa is offered by the journalist Jack Fairweather, who described him as 'a cantankerous sixty-eight-year-old with no power base in Helmand yet with far-ranging and obscure gripes against many of the region's tribes'.[38] The US embassy similarly noted that while Wafa had 'hit the ground running' in January 2007 'with his tribal outreach efforts', by March he had lost interest and rarely left Lashkar Gah. American diplomats observed how 'On more than one occasion the Deputy Governor noted that Wafa was an outsider who did not know the tribal dynamics of Helmand' and that Wafa's 'imperious approach leaves little room for improving local governance'. Increasingly, Wafa looked to British forces as the solution, and insisted on 'robust military operations across the province as the prerequisite to political outreach'.[39]

In the absence of reliable, capable and committed Afghan security forces, there was nobody to stop the Taliban returning to those areas supposedly 'cleared' of insurgents once British forces moved on to the next offensive operation. The cranky and disengaged provincial governor did not help in terms of persuading tribal elders to resist the Taliban. This lack of progress led a frustrated Lorimer to tell journalists that British operations in Helmand were like 'mowing the lawn'.[40]

For eighteen months the British Army and Royal Marines had attempted to defeat the Taliban through major combat operations. The conflict got progressively more intense. The number of recorded major engagements with enemy forces increased from 537 during 16 Brigade's tour, to 821 during 3 Brigade's, then 1,096 during 12 Brigade's.[41] On their respective tours, 16 Brigade fired 479,236 rounds, 3 Brigade 1.295 million, and 12 Brigade 2.474 million.[42] No matter how much ammunition was expended by British forces, the Taliban kept fighting. Many of those Taliban killed were 'accidental guerrillas', that is, locals who had been driven to take up arms to resist oppressive local authorities and the British who were backing them.[43] Richard Dannatt would later admit that 'in the early days we probably wound up – maybe still are – killing lots of farmers'.[44] At the same time, civilian fatalities from the conflict steadily mounted across Afghanistan, rising from under 1,000 in 2006 to well over 1,500 in 2007. ISAF was responsible for only about a quarter of these in both years.[45] However, this did not stop President Karzai from becoming increasingly fed up. He had been complaining in private to US and British commanders about civilians being killed in NATO operations since 2005.[46] In 2007, he went public.

On 23 June 2007 Karzai was told that twenty-five civilians had been killed in NATO air strikes on Deh Adan Khan, the village near Gereshk that had supposedly been cleared of Taliban by 12 Brigade just two months before. This was the final straw. The furious president called a press conference to denounce NATO forces, declaring that 'innocent people are becoming victims of reckless operations'.[47] The NATO civilian spokesman in Kabul and former British Army officer, Nicholas Lunt, promptly went on the BBC and Al Jazeera to admit that 'President Karzai has a right to be disappointed and angry. We need to do better.' For this, he got a dressing-down the following morning from an angry McNeill, who told Lunt that 'the only person I report to is the US President'. Lunt disagreed: his view was that 'if you go around killing large numbers of Afghans you're really setting yourself up for failure'. Five days later, NATO air strikes killed a large number of civilians in Heyderbad, another village near Gereshk. Initially, the Afghan government reported that forty-five civilians had been killed; ISAF disputed this, believing the figure to be twelve. Eventually the head of 3/205 Brigade went to Heyderbad and established the death toll to be between twenty-five and thirty. It transpired that the air strikes were nothing to do with ISAF but had been carried out to rescue an American unit that had been conducting a raid under the Operation Enduring Freedom mission. Of course this distinction was lost on Helmandis, who blamed the British.[48]

London could see that too many civilians were being killed in Helmand. In response, PJHQ tightened up the rules of engagement (ROE) for British forces in Afghanistan. Previously, they had been operating under Rule 429, which permitted indiscriminate use of artillery and air power in support of planned operations, and Rule 421, which required British forces at all other times to make positive identification of targets as armed and showing hostile intent before they could be engaged with lethal force. Under English criminal law, British troops also had the right to use force in self-defence. In July 2007, PJHQ introduced Guidance Card Alpha as the standing ROE for all British forces in Afghanistan. This permitted the use of deadly force only against targets that were 'committing or about to commit an act likely to endanger life and there is no other way to prevent the danger'. Task Force Helmand could apply to PJHQ for specific exemptions to Guidance Card Alpha, if they wished to conduct a major operation under Rule 429.[49] It would be four years before the first British soldier faced criminal charges for breaching Guidance Card Alpha.[50] While the tightening of British rules of engagement was welcome from an Afghan perspective, clearly it was time for a whole different approach.

POPULATION-CENTRIC COUNTER-INSURGENCY

With the campaign in Iraq dragging on longer than expected, the British Army ran out of brigades to send to Helmand. Of the army's seven deployable brigades, five were committed to maintaining a brigade-plus-sized force in Iraq. Only 16 Air Assault and 12 Mechanised were available for Helmand, along with 3 Commando Royal Marines. It took at least two years for a brigade to go through the cycle of recovery from theatre, recoup, retrain and redeploy again. This meant that there was no brigade available to deploy for Operation Herrick 7, the fourth campaign tour covering the period from October 2007 to April 2008.

To fill the gap, the British Army sent a brigade that was never intended to conduct combat operations. The Army Board had agreed in February 2006 to turn 52 Infantry Brigade, based in Edinburgh, from a type B brigade, which is a regional brigade responsible for providing logistical and administrative support to regimental battalions at home, into a type A brigade, which is a brigade capable of deployment on operations overseas. The idea was for it to be the army's lead brigade on post-conflict stabilisation and security sector reform. The commander, Brigadier Andrew Mackay, had developed a reputation in this area, having been in charge of the coalition programme to reform the Iraqi police in 2004. Mackay had previously been an officer in the Hong Kong police before joining the British Army. In its new role, 52 Brigade was assigned to lead the UK military mission to help reform the Lebanese Armed Forces.[51] But in the summer of 2006, the British Army realised that it was going to have to find a new brigade to send to Helmand a year later. In the autumn, 52 Brigade was notified that it would deploy to Helmand, and the brigade headquarters underwent a rapid expansion from 15 to 175 officers. The proposal to reallocate 52 Brigade for this purpose had met fierce opposition from some in Army Headquarters. There was also debate about replacing Mackay as commander should 52 Brigade be deployed. At the age of fifty, Mackay was the oldest brigade commander in the British Army. Some wondered if he was up to the job.[52]

Under 52 Brigade came a further rise in British troop numbers in Afghanistan to 7,750 personnel, up from 6,500 under 12 Brigade. Included in this was a significant increase in capability provided by an armoured infantry company, equipped with fifty Warrior infantry fighting vehicles, which arrived in time for the final month of 12 Brigade's tour. Task Force Helmand was divided into three main zones. Battlegroup North, formed of 40 Commando Royal Marines, covered Sangin, Now Zad and Kajaki. Battlegroup South, formed of the Household Cavalry Regiment and the Royal Gurkha Rifles, held the southern defensive line in Garmsir. Battlegroup Centre, covering the key ground around Gereshk, was due to be given to 1st Battalion the Coldstream Guards. The Danes had a company in this area, which the Danish government decided to increase to an infantry battalion. Thus, in the interest of alliance politics, it was decided to give Battlegroup Centre to the Danes. 52 Brigade was informed just weeks before it was due to deploy. The Coldstream Guards were bitterly disappointed. Mackay recalls that the 'Guards network' was mobilised to try and reverse the decision. On the brigade's final mission rehearsal exercise just prior to deployment, he was visited by General Redmond Watt, then Commander-in-Chief of Land Command (the number two in the British Army) and former general officer commanding the Guards Household Division, who lobbied for the Coldstreams. Mackay was furious at this attempted end run. He pulled the Coldstreams out of the exercise and, as he put it, 'read them the riot act'.[53] The battalion was broken up into different functions within Task Force Helmand. 52 Brigade also deployed with 2nd Battalion the Yorkshire Regiment (2 Yorks), who were assigned the OMLT role, mentoring 3/205 Brigade.

52 Brigade was bigger and better resourced than any previous brigade deployed to Helmand. For all this, there were still serious equipment shortfalls. In a frank memorandum to the MoD, Mackay offered some ground truths, warning of a 'grave crisis' due to so much of the equipment used by his troops being 'tired, limited, and failing regularly'. This even included the much-vaunted Mastiffs: in his post-operation report, Mackay notes that 'I had only sixteen out of thirty-five Mastiffs on the road because parts were just not there'.[54] In the British Army, it is invariably the majors that find creative ways to get things done. An exasperated Mastiff company commander, Major Richard Slack, contacted a factory in Coventry, via satellite phone from the Helmand desert, in order to source spare parts. For other items, Mackay's deputy chief of staff, Major Nick Haston, ended up buying them over the Internet using his own credit card.[55]

Especially problematic was the new Bowman digital radio communications system. Bowman was introduced in 2005 to replace the old analogue Clansman tactical radio. The entire British Army was switched over to the new system and more than 90,000 Bowman radios were acquired at a total cost of £2.5 billion. The Bowman system was supposed to offer a secure tactical network for encrypted audio, text and image communications. Bowman was no different from every other large-scale IT programme, which is to say that it suffered from overpromise and underperformance. British troops found Bowman radio sets too heavy, too bulky and too unreliable. The batteries kept running low and so troops out on long patrols had to turn off their radio sets to preserve power. Even worse, the radios had very poor range in the dense Green Zone, often no more than a few hundred yards. The function that enabled Bowman sets to be used to track friendly forces also failed. To cap it all off, the electronic counter-measures on the Chinooks were inclined to wipe the pre-programmed encrypted frequencies on the radios, rendering them utterly useless for disembarking troops. In the grim humour of disgruntled soldiers, Bowman soon stood for 'Better Off With Map And Nokia'.[56]

52 Brigade deployed, much like 16 Brigade and 3 Brigade, in a strategy vacuum. Mackay received higher military guidance from the Chief of the Defence Staff and PJHQ for his role as commander of British Forces in Afghanistan. However, there was no clear UK national strategy for the Helmand campaign. Mackay later reported that 'the advice I obtained from the FCO in London was vague to the point of being meaningless'.[57] Indeed, doing the rounds in Whitehall prior to deployment, visiting the Cabinet Office, Foreign Office, Department for International Development and MoD for briefings, Mackay was struck by the 'sense of defeatism'. In essence, Whitehall was hoping that Mackay would find a way to 'muddle through'.[58]

When he arrived in Helmand, Mackay was dismayed by what he found: 'half of it was trashed'.[59] There was massive displacement as locals fled district centres to escape the fighting between the British and the Taliban. Now Zad had become a ghost town; the entire population had moved to the desert. Similarly, 'Sangin was a disaster' as the town centre had been destroyed by British artillery and NATO air power. One of Mackay's staff officers told a journalist, 'we have gone backwards. We have created rubble, and a load of blokes died clearing green zones, which is utterly pointless.'[60] Mackay was clear in his own mind that the British Army could not kill its way to victory in Helmand. To emphasise the point he banned the use of enemy body counts as 'a particularly corrupt measure of success'.[61]

Drawing inspiration from traditional counter-insurgency theory, Mackay proposed a different approach to the Helmand campaign, moving from one focused on defeating the insurgency to one that concentrated on winning over the local population. In his operational design, Mackay declared that 'unless we retain, gain and win the consent of the population within Helmand we lose the COIN [counter-insurgency] campaign'. In sum, the population, and not control of territory, was the 'prize' both sides were fighting for. It followed that there was little point in capturing territory if, as in Now Zad, the population had left it. This approach rested on a new way of thinking about the primary purpose of military operations, which was not to defeat enemy forces but enable the government to connect with the people. Put another way by Mackay in his operational design, 'military action is secondary to the political one, its primary purpose being to afford the political power enough freedom to work safely with the population'.[62]

Also informing Mackay's approach were the American military's new ideas about counter-insurgency.[63] When the Sunni insurgency started in Iraq, the US military turned to the British Army for advice. Britain's campaign in Malaya from 1948 to 1960 was considered one of the very few counter-insurgency successes in modern history. There was a sense in the early 2000s, on both sides of the Atlantic, that counter-insurgency was somehow in the DNA of the British Army. Reinforcing this view was a best-selling book published in 2002 in which US Army Colonel John Nagl contrasted British success in Malaya with American failure in Vietnam, and which seemed to underline the notion that the British Army was naturally good at counter-insurgency and the Americans needed to play catch-up.[64] Such an idea was plain nonsense of course, and revealed as such by growing evidence of British failure in Iraq from 2004 to 2006.[65] Over the same period, under the pressure of looming defeat, a number of US Army and Marine brigade commanders developed new counter-insurgency tactics in the Sunni heartland of Iraq.[66] Leading the effort to capture these innovative tactics in a new doctrine was General David Petraeus, who as commander of 101st Airborne Division had employed classic counter-insurgency techniques to stabilise the northern Iraqi city of

Mosul in 2004. Acclaiming his efforts to 'win Iraqi hearts and minds', *Newsweek* put Petraeus on its cover in June 2004 under the title: 'Can this man save Iraq?'[67] Petraeus was then appointed to lead the newly formed multinational Security Transition Command – Iraq, with responsibility for developing Iraqi security forces. It was here that Mackay met Petraeus and worked as one of his senior deputies. On his return to the United States in early 2006, Petraeus sought to produce a new counter-insurgency doctrine in record time. Army field manuals can take years to produce as drafts must be approved by many constituencies within the military. In stark contrast to normal practice, FM 3–24 *Counterinsurgency Field Manual* was written, agreed and published within a year.[68]

Petraeus sent Mackay a pre-publication copy in December 2006. Mackay recalls reading through it and thinking: 'This is it!' He had copies distributed to all of his brigade staff and subordinate commanders.[69] An important message that Mackay took from FM 3–24, and one that gelled with what he found in Helmand, was that excessive use of military force in counter-insurgency is often counter-productive. As he noted in his operational design, 'The more force is used the less effective it is and counter intuitively the more we engage in force protection the less secure we may be.'[70] Force protection includes keeping troops in big bases and in armoured vehicles to minimise their exposure to battlefield risks. Such an approach also prevented troops from developing ties with local people, which could end up reducing local support for the insurgency.

The core conceptual innovation that Mackay took from FM 3–24 was that of 'clear–hold–build' as the key phases in counter-insurgency operations. 'Clear' involved offensive operations to push insurgents out of a particular area; security forces then had to remain to 'hold' the area, so as to create the security conditions for development activities to 'build' services and infrastructure, in order to demonstrate to the local population that they were better off siding with the government than the insurgents. Whereas 12 Mechanised Brigade's approach had focused on the 'clear' phase, 52 Brigade's would focus on the 'hold'.

When 52 Brigade arrived, they found that 12 Mechanised Brigade had 'created a rash of FOBs in response to re-infiltration of Taliban' as well as a 'host of Patrol Bases throughout the AO [area of operations] from Garmsir in the south to Musa Qala in the north'. Most of these were located outside of towns with the purpose of keeping insurgents away; in essence, to act as 'breakwaters'.[71] The problem with this approach was that British troops were less present in population centres. Moreover, under 12 Mechanised Brigade, companies would rotate through FOBs and patrol bases as required for combat operations. Mackay remedied this by deploying battlegroups and companies to particular FOBs for their entire tour in order to demonstrate an enduring presence and also to develop 'an intimate knowledge of the ground, the local nationals and the pattern of life'.[72] In practical terms this meant turning some patrol bases, which were very austere and through which companies would rotate, into bigger FOBs that could accommodate a unit for six months. It also meant moving some bases closer to population centres. As the brigade plans officer explained, 'locals had something of a "castle on the hill" mentality', and 52 Brigade found that by having a proper persistent presence 'locals begin to engage [with] the British and provide information'.[73]

Previous British brigades understood the importance of engaging in activities to win over local support; these were called 'influence operations', and could include the use of demonstrations of force as well as 'softer' activities, such as meetings with local elders, building schools, rebuilding damaged infrastructure, and so forth. However, Mackay was to give 'influence operations' far more prominence, making it central to his operational design, and committing more resources to supporting such activities. Thus, he created new teams dedicated to planning influence operations and assessing their effectiveness, including special two-man teams deployed down to rifle companies (these were called 'N-KETs' or Non-Kinetic Effects Teams), as well as larger Development and Influence Teams, up to twenty strong, assembled as required for specific missions.[74]

The British Army had well-established tools for planning combat operations and through Battle Damage Assessment could determine if combat operations had achieved their objectives. In contrast, there was no methodology to plan what kind of influence operations should be undertaken where, or indeed to measure the effectiveness of such operations. Mackay searched around for ideas and came across a model for targeting soft activities called the Tactical Conflict Assessment

Framework (TCAF, pronounced 'Tee-Caff'), which had been developed by Dr James Derleth from USAID; Derleth had been trying to promote TCAF within the US government but 'no one was interested'. Mackay visited Derleth in Washington in the spring of 2007, and persuaded him to participate in the final Mission Rehearsal Exercise for 52 Brigade six weeks prior to deployment.[75]

Leading on influence operations within 52 Brigade was the head of engineers, Lieutenant Colonel Richard Wardlaw; he would develop TCAF from an 'untested theory' into a tool that troops could use on the ground. Wardlaw had come straight from a tour in Iraq where he had been Chief of Plans for Multi-National Division South East. He had been very frustrated with the US 'traffic light' system for monitoring progress towards Iraqi provincial control. The whole thing was subjective as US commanders 'changed lights pretty arbitrarily' against particular objectives from red (poor progress) to green (good progress). More damningly, the system was 'measuring the wrong things'; it was focused on *outputs* (things built and done) when it should have been focusing on the *impact* of activities on the lives of Iraqis. Wardlaw saw the potential for using TCAF not only to target influence operations but also to assess their impact through a feedback loop.[76]

TCAF was trialled in Lashkar Gah in late October 2007. It consisted of a standard set of questions that patrols were instructed to ask locals in order to understand their views and problems. Up to then, British company and battlegroup commanders had relied on engaging with local elders to understand community priorities. The problem with such 'key leader engagement' was that it failed to accurately capture the concerns of large segments of the population. Regional Command South commissioned public opinion polling by a Kandahar-based company but the polls proved unreliable due to corrupt polling practices; in any case this was too crude a mechanism to capture local-level perspectives. In this context, TCAF looked most promising. The trial was conducted in two areas on the outskirts of Lashkar Gah, which housed camps for persons displaced by the fighting in Helmand, and whose plight had been ignored by the town's mayor. These camps were ideal recruiting grounds for the Taliban. The TCAF trial revealed that the top issue for these displaced people was access to clean water; this concern had been completely ignored by the British PRT.[77]

Once formally adopted following the Lashkar Gah trial, TCAF was pushed aggressively into the field by brigade headquarters. However, as one British officer responsible for implementing it noted, TCAF 'was rolled out too quickly across the whole province, and into areas that weren't ready'. This was because interaction with locals worked fine in the provincial capital but was far more problematic in places like Sangin and Musa Qala where 'locals don't want to be seen chatting away happily to soldiers'. TCAF could also backfire. Asking locals about their main concerns implied that action would be taken to address them. Where remedial action was not taken local communities became understandably hostile, especially when repeatedly asked the same questions by the same soldiers as they conducted iterative TCAF surveys.[78] For all these problems, TCAF was the best effort by a British brigade in Helmand to understand the needs of a population, on behalf of whom they were fighting.

RETAKING MUSA QALA

It all started with a misunderstanding. In late October, a Taliban commander in northern Helmand called Mullah Salaam contacted President Karzai offering to change sides and retake Musa Qala. Karzai immediately seized on what he thought was a wonderful opportunity. The president seemed to be dealing with a major Taliban figure from the Alizai tribe in northern Helmand, who was the brother of Mullah Zakir, then detained at Guantánamo; Zakir would soon be released and within three years become the head of the Taliban Military Commission. Mullah Salaam had gone to the same madrasa as the pro-government Alizai leader, Sher Mohammed Akhundzada. Reconciliation with Mullah Salaam therefore promised to unite the warring sub-tribes of the Alizai in northern Helmand and align them with the government. Yet it later transpired that Karzai was talking to an altogether different Mullah Salaam. This was not the brother of Mullah Zakir but a minor Taliban commander with only fifty or so men under his command. Alarm bells should have rung when this Mullah Salaam began asking for guns and assistance because the Taliban had surrounded his compound: an unlikely request for a great Taliban commander.[79]

Initially, the Americans and British also welcomed this opportunity, albeit far more cautiously. McNeill had been unhappy with the British withdrawal from Musa Qala, and the collapse of the deal and the Taliban taking of the town came as no surprise to him. The British ambassador, Sherard Cowper-Coles, had started to advocate working with tribes to raise community-based militias to defend villages across Afghanistan. Mullah Salaam offered the chance to trial this idea in Helmand. British special forces quickly got a satellite phone to Mullah Salaam, which the Taliban leader, who had the gift of the gab, used to great effect in winning over Karzai. By early November, ISAF had figured out that whoever Salaam was, he was not a great Taliban commander. 'He has got fifty-five fighters, tops,' McNeill told Karzai, 'he's a lightweight.' By this stage, Mullah Salaam had persuaded the presidential palace otherwise. The head of the Afghan National Security Directorate proclaimed this 'a chance to break [the Taliban] backbone' and end 'tribal resistance in northern Helmand'. Karzai told McNeill and Cowper-Coles, 'we must help Salaam without question in any circumstances!'[80]

Originally, 52 Brigade had no intention of pushing back into Musa Qala district. Like 12 Mechanised Brigade, the focus of their campaign was to be the town of Gereshk and the Upper Gereshk Valley. All this changed because of Mullah Salaam. In response to pressure from Kabul, Mackay deployed his Scots Guards armoured infantry company of fifty Warrior vehicles and some 250 soldiers to northern Musa Qala on 2 November, to loiter just outside Mullah Salaam's village. Also in support were a squadron from the King's Royal Hussars of eighteen Mastiffs, who would secure the logistical route to Musa Qala, and a troop of three 105mm guns from the Royal Artillery. The Mastiffs were to prove their worth: the squadron endured fourteen IED strikes during the operation without suffering a single serious casualty. In addition to protecting Mullah Salaam, this operation was intended to put psychological pressure on the Taliban in advance of a possible offensive to retake the town. Consistent with his overall 'influence approach', Mackay hoped to intimidate the insurgents into leaving the area so as to lessen the likely battle for Musa Qala.[81]

The Taliban response was not long in coming. Within a week there was a spike in insurgent activity across Helmand. Military intelligence reported numbers of Taliban fighters entering the province in the

south from Pakistan and coming down from the north. On
9 November, the Taliban launched simultaneous attacks against 40
Commando Royal Marines operating out of FOB Inkerman, north of
Sangin, and against the Royal Gurkha Rifles in Garmsir. This was the
most intensive fighting seen in Helmand for two months. On one day
alone, 52 Brigade suffered fourteen casualties in the Upper Sangin
Valley, with five requiring medical evacuation to the UK. In response,
Mackay decided to ratchet up the pressure on Musa Qala. While he
had yet to receive a formal order from ISAF headquarters, it was clear
that the decision had been reached to retake the town. However, the
Afghan and American forces necessary to support the operation would
not be available before mid December. Meanwhile, with the Scots
Guards probing the north-east of Musa Qala town, Mackay decided
to deploy his Brigade Reconnaissance Force of eighteen WMIKs to
do likewise on the north-western flank. As Mackay later reflected,
these forces began 'almost daily contact with enemy forces'. At the
same time, he was told by British General Jacko Page, commander
of ISAF Regional Command South, that 'at this stage there is more
political work to be done on Musa Qala'.[82]

This is where Michael Semple, an expert on Afghan history, culture
and politics from Dublin, came in. Rory Stewart, the former British
diplomat and adventurer, describes meeting Semple in a remote Afghan
town in early 2002, shortly after the fall of the Taliban:

> A crowd of 100 watched a Hercules plane land and Semple emerge – a
> tall, broad-shouldered figure with a great shaggy light-coloured beard,
> dressed in local shalwar kameez. He proceeded to give a compelling
> speech about the new government in rapid, fluent, colloquial Dari with
> only a hint of an Irish accent.[83]

Semple, who was equally fluent in Pashto (the language of southern
and eastern Afghanistan), worked for the European Union to support
Afghan government efforts to reconcile with and reintegrate former
Taliban.

In May 2005, the Karzai government had launched an Independent
National Commission for Peace, headed by Professor Sebghatullah
Mojadedi, to provide the framework for these efforts. Under the
Strengthening Peace Programme run by the commission, individuals

who formally left the insurgency received a certificate of reconciliation, which was supposed to prevent them from being harassed by
police and local officials. In practice, however, this certificate frequently
failed to prevent continued harassment by corrupt officials and pro-
government tribal rivals. The commission also failed to raise sufficient
funds to launch a programme of economic rehabilitation activities
to support reconciliation and reintegration. All the same, 4,634
ex-combatants had entered the Strengthening Peace Programme by
October 2007.[84]

Whereas the Independent National Commission was focused on
the reconciliation and reintegration of *individual* combatants, Semple
was interested in bringing whole tribal networks over to the government side. In mid 2007, he had a major success when he persuaded
six Taliban commanders, including Barakzai chiefs Mullah Qassim and
Mullah Bashir, to reconcile with the government; with them came
around 150 Taliban fighters. By this stage Semple was formally deputy
head of the EU mission to Afghanistan. His big idea was to integrate
this Taliban group with the Afghan police in Gereshk, giving the
Taliban checkpoints to man, and having Taliban and police conduct
joint patrols. The Helmand provincial chief of police, Nabi Jan Mullah
Khel, who had met 'the Group', as they became known, was supportive.
Many members of the Group were actually Hizb fighters and
commanders from the former 93rd Division, as were many members
of the local police. So the idea of integrating the two forces was
perfectly feasible.[85] The Coldstream Guards helped the Taliban to
establish legitimate security checkpoints. In fact, British military
mentors preferred working with the reconciled Taliban to the Afghan
police and army; they found the Taliban more polite, competent and
reliable.[86] Support was also found in the Afghan Ministry of Interior
in Kabul, with the new first deputy minister, Hamid Khalid, who was
a fellow Barakzai. Khalid arranged for Karzai to meet with the Group
in Lashkar Gah; and the president came away declaring it to be 'the
most encouraging reconciliation effort I've seen in Afghanistan'.[87]
Semple worked behind the scenes to see if the success in Gereshk
could be replicated in Musa Qala.

The final decision to launch the ISAF offensive against Musa Qala
was taken on 17 November, while Cowper-Coles was on leave back
in the UK; the British ambassador had come to doubt the wisdom of

the operation. Once Cowper-Coles was out of the country, McNeill wasted no time in ordering Mackay to proceed. By late November, US special forces and the Brigade Reconnaissance Force were probing Taliban defences on the outskirts of Musa Qala. The British made no secret of their troop movements in the hope of coercing the Taliban into retreating. However, what was kept secret was that British forces would not deliver the hammer blow. Rather, this task was given to Task Force 1 Fury. The plan was for three companies of US para-troopers to assault Musa Qala, each from a different direction, with 52 Brigade securing the perimeter. When the Taliban were defeated, 3/205 Brigade would enter the town and ISAF forces retreat into the shadows so as to put an Afghan face on the victory. In pre-operation planning, US and British planners disagreed on the rules of engage-ment. Mackay's intent was to avoid another Now Zad. His staff declared that all air strikes into Musa Qala had to be approved by Regional Command South in Kandahar. The commander of Task Force 1 Fury thought this was a crazy idea, especially 'if my guys are taking fire'. British officers were told that in such circumstances, US forces would use 'anything and everything to hit the target'.[88]

On 23 November, Cowper-Coles returned from England to discover that the operation had been given the green light and was rapidly moving forward. He was somewhat perturbed, especially as it would occur at the same time as the first visit to Afghanistan by the new British prime minister, Gordon Brown. Cowper-Coles worried that this coincidence might be misinterpreted as political opportunism by Number 10 and denounced as such in the British press. There was also the prospect of the joint press conference with Brown and Karzai being derailed if the operation went badly and there were significant civilian casualties, as in such circumstances Karzai could be relied upon to publicly complain about careless military action by NATO forces. Either way the operation in early December risked overshadowing a planned big speech to Parliament on the prime minister's return from Afghanistan, in which Brown would unveil his new strategy for Afghanistan.[89] Mackay tried to reassure Cowper-Coles, telling the British ambassador in confidence that he would make sure the oper-ation 'would not be overly kinetic while the PM is visiting'. Cowper-Coles copied this reassurance back to the Foreign Office in London, which irked Mackay, not least because he had no actual intention of changing the conduct of a military operation simply to suit the prime minister's travel plans.[90]

In early December, the British vice closed tightly around Musa Qala. An armoured battlegroup comprising the Scimitars of the Household Cavalry and Mastiffs of the King's Royal Hussars took up position north-east of the town. On the westward side was the Scots Guards armoured infantry company with their Warrior vehicles, and the reconnaissance force of the Coldstream Guards. 40 Commando battle-group provided the southern blocking force. The Taliban vowed 'to fight to the death' for Musa Qala. The *Daily Telegraph* quoted one anonymous Taliban commander as saying: 'I have 300 Mujahidin with me. We have brought our best artillery. We have anti-aircraft guns in place to attack the helicopters.' Mackay had hoped the show of force would scare the insurgents into fleeing. The flash from secret intelligence on the eve of battle suggested otherwise. It simple stated: 'Enemy will fight.'[91]

A fleet of twenty-one Chinooks dropped three companies of US paratroopers within marching distance of Musa Qala on 7 December, and march they did overnight to assault the town early the following morning from three different directions. Every available ISAF air asset – including Apaches, Predator drones, Harriers, F-16s, F/A-18s, B-1B bombers, AC-130 gunships, and British and US surveillance planes – was tasked to support the operation. Directing the 'high-density airspace control zone' above Musa Qala was Squadron Leader Simon Tatters and his team of British air controllers. In addition to ensuring that aircraft did not fly into or drop ordnance on one another, they had to plot flight paths for artillery strikes as well. At one point, a US Air Force general, who had arrived unannounced in the airspace over Musa Qala in his own personal jet fighter, was sent packing. The Predator drones also proved challenging for British air controllers, as many belonged to the CIA or US special forces who operated outside the ISAF chain of command. A member of Tatters' team lost it with a pilot of one particularly troublesome drone: 'What the fuck are you doing to me? You're in my airspace. YOU'RE IN THE WAY.' The drone pilot back in Nevada failed to appreciate the gravity of the situation, telling the British officer to 'lose your attitude dude'.[92]

On the evening of 8 December Mackay arrived on Roshan Hill – so named after a mobile phone tower on the hill belonging to the Afghan telecommunications company Roshan – overlooking Musa Qala town to personally oversee the operation. *The Times* reported that 'he spent ten days supervising the attack' from Roshan Hill. It was unusual for a brigadier to be so close to the battle; at one point his forward deployed headquarters came under Taliban mortar fire, and Mackay's driver ended up shooting two insurgents.[93] Mackay understandably wanted to keep a close eye on the operation to ensure that the risks to civilians were minimised.

Task Force 1 Fury was true to its name. A highly experienced and professional combat formation, it overcame Taliban defences within twenty-four hours. The Taliban put up a tough fight, but organised resistance was quickly dealt with by precision air strikes. Insurgents attempting to retreat in darkness were easily tracked and mercilessly gunned down by AC-130 Spectre gunships; around fifty were killed this way. ISAF intelligence intercepted messages from Taliban commanders who had long since fled the scene encouraging their men to continue the fight. In the closing stages of the battle, US and British special forces moved in to hunt down the remaining Taliban fighting units. When British intelligence pinpointed the final Taliban 'command node' in the town, two AC-130s swooped in to reduce the compound to dust. The US military later informed the press that the Taliban deputy governor of Helmand had been killed.[94]

On 11 December, the 2 Yorks battlegroup escorted 3/205 Brigade into the town. The British and Afghan soldiers proceeded with caution, wary of Taliban booby-trap bombs and any remaining snipers. Waiting on the edge of the town were US and Emirati special forces, ready to rush in at the first sign of trouble. As they moved from compound to compound, British troops found an elaborate network of fortified fighting positions and connecting trenches, as well as a series of bomb-making factories. Lieutenant Dan Hopwood of the Royal Engineers told *Sunday Times* journalist Stephen Grey that it was 'the largest find of IEDs and explosives that we've seen in Helmand'. They also found a massive amount of drugs. Over twelve tonnes of sticky brown opium resin was discovered in two compounds; processed into heroin, this would have fetched many millions of pounds on Western streets. British soldiers were ordered to destroy any opium stockpiles they uncovered. This was going to cause a problem since the two main occupations for males in Musa Qala were fighter and opium poppy farmer. As one farmer warned Grey, 'if the British and Americans destroy the poppy, everyone will leave and join the Taliban'.[95]

By 12 December, British and Afghan forces had secured the town centre. The British then hid their vehicles and persuaded reluctant US troops to do likewise, so only Afghan forces would be visible to the press. A convoy of Afghan army pickup trucks then drove into the town, and the head of 3/205, Brigadier Mohaydin, claimed the reoccupation of Musa Qala as an Afghan victory, just as Mackay had planned. On the ground to witness everything, Grey observed how the town's residents began to return soon after the arrival of the Afghan army. 'Tractors, pick-up trucks and cars started bringing people home.' With them came stories of the brutal rule of the Taliban in Musa Qala, including the hanging of four traitors and thieves. One of the men had had his head cut off and put on a spike on the road into the town as a warning to others.[96]

Semple was crucial to the British success in Musa Qala. Working behind the scenes and making use of his many contacts, he had persuaded a number of major Taliban commanders to stay out of the fight for Musa Qala. The National Directorate of Security estimated that as many as eight hundred insurgents in northern Helmand did not join in the defence of Musa Qala; Semple puts the figure closer to four hundred. For Semple, it was vital to find something honourable for these Taliban fighters to do if this temporary success was to be turned into a more sustainable reconciliation. In a meeting between Semple, Hamid Khalid and another deputy interior minister, Munir Mangal, the idea of a 'training camp' was developed, where demobilised Taliban would receive a six-week 'life skills' course to ease the reintegration into civilian life. 52 Brigade was briefed on the idea and British Army engineers set to work finding a suitable site for the camp and planning its construction.[97]

On 18 December, Semple visited Lashkar Gah to update Mackay and Cowper-Coles on how his plan was progressing; he also spoke to Governor Wafa in a separate meeting. Semple had hitched a lift on a UN helicopter with Mervyn Patterson, a fellow Irishman and chief political officer in the UN mission to Afghanistan. Travelling with them was General Naquib Stanikzai, the former commander of the Taliban air force and a key partner in Semple's reconciliation efforts.[98] Mackay and Cowper-Coles liked what they heard but at the second

meeting at the provincial governor's residence Semple had barely
begun to outline his plan when Wafa began shouting and accusing
him, Patterson and Naquib of plotting to train the Taliban. Wafa had
Naquib arrested on the spot and Semple and Patterson were confined
to their guest house in Lashkar Gah. When a large sum of cash was
confiscated from Naquib, Wafa claimed that Naquib was carrying
$150,000 to give to 'terrorists'; in fact, it was $18,700 provided by
the British embassy to cover the costs of the ex-Taliban Group in
Gereshk. Semple was horrified. Wafa's behaviour was not only a grave
breach of Afghan norms of hospitality, Semple had also successfully
campaigned in Kabul to increase Wafa's 'operational funds' as the
governor of Helmand; Semple saw this as the price of doing business
in Helmand. He notes that 'normally when you get to this stage in
Afghan terms [in a relationship], and people disagree with you, they
find a gracious way to do so'.[99]

Wafa called Karzai, claiming that he had caught Semple and
Patterson trying to give aid to the Taliban. Incredibly, Karzai believed
this paranoid fantasy. On Christmas Eve he declared Semple and
Patterson (who had nothing to do with Semple's scheme) *persona non
grata* and gave them forty-eight hours to leave the country. Some
Afghan officials began to spread false rumours that Semple and
Patterson had been working for British intelligence. Karzai's official
spokesman told the press that both were being expelled for engaging
in 'unauthorised activities'. Semple's superior, the EU special representative to Afghanistan, Francesc Vendrell, admitted that he did not
really know what Semple was up to in Helmand, but all the same he
was quick to dismiss the allegations as 'preposterous'.[100] Then, on
25 December, Mullah Qassim and Mullah Bashir were placed under
arrest and the ex-Taliban Group were disbanded. The head of the
British mentor team in Gereshk, Captain Rob Sugden, phoned
the commander of the Coldstream Guards OMLT, Lieutenant Colonel
George Waters, to alert him to what had happened. Waters response
was unequivocal: 'fuck, fuck, fuck!' 'Are we all going to end up in
court?' Sugden asked.[101]

Cowper-Coles cut short his Christmas holidays and scrambled back
to Kabul to deal with the unfolding crisis. On 29 December, he went
to the presidential palace for what he had hoped would be a 'frank
heart-to-heart with the President'. Instead, Cowper-Coles faced a

packed room, with Karzai surrounded by his closest advisers, security ministers and military chiefs. The president unleashed a barrage of complaints about British interference in Afghanistan, and in particular about Semple scheming to train the Taliban. Yet Cowper-Coles had come prepared and brought proof that Semple had proceeded with official Afghan support. He notes in his memoirs:

> To the President's mounting astonishment, I produced photocopies of papers signed by some of those present in the room, including the Deputy National Security Advisor, who happened also to be Karzai's brother-in-law. It was clear that none of those present had dared tell an enraged President that not only had they known about the project, but they had also authorised it.[102]

Karzai did not change his mind, however; Semple and Patterson remained banished from Afghanistan.

For all of his good work, Semple had fallen foul of Afghan corruption and international politics. He believes that Wafa 'saw reconciliation as a cash cow that he should drink from'. From Wafa's perspective, the problem with Semple's scheme to reintegrate former Taliban in Musa Qala was that there was no obvious way to cream off money. Adding to the problem, Nabi Jan Mullah Khel was replaced in December by Hussein Adi Wal as provincial chief of police for Helmand. In Semple's words, Adi Wal was 'more of a creep' and, unlike Khel, not remotely interested in reconciliation.[103]

LOSING HEARTS AND MINDS

Mackay had arrived in Helmand to find it devastated by British operations. To be sure, British forces had prevented the Taliban from sweeping in and seizing complete control of the province. However, the downside of this was that far from improving security, the British presence had contributed to an intensification of the conflict. Thus more than any previous British brigade, 52 Infantry Brigade put effort into minimising the impact of military operations on the local population, and supporting the civilian-led attempt to improve governance and public services in Helmand – in other words, into 'winning hearts and minds'. But the incompetence and corruption of local political partners, the tenacity of the Taliban insurgency and misguided attempts to eradicate poppy fields in Helmand all undid British efforts to gain local support.

The British were trying to bring Western-style democracy and rule of law to a society whose customs and rules resembled those of feudal Europe of the Middle Ages. Notwithstanding the introduction of national elections in Afghanistan, the country was essentially an oligarchy where wealth and power were channelled through familial, mujahedin and smuggling networks that worked with or criss-crossed tribal structures. This was particularly pronounced in the southern provinces like Helmand, where reforms from Kabul had little effect and governors and police chiefs treated their districts as personal fiefdoms.

Thus the story of Musa Qala could not end well. Initially, 52 Brigade made all the right moves. Once the Afghan flag flew in the town on 12 December 2007, a British Military Support and Stabilisation Team arrived to implement a £3 million development programme to repair roads, renovate the town's medical clinic and rebuild the school.[104] As Mackay later noted, 'fifty percent of our planning for that operation [to retake Musa Qala] was for stabilization'.[105] The purpose was to demonstrate to locals the benefits of living under government rule. In early January 2008 Mullah Salaam was appointed the new governor of Musa Qala. Salaam asserted that the Taliban were divided in the district and that he had the backing of the larger group. There was no evidence to support this claim. Nonetheless, the presidential palace suggested that his appointment would facilitate reconciliation with Taliban groups in northern Helmand.[106] Karzai was famously full of contradictions, so this may have been the president's sincere hope, despite his expulsion of Semple, who had done more than anybody to advance reconciliation in Helmand. Salaam did initially win over locals, playing gracious host to local elders and travelling from village to village to promote the virtue of working with the government. It was his eloquence as a public speaker that persuaded the British that Salaam would make a reasonably good governor of Musa Qala. As one officer told a *Times* journalist, 'we have in him a credible governor who is making an impression upon us and the people'.[107]

Within a few months, however, Salaam's popularity had plummeted. He proved to be an ineffective and largely uninterested district governor. Salaam also began to compete with Abdul Wali Koka, the district chief of police; the two men were from rival Alizai sub-tribes. As Mike Martin notes, 'their militias clashed regularly, and even though it was inappropriate for Salaam to have a militia as district governor, it became very difficult to remove his as he was a high-profile reconciled "Talib"'.[108] In May 2008, the US embassy reported that Salaam's 'refusal to control his private militia, which includes his son, has angered many people'. US diplomats noted that around fifty locals from Salaam's home village of Shah Kariz gathered outside Musa Qala town to complain about 'illegal tax collection and unlawful land seizures' by Salaam's militia. Making matters worse, Salaam refused to meet with this delegation and instead sent his son to deal with them.[109] Salaam also went down in British estimation, and not only for what transpired to be his poor qualities as a governor. Like all Afghans in rural areas Salaam would defecate in the open, but he had the unsavoury habit of doing it directly outside the building housing British troops in the district centre. In the end, as one British diplomat observed, Salaam 'was loathed by pretty much everybody'.[110]

Adding to Afghan and British woes was a resilient and resourceful insurgency. The final three months of the brigade's tour proved especially challenging. The Danes in Battlegroup Centre struggled to prevent the Taliban from encroaching into Gereshk. In March, a suicide bomber blew himself up in the town, killing two Danish soldiers and one Czech soldier. Later that month two more Danish soldiers were killed, shot in separate incidents just five days apart. Things had got so bad that Danish Defence Command ended up sending a platoon of sixty-tonne main battle tanks to give their battlegroup more firepower.[111] Towards the end of their tour, the Royal Marines lost two men to an IED strike in Kajaki, while another marine on patrol south of Sangin lost an arm and both his legs when he stepped on a mine.[112] Even after Musa Qala had been retaken, therefore, large numbers of Taliban remained present in northern Helmand. The pressure on the British outpost guarding Kajaki Dam was 'relentless at times', and government control in Musa Qala never extended beyond a few miles from the district centre.[113]

The Taliban were able to draw support from growing popular discontent at Afghan government efforts, with international backing, to eradicate opium poppy in Helmand. Each year at harvest time, government tractors would be sent to destroy poppy fields. The Karzai government had good reasons to target the poppy economy, not least because Taliban taxation of this industry was a significant source of revenue for the insurgency. Indeed, 25 per cent of all opium produced in Afghanistan in 2005 came from Helmand. As provincial governor, Sher Mohammed Akhundzada had launched his own eradication effort for the 2002–3 growing session, which had resulted in a striking 50 per cent reduction of poppy cultivation, mostly in central Helmand. As we have seen, he was later accused by the British of being heavily involved in the drugs trade after they found nine metric tonnes of opium paste in his compound; it was perhaps not a coincidence that under his term as provincial governor there was a significant increase in poppy cultivation in his Alizai tribal lands of northern Helmand. In any case, Sher Mohammed Akhundzada could not repeat the success of the 2002–3 campaign, claiming that the failure of the Afghan government to deliver promised development assistance had undermined his ability to win the necessary support from local officials to support his eradication effort. Thus, poppy cultivation in Helmand trebled from around 26,500 hectares in 2004–5 to over 69,000 hectares in 2005–6. Helmandis feared that this was about to change with the arrival of the British. As the British colonel who deployed to Helmand in November 2005 ahead of the British task force noted: 'It was very hard to convince people that we weren't coming in to eradicate poppy. That's what they thought, everywhere I went. They envisaged helicopters and lines of troops destroying their crops.'[114]

From the perspective of Helmand's rural population, poppy cultivation brought many benefits. It provided an important source of capital and social advancement for farming families, access to land for tenant farmers who would grow food crops as well as cash crops like poppy, and wage labour opportunities for the wider population during harvest time.[115] To be sure, there was also a dark side to poppy farming. Many farmers borrowed hundreds and even thousands of dollars from drug smugglers to buy the poppy stalks. Such loans would be repaid in opium paste when the crop was harvested, and it was common practice for a farmer to offer a daughter as collateral. If the poppy crop failed or was eradicated, such 'loan brides' would have to be surrendered to a life of servitude and sexual abuse, and the farmer and the rest of his family faced ruin. The British military understood how damaging this fear could be to their counter-insurgency efforts in Helmand. At the same time, they could not ignore the fact that Britain was formally the 'lead nation' on counter-narcotics for Afghanistan. Thus, British commanders tried to walk a fine line between supporting the government and reassuring local communities. The result was a confusing message that pleased nobody. Typical of this was Colonel Messenger's statement to a shura of provincial councillors and mullahs in Lashkar Gah in March 2006: 'No UK military personnel will be eradicating poppy; however part of the UK mission is to support the government in its counter-narcotic efforts.'[116]

In its five-year counter-narcotics strategy produced with British assistance in 2006, the Afghan government clarified that its 'drug control policy is not eradication-led'. Rather it was pursuing 'targeted ground-based eradication' in order to incentivise farmers to move away from the poppy crop. In emphasising 'manual or mechanical ground based means' of eradication, the Karzai government was indicating that there was no intention of introducing aerial spraying of fields with chemicals to destroy the poppy crop.[117] Some powerful voices within the US government favoured aerial spraying, including the US ambassador from 2007 to 2009, William Wood, who was so vocal in his support for aerial spraying that he came to be known as 'Chemical Bill'. Nonetheless, supporting the Afghan counter-narcotics strategy was a US-funded and -trained national Afghan Eradication Force, comprising tractors and all-terrain vehicles, which could be dispatched from Kabul to those provinces where insufficient local eradication was taking place. Costing $60 million a year, the Afghan Eradication Force spent almost all of its time in Helmand.[118]

Matching this eradication effort was a plethora of schemes by aid agencies, the British and other governments, and the United Nations Office of Drugs and Crime, to encourage farmers to move into 'alternative livelihoods'. Vast sums were spent on promoting these livelihoods: according to UN figures, $490 million in 2005–6 alone. However, there was no attempt to develop a common and holistic understanding of the political economy of poppy production, and accordingly international, Afghan and non-governmental efforts were fragmented and strikingly ineffective.[119] One large scheme funded by USAID to divert local wage labour towards improving Helmand's irrigation system fell apart as the province became increasingly dangerous in 2005 and 2006.[120] Other schemes were simply hare-brained, including a project funded by DFID and managed by Mercy Corps to get Helmandis to grow mushrooms. Fifteen women, each with a male chaperone, were sent to Peshawar to be trained in mushroom cultivation. Yet attempts to sell the crop failed miserably: Helmandis had never seen mushrooms before and had no idea what to do with them. Similarly, USAID spent $34.4 million in a failed attempt to promote cultivation of soya beans, which was another crop that Afghans had never heard of.[121]

After a hiatus under Akhundzada and Wafa, poppy eradication restarted with gusto under Daoud, who introduced fairly randomised targeting of poppy fields in central and northern Helmand in 2006. At the same time, the Afghan Eradication Force was operating in southern Helmand, but coordination between the two efforts was poor to non-existent. By mid March, Daoud's own force had eradicated 1,350 hectares of poppy crop.[122] While this was only about 2 per cent of the total poppy crop in Helmand, it was enough to aggravate local communities. As Antonio Giustozzi notes, 'support for the Taliban in the villages was immediately boosted'.[123] Rather than 'incentivise' the pursuit of alternative livelihoods, poppy eradication invariably drove farmers and agricultural labourers into the arms of the Taliban. After watching the Afghan Eradication Force destroy his poppy crop, one local farmer told the American mentors: 'We're poor – we're not with the Taliban or anything. You've made a big mistake. Now we'll grow more against you.'[124] Ironically, local resentment was directed as much towards the British military, even thought they had nothing to do with the government's eradication efforts. According to one group of elders from Nad-e Ali district, 'We thought the British were trying to kill us with hunger – they destroyed our opium, but didn't give us even one afghani [the Afghan currency]. That is why people decided to join the Taliban; they needed someone to defend them.'[125] Thus, what the British dimly saw as growing support for the Taliban in central Helmand was, from the locals' perspective, a popular revolt against the British who threatened the livelihoods of the common people.[126] Either way, the British failed to register the extent to which the people of central Helmand had turned against them. Task Force Helmand was about to get a rude awakening.

7

The Campaign Flounders

What struck Hugh Powell most was the incredible heat, as he stepped off the back ramp of a Chinook helicopter in Lashkar Gah to take up his new post as head of the Helmand Provincial Reconstruction Team in early June 2008. Powell had flown straight from Britain with only a short stopover in Kabul. In the capital the temperature was in the low thirties; it was twenty degrees hotter in Helmand. A rising star in Whitehall, Powell arrived in Helmand with an impressive political pedigree as the son of Charles Powell, Chief of Staff to Prime Minister Margaret Thatcher, and nephew of Jonathan Powell, Chief of Staff to Prime Minister Tony Blair. He had been head of the Security Policy Directorate at the FCO when the Helmand job came up. Powell was driven to apply for the post by a 'combination of curiosity and wanting to test oneself'. Moreover, he had joined government 'to tackle the most pressing issues of the day'.[1] Few foreign policy issues were more pressing for Britain in 2008 than the campaign in Afghanistan, which appeared to be adrift.

A large cross-government team had been assembled in early September 2006 to review the UK's Joint Helmand Plan. Reporting to British ministers six weeks later, the review noted a litany of problems. The PRT was desperately short of civilian staff, and lacked secure means of communication and the ability to move around the province. Moreover, provincial government was dysfunctional, and the insurgency was 'more vigorous and complex than expected' and probably made worse by British operations. The review found that only ten of the eighty-nine three-month targets set in June 2006 had been achieved. Nonetheless, the review concluded that the Joint Helmand Plan 'remains substantially sound'.[2]

David Slinn, who had become head of the PRT in January 2007, took a different view. For him the plan was 'in tatters'. The message from Whitehall was unsympathetic. The PRT were told to 'get delivering', but with only eight civilian staff and no way to get around, it was hard to see what could be done. As one PRT official noted, 'we had no idea what was going on outside the wire'. Adding to the problem was Governor Wafa, who 'did not share our plan' and, in general, was 'contemptuous of the international community'.[3]

In late 2007, as 52 Brigade took over the campaign, the Post-Conflict Reconstruction Unit sent a team to Lashkar Gah to conduct another review of the Joint Helmand Plan. Working together, the PCRU and planners from 52 Brigade produced a wholly new two-year plan called the Helmand Road Map. The new plan added a dose of reality: the emphasis would be on creating 'good enough' government, public services and infrastructure for Helmand. The Joint Helmand Plan had taken a top-down and state-centric approach to capacity building in the province. The Helmand Road Map added a bottom-up dimension, with a focus on stimulating local governance structures, promoting dialogue with local communities, and enabling provincial and district government to connect with the line ministries in Kabul. The Helmand Road Map envisaged political officers and stabilisation advisers being deployed to forward operating bases in Lashkar Gah, Gereshk, Sangin, Musa Qala and Garmsir to work with district authorities to improve the delivery of public services and win the support of local populations.[4] Crucial to this 'consent-winning activity' was consultation with local communities, through representative bodies, to ensure that the distribution of international development aid was seen to be equitable by the various sub-tribal networks (to avoid creating 'winners' and 'losers') and that the public works funded by such aid met local needs.[5] Some big aid projects had proceeded without local consultation and produced farcical results. In one such example, in 2007, the PRT hired local contractors to build a 'Park for Women' on the outskirts of Lashkar Gah at a cost of £420,000. A member of the PCRU team recalls that 'the park was very much on the edges of an active warzone, and once opened within a week there were men with RPGs wandering around the park'. One local woman observed that 'women would not go so far from home' or socialise in public as 'that culture does not exist here'.[6] All the while, many thousands displaced by the conflict in Helmand were living in miserable conditions in the camps surrounding the provincial capital.

By late 2007, Whitehall had finally woken up to the fact that the civil–military effort in Helmand was floundering. Not helping matters was bickering between the PRT and Task Force Helmand. The PRT complained that they were not consulted about military plans and operations, while Task Force Helmand was unhappy about the lack of civilian presence on the ground. Military officers also grumbled about the 'six-day week' and frequent rest and recuperation home breaks taken by civilians. The Whitehall response, hammered out by Adam Thomson as Director for South Asia and Afghanistan at the FCO, General Peter Wall as Deputy Chief of the Defence Staff (Commitments), and Cowper-Coles was twofold. First, there would be, in effect, a civilian surge in Helmand. Thus, in the brief period from February to June 2008 when Michael Ryder, former deputy UK ambassador to Afghanistan, temporarily stepped in as head of the PRT, its staff shot up from thirty to sixty. Second, a senior civil servant would be appointed to take overall charge of the Helmand campaign, to manage the uplift in civilian effort and drive forward greater civil–military integration. Equivalent to a major general, this civilian would outrank the brigadier in command of Task Force Helmand. That new senior civilian lead was Hugh Powell. Small wonder that when he arrived in Helmand in June 2008, Powell felt 'the burden of expectation'.[7]

INTO THE SNAKE'S HEAD

In March 2008, the Paras returned to Helmand. The new commander of 16 Air Assault Brigade, Brigadier Mark Carleton-Smith, was determined that the brigade would conduct a very different counter-insurgency campaign from the enemy-focused approach it had taken in 2006. In preparing his brigade for deployment, he made clear that 'the people were the prize'. He emphasised that the main task was 'to improve the sense of security for the people – not just physical security but their human security in the round. It's all about effective governance, rule of law and the provision of basic necessities of life.'[8] Carleton-Smith later recalled that 'I wanted to dispel any danger that

16 Brigade might have confused the intensity of the fighting on
Herrick 4 with the nature of the campaign we were seeking to prosecute'. Carleton-Smith was clear that the goal was 'to undermine
[Taliban] strategy, rather than merely fight their forces'. Since the
Taliban's strategy 'seemed to be one of influence, intimidation and
the provision of parallel shadow government', he determined that
16 Brigade's campaign would seek 'to marginalise their influence in
the centres of population by improving relations between the fledging
Afghan government and the people'.[9] In short, there would be far
less fighting. The commander of 3 Para, Lieutenant Colonel Huw
Williams, remembers Carleton-Smith telling his troops that they
'should consider sometimes withdrawing from a battle which we
could win but which would have no strategic effect'.[10] This way of
thinking did not come naturally to the Paras.

With the British civilian surge in Helmand and the arrival of Powell,
it was a good time for the commander of Task Force Helmand to get
serious about supporting the political engagement and reconstruction
effort in Helmand. It helped that Carleton-Smith and Powell were
both Old Etonians, and in this sense spoke the same language. To
support closer civil–military integration in Helmand, Carleton-Smith
moved his brigade planning cell from his task force headquarters into
the heart of the PRT, reasoning that given the political focus of the
campaign, 'the best ideas would come from the PRT whilst the military
[would] bring planning discipline'.[11] Task Force Helmand and the PRT
occupied two different buildings in the British main operating base in
Lashkar Gah: while only a couple of minutes' walk from one another,
each building was access-controlled and had manifestly different
working cultures which discouraged the two-way traffic of people
and ideas. It was hoped that this would be addressed by moving military planners into the PRT. For his part, Powell recognised that the
PRT needed to lift its game considerably, 'to go on headquarter
settings'. At the same time, he defended the civilian pace of the PRT,
given the far longer periods served by civilians – between eight and
eighteen months as against six months for British troops. Civilians
would simply burn out if they worked the seven-day weeks and
fourteen-plus-hour days of the military. The PRT also worked at a
slower pace in order to synchronise with Afghan partners, something
that the military were not always sensitive to. When Powell explained

this to one senior US Marine officer he was told, 'Sir, the US Marine Corps will not be held up by the Afghans.'[12]

It so happened that in terms of Afghan partners, the situation looked encouraging. Under pressure from the British, Karzai once again replaced the governor of Helmand, this time finally appointing somebody capable of doing a decent job. In a supremely ironic move, Wafa was appointed to the presidential palace as a sort of ombudsman in charge of dealing with public complaints about corrupt and shoddy administration. As his replacement, Karzai appointed Gulab Mangal, a technocrat who had started out as a Soviet-trained political commissar in the Afghan army under the Communist regime. He had previously been governor of Paktika province from 2004 to 2006 and Laghman province from 2006 to 2008, in eastern Afghanistan. Offering the diplomat's perspective, Cowper-Coles suggests that Mangal's 'greatest quality was that he always gave the impression of being serenely competent ... He calmed worried visitors, whom Wafa had merely alarmed.'[13]

Carleton-Smith's espoused campaign approach, emphasising the importance of securing the people and avoiding unnecessary combat, was similar to Mackay's. However, it is not clear that he drew inspiration from or even sought to build on 52 Brigade's campaign. In preparing for command of Task Force Helmand, he did not consult with Mackay. Rather Carleton-Smith recalls that he dusted off old lecture notes and essays written on counter-insurgency from when he was at staff college in the early 1990s, as well as reading FM 3–24.[14] Carleton-Smith's background was also very dissimilar to Mackay's. For a start, at forty-two, he was the youngest brigadier in the British Army. Typical of commanders of 16 Air Assault Brigade, he also had extensive prior experience in British special forces, including command of 22 SAS Regiment. When it was decided that Britain would deploy to Helmand, PJHQ tasked 22 SAS Regiment to conduct a recce of the province from April to May 2005. Carleton-Smith personally led this review. He found a province largely at peace thanks to the brutal rule of Sher Mohammed Akhundzada and a booming opium-fuelled economy that benefitted the pro-government warlords, drug barons and the Taliban alike. Reporting back to the Ministry of Defence in June, Carleton-Smith warned against removing Akhundzada and against the deployment of a large British force which would likely cause conflict where none currently existed.[15] This advice was ignored.

Returning in 2008, Carleton-Smith felt that 16 Brigade was confronting 'a coalition of the angry': this was an insurgency made up in large part of 'the disenfranchised and disillusioned' and not, as commonly claimed, ten-dollar-a-day Taliban who would be less motivated to fight. Hence, his instinct was to avoid unnecessary fighting. 16 Brigade's operational design included some familiar themes, such as the importance of security forces being present in population centres, and the need to improve ISAF support to Afghan forces. The core concept was 'to go deep not broad', and to focus on existing district centres held by the Afghan government, rather than trying to capture new ground. This concept accorded with the instruction Carleton-Smith received from the Chief of Joint Operations, General Nick Houghton, which was 'don't spread yourself too thinly'. PJHQ were understandably concerned that with each brigade tour 'we were responsible for more of Helmand'.[16]

16 Brigade deployed with more troops and resources than any previous brigade; in all, Carleton-Smith commanded six battalions. Nonetheless, and notwithstanding Houghton's injunction, the brigade was spread pretty thinly across four areas and nineteen bases: 2 Para were assigned Battlegroup North, 5th Battalion the Royal Regiment of Scotland (5 Scots) were designated Battlegroup North-West, 2nd Battalion the Royal Regiment of Scotland (2 Scots) became Battlegroup South, and Battlegroup Centre was held by the Danish battalion. 5 Scots were so dispersed that there was a distance of nearly a hundred miles between the battalion's southernmost and northernmost companies, and they had to be reinforced with a company from 4th Battalion the Royal Regiment of Scotland. Also deploying with 16 Brigade was 1st Battalion the Royal Irish Regiment, who were given responsibility for guarding Kajaki Dam and for mentoring the Afghan army's 3/205 Brigade. The Royal Irish had to provide teams to support the Danish battalion as well. To fill all these requirements, the Royal Irish ended up mobilising 116 reservists, more than any other British Army battalion on Operation Herrick. Finally, 3 Para acted as the Regional Battlegroup. Formally under Regional Command South, 3 Para had prepared for deployment along with the rest of 16 Brigade and spent most of its time in southern Afghanistan supporting Task Force Helmand.[17]

Right from the beginning, 16 Brigade was pulled off its plan. ISAF had long realised that southern Garmsir was one of the major entry points for insurgents coming in from Pakistan; Taliban recruits crossing over from Balochistan would practise their combat skills by attacking the British company besieged at FOB Delhi in Garmsir district centre, before continuing on to their assigned districts in Helmand. In March 2008, just as 16 Brigade was taking over from 52 Brigade, General McNeill decided it was time to close this Taliban 'gateway' into southern Afghanistan. US Central Command agreed and committed the 24th Marine Expeditionary Unit (24 MEU), the theatre reserve for the Middle East and South Asia, to the task. 24 MEU consisted of a reinforced 1,200-strong US Marine infantry battalion – the 1st Battalion, 6th Marine Regiment (the 1/6) – which in classic US Marine fashion deployed with its own artillery and dedicated air power. In fact, much to the envy of the Paras, 24 MEU arrived with as many fighter-bombers, helicopter gunships and transport helicopters as the entire 16 Air Assault Brigade. McNeill directed 24 MEU to re-establish FOB Rhino in southern Garmsir, which was the old Saudi airstrip occupied by the US Marines in late 2001, to provide a staging post for interdicting Taliban supply lines from the Pakistani border. In order to do this, 24 MEU would also need to clear the Taliban from their strongholds in the villages of Hazar Joft, Amir Agha and Darveshan, just south of Garmsir district centre. The marines took to calling this area 'the Snake's Head' as this was what it resembled on a map. Before 2006, this had been one of the most fertile and heavily populated areas of Helmand. However, most civilians had since abandoned their homes, fields were no longer intensively farmed, and the majority of shops in the bazaars had closed down. Civilian life had been made impossible by the fighting.

Ryder, the head of the PRT, was none too pleased with this plan and fired off an email saying as much to the FCO in London. He feared that the US Marines would go into Garmsir in 'shock and awe mode', leave a path of destruction in their wake, and that the under-manned British task force would be left to pick up the pieces. This was a fair concern given the reputation of the US Marine Corps, and the simple fact that 24 MEU was only on loan to ISAF. Carleton-Smith should have been equally concerned, given that the proposed MEU offensive ran contrary to his own campaign plan to 'go deep not broad'. However, he sided with McNeill. The debate in Whitehall went on for weeks while 24 MEU sat impatiently in Kandahar airfield.

Having seen the US Marines in action in Iraq, especially in Fallujah where they all but demolished the city in late 2004 in order to clear it of insurgents, some in the British Army also worried that 24 MEU might make matters worse with their overly aggressive tactics. As one British officer put it, it was rather like inviting relations 'from the wrong side of the tracks' to one's party.[18]

In April, McNeill visited Lashkar Gah to try and break the logjam. In a meeting also attended by Carleton-Smith and Ryder, Mangal made it clear to McNeill that clearing the Taliban from Garmsir was a top priority. He told the ISAF commander that 'without control of the south, and the border with Pakistan, we will never establish enduring stability in Helmand'. With McNeill, Mangal was pushing at an open door. By the end of April, with debate still rumbling in Whitehall, McNeill's patience had run out. He ordered the commander of 24 MEU, Colonel Peter Petronzio, to proceed with Operation Azada Wosa, adding that he wanted the marines 'to stir it up in Garmsir … and get some defeating done'.[19]

Each side underestimated the other. As Carter Malkasian notes, 'Years of fighting a lone outnumbered British company had left [the insurgents] over confident.' Little did the Taliban know that they were about to be hit by a battle-hardened US Marine infantry battalion: the 1/6 had been involved in heavy fighting in the Iraqi city of Ramadi in 2006 and 2007. Most of those who saw combat in Iraq where still in the battalion when it deployed to Afghanistan.[20] A Taliban cadre later told Malkasian: 'Our leaders ordered us not to retreat … We thought that we must fight. We did not realize how strong the Americans would be.' For their part, the US Marines expected Taliban defences to crumble. According to the battalion intelligence officer, Major Carl McCleod, 'we were told that the insurgents would fight for a few days and then they would scatter, but that's not what happened'.[21] Because the Taliban stood their ground, 24 MEU faced at least six hundred fighters when they pushed into the Snake's Head. One Taliban commander later confirmed that among these 'were lots of foreign fighters not only from Pakistan, there were also Arab, Uzbek and Chechens' who were 'very experienced' and 'very good fighters'.[22]

The Taliban defences comprised an interlocking series of trenches, reinforced bunkers and hidden fighting positions some five hundred yards from the district centre, with strongholds at the villages of Amir

Agha and Jugroom Fort further south in the Snake's Head. Thankfully, the insurgents in Garmsir made little use of IEDs in early 2008, relying instead on RPGs, mortars and machine guns. The Taliban expected the marines to sweep southwards out of the district centre. Instead, 24 MEU began their offensive with a flanking attack from the east, taking the insurgents off guard and establishing patrol bases in Hazar Joft. For much of May the marines battled Taliban fighters as they pushed into Hazar Joft and down to Darveshan. They engaged in 170 firefights with groups of insurgents, ten to twenty strong. Taliban fighting groups constantly tried to outflank marine units. US Marine helicopters faced volleys of RPGs and intense machine-gun fire as they tried to provide support to marine infantry. 24 MEU gave as good as it got. All day long insurgent positions were pounded by marine artillery and from the air. In one attack by a group of ten Taliban, marines responded with sixty mortar rounds and twenty 155mm artillery rounds. As the marines gradually fought their way south through the Snake's Head, the Taliban reinforced their defences around Amir Agha. 24 MEU spent the latter half of May battling and defeating the hundred-strong insurgent force there. It was tough going, especially as Taliban fortifications were able to withstand direct hits from artillery and air strikes. Eventually by 25 May, the marines had cleared all Taliban from Amir Agha and the way was open to take on Jugroom Fort.[23]

Up to this point, Operation Azada Wosa had been almost entirely a US Marine affair. At the start, the company from 5 Scots based at FOB Delhi provided assistance by securing the left flank of 24 MEU and enabled 'forward passage of lines' (whereby one friendly force moves through ground held by another). Thereafter, the US marines did all the fighting until it came to the final assault on Jugroom Fort, where some forty Taliban were well entrenched. It was a formidable objective – a previous attempt by the Royal Marines to attack Jugroom Fort in 2007 had ended in disaster. A US Marine company and the 5 Scots fought their way down from the district centre through remaining Taliban defences along a four-mile route between the Helmand River and the main canal. The British were amazed at the boldness of US Marine forces as they accelerated along the roads in armoured vehicles. British units would routinely stop to search likely vulnerable points such as bridges for IEDs. The marines didn't bother, not wanting to slow down. As one British corporal observed, 'they're just driving along and crossing their fingers they won't get blown up'.[24] When they arrived at Jugroom Fort a fifty-strong marine platoon was given the task of blasting their way into the fort complex and clearing it room by room.

The Taliban suffered a terrible defeat. Based on multiple interviews with Taliban participants, Malkasian concludes that the loss of the Snake's Head 'broke the Taliban' in Garmsir. One senior Taliban commander told Malkasian that 'the Taliban did not fear the British. They never held anything. The Taliban feared the Marines. The Marines came and stayed and hunted them down.' The Taliban provincial governor, Mullah Naim, ordered a general retreat from Garmsir, and a fleet of cars was dispatched from Pakistan to collect the Taliban district governor, Mullah Obaid Rahman, and other senior commanders. The US Marines reckoned that they had killed around five hundred insurgents against the loss of one of their own. ISAF estimates of enemy dead are often on the high side. However, marine snipers alone, who do accurately record kills, accounted for over eighty Taliban dead. As Malkasian notes, even this lower number makes 'Naim's stand against the 24 Marine Expeditionary Unit the worse defeat suffered by any force in the recorded history of [Garmsir] district'.[25]

In private, Foreign Office officials complained about the US Marine capture of Garmsir, which rather inconveniently highlighted the shortage of British troops in Helmand. This churlish view was robustly challenged by Cowper-Coles, who told civil servants in London that they should be 'rejoicing' at a great victory.[26] In public, Garmsir was quickly claimed as a British success.[27] A string of high-profile British VIPs – including the Foreign Secretary, the Development Secretary and the Chief of the Defence Staff – flocked to Garmsir, as Cowper-Coles puts it, 'rather like Churchill following British forces into Normandy and across the Rhine'.[28] In the end, CENTCOM agreed to let 24 MEU stay in Garmsir until September 2008, when they were replaced by B Squadron of the Queen's Dragoon Guards under the incoming 3 Commando Brigade, as well as by a 200-strong Afghan army battalion and two Afghan border police battalions of 150 men each. A ring of British and Afghan patrol bases was thrown around the Snake's Head, and behind these defences life returned to normal for over 50,000 Afghans.[29]

THE DAMN TURBINE

The centrepiece of 16 Brigade's tour was Operation Oqab Tsuka (Pashto for 'Eagle's Summit', named after the eagle on the 16 Brigade shoulder patch). This was a massive operation, involving most of the brigade, to transport a third turbine to Kajaki Dam – rather confusingly called Turbine Two because it was due to occupy a vacant space between Turbines One and Three. This was part of a USAID project to refurbish the dam that was started in 2002, costing $128 million. With repairs to the dam and the installation of an additional turbine, electricity output would increase from 3 to 150 watts and provide enough power for 1.7 million homes in southern Afghanistan.[30] However, here too there was a contradiction with 16 Brigade's campaign plan, which according to the brigade planning staff was closely aligned with the Helmand Road Map and therefore was supposed to ensure reconstruction activities responded to local priorities. The Turbine Two project was of great symbolic importance to the US State Department but from the British perspective it was 'pointless'. As one senior British official noted, 'There was no discernable benefit for Helmand.' It would take at least eighteen months to install Turbine Two, most of the additional power was actually for Kandahar, and even this longer-term benefit was dependent on securing the power transmission lines from Kajaki to Kandahar, which British officials considered to be a 'real challenge'.[31] For these reasons, Cowper-Coles and Powell were both strongly opposed to the operation, as it would significantly distract Task Force Helmand from other duties essential to delivering the Helmand Road Map.

Once again, Carleton-Smith sided with the American view. He never received a formal order from ISAF headquarters to execute the mission. However, he was under intense pressure from the new ISAF commander, General David McKiernan, and from US Ambassador Bill Wood to get on with it. 16 Brigade had already been shown up by 24 MEU, and more US Marines were on their way to Helmand. Carleton-Smith told 2 Para, who had been given the task of preparing the ground for the turbine to be transported from Sangin to Kajaki: 'Right. Gentlemen … The Americans are coming! We risk being put in a corner, sidelined and forgotten. The Americans think we're wet and present only problems.'[32] Carleton-Smith assumed that the Turbine

Two project 'was driven by DC politics' and that 'USAID was trying to demonstrate progress'. However, he didn't question McKiernan's 'overarching strategic intent'. As he saw it, 'my job was to find solutions'.[33]

It was not going to be easy. The turbine components, weighing two hundred tonnes in total, would need to be transported in seven heavy equipment transporters; these were designed to move Challenger main battle tanks on smooth German motorways. By the time escorts were added, the convoy would number around a hundred vehicles. Given the great weight the seven transporters had to carry and that they were not designed for uneven road surfaces, the whole convoy would end up crawling along at around two miles per hour. The turbine components, manufactured in China, arrived at Kandahar airfield on a gigantic Antonov AN-224 transport plane. The convoy was due to leave the airfield on 27 August, travel west along Highway 1 and at Gereshk turn onto Route 611, which ran north up to Kajaki. This is where things would get tricky. Route 611 got increasingly more dangerous, especially in the Upper Sangin Valley where it was lined with pro-Taliban villages and consequently was one of the most mined roads in Afghanistan. British planners estimated that as the convoy crawled along, it would take an additional seventy-five hours to clear the route ahead of IEDs. In other words, the Taliban would have ample time to mass forces for multiple ambushes of the slow-moving convoy. The British attempted to buy off tribal elders along the route, so as to get locals to suspend their support for the Taliban while the turbine passed through their villages. But the elders feared Taliban retribution and refused British bribes. 16 Brigade planners ran a computer simulation in early July which predicted that over fifty British troops would be killed if the turbine was taken up Route 611. In brigade headquarters they began to call the mission 'Operation Certain Death'.[34]

The Pathfinders Platoon, along with a detachment of Afghan special forces, were sent east of Route 611 to reconnoitre for insurgent threats and also to investigate any possible alternative convoy routes. After a week of going from village to village, speaking with locals, they struck gold. The Pathfinders discovered a well-used track north-west of Ghorak district. When they questioned drivers, the Pathfinders discovered that this back road was used by locals travelling between

Gereshk and Kajaki seeking to avoid the hazards of travelling on Route 611. A recce troop from the Royal Engineers was sent to check out the dirt road and they confirmed that it was suitable for heavy traffic. Dubbed 'Route Harriet' by brigade planning staff, Turbine Two would travel up this back road to Kajaki.[35]

Lieutenant Colonel Rufus McNeil, commanding officer of 13 Air Assault Support Regiment, was placed in charge of the convoy, which set out from Kandahar airfield on schedule on 27 August. McNeil later recalled that 'Early signs were not good. Within one mile of leaving tarmac roads we broke our first trailer and found our first mine. This very much set the tone.'[36] Meanwhile, Task Force Helmand launched a number of deception operations along Route 611 to keep the Taliban occupied, which included sending out a dummy convoy of twenty trucks from Gereshk escorted by the Danish battlegroup. Overall, Operation Oqab Tsuka involved some 4,000 British, American, Canadian, Danish and Afghan troops. A formidable security screen was thrown around the slow-moving convoy, with Pathfinders in their fast-moving Jackals protecting the flanks, WMIKs and Mastiffs providing close protection, and Canadian armoured vehicles guarding the front and rear. Vectors carrying IED disposal teams and armoured diggers cleared the route ahead. The convoy proceeded in four parcels in order to stop vehicles bunching up and causing a traffic jam. Setting off twenty-four hours ahead was a squadron from the Queen's Royal Lancers in Vikings, sent to secure Ghorak Pass, which was the main choke point along Route Harriet. Flying overhead were surveillance planes, drones and helicopter gunships. British special forces patrolled the mountains along the route. A SEAL team from the US Navy reserve, Task Force 71, was also assigned to support the operation. This was not wholly welcomed by the British, who worried that these trigger-happy reservists would compromise the mission; they were therefore assigned over-watch duties in mountains as far away as possible from the convoy.[37]

The British had gone to great lengths to keep secret the actual route being taken by the convoy. But it was hard to miss. The convoy stretched for six miles and created a massive dust cloud as it trundled along the barren Kandahar plain. Electronic intercepts of Taliban communications suggested that some insurgents were lying in wait ahead, but lacking any cover from the helicopters, they were scared to attack. Thus the journey up Route Harriet was uneventful. However, the convoy would need to join Route 611 for the final 4.5 miles, and pass through two pro-Taliban villages, Kajaki Sofla and Kajaki Olya, in order to reach the dam. Intelligence estimated there were around two hundred insurgents in Kajaki district and drones showed the Taliban reinforcing their fighting positions around two complexes of trenches, bunkers and compounds called 'Big Top' and 'Sentry Compound'.

Talks were undertaken with village elders in an attempt to avoid a confrontation. They were offered $25,000 to ensure peaceful passage for the convoy, which it was explained would bring more electricity to Helmand. But the local Taliban were suspicious that the British were actually bringing in a 'super-gun' and refused to allow the deal to go through. In anticipation of a fight, the Regional Battlegroup (3 Para) had been flown to FOB Zeebrugge in Kajaki, along with an Afghan army *kandak* and their Royal Irish mentors. Local civilians were advised to stay out of the way.

On 26 August, the Paras began their assault. Taliban defences were pounded by mortar and artillery rounds and air bombardment. As British and Afghan infantry cleared Big Top and Sentry Compound two days later they discovered well-constructed bunkers, which explained how the Taliban had been able to withstand ISAF artillery and air power for so long. The Paras reckoned that about a hundred insurgents had been killed or injured. However, in the meantime the convoy got stuck at the end of Route Harriet. It turned out that the road did not actually join Route 611; instead it simply ended by a deep wadi, beyond which was a goat track leading up a hill. Fearing that the Taliban were massing for a counter-attack, the Royal Engineers worked through the night to build a road over the hill to connect Route Harriet and Route 611. In the early hours of 2 September, after a five-day journey, the convoy finally arrived at the dam.[38]

Operation Oqab Tsuka was hailed as a 'triumph' by the British press.[39] Lieutenant Colonel McNeil told reporters that 'if you want a mark in the sand for Afghan reconstruction, then this is it'.[40] But the story does not end well. Two months later, the Chinese team that were supposed to assemble Turbine Two fled Kajaki, claiming that they were at risk of being kidnapped by the Taliban, despite being guarded by 150 private security contractors and a British infantry company. In October 2009, USAID formally suspended the Turbine Two project. Two years later the White House directed USAID to complete the installation at an anticipated cost of $75 million. Still, Turbine Two was never installed, principally because Route 611 was too insecure to transport the three hundred tonnes of cement and six hundred tonnes of aggregate that were required for the installation.[41] In September 2015, the Taliban overran Kajaki district and all work on Turbine Two had to be abandoned.[42]

16 Brigade had spent months planning and preparing for Operation Oqab Tsuka and units from across Task Force Helmand were re-tasked to support it. Thus, as one PRT official later noted, 'Kajaki was a huge distraction for our work in Gereshk,' which successive brigades had identified as the key ground in Helmand.[43] To his credit, on looking back, Carleton-Smith recognised that while 16 Brigade had pulled off 'an impressive tactical operation', it was an 'underwhelming strategic operation'. He also recalled being 'left bemused by the lack of interest by [the ISAF commander] in the operation'. Having pushed 16 Brigade to undertake the task, McKiernan 'never asked how it went'.[44] Washington was no more appreciative. Ignorant of the tactical challenges involved, US National Security Council officials could not understand why the British were making 'such a big deal' of the turbine move. They also 'didn't understand why it took so long'. One US official compared it to watching the Space Shuttle as it inched its way out of the Kennedy Space Center.[45]

At the end of his tour Carleton-Smith was more realistic as to what could be achieved. Going into Helmand, he had declared that British forces had reached a 'tipping point' against a weakened and demoralised insurgency.[46] On leaving Helmand, he struck a very different note, telling reporters in October 2008: 'We're not going to win this war.' Instead, he said, the purpose of the British campaign must be to reduce the conflict to 'a manageable level of insurgency that's not a strategic threat and can be managed by the Afghan army'. He further suggested that 'If the Taliban were prepared to sit on the other side of the table and talk about a political settlement, then that's precisely the sort of progress that concludes insurgencies like this'.[47] On both points, he was entirely correct. He was also echoing a growing view within the British government, still only privately expressed, that the war was unwinnable, and that it might be time to start considering tentative talks with the Taliban. However, in the United States, political support for the war had yet to wane. Indeed, quite the opposite was the case. A new president would shortly be elected with the mandate to refocus US military effort on what he declared to be the central front in the Global War on Terror – Afghanistan. Besides, the Taliban weren't ready to talk either.

BACK FROM THE BRINK

In late September 2008, 3 Commando Brigade deployed to take over from 16 Brigade as Task Force Helmand. Much like the Paras, the Royal Marines expected to be engaged in less fighting than last time they were in Helmand. The brigade's study day in May, to intellectually prepare officers for deployment, focused on how to 'de-escalate the conflict' and how to 'balance the risk to civilians and risk to the mission'. The purpose of the study day was to develop a consensus across all company and platoon commanders on this issue. Similarly, pre-deployment training focused heavily on rules of engagement and on 'judgemental training' regarding when and how to use force. This was a major priority for the brigade commander, Brigadier Buster Howes, who was concerned about the tactical aggression of British troops. As one senior brigade officer noted, 'when push came to shove, we felt that the knee-jerk reaction was to go kinetic'.[48] Following the final mission rehearsal exercise for 3 Brigade in July, Howes drafted his operational order which emphasised that troops were not to use force 'unless absolutely necessary'. He further decided not to restate the ISAF commander's tactical directive on restraint in the use of force, as might be expected, because 'it didn't take it far enough'.[49]

For the previous two years the level of insurgent activity had been seasonal, spiking in the summer months once the opium crop had been harvested, and declining over the winter months when the weather made life difficult for insurgents and soldiers alike. Thus, even though 16 Brigade had ended up fighting more than expected on their second outing in Helmand, it was not unreasonable for 3 Brigade to hope for a 'less kinetic' tour. Unfortunately, insurgent behaviour did not conform to Royal Marine expectations; as always, 'the enemy gets a vote'. Within a couple of days of 3 Brigade taking charge, the Taliban launched a major assault against Lashkar Gah, their most audacious of the conflict. The Royal Marines spent the next six months battling the insurgents. By the end of their tour, 3 Brigade had suffered forty-two dead, the highest losses of any British brigade up to then.

Howes never made it to Helmand. He fractured his pelvis in a waterskiing accident while on holiday just a month before deployment. Brigadier Gordon Messenger was appointed in mid September to replace him. As co-author of the original Joint Helmand Plan in late 2005, Messenger would agree with the emphasis in brigade planning and preparations on military restraint, and on providing support to the governance and development lines of operation. Indeed, in reflecting on the lessons of his tour, Messenger would note that the 'spread of governance, allied to the development of capacity at the District level, must be viewed as the principal purpose of our security effort'.[50]

Central Helmand was not exactly a blind spot for 3 Brigade but it was not a priority either. The brigade had been given some 'non-negotiable tasks' under Operation Tolo, a countrywide operation by ISAF Command, to direct military resources towards the deepening of Afghan government, which included supporting voter registration and poppy eradication in central Helmand.[51] However, in late 2008 British military and civilian effort was focused on Gereshk, Sangin and Musa Qala in northern Helmand and on Garmsir in southern Helmand, and this was reflected in the force laydown for 3 Brigade. 45 Commando replaced 2 Para as Battlegroup North, with responsibility for Sangin, the Upper Sangin Valley and protecting Kajaki Dam. 2nd Battalion the Royal Gurkha Rifles replaced the 5 Scots as Battlegroup North-West, with responsibility for Now Zad and Musa Qala. The Danes still manned Battlegroup Centre, with responsibility for Gereshk. Battlegroup South, newly formed to take over from 24 MEU in Garmsir, was assigned to 1st Queen's Dragoon Guards. 1st Battalion the Rifles took over from the Royal Irish in the OMLT role. Finally, 42 Commando deployed as the Regional Battlegroup, tasked by Regional Command South to support ISAF operations right across southern Afghanistan; much like 3 Para, they spent most of their time in Helmand.[52]

As in previous tours, British forces were desperately stretched and so battalions were dispersed over a large area, with some broken up altogether. Thus, only one company from the Gurkha Rifles was in

Musa Qala, and so Battlegroup North-West was augmented by a
Warrior armoured infantry company from 1st Battalion the Princess
of Wales Royal Regiment, and a Mastiff squadron from the Queen's
Dragoon Guards. Of the remaining three Gurkha infantry companies,
one was assigned to mentoring the Afghan police in Lashkar Gah,
another to Battlegroup South, and the third was broken up into
platoons and given a variety of tasks. No battalion was assigned to
south central Helmand. Instead, an ad hoc force protection group
with responsibility for Lashkar Gah and Kabul was formed from the
remaining troops: a company from the Regional Battlegroup, a platoon
from 1 Rifles, and a team from 2nd Battalion the Prince of Wales
Royal Regiment.[53] In short, the British had very few troops guarding
Lashkar Gah.

As one brigade staff officer recalls, 10 October started as a
'completely normal day'. The formal transfer of authority for Task
Force Helmand from 16 Brigade to 3 Brigade had occurred just two
days before. The final campaign plan had just been submitted to
Messenger for approval, and the brigade staff were preoccupied with
the problem of how to resupply a small team from 21 SAS Squadron,
who were mentoring the Afghan police in Nad-e Ali. Shortly before
6 p.m. that evening, the brigade was warned by the National
Directorate of Security that two massive groups of Taliban, together
numbering up to a thousand fighters, were converging on Lashkar
Gah. Intercepts of insurgent radio chatter suggested that they intended
to overrun the governor's compound before moving on to the provincial jail in order to release Taliban prisoners. The brigade intelligence
cell had to quickly determine how seriously to take this threat; as
one officer noted, given 'Afghan maths' one usually had to 'divide by
ten' when it came to estimates of enemy forces. A British Watchkeeper
drone and a pair of Apache gunships were scrambled to investigate.
A ninety-strong column of insurgents was identified approaching from
the south. Full-motion video beamed back to the Joint Operations
Centre in Task Force Helmand headquarters showed that they had
heavy machine guns and RPGs and were 'moving in disciplined
fashion'. Shortly before 7 p.m., the Taliban fired a number of 107mm
rockets into the centre of Lashkar Gah and the PRT compound, and
3 Brigade received reports that Governor Mangal's compound was
taking mortar fire.[54]

The attack on Lashkar Gah should not have come as a shock to 3 Brigade. From May 2008 onwards, 16 Brigade had received multiple reports from the Afghan police about increasing Taliban infiltration of Nad-e Ali and Marjah, respectively just west and south-west of Lashkar Gah. When 21 SAS were sent to assist the Afghan police in Marjah, British special forces arrived just in time to see the police hurriedly flee the area, abandoning their own injured as they drove off. However, Afghan reporting of the threat was generally dismissed. It is likely that the British saw the hand of the former provincial chief of police, Abdul Rahman Jan, behind these reports and figured that they were intended to discredit Mangal, as the new provincial governor.[55] Thus, a British intelligence report on Nad-e Ali and Marjah from 19 August concluded that 'there are spurious reports of gathering enemy forces in these areas to attack Lashkar Gah'.[56] 16 Brigade did warn 3 Brigade that 'the security situation in Marjah and Nad-e Ali was deteriorating',[57] but clearly, the scale of the threat was grossly underappreciated as reflected by force laydown of 3 Brigade. It was also reflected in the distribution of surveillance and intelligence assets, which were concentrated on the Upper Sangin Valley and Garmsir. As one brigade officer noted, central Helmand was an 'information black hole'. Hence the Royal Marines were caught off guard.[58]

It later transpired that the Taliban had launched a three-pronged assault on Lashkar Gah involving up to four hundred insurgents. A large group of fighters was seen heading towards the Bolan Bridge, the main crossing over the Helmand River from Nad-e Ali into Lashkar Gah, and situated right next to the prison. 3 Brigade was desperately short of troops to defend the provincial capital. Messenger later confirmed that 'the number of troops I was able to put beyond the wire totaled the grand sum of twelve'.[59] These were immediately dispatched in three Snatch Land Rovers to Mangal's compound north of Bolan Bridge. The brigade headquarters staff put down their pens and picked up their rifles to man the defences of the PRT compound. The Taliban never made it as far as the PRT. Three passes by an Apache gunship wiped out one large column of insurgents. As the Afghan police scrambled to defend their posts, more Apaches arrived overhead, as did American Predator drones and a B-1B bomber. Some small groups of Taliban tried to infiltrate Lashkar Gah. Those that were spotted by drones did not get far; fifteen insurgents were killed by an Apache as they attempted to approach from the east. Shortly after 1.30 a.m., Afghan police defending the Bolan Bridge were attacked by around 150 Taliban approaching from two directions. Thirty minutes later Task Force Helmand headquarters received reports that the attack had been repulsed and that the insurgents were in retreat. Around the same time, an Apache gunship spotted another group of 150 Taliban, this time attacking the Afghan police checkpoint guarding the eastern approach to Lashkar Gah, on the main road from Kandahar. The insurgents sought cover as the gunship opened fire with its 30mm chain gun, but there was nowhere to hide from the Apache's night vision. By 4 a.m., the Taliban had realised that their assault had failed. Through intercepts of enemy communications, the British were able to overhear insurgent commanders ordering their forces to retreat.[60]

This was yet another catastrophic defeat for the Taliban. Working from video feeds from drones and gunships, and human intelligence from the National Directorate of Security, 3 Brigade estimated that around seventy-five insurgents had been killed and the same number wounded.[61] ISAF air power could have continued to attack the retreating Taliban. However, Messenger conferred with his senior staff and weighing 'the legality, morality and utility of continuing the killing' decided to let the insurgents flee. British and American drones followed Taliban vehicles as they drove to Babaji, Nad-e Ali and Marjah, dropping off insurgents at their family compounds along the way. This enabled 3 Brigade to build an excellent intelligence picture of Taliban disposition in central Helmand.[62]

In the aftermath of the attack, troops were rushed to reinforce Lashkar Gah. A company from the Regional Battlegroup (42 Commando) was flown in from Kandahar airfield on 12 October. In the days that followed, Kabul sent one thousand extra Afghan troops by redeploying 5th Brigade, 302 Corps to Lashkar Gah. The spectre of Iraq hung over the discussion about what to do next. One option was to move Task Force Helmand headquarters to the more secure location of Camp Bastion. However, it was felt this would be akin to the British withdrawal from Basra Palace in September 2007, a strategically disastrous move in retrospect which surrendered Basra city to the Shia insurgents of the Mahdi Army. This, in turn, led to Operation Saulat al-Fursan (Arabic for 'Charge of the Knights') in March 2008, when the frustrated Iraqi prime minister, Nouri al-Maliki, ordered the Iraqi Army to retake control of Basra city from the Mahdi Army; a tactically successful operation for the Iraqi Army, it was nonetheless deeply embarrassing for the British military. The Afghan reinforcements rushed to Lashkar Gah suggested how a similar situation could easily unfold in Helmand. One Royal Marine staff officer recalled how in Task Force Helmand headquarters, 'Everyone was thinking "Charge of the Knights".'[63]

Messenger's campaign plan, which had only just been finalised, was 'stuck in a bin', and his headquarters set about producing a wholly new plan focused 'on retaking central Helmand'. Accordingly, the centrepiece of 3 Brigade's tour was Operation Sond Chara, a major offensive to 'secure' Nad-e Ali. (The Royal Marines understood Sond Chara to be Pashto for 'Red Dagger', after the insignia on the Royal Marine Commando badge; the correct translation is actually *Sura* Chara.) Nad-e Ali is a heavily irrigated district, thanks to the work of the US-funded Helmand and Arghandab Valley Authority, which created a network of canals and waterways in central Helmand in the 1950s and 60s. The district is bounded by four major waterways: the Helmand River to the east, the Nahr-e Bughra Canal to the west, the Shamalan Canal to the north, and the Trikh Zabur Canal to the south. Operation Sond Chara focused on the area, roughly 120 square miles, framed by these major waterways. The district is heavily criss-crossed with smaller canals of varying width and depth, making it very difficult for vehicles and infantry to traverse. Not surprisingly, given the land is so well irrigated, Nad-e Ali is a heavily populated district, with some 30,000 people and a patchwork of around fifty tribal groups. It contains three walled villages, or *kalays* – Khushhal Kalay and Shin Kalay in the west and Zarghun Kalay in the north-east – as well as a large number of non-walled villages, including Baluchan, Chah-e Mirza and Chah-e Anjir in the north of the district. At the heart of Nad-e Ali town lies an old crumbling fort, in the shadow of which the main bazaar is located. The new British headquarters in Nad-e Ali would be built on the site of this fort by the Royal Engineers. However, FOB Shawqat, as it was called, would not be ready for use until the summer of 2009.[64]

In all, some 1,500 troops were rustled up for Operation Sond Chara. The main units were the Regional Battlegroup (42 Commando), two British infantry companies, an Estonian mechanised company, and a mechanised company from the Danish Jutland Dragoons Regiment. Also in support was a troop of sixty-tonne Danish Leopard 2 main battle tanks. The British Army had decided not to deploy any of its Challenger 2 main battle tanks to Helmand, but working alongside the Danes from November 2007, the British had begun to appreciate the value of main battle tanks in counter-insurgency, both in terms of delivering precise and overwhelming fire, and the psychological effect they had on insurgents: radio intercepts showed that the Taliban were terrified of tanks. One British commander observed approvingly: 'There is much to be said for the persistent loitering menace of a main battle tank sitting in over-watch: it intimidates insurgents and reassures both coalition forces and local nationals.' The experience of the Danes persuaded the US Marines to deploy seventeen M1A Abrams main battle tanks when they took over northern Helmand from the British in late 2009. The British Army later admitted: 'The UK's decision not to deploy tanks to Helmand province was out of step with all our significant coalition partners.'[65]

D-Day for Operation Sond Chara was 7 December 2008. The offensive began with a combined force of Danish Leopard 2 main battle tanks and British Scimitar light tanks conducting feinting attacks into western Nad-e Ali, in the area between Shin Kalay and Khushhal Kalay, in order to draw insurgents away from the centre of the district. The Taliban fired a number of unguided 107mm rockets at the tanks, without making an impact. Devastating fire was returned by the Danish and British tanks. Simultaneous operations were conducted to keep the Taliban occupied in neighbouring areas so as to prevent them from sending reinforcements to Nad-e Ali. Thus the Brigade Reconnaissance Force seized crossing points in south-west Marjah, commandeered compounds nearby, and conducted fake helicopter drops to suggest that a larger British force was arriving. Mangal played his part, informing the Helmand chief of police that the British had begun a major offensive in Marjah. British intelligence tracked this information as it was immediately passed on to Abdul Rahman, who in turn told the Taliban.[66]

The operation lasted eighteen days. The weather conditions were miserable: British troops endured days of pouring rain, and had to wade knee-deep in mud and across freezing waterways. Armed resistance was stiffest from the walled villages of Khushhal Kalay, Shin

Kalay and Zarghun Kalay. The British would later realise that what they took for insurgents in Shin Kalay were, in fact, Kharoti tribal militia engaged in a struggle against the Noorzai, who dominated the ranks of the corrupt Afghan police in Nad-e Ali. After two hours of fighting, by which time seventeen militiamen had been killed, it became clear to the Kharoti that this was a determined attack by the British. The elders instructed their militia to stand down in order to save their village from further destruction. The villagers were dismayed that the British 'entered the village with the Noorzai police in tow'; while the British thought there were supporting the Afghan government they had in fact taken sides in an inter-tribal conflict.[67]

In contrast, Zarghun Kalay *was* a pro-Taliban village, and insurgents mobilised to defend it. The oral historian Mike Martin, who served with the British Army on Operation Sond Chara and subsequently interviewed village elders, writes that 'A shout went out to other communities across central Helmand that the Angrez were coming and the village needed help defending itself. Groups came from far afield as Nawa and the fighting was chaotic with many commanders operating against the British.'[68] After two days of intense fighting, during which Taliban positions were attacked by Apache gunships and pounded by Harriers and British artillery, the village fell to ISAF forces. The Taliban had suffered heavy casualties but so did the villagers, including several members of one family who were killed by a British bomb.

At the same time as the battle for Zarghun Kalay, further to the east the Estonian mechanised company moved into the village of Chah-e Anjir. When they arrived, the Estonians were surprised to discover that a handful of policemen had somehow managed to keep the Taliban out of the village. The British were mystified by this, not realising that the Aghezai clan who controlled Chah-e Anjir, and its highly profitable drugs market, had familial links to both the provincial police and the Taliban shura for the district and managed to keep the village out of the fighting. Operation Sond Chara ended with Juliet Company of 42 Commando pushing into Chah-e Mirza. Here, too, there was no resistance. With control of Chah-e Anjir and Chah-e Mirza, the British were able to establish patrol bases along the line of the Shamalan Canal, and at a key crossing over the Nahr-e Bughra Canal.

With Nad-e Ali 'secured', the British and Mangal set about bringing Afghan government to the district. The former Noorzai police chief of Garmsir and Gereshk, Habibullah Khan, who had also been a police officer under the Communist regime, was brought out of retirement and appointed the new district governor of Nad-e Ali. In comparison to the other governors in Helmand, Habibullah was relatively competent, hard-working and fair-minded (except when it came to the Kharoti of Shin Kalay). A new district community council of twenty-five elders was formed, consisting mostly of former mujahedin commanders. At British insistence, the community council included some representatives who had links to the Taliban, as a key purpose of the council was to draw those who were pro-Taliban into political dialogue with Afghan political authorities.

Following the conclusion of Operation Sond Chara, the Regional Battlegroup withdrew and the newly formed Battlegroup Centre-South struggled to maintain freedom of movement in the district. The fast pace of Operation Sond Chara meant that it was difficult for the Taliban to lay IEDs in the paths of ISAF units; only eleven were found. However, it was easy for insurgents to ring British patrol bases with these devices. Thus, as Martin notes, 'Within weeks, the British were hemmed in their bases,' which made patrolling and resupply very difficult. The area from Shin Kalay down to Khushhal Kalay became once again 'a no-go zone for the government and the British'.[69] Judged in the context of what the situation had been in Nad-e Ali before the operation – no Afghan government presence, no reconstruction, just a small beleaguered British patrol base – Sond Chara was a modest success. Or perhaps more accurately, it was a necessary first step. As one senior PRT official later noted, 'What Sond Chara did was to establish a lodgement, a district governor and stabilisation adviser from day one ... [and] set the conditions for later success.'[70]

Less successful was the counter-narcotics effort under 3 Brigade. The Royal Marines place the blame squarely on the Poppy Eradication Force for being 'poorly targeted, poorly led, and not really effective'. One aim of Operation Sond Chara was to secure the district for counter-narcotics operations, but the Poppy Eradication Force refused to operate in Nad-e Ali due to security fears. The Royal Marines concluded that the force was pretty useless as 'they didn't provide the stick we needed, all they did was to stir up trouble'.[71] The problem, well appreciated by battlegroup and company commanders, was that eradicating poppy risked turning the population against ISAF and the Afghan government, especially in the absence of a compensation scheme and an effective alternative livelihoods programme. Thus, while there were some targeted raids against the opium production facilities of pro-Taliban growers, generally British troops did not interfere with poppy farming. Indeed, on one occasion, in order to reassure the locals, British soldiers took part in an impromptu lesson on how to harvest poppy. The Foreign Office counter-narcotics team were horrified when they found out.

Foreshadowing what would become the greatest threat to ISAF forces, 3 Brigade saw a huge increase in the number of IEDs over their tour. Sangin was particularly bad, where the number of IEDs found doubled between the first and final months of 45 Commando's tour.[72] Overall, there was a 40 per cent increase in IEDs that were found or exploded during 3 Brigade's tour, and IED strikes accounted for 63 per cent of brigade casualties. After six months, Helmand had worn down 3 Commando Brigade – 1 per cent of its soldiers had been killed and 4 per cent wounded in action. The brigade had also suffered 379 losses to disease and non-battle injury, amounting to 8 per cent of brigade strength. In the absence of a casualty replacement system that exists in the US Army and Marine Corps, 3 Brigade experienced the same challenges of previous British brigades in sustaining force levels as losses mounted during its tour, especially given that at any time a further 3 per cent of military personnel were on leave.[73]

THE BATTLE FOR BABAJI

Next up for the British was 19 Light Brigade, who formally took over from 3 Commando Brigade on 10 April 2009. More than any previous brigade, 19 Brigade sought to build on their predecessor's campaign. For Brigadier Tim Radford, the incoming commander of Task Force Helmand, 'continuity' would be the watchword for 19 Brigade's tour, and this meant 'continuing the focus on central Helmand'. Radford's operational design also emphasised the virtue of importing counter-insurgency methods from the latest US military doctrine, FM 3–24. This might suggest an approach that focused primarily on winning the hearts and minds of the population rather than on killing insurgents. However, Radford had something else in mind. The centrepiece of his campaign was a major offensive called Operation Panchai Palang (Pashto for 'Panther's Claw', so named after the panther insignia on the 19 Brigade badge) to continue what 3 Commando Brigade had started: to push the Taliban out of central Helmand. Radford later recalled that 'Mullah Omar declared central Helmand to be his main effort and so we decided to meet him with force'. Looking back on the operation, Radford added that 'this is when we gave them a good hiding'.[74]

Once again British forces were severely stretched across Helmand, making it difficult to mass the units necessary for Operation Panchai Palang. 19 Brigade deployed with five infantry battalions and a cavalry regiment. 2nd Battalion the Rifles (2 Rifles) and 2nd Battalion the Royal Regiment of Fusiliers were both committed to holding north and north-west Helmand, while 2nd Battalion the Mercians (2 Mercians) was broken up to provide OMLTs for the Afghan army. This left potentially three major units for Panchai Palang. 2nd Battalion the Welsh Guards would be involved as Battlegroup Centre-South. But to pull off the operation, Radford also needed the Light Dragoons cavalry regiment who were holding the southern districts of Nawa and Garmsir, as well as 3rd Battalion the Royal Regiment of Scotland (3 Scots), who deployed as the Regional Battlegroup under Regional Command South, and therefore lay outside Radford's direct chain of command.

The arrival of the 2nd Marine Expeditionary Brigade gave Radford hope. Ten thousand US Marines were flooding into southern and northern Helmand, half of whom were arriving by the summer of 2009. On meeting Radford, the marine commander, Brigadier General Larry Nicholson, wanted to know: 'Where's the worse place you've got?' Radford pointed to Sangin as the deadliest district for ISAF forces, and Marjah as an area that had been completely taken over by the Taliban. Nicholson's response alarmed Radford: 'That's easy then. We'll go to Marja.' From the British perspective, this was a really bad idea as it would drag ISAF resources away from central Helmand. Radford was able to persuade Nicholson to hold off on Marjah and deploy instead to Nawa and Garmsir, which would release the Light Dragoons for Operation Panchai Palang. The marine general was fine with this, 'Provided there's a fight to be had.'[75]

A different Nicholson, US Army Brigadier General John 'Mick' Nicholson, would free up the Regional Battlegroup (3 Scots) for Radford. Inexcusably but rather helpfully as it turned out, the Dutch commander of Regional Command South, Major General Mart de Kruif, went home on leave for two weeks on the eve of Operation Panchai Palang, leaving the highly capable Nicholson to take charge as his deputy commander. Nicholson was universally liked by the British, both for his pragmatism and because it was he who persuaded McKiernan to reorder ISAF main effort from the east to the south of Afghanistan. Hugh Powell said of him: 'You went to Nicholson when you wanted to work the US system.'[76] Mick Nicholson committed the Regional Battlegroup and much else besides to support Operation Panchai Palang.

The purpose of the operation was to clear insurgents from an area which lay ten miles north of Lashkar Gah, in between Nad-e Ali and Nahr-e Seraj districts, and from which the Taliban had been mortar-bombing the provincial capital. The British mistakenly referred to this area as 'Babaji', when in fact the area of operations for Panchai Palang also included the adjacent areas of Malgir and Spin Masjid. The Afghan government had yet to show its presence there and the twenty or so villages in Babaji, Malgir and Spin Masjid were self-governing. This area was dominated by the Barakzai tribe and by any standards was very backward; there were no schools and no medical clinics. The main warlord had been a former Hizb-i Islami commander named Haji Kaduz, who had received payments from the British to keep the Taliban out. However, his militia had been demobilised under the 'Strengthening Peace Programme' in 2008 and Kaduz had been coerced out of the area. According to a reliable source who has spoken to residents in the area, the Afghan National Police then 'tried to take over [Kaduz's] racket', but their behaviour so appalled locals that 'the population turned to the Taliban to get rid of them'.[77] Radford declared that Operation Panchai Palang would 'liberate' the 80,000 inhabitants of 'Babaji' from Taliban rule, and enable them to vote in the upcoming 2009 presidential elections. Since the Taliban had been invited in to deal with the ravages of a militia previously paid by the government, and given that almost everybody in Babaji, Malgir and Spin Masjid was involved in opium production, locals had little reason to welcome the arrival of the British and their seemingly hollow promises of a better life under the Afghan government.

Together, Babaji, Malgir and Spin Masjid occupy a lush area of Green Zone between Lashkar Gah and Gereshk that is triangular in shape and, much like Nad-e Ali, is bordered by major waterways. The Nahr-e Bughra Canal runs along the north and the Helmand River to the south, and the two meet at the eastern end of Spin Masjid. The triangle is completed with the Shamalan Canal forming the western side. Radford's plan was to control access across these waterways and trap the Taliban inside. The Welsh Guards would secure the Shamalan Canal, the Regional Battlegroup (3 Scots) the Nahr-e Bughra Canal, and two mechanised companies from the Danish battlegroup the eastern end of Spin Masjid. The Light Dragoons would then be inserted in the eastern tip and move westwards down the spine from Spin Masjid, first to Malgir, and then on to Babaji, clearing insurgents in their path. In effect, the Light Dragoons would be the hammer and the Welsh Guards would act as the anvil. Once cleared of Taliban, the area would be turned into a 'gated community' by establishing checkpoints manned by Afghan police to control access across the canals. Some 3,000 troops were massed for Operation Panchai Palang, including a number of Afghan army companies from 3/205 Brigade. Task Force Helmand estimated that there were around 350 insurgents in 'Babaji' and the operation was planned to take five weeks, so the odds looked good. However, it proved to be a terribly hard slog along IED-infested routes and, for the British, it would be the bloodiest offensive of the Helmand campaign so far.

Operation Panchai Palang began on 19 June with a midnight air assault against the main southern crossing point of the Nahr-e Bughra Canal on the Loy Mandah Wadi. Twelve Chinook helicopters – the entire British fleet in Afghanistan plus six more provided by the US Marine Corps – dropped 340 men from 3 Scots onto the target. The Taliban were taken completely by surprise. The only insurgents present were fifteen unlucky men who were spotted near the landing zone carrying weapons including a belt-fed machine gun. These were promptly engaged and killed by gunships circling overhead. 3 Scots then advanced on the nearby village of Lashkah Kalay, which contained the main drugs bazaar for the area. Part of their mission was to win local hearts and minds, and to this end they brought with them a box of 'consent-winning goods': pencil cases, school bags and the like. They found the village utterly deserted; everybody had fled. This came as little surprise. 19 Brigade had extensively warned locals in Babaji, Malgir and Spin Masjid that British and Afghan troops were going to arrive in large numbers, precisely in order to give civilians a 'golden bridge' to leave before the battle started.[78] The insurgents had heavily mined the village; the British discovered thirty-five IEDs. On the fourth day, 3 Scots finally found an old man, and tried to persuade him to get other local elders to meet with them. The old man was blunt, telling British officers that 'last year a big British bomb in Nowzad killed 600 people'. While this number was a gross exaggeration, it nonetheless got to the heart of the matter: so far, all the British had brought to Helmand was destruction. Besides, the man noted, 'I'm eighty years old and I have seen many governments and none of them have been any help. Why should I believe that this one will help?'[79]

With support from the Royal Engineers, 3 Scots established a patrol base at the Loy Mandah crossing, which they called PB Wahid. The Taliban spent two days attacking the base; at one point a group of insurgents came within a hundred yards. These attacks were seen off with machine-gun, mortar and artillery fire. Thereafter, the Taliban held off but a pair of insurgent marksmen spent the next two weeks taking daily potshots at PB Wahid, until they were ambushed and killed by a British patrol.[80]

On 25 June, the Welsh Guards moved into position. The operation began with the Prince of Wales's Company securing Chah-e Anjir, on the southern end of the Shamalan Canal – the same village that had been 'secured' a few months before by the Estonian mechanised company for Operation Sond Chara. The British drove into the village in a convoy of Vectors and Vikings and were pleasantly surprised to find that it was free of Taliban; the British still had not realised that the Aghezai clan who controlled the village had links with both the government and the Taliban (as did many villages in Helmand). This time the British stayed, establishing PB Shahzad in a run-down complex that originally belonged to the Helmand and Arghandab Valley Authority.

The second phase of Operation Panchai Palang involved the Welsh Guards advancing northwards up along the Shamalan Canal to provide a block to stop insurgents from fleeing south out of the 'Babaji' area of operations. The plan was for 2 Company to proceed on a raised track called Route Cornwall which ran directly along the west side of the Shamalan Canal, destroying or blocking thirteen identified crossing points as they went and thereby sealing the canal. Aerial photography had failed to show how narrow Route Cornwall was, thus it was not possible for Scimitars to provide flank protection as originally planned for the convoy of Mastiffs and Vikings, which trundled along as guardsmen proceeded ahead on foot sweeping for IEDs. To make matters worse, the track was far more raised than expected, six feet above the canal. Not only did this leave the convoy terribly exposed, it also provided a treacherous drop into the canal below. In some places, Route Cornwall was little wider than a Mastiff. If an armoured vehicle fell into the canal, it would sink like a stone and those inside risked being drowned. One soldier recalled that 'the canal filled us with dread'.[81]

It was not long before the Taliban began to launch coordinated attacks from both sides of the canal. Cars and motorcycles dropped off insurgents ahead of the convoy, and collected the injured. British rules of engagement prevented Apache gunships overhead from firing on vehicles carrying injured fighters. To the guardsmen battling them, the insurgents appeared to be well-trained foreign fighters, swiftly moving from one defensive position to the next. The one saving grace was that there were no IEDs along Route Cornwall; it transpired that the Taliban had expected the British to move up along the eastern side of the canal, which had been mined instead.

All was different on the second day, however. Overnight, the Taliban seeded Route Cornwall with IEDs and thereafter the British convoy's speed was reduced to a painfully slow crawl. At one point, it was decided to move the battlegroup's Recce Platoon forward in a troop of Vikings to provide cover for the convoy. The members of the Royal Tank Regiment manning the Vikings had been driving for almost thirty hours, ferrying troops and supplies from FOB Shawqat to PB Wahid, and up and down the canal. Disaster struck when one of the Vikings tried to squeeze past another vehicle that was parked on the route. The exhausted driver miscalculated, causing his Viking to roll over and into the Shamalan Canal. Fortunately, nobody drowned because the canal was not as deep as expected and thanks to the quick actions of guardsmen nearby, but eight members of Recce Platoon and the two Viking operators had to be medically evacuated. That the canal turned out to be only about five feet deep was lucky for those in the Viking, but it also meant that it could be crossed almost anywhere by insurgents. This made a mockery of the Welsh Guards' mission to 'seal' the Shamalan Canal by blocking the crossing points. Back at battlegroup headquarters, officers watched in disbelief as video feed from a drone showed insurgents crossing the canal at will.[82]

On 2 July, the Welsh Guards' commanding officer, Lieutenant Colonel Rupert Thorneloe, was killed by an IED. With 2 Company struggling to make progress along Route Cornwall, Thorneloe had decided to hitch a lift with the next supply convoy going up to 2 Company in order to check things out for himself. Thorneloe believed strongly that commanders should share the risks of troops on the front line; not surprisingly, Thorneloe was much loved by his men. Thus, he insisted on travelling in the lead Viking of the convoy and on joining the four-man squad that would have to sweep the route for IEDs. Half a mile out from PB Shahzad along Route Cornwall, that leading vehicle struck an IED, killing Thorneloe and the driver. With tears streaming down his face, Colour Sergeant Dai Matthews yelled at two soldiers extracting Thorneloe's severed corpse from the Viking, 'That's my colonel. Be careful with him!' Later, the three most senior officers on the scene carefully picked through the Viking wreckage for body parts: DNA tests would be carried out at the John Radcliffe Hospital in Oxford so each body part could be buried with the correct corpse.[83] Thorneloe was the first British Army battalion commander to die on the battlefield in twenty-seven years, and only the second ever in the entire history of the Welsh Guards. His death reverberated through the regiment, Task Force Helmand and the Ministry of Defence; he had previously served as military assistant to the Defence Secretary. Speaking for many in his role as Colonel-in-Chief of the Welsh Guards, Prince Charles described Thorneloe's death as 'completely heartbreaking'.[84]

It also highlighted the growing risk from IEDs, which had become the insurgent's weapon of choice. The first week of July alone would see fifteen British troops killed across Helmand, most from IEDs, and a further fifty-seven were wounded in action in the first fortnight of July. During the summer of 2009, the medical staff in the British field hospital at Camp Bastion treated over six hundred patients, civilians as well as soldiers of all nationalities, for a range of injuries ranging from battle shock and heat exhaustion to amputations and bullet wounds. Throughout July the surgical team at Bastion was operating on up to four wounded patients a day, each of whom would need post-operative intensive care from the nursing staff.[85] Doctors and nurses worked incredibly long hours to provide the best possible care for the sick and injured. This is captured in the hospital diary of one patient, Lieutenant Mark Evison of the Welsh Guards, who was rushed to Camp Bastion after being shot on 9 May. The Territorial Army nursing major who took charge of Evison when he arrived in intensive care following surgery stayed by his side for the next nine hours. When Evison used up the hospital supply of his blood type, everybody on the medical team donated. The senior nurse who had been in the operating theatre that morning when Evison was in surgery returned in the evening to give him a blood transfusion; she wrote in his patient diary, 'I've donated many, many times over the years – but you've been the first patient I've been privileged to see actually receiving my blood – it's trickling through as I write this!!'[86] Evison died three days later. By the end of July, British medical staff at Camp Bastion were so exhausted that a US military surgical team had to be drafted in to help.[87]

Two days after Thorneloe's death the next phase of Operation Panchai Palang began when the two Danish mechanised companies secured an entry point into the eastern corner of Malgir. As they roared into view, the Danish Leopard 2 main battle tanks discouraged the Taliban from putting up any resistance. The Light Dragoon Battlegroup then passed through the Danish lines and proceeded into Malgir. With them went 25 Field Squadron Royal Engineers, whose job it was to clear a path through the heavily cultivated land, across numerous ditches and other obstacles, for the Scimitars and Mastiffs. The Taliban had seeded the area with IEDs and launched ambush after ambush against the slowly advancing British force. On the first day, B Company took multiple casualties from a Taliban ambush and the Light Dragoons had advanced a mere four hundred yards into Malgir. The following day, A Company got bogged down within thirty minutes of setting out, taking seven casualties in a Taliban ambush; by the end of the day, they had pushed the insurgents back by only two fields. By the third day, 19 Brigade decided to unleash ISAF air power in order to break Taliban resistance. This did enable the Light Dragoons to advance a little faster but progress was still painfully slow as British infantry had to sweep every step for IEDs, and the Taliban continued to lay on ambush after ambush.

By the second week, things picked up and the Light Dragoons were advancing half a mile per day. As they pushed into the centre of Babaji, groups of insurgents behind them began to harass the supply lines. The Danes and British special forces moved into Malgir to deal with this threat and in the meantime a company from 3 Scots was dropped by helicopter into central Babaji to protect the right flank of the Light Dragoons. In the final phase of Operation Panchai Palang, launched on 20 July, the Light Dragoons, who had become stuck midway in Babaji, made one last push towards the Shamalan Canal. Radford threw all available forces into this final offensive, which included moving an infantry company down from Musa Qala at short notice. 3 Scots launched another assault by helicopter on insurgent defences in western Babaji, and an armoured infantry company from 2nd Battalion the Royal Welsh also swept in with over twenty Warrior infantry fighting vehicles. On 25 July, with the Light Dragoons still short of their objective, Radford called Operation Panchai Palang to a close.[88]

So ended the bloodiest month of the war for British forces. Radford recognised that it has been 'an incredibly hard fight'.[89] Twenty-two British soldiers were killed in July 2009, although Operation Panchai Palang accounted for only ten of these deaths, which highlighted the Taliban attacks on ground-holding battlegroups elsewhere in Helmand as military assets were focused on Babaji. Thus 2 Rifles were left on their own to tackle a vicious insurgency in Sangin. Over their six-month tour, 2 Rifles found over two hundred IEDs; twenty-four riflemen were killed and another eighty were wounded in action, with the bulk of these losses caused by IEDs. The level of attrition was so bad that for the first time during the Helmand campaign the British Army had to send battle-casualty replacements, and an infantry company from 3rd Battalion the Duke of Wellington's Regiment was deployed at short notice to join the 2 Rifles battlegroup. The attrition of units that participated in Operation Panchai Palang was also terrible. One company in the 2 Mercians suffered 50 per cent losses, while one troop from the Light Dragoons which started their tour with thirty-four men were left with eleven at the end; three had been killed and twenty were wounded in action. Overall, 19 Brigade suffered the

highest casualties of any British brigade in Afghanistan, with 78 dead
and 328 wounded. The daily losses in Babaji, Sangin and elsewhere
caused troop morale to plummet. Soldiers were understandably terrified; some refused orders to advance or to go out on patrol, and cases
of battle shock and non-battle casualties (such as soldiers reporting
stomach ailments) shot through the roof. Back in Britain, military
chiefs began to worry about the army breaking in Helmand. It did
not break, but it came back battered.[90]

Gordon Brown hailed Operation Panchai Palang as a success. The
prime minister noted that the efforts of British troops had been 'nothing
short of heroic'. He also recognised that 'there had been a tragic human
cost. But this has not been in vain.'[91] The evidence suggested otherwise.
To be sure, a large number of insurgents were killed in the summer
and autumn of 2009, even if the figure of 3,000 enemy dead claimed
by 19 Brigade is somewhat doubtful. However, 19 Brigade never fully
cleared and was unable to hold Babaji. The Light Dragoons did not
reach the Shamalan Canal as they were supposed to; instead their
offensive stalled about two-thirds of the way across Babaji. The
insurgents were pushed into an area east of the Shamalan Canal that
the British called the Babaji Pear. West of the Shamalan Canal was an
area called the Chah-e Anjir Triangle (or the 'CAT') which was also
thick with Taliban. The Welsh Guards were originally supposed to clear
it but Thorneloe had refused to do so, telling Radford that he only had
enough troops to secure the Shamalan Canal itself. From the CAT and
the Babaji Pear, the Taliban continued to threaten Nad-e Ali district
and Lashkar Gah. British and Afghan forces were also unable to prevent
the Taliban from traversing Babaji, and in August five British troops in
Babaji were killed by insurgents. Speaking to the journalist Toby
Harding about Operation Panchai Palang, a Taliban commander in
Nad-e Ali district noted that 'these big operations with grand names
have not been successful'. Mullah Abdul Aziz Hamdard went on to
observe that the British 'may take over the centre of a village but the
edges and the fields are ours'.[92]

Equally troubling was the shambolic presidential election on
20 August 2009. A major aim of Operation Panchai Palang had been
to create the security necessary for locals in Babaji to vote in the
election; Operation Sond Chara had had a similar aim in Nad-e Ali.
Given that the rural population in Helmand was largely illiterate,

votes were cast by fingerprint using indelible ink. This made it easy for the Taliban to threaten to cut off the fingers of anybody who voted, and to follow through on this threat. When asked if he thought the election would go well, the head of the Afghan Election Authority in Helmand was blunt in his response: 'No.'[93] In the end there was massive electoral fraud, making a mockery of the whole exercise. Only around 150 people registered to vote in Babaji. Nad-e Ali was only marginally better, with 625 people registering to vote out of a population of many thousands. On the evening of the election, the local head of the supposedly Independent Election Commission (appointed by Karzai) claimed that 50,000 people had voted in Helmand. Three days later that figure had climbed to 110,000, which is a staggering turnout given that the total population of Helmand was no more than 800,000. Already a week before the election, *The Times* reported that President Karzai's supporters were buying up votes in Helmand.[94] In the days that followed, Karzai's main rival, former Foreign Minister Abdullah Abdullah, would accuse the president of engaging in 'widespread rigging' of the election. *The Times* accurately concluded that 'the scale of the alleged fraud now threatens to undermine the entire election process'.[95] This raised questions regarding the sacrifice of British troops in Helmand and indeed the whole British enterprise in Afghanistan.

THE MARINES ARRIVE

British military chiefs were anxious about the US Marines flooding into Helmand. They worried that the 2nd Marine Expeditionary Brigade might compete with Task Force Helmand for battle space and Afghan partners. Most of all they were concerned that the US Marines would steal the show. On the other hand, the British had come to realise that they needed help if they were to turn the situation around in Helmand. Ten thousand marines would make a big difference, and with the marines came the one thing the British desperately needed: more helicopters. The 2nd Marine Expeditionary Brigade deployed with twenty times more helicopters than Task Force Helmand. Moreover, under Brigadier General Larry Nicholson, the marines were prepared to play nice.

Thus Nicholson agreed to focus on Garmsir instead of Marjah, and to synchronise the marine offensive in southern Helmand with Operation Panchai Palang. Launched on 2 July, Operation Khanjar involved around 4,000 US Marines and over 600 Afghan soldiers. *The Times* noted how 'heavily armed marines, backed up by drones and fighter jets', swept into southern Helmand in 'a spectacular show of force, contrasting strongly with the British lack of equipment'.[96] Operation Khanjar had three objectives: to secure Nawa district; to extend control in Garmsir, by advancing further into the Snake's Head; and to seize Khaneshin district in the south. Khaneshin was a remote, arid and sparsely populated district on the border with Pakistan, which had been of little interest to ISAF up to then. The US Marines believed that by putting a force in Khaneshin, they would be able to disrupt Taliban smuggling routes into Helmand from across the border. The 1st Battalion, 5th Regiment (the 1/5) had little trouble taking control of Nawa district centre: the Taliban melted away when the marines arrived. Similarly, the 2nd Light Armored Reconnaissance Battalion was able to drive in unopposed to Khaneshin district centre; the arrival of a huge convoy of seventy armoured vehicles doubtless discouraged local Taliban from attacking.[97]

The push into the Snake's Head by the 2nd Battalion, 8th Regiment (the 2/8) was altogether more difficult. Leading the 2/8 was a tall, tobacco-chewing Anglophile, Lieutenant Colonel Christian Cabaniss. Determined to enculturate his headquarters staff in FOB Delhi, Cabaniss made them watch classic British comedy at evening meal-times; they worked their way through *Monty Python* and *Fawlty Towers* over the summer, and by the autumn were on to the *Yes Minister* series. Aside from FM 3–24, Cabaniss's handbook was Colonel C. E. Callwell's Edwardian guide to *Small Wars: Their Principles and Practice*, published by the British War Office in 1906. Cabaniss preached the importance of understanding culture and connecting with the people, but his marines also had a lot of hard fighting to do.[98]

When the 2/8 moved into Garmsir in early July to release the Light Dragoons for Operation Panchai Palang, the Taliban responded by attacking the patrol base line at Amir Agha. Cabaniss felt that the Taliban were testing the 2/8; they would soon experience US Marine mettle. Nicholson had ordered Cabaniss to clear nine miles into the Snake's Head. Three companies of marines pushed six miles south on foot to seize the village of Kuchinay Darveshan, while another company conducted an assault by helicopter into a village called Mian Poshtay lying a further three miles to the south. Marine intelligence estimated that there were around a hundred Taliban in each village, with a further hundred at the main Taliban bazaar of Lakari, three miles south of Mian Poshtay. It took a week for the marines advancing on Kuchinay Darveshan to break through Taliban IED belts and defences. Landing by helicopter in Mian Poshtay, Echo Company also encountered fierce resistance and the battle that broke out in the bazaar would last for two days.

The marines slowly pushed the insurgents out of Kuchinay Darveshan and Mian Poshtay. They fought daily battles against groups of insurgents, and made heavy use of artillery and air strikes to dislodge Taliban from compounds. Cabaniss recalled that 'enemy forces had been trying to push us out of [Mian Poshtay] all July and most of August'.[99] As is their way, the 2/8 responded by taking the fight to the enemy. Fox Company, with support from 3 Scots, were dropped by helicopter into Lakari village, deep in Taliban-held territory. This was a temporary measure designed to stop a new Taliban front line from developing south of Mian Poshtay.[100] But this was a forlorn hope, for while the US Marines did manage to create 'security bubbles' around Kuchinay Darveshan and Mian Poshtay, the Taliban ringed each with IED belts and trench lines. Moreover, even within these security zones, the Taliban were able to freely move about unarmed, right under the noses of the marines, and intimidate the local population. As a result, local elders refused to meet with marines for fear of retribution, and locals refused to accept payments from marines, even for damaged property.[101]

The 2nd Marine Expeditionary Brigade brought massive force to bear on southern Helmand yet they did so cleverly. The 1/5, the 2/8 and the 2nd Light Armored Reconnaissance Battalion were led by commanders who understood that developing governance and building up Afghan security forces were as important as fighting the Taliban. Each day, marine officers spent many hours patiently having tea with local elders and Afghan officials. Typical on this score was Cabaniss, who had read and thought deeply about counter-insurgency and had perfected the art of speaking softly and carrying a big stick. While his marines pursued a tough and relentless campaign against the Taliban in the Snake's Head, at the same time they put effort into building relationships with local communities and Afghan partners. The 2/8's secret weapon in this was Carter Malkasian. Employed by the US State Department to be the district political officer, Carter had a doctorate in history from Oxford, was the lead expert on counter-insurgency at the US Centre for Naval Analysis, and had previously worked as a political adviser to the US Marines in Iraq. Within weeks, local elders would turn up at the gates of FOB Delhi asking to speak with the slightly built and mild-mannered 'Carter Sahib', a term of honour and respect very rarely extended to Westerners in Afghanistan. The *Washington Post* noted that

> The adoration [towards Malkasian] stems from his unfailing politeness (he greeted people in the traditional Pashtun way, holding their hands for several minutes as a series of welcomes and praises to God were delivered), his willingness to take risks (he often traveled around in a police pickup instead of in an American armored vehicle with a squad of Marines), and his command of Pashto, the language of southern Afghanistan (he conversed fluently, engaging in rapid-fire exchanges with gray-bearded elders).

Brigadier General Larry Nicholson would later declare that 'We need a Carter Malkasian in every district of Afghanistan', adding that 'You can surge troops and equipment, but you can't surge trust. That has to be earned – and that's what Carter did.'[102] Carter would end up spending two years in Garmsir working alongside the US Marines. And yet for all these advantages – the sheer power and determination of the 2nd Marine Expeditionary Brigade, an approach to counter-insurgency that focused on working with local communities, and Carter Malkasian to provide the seed of trust to make such collaboration possible – the US Marines struggled to push the Taliban out of southern Garmsir.

THE HOME FRONT

British public opinion turned decisively against the war in Afghanistan in 2009. When the war started in October 2001, polls revealed that 56 per cent of the British people thought the military campaign against al-Qaeda and the Taliban would be effective, while 33 per cent believed that it would not. By July 2009, those figures had been almost reversed, with only 38 per cent believing that the campaign would be effective, and 57 per cent convinced that it would fail.[103] The public tends to 'rally round the flag' at the onset of military involvement in an armed conflict;[104] however, if a war drags on, support will invariably waiver and critical voices will gain more political traction. Scholars continue to debate the causes of this fall in public support; some argue that wars become unpopular when there are mounting numbers of casualties, while others contend that the public will lose faith in a war when it appears to be going nowhere.[105] Unfortunately for the British government, both conditions coexisted with the war in Afghanistan in 2009. By that time the British military had been involved in the country for eight years, and large numbers of British troops had been fighting in the south for three years. Since 2007, a succession of British task force commanders had ended their tour by claiming that the Taliban had suffered some kind of defeat, and that some kind of 'tipping point' had been or was close to being reached in the campaign, and yet the insurgency continued to rage in Helmand and across the country. Allied to this, British war dead mounted with each brigade tour. The number of killed in action almost doubled between late 2008 and late 2009, from forty-two under 3 Commando Brigade to seventy-eight under 19 Light Brigade.

By this stage, the Ministry of Defence had a well-developed process for dealing with fatalities in Helmand. Under Operation Minimise, all communications to Britain were suspended for troops so that no news got out until the next of kin had been notified. A silence and an almost tangible gloom would descend on Camp Bastion whenever the tannoy declared 'Op Minimise' to be in force. A notification officer (sometimes two) would be dispatched immediately to tell the spouse, partner or parents of the dead soldier or marine. As might be expected, people reacted in different ways to the news. One widow later recalled how she 'slammed the door in their faces' and locked it. 'I thought if I locked them out I could lock out what they had to say.'[106] A senior member of the army's bereavement service observed that 'Notifying a family is possibly the toughest job in the British Army, and it is rare for a Notification Officer to walk away not haunted by the family's first responses of incomprehension, disbelief, and agony'. The job of the notification officer was simply to break the bad news and then leave; the army's thinking was that 'after the notification has taken place the family will never want to see the officer again, that they should leave quickly and without a trace'.[107] Within hours, a visiting officer would arrive, whose role it was to help the family to liaise with the Ministry of Defence and other agencies, and to navigate through the process of repatriating and burying their loved one.

A few days after the notification, families were invited to attend the repatriation ceremony for the body as it arrived back in Britain. This ceremony, in which the body of the fallen service member was received respectfully by an honour guard, was introduced in 2003 and modelled on US military practice; previously, the bodies of dead service personnel had been buried overseas or were brought back in shipping containers to be collected quietly by privately hired hearses. As one who attended many British military repatriation ceremonies noted:

> It is difficult to find the words to capture the atmosphere at the ceremony. Sadness, pride, and disbelief have become indistinguishable emotions felt by hundreds of people. But it is the families who are the most distinct, their grief uncontrollable, often helped to stand as their bodies buckle under the weight of their hearts breaking.[108]

A more informal and very public repatriation ceremony spontaneously emerged in 2009. Due to runway repairs at RAF Brize Norton, returning war dead had been flown into RAF Lyneham since 2007. As the cortège drove through the Wiltshire market town of Wootton Bassett locals began to line the high street to pay silent respect. In May 2009, locals gathered for the sixteenth time to honour the fallen, as the bodies of four slain soldiers were driven through the town. As one retired veteran on the scene put it, 'There's not enough respect for soldiers. If only you could take the spirit here in Wootton Bassett and connect it with the rest of the country.'[109] Press coverage of the Wootton Bassett spirit led to growing crowds, as people came from across the country to express support. On 14 July, a huge crowd turned out as the bodies of eight British soldiers were driven through the town. In a very public display of emotion, many threw flowers on the passing hearses. This led some locals to complain that the 'atmosphere of dignified respect' had been lost as 'grief tourists' descended on the town and turned the public ceremony into a 'three-ring circus'.[110] This debate aside, it seemed to the Chichele Professor of War at Oxford, Hew Strachan, as if Wootton Bassett had somehow come to 'carry the burden of national commemoration for the country as a whole'.[111]

While the public became more vocal in their support for 'our boys in uniform', support for the war plummeted over the summer of 2009. In a YouGov poll commissioned by *Channel 4 News* in late October, 84 per cent of respondents believed that British forces were not winning in Afghanistan, and 62 per cent wanted all British troops to be brought home as soon as possible or within the year.[112] Two weeks later, the public view had grown even more strident with 73 per cent wanting troops brought home.[113] Despite this, British troop numbers increased over this period as Gordon Brown came under intense political pressure to pour resources into a war that privately he did not believe in.

The prime minister was far from alone in his scepticism towards the military campaign in Afghanistan. By late 2008, the three most senior ministers responsible – Des Browne as Defence Secretary, David Miliband as Foreign Secretary and Douglas Alexander as International Development Secretary – agreed that far more effort needed to be put into finding a political resolution to the conflict. In October 2008, Des Browne resigned and was replaced by John Hutton. Hutton viewed things entirely differently. He thought that the Cabinet was failing to back the military and in particular that the prime minister 'was an extremely reluctant war leader'. He felt that military success was possible and entered office 'with a strong sense that there was not sufficient [military] strength in Afghanistan'.[114] On military advice, Hutton sent several requests for troop increases to the prime minister, all of which were turned down. In the aftermath of the global financial crisis, the government spent £37 billion on bailing out three high street banks in late 2008, and billions more on major public works in an attempt to spend Britain out of the worst recession in decades. In this context, the Treasury refused to spend more on military operations overseas. In December, Brown finally agreed to send three hundred more troops to Helmand. This fell far short of what Hutton had requested, and British chiefs now tried to get the Americans to put pressure on the prime minister. The US commander of NATO, General John Craddock, told the *Sunday Times* that 'I don't think 300 more, if you are talking about Helmand province, will do the trick'. One senior

US defence official put the matter more bluntly, telling the newspaper that Washington was wondering if the British 'have the stomach for Afghanistan'.[115]

The newly elected US president, Barack Obama, used the London G20 Summit in March 2009 to personally press Brown to send more British troops to Afghanistan. The US National Security Council emailed Number 10 in advance to advise that Obama 'would very much hope that [Brown] would commit to two additional battlegroups'. The prime minister was furious at British military chiefs for going to the Americans behind his back. In April, he agreed to send seven hundred soldiers to bring British troop numbers in Afghanistan to 9,000 but only to provide security for the Afghan presidential election; afterwards, British forces would revert back to the 8,300 troop cap.

Relations between the prime minister and military chiefs broke down completely over the summer of 2009. In June, Hutton was replaced in a Cabinet reshuffle with Bob Ainsworth; by that stage, Hutton was barely on speaking terms with Brown. Ainsworth likewise came in with proposals for troop increases, only to have Brown snap at him that the war was already costing Britain £3 billion a year. In addition to having dysfunctional relationships with successive Defence Secretaries, the prime minister also proved to be a terrible chair of the National Security, International Relations and Development Subcommittee (NSID) of the Cabinet, which was formally responsible for the strategic management of Britain's war effort in Afghanistan. Brown often arrived late and spent meetings scribbling notes to his advisers instead of paying attention to ministers as they discussed matters of state. One senior official complained that 'NSID meetings were a charade' that 'became more and more detached from reality'.[116]

Relations between Brown and Dannatt as Chief of the General Staff were especially poisonous. Downing Street considered Dannatt to be a troublemaker because of his agitation for more troops and in consequence, when he had expected to be promoted to Chief of the Defence Staff, the prime minister simply extended the term of the incumbent, Air Chief Marshal Jock Stirrup. Dannatt understandably took umbrage at this, and the fact that he was not a member of NSID. Since the PM only ever consulted the Chief of the Defence Staff, he only ever received military advice on Afghanistan (and Iraq) from an airman. Dannatt was reduced to ambushing Brown on Horse Guards Parade one morning in early 2009, to make the case in person for more troops to support Operation Panchai Palang.[117] The temporary uplift subsequently announced by Brown fell far short of the 2,000 troops that Dannatt had in mind.

As British casualties grew over the summer of 2009, Dannatt went public with his concerns to Tory MPs and journalists, declaring on 12 July that 'If we are going to fight this war as it needs to be fought, we need a properly-resourced army'. It was unprecedented for a serving military chief to openly criticise the government but Dannatt was utterly fed up and only a month from retirement anyway. The columnist Max Hastings noted that he had 'written about the Army for forty years and I've never known such bitterness' towards the government.[118] An argument over troop numbers soon morphed into one over inadequate equipping of the forces. Thus, the Shadow Defence Secretary, Liam Fox, followed Dannatt's public criticism by accusing the prime minister of 'the ultimate dereliction of duty' for sending British troops to fight without the equipment they need to combat the threat from IEDs, in terms of suitable armoured vehicles and more helicopters.[119] In fairness, the government had ordered hundreds of new blast-proof vehicles (Mastiffs, Ridgebacks and Wolfhounds) in 2008. On helicopters, the record was not so good. Despite repeated complaints from British commanders in Helmand, the Ministry of Defence had failed to provide more heavy-lift transport helicopters. The Royal Air Force had eight Chinooks specially designed for use by special forces that were sitting around unused because the US government refused to release the software necessary to make them operate. The decision was taken to strip out and retrofit these helicopters for use in Afghanistan, and to urgently buy seven Merlin helicopters second-hand from Denmark. However, these additional helicopters did not actually arrive in Afghanistan until 2010. To plug the gap, the Ministry of Defence sent medium-lift Sea King helicopters to Helmand; as the name suggests, Sea Kings are designed to operate over the cold waters of the Atlantic and they really struggled in the heat of the Helmand summer.[120]

On Dannatt's final visit to the troops in Helmand in mid July, the press reported how he was forced to fly around on a US helicopter. When asked about this, Dannatt told reporters: 'Self-evidently … if I moved in an American helicopter, it's because I haven't got a British helicopter.'[121] Actually, the army chief was far less concerned about helicopters than he was about troop numbers and the 'lack of energy and investment' in developing a range of counter-IED capabilities; the Americans in contrast had invested in a multibillion-dollar effort.[122] Dannatt returned from Helmand with 'a shopping list' for the government, at the top of which were 'more boots on the ground' and more funding for counter-IED.[123] Labour ministers were nonplussed, angrily criticising Dannatt for 'playing politics'.[124] This row between the army and the government spilled over into Westminster, with the Commons Defence Committee rushing out a highly critical report on the shortage of helicopters.[125] Under immense pressure from the news media, the prime minister appeared before the committee for a public grilling on the helicopter issue.[126]

This embarrassing spectacle underlined how Brown had lost control over the Afghan campaign. This had already been evident a fortnight before when the prime minister was away at a G8 Summit in Italy and his team were notified of Thorneloe's death. At first, they failed to appreciate that the story was getting 'wall-to-wall coverage' back home. However, it did add to Brown's creeping sense of doubt about the Helmand campaign. When he arrived back in the UK, he decided to go straight to PJHQ for an impromptu briefing on Operation Panchai Palang. He was shocked to be told by the Chief of Joint Operations, Air Marshal Stu Peach, that the unprecedented number of dead and wounded returning from Helmand 'were within our expected range'.[127] Brown's team focused on the immediate media storm over casualties and helicopters, missing the larger problem, namely the absence of political-strategic direction over the military campaign. This point came home to Hutton when he visited 19 Brigade in April 2009 and found that 'strategy was largely left to the military'. In reality, NSID had no actual oversight of the Afghan campaign, and hence ministers were 'never consulted on whether we should do a big push' in central Helmand.[128]

In this context, one would at least hope that the British Army was focused 100 per cent on the success of the Afghanistan campaign. However, even as late as mid 2009, they were not. When he took over as Commander-in-Chief of Land Forces (the number two in the British Army), General Sir David Richards was stunned to discover the level of apathy in the army about the Afghanistan campaign. He later recalled that 'it was clear to me that a lot of the Army was "in denial" that we were in a war'.[129] As another senior officer put it, the army at home was 'at work' and only the army in Afghanistan was 'at war'.[130] As a former ISAF commander, Richards was strongly committed to what he viewed as a 'war of necessity' in Afghanistan. In addition, where Dannatt worried mostly about the British Army 'being broken' by the Afghanistan war, Richards was more concerned about the consequences of failure. In January 2009, therefore, Richards launched a campaign to 'put the army on a war footing'. Named Operation Entirety, it was, as Richards later observed, 'in part to capture the need for the whole army to view [the war] as main effort and not just those deploying in Afghanistan'.[131] When he succeeded Dannatt as Chief of the General Staff in August 2009, Richards was able to champion the case for making the Afghanistan campaign the 'main effort' across the whole of the Ministry of Defence. This had beneficial effects in terms of redirecting defence programmes and resources towards supporting the war effort.

Consistent with the lack of defence leadership up to 2009, military strategy was delegated to field commanders, resulting in an inconsistent campaign as successive brigades did their own thing. This problem had been ongoing from the beginning, and in consequence every six months the campaign took a new direction. Moreover, however much incoming British commanders emphasised the importance of demonstrating military restraint and supporting the development of government, every brigade ended up focusing on the conduct of major combat operations – even 52 Brigade. Locals looked on wearily as the fighting raged in their towns and across their fields. While civilian casualties mounted in Helmand and the war dragged on, public support for the campaign collapsed back home. Furthermore, in Helmand, British support for the corrupt police and for clumsy poppy eradication efforts proved a boon for Taliban recruitment.[132]

The Afghan campaign desperately needed strategic direction, and ideally this would come from political leaders working in constructive dialogue with military chiefs.[133] Clearly this was near impossible under Brown, given his dysfunctional leadership style and terrible relations with military chiefs. This now raised the urgent question of who would provide the direction necessary to turn around the floundering British and ISAF war effort.

8

American Surge

It fell to the Americans to get the war in Afghanistan back on track. During the 2008 presidential election campaign, the Democratic candidate Barack Obama was pretty strident in his views on the conflict. He saw Afghanistan as a war of necessity for America in contrast with Iraq, which he considered to be a misguided war of choice. Speaking at the Woodrow Wilson Center in Washington DC in July, Obama declared that 'the central front in the War on Terror is not Iraq, and it never was'. Instead, the focus should be on 'taking the fight to al-Qaeda in Afghanistan and Pakistan'.[1] During his first visit to Afghanistan in late July, Obama used an interview on CBS television to present his assessment of the situation as 'precarious and urgent', and to hammer home his central criticism: 'I think one of the biggest mistakes we made strategically after 9/11 was to fail to finish the job here … We got distracted by Iraq.' This was a consistent theme throughout Obama's election campaign. In the first presidential debate with his Republican rival, John McCain, in September 2008, Obama was asked if more troops needed to be sent to Afghanistan. His answer was clear: 'Yes, I think we need more troops. I've been saying that for over a year now. And I think we have to do it as quickly as possible, because it has been acknowledged by the commanders on the ground that the situation is getting worse, not better.'[2]

Obama won a landslide victory in the election, with almost 53 per cent of the popular vote and more than twice as many votes from the electoral college as McCain. Eleven days before his inauguration, he sent Vice President-Elect Joe Biden on a fact-finding trip to Pakistan and Afghanistan. In a heated discussion over dinner in Kabul with President Karzai, Biden complained about the lack of progress on Afghan government corruption and Karzai's failure to rally public support among his people for the war. Karzai, in turn, complained about ISAF's failure to minimise civilian casualties. The meal ended with Biden throwing down his napkin and storming out. His visit to ISAF headquarters was no more reassuring. The best that McKiernan could say was that 'we're not losing'. He reported positive signs in Regional Command East but a rapidly deteriorating situation in Regional Command South. When pushed by Biden, McKiernan had no plan to improve things in the south beyond asking for more troops.[3] On departing, Biden shook the ISAF commander's hand and said: 'I'm looking forward to working with you.'[4] Six months later, McKiernan would be fired.

OBAMA'S NEW STRATEGY

Biden brought back a gloomy assessment for Obama. The war completely lacked strategic direction, and was being waged 'on autopilot'. There was no shared vision in ISAF of why and how the war was being fought. As it happened, the outgoing Bush administration had reached a similar conclusion. In late November 2007, one of the final National Security Council meetings under Bush was convened to consider the findings of a high-level review undertaken by Lieutenant General Douglas Lute, the 'war czar' appointed to oversee both wars in Iraq and Afghanistan for the White House. The review had lasted months and had been conducted by a senior inter-agency team from the Defense and State departments and the CIA. It found the Afghan government and security forces to be woeful partners; that ISAF and US forces were fighting multiple disjointed wars; and that the Taliban insurgency was growing in strength, especially in the south. The report concluded: 'We're not losing, but we're not winning, and that's not good enough.'[5]

In a highly unusual move, Obama asked Robert Gates to stay on as Secretary of Defense, making him the only individual to hold this office in both Republican and Democratic administrations. Gates had proven to be a non-ideological Defense Secretary, and immensely effective in getting the Pentagon to shift focus from preparing for future wars to winning the war in Iraq.[6] Obama also kept Lute on as the war czar in the White House. At the same time, the new president commissioned a fresh strategic review of the Afghanistan war to be undertaken by Bruce Riedel, a senior fellow at the Brookings Institution. Riedel had almost thirty years' experience in the CIA, Defense Department and White House, ending up as senior adviser on South Asia for President Bill Clinton. He had also worked on the national security team for Obama's election campaign. In late 2008, Riedel published a book in which he argued for a 'vast increase' in the US military, diplomatic and economic efforts in Afghanistan. He called for these efforts to 'extend into Pakistan', and through pressure and persuasion to get Pakistan to 'crack down aggressively and system-atically on all terrorists' operating from its territory.[7]

In January 2009, there were 34,000 US troops in Afghanistan – 19,000 dedicated to the Operation Enduring Freedom mission and 15,000 assigned to ISAF. There were a further 32,000 troops from forty-one other nations serving in ISAF. When he came into office, Obama inherited a request for 30,000 additional US troops from McKiernan. At the first National Security Council meeting chaired by the new president on 23 January 2009, the chairman of the Joint Chiefs of Staff, Admiral Michael Mullen, and the commander of US Central Command, General David Petraeus, both urged for quick presidential approval of this request in order to get the troops deployed in time for the 2009 summer fighting season. When he had campaigned for more troops to be sent to Afghanistan during the presidential election, Obama had in mind only about half this number. Moreover, he did not want to approve the troop uplift in Afghanistan until he was able to announce troop drawdowns in Iraq, and before a new strategy for Afghanistan had been settled. Echoing what was happening in Britain, a fault line rapidly emerged in the Obama administration between military chiefs and the White House on the question of troop numbers. Vice President Biden, the White House Chief of Staff, Rahm Emanuel, the National Security Advisor, General James Jones, and his deputy, Tom Donilon, all pushed back strongly against the 30,000 number. The Pentagon came back with a revised figure of 17,000, this being the actual number of troops that they could get to Afghanistan by the summer. The president still wanted to wait for the conclusion of the Riedel review before authorising this deployment. However, following a National Security Council meeting in mid February, he agreed for it to go ahead when almost everybody around the table, including Gates, Secretary of State Hillary Clinton and Riedel argued in favour of it. Biden remained opposed.[8]

According to Bob Woodward's 'inside story' of the decision-making on Afghanistan, Obama was persuaded by the need to get troops on the ground in order to secure the 2009 Afghan presidential election. Riedel is quoted as saying to the president: 'with more troops on the ground in August, your capacity to have a real election will increase. If you don't do it, you may find yourself in August unable to hold an election.' In a later interview with Woodward, the president confirmed that 'there were strong warnings, both from the military as well as our intelligence agencies, that if we did not bolster security in Afghanistan rapidly, that the election might not come off and in fact you could see a country that splintered'. However, as Woodward correctly notes, the 2nd Marine Expeditionary Brigade comprising the first 10,000 reinforcements would go to sparsely populated Helmand 'to provide security in a place with few voters'.[9] In his memoir, Gates provides a frank admission that this deployment was as much about institutional politics as war strategy. The commandant of the US Marine Corps, General James Conway, was keen to get his troops out of Iraq and into Afghanistan. He also required that all marine forces deploy into a single area of responsibility, where they could operate independently from the US Army, and indeed largely independently from ISAF headquarters. As Gates notes, 'Only Helmand fit Conway's conditions.'[10] This was fortuitous for the British, who needed all the help they could get.

Flanked by Gates, Clinton and other senior members of his national security team, the president unveiled the administration's 'comprehensive, new strategy for Afghanistan and Pakistan', based on the findings of Riedel's review, on 27 March 2009.[11] He described the situation in Afghanistan as 'increasingly perilous', further noting that '2008 was the deadliest year of the war for American forces'. Obama reminded the nation of the continued threat that made the war necessary: 'If the Afghan government falls to the Taliban, or allows al-Qaeda to go unchallenged, that country will again be a base for terrorists who want to kill as many of our people as they possibly can.' He articulated 'a clear and focused goal' for the war: 'to disrupt, dismantle and defeat al-Qaeda in Pakistan and Afghanistan, and to prevent their return to either country in the future'. Central to the new strategy was linking the war in Afghanistan with the problem of terrorists operating from safe havens in Pakistan. The president was clear: 'Pakistan must demonstrate its commitment to rooting out al-Qaeda and the violent extremists within its borders.' Since 2001, the United States had given over $12 billion in security assistance and economic aid to Pakistan, notwithstanding growing evidence that elements of the Pakistani military were providing support to insurgents in Afghanistan.[12] In a private briefing at the White House in advance of the public unveiling of his new strategy, the president told congressional leaders that 'the era of the blank check is over' for Pakistan.[13] All the same, to induce Pakistan's cooperation, the Obama administration was promising a five-year package of military assistance for counter-insurgency operations amounting to $1.5 billion per annum.[14] For Afghanistan, the strategy would focus on accelerating the growth of the Afghan police and army, reducing corruption and improving Afghan government, and persuading ordinary people to leave the insurgency. To support this, the president announced that an additional 4,000 military trainers would be deployed. Obama also confirmed that there would be 'a dramatic increase in our civilian effort', declaring that 'to advance security, opportunity and justice, not just in Kabul, but from the bottom up in the provinces, we need agricultural specialists and educators, engineers and lawyers'.

The Riedel review findings and new strategy had been debated by the National Security Council over a series of meetings between 12 and 20 March. Clinton was enthusiastic in her support for the proposed strategy. She was firmly persuaded of the need to win over Afghans by improving the competency and thereby legitimacy of Afghan government, and to this end she recognised the need for a sustained counter-insurgency effort.[15] Of the principal decision-makers, only Biden spoke out against the proposed strategy for Afghanistan and Pakistan. He argued strongly that instead of increasing its military and civilian efforts in Afghanistan, the United States should pursue a 'counterterrorism plus' strategy focused on hunting down al-Qaeda in Pakistan.[16] In approving the new strategy, the president rejected 'CT plus', but given that it was proposed by the vice president, it remained on the table as a potential alternative to the counter-insurgency campaign that was about to be pursued with renewed vigour. In the meetings Gates was supportive even though privately he was 'deeply skeptical of two fundamental elements' of the new strategy. Based on the experience of Iraq, he thought it most unlikely that sufficient civilian advisers would be forthcoming from the State Department, the Department of Agriculture and USAID. He also doubted that 'we could persuade the Pakistanis to change their "calculus" and go after the Afghan Taliban'. Time would prove him right on both counts.[17]

PROTECTING THE PEOPLE

It fell to the ISAF commander to come up with an operational plan to implement the new strategy. The problem was that Gates had lost confidence in McKiernan. For over a year, the Defense Secretary had seen the war turn around in Iraq. Central to this success was the synergistic effect of the surge of US forces into Iraq in 2007 combined with the 'Sunni Awakening', when Sunni insurgents rose against their former al-Qaeda allies and instead joined US-funded militias.[18] But equally important was the eagerness of US battalion commanders to introduce new counter-insurgency tactics on the ground.[19] Crucially, this eagerness was matched by commanders at the top, generals such as David Petraeus as the coalition commander and Stanley McChrystal as the commander of US special operations in Iraq, who embraced new tactics and were prepared to reorganise their forces to best exploit them.[20] Gates and Mullen both felt that McKiernan was too conventional; in their fortnightly videoconference with ISAF headquarters, it was clear that McKiernan was not on top of the wider stabilisation and reconstruction effort. One senior defence official later reflected that 'when you judge McKiernan by Petraeus standards, he looks old school by comparison'.[21]

Not surprisingly, the Defense Secretary's disquiet was shared by Petraeus, who, as commander of US CENTCOM, was responsible for overseeing the wars in Iraq and Afghanistan. Both recommended that McKiernan be replaced with McChrystal, who had left Iraq in the summer of 2008 to take over as director of the US Joint Staff. He continued to innovate in that role, creating a Pakistan–Afghanistan Coordination Cell staffed by officers with multiple tours in the region to leverage their expertise for defence planning and policy.[22]

Mullen flew to Kabul in late April to persuade McKiernan to step down one year before he was due to do so. When McKiernan refused to go, Gates went out on 6 May to fire him.[23] Five days later, Gates announced that McChrystal was taking over as commander of coalition and US forces in Afghanistan, and in this role would be promoted to a four-star general. At the same time Lieutenant General David Rodriguez was appointed to take charge of a new three-star headquarters, ISAF Joint Command (IJC). This arrangement, which followed a similar model in Iraq, would have a four-star command dealing with the 'up-and-out' aspects of the war, such as relations with the host nation government and the governments of coalition partners, and a subordinate three-star command dealing with the 'down-and-in' aspects of day-to-day management of the war. McKiernan's resistance to adopting this command structure had contributed to his downfall. In announcing the changes, Gates told the Pentagon press corps: 'our mission there requires new thinking and new approaches from our military leaders. Today we have a new policy set by our new president. We have a new strategy ... I believe that new military leadership also is needed.'[24]

In his confirmation hearings before the US Senate Armed Services Committee at the beginning of June, McChrystal outlined what would become the key elements of his strategy for success in Afghanistan.[25] The first was the importance of winning over the Afghan people and, to this end, the imperative to protect them from the effects of the war. McChrystal was acutely aware that, just a month before, an American air strike against insurgents who had taken refuge in a village had killed a large number of civilians. At the time, the Afghan government claimed 140 civilians had been killed; an investigation later estimated that around ninety civilians had died. He also knew that 2008 had been the deadliest year so far in terms of civilians killed in the war.[26] McChrystal told senators that 'central to counterinsurgency is protecting the people'. He stressed:

This is a critical point. It may be *the* critical point. This is a struggle for the support of the Afghan people. Our willingness to operate in ways that minimize casualties or damage, even when doing so makes our task more difficult, is essential to our credibility. I cannot overemphasize my commitment to the importance of this concept ...

although I expect stiff fighting ahead, the measure of effectiveness will *not* be the number of insurgents killed, it will be the number of Afghans shielded from violence.

The second element was the importance of a 'holistic counterinsurgency campaign' combining security, diplomatic and development lines of operation in collaboration with inter-agency partners. Thus, McChrystal stated that military operations 'must be subordinate to efforts to protect the people and set conditions for governance and economic advancement'. The third element of McChrystal's strategy was to focus on developing Afghan police and army forces of sufficient size and quality to provide internal security of their country. McChrystal considered this the 'highest priority security task'.

The questions that followed from senators threw up two key issues that would produce increasingly tense relations between the White House and McChrystal's command in Kabul in the months ahead. First and foremost was the question of troop numbers. Senator John McCain noted that there was 'reportedly' an outstanding request from McKiernan for an additional 10,000 troops in 2010. He asked McChrystal: 'do you expect to renew this request, alter it or rescind it?' The general responded that he would 'have to make an assessment on the ground'. McCain pushed: 'What is your initial assessment? Do we need the additional 10,000?' McChrystal kept his cards close to his chest. 'Sir, I'm just not sure at this point.' The other issue was time. In his testimony, McChrystal told senators that he recognised that 'we need to start making progress within about the next 18 to 24 months'. However, in office calls to members of Congress in advance of deploying, he was told repeatedly that he had 'at most, a year to show convincing progress'.[27] Progress on this timescale was wholly unrealistic given what McChrystal would later characterise as the 'often glacial speed of counterinsurgency'.[28] These two issues would come to dominate American civil–military politics of the war.

McChrystal arrived in Kabul on 13 June 2009 to take command of ISAF. Arriving with him was a small team of handpicked innovators to help him shake up ISAF. He brought in Major General Mike Flynn to take over ISAF intelligence, which was floundering and not fit for purpose. Flynn had transformed the intelligence arm of the US special operations task force under McChrystal in Iraq. In January 2010, he would publish a policy paper that was openly critical of the intelligence structure he inherited, and called for a complete reorganisation of intelligence gathering and analysis in ISAF.[29] McChrystal recruited British General Graeme Lamb to lead a renewed effort to 'reintegrate' Taliban fighters, that is, to persuade them to abandon the insurgency. McChrystal had first met Lamb in 1991, when the two collaborated on a joint US–British special forces operation hunting down Scud missiles behind enemy lines in Iraq during the Gulf War. They worked together again in Iraq in 2006–7, when Lamb arrived to take command of British forces and McChrystal was leading the US special operations effort. McChrystal also brought in Colonel Chris Kolenda to lead on a major assessment of the Afghanistan campaign, and on drafting key strategy documents. As a task force commander, Kolenda had led a brilliant counter-insurgency campaign in Kunar and Nuristan provinces in eastern Afghanistan in 2007–8. On his return to Washington, he had been appointed to serve as the chief military adviser to the Riedel review. Another key adviser was Lieutenant Commander Jeff Eggers, a US Navy SEAL with service from Iraq, who had been chief of counterterrorism on the Joint Staff. He was serving as Mullen's strategic adviser when McChrystal poached him.[30]

From its modest origins in December 2001, ISAF headquarters had grown to occupy almost a square mile. As McChrystal describes it well in his memoirs: 'the ISAF compound was a crowded hodgepodge of buildings and trailers connected by twisting, casbah-like alleyways'. The command was dotted with flags; in a coalition of forty-two nations, most countries had their own accommodation blocks. Behind its high blast walls and heavily guarded gates, ISAF headquarters was a sort of shabby 'emerald city'. Hundreds of ISAF staff officers, far removed from the daily realities of the war, laboured therein to produce and analyse a growing mountain of documents. Given security restrictions, few ISAF staff officers were able or inclined to venture beyond the compound walls to talk to Afghans. Even fewer Afghans were allowed in to talk to their ISAF allies. Some weeks after McChrystal arrived, the chief of operations for the Afghan army, Lieutenant General Sher Mohammad Karimi, was denied entry to the ISAF compound, even though he had an invitation from the new ISAF commander to attend a meeting for Afghan partners.[31] McChrystal set out to change this but it would take time.

The day after he arrived, McChrystal put on his dress uniform and went to pay his respects to Karzai. The meeting went well and laid the foundation for what would be the strongest relationship that any ISAF commander had with the Afghan president. On 18 June, McChrystal set off on a week-long 'listening tour' of Afghanistan. From the beginning, and contrary to US military regulations, he adopted the habit of not wearing body armour or carrying a weapon when travelling off base. McChrystal did so in solidarity with the Afghans he met and those who saw him on the news media. McChrystal toured each of ISAF's five regional commands in turn: RC-Centre in Kabul, RC-East in Bagram, RC-South in Kandahar, RC-North in Mazar-e-Sharif and RC-West in Herat. In RC-East, he visited the US brigade task force in Khost. The brigade commander told him that 'the number one complaint from Afghans is that the Afghan government doesn't deliver on promises'. In Mazar-e-Sharif, he was shocked by the excessive emphasis on protecting ISAF forces. He observed an ISAF convoy 'forcing Afghan drivers off the road and pointing weapons at an Afghan family', and noted that such behaviour 'endangered and insulted the population whose support we needed'.[32] Among the other key themes that emerged for McChrystal from this battlefield tour were the problems caused by corrupt Afghan government, an undersized Afghan army, and poorly trained, equipped and led Afghan police. Equally worryingly, he found chronic disunity of effort within ISAF itself. The security force lacked 'a unified theory of victory' and 'campaign design' to achieve it. Instead, the five regional commands and the brigade task forces within them were focused on waging their own tactical campaigns.[33]

In fact, ISAF did have a campaign plan. Moreover, in 2008 McKiernan's command had updated the plan inherited from his predecessor, General Dan McNeill. McNeill had a traditional military plan focused on killing the enemy and capturing territory. Contrary to the concerns back in Washington that McKiernan was 'too conventional', his plan sought to shift the focus to providing security for the Afghan population. It adopted the 'clear–hold–build' concept of operations from FM 3–24, and to this, McKiernan added 'shape' as the first phase of operations. 'Shape' can involve use of special forces or precision air strikes to disable insurgent command and control, before an operation to 'clear' insurgents from a particular area. But it also involves, and this is what McKiernan had in mind, engaging with local leaders and elders to explain what operations are about to be conducted, why such operations are necessary, and how this will benefit their communities. The McKiernan plan was developed in collaboration with United Nations Assistance Missions to Afghanistan (UNAMA) and the general staff of the Afghan Ministry of Defence, especially with General Karimi. ISAF planners also collaborated with the regional commands, but here they faced considerable pushback. The Germans in RC-North and the Italians in RC-West were not at all keen on adopting a counter-insurgency approach. As far as they were concerned, they were engaged in peacekeeping operations, and they had no plans to 'clear' insurgents from their area of operations, let alone 'hold' that ground afterwards. The US Army in RC-East was entirely comfortable with the new concept of operations but they had their own ideas for their area of operations and were not prepared to subordinate these to the ISAF plan. Only the British and Dutch staff in RC-South were prepared to embrace the new approach.[34] Thus, while the McKiernan plan was unveiled with much fanfare in August 2008, at a ceremony attended by ISAF commanders and Afghan police and army chiefs, it did not have buy-in across ISAF and was largely ignored by the various national task forces on the ground.[35]

McChrystal came in with a mandate to turn things around in Afghanistan. So it is hardly surprising that his team found the existing campaign plan to be inadequate. Strategic guidance for the new plan was provided by the president's speech of 27 March, which had clarified US war objectives, and the Riedel review, which set out a number of key priorities. NATO also had a 'strategic vision' for the war, outlined in its Comprehensive Strategic Political-Military Plan, which had been approved by alliance heads of state at the Bucharest Summit in April 2008. The strategic vision outlined four key themes focusing on the need for a long-term commitment by the alliance, stronger Afghan leadership, better international coordination, and a regional approach that included Pakistan.[36] The NATO plan was mostly aspirational and short on essential detail, in no small part because certain states were opposed to key aspects of any realistic plan. Thus, France and Spain 'took a hard line' against including counter-insurgency as a key mission in the plan, and France and Germany opposed giving ISAF a role in training the Afghan police (for fear this would undermine the European Union's Police Mission to Afghanistan).[37] Accordingly, McChrystal's team found the NATO strategic plan to be pretty useless as a source of guidance for their redrafting of the ISAF campaign plan.[38]

McCHRYSTAL'S CAMPAIGN ASSESSMENT

As McChrystal left Washington, Gates tasked him with conducting a strategic assessment of the campaign and to report back within sixty days. McChrystal used this process to generate his own campaign plan. To assist in the task, he assembled a team of civilian experts including Steve Biddle, Anthony Cordesman, Fred and Kimberley Kagan, Andrew Exum and Catherine Dale. Biddle was a senior fellow of the Council on Foreign Relations; a former professor at the US Army War College, he was widely respected as the leading social scientist of his generation working on military affairs.[39] Cordesman was professor of strategy at the Center for Strategic and International Studies in Washington, and former director of intelligence assessment in the US Department of Defense. The Kagans were something of a power couple on the US think-tank scene: Kimberley Kagan was founder and president of the Institute for the Study of War, and Fred Kagan a fellow at the conservative American Enterprise Institute. Biddle, Cordesman and the Kagans had all served on similar assessment teams for Petraeus in Iraq. Exum was a fellow at the Center for a New American Security and a PhD student in war studies at King's College London; possessing a slow Tennessee drawl and a sharp mind, he was a former US ranger who had served with multiple tours in Afghanistan and written a best-selling book about it.[40] Dale was lead analyst on military affairs for the US Congressional Research Service and had previously been a political adviser to US forces in Iraq; forever in motion, she brimmed with energy and ideas. The civilian team were assembled hurriedly in late June and given a month to produce a draft assessment. McChrystal asked them to go back to basics, and among the exam questions he gave them was: 'Is this mission doable, and if so, what changes in strategy and policy are needed to succeed?' One team member recalls that this was 'pretty ballsy' of McChrystal, noting that 'senior commanders rarely ask questions that might produce answers they do not want'.[41]

The civilian team travelled around Afghanistan but security restrictions imposed by the regional commands prevented them from getting out much to talk to troops and ordinary Afghans. Exum would later blog about his frustration at being driven around Mazar-e-Sharif, a largely secure city in the north, in a German armoured convoy 'whereby I could only observe Mazar and the Afghans themselves through a narrow two inch by four inch slit of bullet-proof glass'. He likened it to 'seeing Afghanistan through a periscope'. This problem was not confined to the German sector. The assessment team were wrapped in cotton wool everywhere they went. Exum captured this experience in a one-page memorandum to McChrystal entitled 'Touring Afghanistan by Submarine'.[42] Like McChrystal, the team also experienced excessive concern with force protection, resulting in behaviour that was alienating locals, such as barging through civilian traffic in armoured vehicles.[43]

The assessment team conducted an extensive review of intelligence and field reports (the Kagans, in particular, spent an enormous amount of time doing 'deep-drives' into the intelligence data), interviewed a large number of staff officers in ISAF headquarters and all the regional commands, and held discussions with senior Afghan police and army officers. This was a major endeavour. At the same time McChrystal commissioned several specific studies by ISAF staff on key challenges, such as strategic communications, civilian casualties and detainee operations, which all fed into the campaign assessment. The initial draft was written by Kolenda, and then pored over line by line for corrections and revisions by the civilian team.[44] The final draft was edited by Kolenda and Eggers, working closely with McChrystal.[45] The final document therefore captured a huge collective effort.

The report was far from encouraging. It found that the war was in stalemate. Moreover, 'many indicators suggest the overall situation is deteriorating'. It concluded that 'trying harder' would not produce campaign success; rather a new strategy and more resources were needed. The assessment called for a new population-centric counter-insurgency strategy. 'Our strategy cannot be focused on seizing terrain or destroying insurgent forces; our objective must be the population.' It identified government corruption as being as great a threat to the Afghan people, and therefore campaign success, as the insurgency. It called for a fundamental shift in ISAF's operational culture to one that 'puts the Afghan people first'. For this, ISAF was going to have to get a lot closer to both the Afghan security forces and the population. The report noted that 'preoccupied with force protection, we have operated in a manner that distances us, both physically and psychologically, from the people we seek to protect'. Accordingly, ISAF had to 'shift its approach' in order to 'bring security and normalcy to the people' by shielding them from government abuse as well as insurgency violence. This would require ISAF forces to accept more risk, to 'spend as much time as possible with the people, and as little time as possible in armored vehicles or behind the walls of forward operating bases' in order to build the relationships, and create the 'perception of security', necessary to win over local support for the Afghan government.[46] Crucially, this new approach would require ISAF forces to exercise more restraint in how they used force so as to reduce civilian casualties and collateral damage. Thus, McChrystal issued a revised tactical directive with a general injunction to scrutinise more carefully and limit the use of force, and prohibiting the use of artillery or aerial bombardment against residential compounds except in a few prescribed circumstances.[47] Some structural changes were also identified as needed to improve unity of command within ISAF and the unity of effort by all international partners, including ISAF, UNAMA and the various international civilian agencies. The planned formation of IJC under General Rodriguez was designed to address disunity of effort within ISAF. NATO also decided to appoint a senior civilian representative to work in partnership with the ISAF commander, in order to better coordinate the international aid effort.

The report outlined the 'four fundamental pillars' of McChrystal's strategy. First was the aim to accelerate the growth of Afghan security forces and develop them better through much closer partnering with ISAF forces. Numbering under 90,000 soldiers at the time, the ANA was due to grow to 134,000 by the autumn of 2011; this target was brought forward by a year and a new target was set of a final strength of 240,000. No objective was set for the Afghan National Police but these also would grow hugely in number. Second, as much priority would be placed on developing effective and accountable Afghan governance as on defeating the insurgency. Third, it was necessary to 'reverse the insurgency's momentum' through military operations in order to buy time for the invariably slower improvements in governance to occur. Fourth, the report acknowledged the need to prioritise resources and effort in 'critical areas where the population is most threatened'; ISAF would go on to identify eighty such 'key terrain districts', out of the 340 districts in Afghanistan.[48]

Already in his testimony to Congress in June McChrystal had identified the need to focus more on protecting civilians and on developing the Afghan security forces. However, the campaign assessment threw up new problems and had clarified McChrystal's thinking in several respects. The assessment team highlighted a blind spot of ISAF military planners, namely, the political dimension of the conflict. As one senior ISAF adviser notes, they introduced 'the key idea of the Taliban as a political and social organization, not just an armed group'.[49] Hence, the assessment concluded that Taliban shadow government was as much of a threat as Taliban fighting forces, and that the focus of the ISAF effort on the annual insurgent 'fighting seasons' in the warmer months missed the bigger picture of 'a year-round struggle, often conducted with little apparent violence, to win the support of the people'.[50] This, in turn, led to an emphasis on the importance of governance in the ISAF campaign. Here, too, the assessment team introduced an important conceptual innovation by distinguishing between 'government' and 'governance': the former comprising the top-down formal political institutions of the Afghan state, and the latter the bottom-up political customs and arrangements of Afghan society. Empowering local governance was critical to the conduct of counter-insurgency by ISAF forces. As a senior ISAF adviser observed, 'the conventional wisdom was that "government" was a State Department function. The whole idea of ISAF being involved was radioactive in NATO. The emphasis on placing "governance" on a par with security [in ISAF planning] was revolutionary.'[51] Drawing this important distinction, and illustrating the security implications of weak and bad government, demanded of ISAF to get involved in politics, specifically in reducing corruption and improving the accountability of Afghan government.

The rapid expansion in ANA numbers proposed in the campaign assessment would increase the need for more effective mentoring, as growing the army faster would invariably mean taking in weaker recruits and pushing them through training more quickly; basic training for Afghan soldiers was now reduced from ten to eight weeks.

At the time there was huge variance in practice when it came to ISAF's mentoring of the ANA; and the Afghan police was still being mentored by EUPOL (European Union Police), even though it became increasingly obvious that the small EUPOL mission lacked the resources for such a mammoth task. In response, McChrystal came up with the concept of 'embedded partnering', which would involve much deeper integration of ISAF and Afghan security forces into a single combined force. To implement this concept, McChrystal directed that 'ISAF will partner with ANSF [Afghan National Security Forces] at all levels – from government ministries down to platoon level' in order to 'live, train, plan, control and execute operations together'.[52]

Even before the campaign assessment was concluded, in late June, McChrystal notified Gates that the situation was far worse than expected. He was especially concerned about southern Afghanistan, much of which was 'not under our control'. The message was not new; Biden had brought back the same assessment from his first visit to Afghanistan as vice president-elect in November 2008. But the scale of the problem had not been appreciated in Washington. McChrystal told Gates that in Helmand province, five of the thirteen districts were under Taliban control.[53] He reported that the British had been unable to stop the insurgency from making 'serious inroads' in the province. The new ISAF commander's perception at the time, later recalled in his memoir, was that 'the insurgency was … strong enough that British forces were challenged to move outside the network of small bases they had established'.[54] Most worryingly, 'the Taliban had captured districts closely encircling Lashkar Gah, giving them a perch from which to seriously threaten the provincial capital'.[55]

The assessment team also had deep concerns that ISAF intelligence had underestimated the extent of insurgent pressure on Kandahar city.[56] Overall, ISAF intelligence was found to be far too enemy-centric and so gave the command little inkling of how things looked from the perspectives of ordinary Afghans. Thus, ISAF was unable to assess if the Taliban's campaign of fear and intimidation was working in key provinces and districts. As one member of the assessment team put it: 'We could already be losing Kandahar but we don't know it because we don't have enough contact with the population to know what the hell is going on in the city.'[57] Under Mike Flynn, ISAF intelligence would attempt to focus more on the population and on Afghan politics.

In mid July, Mullen visited Afghanistan and returned to tell an alarmed Gates that McChrystal might request as many as 40,000 additional troops. Gates was incredulous that McChrystal could believe that the president would agree to such a massive increase in forces, especially as Obama had already approved an additional 21,000 troops for deployment to Afghanistan since coming to office seven months before. Gates arranged a secret meeting with McChrystal and Rodriguez on 2 August at an air force base in Belgium; Mullen, Petraeus and US Admiral James Stavridis (the Supreme Allied Commander of NATO) were also present. The meeting reviewed the campaign assessment and then focused on the question of troop numbers. Gates's perspective was heavily influenced by the Soviet experience in Afghanistan. He was concerned 'about reaching a "tipping point" where the size of our presence and our conduct turned us into "occupiers"'. However, Gates's view on this would change later that month when he read an essay by Fred Kagan entitled 'We're not the Soviets in Afghanistan' which highlighted the brutal tactics employed by ill-disciplined and increasingly beleaguered Soviet forces. Kagan had been a prominent proponent of the surge in Iraq, and in his essay he made the case for a similar surge in Afghanistan.[58]

Crucially, the meeting enabled Gates to give the new ISAF commander a political steer. He was told to make sure the campaign assessment focused explicitly on implementing the broader strategy set out by Obama in March. Hence 'President Obama's strategy to disrupt, dismantle, and eventually defeat al Qaeda and prevent their return to Afghanistan' was invoked in the second sentence of the report as having 'laid out a clear path of what we must do'. Also invoked as a key guide for the revamped ISAF campaign was NATO's Comprehensive Strategic Political-Military Plan, even though in actuality McChrystal's team found the NATO plan pretty useless.

McChrystal's campaign assessment and the implications for American strategy for Afghanistan were debated exhaustively by the Obama administration throughout September and October 2009. In sending McChrystal's assessment to Obama on 10 September, Gates wrote to the president that in light of the perilous situation in Afghanistan, 'the debate and decisions – including over resources – I had hoped could be delayed until early next year when we might be able to show some progress are, unfortunately, upon us now'.[59] This debate occurred against a backdrop of worsening relations between the White House and the military. In a series of press interviews and public statements, Mullen, Petraeus and McChrystal all declared that the counter-insurgency strategy would fail without significantly more troops. They also dismissed 'CT plus', which Biden was continuing to push as a cheaper option. To top it all off, McChrystal's classified assessment was leaked to the *Washington Post*; its lead article on 21 September noted that the assessment 'repeatedly warns that without more forces and the rapid implementation of a genuine counterinsurgency strategy, defeat is likely'.[60] Understandably, White House officials reacted with growing anger at what they perceived to be a blatant attempt by the military to push the president to bankroll McChrystal's strategy.[61]

The cost implications were staggering. In a secret memorandum to Gates at the end of September, McChrystal submitted his formal request for 40,000 additional troops. The president was told by his budget advisers that this would cost around $50 billion a year, and take the ten-year cost of the war to over $1 trillion.[62] The president wanted to know how sending more forces to Afghanistan served US interests: it was proving difficult to articulate the national security case for American troops to fight and die in Afghanistan. Debate on Afghan strategy and troop numbers would drag on into November. In the meantime, ISAF was preparing to launch massive offensives in Helmand and Kandahar in the new year, in order to push the Taliban out of their strongholds in southern Afghanistan.

9

Showdown

It was a clever public relations exercise. In September 2009, a delegation of six British Muslim leaders was invited by the Foreign Office to visit Afghanistan. The official purpose of the trip was supposedly 'to challenge [foreign] misconceptions about the reality of life for Muslims in Britain'. Given the political fallout from Iraq, a war that many British Muslims saw as one waged by their own government against fellow believers, the trip was as much to challenge British Muslim misconceptions about what their country was doing in Afghanistan. It was a chance for the UK government to demonstrate how its diplomats and stabilisation advisers, assisted by the armed forces, were helping the Afghan government and people to rebuild their country after decades of war.

After a full day of briefings at the PRT in Lashkar Gah, the delegation was to be taken to the nearby district of Nad-e Ali, to meet with locals and 'to get a glimpse of life on the frontline'. While far from naive about the challenges in Afghanistan, the visitors were inspired by what they heard and saw, and looked forward to speaking with ordinary Afghans. Accompanying the delegation were PRT officers, a handful of journalists, and a heavily armed close-protection team. Even though Nad-e Ali district centre was only ten miles away, the party was to travel via Chinook as the roads were too dangerous. Taking no chances, the Chinook flew low, swerving and tilting in order to avoid possible enemy fire as it left Lashkar Gah; buzzing overhead like fearsome wasps were two British Army Apache gunships, acting as escorts for the short flight.

The helicopter flew directly into FOB Shawqat, where 1st Battalion the Grenadier Guards was headquartered as Battlegroup Centre-South. On arrival, the Muslim delegation received yet another briefing, this time in the clipped tones of Guards officers; for most visitors to Afghanistan, the greatest danger they faced was death by PowerPoint. Finally, the delegation was allowed 'out of the wire'. The party was taken to a newly reopened school just three hundred yards away on the site of what was previously PB Argyll. One journalist was none too impressed. 'Oh God, not another fucking school,' he muttered. Minutes later, the district governor, Habibullah Khan, rolled up in his Toyota Land Cruiser to meet with the delegation. It later transpired that the school had been officially 'opened' four times already by Afghan authorities for the benefit of visiting dignitaries. Still, the school was full of eager pupils, much excited by the foreign visitors. The British Muslim leaders spoke with the teachers and addressed the children. Outside, the journalist chatted with some pupils. 'Why are there no girls in the school?' he wanted to know. To the boys, this seemed a stupid question. Their sisters would never be allowed to attend a school so close to the *kafir* (infidel) base.

A short wander through the district centre took the party to the governor's compound for lunch. The meal had been paid for by the British PRT, but all the same Habibullah was a gracious host. Afterwards, the visitors were taken to witness the distribution of wheat seed to local farmers. This was part of the PRT's Alternative Livelihood Programme, designed to wean them off growing poppy. It appeared to be a good demonstration of the programme, as farmers formed an orderly queue to receive sacks of wheat seed. In fact, it was all for show: somebody had forgotten to send the relevant paperwork, and so the farmers had to give back their sacks once the British delegation had left the scene.

Midway through the wheat seed distribution, the party of visitors with their British close-protection team was suddenly surrounded by a larger group of Afghan paramilitaries, who it transpired were the provincial governor's bodyguards. Gulab Mangal's visit to Nad-e Ali took everybody by surprise, but it delighted the visiting Muslim leaders nonetheless. They pushed onto the stage to join Mangal, who began to address a growing crowd of Afghan locals. Compared to his predecessors, Mangal was a competent and popular governor, and therefore a key target for the Taliban. The British close-protection team were far from pleased by his unannounced appearance and very soon an explosion and gunfire in the district centre brought the visit to an abrupt end. The visitors were instructed by their bodyguards to walk 'calmly but quickly' back to base. The retreat was certainly quick.[1]

The incident revealed that the situation was far from well in Nad-e Ali. Since they had first entered the district a year ago, the British had spread out to over a dozen patrol bases and checkpoints. Three patrol bases – PB Silab, PB Pimon and PB Wahid – were supposed to control the main access points to the district from across the Nahr-e Bughra Canal. In reality, operating from strongholds in the northern and southern reaches of Nad-e Ali, the Taliban had freedom of movement across much of the district. The insurgents had planted IED belts around British bases, making movement out of them a treacherous and time-consuming business, and a number of checkpoints were completely cut off, requiring resupply by helicopter. The Taliban were able, at will, to threaten the district centre. But all of this was about to change.

THE STEAL

When he visited 19 Brigade during Operation Panchai Palang, McChrystal was troubled by what he saw. The British were focused on fighting the Taliban in central Helmand, and not on protecting the population and supporting governance. As one American officer who accompanied McChrystal observed, the British task force was 'just focused on security', and in the PRT, 'governance people were doing governance stuff, and development people doing development stuff, and never the twain shall meet'. Analysis undertaken by McChrystal's campaign assessment team of one British battlegroup revealed ninety-three 'escalation of force' incidents between April and June 2009, where soldiers fired on approaching vehicles or people perceived to be a threat, resulting in over two hundred civilian casualties. Not one of these incidents involved a suicide bomber.[2]

In July 2009, within a month of taking charge, McChrystal issued a new tactical directive to all ISAF forces in which he declared: 'Gaining and maintaining [the support of the Afghan people] must be our overriding operational imperative and the ultimate objective of every action we take.' Accordingly, his tactical directive introduced new measures to restrain the use of force by ISAF. Air strikes against residential compounds were 'expressly prohibited', with strict rules for very few exceptions. Where ISAF troops faced deadly fire from compounds, the directive instructed that they withdraw rather than call in an air strike. Where withdrawal was not an option – for example where an ISAF patrol was pinned down – an air strike would be permitted provided there were no civilians in the compound. The Taliban quickly learned to exploit ISAF's new rules of engagement, such as by firing from compounds occupied by families. Under McChrystal, ISAF and Afghan units were partnered at all levels and became a 'combined force'. Reinforcing this, the tactical directive banned ISAF forces from conducting operations without Afghan partners, and required that where entry to residential compounds was necessary, Afghan soldiers or police were to go in first.[3] The British called this 'the Green Knock'.

This tactical directive arrived too late to influence Operation Panchai Palang, which was in full swing by July. But it profoundly shaped the plans and conduct of operations by 11 Light Brigade, which took over command of Task Force Helmand from 19 Brigade on 10 October 2009. In explaining the nature of the campaign to his troops, the incoming task force commander, Brigadier James Cowan, explicitly drew on McChrystal's 'Counterinsurgency Guidance' to subordinate commanders, which emphasised that the Taliban could not be defeated militarily: 'an insurgent cannot be defeated by attrition; its supply of fighters, and even leadership, is endless'. Rather, the primary task of ISAF was to 'win the trust and support' of the Afghan people for their government, by protecting them from violence and corruption, and denying the insurgents 'influence and access' to the people. The difference in approach would soon be obvious in Sangin. As Battlegroup North under 19 Brigade, 2 Rifles had called in over 2,700 rounds of supporting artillery fire, of which almost 2,500 were high explosive. As Battlegroup North under 11 Brigade, 3 Rifles called in just 225 artillery rounds, of which only 41 were high explosive.[4]

Sangin continued to be an immensely challenging area for British forces, and held a grim totemic quality as the place where one-third of British troops killed in Afghanistan lost their lives. However, central Helmand would be the focus on 11 Brigade's campaign, as it had been for its predecessors. And there was still much to do. The Taliban continued to control the northern end of Nad-e Ali, with a major logistical hub at Showal, where the Taliban shadow district governor, Mullah Ahmed Shah, was based. They held the southern edge of the district as well, with a stronghold in the village of Saidabad. There were also large numbers of Taliban in Marjah, just below Saidabad. (President Karzai would turn Marjah into an independent district of Helmand in 2010.) Marjah fell into the newly expanded area of operations for the 2nd Marine Expeditionary Brigade, which formed Task Force Leatherneck. With the Taliban entrenched in northern Nad-e Ali and in Marjah, central Helmand became the main focus for the ISAF campaign in the south.

RC-South was in charge of planning and overseeing this effort. The command rotated every year between the three main ISAF troop-contributing nations to the region – Britain, Canada and the Netherlands. In September 2009, it was Britain's turn to take over again. The new commander, Major General Nick Carter, was clear that the campaign was 'principally a battle for people's minds'. Accordingly, his main focus was on protecting the people and on supporting Afghan government.[5] To clear the insurgents from central Helmand would require a massive offensive, which was designated Operation Moshtarak. For Carter, the challenge was how to conduct this offensive in such a way as to avoid big battles, bloody losses, and civilian death and displacement.

The answer was provided by the Grenadier Guards, who took over from the Welsh Guards in September 2009 as Battlegroup Centre-South. Local support was crucial to the Taliban's ability to operate in Nad-e Ali; villages paid tax to the Taliban, and provided food, cover and information for the insurgents. Colonel Roly Walker, commander of the Grenadier Guards, worked out that if local elders were persuaded to withdraw this support, then the Taliban could be levered out of villages without too much fighting. In the context of the 'shape–clear–hold–build' construct of counter-insurgency doctrine, Walker called this 'consent-based clear'. It would later be called 'the steal' – the task was to steal ground from right under the Taliban's noses.[6]

The situation in Nad-e Ali was so unstable that overland resupply of the district centre from Camp Bastion required a three-day operation using most of the battlegroup to secure the route from the canal crossing at PB Silab to FOB Shawqat. Walker got British combat engineers to build a new crossing at the closest point between the district centre and the Nahr-e Bughra Canal. This new route went through the village of Shin Kalay, home to the Kharoti tribal community. Habibullah had told the British that Shin Kalay was a 'Taliban village', but behind the villagers' sympathies for the Taliban was a long-standing conflict between the Kharoti and the Noorzai, who dominated the district government and the police; Habibullah himself was Noorzai. Predatory behaviour by the police in particular had turned the Kharoti towards the insurgency. As one elder put it: 'Every Kharoti who is a Talib, is a Talib because of police brutality.'[7] One way or another, Shin Kalay had to be secured for Walker's proposed new route to work. In shuras with the local elders, the Grenadier Guards explained that they would be bringing convoys through Shin Kalay on a regular basis. The elders were given a choice: stand down their militia and encourage non-local Taliban to leave, or face the prospects of repeated battles every time a British supply convoy was passing through. The villagers were also given a carrot: the considerable convenience of the new crossing point right next to their village. The elders were persuaded, and the British were able to establish a checkpoint in the village without facing any Taliban resistance. As Walker later recounted, 'We talked our way into Shin Kalay.'[8]

This operation had improved security for the district centre. But the Taliban were well embedded in north-west Nad-e Ali, in Chah-e Mirza and the surrounding villages of Zorobad, Baluchan and Noorzoy Kalay. A line of Taliban dug-ins guarded the routes into these villages, and they controlled the one accessible crossing of the Nahr-e Bughra Canal; the other, nominally controlled by the British at PB Pimon, was completely surrounded by insurgents. Between Chah-e Mirza and Babaji, in the northernmost tip of the Nad-e Ali district, was Chah-e Anjir. This area, triangular in shape, was where many insurgents had retreated to after 19 Brigade's offensive pushed them out of Babaji. ISAF intelligence estimated there were up to 90 insurgents in Chah-e Mirza and around 175 insurgents in Chah-e Anjir. Walker knew that Task Force Helmand was scheduled to undertake a major clearance operation of the Chah-e Anjir Triangle as part of Operation Moshtarak, and he was concerned that this would result in insurgents being driven south into Char-e Mirza, from where they would threaten the district centre. Walker got approval from brigade headquarters for a major operation to clear the insurgents out of Char-e Mirza, so as to create a 'hard shoulder' on the border with the Chah-e Anjir Triangle in advance of Operation Moshtarak.

Launched on 18 December 2009, Operation Tor Shpa'h was to last four weeks and involve 450 British troops, 100 Afghan soldiers and police, and two long patrols from Afghan Task Force (ATF) 444. As the Afghan special operations group for Helmand, ATF 444 was in very high demand in Helmand; 'every unit in Helmand wants to work with them because they are such a fantastic asset' was how one British defence official put it.[9] Mentoring AFT 444 in the field was a company from the Special Forces Support Group, which had been formed in 2006 when 1st Battalion the Parachute Regiment was converted into a British version of a US Army Ranger battalion. In Iraq, the Special Forces Support Group provided cordons and on-call firepower for SAS and SBS raids. In Afghanistan, working alongside ATF 444, they went after Taliban commanders and bomb-makers. They took some satisfaction in the task: as one soldier put it, 'killing the enemy in the close battle is exactly what we joined up to do'.[10]

Operation Tor Shpa'h started with the Grenadier Guards and ATF 444 slowly advancing up from Shin Kalay in order to 'find and fix' the insurgent defence. 'It was like Normandy' was the impression of the British deputy commander of Task Force Helmand, who visited Nad-e Ali two days into the operation: 'You couldn't move for armoured vehicles. There were Vikings and Mastiffs everywhere.'[11] This cautious advance revealed major weaknesses in insurgent command and control. There was only one Taliban commander in the area, whose capacity to deal with the unfolding battle was soon overstretched. Taliban logistics also appeared to be weak, as insurgents typically ran out of ammunition after a few hours. The Grenadier Guards found that the insurgents 'were constantly trying to get us to fire on civilians by putting civilians between our and their fire lines'.[12]

After ten days, ISAF launched two simultaneous night-time assaults by helicopter over insurgent front lines and directly onto Taliban strongholds. In the early hours of 28 December, a pair of Royal Air Force Chinooks dropped A Company from the Royal Welsh battlegroup and their ATF 444 partners directly into Noorzoy Kalay. At the same time, a third Chinook dropped a British and Afghan special operations group onto the Taliban command position near Baluchan. Only just arrived in Helmand, the Royal Welsh were assigned to be the Regional Battlegroup. This was A Company's first trip outside Camp Bastion. Once on the ground, they followed standard tactics, which were to use their Vallon metal detectors to clear a route up to the nearest compound so their Afghan partners could do 'the Green Knock', and pay the owner handsomely to clear out for the duration of the operation; the standard payment in 2009 was 50,000 afghanis, about $1,000. The Royal Welsh now had a foothold in Noorzoy Kalay.[13]

British and Afghan ground forces then moved up to complete the clearing of Noorzoy Kalay and Baluchan, and lift the siege of PB Pimon. Insurgents were caught in a pincer movement as B Company of the Royal Welsh swept in on Jackals from the Helmandi desert. A light armoured vehicle able to travel at fifty miles per hour off road, and packing two heavy machine guns and a grenade launcher, the Jackal was designed for precisely this kind of rapid ground assault. Introduced for Afghanistan, the British military would end up buying five hundred Jackals. Finally, on 29 December, a company from the Grenadier Guards, operating with ATF 444, cleared the insurgents out of Zorobad. ISAF intelligence had estimated that the villagers in Noorzoy Kalay and Baluchan were giving reluctant support to the Taliban, and so could be persuaded to side with the government instead. Following the model of Shin Kalay, heavy 'messaging' had preceded the operation to advise local elders that an overwhelming force was on its way to secure Chah-e Mazir. This message was passed straight on to local Taliban commanders and had the desired effect. The insurgents retreated in advance of British and Afghan forces, and put up only sporadic resistance. Hot on the heels of military operations, Habibullah held shuras with locals in Baluchan on 28 December, and in Zorobad and Noorzoy Kalay on 30–31 December.[14]

Tor Shpa'h was, in effect, the dry run for Operation Moshtarak. Task Force Helmand headquarters had deliberately downplayed Operation Tor Shpa'h in advance so as 'to avoid the impression that it would be another Panchai Palang', that is, another big battle in central Helmand. They were also unsure if Tor Shpa'h would be a success. In the event, the operation demonstrated that working through local elders, the Taliban could be coerced into surrendering ground without the necessity for major combat operations. Satisfied that this approach worked, Task Force Helmand headquarters 'promoted Tor Shpa'h up through RC-South and PJHQ as an example of how [Moshtarak] could be done'.[15] They were pushing at an open door. Carter had visited FOB Shawqat just before Tor Shpa'h and was impressed with Walker's concept of operations. Carter ended up pointing to Tor Shpa'h as the 'clear example of how he wanted Moshtarak to proceed'.[16]

MORE AMERICANS WILL DIE

The 2nd Marine Expeditionary Brigade was in full swing by the time Carter took command of RC-South. The marines had cleared large tracts of the southern districts of Nawa and Garmsir over the summer in Operation Khanjar. Next on their list was Marjah, which lay between their area of operations in southern Helmand and that of the British in central Helmand. McChrystal encouraged the 2nd Marine Expeditionary Brigade to push on as he needed a quick win to build political capital in Washington. Marjah was scheduled to be cleared by the marines in late November when Carter arrived and put everything on hold.[17]

For Carter, Kandahar and not Helmand was the key terrain for the ISAF campaign in the south. This view was shared by the British deputy commander of ISAF, Lieutenant General Nick Parker, who recalled that 'the analysis clearly showed that Kandahar was more important'.[18] Next door to each other, the two provinces were of similar size, in terms of land and population. However, Kandahar contained Afghanistan's second-largest city and was the birthplace of the Taliban. Carter's problem was that there were far more ISAF forces in Helmand. His command spent November trying to refocus ISAF effort on Kandahar. In the meantime, working with the Afghan army planners and the regional commands, ISAF Joint Command produced the ISAF operational plan. The 'main effort' of the whole ISAF–ANSF campaign in 2010 was identified as providing government and development in Kandahar and security in Helmand. But the plan left open the order of which to tackle first: Kandahar or Helmand.[19]

RC-South headquarters attempted in vain to get the US Marines to divert some forces for an ISAF offensive in Kandahar. Formally, the 2nd Marine Expeditionary Brigade did not fall under the ISAF chain of command at the time, but rather reported to a three-star marine general in CENTCOM. This was one of several concessions that James Conway, the commandant of the US Marine Corps, had secured from the US Joint Chiefs of Staff, in sending his marines to Afghanistan. The other chief concession was that US Marines would operate in their own contiguous area of operations, where marine ground forces could be supported by their own dedicated aviation.[20] With the US Marines not budging, RC-South headquarters tried to get British forces to shift from Helmand to Kandahar.[21] Rumours rippled across the British Army. Preparing for deployment back in the UK, the Scots Guards wondered if Task Force Helmand 'would move lock, stock, and barrel to Kandahar'.[22] This was an even more forlorn hope than moving the marines. Given the British investment in Helmand, financially with the huge base at Camp Bastion, and politically with the sacrifice of British lives, there was little chance that the British government would agree to it.

On 1 December 2009, President Obama made a major speech 'on the Way Forward in Afghanistan' that pretty much sealed things. The White House chose a highly symbolic setting, with Obama giving a televised address to the nation in front of thousands of army cadets at the US Military Academy at West Point. The president announced the completion of his three-month-long review into the Afghanistan war, which led him to conclude that 'it is in our vital national interest to send an additional 30,000 troops to Afghanistan'. These three additional brigades were to be deployed at 'the fastest possible pace' in early 2010. By this stage, there were 68,000 US troops in Afghanistan; this surge would take US force levels to almost 100,000. But this would not be an open-ended commitment, especially as the extra forces were 'likely to cost us roughly thirty billion dollars' a year. Hence, Obama also announced that 'after eighteen months, our troops will begin to come home'.[23] 'OBAMA ADDS TROOPS, BUT MAPS EXIT PLAN' was the *New York Times* headline the following day.[24]

The July 2011 deadline for the start of the US force drawdown came as a complete surprise to ISAF headquarters. 'He said what?' was the general reaction among groggy ISAF staff, watching the president's speech live in the early hours of 2 December in Kabul.[25] It meant that the three extra brigades would not have much time to make a difference. While this sent a clear and useful message to the Afghan government, that they could not rely indefinitely on the United States to protect them, it sent an equally clear and less helpful message to the Taliban, that all they had to do was hold out until the summer of 2011 when the Americans would start to leave.

McChrystal had been confidentially forewarned of the president's decision. Two days before, Obama had held a videoconference with the ISAF commander. The president made clear that he was giving ISAF a short-term surge of American troops in order to reverse the Taliban's momentum, and to buy time for Afghan forces to grow and take charge of security. The military had long told the president that areas cleared of insurgents would be ready to hand over to Afghan security forces in two years. As the 2nd Marine Expeditionary Brigade arrived in Helmand in the summer 2009, Obama figured that American forces could begin drawdown and return home from Afghanistan in the summer of 2011.

McChrystal, like Defense Secretary Gates, felt able to sign up for this timetable on the understanding that the transfer of security to Afghan responsibility would be 'conditions-based' – that is, based on an assessment of security and governance conditions in each district and province.[26] However, it was clear that in reality US forces would start coming home in July 2011 no matter what. In this respect, the president had a far better sense of the national mood than the US military. Public support for the surge itself was reasonably high at 59 per cent according to CNN polling. But this was against a background of declining support for the war, which had dropped from 50 per cent in May 2009 to 41 per cent in July, and never climbed above 46 per cent for the rest of 2009.[27]

In addition to asking for more US troops, McChrystal had also recommended that Afghan National Security Forces be increased to 400,000, comprising 260,000 soldiers and 140,000 police. At the time the ANA stood at 92,000 and had been approved to grow to 134,000, and the Afghan National Police consisted of 84,000 men. Obama refused to sign off on the 400,000 target given the huge expense, nor was he prepared to agree to an end strength for the Afghan National Security Forces. He simply instructed ISAF to train as many Afghan soldiers and police as possible over the next two years.[28]

The Obama announcement meant two things for the campaign in the south. First, by the summer of 2010 there would be more American and Afghan forces, starting with more US Marines for Helmand followed by a US Army brigade for Kandahar. Second, there was added pressure on ISAF for early successes in the south, to show how the larger forces were making a difference. Both reinforced the logic of focusing on central Helmand in early 2010 – given that US Marine numbers there were due to double to 20,000 – and then shifting to Kandahar over the summer. An added consideration was the threat to Lashkar Gah from insurgent forces in Nad-e Ali and Marjah, creating the ever-present risk of another spectacular attack like the one carried out in October 2008, which would undermine any claim that ISAF was reversing Taliban gains. In contrast, as McChrystal recalls, Kandahar city 'wasn't besieged or in imminent danger of failing'.[29] Thus, by December 2009, it was decided to make central Helmand the main effort of the ISAF campaign in early 2010, with the purpose of inflicting 'a strategic defeat' on the Taliban and thereby creating 'campaign momentum'.[30]

On 8 December, McChrystal testified before the Senate and House Foreign Relations committees in support of the surge outlined in the president's speech. He did so alongside the US ambassador to Afghanistan, Karl Eikenberry. Both put on a show of being in sync with one another; glancing over at Eikenberry, McChrystal claimed that 'the person I listen to most is about three feet to my right'.[31] In reality, relations between the two had completely collapsed when Eikenberry sent a cable to the president in early November opposing any further deployment of US forces until the Afghan government cleaned up its act and got a grip on corruption.[32] Eikenberry was a retired lieutenant general in the US Army, who had previously served as a commander of Combined Forces Command in Afghanistan in 2007, so he was not shy about drifting into McChrystal's lane.

A few days before these congressional hearings, NATO partners agreed to deploy 7,000 more troops, including 500 from Britain.[33] This went some way to assuaging the concerns in Congress that McChrystal was not getting the full 40,000 troops that he had originally requested. However, the chair of the Senate Armed Services Committee, Senator Carl Levin, put his finger on the real problem: 'Our Achilles heel in Afghanistan, in the words of one Marine company commander, is not a shortage of US troops. It's a shortage of Afghan troops.' Levin correctly noted that it would be up to Afghan forces to secure the ground cleared of Taliban, and yet the ratio of US Marines to Afghan troops and police in Helmand was five to one.[34] The situation was about to get far worse as US Marine numbers were set to almost double, which raised the prospect of British and American units competing for Afghan partners.

Much like Obama, Downing Street was worried about the apparent lack of progress in the Afghanistan campaign, especially after the shambles of Operation Panchai Palang. Prime Minister Gordon Brown visited Camp Leatherneck on 30 August to receive a verbal briefing from the ISAF commander on the findings of his campaign assessment; this was eleven days before the campaign assessment report was sent to President Obama. Headlining his report, McChrystal described the situation in Afghanistan as 'deteriorating but winnable'. Brown cautioned McChrystal against offering 'too bleak' an assessment, as this could further undermine public support for the war. He told McChrystal that the British domestic audience, and those of other allies, needed to see progress in the campaign on a 'month-to-month' timeline, 'not year-to-year'.[35]

Brown was right to worry. Much like in the United States, British public opinion had turned decisively against the war in the summer of 2009, after the heavy British losses in Panchai Palang. Not surprisingly therefore, he was keen to play up the prospects for progress and a prompt withdrawal of British forces from Afghanistan. Following Obama's West Point speech, the prime minister said that he expected security responsibility in some Helmand districts to be transferred to Afghan security forces by the end of 2010. This positive message was echoed by the outgoing British deputy commander of ISAF, Lieutenant General Jim Dutton, in an op-ed for the *Guardian* newspaper. Citing improved access to education and health care across Afghanistan, and the extra forces being sent by the United States and NATO partners, Dutton declared 'failure should not be contemplated; we must maintain our resolve'.[36] Dutton's successor was less sanguine. With refreshing honesty, Parker told the *Daily Telegraph* that ISAF knew it had 'lost the initiative' and that the Taliban had enjoyed more success in recent years. Of the prime minister's suggestion that security transition to Afghan hands in Helmand could occur by the end of 2010, Parker simply said that it was 'very foolish to start setting deadlines for something as critical as that'.[37]

Weighing heavy on Parker's mind was a grim milestone: the hundredth British soldier to die in Afghanistan was Lance Corporal Adam Drane of the Royal Anglians, who was shot and killed in Nad-e Ali district on 7 December 2009.[38] With the prospect of major offensives in Helmand and Kandahar, British troops and their American and Afghan allies were facing a tough year ahead. In his op-ed Dutton had refuted the notion that 'more troops will generate more violence'.[39] The Taliban promised otherwise. As a senior insurgent commander told the BBC: 'Obama is sending more troops to Afghanistan and that means more Americans will die.'[40]

PREPARING THE OFFENSIVE

Planning for Operation Moshtarak began in earnest in December 2009. Once it was decided that central Helmand would be dealt with before Kandahar, the question arose of which part of central Helmand to tackle first. The British Ministry of Defence was worried that the US Marine offensive in Marjah would be a rerun of Panchai Palang, with heavy fighting and casualties, and so it wanted to disassociate this from the British 'steal' of the Chah-e Anjir. However, ISAF intelligence assessed that there was significant risk of insurgents being displaced into northern Nad-e Ali if the Marjah operation was undertaken first, and vice versa. Accordingly, RC-South headquarters decided to conduct both operations simultaneously. This would also create a more credible impression that ISAF was regaining momentum in the war.[41]

More so than any other major ISAF operation, governance had primacy in Moshtarak. This was emphasised in the formal operational order issued by Carter in mid January 2010. A number of practical implications flowed from this. It meant that the operation would be shaped by the preferences of Mangal as the provincial governor and Habibullah as the district governor of Nad-e Ali. Thus, as one ISAF planner put it, 'the most important question for commanders when approaching operations was "is this what the provincial governor or DG wants?"' Moreover, commanders were told that in the conduct of operations 'governance is at the tip of the spear'. Carter understood that key to holding areas cleared of Taliban would be the rapid establishment of local governance and funding of projects to improve the lives of local people.[42]

By this stage it was uniformly understood within the British Army that success in counter-insurgency ultimately depended on persuading local people that they would be better off with the government than with the insurgents. For this to happen, there had to be a degree of security, but even more there had to be some governance at the local level. In a counter-insurgency context, building local governance was primarily about connecting people with national government. This was especially important in Afghanistan, where 80 per cent of the population live in the countryside and therefore far away from the reaches of Kabul. For most Afghans, the central government was largely absent from their lives.

There were two main problems here. One was the reluctance of Afghan government line ministries – the ministries for agriculture, rural development, education, public health and justice – to visit remote districts. The other was the lack of trained local government officials. Often officials appointed to remote districts never even turned up, although they drew their salaries nonetheless. When the deputy head of the Afghan Independent Local Governance Directorate visited Nawa district in Helmand in November 2009, he found only the district governor and his executive officer present; the other fifty-seven officials on the payroll were nowhere to be seen. The absence of effective local state governance created an opportunity for the Taliban to offer shadow government instead.

In response, ISAF Joint Command and the Local Governance Directorate came up with a plan to rapidly improve security and local government in eighty 'key terrain districts'; these were particularly important districts in terms of being population centres or economic hubs, and it was here that the insurgency was rife.[43] Called the District Delivery Programme, it would see a major injection of resources and newly appointed officials in districts cleared of insurgents by ISAF and Afghan security forces. This programme was to be funded by USAID and the British Department for International Development, and was intended to run alongside other USAID efforts to improve governance and agricultural output in rural areas. Central to the design of the programme was the collaboration with provincial and district governors, as well as consultation with local communities, to produce tailored packages that met local needs.[44] The District Delivery Programme would provide the platform for enhanced support to local government in Nad-e Ali and Marjah in support of Operation Moshtarak.[45]

Selling Moshtarak to audiences in Helmand and Kabul, as well as back home in London and Washington, was another key aspect of the preparations for the operation. In Helmand, the main message was that ISAF and Afghan security forces were coming to stay in Nad-e Ali and Marjah, and that life would be better afterwards. There was some truth to this: locals from Marjah visiting the nearby district of Nawa in late 2009 could readily see the improvements that followed, with more trading and better public services, when the Taliban were pushed out by the US Marines. But RC-South command realised that the operation 'also had to be fought in Kabul'.[46] Hence, a coordinated public relations effort was undertaken by ISAF Command. McChrystal would regularly meet with President Karzai, and likewise Rodriguez with the Afghan defence and interior ministers, to keep them on side.

Within 11 Brigade headquarters, there was an acute awareness of the need also to 'prepare people back home'. The deputy commander of Task Force Helmand had been assistant director for strategic communications in the Ministry of Defence at the time of Operation Panchai Palang. He saw at first hand that 'people weren't expecting how it would go down': that is to say, they were not expecting such fierce fighting and quite so many British casualties.[47] This time, far more effort was put into preparing the British political establishment and public. The Ministry of Defence decided to explain to the media, in some detail, how the operation would be conducted in such a way as to minimise the risk of casualties.

Mirroring these political preparations was a huge military effort. In advance of Operation Moshtarak, the ANA began to mass forces in Helmand. Five *kandaks* from neighbouring provinces were redeployed to Helmand. Two Afghan commando *kandaks* were also sent to Helmand, and the Ministry of Interior sent nine hundred Afghan National Civil Order Police. The Afghan Ministry of Defence also raised sixteen new infantry companies and stood up a new brigade for Helmand, designated 3/215 Brigade. However, foot-dragging by Afghan officials meant that 3/215 was only formed two weeks before the launch of the operation. Led by Colonel Sherin Shah, it was based in Camp

Shorabak near Camp Bastion, even though it was due to partner with
Task Force Helmand based in Lashkar Gah.

The word *moshtarak* means 'together' in Dari, and the name for
the operation had been chosen to underline the central importance
of partnership with the Afghans. In his command direction to ISAF
forces, Carter identified partnership with Afghan security forces as
'the glue' that held the operation together.[48] In Operation Panchai
Palang, ISAF and Afghan army units had met each other for the first
time when boarding helicopters to fly into combat. Things would be
done differently this time. As ordered by RC-South headquarters,
British and Afghan forces assembled in Camp Bastion in advance of
the operation, to train together and to rehearse tactical plans.[49] By
one account, some of the training was 'laughably simple': 'Troops
went to the flight line in Bastion, where a Chinook was parked. They
got on. Then went back to their tents.'[50]

OPERATION MOSHTARAK

The Taliban saw the ISAF offensive coming. They were meant to.
Following the model of Tor Shpa'h, RC-South authorised 11 Brigade
to tell local elders about the operation in some detail, working
through Habibullah to get the message out. Initially, the idea of
'telegraphing' the offensive had been ruled out on the grounds that
ISAF would be giving up the element of surprise. However,
RC-South felt it more important that locals be reassured that this
operation would not be like the previous ISAF offensives in Babaji
and Marjah in 2009. This time, ISAF and Afghan security forces
would stay on and improve the lives of locals. British commanders
also knew local elders would alert Taliban commanders – indeed,
they banked on it – that a massive force was heading their way in
the hope that the insurgents would withdraw.

The 'shape' phase of Moshtarak also involved preliminary operations to probe insurgent defences. In three pulses in January 2010, D
Company of the Royal Welsh roamed through Babaji moving towards
the Shamalan Canal. The purpose was to 'unmask' insurgent capabilities and defensive positions in preparation for the push into the Chah-e
Anjir Triangle. As before, jittery Taliban commanders gave away their

locations through radio and mobile communication. Many commanders simply fled, and those that did not were captured by British special forces. Before the offensive had even begun, therefore, the British had eviscerated Taliban tactical command in the Chah-e Anjir Triangle; in all, around thirty insurgent commanders were killed or captured. Intercepts of insurgent communications revealed that the Taliban shadow provincial governor, Mullah Ahmed Shah, had fled the scene. They also confirmed the presence in Saidabad of a thirty-strong fighting group, a sort of Taliban quick reaction force, which was preparing to move north to support the insurgent defence of Chah-e Anjir. This underlined the importance of pinning down Taliban forces in the south of Nad-e Ali, in Khushhal Kalay and Saidabad, to prevent them from disrupting the ISAF offensive.[51] Ten days in advance of the start of Moshtarak, a company of Scots Guards was lifted by helicopter into Saidabad. After a week of heavy fighting, the Guards estimated they had killed forty insurgents. At the same time, a company of Grenadier Guards advanced in armoured vehicles into Khushhal Kalay, where they faced only fragmented resistance. With these two operations, 11 Brigade had put in place a southern block for Operation Moshtarak. Across Helmand, British battlegroups in Gereshk, Sangin and Musa Qala were instructed to limit their own operations for the first three days following the Moshtarak offensive, so Task Force Helmand could focus its attention and resources (such as intelligence and air support) on Moshtarak. Thereafter, they were to increase patrolling in order to deter insurgent displacement from Nad-e Ali. Everything was now ready for D-Day, which was set for 12 February. Well, almost everything.

Operation Moshtarak was to have 'an Afghan trigger'. It was to be the first major ISAF operation approved by President Karzai. Yet D-Day came and went without Karzai giving his approval. Thousands of British, American and Afghan troops were waiting in bases across Helmand. For one British company commander, this proved to be a blessing in disguise. 'We were actually relieved as with all the rehearsals and battle prep we were all shattered. The 24-hour delay allowed us all to get some rest and fine-tune the plans before we set off.'[52] However, Task Force Helmand was anxious because the weather was due to turn the following day and could cause a 72-hour delay in the operation.[53] McChrystal now requested an urgent meeting with the president. Karzai appeared bewildered to find a major offensive held up by waiting for his say-so. 'General McChrystal,' he said, 'you'll have to forgive me. I've never been asked to approve this kind of operation before.' One senior British officer, who had served as an ISAF adviser to the Afghan National Security Council, would later reflect that this kind of dithering was 'bloody typical' of Karzai.[54] McChrystal offered a more diplomatic view in his memoir, suggesting that Karzai was understandably reluctant, 'fearing it was a charade to put a fig leaf, or "Afghan face", on what was still an entirely Coalition-controlled operation'. But McChrystal, like Carter, was completely serious about the need for ISAF to follow Afghan political direction. His reasoning was compelling: 'ISAF could never win the war; the Afghans must do that. And they couldn't win it until they owned it. That ownership started at the top.' McChrystal waited patiently for Karzai to deliberate with his ministers and generals. Then Karzai gave his approval. D-Day was reset.[55]

In the early hours of 13 February, British and Afghan troops boarded dozens of helicopters for the short flight to northern Nad-e Ali. Arriving in three waves of thirty-six helicopters each, the entire assault force was on the ground in the Chah-e Anjir Triangle by daybreak. Simultaneously, the 2nd Marine Expeditionary Brigade arrived in Marjah on a fleet of sixty helicopters, some flying from Camp Bastion and some from Camp Dwyer, the US Marines' main base in southern Helmand. The Moshtarak offensive had started. It would involve 1,200 soldiers from Task Force Helmand, 3,000 US Marines and 4,400 Afghan troops.

The plan was for three companies of the Royal Welsh battlegroup to air assault with their Afghan partners onto the Taliban-held villages of Naqilabad Qalay and Showal in the Chah-e Anjir Triangle; the fourth company was to air assault onto an insurgent position in the 'Babaji Pear', just east of the Shamalan Canal. A company of Coldstream Guards and a company of Estonians with their Afghan partners were to seize control of all crossing points on the Shamalan Canal in order to stop insurgents fleeing from Chah-e Anjir into Babaji. Remarkably, 11 Brigade were repeating the mistake made by 19 Brigade in overestimating the depth of the Shamalan Canal.

Even though the Taliban had been alerted to the offensive by the advance messaging, ISAF was able to achieve some tactical surprise through aviation 'shows of force' to draw the insurgents away from helicopter landing sites. ISAF also flooded Nad-e Ali and Marjah with surveillance and reconnaissance assets – unmanned drones and jet fighters with surveillance pods – in order 'to detect enemy force distribution'.[56] With their field commanders captured or having fled, the Taliban in Chah-e Anjir were in complete disarray. The British found insurgent response to be 'exceptionally muted' with only sporadic gunfire. After just one day, the Taliban effectively conceded defeat: at midday on 14 February, the Taliban military commission in Quetta issued an order to all fighters to hide their weapons and avoid direct battle with ISAF forces.[57]

THE BATTLE FOR MARJAH

Marjah was an altogether tougher proposition than Chah-e Anjir. It had been in Taliban hands since the summer of 2008. The circumstances under which this happened are murky. Until recently, it was widely believed that local opium farmers had allied with the Taliban in order to protect their fields from Governor Mangal's poppy eradication programme.[58] More recently, it has emerged that the former police chief of Helmand, Abdul Rahman Jan, in fact 'invited' the Taliban into Marjah after his own poppy fields had been targeted by Mangal, causing him to lose 20 per cent of his poppy crop. In retaliation, and to protect his fields from further eradication, Abdul Rahman negotiated a deal with the Taliban shadow governor of Helmand 'whereby the "policeman" guarding the checkpoints in Marjeh would become "Taliban" and other Taliban would be allowed into Marjeh'.[59] Either way, Marjah was one of the main production and processing centres for opium in Helmand. By 2010 there were almost 190 'factories' in the area, where opium paste was processed into heroin, and from which the Taliban were earning $200,000 per month in tax.[60]

As in northern Nad-e Ali, the offensive in Marjah was preceded by telling local elders that ISAF was coming, and to encourage the Taliban to flee. However, as Habibullah's contacts in Marjah were not as good as in northern Helmand, RC-South resorted to leaflet drops to get the message out; this was a pointless exercise, however, since virtually all residents in Marjah were illiterate. At the same time, US Marine reconnaissance units operating alongside Afghan special forces conducted probes into Marjah to get eyes on the ground. ISAF intelligence had assumed that the residents in Marjah were rich on the proceeds of the drug trade. The ground reconnaissance reported back a very different picture: most residents were poor tenant farmers working fields belonging to wealthy landowners, many of whom were living in Lashkar Gah. Since these people had not prospered under Taliban rule, ISAF now felt confident there would be no popular support to help the Taliban resist the arrival of ISAF and Afghan forces.[61] However, it was still proving difficult for ISAF to get its message out to the residents of Marjah. In a last-ditch effort, around 350 elders from the main tribes in Marjah were assembled in Lashkar Gah to meet with the Afghan interior minister, Hanif Atmar, on the eve of D-Day. Voicing what many thought, one elder said: 'Yes, we want this operation in our area, but do not leave, as you have in other areas, and let the Taliban back in.'[62] The problem was that these elders were actually based outside of Marjah and it was not clear if they spoke for the residents.[63] In early February, US SEAL teams conducted raids to capture or kill Taliban commanders in Marjah. In what was most likely an overestimate, the *Sunday Times* reported subsequently that there were up to a thousand Taliban holed up in the area. One Taliban commander spoke to the newspaper via satellite phone, declaring that he and his 120 fighters would fight to the last.[64] The *New York Times* reported another Taliban commander as claiming that his men had planted 'thousands of mines' on Marjah's roads and paths. 'The Afghan and foreign soldiers always use footpaths while they walk and do their patrols,' said Mullah Mir Azar. 'That's why we have paid such close attention to them.'[65]

In the early hours of 13 February, wave after wave of helicopters dropped hundreds of US Marines and Afghan soldiers into Marjah. All told, 1,500 US Marines of the 1 Battalion, 6 Regiment (1/6) descended on the area in this predawn air assault, with 1,500 Marines from 3/6 following behind. By the end of D-Day, the Marines had seized control of the northern half of Marjah, including one of its two main bazaars.[66] As in the Chah-e Anjir Triangle, the Taliban did not contest the initial ISAF assault. There was some spirited resistance around noon on the first day, but this soon ended when a B-1B bomber flattened an insurgent compound with a 500-pound bomb.[67] One journalist on the ground noted that 'the Marines had expected another Fallujah, with hundreds of hard-core militants ready to fight to the death. What they got instead was Baghdad – the bad guys melted back into the population or fled.'[68]

The insurgents made it hard going, however, since they used IEDs, ambushes and sniper fire to harass advancing marines and Afghan troops. As they moved into Marjah, marines struggled to identify the key buildings. The 1/6 set up base in a compound they thought was a former police station but turned out to be a former school. When Karzai found out he was incensed. He gave the marines forty-eight hours to clear out; McChrystal bought them another two days.[69] On day two of the offensive the rules on using air strikes were tightened up when twelve civilians, all members of the same family, were killed after their compound was hit by an American missile. Thereafter, calls for air support from frustrated marines, taking fire from compounds or seeing insurgents move into position to ambush them, would be mostly denied by RC-South. The Taliban took advantage of ISAF rules of engagement, sending women and children onto the roofs of buildings from which they would fire on US and Afghan forces.[70] By day three the marines had seized the centre of Marjah and its second bazaar. They had to move across open muddy fields, in order to avoid booby-trapped paths, which made for slow and dangerous progress; insurgent sharpshooters constantly caused marines and Afghan troops to dive to the ground or dash for whatever cover they could find. Marines would return heavy automatic fire but insurgent sharpshooters proved remarkably difficult to take out. All the main routes, crossroads and bazaars in Marjah had been secured by the end of the third day, by which time some marine platoons were running out of ammunition.[71] By day four, insurgent resistance had tapered off, civilians began to move around more freely, and convoys of Afghan police were brought in to begin the 'hold phase'. The US Marines had estimated that there were four hundred insurgents in Marjah, half of whom had been chased out or killed by mid February.[72]

THE RULE OF THREE

Everybody expected it to be difficult to 'hold' territory seized from the Taliban. Hence, 11 Brigade put an immense amount of preparation into it. Through 'persistent security presence', and using checkpoints and control of canal crossing points, 11 Brigade intended to create a series of 'protection communities' in Nad-e Ali. These would keep insurgents out of populated areas and enable governance to grow. Yet the main challenge was generating a sufficient security force to ensure this persistent presence. Northern Nad-e Ali was divided into a number of operational 'boxes', each with a population of about 12,000 people. It was estimated that at least three hundred soldiers and police would be needed to secure a populace of this size. In light of this, British Army, Afghan army and Afghan police units were to work together in the same operational box, at company and platoon level. James Cowan called this 'the Rule of Three'.[73]

One major problem with this concept of operations was the unreliability of the Afghan police in Helmand. They were few in number and many of them were high on drugs; they also had a reputation for robbing locals and raping children. ISAF had a rolling programme to clean up Afghan police units in key districts, with the suitably anodyne name 'Focused District Delivery Program': entire police units would be taken out of their locality, drug addicts would be weeded out, and the whole unit retrained. When the Gereshk police force was taken to the Kandahar regional training centre under this programme in 2008, 119 out of 130 policemen tested positive for drugs.[74] It was obvious that the EUPOL mission in Helmand had singularly failed to develop the police. The lightly armed EUPOL trainers could not be blamed; it was simply too dangerous for them to leave the main base in Lashkar Gah in order to train the police on the ground. In response to this situation, Cowan had established an interim Helmand police training academy, which was up and running by early December 2009. Every fortnight it was churning out 150 trained police officers, and it produced 450 newly minted officers in time for Operation Moshtarak.[75] Many of these new police ended up deserting; of the first hundred sent to Nad-e Ali, half had disappeared within a few weeks.[76] Nonetheless, the Helmand police academy was crucial to turning things around in Nad-e Ali, which like many other districts in Afghanistan suffered from appalling police corruption. Moreover, following Moshtarak, the British were able to put pressure on Kabul to change the provincial chief of police in Helmand and the district chiefs of police in Nad-e Ali, Gereshk and Sangin. Still, even months after Operation Moshtarak, Afghan officials in Helmand admitted that there was still much work to do, as corrupt mid-level police commanders continued to control the checkpoints and so were in prime position to extort money from locals.[77]

The ANA was more reliable than the Afghan police but here too there was a problem with numbers. One British mentor calculated that only about 45 per cent of the 3/215 manpower was actually available to deploy. Soldiers were deserting in large numbers. As one British Army mentor observed, 'When an Afghan soldier goes on leave, you are unlikely to see him return.' So whereas a British infantry company was 120 strong, the typical ANA company comprised only around 50 soldiers.[78] The basic flaw, then, with the Rule of Three was that there were not enough Afghan soldiers and police (even with the interim police academy) for it to work. For this reason, some ISAF officers thought the Rule of Three was 'doomed from the beginning'.[79]

Despite this, working alongside Afghan soldiers and police, 11 Brigade was able to improve security in Nad-e Ali. The atmosphere on the ground and key indicators – such as the number of shops open in the bazaar and the number of children attending school – all suggested that local people felt that security in the district had improved.[80] In one survey of five hundred callers to Radio Nad-e Ali, 95 per cent of respondents felt that life was 'better or very much better' in the district following Operation Moshtarak.[81] By the end of their tour, 11 Brigade had seen an 85 per cent drop in 'significant activities' involving insurgents (called SIGACTS in military jargon, and meaning an incident involving a gun battle or explosion) in Nad-e Ali: at its height, there were 150 SIGACTS per week in Nad-e Ali; this had fallen to two per week by March 2010.[82] One of the reasons might have been the beginning of the poppy harvest. All the same, this was an impressive downturn in armed violence.

Development activities were as important as persistent security operations. In military doctrine, the 'hold' and the 'build' were identified as distinct and sequential phases of counter-insurgency operations. In reality, however, the two were intertwined and simultaneous. The key to keeping insurgents out of a village was by showing the locals that they would be better off under the government, by funding development projects and public services. As Lindy Cameron, the then head of the Helmand PRT, observed, 'Counter-insurgency is very

political: it is really about delivering on promises to expectations.'[83]
To support this effort there was intense planning and preparation
between the PRT and the task force, so much so in fact that the British
Army had to lend the PRT a team of military planners so they could
keep up with the blizzard of activity.[84] The package for Nad-e Ali and
Marjah, agreed and funded under the District Delivery Programme,
would see $3 million of aid injected into the district.[85] The Helmand
PRT also committed another £8 million in the first six months of
2010. These funds were spent on various projects which gave employment to local people: projects such as new public buildings, paving
and lighting for bazaars, and digging wells and cleaning out canals.
Crucially, the District Stabilisation Team in Nad-e Ali understood the
importance of empowering local governance. They made sure that
PRT funding was routed through the District Development Shura,
thereby allowing locals to decide how these funds were invested in
their own communities.[86]

THE GOLDEN HOUR

Things did not go so well in Marjah. In part, this reflected the nature
of the challenge. As the deputy commander of RC-South observed,
'We were eighteen months along in Nad-e Ali, whereas Marjah was a
black hole beforehand.'[87] The US Marines struggled, and failed, to keep
the Taliban out of Marjah. In part this was because many Taliban,
who were local, never left: they simply stashed their weapons and bided
their time. In late April and early May, they began to beat and intimidate the inhabitants to stop them taking money from the Americans
and supporting the Afghan government. They also intensified their
attacks on the marines. Locals were helpless to stop this. One farmer
explained to the *New York Times*:

> We know who the Taliban are. When they attack the police or the
> Americans, they put down their weapons and sit down with ordinary
> people. We cannot say a word against them, they know us and we
> know them pretty well. We know Taliban are killing people and threat-
> ening people, but we cannot stand against them, or tell Americans or
> police about their whereabouts.

Many civilians simply fled. The Afghan Red Crescent Society estimated that 150 families escaped Marjah in the first two weeks of May 2010. The marines fought fire with fire, but this made matters worse for the residents. According to one farmer who left Marjah, 'every day they were fighting and shelling'. He added: 'we do not feel secure in the village and we decided to leave. Security is getting worse day by day.'[88] Returning to the district in late May, this was also one journalist's impression: 'Marjah had grown more violent and deadly than it had been in the first month' of Moshtarak.[89]

All of this could have been anticipated. And yet, the 2nd Marine Expeditionary Brigade appears to have put less effort into preparing for the 'hold' phase than 11 Brigade. Unlike the British, the US Marines made no attempt to integrate their planning with the Helmand PRT. The marines asked the PRT District Stabilisation Team for Marjah to attend their mission rehearsal sessions at Camp Dwyer just one week before D-Day; this was the first time the PRT team met the commanding officers of the 1/6 and 3/6 Marines. No wonder PRT officials 'got the impression that [US Marine] planning for stabilisation was very last-minute'.[90] Of course, this may be down to organisational culture: the US Marine Corps famously likes to do everything for itself, and the 2nd Marine Expeditionary Brigade would have brought more resources, in terms of money and personnel, than what was at the disposal of the Helmand PRT. The marines may have figured that they didn't really need the PRT.[91]

What they did need was a capable governor for Marjah. The man appointed by Karzai was presented as a respected Pashtun elder who had lived in Marjah as a youth. It subsequently transpired that the sixty-year-old Haji Zahir had served four years in a German jail for attempted murder, before being deported to Pakistan in 2003.[92] British and American diplomats in Helmand discovered this only after Moshtarak had started, when they heard disturbing rumours and contacted Interpol. Since there was nothing they could do about it, they reassured themselves that 'the position of sub-district governor is a low-level position, and Mangal intended Zahir's appointment to be on a temporary basis'.[93] If true, this was hardly encouraging.

Making matters worse was Zahir's late arrival in Marjah. One of the key lessons that RC-South drew from previous operations was that in the 'hold phase', there was a '"golden hour" for the delivery

of promises' in terms of security and governance.[94] Thus, RC-South
planners sought to have government officials on the ground as soon
as possible after the clear phase had been completed, to hold shuras
with local elders. For some reason, Haji Zahir did not arrive in Marjah
until nine days after the launch of Operation Moshtarak. Thus, district
government was slow to get going in the town. According to a senior
stabilisation officer at RC-South headquarters, 'Two weeks in, the US
Marines were asking "Where are the governance and stabilisation
bits?"'[95] They did not wait for government to appear. Marine civil
affairs units pushed aggressively to get projects off the ground, to
give employment to locals and improve their environment. In this
way 'the Marines were pretty good at making it look like the district
governor was delivering'.[96] By early March, Haji Zahir was still
struggling to get his office up and running. Incredibly, it also turned
out that he did not speak Pashto and so 'had to use a translator, much
to the annoyance of locals'.[97] One marine civil affairs officer
noted that the local view of the new district governor was 'definitely
mixed'.[98] The golden hour had passed, and Haji Zahir had missed it.

SIGNALS INTELLIGENCE

Operation Moshtarak had underscored a key vulnerability for the
Taliban, namely insecure communications. Taliban leaders were
pinpointed through their radio and mobile communications, and
targeted for drone strikes or commando raids. ISAF intelligence was
also able to gauge the state of crumbling insurgent defences by
listening to radio communications between Taliban fighters, which
ISAF called 'i-comm chatter'. All of this should come as no surprise
to any informed Western observer. Modern militaries spend vast
sums on securing their battlefield communications.[99] This kind of
technical capability was well beyond the means of the Taliban, who
instead just used normal CB radios. Equally, it is hardly surprising
that British intelligence were able to monitor Taliban mobile phone
communications, given recent revelations about the activities of
Government Communications Headquarters (GCHQ), Britain's
signals intelligence agency, and its American equivalent, the National
Security Agency. By 2009, GCHQ had deployed a number of

personnel to Helmand and established 'listening posts' in the main British bases; mobile phone communications intercepted in the field were analysed by a ninety-strong team back in Britain at GCHQ headquarters in Cheltenham.[100]

How aware were the Taliban of this vulnerability, and what did they do in response? Interviews with thirty-seven Taliban field commanders from across Helmand conducted a year after Operation Moshtarak provided fascinating insights on these questions. Only four interviewees dismissed this threat as 'rumours and propaganda' on the grounds that 'if they [the British and Americans] could discover and listen to our radio and telephone conversations then they could [have] killed all the Taliban by now'.[101] Or, as another commander put it, 'They are well-equipped people but still their machineries are not working well against mujahedin.'[102]

Yet most insurgent commanders probably knew that the enemy could listen in on their radio communications; anecdotal evidence even suggests that insurgents attempted to use this to their advantage. The journalist Ben Anderson witnessed one such incident in 2007, when Afghan soldiers tuned in to Taliban frequencies. The claims made by the insurgents that they were about to storm the patrol base with four hundred fighters were so outlandish that Anderson assumed the Taliban 'were being deliberately misleading'. The Afghan soldiers were not fazed, and began to taunt the Taliban about a battle they had just lost. 'Come back tomorrow without the planes and helicopters and we'll show you how to fight,' the insurgents retorted. 'We'll kick your ass the same way,' replied one Afghan soldier, much to the amusement of his comrades.[103]

It seems that most Taliban commanders also understood that the British and Americans had the ability to listen in on mobile calls. Some interviewees saw this as a 'big problem',[104] and a number of commanders in Kajaki and Marjah districts in particular appear to have abandoned technology for really important communications, sending a letter or a messenger instead.[105] However, many of the commanders were surprisingly relaxed, trusting in their countermeasures or simply placing their faith in God. Four interviewees talked about their use of Thuraya satellite phones, which they believed to be impossible to intercept; ironically, these were even easier to track.[106] Other counter-measures included keeping mobile phones off most of the time, frequently changing numbers, not registering SIM cards, and commanders using the phones of ordinary fighters in their group.[107] Some interviewees referred to the use of codes. 'When we are talking on mobile or radio, we have secret words … even if the British and Americans bring all their technology, they won't understand our words.'[108] Insurgents appeared to have been trained in the use of coded communications. 'We learned from our trainers how to use our radio and mobile, and also learned some secret words to use when we are talking on phone or radio.'[109] In this respect, one commander in Kajaki district, in the far north of Helmand, referred to training provided by 'Iranian engineers'.[110] Shia Iran had had frosty relations with the Sunni Taliban regime in the 1990s, but found common cause with the insurgents when the US and Britain invaded Afghanistan, and so it provided weapons and other material support to the Taliban insurgency in Helmand. But mostly, especially in central and southern Helmand, the trainers would have been from Pakistan Army intelligence. For all their training, according to one British source, most of the Taliban code words were laughable, such as 'where is the watermelon?' and 'bring the big thing'.[111]

A handful of commanders simply invoked the will of God. 'They [the British and Americans] have lots of possibilities and modern technology in their hands, but we don't care because we are standing against them with the full trust of God, and if God supports us, any kind of their technology will fail.'[112] What Operation Moshtarak showed was that the Taliban were sorely misguided to think that anything, even God, could stop the British and Americans from following their communications, and using this to devastating effect.

A BLEEDING ULCER

For all its tactical success, Operation Moshtarak was ultimately a strategic disappointment for ISAF. The inconvenient fact was that, for McChrystal, Marjah mattered the most. He had played up Moshtarak because he needed a big win to demonstrate to the White House the benefit of the surge, and to show the American and Afghan people that his new 'population-centric' counter-insurgency strategy was working. In the days leading up to the operation McChrystal had told the world's media: 'We've got government in a box, ready to roll in.'[113] He was talking about Marjah, where there had been a complete absence of Afghan government, and not about the extension of existing government in Nad-e Ali to the northern reaches of that district. Marjah was to be the key test of his strategy.[114] The action there was also going to grab all the attention, since that's where the US Marines were heading. As one senior US policy adviser put it: 'Marjah was the bright shiny object that everybody was focused on.'[115]

As the situation further improved in the British sector in northern Nad-e Ali, it got steadily worse in Marjah, with growing intimidation of local farmers and increasing attacks on Afghan and ISAF forces. McChrystal's patience was wearing thin. On a visit to Marjah in May, he barked at a marine colonel who asked for more time: 'How many days do you think we have before we run out of support from the international community?' Later, in a meeting with senior ISAF and Afghan generals and officials to review campaign progress in the south, an utterly exasperated McChrystal said of Marjah: 'This is a bleeding ulcer right now.'[116] In large part, however, this was a problem of McChrystal's making. RC-South felt that 'government in the box' was an 'unhelpful' metaphor, in that it created wholly unrealistic expectations that would be impossible to fulfil.[117] This view was shared by one senior official in Governor Mangal's office who 'completely disagreed with the idea of government in a box in Marjah', noting that 'it takes time to change people'.[118]

In his operational order to British and US Marine forces, Nick Carter had specified 'protecting the people' as the 'main effort' for Moshtarak. Yet the operation had mixed results. The marines killed an estimated sixteen to twenty-eight civilians in Marjah;[119] in contrast, there were no civilian casualties in the British sector. The fact that more civilians died in Marjah than in northern Nad-e Ali might have been due to more aggressive tactics by the marines, but equally it could simply have been down to the insurgents putting up stronger resistance, in particular making more widespread use of civilians as human shields. Certainly Marjah proved more deadly for ISAF: sixteen marines were killed in Marjah as against four British troops in Nad-e Ali. The relatively low number killed belies a far heavier toll for Moshtarak: by early March, over 730 casualties had been evacuated by helicopter for emergency medical treatment, including British and

American troops as well as Afghan soldiers and civilians. Forty-four per cent of these had suffered life-threatening injuries, including the loss of one or more limbs.[120]

In both the Chah-e Anjir Triangle and Marjah, Mangal had encouraged locals to stay put in their compounds while British, American and Afghan forces pushed the Taliban out. Understandably, many people ignored the advice. Anticipating this, reception centres were set up outside Lashkar Gah for people fleeing the fighting. The United Nations humanitarian agency estimated that Moshtarak produced as many as 3,800 internally displaced persons (although these figures may have been inflated by migrant labourers); of these, only 1,400 had returned to their homes in Nad-e Ali and Marjah by May.[121]

Moshtarak was also supposed to be a showcase for Afghan-led security. For Whitehall and Washington this was crucial. Just weeks before the operation, on 28 January 2010, the British government had hosted an international conference in London on the future of Afghanistan, at which a rough timetable was agreed for Afghan security forces to assume responsibility for whole provinces. The prime minister was pushing as hard on this as President Obama; Brown had announced in November 2009 that he expected at least five provinces to be handed over to the Afghan security forces within a year.[122] But how ready were they?

ISAF made a big deal about Operation Moshtarak being Afghan-led, but in truth it was not. It may have had 'an Afghan trigger', and even a couple of Afghan bullets, but it was an ISAF gun and shooter. British and American planners produced the operational and tactical plans for Moshtarak. Afghans provided some input, especially in identifying 'key targets', but they did not lead the planning. Rather, as one ISAF officer later revealed, 'There was frenetic planning at ISAF level and once the plan was developed, Afghans were brought in.' Indeed, when Task Force Helmand briefed the plan to 3/205 Brigade in late December 2009, the Afghan brigade commander, General Mohadin, became 'very difficult' because 'he was annoyed at not being included' in producing the plan.[123] Moreover, once the operation got under way, British and US battlegroup commands took over the running of things.

Standing next to his ANA partner, Brigadier General Larry Nicholson, the US Marine commander in Helmand, told reporters: 'There's a brotherhood there, of great trusting and cooperation between us. And this isn't fluff. This isn't talk. This is the real deal. The marines have great respect for the Afghan army and I think it's reciprocal.'[124] That was not how things looked on the ground. Marines were disgusted by the laziness of Afghan soldiers, who would endlessly smoke marijuana at night and rise late in the morning. Afghan company commanders would refuse to join their men on operations. Whenever they came under fire, Afghan soldiers would empty their guns in the general direction of the insurgents, without bothering to aim – 'spray and pray' the marines called it. In his first-hand account of US Marine operations in Marjah, the *Washington Post* journalist Rajiv Chandrasekaran exposes the fiction that 'Afghan officers were helping to plan day-to-day operations and leading the fight', as suggested by ISAF and Afghan officials in Kabul. He notes that the Afghan army *kandak* partnered with the 1/6 Marines had only 'just finished its basic training, and its men, most of whom were illiterate, lacked the skills to organize even the simplest missions'.[125] Indeed, partnering between the US Marines and Afghan soldiers did not go to plan. They were supposed to assemble and train together in advance, either at Camp Bastion or Camp Dwyer. But instead, as an ANA post-operation report notes, American and Afghan units 'met for the first time in Marjah'. The report notes how this led to poor integration as 'nuances in movement techniques were not known, which caused units to be tentative when encountering Taliban forces during initial operations'.[126] In his HBO documentary *The Battle for Marjah*, Ben Anderson shows what happened on the ground. As the marines cleared suspected Taliban compounds in Marjah, Afghan soldiers were supposed to go in first, as directed by McChrystal. Yet the Afghan soldiers were understandably nervous about this. Marines yelled at them: 'Go, go, get the fuck in there!' As they cautiously approached the compound door, reluctant Afghan soldiers were suddenly grabbed and used as human battering rams by marines who piled in behind them.[127]

The British were more sanguine about their Afghan partners. British mentors noted that while the ANA were far less capable than ISAF, they could be fearless in a firefight and were 'absolutely fantastic at finding IEDs', the cause of 80 per cent of ISAF and ANSF casualties during Moshtarak.[128] While not all Afghan troops were eagle-eyed when it came to spotting IEDs, some were spectacularly good at it:

on the first day of Operation Moshtarak, Afghan forces found forty-five IEDs in Showal.[129] Not surprisingly, Afghan troops were also better than Western troops at distinguishing insurgents from ordinary farmers. British troops were also amazed to find that when shot at by insurgents, 'the Afghans were happy to stand up and walk towards firing points, letting go with their American-supplied M-16 rifles'.[130] This was not always welcome, however, especially when it risked causing friendly force or civilian casualties; British officers found that Afghan troops did not really get the concept of 'courageous restraint'.

Like the US Marines, the British did find that Afghan soldiers could be lazy, refusing to patrol in the afternoon when it was hottest, and that some Afghan commanders simply would not join their soldiers on operations. However, some were involved closely in the planning process, and 'frequently their input to the plan would identify particular areas of cultural sensitivity close to target locations and steer the process to minimize impact on the local community'.[131] All the same, perhaps the greatest ANA weakness was its leadership. One senior British mentor reckoned that there were only four good officers out of fifty in 3/215 Brigade. He found that Afghan officers displayed 'gross ambivalence' towards their own soldiers and 'don't seem to care about the outcome of the war'.[132] The British overcame this weakness in Moshtarak by partnering in advance at Camp Bastion, and striving for continued sub-unit integration through the Rule of Three.[133] In this way, British strengths made up for Afghan shortcomings.

The bottom line was that the ANA was nowhere near ready to take over from ISAF. Following Moshtarak, one senior adviser on counter-insurgency concluded that the Afghan troops 'will do the fight, if you can get them to the fight'.[134] This was a good summary of Afghan capability at the time. It had been agreed at the London conference in January 2010 that the Afghan security forces would progressively take charge in a year's time. Operation Moshtarak suggested that this timetable looked pretty optimistic.

Undefeated

Nad-e Ali in the late spring of 2010 was a place transformed. Visitors from Britain could stroll freely through the district centre where previously they had needed to be surrounded by a phalanx of heavily armed bodyguards and trailed by armoured cars. The district governor's compound was a hive of activity with locals bringing their problems to officials where before there had been hardly any officials for them to meet. The District Community Council was in regular session, making decisions on how thousands of pounds of British aid was to be spent. The District Security Shura also met regularly, with the Afghan army commander and district chief of police working together under the authority of the district governor to take responsibility for securing their own district; previously, Afghan soldiers and police in the district centre would communicate with one another using the medium of fistfights, and occasionally through an exchange of gunfire.[1]

With good reason, there was a renewed sense of optimism as 4 Infantry Brigade took over from 11 Brigade in April 2010. Sangin remained immensely challenging for British forces, as did Marjah for the US Marines, but central Helmand looked largely secure as did southern Helmand under the 2nd Marine Expeditionary Brigade. Crucially, Operation Moshtarak had brought much more freedom of movement for locals, who could now travel between Lashkar Gah and Gereshk without fear of attack. For the new commander of Task Force Helmand, Brigadier Richard Felton, all that was left in terms of military action in central Helmand was some 'tidying up [of] the edges'. Indeed, a key priority for Felton was to avoid the big battles that had characterised previous tours by British brigades. Hence, he declared at the outset that there would be 'no totemic operations', and he imposed tight restrictions on the use of force in order to minimise the risks of collateral damage by British forces. One battlegroup commander recalled how '"courageous restraint" was hammered into us in pre-deployment training'. In the context of the intent to progressively hand over responsibility for security to Afghan forces, Felton correctly identified partnering as 'the tactical centre of gravity' in the campaign.[2]

The optimistic mood was similarly felt by 1st Battalion the Duke of Lancaster Regiment (1 Lancs), taking over as the British battlegroup for Combined Force Nad-e Ali; in line with the new emphasis on partnering with the Afghan police and army, British battlegroups in Helmand had re-formed as 'Combined Forces'. Following Operation Moshtarak, the Taliban had been pushed to the edges of the area. British intelligence identified up to seventy insurgents in Saidabad in southern Nad-e Ali, and insurgents were also still active in the Chah-e Anjir Triangle in northern Nad-e Ali. Over the summer, British and Afghan troops focused their operations on these remaining pockets of Taliban. The largest such operation was launched in August 2010 against Taliban-held Saidabad. The Taliban were thrown off guard when a company of US Marines moved up from Marjah to threaten Saidabad, thereby distracting the insurgents from the actual assault by a British infantry company ferried in on eight helicopters. Taliban defences rapidly collapsed, with insurgents fleeing east to Nawa district. The Hazara tribe who lived in the village were glad to be rid of the Taliban, and obligingly told the arriving British where the insurgents had buried IEDs.[3]

In Babaji, where the Taliban had encircled patrol bases with IEDs, things were more taxing for British troops. A reporter for the *Sun* newspaper visiting one British outpost was warned: 'walk out there on your own and you would be dead in seconds. That field is full of IEDs.' Never cleared of Taliban, the Babaji Pear was particularly bad for the Scots Guards company deployed there, who spent April to October 2010 receiving daily fire from insurgents. By the end of the tour, this one company of guardsmen had got involved in 650 gunfights and expended 350,000 rounds of small arms ammunition keeping the insurgents at bay. It proved to be a more difficult tour for 4 Brigade than anticipated at the outset, with fifty-five soldiers killed in action and a further four hundred injured.[4] British ministers promised that the handover of security responsibility to Afghan forces would be 'conditions-based'. However, the persistently high rate of British casualties strongly suggested that the conditions were not suitable to begin the phased withdrawal of Western combat power from Helmand.[5]

THE GLOVES COME OFF

With the British continuing to struggle in Helmand as the summer wore on, General David Petraeus arrived to take charge of the overall war effort in Afghanistan. In a remarkable turn of events, McChrystal had been fired by Obama in late June, when he was quoted making derogatory remarks about Vice President Biden (whom he referred to as 'Bite Me') and other senior civilian officials in a lengthy profile for *Rolling Stone* magazine. Entitled 'Runaway General', the article portrayed McChrystal as a loose cannon who had scant regard for the US civilian leadership.[6] Set against all that McChrystal had achieved in terms of invigorating and giving strategic direction to the Afghanistan war effort, the *Rolling Stone* profile and its consequences were grossly unfair. However, Obama was already disillusioned with the way that McChrystal had used the news media to influence administration policy on troop numbers for Afghanistan. McChrystal's command and career were terminated in a twenty-minute meeting with the president on 23 June.[7]

As commander of US and multilateral forces in Iraq from 2007 to 2008, Petraeus was credited with turning around a losing war. In October 2008, he had taken charge of CENTCOM based in Tampa, Florida, which was responsible for overseeing the Iraq and Afghanistan wars. By wanting him to return to a field command, Obama was asking Petraeus to take a step down in the military hierarchy for the sake of his country. He was expected to bring better political skills than McChrystal and more willingness to work with civilian policymakers.[8]

What was not expected was a change in campaign strategy, especially as the population-centric approach to counter-insurgency introduced by McChrystal had originally been developed by Petraeus in Iraq. Yet as commander of US Joint Special Operations Command from 2003 to 2008, McChrystal had also developed a whole new approach to the secret fight against insurgent networks involving better fusion of intelligence from multiple sources, and far closer integration of intelligence, special operations and counter-insurgency forces. At the heart of this new approach was a faster 'targeting cycle' powered by the rapid exploitation of intelligence.[9] Where previously it would take days for special operations forces to receive intelligence and prepare for raids, the cycle was radically compressed: intelligence gathered on a raid was analysed immediately so the special operations team could be sent directly on to the next target. This prevented insurgents from being tipped off and going to ground. It also increased hugely the tempo and thereby number of operations. The result was a massive kill/capture campaign conducted by US special operations forces in Iraq, which was a crucial and underappreciated element in how a losing war was turned around over 2006–8. The same techniques were brought to Afghanistan when McChrystal assumed command in mid 2009.[10] As one of his staff officers noted, McChrystal 'ramped up the SOF campaign to industrial scale'. This resulted in a fivefold increase in the tempo of special operations against high-value targets in Afghanistan. However, McChrystal did not 'make a big deal of this' because he wanted to focus ISAF's attention on the imperative to reduce civilian casualties, and demonstrate to the Afghan president and public that international forces were responding to their concerns.[11]

Yet one year on, the priority had changed from reassuring the Afghans that ISAF would show more care towards civilians, to reassuring Washington that the surge forces were being put to good use and that the tide was turning in the war. Petraeus already signalled this shift in his confirmation hearing before the Senate Armed Services Committee in late June 2010, when he told senators that 'focusing on securing the people does not, however, mean that we don't go after the enemy; in fact, protecting the population inevitably requires killing, capturing, or turning the insurgents'.[12] In his commander's guidance issued to ISAF forces in August 2010, Petraeus confirmed McChrystal's emphasis on the Afghan people as the centre of gravity in the campaign, and on the need to exercise discipline in the use of force. At the same time, ISAF troops were told to 'get your teeth into the insurgents and don't let go. When the extremists fight, make them pay.'[13] Thus, 'relentless pursuit' replaced 'courageous restraint' as the watchword of the campaign. This was welcomed by many in ISAF, especially hard-pressed US commanders in eastern Afghanistan, who resented the priority given to protecting civilians over defeating enemy forces. The overall message was clear: the gloves are coming off.

For Petraeus, this meant lifting the curtain on the secret war being aggressively waged by ISAF special operations forces in Afghanistan. He began to brief the '90 Day roll-up' from the kill/capture campaign back to Washington and to dignitaries visiting Kabul. The figures were certainly impressive. In the ninety days up to 23 September 2010, 285 insurgent leaders had been killed or captured, and over ten times this number of Taliban foot soldiers.[14] Petraeus pointed out that this 'staggering operational tempo' was 'three to four times higher' than the speed of special operations at the height of the surge in Iraq.[15] The new approach was not uncontroversial. While he avoided the language of enemy body counts, this was essentially what Petraeus was offering as proof of progress in the campaign. This approach had infamously failed to work for General Westmoreland in the Vietnam War – although he had only given Washington what it then wanted: some quantifiable way of *measuring* progress in the war.[16]

Invariably, ordinary Afghans were targeted by mistake and hauled off to American-run detention facilities for interrogation, while civilians were killed and injured by accident. ISAF conducted the raids at night, both because it conferred an advantage on special operators equipped with night-vision goggles and to reduce the risk to civilians from gunfights with Taliban. ISAF tightened up procedures in other ways too to minimise the risks to civilians, but the sheer scale of the night raids, with an average of twenty conducted each night across the country in 2010, meant that many innocents were killed, injured or detained.[17] American and allied special operators were accompanied on the raid by Afghan troops – sometimes these were Afghan special forces, and sometimes they were irregular Afghan militia. However, this did nothing to lessen the sense of public outrage among ordinary Afghans who were profoundly affronted by the idea of Western soldiers barging into Muslim homes at night. By November 2010, Karzai was openly demanding that ISAF stop conducting night raids. Under the terms of the Military Technical Agreement, though, he was unable to prevent ISAF from conducting any military operations that it deemed necessary on Afghan soil. Moreover, the Obama administration supported the raids as an essential plank of the strategy now being pursued by Petraeus.[18]

Aside from the headline figures, everything surrounding the kill/ capture campaign was necessarily shrouded in secrecy. However, the German news magazine *Der Spiegel* was able to provide some insight into the Joint Prioritized Effects List (JPEL), as it was officially called, based on secret NATO documents posted on Wikileaks. At any time, around 750 individuals were on that list. Each target would be assigned a code name, a priority level and an approved action – to be killed, captured or observed. In 2010, ISAF even added the governor of Balkh province in northern Afghanistan, Atta Mohammad Noor, to the JPEL for observation, which made him an intelligence priority. The *Spiegel* report also revealed how targets were tracked by US drones and British surveillance planes, flying overhead and constantly listening out for insurgent telecommunications. GCHQ and the NSA maintained data-banks of known Taliban mobile phone numbers. Once a phone was switched on, voice recognition software would be used to produce a positive identification of a target. As we have seen, the Taliban were highly vulnerable to interception of their mobile phone communications. If the phone user identified himself, this was sufficient to proceed with the approved action. Where this involved a strike mission, likely collateral damage would be estimated, and where this endangered the lives of ten or more civilians, only the commander of ISAF could give the go-ahead. Consistent with the law of armed conflict, approval could still be given if the target was sufficiently important. The *Spiegel* report gives the example of the targeted killing of a mid-level Taliban leader in Helmand, code-named 'Doody' (his actual named was Mullah Niaz Mohammed), in February 2011. A British Apache gunship was tasked with executing the target. Tragically, the Hellfire missile launched by the Apache missed and killed a child instead; the gunship then used its 30mm cannon to kill Doody. The Taliban leader was assigned priority level 3 on JPEL, meaning that he was not that important.[19]

British newspapers also drew on Wikileaks data to reveal the existence of a joint SBS/SAS task force based in Kandahar and dedicated to conducting operations against targets on the JPEL.[20] As the *Spiegel* report showed, British Apache gunships were frequently assigned to support this British task force, as were Predator drones. Working alongside the Americans in Iraq had profoundly changed the way British special forces operated. Initially British military chiefs had been sceptical about the Americans' industrial approach to the kill/capture campaign in Iraq; according to one British special forces officer, his superiors back in London were 'very sniffy of the American way of doing things'.[21] The commander of 22 SAS Regiment from 2005 to 2008, Lieutenant Colonel Richard Williams, disagreed with this attitude, and under his command the SAS attempted to match the new American tempo of kill/capture missions in Iraq.[22] One inside source told the *Telegraph* in late 2010 that 'the SAS are bringing all the strike operational experience they learnt from Baghdad to Afghanistan. They are not waiting for goldplated intelligence to launch strikes, they are just really going for it.' It was further claimed that British special forces had 'removed from the battlefield' sixty-five of the 240 senior Taliban commanders on the JPEL.[23]

Certainly British special forces had a spectacular success when they killed the Taliban commander for southern Afghanistan, Mullah Dadullah Lang, back in May 2007. Mike Martin describes Dadullah as 'an exceptionally charismatic commander who was known [to Afghans] as the "lame Englishman" … because he had one leg and was incredibly devious'. Martin notes how when Dadullah arrived in a particular area in Helmand, 'his presence alone would increase the attacks against the government and the British'.[24] According to Carter Malkasian, the British learned that Dadullah was holding a meeting in Garmsir with senior Taliban commanders and an SBS team was sent by helicopter to capture him. Dadullah was killed in the gunfight ensuing when the SBS burst into the compound where the meeting was taking place.[25] This was unquestionably a great loss for the Taliban.

Petraeus hoped that by showing tangible progress through the kill/capture campaign, he could buy time with political leaders back home. Using an American sports metaphor, he told his staff officers that he was seeking to 'put back time on the shot clock', meaning that he hoped to persuade the White House to extend the deadline for the withdrawal of the US surge forces. However, Obama was not impressed. He told his National Security Council in March 2010 that he intended to begin the transition to Afghan security forces in July 2011. The president warned that he would 'push back very hard' at any suggestion of delay. By now, Obama's relations with Petraeus had soured. He had not expected Petraeus to adopt the same line as McChrystal, which was to argue for more troops and more time. He issued a thinly veiled warning knowing that the message would get back to Petraeus: 'If I believe that I am being gamed ...'[26]

Petraeus also hoped that by eviscerating the mid-level leadership of the Taliban, the kill/capture campaign would cause the insurgency to fracture, just as it had done in Iraq. Indeed, this had been McChrystal's intent as well and the expectation was widely shared within the US military. As one senior officer from CENTCOM put it, 'Show me an organisation that can function when its entire middle layer of management is wiped out.'[27]

Yet there was little evidence of the Taliban falling apart. Indeed, quite the opposite. Across the whole of southern Afghanistan, ISAF and Afghan casualty rates continued to climb, with the number of killed and injured more than doubling over the 2010 summer fighting season; the monthly rate reached more than six hundred in August 2010.[28] This was not an insurgency running out of steam.

A POPULAR UPRISING

Under McChrystal and Petraeus, widely recognised as two of the most talented and capable American war commanders of recent times, NATO resources were concentrated as never before on defeating the Taliban. In 2010, Helmand was designated ISAF main effort and the place to inflict a 'strategic defeat' on the Taliban. The two most powerful NATO task forces in Afghanistan – the British-led Task Force Helmand and the 2nd Marine Expeditionary Brigade – were committed to the fight. Yet ISAF failed to deliver the killer blow. Instead, the Taliban were dislodged from central Helmand for a limited time, with many fighters escaping to the northern districts. The fighting around Sangin would rage throughout 2011 and 2012, and in Nad-e Ali, the Taliban began to return.

Why were the Taliban not defeated? The insurgency drew strength from a myriad of local conflicts between rival kinship networks and sub-tribal groups over land, water, drugs and government largesse. The Taliban proved highly skilled at exacerbating and exploiting these conflicts in order to expand their influence. As we saw, helping the

Taliban cause was the return of corrupt warlords in the new guise of officialdom under the Karzai regime. Similarly, the arrival of the British in Helmand gave the Taliban a convenient rallying cry for their struggle, namely jihad against the foreign invader. Thus northern deployment of British forces into Now Zad, Sangin and Musa Qala in 2006 had become a magnet, drawing Taliban in from surrounding districts and provinces. Likewise, the deployment of British forces down south into Garmsir had drawn in ever more insurgents across the border from Pakistan. Indeed, the Taliban leadership in Quetta decided to launch a major assault led by Mullah Dadullah against the NATO forces deploying south into Helmand and Kandahar in 2006. The main Taliban defensive line was just south of Kandahar, but large numbers of fighters were also dispatched into Helmand to take on the British.[29]

Complicating matters enormously for the British task force was the ramshackle counter-narcotics programme, formally led by the British government but mostly pushed by the Afghan government with strong US backing. British commanders were reluctant to get involved, fully appreciating that this was not the way to win local hearts and minds. And yet they did enough to make many Helmandis angry. Thus, British support of poppy eradication triggered a popular revolt in Nad-e Ali in 2007. According to one local elder, 'When they started destroying the opium fields, the people – landowners, farmers, poor people, everyone – became angry. And they started fighting.'[30] The British did offer compensation for the destruction of poppy crop but this scheme was administered by corrupt local officials, which meant that the farmers got nothing.[31] In 2008, it was decided to target eradication efforts against the poppy fields of warlords, in particular against Abdul Rahman Jan, who had been removed as provincial chief of police. This made matters even worse. Through his patronage network, Abdul Rahman still controlled the police in central Helmand and he retaliated by allowing the Taliban to return and take control of Marjah.[32] The Taliban promised to protect landowners and farmers from having their poppy crop destroyed, and thereby won over local support. Indeed, the drugs industry in southern Afghanistan became a major source of income for individual Taliban commanders and for the movement as a whole, through taxation of poppy crop, and opium production and trafficking.[33]

Young Helmandi men flocked to the Taliban. Recruitment had started before the British arrived, in 2004–5 when the Taliban began to reorganise in Helmand, but the British presence made it far easier for them to recruit local fighters.[34] Where villages welcomed the Taliban, the insurgents encouraged local young men to join up in order to 'free their villages' from foreign invaders.[35] As one Taliban recruit recalled, 'When the Taliban came new to our district, there were not enough fighters, they told us to make groups of ten to fifteen and come to them, and they would give us weapons and supplies to fight against the foreign [i.e. British] fighters.'[36] These young men were in effect forming 'pals platoons'.[37] In the mid 1990s, the Taliban had forcibly recruited young men to fight against the Northern Alliance; ten years on, they knew they could not afford to alienate the local communities on which they depended for support.[38] Accordingly, they relied on persuasion and social pressure.[39] As one local elder recounted: 'The Taliban come and ask each house for their sons. Not forcing them, but telling them, asking them, "How Muslim are you? Why are you not doing jihad?"'[40] In some cases Taliban recruiters made multiple visits to people's homes to pile on the pressure.[41] In pro-Taliban areas, where a family had more than one adult son, there was almost an expectation that one of them would join the Taliban.[42] Madrasas were also an important source for Taliban recruitment. Taliban commanders particularly targeted three main madrasas in Sangin where many hundreds of students who were taught Islamic subjects also received 'military lessons and trainings'.[43] According to one commander, the Taliban in Sangin treated the madrasa students as a source of auxiliary 'ready-made forces' for emergencies.[44] As an added bonus for the insurgents, madrasas were generally exempt from raids and attacks under ISAF rules of engagement.

Helmandis had a range of motives for volunteering to join the Taliban. Many claimed to be appalled by the 'cruelty of the Americans and British'.[45] Afghans objected to Western troops barging into residential compounds, and especially to the night raids by American and British special forces, which they considered a grave insult to their religion and culture.[46] Some joined the insurgency to take revenge on the Americans and British for the death of a family member or friend; one Taliban fighter joined up after 'being beaten up badly' by British troops.[47] Amazingly, many Afghans believed that British soldiers were returning to 'settle scores' from the Anglo-Afghan Wars, in particular their defeat at the Battle of Maiwand in 1880.[48] Most important of all was the sense that they were signing up to wage jihad on occupying foreigners; as one Taliban put it, all Afghans had an 'Islamic duty to fight against the *kafirs*'.[49] This was a powerful narrative for the Taliban, providing a crucial social resource for motivating fighters.[50] Needless to say, the call to jihad was especially strong in those communities where local mullahs supported Taliban recruitment.[51] Indeed, recognising the importance of mullahs in shaping local opinion, the Taliban systematically targeted those religious leaders in the southern provinces that spoke out against them.[52] They also imported new mullahs, young zealots from Quetta and Peshawar indoctrinated in Taliban ideology.[53] Of course, more mundane and material motives were at play in the recruitment process as well. For some young men, the Taliban offered a way out of unemployment and the boredom of rural life. As one elder observed, 'They were jobless, the young. They didn't talk to the mullahs, they went straight to the Taliban. They saw it as work.'[54]

THE TALIBAN ADAPT

The arrival of NATO forces in southern Afghanistan in 2006 was a mixed blessing for the Taliban. On the one hand, it made it easier for them to mobilise local support for a jihad against the Karzai regime and its foreign backers; on the other, NATO forces frustrated Taliban attempts to overrun district centres and cause the collapse of the fledgling Afghan government in the rural south. As time went on, the Taliban came under increasing pressure as NATO poured ever more resources into the Afghanistan war. Drawing on fifty-three interviews with Taliban commanders and fighters in Helmand in 2011–12, and over forty interviews with Taliban commanders and cadre elsewhere in Afghanistan and Pakistan, Antonio Giustozzi and I were able to reconstruct the Taliban campaign in Helmand. We uncovered how the Taliban adapted to an increasingly capable ISAF. At the strategic level, the Taliban leadership introduced a number of measures to strengthen command and control of fighting groups. At the tactical level, the Taliban moved to greater use of classic guerrilla methods – ambushes, sniper fire and bombs – and training was provided for fighters to support this shift in tactics.

In the early days of the insurgency from 2004 to 2006, the Taliban were organised in a series of fighting groups of between twenty and fifty men, with most linked to a particular patronage network – called a *mahaz* or 'front' – on the basis of personal relations; the Taliban had organised along the same lines during the Soviet War. These Taliban fronts, the larger of which stretched across several districts and even provinces in southern and eastern Afghanistan, were arranged around a number of prominent figures. Formally, Taliban *mahaz* came under the authority of the Quetta Shura, but in reality the *mahaz* leaders acted independently of the shura and of each other. As one Taliban commander noted many years later: 'At that time, all the network commanders misused their positions, they thought they were kings.'[55] In some cases, cooperation between networks was precluded by rivalry between *mahaz* leaders. The most famous fallout was between Mullah Dadullah, the powerful southern commander, and Mullah Abdul Ghani Baradar, the deputy head of the Taliban. Many Taliban believe that Baradar betrayed Dadullah to the British, and Dadullah's people got their revenge by betraying Baradar to the Pakistani intelligence service, who captured him in 2010.[56] The whole front could be destabilised with the death of its leader. In the case of Baradar's *mahaz*, 'many of his commanders went to Pakistani and left the movement'.[57] The limited capacity of the *mahaz*-based system to foster cooperation between insurgent fighting groups inhibited the Taliban's tactical effectiveness and strategic flexibility, and prevented the Taliban from achieving any big wins in their much heralded spring offensives.[58]

In response to this, the Taliban resorted to dispatching large numbers of fighters from Pakistan who could be deployed wherever needed in Afghanistan. In parts of Helmand, elders recall the predominance of Punjabi speakers in the early years of the insurgency.[59] One elder remembers that when Taliban came knocking on the door for food, they could not speak Pashto.[60] Another elder in Garmsir even notes that 'because there were loads of Punjabis, the locals didn't fight'.[61] A third recalls, 'I was a doctor in Now Zad at that time, and the Taliban brought their wounded to me for treatment. I saw wounded fighters who couldn't speak any Pashto … most of the foreign Taliban were from Pakistan, Iran [or were] Arabs.'[62] However, this system proved of limited effectiveness except in the presence of a weak adversary that could be overwhelmed by human waves of fighters, such as Afghan police checkpoints. It may be telling that no ISAF base was ever overrun by the Taliban. An added problem was that these foreign fighters were not suited for guerrilla warfare. They were not able to blend easily into the local population, and they fought without care for local concerns. As one Taliban commander notes: 'In the time of Mullah Baradar, there were more Pakistani fighters in the front line ... But now we don't let them come because they disturb the [local] people a lot.'[63]

Accordingly, the emphasis shifted to recruiting local fighters. This led to a drastic reduction in the number of foreign Taliban in Helmand after 2010, with those remaining being increasingly used in more specialised roles, mostly acting as technical advisers. In Sangin, for example, some fighting groups had 'Punjabis' making IEDs and acting as trainers.[64] The picture is strikingly similar in Musa Qala, Nahr-e Seraj, Now Zad and Garmsir.[65] And large groups of foreign fighters could still be sent from Pakistan for particular operations or to enforce Taliban authority in rural areas.

Between 2005 and 2008, the Quetta Shura sought to improve the ability to concentrate force without challenging the entrenched networks of the old system. Fighting groups began to be moved across districts while staying within their home *mahaz*; for example, a commander affiliated with Mullah Baradar would move with his fighters to another area where Baradar had people.[66] This development might have facilitated the large-scale penetration of Helmand by the Taliban in 2005–6, with groups of fighters originally mobilised in Baghran (in the extreme north of the province) and Garmsir (in the south) being moved into the more central and heavily populated districts.[67] On at least one occasion the Taliban managed to amass around 2,000 fighters from Mullah Dadullah's *mahaz*, for the Battle of Pashmul around Kandahar in September and October 2006.[68] This noteworthy example aside, by 2008 the Taliban leadership came to realise that this attempt to reform the *mahaz* system was not working. Anecdotal evidence from Helmand illustrates the problem. In Kajaki, for instance, an Afghan interpreter hired by the British to listen to Taliban communications 'described almost comical attempts by different commanders to shirk combat and foist the responsibility on other commanders'.[69]

In response, the Taliban leadership council created two military commissions, one based in Quetta and the other in Peshawar. In principle, these two commissions divided territorial responsibility for Afghanistan, with Quetta being in charge of west, south and north, and Peshawar of south-east, east, north-east and the Kabul region. However, these regional military commissions had little control over insurgent field commanders and fighting groups, who owed allegiance to their parent *mahaz*, from whom they received funds and supplies. The Peshawar Military Commission included the formidable Haqqani network, a terrorist organisation based in south-eastern Afghanistan which is formally tied to the Taliban.[70] The Haqqanis sought to professionalise the Taliban campaign. Through their close links to ISI, the Haqqanis also ensured that most resources from the Pakistan Army went to the Peshawar Military Commission. Thus, over time, the commission began to exert influence over the entire Taliban war effort.

From around 2009, the Peshawar Military Commission negotiated deals with a number of key Taliban leaders, leading to the creation of a more formalised system of subordinate military commissions at provincial and district level across Afghanistan. These were led by *nizami masoul* (military commissioners) and were answerable to the military commissions in Peshawar and Quetta.[71] The actual result was a somewhat cumbersome double chain of command, where a fighting group belonging to a particular *mahaz* would respond to both its parent network and the Peshawar or Quetta Military Commission. As one Taliban field commander explained in 2011, 'When I get orders from the *nizami* commission, I have to check the orders with my *mahaz* commander, who will contact the *nizami* people and discuss it with them in order to confirm.'[72]

This new command system evolved into a balance between local autonomy and central control. Individual commanders maintained their exclusive territorial responsibility, but under the authority of the Quetta Military Commission (in Helmand's case), which was able to intervene in the event of disputes and could regulate redeployment. In the words of one commander, 'Before, if anyone but my network commander had told me to move to another area, I wouldn't have listened. But now we have this *nizami* commission for my area, and whatever they tell me, I have to do it.'[73] Another noted that 'when some small problems come between two Taliban commanders, they are solved by the *nizami* commission in a very short time'.[74] When the rivalry was too serious and the *nizami masoul* was unable to impose discipline, the Quetta Shura would send in a senior mediator ('a Pakistani mullah' from Quetta) to sort out problems among commanders.[75] In later years, the Quetta and Peshawar Military Commissions also relied on Taliban courts to maintain discipline within their ranks.[76] Taliban commanders, cadres and courts were all guided by *layeha* (or codes of conduct), periodically issued by the Quetta Shura from 2006 on, which provided authoritative guidance on how the Taliban should organise, train and act (especially towards the civilian population), and rules regarding the treatment of spies and prisoners, and what may and may not be attacked.[77]

Another innovation that was supposed to strengthen the hand of the two military commissions was the rotation of Taliban field commanders and officials. This should have professionalised what had been until then charismatic leaders of small groups of personal followers; it was intended to reduce the risk of corruption as well. According to one commander, the Quetta Military Commission 'don't want Taliban fighters to become too powerful in one area and to start abusing the people'.[78] This experiment in rotation was probably also meant to prepare the ground for greater centralisation, by separating commanders and the rank and file and dissolving bonds of personal loyalty. When first introduced around 2009–10, the rotation system worked for a while but it quickly fell into disuse. One Taliban commander recalled in 2011 that 'before there were lots of rotations in the Taliban system. A commander of Taliban rotated every four or five months but now they rotate almost every two years.'[79] Indeed, this seems to have been the case across Helmand.[80] As another Taliban commander observed: 'It is the policy of the war that one person cannot stay in one place for a long time, that is why we change our places and it is the *nizami massoul* who brings such changes and makes decisions. But these days due to a very hard situation, we cannot move a lot and rotation has also decreased or somehow stopped.'[81]

The intensification of the kill/capture campaign against Taliban commanders contributed to this failure of the rotation system, as they were 'targeted by American drone attacks while they were moving from one district to another district'.[82]

WEAPON OF CHOICE

The more centralised control of fighting groups might have fallen short of the Taliban's expectations, but it nonetheless allowed for more systematic training of the field units. This occurred against the background of a shift towards greater use of guerrilla warfare tactics by the Taliban. As one commander noted, 'It's clear for everyone that we have changed our tactics in our fighting; we are not fighting face-to-face a lot.'[83] The Taliban made wide use of fairly conventional infantry assaults in 2006–7, in an attempt to overrun British outposts. The exact number of Taliban killed in action over this period is unknown; British defence intelligence calculated it in the thousands.[84] Even accepting the tendency to overestimate numbers of insurgents killed, it seems likely that in the face of considerable attrition, Taliban groups adapted their fighting methods. They still engaged in occasional large-scale attacks, including the spectacular attempt to overrun Lashkar Gah in October 2008. However, it would appear that in 2010, the Quetta Military Commission issued a general order instructing field units to avoid direct combat and make greater use of IEDs, sniper fire and ambushes.[85]

With a shift in tactics came a new military training regime, re-inforced by directives from the Quetta Military Commission, compel-ling the tactical commanders to undergo this training and receive regular advice on guerrilla warfare. Specialist Taliban teams were also sent from Pakistan to go from village to village in order to provide training in new fighting methods.[86] Taliban commanders seem to accept that training was particularly important in light of the new tactics. As one commander from Sangin put it, 'We need to get training in making bombs, in ambushes and making suicide vests.'[87] And a commander in Garmsir noted how 'our training system has also changed and now we are all focused a lot on … making of *fedayi* [martyrdom] vests, getting ready of *fedayi* bombers and guerrilla fighting'.[88]

The impact of this shift in tactics was noticeable. In 2006, around 30 per cent of all ISAF fatalities were caused by IEDs. This rose to almost 40 per cent in 2007, and from 2008 to 2010, IEDs were respon-sible for well over half of all ISAF troops killed.[89] By late 2008, use of IEDs had quadrupled in Helmand and the British military recognised that these devices had become the insurgent 'weapon of choice'. The number of IEDs detected one way or another (including those triggered) jumped again from around 100 per month in late 2008 to over 450 per month in the summer of 2009, causing four out of every five British fatalities over this period. Looking at July 2009, the worst month of the war for British losses, nineteen of the twenty-two British troops killed lost their lives to IEDs. In 2010, the number of IEDs in Helmand jumped once more, to over five hundred per month, with spikes of over six hundred in February and over seven hundred in March (coinciding with Operation Moshtarak).[90]

The IED played to insurgent strengths. It could be made from all manner of materials, including fertilisers, home-made chemical cocktails, and recovered and recycled munitions, such as old Soviet mines and unexploded ISAF artillery shells and bombs – hence the name, improvised explosive device. The Taliban used a variety of trigger mechanisms, including remotely activated, command wire and pressure-plate. Increasingly, the Taliban put explosives in plastic containers, producing IEDs with little metal or even no metal content – some Taliban bomb-makers would hand-carve components in wood – which were especially difficult to detect. These IEDs typically carried a ten-, twenty- or forty-five-pound explosive charge. Anything below twenty pounds would tear off one or both of the victim's legs; anything above would blow a person to smithereens. British soldiers and marines deploying to IED-infested parts of Helmand, such as Sangin, were resigned to the possibility that they might be wounded by an IED. What they most feared was losing their genitals in a blast. As one soldier stated, 'The first thing everybody checks after they have been blown up is their wedding tackle, that's providing they are conscious.'[91] British troops were intensely drilled in the basics of combat first aid, drills which had to be put into practice in the most challenging situations imaginable: putting tourniquets on the stumps of blown-off limbs, while looking out for secondary IEDs, taking fire from insurgents, and working out how to evacuate the wounded.[92]

In Helmand, IEDs were planted along all routes and at key crossing points used by ISAF and Afghan security forces. In response, British and American troops took to following the least accessible paths, wading along water-filled irrigation ditches and climbing over walls and hedgerows. The Taliban became especially effective at hiding IEDs under paths, and embedding them at knee height in walls or in doorways, making them incredibly difficult to spot. In response, the British Army developed 'ground sign awareness' training for all troops in 2010, as well as employing a range of aerial surveillance capabilities to detect Taliban IED emplacement teams in action. The IED threat severely hindered the mobility of ISAF forces. The average British infantryman in Helmand was carrying around 150 pounds of kit; the bulky Osprey body armour, incorporating ceramic front and back plates, added another 20 pounds. This made it very difficult to move far and fast. By 2008, the Taliban had also started to ring British bases with IEDs, thereby effectively hemming in the troops.

The British deployed to Helmand woefully unprepared for the IED threat. Ironically, the British Army had spent thirty years dealing with IRA bombs (IEDs in all but name) in Northern Ireland but much of this experience and expertise had been lost by the mid 2000s. From 2006 to late 2007, the British Army had only two IED disposal teams for the whole of Helmand. This figure rose to six teams by late 2008, and fourteen teams by late 2009. But even this was nowhere near enough to deal with the huge number of devices that British troops were encountering. Moreover, IEDs became more sophisticated as the Taliban tried to make them difficult to find and defuse. Some were fitted with anti-tamper devices which would kill anybody who tried to move or defuse the bomb. Frequently, unarmed Taliban would watch British IED disposal teams at work from a distance in order to learn British procedure. The bomb disposal officers therefore tried to change their drills to keep the Taliban guessing. The British Army was desperately short of bomb disposal experts, and when they were killed or injured, they proved near impossible to replace; this was, after all, the most dangerous job in Afghanistan. When the British lost three bomb disposal officers just before Christmas 2009 (one killed and two injured), their IED disposal capacity in Helmand suddenly fell by 30 per cent.[93]

The key shift had occurred in 2009 in the British approach to tackling IEDs, when it evolved from being a 'specialist task' for disposal teams, to becoming an 'all arms activity' for all forces. A new metal detector, the German-manufactured 'Vallon', was introduced along with a training package and operating procedure called Operation Barma. 'Barma-ing' a route required six soldiers moving in formation and carefully sweeping ahead in overlapping arcs; as we saw during

Operation Panchai Palang, it could reduce British advances to a slow crawl.[94] To make matters worse, Vallon was useless at detecting IEDs with little or no metal content. As Royal Marine Adam Gunningham, who endured a gruelling tour in Sangin under 40 Commando, during which he lost two friends to IEDs, noted:

> Vallon only picks out 8 of 10 IEDs. When it's a command pull, there's no metal needed. They are just sitting on the end of a wire, dug underground, and when they know you're there, they'll connect the battery. The only way you would spot them is ground signs. Rocks piled up, a change in the colour of the sand, dips in the ground; or sometimes they would put water on top of where it had been disturbed.[95]

With command-wire-operated IEDs, the Taliban operators would try to target those of higher rank, or whose different appearance somehow marked them out as important. Gunningham recalled how on one patrol, the IED was detonated when the fifth person walked over it, a US Marine who was wearing a different uniform from the Royal Marines. 'They targeted the American, he was getting intelligence. We had three injured, including one walking. The American was the worst. I glanced at him a few times, he was a triple amputee.'[96]

In 2008, PJHQ had conducted a major review of the IED threat in Iraq and Afghanistan. Reporting in November that year, the Burley review made a number of major findings and recommendations. It noted that British forces had a 'defensive mindset' and were almost exclusively focused on measures to protect forces in the field from IEDs. In contrast, the US military had a more aggressive approach that concentrated on actively defeating the IED networks, with brigade-sized task forces in Iraq (Task Force Troy) and Afghanistan (Task Force Paladin) charged with exploiting intelligence and forensic material on IEDs, and providing targets for appropriate actions by special operations forces. The British review team visited both US task forces and were impressed with what they saw, concluding that Task Force Troy 'represents current best practice in the C[ounter]-IED fight'. The Burley review was clear: the British military had to adopt something akin to the US approach. It recommended the restructuring of intelligence in Task Force Helmand 'to support the prosecution of effective offensive C-IED operations through: timely exploitation of recovered material, all-source intelligence fusion, and the proactive targeting of IED networks'. It took a year for this recommendation to be implemented with the creation of a new C-IED Task Force in Helmand, supported by intelligence exploitation teams in Camp Bastion (code name 'Torchlight') and at Regional Command South headquarters in Kandahar airfield (code name 'Varsity').[97]

In another emulation of American best practice, Task Force Helmand began to build up a biometric database of Helmandis in areas under Afghan government control. British patrols were sent out to collect digital images, fingerprints and DNA swabs from locals. By mid 2010, Task Force Helmand had generated 17,000 biometric profiles; although this covered only a fraction of the Helmand population, these could be matched against forensic analysis of IED materials. This analysis suggested that there were between twenty and forty Taliban IED emplacement teams at work in Helmand.[98] Under the Talisman Programme, 4 Brigade also deployed in mid 2010 with a new suite of counter-IED capabilities which included Mastiffs fitted with rollers, Buffalo armoured vehicles with an extendable arm, micro-drones for checking out suspicious objects, and Talon remote-controlled robots for IED disposal; the last proved disappointing, however, often breaking down and proving too weak to lift any object over five pounds.[99] By degrees, the new offensive and defensive measures taken by the British and US militaries began to pay off, as the proportion of ISAF troops killed by IEDs fell to below 50 per cent in 2011 and further dropped to around 30 per cent in 2012.[100]

Even these improved odds did not stop the reputed British 'bomb magnet' from being blown up yet again in 2013; yet another blast he walked away from with minor injuries. In total, Warrant Officer Patrick Hyde from 4th Battalion the Rifles survived seventeen IED explosions. On one tour in Sangin from October 2009 to April 2010, he was hit eleven times by IEDs while travelling in Mastiff vehicles, and twice on foot patrol. Hyde received the Military Cross for bravery when he rescued his battalion commander and the Afghan army commander for Helmand, Brigadier General Shirin Shah, from a compound that had been laced with IEDs, after he himself had been wounded in a blast. Depending on how you look at it, Hyde was either the luckiest or unluckiest British soldier in Helmand. For him, IEDs were simply an 'occupational hazard' and he believed that fate was as likely to catch up with him in civilian life. 'I might get run over or fall down stairs. I reckon I will die in a really stupid way.'[101]

UNWILLING ALLY

In addition to exploiting local tensions to mobilise popular support and adapting to growing military pressure from ISAF by employing asymmetric tactics, there is a third crucial reason for why the Taliban proved so resilient in Afghanistan: they had outside help.

Iran provided weapons and bomb-making materials to the Taliban. This was in spite of terrible relations between (Shia) Iran and the (Sunni) Taliban Emirate in the late 1990s, when each provided assistance to anti-regime armed groups in the other's territory; the two sides almost went to war when Iranian diplomats were murdered following the Taliban capture of Mazar-e-Sharif in 1998.[102] Yet on the principle of 'the enemy of my enemy is my friend', Iran gave support to the Taliban fight against the British in Helmand, just as Iran was backing the Mahdi militia in its war against the British in Basra. The British were worried in particular about Iranian-supplied heavy machine guns that could shoot down helicopters, and explosively formed projectiles, which were roadside bombs able to target vulnerable spots on armoured vehicles. British intelligence tried to keep tabs on these dangerous Iranian weapons as they came into Helmand.[103]

However, a far greater problem was Pakistan, a country that was supposed to be an ally in the US-led war against the Taliban and al-Qaeda. Following the 9/11 attacks and under heavy pressure from the Bush administration, Pakistan had formally broken with the Taliban, and provided support to the US invasion by permitting American and British forces to fly through its airspace and operate from its airbases. When the Taliban Emirate collapsed, the Pakistani authorities also apprehended large numbers of foreign jihadis as they fled across the border from Afghanistan. These were handed over to the Americans, and promptly sent to the US detention camp at Guantánamo Bay for interrogation. However, nothing was done to

stop the Afghan Taliban from reconstituting itself in Pakistan and
launching attacks into Afghanistan from 2003.

All of this happened with the complicit if not active support of
the Pakistani Inter-Services Intelligence agency. Indeed, according to
one account, the ISI met with exiled Taliban leaders as early as
December 2001 'to reiterate their support for the Taliban' and to
discuss 'how to agitate against Hamid Karzai's new government'.[104]
As the war took off against Afghan and Western forces, the Taliban
were allowed to operate from camps in the Federally Administered
Tribal Areas (FATA) and the Western province of Baluchistan; some
critics claim that the ISI actively provided logistical support for these
camps.[105] The Taliban were also freely allowed to raise funds and to
recruit fighters in Pakistan. Moreover, as our interviews with Taliban
revealed, the ISI provided military assistance and training to them, in
particular with bomb-making materials and expertise. Afghan intelligence claimed that several ISI agents had been killed or captured
operating undercover as Taliban commanders and directing the
fighting on the ground. For Amrullah Saleh, the long-standing chief
of the Afghan National Security Directorate, the evidence was clear:
'The reality is [that] Pakistan is a lethal deceptive terrorist-sponsoring
state. Without Pakistan's support Taliban don't exist for a day. NATO
is fighting a Pakistan proxy.'[106]

Pakistani officials robustly denied charges that the Pakistan Army
continued to provide material support to the Taliban following 9/11.
They claimed not to know the location of Afghan Taliban leaders.
Western intelligence suggested otherwise: that the ISI carefully tracked
them and even attended meetings of the Taliban leadership council.
The Pakistan Army is on slightly safer ground when it complains about
the porosity of the Afghan–Pakistani border, which runs for over 1,500
miles and has innumerable crossing points. Complicating matters is
Afghanistan's refusal to recognise the legality of the Durand Line, which
cuts through Pashtun tribal lands and forms the basis for the modern
Afghan–Pakistani border. For this reason, Afghanistan rejected Pakistan's
suggestion that portions of the border be fenced and mined.[107] Pakistan
reasonably protested that it had attempted to secure the border region,
pouring some 140,000 troops into FATA and Baluchistan. However, the
Pakistan Army was grappling with rising tribal militancy in these areas
from 2004 to 2007 and so could ill afford to start a conflict against the

Afghan Taliban, even if it were inclined to. By 2007, following a number
of attacks on Islamabad and Karachi, Pakistani tribal militancy came to
be seen as a direct threat to the state and the Pakistan Army launched
a series of major offensives against the Pakistani Taliban in FATA. Thus,
preoccupied, the army was even less inclined and able to take on the
Afghan Taliban.[108]

At best, then, Pakistan was a very unwilling ally of the West. At
worst, it was double-dealing.[109] The Bush administration had bought
off Pakistan handsomely. In addition to lifting sanctions that had been
imposed following a series of nuclear tests by Pakistan in 1998 and
the military coup that brought President Musharraf to power, the
Bush administration helped Pakistan to renegotiate its loans with
international creditors (including the International Monetary Fund).
It also gave Pakistan a $5 billion aid package over 2002–7, and agreed
to a further $6 billion for allowing US military supplies to transit
through Pakistan. So, as well as the threat of American ire – senior
Pakistani officials were told in no uncertain terms on 12 September
2001 that 'either you are with us or against us' – Pakistan had other
good reasons to give full support to America's (and Britain's) war
against the Taliban. Yet it failed to do so. Why?

The simple fact is that the Pakistan Army which ruled the country
under Musharraf had more compelling strategic and political reasons
for not going after the Afghan Taliban. In terms of strategic calculations, Pakistan views the Afghan Taliban as its proxies in the ongoing
struggle for power in Afghanistan. The key context here, as noted
by Anatol Lieven, is 'the growing conviction that the West is going
to fail in Afghanistan, and will eventually withdraw, leaving anarchy
and civil war behind', just as the Soviets did in 1989. 'In the resulting
civil war, it is believed, every regional state will have its own allies –
and so must Pakistan.'[110] This raises the related Pakistani concern
about growing Indian influence in Afghanistan. Pakistan was suspicious of the pro-Indian leanings of the Afghan political leadership
given the dominance of Tajiks in the government, who the ISI
consider to be India's 'Afghan protégés'.[111] Pakistan had equal reason
to be concerned about the new Afghan president, who had been
educated in India.[112] To Ambassador Cowper-Coles, it was quite
obvious that not only was Karzai 'viscerally anti-Pakistan, he was
profoundly pro-Indian'.[113] Moreover, Pakistani intelligence claimed to

have evidence that India was stirring up trouble by providing assistance to Baluch separatists; stoking this fear, the Pakistani press frequently published fallacious reports of Indian consulates being opened in Afghan provinces bordering on Pakistan.[114] The Taliban, and especially the Haqqani network, was therefore supposed to provide Pakistan with the means to counter the growth of Indian influence in Afghanistan.[115] This was demonstrated in July 2008 when the Haqqanis detonated a massive truck bomb outside the front gate of the Indian embassy in Kabul, killing fifty-eight people, including the Indian military attaché.[116] As the Pakistani interior minister put it, 'RAW [Indian intelligence service] and Afghan intelligence are one, so ISI has no option but to counter it.'[117]

Reinforcing these strategic reasons was the political reality that the Afghan Taliban were very popular among the political class and the public in Pakistan, whereas America was not. It was difficult enough for Musharraf to persuade senior generals in the Pakistan Army that America was a 'wounded bear' following 9/11, and that Pakistan had no choice but to declare its support for Bush's global war on terror. This move went against the prevailing mass sentiment. As Lieven observes, 'the overwhelming majority of Pakistanis – including the communities from which most Pakistani soldiers are drawn – see the Afghan Taleban as engaged in a legitimate war of resistance against foreign occupation, analogous to the Mujahidin war against Soviet occupation in the 1980s'.[118] The 'tilt towards India' by the Bush administration, encapsulated in the 2005 nuclear deal in which the United States formally recognised India as a nuclear power while refusing this status in any matching deal with Pakistan, further aggravated political and public opinion in Pakistan. The onset of CIA drone attacks against al-Qaeda, Haqqani and Taliban operatives in Pakistan a year later poured yet more fuel on the fire. A drone strike against a compound in FATA in January 2006 which killed eighteen villagers was angrily denounced by the Pakistani government; in October 2006, a madrasa in the same village was hit by missiles fired by a US Predator drone, this time killing at least eight people.[119]

President Obama attempted to reset the relationship with Pakistan. He wanted Pakistan to do more: as he told Congress, 'the era of the blank check is over'. Hence, when Pakistan was offered a more generous military assistance package in September 2009 amounting to $1.5 billion per year for five years, there were strings attached. Release of this aid was tied to certification that Pakistan was supporting the US war on terrorism and nuclear non-proliferation, and an assurance regarding civilian control of the military. This latter point was intended to strengthen the civilian government of President Asif Ali Zardari. However, it backfired spectacularly. The Pakistani press decried an American attempt to interfere in Pakistani sovereign matters, and the leadership of the Pakistan Army mobilised political and popular opposition to the terms of the aid package. Secretary of State Hillary Clinton had to travel to Islamabad in October 2009 to avert a full-blown diplomatic crisis.[120] The following year the Pakistan Army was offered an additional $2 billion assistance package.[121] Yet throwing money at the army failed to fix crumbling relations with Pakistan. The gathering pace of CIA drone strikes – increasing from fewer than 20 in 2007 to 33 in 2008, 53 in 2009 and jumping to 118 in 2010 – continued to stoke anti-US sentiment among the masses and the elites in Pakistan.[122] By early 2010, a survey undertaken by Pew Research revealed that two-thirds of Pakistanis viewed America as the enemy.[123]

Then, in late 2010, the CIA found bin Laden. They tracked him down to a private compound in the sleepy city of Abbottabad, sixty miles north of Islamabad. To US officials, it strained credulity that the Pakistan Army did not know where bin Laden was hiding, especially as his compound was only a few hundred yards from the Kakul Military Academy. One inside source told reporter Carlotta Gall that bin Laden had a dedicated ISI handler. In any case, it was clear that the Pakistani police were avoiding the compound, despite the oddly reclusive behaviour of those inside, indicating that this was some kind of ISI safe house.[124] On 1 May 2011, two US SEAL teams launched a raid against the compound, killing bin Laden in the process. Pakistan had not been forewarned: the Obama administration did not trust their ally. When Obama broke the news that evening, there was jubilation in America. The following day, the *New York Times* solemnly reported 'BIN LADEN IS DEAD'; the *Washington Post* quoted the president: 'JUSTICE HAS BEEN DONE'; 'GOT HIM!' declared the *New York Post*; while the other New York tabloid, the *Daily Post*, probably best captured the public mood with its headline: 'ROT IN HELL'.

In Pakistan, the mood was very different. The public was shocked that Americans troops could swoop in undetected. The army became the butt of popular jokes, such as 'Pakistan radar system for sale: 99 dollars. Buy one, get one free (can't detect US helicopters but can receive Star Plus)' – this being an Indian satellite channel. Directly following the US raid, the head of the Pakistan Army, General Ashfaq Parvez Kayani, and the head of the ISI, Lieutenant General Ahmed Shuja Pasha, were called to parliament to explain how American commandos could enter Pakistani territory, conduct a raid and leave unchallenged. Four hundred angry politicians badgered the two generals until 2 a.m. Parliament then passed a resolution condemning the American violation of Pakistani sovereignty and calling for a review of Pakistan's relations with the United States. Most embarrassing of all, it also called for an independent inquiry into whether the military was able to secure Pakistan's borders. It was obvious to Robert Gates that the White House had made matters far worse with its handling of the media: it looked as if America was gloating. 'I have a new strategic communications approach to recommend,' he told the National Security Advisor, Tom Donilon: 'Shut the fuck up.'[125]

Pakistan's retaliation was not long in coming. On 28 June 2011, eight Haqqani terrorists stormed the Inter-Continental Hotel in Kabul, killing eleven civilians and two policemen. On 10 September, a US base in Wardak province was hit by a massive truck bomb, injuring ninety-six, including seventy-seven US soldiers, and killing five Afghans. Three days later, three gunmen seized a tall building under construction in the secure zone in Kabul, and from this vantage point fired on the US and other embassies for nineteen hours. Testifying before a Senate committee a week later, the chairman of the US Joint Chiefs of Staff, Admiral Mike Mullen, had had enough. In a rare public display of what senior US officials really thought, he described the Haqqani network as 'a veritable arm of the ISI'.[126] Things got even worse in November when twenty-four Pakistani soldiers were killed in a US air strike against a suspected militant position in Pakistan from which US forces had taken fire. By this stage, as one senior US State Department official noted, 'the most frequently stated sentiment' in the White House concerning Pakistan was 'we have had it with these guys'. There had been a misplaced belief in the White House that the United States had leverage over Pakistan when in fact it had none. Thus, demands from Pakistan for a formal apology for the incident were brushed aside. One senior US official told the Pakistani ambassador: 'We will never apologise, it will never happen. Get over it.' Pakistan responded by closing NATO supply routes through its territory for seven months, plunging ISAF into crisis and costing the United States $700 million.[127]

British and American policymakers appreciated the countervailing strategic and political pressures that hindered fulsome support from Pakistan. They also hoped that support for the Taliban and the Haqqani network was mostly coming from groups within the ultra-secretive ISI, and not from the Pakistan Army more generally. They understood that ties between the ISI and the Haqqani network were especially strong, formed as they were from the shared experience of waging jihad against the Soviets; and moreover, that the Haqqanis provided support to the ISI-sponsored campaign waged by militants in Kashmir.[128] By 2011, the scales had fallen from Western eyes. According to Brigadier General Mick Nicholson, who had returned to Washington to lead the Pakistan–Afghanistan Coordination Cell in the Pentagon, 'The Pakistanis were playing ten-dimensional chess, and we were not even showing up or aware of the chessboards they were playing on.' Put more plainly by Cowper-Coles: 'we were naïve about ISI, that it was just "rogue elements". All along they hadn't moved once against the Quetta shura.' Yet the West had no choice. The modest support that the United States received from Pakistan, in permitting the CIA drone campaign in FATA and allowing NATO supplies to be shipped in via Karachi, was better than no help at all. And Pakistan could make things far worse for NATO if it wanted to. As ever, Nicholson offered the pragmatic view: 'You just look at the map and the number of madrassas and the number of youth in those madrassas. If they recruit just ten percent of those into the insurgency, we lose.'[129]

HIGH-WATER MARK

The Helmand campaign was at its zenith in 2010. British force levels in Afghanistan had peaked at 9,500 troops, and US Marine Corps troop levels had reached 20,000, with the 1st Marine Expeditionary Force taking over from the 2nd Marine Expeditionary Brigade in Helmand.

In July that year, ISAF Regional Command South was divided in two, with a new command, Regional Command South-West, taking responsibility for Helmand and Uruzgan. The official reason was that this would enable Regional Command South under General Nick Carter to focus on a major offensive called Operation Hamkari to secure Kandahar city and the surrounding districts.[130] The actual reason was that, since they had sent a whole division to Helmand, the US Marine Corps wanted their own regional command; in fairness, given that there were twice as many US Marines as there were British troops in Helmand, it did not make sense for the 1st Marine Expeditionary Force to be under British command.

For Brigadier James Chiswell, the incoming commander of Task Force Helmand in October 2010, the campaign was at 'something of a high-water mark' in other respects too. The British task force had all the equipment it required; for Chiswell, 'it was the end of the era of kit being an issue'. ISAF had excellent aerial and electronic surveillance of the province, and even more importantly, the Helmand provincial government and British-led PRT were both functioning well. Chiswell had taken command of 16 Air Assault Brigade when it returned from Afghanistan in 2008. In preparing the brigade for its third tour in Helmand, he focused in particular on 'the conceptual bit': understanding the utility of force in counter-insurgency. Chiswell had reached the conclusion that 'courageous restraint' had become counterproductive, as it was preventing ISAF from demonstrating to the Afghan population that it could and would decisively defeat the Taliban. Thus ISAF was unable to give locals the confidence to stand up to the Taliban and side with the government. Chiswell recalls a 'penny-drop moment' when the Afghan ambassador explained to him what ordinary Afghans thought of the British – 'that we were just not up for the fight'. To Chiswell, Task Force Helmand was engaged in a 'physical contest' with the Taliban, and the British could not win over local support for the Afghan government unless they demonstrated that 'we are winners on the battlefield'.[131]

Certainly the Taliban understood that it was a physical contest. The commander of 1st Battalion the Royal Irish Regiment (1 Royal Irish), Lieutenant Colonel Colin Weir, described their arrival in Nad-e Ali in September 2010 as 'a literal baptism of fire'. Over the first three days of their tour, 1 Royal Irish had thirty-six 'prolonged engagements' with the Taliban, including 'a determined attack on the district centre'.[132] Weir later recalled that 'we were fighting everywhere in those first weeks; frequently we had four companies in contact at the same time'.[133] Nad-e Ali saw a huge increase in the weekly number of SIGACTS, from fifty to over seventy, during this time. Moreover, there would be no let-up for the first six weeks, until the rate dropped down to between thirty and forty SIGACTS per week.[134] Weir soon figured out that 'the enemy were mounting a vicious riposte to ISAF's attempts to clear them from the area'.[135] In other words, the Taliban were pushing back.

The situation was so bad that ISAF headquarters began to get worried. Petraeus started referring to Nad-e Ali as 'the shoulder of badness', while the district was showing up 'the deepest red' on the ISAF-wide SIGACT map. Chiswell asked the ISAF commander 'to just bear with me' as 16 Brigade were engaged in 'a physical contest for the ground'. This was not, however, a return to 2006 and the unrestrained use of firepower. Chiswell emphasised the importance of 'deep understanding and empathy', telling his subordinate officers 'to seek to understand the red picture [enemy forces] in the context of the white picture [local communities]'. For this reason, he adopted the concept of operations used by Afghan Task Force 444 – 'find, feel, understand, influence'. Influence involved using all the tools at the brigade's disposal, including armed force. Chiswell did not want the brigade to be shy about using force, but at the same time to do so with precision in order to avoid civilian casualties and unnecessary damage to civilian property. Thus, in place of 'courageous restraint', he coined 'front-footed precision' as the watchword for the brigade; it also seemed to be more in step with the new ISAF mantra of 'relentless pursuit'.[136]

This way of thinking was reflected in the approach taken by 1 Royal Irish in Nad-e Ali. The troops had a tough fight on their hands, and they could not afford to take a 'zero-risk approach' to civilian casualties. As Weir reasoned:

> If we withdrew every time we came into contact because we *might* kill a civilian then we would end up withdrawing *every* time because the enemy would make sure civilians were there, and those civilians would also provide a ready-made audience to watch from the grandstand and to see our defeat.[137]

Weir's impression was that it was almost 'like a gladiatorial thing' with the locals watching to see how the British fared. He was determined that when they got into engagements with the Taliban, British troops 'would be the last to leave the battlefield'.[138] At the same time, 1 Royal Irish were careful in how they used force. In particular, they avoided using air strikes: they dropped no bombs in almost a thousand engagements with insurgents over the course of their tour. Where firepower was needed, they called in precision weapons such as Hellfire missiles and GMLRS. They also made extensive use of artillery and mortar fire, which were not as precise as GMLRS but at least caused far less damage to the surrounding area than aerial bombardment. Weir was acutely aware of 'the negative-influence effect of large-yield ordnance' in the populated environs of Nad-e Ali. Put in plain English, it does little for local confidence to see the British bombing the hell out of their district.[139]

Here the revolution in intelligence, surveillance, targeting and reconnaissance (ISTAR in British military jargon) made a huge difference. ISTAR refers to the networking of aerial surveillance (drones and planes), signals intelligence and targeting capabilities, which is intended to enable forces to see and react faster on the battlefield than their opponents. The ISTAR programme was originally designed to equip the British military for future conventional warfare. In 2010, however, the Ministry of Defence decided to refocus their overall ISTAR programme to concentrate on meeting the needs of the Afghanistan campaign. One new technology that exceeded all expectations was the Persistent Threat Detection System, a sixty-foot tethered aerostat (basically a big balloon) kitted out with various surveillance and listening devices. Developed for the US Marines and US Army in Iraq in 2004, a number of these were purchased by Britain in 2010 and operated by the Royal Artillery in Helmand. Helmandis called the aerostats 'frogs' because they were ever-watchful, and 'milky fish', because of their fins and opaque white appearance. The helium-filled aerostats proved impossible to shoot down; hovering 2,000 feet up in the air, they were difficult in hit, and in any case could stay airborne even with bullet holes.[140] Soon they were dotted across Helmand, with one over every British and American forward operating base. Thus by late 2010, the British military had an unprecedented ability to track insurgents across the battlefield. If any group of Taliban attempted to move in the open in Nad-e Ali, the British could see them.

16 Air Assault Brigade used the new ISTAR capabilities to devastating effect. This could most clearly be seen in the Chah-e Anjir Triangle, where the Taliban had returned in force and had laid siege to British patrol bases. As Battlegroup North, 3rd Battalion the Parachute Regiment (3 Para) had the task of clearing insurgents out of the triangle. The commanding officer, Lieutenant Colonel James Coates, came up with a clever way of putting 'front-footed precision' into practice. His battalion used aerostats to systematically track armed individuals, and drew on intelligence to identify those deemed to be particularly dangerous, who were then killed using Apache gunships.[141] 2nd Battalion the Parachute Regiment (2 Para) resorted to more traditional methods when they encountered strong Taliban resistance in Babaji, frequently calling in artillery fire. Here, the Taliban eventually gave up, and 2 Para spent the latter half of their tour in a 'gendarmerie role' rather than battling insurgents.[142]

The British had been conducting precision strikes against leadership targets for some time in Helmand, and as we saw in Operations Tor Shpa'h and Moshtarak, this tactic was used to cause Taliban defences to collapse in advance of major offensives. Chiswell's innovation was to make this central to the brigade's concept of operations. Where previously the headquarters had a single SAS liaison officer connecting Task Force Helmand operations with JPEL operations, Chiswell created a whole team. The precision-targeting cell focused in particular on mid-level Taliban commanders and facilitators; forty-three were killed by 16 Brigade.[143] This significantly reduced the ability of commanders to motivate and lead their fighters, as they were forced to send instructions remotely, calling in orders from Pakistan.[144]

1 Royal Irish spent their entire tour fighting. In late October 2010 they began clearing an area in north-west Nad-e Ali, two miles east of the village of Zarghun Kalay, which the rangers nicknamed 'the Red Wedge' (after its shape). The British checkpoint in the Red Wedge was cut off by Taliban lines. Weir recalls visiting it three times in Ridgeback armoured vehicles and 'taking fire on all three occasions'.[145] The Taliban were also launching attacks into Nad-e Ali district centre from the Red Wedge. After a month of being hunted down by B Company, the Taliban were forced out and the rangers turned their attention to southern Nad-e Ali, and the village of Saidabad and adjacent area of Zaborabad. The rangers battled back and forth with the

Taliban over the winter. In early December, they pushed the insurgents out of Saidabad and reopened the bazaar, only to see it close three weeks later when the Taliban re-infiltrated and intimidated the villagers.[146] In the final operation of their tour in late February, eleven helicopters dropped two companies of rangers into Zaborabad. Yet even such major operations failed to force the insurgents out in the long term.[147]

LEAVING SANGIN

In September 2010, one month before Chiswell assumed command of Task Force Helmand, the 1st Marine Expeditionary Force took charge of Sangin. The US Marines now had complete responsibility for southern and northern Helmand, having taken over from the British in Musa Qala in March 2010. The British Army was keen to pull out of Sangin as it could then concentrate its forces in a smaller area in central Helmand. The idea was first mooted in December 2009 by General Nick Parker, who went to London to argue the case following the announcement that 8,000 more US Marines would be arriving in Helmand as part of the Obama surge. Much to Parker's surprise, this suggestion was overruled by Prime Minister Brown; with the UK general election approaching, Brown wanted to avoid the negative publicity that he feared would follow surrendering such totemic ground.[148]

Brown lost the general election in May 2010 to his Tory rival, David Cameron. A visit by the new prime minister to Camp Bastion in mid June gave Parker the opportunity to explain the logic of giving Sangin to the Americans.[149] He succeeded: four months later, with 'a simple handshake and lowering and raising of flags', 40 Commando Royal Marines handed Sangin over to 3rd Battalion, 5th US Marine Regiment (3/5). It was a low-key affair, with no reporters present – which suited the UK government just fine. The British had lost 106 troops in Sangin, almost a third of all killed in action in Afghanistan.[150] One British officer doubtless spoke for many in expressing 'a mixture of relief and regret' at leaving Sangin.[151]

The US Marines were determined to shake things up in Sangin. The 105mm guns of the British battery in Sangin were replaced with the much more powerful 155mm guns of 3/5. The 1st Marine Expeditionary Force intended to push back Taliban defensive positions well away from the district centre, just as they had done some months before in Musa Qala.[152] The marines felt that the British had spent too much time hunkering in their bases.[153] Off the record, the Americans were pretty contemptuous of the British reluctance to take the fight to the enemy. 'They were here for four years. What did they do?' asked one arriving US Marine officer.[154]

The British had built twenty-three patrol bases in Sangin in an attempt to control the main routes through the town, and especially the notorious Pharmacy Road, which ran from the main British camp on the outskirts of Sangin, FOB Wishtan, into the town centre. Most of these patrol bases had been put in place by 3 Rifles as Battlegroup North in the winter of 2009–10, at a very high price: from a battlegroup of 1,400 soldiers, 30 men were killed and 100 injured.[155] The losses were so frequent that the 3 Rifles commander, Lieutenant Colonel Nick Kitson, put a stop to the sunset service which is traditionally held on the evening of a soldier's death. 'I didn't think it was helpful,' he said.[156]

When 3 Rifles had arrived in Sangin in October 2009, they found British and Afghan forces 'hemmed in by overwhelming numbers of IEDs'.[157] The Taliban planted devices within ten yards of British bases, and every patrol leaving a base took fire.[158] 3 Rifles set out to double the number of patrol bases in order to keep watchful eyes over Pharmacy Road and other routes through the town, thereby making it harder for the Taliban to plant IEDs and significantly reducing the number of battles near Sangin's marketplace and school. This also gave the British more of a permanent presence among the people and helped to normalise their daily lives. Rather than staying on base, British foot patrols increased by 300 per cent under 3 Rifles, and there was a 50 per cent increase in partnered patrols with the Afghan army. Sangin was about the most challenging place to apply the McChrystal mantra of 'courageous restraint'. Yet that is what Kitson did. The number of artillery rounds fired by the Sangin gun battery decreased tenfold under 3 Rifles, in comparison to 2 Rifles battlegroup who had preceded them. Where 2 Rifles had relied heavily on American air power – F15E Strike Eagles and B-1B bombers – to obliterate insurgent firing positions, 3 Rifles avoided dropping bombs in the town. The new approach resulted in a dramatic fall in Taliban attacks by the end of 2009, such that 3 Rifles called in no high explosive artillery rounds from 18 December 2009 to March 2010.[159]

Where 3 Rifles and 40 Commando had focused on securing Sangin town, the US Marines had orders to push into the surrounding area. Much to British dismay, 3/5 abandoned half of the patrol bases that had been created just a year before. One Rifles officer observed wearily that 3/5 'are trying a new approach but it was one tried by us in the past and led to troops being tied to just the outskirts of town and gave the Taliban the chance to plant IEDs virtually wherever they wanted'.[160] On 22 September 2010, the first US Marine foot patrol came under fire within 150 feet of leaving their base; a marine was dead before the patrol had returned. Over the four days that followed, 3/5 lost another eight marines. The US Marines were surprised at the ferocity and tactical proficiency of Taliban attacks[161] and it soon became clear that they had underestimated what the British had achieved in Sangin. The insurgents had skilled marksmen, firing from well-concealed positions in compound walls, and mortar teams that were able to fire highly accurate 82mm shells into bases using a low trajectory to avoid counter-battery radars.[162] Not helping matters for 3/5, Operation Moshtarak had displaced around eighty Taliban fighters from central Helmand into the Sangin area.[163] Nevertheless, the US Marines gave as good as they got. They started patrolling in two-squad formations so as not to be outflanked by Taliban fighting groups. In one engagement witnessed by a journalist, they responded to sustained fire from a Taliban defensive position by bombarding it with artillery and strafing runs from F/A-18 warplanes and helicopter gunships for two hours. Incredibly the insurgents kept firing.[164]

The US Marines certainly made an impression on locals. According to one Sangin elder, they 'were fighting crazily instead of British troops'.[165] Another elder recalled that 'when the American marines arrived in Sangin, they did a miracle fighting; they were fighting more dangerously than Taliban fighters. They pushed back the Taliban in one month, very far away of Sangin district centre.'[166] Taliban fighters radioed back to their commanders in Pakistan that 'marines run towards bullets'.[167] One Taliban commander claimed with a touch of bravado that 'when American troops came into the area, despite of their more experience, more men and latest machineries, we are still upper handed'.[168] However, other commanders from Sangin confirmed that following heavy fighting against 3/5, the insurgents changed tactics, possibly on instruction to avoid direct battle with US Marines.[169]

Invariably civilians got caught in the crossfire. In one of the worst cases, during a prolonged battle in the Upper Sangin Valley on 23 July 2010, the US Marines called in air strikes on insurgents in a compound in the Ishaqzai village of Riga. At least thirty-five civilians were killed. A subsequent investigation by the National Security Directorate concluded that as many as fifty-nine civilians may have perished. Karzai was furious and held ISAF publicly accountable.[170] Relations between Petraeus and Karzai had got off to a bad start; echoing the growing impatience in Washington, Petraeus was far less accommodating towards the Afghan president than McChrystal had been. Incidents such as this contributed further to the deterioration of relations between ISAF headquarters and the presidential palace.

The US Marines paid a terrible price for their efforts to push back the Taliban. Halfway through their seven-month tour, 3/5 had suffered 24 killed and 140 injured out of a battalion of 800 marines. The 136 marines of Kilo Company were hit particularly hard, with 9 killed and 45 wounded.[171] Sure enough, the Taliban infiltrated past marine bases on the outskirts of Sangin, and began to wreak havoc in the town itself. Where 3 Rifles had brought relative calm to the district centre, there were again pitched battles and air strikes among the population under 3/5. The Taliban also planted IEDs just about everywhere. Marine infantry, as British troops before them, were terrified of the devices. One marine told an embedded journalist, 'It scares the crap out of you. I step just in footprints. Someone can say a route's been cleared and I'm still only stepping in footprints … Every intersection we've been in we've either found IEDs or been hit by IEDs.'[172] Much to the bemusement of passing locals, marines would lay a trail of plastic bottle caps along a route for others to follow. Much to the irritation of the Americans, locals would carelessly wander down these routes, overtaking marine patrols as they inched along sweeping for IEDs. The journalist observed: 'Everyone seemed to know where it was safe to walk but no one was willing to explain it to the marines.'[173] By the end of their tour, 3/5 had found 1,315 IEDs.[174]

The marines of 3/5 responded with the same techniques they had
used in Fallujah. Roads were cleared with 350-foot-long line charges,
with five pounds of C4 explosive for each foot. If the marines found
a compound rigged with IEDs, they simply blew up the compound.
One company commander destroyed a mosque that had command
wires running into it. All these structures were first photographed, so
compensation could be paid to the owners.[175] In January 2011, 3/5
decided to reoccupy all the patrol bases they had inherited from the
British and then abandoned. They brought in huge seventy-tonne
Assault Breacher Vehicles to bulldoze their way down Pharmacy Road,
destroying any structure that insurgents might possibly hide behind,
including all compound walls along the route. 'If it casts a shadow, it
gets flattened,' decreed the commander of Lima Company, charged
with retaking the most dangerous mile of road in Afghanistan.[176] By
this stage, many marines were beginning to go deaf from all the
explosions. And many locals were beginning to lose their patience.
One mullah complained bitterly to a young marine platoon commander,
'Your tanks are here for killing. Your cannons are here for killing. Your
planes are here for killing. You haven't brought anything that we like.
All you have brought are the things for death.' The mullah told one
Afghan soldier, 'God willing they will suffer the same fate as the
Russians.'[177]

PEACE IN SANGIN

On 29 May 2010, four months before the US Marines took responsibility for Sangin, a most remarkable thing had happened. As noted
by the British stabilisation officer then in the town, 'a formal offer
of peace with the Upper Sangin Valley was made by eight of the
most influential leaders and was swiftly followed by overtures from
tribal groups in the south'.[178] What created this opportunity and what
happened to it?[179]

The insurgency in Sangin drew strength from the Ishaqzai tribes
mostly located in the Upper Gereshk Valley. As we have seen in
chapter 5, traditionally the Ishaqzai have been the most disenfranchised and downtrodden of the tribal groups in Helmand; unsurprisingly, they sided with the Taliban.[180] The Alikozai, on the other hand,

were well represented in the power structures of Helmand: the provincial head of the National Directorate of Security, the former district governor of Sangin and the district chief of police were all senior Alikozai. Nonetheless, by bringing in other Afghan and foreign fighters, the Taliban were able to coerce the Alikozai in the Upper Sangin Valley into tolerating their presence and activities. The Taliban also drew support from two villages in the valley, Mianroady and Jushaley, which were populated by Ishaqzai and Noorzai tribespeople. Mianroady was especially significant as the birthplace of Mullah Akhtar Mohammad Osmani,[181] the deputy head of the Taliban who had been killed by a targeted ISAF air strike in December 2006.[182] Osmani's madrasa in Mianroady continued to produce Taliban, and was a major centre for preparing suicide bombers.[183] When in 2007 Alikozai tribesmen in the Upper Sangin Valley attempted to push the Taliban out of their lands, the insurgents put down this uprising with ruthless efficiency, chaining the leader to a truck and dragging him face down into the next province. At the time, the Alikozai felt bitterly betrayed by the provincial governor, Asadullah Wafa, and the National Directorate of Security, who 'promised to send us weapons and fighters' but in the end did nothing.[184] Three years on, they were ready to try again.[185]

Underlying the importance of local governance to counter-insurgency, the key factor creating this new opportunity was the appointment of Mohammad Sharif as the new district governor of Sangin. His predecessor, Faisal Haq (described by one British observer as 'a grubby old mujahid'[186]), had made half-hearted attempts to reach out to tribal leaders in the Upper Sangin Valley since 2008. However, as one informed observer notes, Haq 'saw government office often as a mechanism for safeguarding narrow tribal interests rather than promoting a wider reconciliation'. By early 2010, Haq's corruption and incompetence was being increasingly challenged by frustrated local leaders, with both the Mayor of Sangin and the chair of the district community council threatening to resign if he did not go.[187] On 1 March 2010, Haq was replaced by Sharif, a former science teacher and a proven administrator who had been the former deputy district governor of Garmsir. Already three weeks later, the British PRT reported to London that the 'early signs are encouraging. Sherrif [sic] is intelligent, competent, even-handed and keen to learn. He commands respect and affection.' The PRT also noted how Sharif was well supported by a new district chief of police, Haji Umer Jan, and a new district chief of the National Directorate of Security, Saeed Musa, 'both of whom he hand-picked'.[188] In an important sign of the growing legitimacy and popularity of the new governor, the British District Stabilisation Team in Sangin noticed how 'the number of local people coming to meet Sharif in his office outside the ISAF base increased from 5–10 Alikozai per day under Haq, to some 60–70 daily from all local groups'.[189]

Reconciliation with tribal groups aligned to the Taliban was a major priority for Sharif and he wasted no time in getting on with it. As the PRT reported in late March, Sharif 'is looking to explore interest expressed by individuals based in the Upper Sangin Valley with close links to the local Taliban leadership'.[190] The ball had actually started rolling some months back, when a major reconciliation and reintegration conference was held in Kandahar on 6–7 December 2009, convened by the High Peace Council (the formal body appointed by Karzai to take forward reconciliation efforts) and personally endorsed by the Afghan president, who made a brief appearance. Following the conference, the British PRT informed London that the High Peace Council 'offers strong support for Helmand Governor Mangal to begin reintegration work, emphasizing that progress in North Helmand is key for province-wide security' and that 'Mangal returns to Lashkar Gah confident he now (finally) has the level of political cover he requires'.[191] This was vital for the governor, given what had happened to Semple when he tried to facilitate reconciliation with local Taliban in northern Helmand. Mangal was all too aware that Karzai was looking for an excuse to reinstate his old ally Sher Mohammed Akhundzada as Helmand governor. Suitably reassured, Mangal authorised Sharif to make contact with pro-Taliban tribal leaders, working alongside Mangal's security adviser, Abdul Ali Shamsi. Sharif recalls that these contacts involved numerous telephone discussions and informal meetings 'with different groups of the Alikozai in Sangin'.[192]

Sharif and Shamsi explored the earlier offers of peace from some Alikozai contacts, and put pressure on others to withdraw their support for the Taliban. Alikozai elders were warned that the US Marines were planning a major offensive into the Upper Sangin Valley, bringing considerable risks to civilian life and property, but that this could be avoided if the Alikozai cooperated with ISAF and the Afghan security forces.[193] There was also a carrot. Spring flooding in 2010 had caused major damage to the network of canals that irrigated the Alikozai lands north of Sangin town. The Alikozai had asked the Taliban for assistance in repairing their irrigation system. However, the Taliban had no capacity to undertake the complex heavy engineering required, so when this was not forthcoming various Alikozai elders independently began to approach Sharif.[194]

Whether by happenstance or design, over this period a Taliban commander was captured who was very influential among the Alikozai in Sangin. Mullah Karimullah Agha was from the Sayyid tribe, who are revered across the Islamic world as direct descendants of the Prophet Muhammad. As one Taliban commander noted, 'Mullah Karimullah was very important for Taliban, people were obeying to him, and whatever Karimullah told the people, local people accepted that as a message of their religious man.'[195] The Alikozai Taliban commanders insisted on his release before they would conclude a formal peace agreement with the government.[196] Sharif recognised how important it was to confidence-building, and so he got Mangal's permission for Mullah Karimullah to be released.[197]

This was the final critical step that led to a formal agreement signed by the deputy provincial governor (in Mangal's absence) and the Alikozai commanders at a shura on 1 January 2011, witnessed by the head of the British PRT and the US commander of Regional Command South-West. The final agreement had been hammered down over four days of secret talks in mid December 2010 between Sharif, Shamsi and twenty elders 'representing the entire Upper Sangin Valley'. The Alikozai agreed to a long list of government demands: to 'cease combat operations' against Afghan forces and ISAF; 'to disable any IEDs emplaced or notify their locations' to Afghan security forces and ISAF; to 'compile a complete list of all commanders willing to reintegrate and guarantee that they will cease fighting'; to allow Afghan development work to take place (such as continuing Route 611 up to Kajaki Dam); and 'to prevent re-infiltration of the valley by out-of-area insurgents'. For its part, the Afghan government undertook to 'release insurgents recently arrested providing there is a guarantee from elders that they would not again take up arms', and to 'undertake not to harass former insurgents and grant them immunity from arrest from insurgency-related offences'.

'Eleven days after the 1 January agreement, the mood is cautiously optimistic,' the British PRT reported to London. There was evidence that the Taliban were trying to isolate and put pressure on the Alikozai defectors. However, 'The sense on the ground is that Upper Sangin Valley Elders have risked too much for them to turn their backs on the deal'. The PRT planned to deliver on its side of the agreement by undertaking 'small-scale canal clearance and infra-structure projects' and deploying a team of engineers to assess 'irrigation opportunities and health needs' for a large programme of works. At the same time Regional Command South-West planned some 'low-key' reconnaissance operations in the Upper Sangin Valley 'to gauge the local population's readiness to stick to the accord'. Visiting Lashkar Gah for an update in mid January, Petraeus told the British PRT and Regional Command South-West that they 'should do everything possible to build on [the Sangin accord]'.[198]

Despite this, the peace accord gradually broke down in late 2011. Not surprisingly, the Taliban leadership were determined to wreck it through a campaign of assassination and intimidation of defectors. Two Taliban commanders confirmed that they 'got an order from Quetta Shura to kill all those Taliban and elders who were involved in that accord'.[199] Another noted how two Alikozai elders who were key figures behind the agreement were beheaded by the Taliban.[200] According to one highly critical report, the Sangin peace accord also failed because the US Marines and the PRT did not put enough effort into it. The Alikozai honoured their side of the bargain, and SIGACTS plummeted by 80 per cent over the summer of 2011. However, the ANA did not deploy forces to protect Alikozai lands and the PRT failed to deliver the promised programme of works to repair the damage caused by the floods in 2010. Behind this were terrible relations between the 1st Marine Expeditionary Force and the PRT.[201] The US Marines made it clear that they did not welcome interference by civilians in their business, and understandably the PRT came to view Sangin as no longer their problem. A local journalist interviewed in 2013 confirmed that 'due to Afghan government not standing by their promises like construction and making clinics and schools and other buildings, the Alikozai Taliban broke the accord and rejoined with Taliban'.[202]

TALIBAN SHADOW GOVERNMENT

The Sangin accord was made possible by the failure of Taliban shadow government. The Taliban were never good at government. When they were in power in Afghanistan in the 1990s, they provided little beyond security and harsh justice. As the Taliban insurgency took hold from the mid 2000s on, the Quetta Shura appointed provincial and district governors to provide shadow government for areas under a degree of Taliban control. In his 'Commander's Initial Assessment' to Gates in August 2009, McChrystal highlighted the threat from a 'Taliban "shadow government" that actively seeks to control the population and displace national government and traditional power structures'. McChrystal warned that ISAF was overly focused on 'insurgent military operations', which he claimed 'are only a supporting effort' in the Taliban's overall campaign.[203] However, they failed to establish anything like an effective shadow government.

There is one exception. Multiple interviews with Afghan elders confirm the widely held view among Western experts that the one area in which Taliban shadow government is effective is in the administration of efficient, if often harsh, justice.[204] Disputes over land and water were a significant problem for rural communities in Helmand.[205] As one elder commented, 'in two or three hours, [the Taliban] could solve disputes between people. Now in Lashkar Gah, if you have a dispute with someone over one jerib of land, you have to sell twenty jeribs to pay to the courts.'[206] However, growing military pressure from ISAF and the government from 2009 on forced the Taliban to switch from standing courts in fixed locations to mobile courts. 'Now it is different,' one elder noted. 'Judges are hiding; sometimes they meet in people's houses, sometimes in the mountains, sometimes in the mosques. They are more mobile than they used to be.'[207] Nonetheless, the administration of justice continued to be an area where the Taliban were able to provide a public service appreciated by local communities; it also tied locals to the fate of the Taliban in that beneficiaries of Taliban courts had a direct interest in the continuation of Taliban shadow government in their area.[208]

Beyond their courts system, the Taliban never fully invested in developing their rule. The 2010 edition of the *layeha* specifies the structure of Taliban shadow government at provincial and district levels. It also provides for the appointment of non-Taliban, with appropriate skills and ideological commitment, to positions within it.[209] However, in reality, most leaders were selected from among Taliban commanders according to their seniority. One elder from Musa Qala observed, 'There was a district chief, but he didn't have much influence. Most of the power was with commanders who had lots of fighters in the district.'[210] The intensification of the kill/capture campaign meant that Taliban commanders and district chiefs ended up fleeing to Pakistan, from where they would send their orders via mobile phone.[211] Local commanders therefore appeared to have had more influence by virtue of their presence on the ground. As an elder from Nahr-e Seraj noted, 'When people have an issue, they will approach the local [Taliban] commander. They don't know who the district chief is.'[212]

This 'militarisation' of Taliban shadow government did not mean that they stopped advancing political initiatives, but that incipient development of a civilian structure of governance was rolled back. The leadership under Mullah Omar took steps to regulate shadow governors to ensure that they did not undermine efforts to win over local communities, such as banning arbitrary executions and imposing restrictions on attacking education and health officials. However, in the absence of a proto-civilian structure to counterbalance the military chain of command, the implementation of these important political measures was rather erratic. Attacks on schools declined in 2010–11 but did not disappear altogether, and arbitrary killings, while perhaps less frequent, also continued.[213]

The failings of Taliban shadow government provided a key context for the Sangin peace accord. By 2010, the Taliban were struggling to maintain local support in many districts in Helmand, as the people began to see the benefits received by those areas that were pro-government (in terms of better public services and funding for public works). Just as Taliban shadow government was wilting, provincial and district government in Helmand was significantly improving. Conscious of the need to keep the people onside, the 2007 and 2010 editions of the *layeha* provided processes whereby local communities could complain to the Quetta Shura if a provincial or district governor was corrupt or too repressive. The people of Sangin had forced the Taliban leadership to remove two Taliban shadow district governors.

Mullah Abdul Khaleq was removed in November 2009 for allowing Taliban to attack local farmers who had received government wheat seed under the Alternative Livelihoods Programme. Mullah Agha Mohammed Khanon was removed for his 'draconian justice' – he had insisted that a hungry man who had stolen bread had his hands cut off – and for failing to provide assistance following the 2010 floods.[214] Thus, the incompetence and brutality of insurgent officials limited the popular appeal of Taliban rule, as an alternative to the increasingly less incompetent and increasingly more accountable provincial government.

TURNING POINT?

Every British brigade left Helmand declaring that some kind of turning point had been achieved during their campaign. The fact that the war dragged on for so many years suggests otherwise. However, on their third tour in Helmand (and fourth in Afghanistan), 16 Brigade had more reason than most to make such a claim. The second half of their tour saw a dramatic fall in fighting in central Helmand, and local communities openly side with the government. There were many reasons for this, including the failure of Taliban shadow government and the ability of the British to concentrate forces in central Helmand after the US Marines had taken over in Sangin. Just as important was the development over time of a British approach to counter-insurgency that fused intelligence and surveillance with the precise and determined application of force. These elements came together under 16 Brigade's tour in 2010–11, with better exploitation of the ISTAR network and a concept of operations that sought to build local confidence by demonstrating to everybody, local farmers and Taliban alike, that a grim fate awaited insurgents in central Helmand. Moreover, contrary to the approach taken by 11 Brigade, the intent was not to force the Taliban out of the area, but to fight the insurgents and end the battle on British terms. As Colin Weir put it, 'My view was that it was our responsibility to fight and kill our Taliban; I did not want our insurgents to reappear in a different place or time.'[215] The ability of the British to target and kill Taliban commanders made it extraordinarily difficult for the insurgents to conduct significant operations or establish shadow government in central Helmand in 2011.

Crucially, 16 Brigade put equal effort into improving opportunities for rural communities – access to education, health care, the market-place, jobs, and so forth. Here Chiswell was building on a long-standing practice established across several British brigade tours of balancing the use of force with supporting development activities. In this, he identified sub-district governance as a key area where his brigade could complement the work of the PRT in developing legitimate and functional governance in Helmand. This was important because the PRT did not have a presence in rural villages whereas the British Army did through its patrols and patrol bases. Chiswell challenged his company, platoon and section commanders to work with villages in creating inclusive self-governing shuras.

The British Army and Royal Marines had come a long way in five years. An early focus on defeating insurgent forces through extensive use of firepower had been replaced with creating the conditions for local communities to feel able to reject the Taliban and side with the Afghan government. Speaking to an audience back in London in June 2011, Chiswell claimed that 'at all levels, our people absolutely get this counter-insurgency stuff; they get it absolutely right in terms of understanding and the appropriate use of force'.[216] This may not have been entirely true. Based on interviews with British Army personnel returning from operations in Helmand in late 2009 to early 2011, academic Sergio Catignani concludes that 'part of the lower-ranking officers and non-commissioned officers [did not] embrace and internalize the population-centric approach to COIN warfare', in particular the primacy of the focus on protecting the population. Catignani cites an expressed preference for using force among many in the lower ranks, and examples of where units used heavy suppressive fire when engaged with major firefights against insurgents. However, at the same time, he shows how population-centric tactics had become 'enshrined' in British military doctrine and had 'permeated to a certain extent the training regime of the [British] Army'. Moreover, comparing the extent and manner of the use of force by British troops in Helmand in 2006 and 2011, it is difficult to conclude that there was not a significant shift towards population-centric counter-insurgency.[217]

If the campaign did reach a turning point in early 2011, thanks to better British tactics and improved local Afghan government, it was to be short-lived. By the end of 2014, all British forces were due to withdraw from Helmand and the ISAF mission was scheduled to end. All the Taliban needed to do was bide their time.

11

Time Runs Out

On 1 June 2010, David Cameron assembled his military chiefs, foreign policy experts and security officials at Chequers for a policy summit on Afghanistan. Just two weeks before, Cameron had hosted President Karzai for lunch at Chequers in order to underline Britain's commitment to Afghanistan. Thus military chiefs might have been forgiven for thinking that the new PM would be prepared to give them more time and more resources to succeed in Afghanistan. They were, however, very wrong.[1]

Cameron wanted to open up debate on the Afghanistan campaign. He therefore invited some Afghan experts known for their unorthodox views ('wild men', he called them) to present alternative perspectives. The journalist James Fergusson, an Old Etonian and Oxford friend of the prime minister, began proceedings by declaring it 'pointless to put in more troops'. He stated bluntly that it was time to get serious about talking to the Taliban. Fergusson had interviewed several senior Taliban for a book in which he provided a sympathetic account of what they had tried to achieve when they governed Afghanistan before 9/11; he argued that everything became derailed when the Taliban Emirate was 'hi-jacked' by al-Qaeda. Fergusson felt that it was an opportune time to explore peace talks with the Taliban and that the British were in a much stronger position to do this than the United States. The Taliban hated the Americans for the abuses and humiliations inflicted on them and fellow Muslims at Guantánamo. In contrast, they were more accepting of the British. One senior Taliban leader said of the British in Afghanistan: 'You have been coming here for 170 years. We feel we know you.'[2] Fergusson identified, in particular, Mullah Zaeef, the urbane former Taliban ambassador to Pakistan, as a man the West could do business with.[3]

Another one of the 'wild men' was Graeme Lamb, the former director of UK Special Forces. Lamb still thought it was possible militarily to defeat the Taliban; he and Fergusson vigorously disagreed on this point. But recognising the limited political appetite to pour yet more resources into the war, he said that the British government should start thinking about what a deal with the Taliban would look like. Then there was Rory Stewart, also an Old Etonian and Oxford-educated, formerly a British diplomat and Harvard professor, and now a newly elected Tory MP. Stewart famously had walked the length of Afghanistan shortly after the fall of the Taliban.[4] For him, the NATO mission in Afghanistan was a deeply misguided and 'humiliating mess'. Western politicians and officials were hopelessly optimistic about what could be achieved in a country with so many complex challenges and about whose politics and culture they knew so little. Almost ten years on, and despite many thousands of Western diplomats, development officials and military officers having served in Afghanistan (hardly any of whom spoke Dari or Pashto), the West was still largely ignorant about the country and its peoples. Stewart would later write how these foreigners were 'inevitably isolated from Afghan life' by security restrictions on travel, their tour lengths, language barriers, and simply the fact of their foreignness.[5] He advocated a massive scaling back in ambition: reducing troop numbers and 'a turn away from state-building', while continuing to fund discrete development projects in health, education and agriculture.[6]

Cameron was not about to go as far and fast as suggested by his 'wild men', but he had decided that it was time for Britain to make a dignified exit from Afghanistan. His Chancellor of the Exchequer, George Osborne, was horrified at the cost of the war, which was estimated to reach £26 billion by 2015. As far as Osborne was concerned, the sooner Britain got out the better. Public support for the war had also dropped dramatically. In July 2009, just 31 per cent were prepared to support continuing Britain's involvement in the war beyond six months; one year on, that number had fallen to 22 per cent.[7] It was vital, however, that Britain did not cut and run as it had done in Iraq, and equally imperative that the United States was not left in the lurch, especially as political support for the war was also collapsing within the NATO alliance. In January 2010 France announced that it was withdrawing its forces from ISAF, and in

February the Dutch government fell after trying to extend the ISAF mission for its forces, who were pulled out of Afghanistan six months later. Canada was already on schedule to withdraw its combat forces in 2011. These developments reflected the public mood: between 2009 and 2010, public support for the ISAF mission fell from 37 per cent to 30 per cent in Germany, from 32 per cent to 30 per cent in France, and from just over 40 per cent to around 35 per cent in Canada.[8] With regard to the White House, the British ambassador to Washington, Nigel Sheinwald, told the prime minister that 'the direction of travel is they want to get out, without rush, and in an orderly way'. Cameron came away from the policy summit clear in his mind that he had to end Britain's war in Afghanistan before the next British general election in 2015.

Ten days later he flew to Kabul. Speaking alongside Karzai, the prime minister declared Afghanistan to be his top foreign policy concern. In the same breath, however, he said that sending more troops to secure the country 'was not remotely on the UK's agenda'. Cameron made clear that there would be renewed emphasis on speeding up the transition process.[9] The PM then flew on to Camp Bastion to visit British troops in Helmand. There he met with General Nick Parker to sound him out on the idea of setting an end date for the British mission. With military chiefs back home arguing strongly against any deadlines, Cameron wanted to hear the view of the senior British commander in theatre.[10] Parker told him that provided British forces could concentrate on central Helmand and show progress, it would be perfectly sensible to set a date for the withdrawal of British troops.[11] At the time Parker was trying to win Cameron's support for handing over Sangin to the US Marines, and this might explain why he was so agreeable on the question of an end date to the mission. Either way, this was music to Cameron's ears.

In early July, the prime minister made public his thinking regarding 'an end strategy' for Afghanistan. There was nothing new in the general thrust: 'to train up the Afghan army and police, improve the level of governance and security and come home'. What was new was a clear deadline. Talking about British counter-insurgency operations in Afghanistan, Cameron stated that 'this is something we won't be doing in five years'. In short, by 2015, the Afghans would have to secure their own country.[12] This was fine by Karzai, who wanted to assert Afghan control over security transition, which NATO called the *inteqal* process, after the Dari and Pashto word for transition. At a major international conference in Kabul on 20–21 July 2010, Karzai outlined his vision for the phased transfer of all responsibility to Afghan security forces to be completed by the end of 2014. This timeline was endorsed by the North Atlantic Council at the NATO Summit in Lisbon in November, which meant that all NATO combat forces would be withdrawn from Afghanistan by the end of December 2014.[13] The countdown had started.

ENDING ISAF

After the Lisbon decision, ISAF had just four years to grow the Afghan security forces to sufficient size and strength to fight on their own two feet. Initially, some senior officers at ISAF headquarters still hoped that the *inteqal* process could be slowed down to buy more time. But with major NATO partners already leaving ISAF in 2010 and 2011, and both Obama and Cameron determined to end the combat mission by the end of 2014, security transition rapidly became an unstoppable locomotive.

In July 2011, command of ISAF was handed over to US Marine General John Allen, Petraeus having returned to Washington to become the next director of the CIA. Allen had previously been deputy commander of CENTCOM, and before that deputy commander of the 2nd Marine Expeditionary Force in Iraq. He was a low-key and businesslike general; unlike Petraeus and McChrystal before him, Allen was not going to fight the White House over the transition timeline. He declared that 'the time for "big ideas" has passed'. ISAF had to be less ambitious and more pragmatic in order to deliver transition. Hence, Allen directed, 'we need to find what systems the Afghans have in place and leverage and support them toward success'.[14] The new standard would be 'Afghan good enough'.

The set deadline notwithstanding, ISAF still clung to the rhetoric of 'conditions-based' transition. This required ISAF headquarters to understand how the campaign was progressing at provincial and district level. Assessing progress in a counter-insurgency campaign is no easy matter: unlike conventional wars, strategic assessment in counter-insurgency does not lend itself to metrification. Yet this did not stop ISAF from trying.

A complex assessment process had been set up by ISAF Joint Command in late 2009 to support the focusing of ISAF efforts on eighty or so key terrain districts. By 2010 this had grown into a massive exercise whereby seven main lines of effort – the top three being governance, security and development – were turned into many dozens of metrics, with each metric assessed at provincial and district levels and colour-coded in terms of success (red, orange, yellow and green). An internal study for 1st Marine Expeditionary Force, as it prepared to assume responsibility for Regional Command South-West, found the ISAF strategic assessment process so 'riddled with highly visible flaws' that even many within ISAF distrusted it. Among the flaws highlighted in the report were 'promiscuous metric collection', including a bias towards showing progress; there was also the suspicion that many people were just 'making stuff up'.[15] In July 2011, Allen directed that the ISAF assessment process incorporate qualitative reports from subordinate commanders in addition to quantitative data, so as to develop a more 'holistic picture' of the campaign.[16] This did not fix the problem. A report by the RAND Corporation in 2012 found that the ISAF process was still fundamentally flawed. The summaries from field commanders simply added 'uncoordinated and inconsistent subordinate insights' and did not address the 'lack of comprehensive analysis' in the campaign assessment exercise. The report concluded that any centralised assessment process was severely limited in its ability to capture the 'contextual nuance of a COIN campaign'.[17] Thus, for all the talk of conditions-based transition, ISAF headquarters had a poor understanding of how much progress it was making.

Crucially, ISAF struggled to accurately assess the capabilities of the Afghan security forces, the growth of which was accelerated in preparation for transition. The ANA was originally scheduled to grow to 134,000 troops by 2013. This target was brought forward twice: first to 2011, and then to October 2010 under General McChrystal. At a major conference on Afghanistan held in London in January 2010, NATO agreed a new end-strength target for the ANA of 240,000 soldiers by 2014. The growth of the Afghan National Police was to be equally rapid, rising from 109,000 men in October 2010, to 134,000 in October 2011, then 157,000 in October 2012. Growing forces so quickly put considerable strain on those aspects of the army and police that were already most weak – human resource management, leadership, logistics, and infrastructure (including accommodation).[18] Invariably recruiting standards had to be dropped and training packages condensed in order to meet manpower targets. As noted earlier, the Basic Warrior Training course for Afghan army recruits was reduced from ten to eight weeks; Afghan police received just six weeks of basic training.

The ANA in 2010 continued to be dogged by high levels of illiteracy, drug abuse and absence without leave. It was also entirely dependent on ISAF for logistical and fire support: Afghan combat support services was staffed by officers with no background in logistics; few Afghan artillery units and mortar teams had mastered indirect fire, 'relying instead on gradual adjustment of fire based on direct observation'; and the Afghan air force comprised around twenty Mi-17 transport helicopters and no ground-attack aircraft. Most striking of all was the lacklustre commitment of Afghan soldiers, who were generally unwilling to conduct patrols or to man remote outposts.[19] What the Taliban lacked in resources they more than made up for in morale; as one village elder noted, the Taliban 'believe they are doing Jihad and if they kill in the way of Jihad, they go to Heaven'. In contrast, as one Afghan general admitted, the Afghan state had 'a mercenary army'.[20]

The task of growing the ANA fell to the US Combined Security Transition Command – Afghanistan, which was joined in February 2010 by the newly created NATO Training Mission – Afghanistan; both were under the command of the same US general. Since 2005, CSTC-A had both trained the Afghan security forces and assessed their operational effectiveness through the Capability Milestone rating system. There was an obvious institutional bias in a set-up that had, in effect, CSTC-A marking its own homework; not surprisingly, it overestimated the operational efficiency of Afghan forces. This rating system also had all the same flaws of ISAF's other assessment processes, in particular over-reliance on quantitative metrics and unreliable data. In 2009, ISAF Joint Command took over responsibility for assessing Afghan army proficiency. Following a damning report by the US Special Inspector

General for Afghanistan Reconstruction, ISAF Joint Command introduced a new rating system called the Commander's Unit Assessment
Tool, which included subjective assessments of unit proficiency.[21] In
2011, the US Department of Defense reported that of the 204 battalion-
sized units in the ANA, only 147 were 'effective with ISAF assistance
or advisors'. Just one unit was reported as able to operate independently.[22] This number jumped to thirty battalions in 2012, and by mid
2013, ISAF Joint Command reported that five out of the twenty-six
Afghan army brigades were able to operate independently. Outside
observers remained doubtful, however; as one of them noted, the
Afghan security forces 'are completely reliant on the United States or
on NATO for the logistics, for their planning, for their intelligence,
for their air support, for their quick-response forces if they get into
trouble'.[23]

The operational effectiveness of the Afghan police was even more
questionable. The ANP was effectively a paramilitary force responsible for securing urban and rural communities. But as they were
poorly trained and equipped, invariably it fell to the ANA to keep
the insurgency at bay. For the most part, the ANP were a bane
in the lives of ordinary Afghans. They suffered from even higher
levels of illiteracy, drug abuse and corruption than the ANA. An
added problem in southern Afghanistan was the low number of
southern Pashtuns in the police force; by early 2012, southern
Pashtuns made up only 13 per cent of total police recruits.[24] Thus
for villagers in Helmand and elsewhere in the south, the Afghan
police were foreigners. Training of the police recruits was haphazard
at best. As we have seen, in Helmand it languished in the hands of
EUPOL until Task Force Helmand stepped in and under James Cowan
got the Helmand Police Training Centre up and running in preparation for Operation Moshtarak. In a long overdue move, ISAF Joint
Command made 'embedded partnering' with the Afghan National
Police a priority for 2010. However, ISAF Regional Commands
responded with varying degrees of enthusiasm to this instruction.
The US Army-led Regional Command East embraced embedded
partnering, making it central to their 'Combined 24/7' concept of
operations. However, in northern Afghanistan, which saw an alarming
rise in Taliban activity in 2010, the German-led Regional Command
North simply outsourced such partnering to a US Army Brigade

Combat Team, who were immensely stretched, with only two battalions to partner with seven ANP *kandaks* across the whole region.[25]

Given the ongoing challenges with the Afghan police and army, ISAF headquarters became increasingly interested in the potential for locally raised irregular forces to resist the Taliban in rural areas. This also promised to offset the low numbers of southern Pashtuns in the Afghan National Police. Petraeus foresaw the possibility of an Afghan-style 'Anbar Awakening', to mirror what happened when the Sunni tribes in central Iraq rose up in large numbers and joined forces with the Americans to defeat al-Qaeda in western Iraq in 2006–7.[26] As it happened, in Pashtun areas of Afghanistan there was a strong tradition of using locally raised militia (or *arbakai*) to protect villages. However, recent attempts by ISAF to recruit, train and support such irregular forces – the National Auxiliary Police in 2006, the Public Protection Programme trialled in Wardak province in 2009, and the Community Defence Initiative that McChrystal had attempted to launch – had all ended in disaster. To avoid the errors of these previous attempts, a RAND study in 2010 recommended that any initiative to raise local irregular forces should ensure that these would be 'small, defensive, confined to village-level protection and controlled by the [village] Jirga or shura'.[27] It was Petraeus who persuaded a sceptical Karzai to accept the need for locally raised irregular forces. The president agreed to a total force of 10,000 on condition that they be called 'police' and put under the control of the Ministry of Interior.[28]

In formally launching the Afghan Local Police (ALP) programme in August 2010, the Ministry of Interior explicitly noted that 'As a defensive force, ALP are neither equipped for offensive operations nor permitted to grow beyond size in their *tashkil* [i.e. establishment], which is typically 30 per village and 300 per district. Their activity is restricted to the area required for the defense of their own village.'[29] ALP recruits were vetted by the National Directorate of Security and received 60 per cent of the salary of Afghan National Police. They were armed with AK-47 assault rifles and given one light machine gun per six men (but no rocket-propelled grenades). They received three weeks' training from US Army special forces. Once launched, the ALP programme expanded rapidly. By March 2011, 5,400 sites for selecting and training ALP had been established. That same month, Petraeus told the US Senate Armed Services Committee that the ALP was 'arguably the most critical element in our effort to help Afghanistan develop the capability to secure itself'.[30] By 2015, the ALP had grown to around 29,000 men in twenty-nine of Afghanistan's thirty-four provinces, with an approved end strength of 30,000 personnel.

The ALP was not the silver bullet that Petraeus hoped it would be. One independent assessment by a team of US experts in 2013 concluded that the programme had worked well in some areas but 'in other districts, ALP are causing more harm than good'.[31] In Helmand, the ALP proved a mixed success. The US Marines had supported *arbakai* in Marjah since mid 2010, which were funded directly by the 1st Marine Expeditionary Brigade and did not formally come under the ALP programme. However, the Marjah *arbakai* were anchored in the village shura, which made them accountable and gave them legitimacy in the eyes of locals. For two years, the 'Lions of Marjah' proved successful at preventing the Taliban from retaking the district.[32] The first ALP supported by Task Force Helmand was established in the Hazara village of Saidabad in late 2010. It was complicated to set up, requiring approval from ISAF headquarters, the Afghan Ministry of Interior, and the provincial and district governors and chiefs of police; James Chiswell recalls that 'it took ages to close the deal'. Nonetheless, 16 Brigade were determined to do things by the book, if at the risk of appearing 'a bit pedantic' by some in ISAF. Chiswell understood that it was crucial to ensure that the ALP was answerable to the village shura. In this way, the ALP was about much more than just security; here was a way of bringing rural communities into the political process and this, as Chiswell puts it, was 'potentially gold dust'.[33]

The ALP became a major priority for the British in Helmand in 2011 and 2012. The number of ALP sites expanded greatly under 20 Armoured Brigade's mission from October 2011 to March 2012, led by Brigadier Patrick Saunders. There was some concern that in the rush to grow the programme, not sufficient care had gone into ensuring that all ALP units were genuinely local community defence forces as opposed to rebadged warlord militia.[34] British commanders were acutely aware that no two ALP units were alike in terms of social context and how they operated. As Brigadier Doug Chalmers, who commanded 12 Mechanised Brigade from April 2012 to October 2012, put it, 'When you've seen an ALP you've seen just that' – one ALP unit. Chalmers' headquarters looked closely at every ALP unit and

worked with the deputy provincial chief of police to 'weed out' problematic ones and to better integrate them with Afghan National Police
units.[35]

By 2013, there were ten ALP sites mentored by the British and a
further six mentored by US special forces in the Task Force Helmand
area of operations. The Saidabad ALP had become the archetype for
the British, as it was well led and had strong support from the local
community. The ALP in the village of Bayazo, south of Gereshk, was
led by Jan Mohammed (commonly known to the British as 'Jamo'), a
former Hizb-i Islami commander who served in the 93rd Division
under Mir Wali. This was an example of an existing warlord militia
rebadged as ALP, but it did serve effectively to protect local communities from the Taliban. Less successful was the ALP in northern Nahr-e
Seraj under the command of a former Afghan army sergeant called
Rahmatullah. Here was a case of a commander turning bad, and an
ALP unit becoming increasingly separated from and abusive towards
the local population. When US special forces took over the mentoring
of this ALP from the British in 2012, they promptly dismissed
Rahmatullah, although they struggled to find a replacement
commander. Even worse was the ALP located on the boundary of
northern Nad-e Ali and southern Nahr-e Seraj, where the commander,
Lal Mohammed (known as 'Lali'), was related by marriage to the local
Taliban commander, a fellow Barakzai. Such familial links across the
divide were common in Helmand. When a dispute with a local Noorzai
warlord escalated to threaten Lali, he defected to the Taliban, taking
with him intimate knowledge of Afghan police strengths and weaknesses in the area.[36]

Complicated command and oversight arrangements – involving
four deputy ministers and the ALP directorate in the Ministry of
Interior, US Joint Special Operations Task Force–Afghanistan, and
provincial and district chiefs of police – and lack of clarity regarding
the rules for detention and treatment of suspects by ALP opened the
door to abuse. Doubtless adding to ALP disgruntlement was Kabul's
routine failure to provide promised weapons, requested supplies and
agreed pay. A survey of US special forces teams mentoring ALP in
2011 found that 20 per cent of ALP members had committed violent
acts towards civilians. There were widespread complaints of ALP
involved in beatings, kidnappings, extortion, extrajudicial killings and

illegal taxation of the population. This was most likely to occur when, as in Uruzgan, the ALP served local warlords and not the village shura. ALP members in Faryab province were accused of 'raping, looting, and keeping a torture chamber'. One eyewitness in Logar province claimed that the ALP executed forty-five Taliban prisoners. In Baghlan, where the ALP were rebadged members of a warlord's militia, they were involved in the kidnapping and raping of teenage boys, and in arbitrary detention and enforced disappearances of local leaders. The ALP directorate in the Ministry of Interior told Human Rights Watch in 2015 that they investigated all complaints and had imprisoned sixty-five ALP officers on charges. However, in reality, intimidation and the deliberate ignoring of abuses prevented most complaints from coming to light. When the situation got really bad, villagers would form a rival ALP militia to defend themselves against the existing predatory force (as happened in Uruzgan) or they would align with the Taliban (as happened in Kunduz).[37]

Another growing challenge in the latter stages of the ISAF campaign was the rise of 'insider attacks' by Afghan soldiers and police against Western troops, also called 'green-on-blue attacks'. There were only two such attacks in 2007 and 2008, and six in 2009 and 2010. But then the number jumped to twenty-one in 2011 and thirty-six in 2012. The number of ISAF fatalities rose accordingly, from ten in 2009 to fifty-one in 2012.[38] The worst insider attack suffered by British forces occurred in November 2009, when three Guardsmen and two Royal Military Police were killed by a lone gunman at an Afghan police checkpoint near Shin Kalay in Nad-e Ali. One survivor, Lance Sergeant Peter Baily, recalled that 'We had just finished lunch, and most of the soldiers were sitting on a small wall in the courtyard', when a rogue Afghan policeman emptied his AK-47 at the unsuspecting British troops. As in this case, the Taliban frequently claimed credit for insider attacks, even though there were clearly multiple reasons for them, including Afghans becoming enraged by rude or abusive behaviour of their ISAF mentors. Invariably, the attackers defected to the Taliban, raising the suspicion that they were sympathetic to the Taliban from the outset, if not actual Taliban infiltrators. In mid 2011, the US military became so concerned about insider attacks that they dispatched eighty counter-intelligence agents to help improve the vetting of army and police recruits.[39] The Afghan army National Recruiting Centre in

Kabul had itself just eighteen officers vetting potential recruits for ties to the Taliban, as well as other factors making them unsuitable for army service. In 2012, only one in every thirty applicants was rejected.[40]

Insider attacks became 'the signature violence of 2012', according to one US official.[41] While this claim is unpersuasive from an Afghan perspective, it does reveal the political salience of insider attacks for war-weary NATO. In late March 2012, Allen responded by ordering new protective measures for ISAF personnel when in the company of Afghan soldiers and police, including that they be watched by armed comrades who would act as 'guardian angels'.[42] On 18 September 2012, Allen took a step further in ordering a halt to all joint operations and patrols below battalion level 'until further notice'. ISAF headquarters neglected to warn the Afghan government or home capitals of this decision. The Afghan Ministry of Defence initially dismissed reports of this change in policy as 'incorrect'. Even more embarrassing for the British, the previous day the Defence Secretary, Philip Hammond, had told the House of Commons that the insider attack on British forces the weekend before, resulting in the deaths of two soldiers from 3rd Battalion the Yorkshire Regiment, would not 'derail' the essential job of training Afghan forces by British troops.[43] This led to behind-the-scenes scrambling as Whitehall tried to figure out what was going on. The British Chief of the Defence Staff, General Sir David Richards, phoned Allen to come up with a face-saving solution. It was decided that joint patrols and operations below battalion level by British forces had to be agreed by the commander of Regional Command South-West, US Marine Major General Charles Gurganus. The UK Ministry of Defence promptly secured a statement from Gurganus confirming that he approved the current British approach.[44] At their height in 2012, insider attacks amounted to 15 per cent of ISAF killed in action. More damaging still, such attacks sowed distrust and created distance between ISAF and Afghan troops at the worst possible time.

In September 2012, the Taliban launched an audacious attack against the Camp Bastion complex, which had grown to encompass three contiguous camps – the original British-built Camp Bastion, the US Marines' Camp Leatherneck and the ANA's Camp Shorabak – occupying a site the size of Reading. At 10 p.m. on 14 September, fifteen heavily armed insurgents dressed in US Army uniforms cut the wire on the eastern perimeter of the camp. Splitting into three groups, they then launched a coordinated attack on the airfield. US and British quick reaction forces responded within sixteen minutes. The gunfight lasted into the early hours of 15 September, during which two US Marines were killed and eight others wounded, as were eight British troops. Six US Marine Harrier jump jets were destroyed and two more severely damaged; a number of other planes and helicopters were also damaged in the attack. Fourteen insurgents were killed, and the remaining one was captured and interrogated. From this it was ascertained that the attackers had been trained specifically for the mission in a camp in Pakistan for seventeen days; the ISI were almost certainly involved.[45]

ISAF failings contributed to the Taliban success in this attack, in particular the convoluted command arrangements for security of the wider Camp Bastion complex. The British were responsible for protecting Camp Bastion including the airfield; the US Marines were in charge of Camp Leatherneck and the area around the Bastion–Leatherneck–Shorabak complex. This was not the first time that security had been breached: there were nine breaches in 2011 and twelve in 2012, although most were incursions by locals seeking scrap metal. However, there was a spectacular insider attack on 14 March 2012, when an Afghan interpreter drove a vehicle onto the airfield and straight towards Gurganus, as he waited on the runway for the arrival of US Defense Secretary Leon Panetta. The vehicle narrowly missed Gurganus and his staff, and the attacker then set himself on fire. Following this close call, Gurganus directed that a single commander be appointed to take responsibility for the running and security of the wider Camp Bastion complex and airfield. However, this change was blocked by the US–British Executive Steering Group for Camp Bastion, presumably by the British, who did not want to relinquish complete control to the US Marines. Gurganus also requested an additional two hundred US Marines to bolster security of the complex, but none were forthcoming as the 1st Marine Expeditionary Force was drawing down from Helmand in 2012. Primary responsibility for perimeter security therefore fell to UK Number 5 RAF Force Protection Wing, who in turn assigned the tiny Tonga Defence Services contingent to man the guard towers in the British sector. Accordingly, only eleven of the twenty-four guard towers in the Camp Bastion complex were occupied on 14 September; crucially, the guard tower closest to where the insurgents broke in was unmanned. An internal US Army investigation found the two most senior US Marine commanders responsible for this grave breach of security at Bastion. The commandant of the US Marine Corps, General James Amos, requested the resignations of Gurganus and Major General Gregg Sturdevant, commander of the 3rd Marine Aircraft Wing. In stark contrast, no British officer was sanctioned or dismissed. The UK Chief of Joint Operations, Lieutenant General David Capewell, admitted that mistakes had been made by British service personnel but he told the Commons Defence Committee that these 'were not culpable errors'. The British were content to let the US Marines take the blame.[46]

In February 2013, Allen handed over command of ISAF to fellow US Marine General Joseph Dunford. Like Allen, Dunford had no command experience in Afghanistan. However, he did have a highly experienced British deputy in the newly promoted Lieutenant General Nick Carter. Carter was more comfortable navigating Kabul politics and Dunford was sensitive to Washington politics; they were well matched as a pair and formed a close working relationship. Dunford's command identified the confidence of the Afghan people in their own government and security forces as the campaign's centre of gravity; indeed, with the end of the ISAF mission rapidly approaching, the sense of anxiety in Kabul was palpable. ISAF headquarters anticipated that the logistically demanding process of closing down bases and shipping equipment back home (called 'retrograde' in military jargon) would increasingly become the dominant activity for Western forces in Afghanistan in 2014. For the British alone, it would involve shipping 3,345 vehicles and other items of major equipment (including fifty aircraft) and 5,500 twenty-foot equivalent units (called 'TEUs') of material back to the United Kingdom between October 2012 and the end of 2014; by September 2013, around half of this material had been repatriated.[47] NATO was promising to provide enduring support to Afghanistan beyond 2014; that post-ISAF NATO mission was called 'Resolute Support'. However, what Afghans saw were NATO forces packing up and going home. Dunford was acutely aware that, as he put it, 'the video did not match the audio'.[48]

By this stage, the Afghan government was increasingly asserting its sovereign authority. In one sense, growing government confidence was welcome. But this also created tensions, as happened in March 2013 when Karzai banned Afghan forces from requesting ISAF air support because of the civilian casualties this had caused. ISAF was particularly concerned to ensure that the Afghan Ministry of Defence and Ministry of Interior had sufficient capacities to take full responsibility for planning, commanding and supporting the counter-insurgency campaign from 2015. To this end, the ISAF concept of operations under Dunford was to 'go narrow and deep', that is, for ISAF to draw up from the field into Kabul and the regional centres, where resources would be focused in 2014 to support the development of Afghan capacity. However, as US and NATO forces began to leave Afghanistan, ISAF increasingly lost influence with Afghan partners. Already by mid 2013 ISAF headquarters found that the 'Afghan leadership are starting to be dismissive of US leaders', for example, in not recognising US leadership at joint meetings.[49]

ISAF headquarters was also losing touch with what was happening on the ground. It was taken completely by surprise when a large force of insurgents, numbering many hundreds, ambushed an Afghan army patrol in the far north-east province of Badakhshan in late March 2013, killing seventeen and capturing eleven Afghan soldiers. The ANA scrambled to send reinforcements, and Afghan generals had to plead with President Karzai to let ISAF provide air support.[50] After three days of fighting, the Taliban retreated, having lost fifty insurgents. ISAF had handed over responsibility for Badakhshan to the Afghan security forces in 2012 and so this province was 'an ideal testing ground of Afghanistan's ability to secure remote areas on its own'. Two journalists based in Afghanistan concluded that the battle for Badakhshan offered 'a bleak picture of the future'.[51]

On 18 June 2013, the *inteqal* process reached 'Milestone 13', when responsibility for the whole country was formally handed over to the Afghan security forces; in actuality, transition had yet to be completed in around one-fifth of the districts in Afghanistan. Thereafter, remaining ISAF forces would shift to a 'train, advise, assist' mission. With more than a hint of irony, one British journalist reporting on the ceremony in Kabul noted how 'Security was so tight that diplomats and journalists were flown across the city in helicopters, to hear speeches about how effective the army and police were at protecting the country'.[52] By this stage, the United States had spent close to $60 billion building the ANA, and army and police numbers had reached 350,000. The first true test for the Afghan security forces came that spring and summer, as ISAF planned to adopt a far more backseat role during that fighting season to see if Afghan security forces could plan and conduct operations by themselves.[53] Following Karzai's decree, ISAF intelligence worried that without air support, ANA outposts would be vulnerable to wave attacks by large groups of insurgents. Sure enough, a remote Afghan army outpost in Kunar province was overrun by around a hundred Taliban in April, and all thirteen soldiers were killed; this was all the more shocking because the unit came from one of the few battalions in the ANA (3rd Battalion, 5th Brigade) rated by ISAF Joint Command as able to operate independently of ISAF assistance or advisers.[54] The Afghan army was also more vulnerable to IEDs than ISAF forces, as they drove around in Ranger pickup trucks with no electronic countermeasures. ISAF intelligence noted that in areas where ISAF had withdrawn, to attack the unarmed Ranger trucks the Taliban were switching to radio-controlled IEDs with smaller charges, which were far more difficult to detect.[55]

As it turned out, the 2013 fighting season went pretty well for the Afghan security forces. An independent assessment based on extensive field research concluded that 'the Afghan army showed that it can fight well' and that the Taliban 'could not tactically overmatch Afghanistan's soldiers'.[56] To be sure, the report noted many challenges ahead for Afghan security forces: the army was terrible at logistics and maintenance; the police were often outgunned by insurgents; the air force was unable to provide close air support; and the security ministries in Kabul were poor at planning and budgeting. All the same, the report concluded that the Taliban did not have a good campaign in 2013:

> The insurgents were unable to seize and hold large swaths of terrain; they were unable to take and hold district centers or other notable political targets; they were limited in their ability to influence major population centers (occasional high-profile attacks notwithstanding); and they remain generally unpopular among the Afghan populace.[57]

This 'success' came at a terrible cost to the Afghan security forces. Already in late 2012 the Afghan Ministry of Defence spokesman reported that the army was losing over a hundred men per month, and the Afghan police twice that amount.[58] By 2013, the ANA was beginning to lose men at a faster rate than it was replacing them. According to official US figures, between October 2012 and March 2013, the ANA lost 3 per cent of its personnel to combat and desertion *per month*; this amounted to a staggering loss rate of over one-third of the total force per year.[59] Casualties mounted in the summer fighting, with Afghan security forces typically enduring a hundred dead per week. The Afghan Ministry of Defence stopped publishing the monthly death toll because of concerns about the impact on troop morale.[60]

The House of Commons Defence Committee offered a fairly upbeat assessment of the Afghan security forces in 2013. The British Ministry of Defence reported steady progress, noting that 2010 and 2011 'saw for the first time, large scale operations planned and led by the ANSF, with ISAF providing support with an increasingly lighter touch', and that in 2012 'there were no requests for ISAF to support the ANSF in delivering security within the transitioned areas'. In 2012, security responsibility for Lashkar Gah and Nahr-e Seraj (containing the key town of Gereshk) had been transferred to the Afghan security forces. It was reported that Regional Command South-West saw a 3 per cent decrease in attacks by the Taliban in 2012. Doug Chalmers told the Defence Committee that while armed violence in central Helmand 'has only dipped very slightly', it has 'been displaced out of the market town areas and the deeply farmed areas, more into the dasht or the desert areas', and this had allowed confidence to grow among the population. Committee members visited Helmand, where they were told by the commander of 3/215 Brigade, Brigadier General Sherin Shah, that the ANA still lacked crucial intelligence, medical, air support and counter-IED capabilities. Various British government and military officials assured the Defence Committee that these capabilities would be developed to an appropriate level in the Afghan army in 2014.[61] This never happened.

Nonetheless, the British withdrawal from Helmand began on 19 August 2013, when the headquarters of Task Force Helmand was moved from Lashkar Gah to Camp Bastion. Philip Hammond told reporters that this move was made possible by the 'growing capability of the Afghan security forces our troops have trained'.[62] Then, on 27 February 2014, the British PRT in Lashkar Gah was formally closed. A British embassy spokesman told reporters: 'It is desirable and right that the Afghans take increasing responsibility for their own future prosperity and security. We will continue to support them as they do so.'[63] Obviously, British support would thereon be from more of a distance. On 2 April 2014, Task Force Helmand was disbanded and command of remaining British troops in Helmand was transferred to Regional Command South-West (led by a US Marine general with a British deputy).[64] Finally, on 28 October, Camp Bastion was handed over to the ANA, and the last three hundred British soldiers in Helmand were flown to Kandahar airfield along with five hundred US Marines. To discourage parting shots from the Taliban, US and British jets, drones and helicopters patrolled the skies above. Aside from these heightened security measures, as with all the previous stages in Britain's withdrawal, the Bastion handover was done with minimum fuss and fanfare.[65] A few hundred British military personnel remained in Kabul in non-combat functions, principally to support the ISAF headquarters and to staff the officer-training academy on the western outskirts of the city, established and funded by the United Kingdom (and colloquially called 'Sandhurst in the Sands').[66] But basically, for the British, the war was finally over. For Afghans, it raged on.

THE KARZAI PROBLEM

By 2009, Karzai, once the darling of the international community as a cosmopolitan Pashtun leader, had become a problem for the West. This was not because he kept publicly berating ISAF for conducting night raids and for causing civilian causalities, although this did irk successive ISAF commanders; nor even because of his infamous temper and mood swings. It was because he had done nothing to stop endemic corruption and cronyism from gripping the new Afghan state.

According to Vali Nasr, a regional expert and former senior adviser to the US State Department on Afghanistan, 'The shine had come off Karzai even before Obama took office.' US officials and members of Congress increasingly viewed Karzai as a 'venal, corrupt, and unreliable partner, and as such the chief reason why the Taliban were doing so well'.[67] The problem was thrown into stark relief by the staggering extent of fraud in the Afghan presidential election in August 2009, most of it committed by the Karzai camp. In the lead-up to the election there were numerous reports of voter registration cards for sale on the black market; on the eve of the election, a BBC reporter was offered a thousand such voter cards for sale at $10 apiece.[68] People were commonly registered at multiple polling centres, and men collected stacks of voting cards for female relatives who did not exist. Possibly more worrying, the instruments of the state were harnessed for Karzai's presidential campaign. Supposedly impartial election officials were tacitly if not openly pro-Karzai, including all seven members of the so-called Independent Elections Commission who were personally appointed by Karzai. In rural areas, pro-Karzai strongmen coerced locals to voting for the incumbent president. And there was industrial-scale stuffing of ballot boxes. With the Taliban delivering on their threat to attack polling stations across the country, only a fraction of the registered voters in Helmand turned out to vote. Yet mysteriously, large numbers of votes were cast. Independent election monitors deemed it too dangerous to visit polling stations in rural parts of the province. A journalist working for the *Independent* witnessed election officials in Nad-e Ali 'counting piles of ballot papers, without even checking the choices, simply declaring the votes had been cast for incumbent president Hamid Karzai'.[69]

It took weeks to sort out the results. In mid September, over one million votes had been invalidated as fraudulent; two-thirds of these had been cast for Karzai. Based on the remaining 5.6 million valid votes, the Independent Elections Commission declared Karzai the winner with over 54 per cent of the vote, as against just under 28 per cent for his main rival Abdullah Abdullah. Abdullah was quick to accuse the president of rigging the election. It was a moment of high crisis in Kabul. With Abdullah calling on his supporters not to recognise the legitimacy of the election result, the international community feared open conflict between Abdullah's Northern Alliance backers and the Pashtun power-holders backing Karzai. US diplomats briefly tried to broker a power-sharing deal between Karzai and Abdullah.[70] Meanwhile the United Nations-sponsored Electoral Complaints Commission (with two Afghan and three international officials) investigated the 740 most serious cases of ballot-stuffing, leading to more votes being invalidated and lowering Karzai's overall vote to 49.67 per cent, bringing it to just below the 50 per cent threshold for re-election.[71]

The United States put immense pressure on Karzai to accept the necessity for a second-round run-off election, dispatching US Secretary of State John Kerry in late October to twist his arm: Kerry arrived just in time to see off a ruse by the Independent Elections Commission to certify that Karzai had achieved the required 50 per cent of votes in the first round.[72] The second round was scheduled for 7 November, but Abdullah pulled out on 1 November because Karzai refused to take measures to improve transparency in the run-off, including replacing the head of the Independent Elections Commission. The following day, Obama called Karzai, ostensibly to congratulate him on his re-election, but actually to admonish him for his failure to tackle corruption. Obama told Karzai that he would have to do more; that 'the proof is not going to be in words; it's going to be in deeds'.[73]

If Obama expected Karzai to eat humble pie, he was to be sorely disappointed. Karzai was furious at what he saw as American attempts to unseat him from power. Already in early July 2009, the US ambassador, Karl Eikenberry, reported back to Washington that 'Incredulously, Karzai appeared to accept so-called rumors that the US and Iran were working together to support Abdullah against him'. At a meeting with Afghan national security ministers and senior officials attended by Eikenberry, Karzai declared that 'the US had actively encouraged Abdullah, Ashraf Ghani, and Zalmay Khalilzad [the Afghan-born former US ambassador] to run for the presidency'.[74] In late September, the US deputy head of the UN mission in Afghanistan, Peter Galbraith, was fired when he openly criticised the UN for failing to challenge Karzai on election fraud.[75] Behind this principled stance by a US diplomat, Karzai would doubtless have seen an American power play, as Galbraith was a close associate of Richard Holbrooke, the US special representative for Afghanistan and Pakistan. Just days after the election, well before all the votes had been counted, Holbrooke attempted to persuade Karzai publicly to accept the necessity for a second round of voting. For Karzai, this was yet another example of the Americans siding with Abdullah.[76]

In early November, the head of the UN mission, Kai Eide, called on Karzai to appoint 'competent reform-orientated personalities' in his new administration, and to wage 'a vigorous fight against corruption'. Karzai promptly pushed back. In a sharply worded rebuke, his foreign minister accused Eide and 'some political and diplomatic circles and propaganda agencies of certain foreign countries' of disrespecting Afghanistan's national sovereignty 'by issuing instructions concerning the composition of Afghan government organs and political policy of Afghanistan'.[77] This incident served to underline Eikenberry's overall assessment, sent in a secret cable to Washington around this time, that Karzai 'is not an adequate strategic partner' and that he 'continues to shun responsibility for any sovereign burden'. Eikenberry's criticism extended beyond Karzai to the Afghan polity as a whole; he stated that the country had 'little to no political will or capacity to carry out basic tasks of governance'.[78]

Relations between the international community and Karzai continued to deteriorate in 2010. The year got off to a bad start when Eikenberry's highly critical cable about Karzai was leaked by the *New York Times*.[79] Where Bush had been warm towards Karzai and frequently in contact with the president through weekly video teleconferences, Obama was cold and distant. Sensitive to this fact, McChrystal went to great lengths to develop a strong relationship with the Afghan president.[80] McChrystal had been chipping away at the corruption problem, working with the new NATO senior civilian representative for Afghanistan, Ambassador Mark Sedwell. In February 2010, the two issued 'anti-corruption guidance', instructing ISAF forces to look out for and take action against corruption; in reality there was little ISAF officers could do beyond shaming and persuading corrupt officials to change their ways, and if this failed reporting them to Afghan authorities (who were themselves invariably corrupt).[81] Following the growing international pressure for the second Karzai administration to get serious about corruption, Petraeus decided to make it a top priority for his command. He appointed Brigadier General H. R. McMaster, a rising star in the US Army, to be the ISAF lead on a new inter-agency task force on transparency and corruption.[82]

The main British contribution to the fight against corruption was in creating an Afghan criminal investigation unit called the Major Crimes Task Force, whose remit included corruption. It was mentored by officers from Scotland Yard. The very first case for the task force was a pretty good indicator of what was to come. Given that Britain had the lead on counter-narcotics, the mentors decided that the first case ought to reflect this. The task force therefore arrested an Afghan border police officer involved in taking bribes from drug smugglers and arranged for the suspect to be held in an Afghan detention facility in Kandahar. The Afghan interior minister, Hanif Atmar, was furious and threatened to fire the head of the detention facility for agreeing to hold the police officer. In order to defuse a growing diplomatic crisis, British officials agreed to brief Atmar in advance before the Major Crimes Task Force arrested any future suspects; in effect, this would enable Atmar to take pre-emptive action to protect officials in his network. Thus when the task force tried to move against the Afghan border police chief in Kandahar, numerous obstacles were put in their way and the case was eventually dropped.[83] Yet comparatively speaking, Atmar was one of the most capable and least corrupt political leaders in Afghanistan. As the minister for reconstruction and rural development from 2002 to 2006 he had played a central role in securing large amounts of international aid for his country and he ran one of the more effective ministries in the first Karzai government.[84]

The Major Crimes Task Force lasted barely a year. When in July 2010 they arrested Mohammad Zia Saleh, a top official in the office of the Afghan national security adviser, on bribery charges, Karzai responded by dismantling the task force. The two prosecutors on the Saleh case were demoted and reassigned, the deputy attorney general who had signed the arrest warrant was accused of espionage and forced to flee the country, and Saleh was released. It later emerged that the CIA were somehow tied up in shady dealings in the presidential palace. The agency had been paying Karzai millions of dollars in cash each year and their bagman was Saleh. Even as Saleh was being investigated by the Major Crimes Task Force, the CIA remained silent about this, not even telling Petraeus or the US ambassador.[85] Relations between Petraeus and Karzai collapsed over the Saleh affair.[86] Petraeus came away completely disillusioned about what could be achieved in terms of combating corruption in Afghanistan. In September, he issued commander's guidance on reducing corruption caused by ISAF contracting practices,[87] but otherwise, decided to devote his energies to intensifying the kill/capture campaign.[88]

Afghanistan had become the third most corrupt state in the world by 2010, according to the non-governmental watchdog Transparency International. In a survey of surveys, the watchdog found that 60 per cent of Afghans polled reported that corruption had got worse over the past three years.[89] Moreover, the United Nations Office on Drugs and

Crime reported in 2010 that corruption had overtaken insecurity and unemployment as the greatest concern for Afghans.[90] In fairness to Karzai, he was not wholly to blame. By pouring money into Afghanistan, the international community had helped to create a kleptocratic state. One study into the international development effort in Afghanistan concluded that 'The money flow simply overwhelmed the country's social and institutional capacity to deal with it in a legal and socially acceptable manner'. Afghanistan was particularly susceptible as a country with weak formal government institutions and 'the predominance of social norms and practices that favour patronage and clientalism in social exchanges'. Huge contracts for development activities and military infrastructure created 'a bidding frenzy' among Afghans, and in turn fantastic opportunities for officials to skim money. The US Defense Department alone authorised $11.5 billion of contracts for 2007–9.[91] From 2009 to 2011, at the height of the US military surge, American units spent around $2 billion on 'small' humanitarian and infrastructure projects, all locally contracted work, under the Commander's Emergency Response Program.[92]

In the rush to 'build capacity' in Afghanistan, the international community ruined the Afghan economy and the prospects for sustainable and effective government. The international military presence sent massive amounts of money flowing in multiple directions, to rent land, build facilities and buy supplies for bases, and to hire security guards and other general services. In Helmand, for example, the British supported warlords by paying them rent for the land on which were constructed FOBs and PBs; some of these landlords paid subsidies to the Taliban, and so in this roundabout way, the British ended up funding the Taliban. These kinds of antics fuelled the surprisingly pervasive and persistent myth in Helmand that the British were covertly supporting the Taliban. Mike Martin has observed how 'almost all Helmandis sincerely believe that the UK is working with the Taliban' for any number of reasons, including keeping Islam divided and weak in Afghanistan, revenge for Maiwand, wanting to re-establish the British Empire, and stealing Helmandi uranium. Reinforcing the myth, many Afghans believed that Britain was powerful enough to crush the Taliban at any time, had it wanted to. Martin notes that 'This is not a fringe conspiracy theory ... I have heard it from farmers, senior rival leaders, senior Hizb-i Islami figures, Helmandis with tertiary education, ANP

officers of Colonel and above rank, a Helmandi senator, and (reportedly) Hamid Karzai.'[93] Suffice to say that the guidance issued by Petraeus
on reducing corruption in ISAF contracts was too little too late.

By now the political economy of Afghanistan was profoundly
corrupt. It was a state in which economy activity and access to public
goods was fuelled by bribery. It was commonly believed that power-
holders at the top, including Karzai, distributed capital (most of it
recycled international funds) to their respective networks of supporters
and thereby stayed in power. Yet a leading expert on corruption, Sarah
Chayes, argues that this view of the structure of corruption in
Afghanistan is entirely wrong. Drawing on an insight first offered by
Colonel Chris Kolenda, the special adviser to McChrystal and Petraeus,
she believes that 'Karzai was not, as the conventional wisdom had it,
doling out patronage. He wasn't distributing money downward to buy
off potential political rivals.' Rather, money was flowing *upwards* in
'the form of gifts, kickbacks, levies paid to superiors, and the purchase
of positions'. The key insight is that almost every public position in
Afghanistan, from police sergeant to provincial governor, was purchased
and so required regular payment to higher-ups. Thus international
funds that came into Afghanistan to pay for public works and salaries
were siphoned off at multiple points by corrupt officials and passed
upwards through payments from subordinates to superiors and eventually to the elite at the top, from where it was transferred to offshore
accounts. In this way very large quantities of international aid for
Afghanistan ended up in banks in Dubai.[94]

Corruption undermined the counter-insurgency campaign in two
ways. First, it had a direct and negative impact on the effectiveness of
the Afghan police and army. Here promotion was dependent on
patronage and purchase, rather than merit. For those seeking to get
ahead, competence in their job was irrelevant; what mattered were
connections and the ability to generate cash. For army officers it meant
skimming soldiers' pay and stealing whatever they could get their hands
on, such as fuel and supplies.[95] Police officers also raised income through
illegal taxation and ransom of illegally detained civilians. Second, corruption undermined public support for the security forces, especially the
police. The British military presence reduced the worst police excesses
in Helmand – such as the kidnap, murder and rape of civilians – but
no amount of mentoring or training would prevent police corruption

when officers depended on it for their livelihoods, and many had to make regular payments to keep their positions. Opinion polling by the Asia Foundation shows that across Afghanistan as a whole, public confidence in the police improved over time: from 2008 to 2013, over 80 per cent of those polled expressed confidence in the Afghan National Police.[96] However, as this book has shown, extensive interviews of locals in Helmand reveal a different picture, that is, of the police as a blight to be endured or, where possible, resisted by force.

In Kabul, matters continued to go from bad to worse. In late 2010 Kabul Bank collapsed amid allegations that all of its reserves had been embezzled, and it went into receivership in mid 2011. Kabul Bank was the main commercial bank in Afghanistan, through which the US government channelled hundreds of millions of dollars to pay the salaries of Afghanistan's public servants, including the army and police. International donors, including the UK Department for International Development and the World Bank, suspended funding for Afghanistan for almost a year while the matter was investigated. In November 2011 the investigation revealed that $935 million had been looted from the bank – amounting to 6 per cent of total Afghan gross domestic product – most of it in unsecured 'loans' to nineteen powerful individuals, one of whom was the president's brother, Mahmood Karzai. In scenes straight from a Hollywood movie, stacks of cash had been smuggled out in the food carts of a commercial airline funded by the bank. Most of the stolen funds ended up in the Gulf, as well as in banks and assets in twenty other countries, including Britain and the United States. Only $225 million was recovered.[97] At the centre of the scandal were the bank's chairman, Sherkhan Farnood, and its chief executive, Khalilullah Ferozi; both had been arrested in the summer of 2011 but soon let out on day release. Ferozi was refusing to assist in recovering the looted funds if he was convicted. Farnood threatened to reveal 'many cases and documents regarding Mr Mahmood Karzai and Karzai's family and their businesses'.[98] In 2013, both men were found guilty of the lesser charge of 'breach of trust', sentenced to five years in jail (when prosecutors had sought twenty years for each), and ordered to repay hundreds of millions of dollars in embezzled funds; however, there was no court order to confiscate the bulk of the funds held in their offshore accounts.[99]

Karzai's grip on power ever tightened in the years following his re-election in 2009. He used the authority invested in the president to hire and fire officials, right down to district officials, to keep everybody in line. Thus, while senior officials in the Ministries of Defence and Interior would complain privately to ISAF headquarters about Karzai, nobody would dare speak out. In early 2013, Karzai turned up the heat on his anti-ISAF rhetoric. During the first visit to Afghanistan by the new US Defense Secretary, Chuck Hagel, in March, Karzai went off on a bizarre rant, declaring that America and the Taliban were working together to destabilise the country. He claimed that a day earlier two major suicide bombings had been carried out by the Taliban acting 'in the service of America'. Hagel's meeting with Karzai was quietly dropped from the Defense Secretary's schedule.[100]

It had become impossible for ISAF to work with Karzai. The previous month the president had banned the army and police from calling in NATO air strikes. This provoked uproar in the Afghan Ministries of Defence and Interior, and consternation in ISAF head-quarters. It was no wonder that Afghan police and army generals were so upset; in many situations, the timely arrival of ISAF air power had saved army and police units from being slaughtered by the Taliban.

Then, in March, Karzai publicly suggested that Afghan forces might take unilateral action to seize control of Parwan Detention Facility at Bagram; the US military was dragging its heels in handing over full control of the facility, fearing that the Afghan authorities would end up releasing prisoners who had been apprehended attacking ISAF and Afghan forces. (Sure enough, they would do so after taking over the facility in early 2014.[101]) Dunford responded by quietly putting ISAF on security alert.[102] The assessment from ISAF intelligence was that Karzai was deliberately trying to provoke a crisis to disrupt, or even create a pretext for delaying, the presidential elections scheduled for the spring of 2014.[103] These elections would see Karzai removed from power: under the terms of the Afghan constitution, no indi-vidual may serve more than two terms as president. Kabul insiders suggested that there was method behind Karzai's apparent madness: that he was vilifying America in order to shape his political legacy. As one Afghan observer put it, 'he wants to be remembered as the guy who kicked out the foreigners' rather than the person put in power by America.[104]

In 2013, ISAF was focused on security transition – in particular, on managing the withdrawal of Western combat forces, and on ensuring that the Afghan security forces had a good summer campaign. However, most of Kabul concentrated on the impending political transition to a post-Karzai government. When asked which mattered more, security transition or political transition, even senior officers in the Ministries of Defence and Interior opted for the latter.[105] Dunford understood the importance of the upcoming presidential election and preoccupation of Kabul's political and security elite with it.[106]

At the same time, he was clear that ISAF headquarters would not get involved in Afghan politics, and this induced ISAF caution when it came to the 2014 elections. Dunford was especially concerned to avoid repeating the breakdown in relations that occurred with Karzai over the 2009 elections. He also had a particular reason to keep Karzai sweet. The United States and Afghanistan had yet to conclude a Bilateral Security Agreement (BSA) that would provide the legal basis for US troops to remain in Afghanistan beyond the end of ISAF. Critically, for the United States, the BSA needed to provide immunity for US military personnel from Afghan law (although American troops would still be accountable for their actions under US military law). The BSA would provide the template for a Status of Forces Agreement that would cover all NATO forces. The US government and ISAF headquarters expected Karzai to be difficult on this issue, but they failed to appreciate just how difficult he would be.

In mid October 2013, Kerry visited Kabul to thrash out the basic terms of the BSA with Karzai. In the joint press conference that followed, the president recounted the story of a young girl he had met two weeks before who had been gravely injured and 'lost her whole family' in an ISAF operation. He stated that a key Afghan demand in the talks with Americans was that in future 'foreign forces will not search the homes of the Afghan people' and 'will not attack – will not conduct any sort of ground attack or air attack on the Afghan homes'.[107] Karzai was due to take the draft BSA to a Loya Jirga for ratification in late November. Since the 2,500 delegates would be selected by the presidential palace, Western observers expected the meeting to do Karzai's bidding and wave the deal through. But things did not turn out as expected.

The Loya Jirga recommended that the BSA be signed. However, Karzai stunned everybody by telling delegates that he would not do so, and suggesting that it should be signed after the presidential elections in April 2014. US and NATO officials had made clear that this would be too late, as it would not leave enough time for post-ISAF planning, which could only start when the BSA was in place. Returning to a familiar theme, Karzai told the Loya Jirga: 'From this moment on, America's searching of house, blocking of roads and streets, military operations are over [*sic*], and our people are free in their country.' Many delegates were horrified, as the Obama administration had threatened a total US military pullout if there was no BSA. This was not an empty promise as failure to conclude a similar deal had led to the withdrawal of all US forces from Iraq. The British government adopted the same line, with the Defence Secretary declaring: 'There will be no British forces on the ground in Afghanistan if there is no bilateral security agreement.'[108] With the US Congress increasingly exasperated by Karzai's behaviour, not signing the BSA also threatened billions of dollars in US funding for the Afghan security forces. Karzai thought the Americans were bluffing; his spokesman told reporters that 'we don't believe there is a zero option'. On a note of high drama, the Loya Jirga closed with Sebghatullah Mojadedi, a Karzai ally and the Loya Jirga organiser, taking the podium after Karzai and declaring that if the BSA was not signed within three days 'I will resign my position and seek refuge in another country'.[109] The US National Security Advisor, Susan Rice, immediately flew to Kabul to try to get the Afghan president to change his mind. But Karzai refused to budge.[110] He left the BSA for his successor to deal with.

The 2014 presidential election was a pretty undignified scramble for power. Twenty-seven candidates submitted nominations by the October 2013 deadline; some drove into the centre of Kabul in long convoys of armed men. Sixteen of these were subsequently disqualified by the Independent Elections Commission, leaving eleven in the race. There was a lot of deal-making behind the scenes and Karzai, the deal-maker in chief, appeared to offer his support to several rival candidates. The lead candidates were Abdullah Abdullah, trying for a second time, and Ashraf Ghani, the former finance minister; Ghani had also run in the 2009 presidential election, when he received only 3 per cent of the vote. Ghani had some very odd bedfellows; the

technocrat ran a strong anti-corruption campaign, yet chose the brutal
warlord Dostum as his running mate, who was supposed to bring
the Uzbek vote. Abdullah got 45 per cent of the vote in the first
round held in April 2014, and Ghani received 32 per cent. Everybody
else was knocked out for the second round, with most of the significant candidates endorsing Abdullah. Abdullah claimed a mixed
heritage – to be both Tajik and Pashtun – but he was fooling no one:
as the former foreign minister of the Northern Alliance, he was
widely seen as the Tajik candidate. Most of the Pashtun candidates
who lost in round one offered their support to Abdullah, doubtless
fearing the anti-corruption drive promised by Ghani. Nonetheless, it
was expected that much of the Pashtun vote would transfer across
to Ghani in the run-off.[111]

Abdullah was unpleasantly surprised by the result of the second
round of voting in late June: Ghani received 56 per cent of the vote.
Significantly, the total number of votes cast increased from 6.6 million
in the first round to almost 8 million in the run-off election. In the
process, the number of votes cast for Ghani more than doubled. It
seemed that an army of 'ghost voters' had magically turned out for
Ghani in the second round, especially in the Pashtun-dominated provinces of Paktika, Paktia and Khost (where Ghani's election campaign
was managed by the canny former Helmand governor, Gulab Mangal).
There was fraud on both sides but, as in 2009, it was much more
frequent in the Pashtun camp. For Tajiks, it was final proof, if proof
were needed, that they would never be able to win power by the
ballot box in Afghanistan.[112] Once again, Abdullah challenged
the result, claiming there had been 'blatant fraud'. Large protests
broke out in Kabul, and for some nervous ISAF commanders the
ever-present spectre of civil war loomed into view.[113] Once again,
Secretary Kerry was dispatched to mediate.[114] The Independent
Elections Commission announced on 19 September that Ghani was
the winner, and hours later Ghani and Abdullah signed a power-sharing
agreement that would see Ghani and Abdullah form a 'National Unity
Government', with Ghani as president and Abdullah appointed to a
prime ministerial-type position, formally called the chief executive
officer of Afghanistan.[115] Under the agreement, posts in the new
National Unity Government would be divided up between the Ghani
and Abdullah camps; months of wrangling followed as both sides

argued over who got what. It took three months for Ghani and Abdullah to agree on a list of twenty-seven ministerial appointments to be sent to parliament for approval – a process that would involve extensive deal-making and bribing of parliamentarians.[116] There were also twenty-five provincial governors to appoint, and hundreds more government appointments to agree (including ambassadorships). Two years on, many of these roles remained unfilled. As the squabbling went on in Kabul, the National Unity Government effectively ground to a halt.[117] However, one thing that Ghani and Abdullah did agree on was the need to keep US troops in Afghanistan: ten days after coming into office they signed the BSA.[118]

THE FALL OF KUNDUZ

On 28 September 2015, the fifth largest city in Afghanistan fell to the Taliban. Some 5,000 Afghan soldiers, police and militia were protecting the northern city of Kunduz, but these quickly retreated as hundreds of Taliban swept into the city to join up with insurgents who had infiltrated beforehand. This was a hard-won victory for the Taliban. Pouring fighters into the north, they had by degrees taken control of the districts around the city over the past two years, even compromising on their usual austere rule in order to win over local support.[119] The Afghan government vowed to quickly retake Kunduz, but the army had to fight through Taliban-held territory surrounding the city.[120] Supported by US air strikes and special forces, Afghan commandos began to clear the Taliban out of the city on 1 October.[121] It took them two weeks.[122] In seizing Kunduz, the Taliban had achieved a key stated objective of their 2015 campaign, which was to capture a provincial capital, albeit temporarily. Appearing before the Senate Armed Services Committee a few days afterwards, the then commander of ISAF, General John Campbell, 'absolutely' agreed with John McCain when the senator observed that 'from a PR standpoint, it was a rather significant victory for the Taliban'.[123] This was something of an understatement.

Kunduz provided a window into Afghanistan's future, and it did not look encouraging. The 2014 fighting season had not gone well for the Afghan police and army, who were increasingly left to their own devices as NATO forces devoted ever more attention to pulling out of Afghanistan. At the height of US force levels there were more than eight hundred bases in Afghanistan; by early 2014 this number had fallen to below eighty, and it would decrease to below thirty by October 2014.[124] Reflecting the worsening situation across the country, civilian fatalities from the conflict rose by 20 per cent, from under 3,000 in 2013 to more than 3,600 in 2014.[125] In the south, the Taliban launched large-scale assaults in several districts in Helmand province. In late September, they overran Sangin, capturing everything except the district centre and central bazaar; it was six months before the Afghan army launched a counter-offensive supported by NATO air power to retake some lost ground. In October, the Taliban twice attacked Lashkar Gah with massive suicide bombs. According to one estimate, the Afghan security forces suffered close to 1,300 killed in Helmand alone between August and December 2014, which amounted to almost a quarter of total security forces losses in the country that year. Elsewhere the Taliban seized villages in Uruzgan and Ghazni, and in the provinces of Wardak, Kapisa and Logar surrounding Kabul, which enabled them to ambush Afghan army convoys along the Kabul to Kandahar highway that were ferrying reinforcements for Sangin. The Taliban also made major gains in the north. In August 2014, insurgent forces were reported to be just three miles from Kunduz city. By January 2015 local officials admitted that the Taliban had 'effectively surrounded' the city.[126]

The United States had planned to reduce its remaining forces in Afghanistan from 9,800 down to 5,500 by the end of 2015. This plan was quietly scrapped in the face of growing concern in Washington about the ability of the Afghan security forces to check a Taliban resurgence. The start of the Taliban's offensive in 2015, officially launched on 24 April, saw an immediate spike in armed activity, with a 45 per cent rise in insurgent-initiated attacks, leading to a 33 per cent increase in Afghan police and army casualties over the following month.[127] The 2015 offensive saw the Taliban make gains in Helmand and Uruzgan in the south, and Kunduz, Faryab and Badakhshan in the north.[128] During three months of near-continuous fighting in north-east Uruzgan, the Taliban decimated local pro-government militia forces. Here, as elsewhere, abusive behaviour by Afghan National Police and Afghan Local Police – including the rape of children and murder of civilians – turned local communities against the government and gave the Taliban an easy inroad to the district.[129] In neighbouring Helmand, the Taliban captured two districts, Now Zad in late July and Musa Qala in late August. Afghan security forces retook Musa Qala four days later, following a major battle in which some two hundred Taliban were reportedly killed. However, the army left after only one day and the Taliban promptly recaptured the district centre. Musa Qala finally returned to government control when the Taliban decided to pull out to attack neighbouring Kajaki district.[130] A report by the Afghan Analysts Network in September 2015 estimated that of the fourteen districts in Helmand '8 are under full or significant Taliban control'.[131]

Elsewhere, the Taliban launched their most spectacular attack in Kabul in June, when a massive car bomb was exploded outside the fortified Afghan parliament and seven gunmen attempted to storm the building; the attack was timed to coincide with parliamentary debate over Ghani's nominee for minister of defence, Mohammed Masoom Stanekzai.[132] And in July, the Uzbek warlord and Afghan vice president, General Dostum, rushed to Faryab to mobilise his tribal militia to prevent a large Taliban force, reported to be up to 5,000 strong, from overrunning the province.[133]

There were significant failings by the Afghan security forces in the defence of Kunduz, in particular the lack of coordination between the ANA and the Afghan Civil Order Police in separate garrisons on either side of the city. The fall of Kunduz also illustrated the fault lines in the National Unity Government as much as failings of the Afghan security forces. The rivalry between the Ghani and Abdullah camps was played out in Kunduz with the provincial governor, a Pashtun appointed by Ghani, at loggerheads with the deputy provincial governor and the provincial police chief, both Tajiks appointed by Abdullah.[134] The governor was unable to rein in abuse by the ALP, who were protected by the police chief. Thus, attempts to clear surrounding districts of Taliban became opportunities for the ALP to go on 'a looting rampage' and, much like Uruzgan, this made it easy for the Taliban to consolidate their hold over such areas.[135] The population in Kunduz also grew increasingly disillusioned by ineffective and corrupt provincial government. Unusual in provinces in the north, Kunduz has a sizeable Pashtun population and the Taliban shrewdly exploited this ethnic geography. For their infiltration, they sought help from migrant Pashtuns in the city and surrounding villages. Many residents cooperated with Taliban infiltrating the city in advance of the offensive. As the *New York Times* reported, 'even pro-government residents and Afghan security officials now admit that part of the assault on Kunduz started from within the city: Many of the Taliban fighters had been hiding in people's homes before they launched an inside-out offensive'.[136] The Taliban attempted to replicate the success of Kunduz elsewhere. In the weeks following their capture of the city, they massed thousands of fighters in attempts to overrun the provincial capitals of Faryab and Ghazni. Fortunately in both cases they were repulsed by Afghan security forces.[137]

The following year brought yet more woe for the Afghan government. The US Defense Department reported that there were ten high-profile attacks in Kabul and fifty elsewhere in Afghanistan in the first six months of 2016. This was in fact a 41 per cent decrease in such attacks over the same period the previous year, which the US Special Inspector General for Afghanistan Reconstruction attributed to a different focus in the Taliban's campaign for 2016, away from Afghan government targets and towards district administrative centres. Overall, US forces in Afghanistan Command reported that around 65 per cent of the country's 407 districts were under the government's control at the end of May 2016, down from over 70 per cent in January of that year. According to the Ministry of Interior, four of Helmand's fourteen districts were under serious threat from insurgents.[138] This was almost certainly a gross underestimation. The Taliban had already almost completely overrun the northern districts of Baghran, Musa Qala, Kajaki, Now Zad and Sangin in 2015.

In 2016, the insurgents nearly captured Lashkar Gah. In early May, they stormed police checkpoints on the approaches to the city from Babaji, killing fifteen Afghan policemen.[139] Then in late May, up to four hundred fighters descended on the provincial capital, capturing yet more police checkpoints and causing the outer ring of defences to collapse. The regional chief of police told Reuters news agency that around fifty police officers were killed and another forty injured over two days of fighting. Gunfire and artillery resounded throughout the city causing panic among residents. NATO bombers and gunships along with US special forces were scrambled to repulse the attack. The Taliban got to within a mile of the provincial capital before they were beaten back by air power.[140] The police chief in Helmand told the *New York Times* in early August that over the past few weeks, NATO had conducted six or seven air strikes per day, and that without this level of bombing, 'the Taliban would have control of the provincial capital'. At the time of writing, the city remains cut off and under siege. The main road connecting Lashkar Gah to Kandahar is heavily mined, and residents have evacuated in droves along alternative routes that are controlled by Taliban checkpoints.[141]

It was anticipated that the Taliban would make Helmand a major focus of their 2016 campaign. In preparation, US forces returned to the province, deploying a 500-strong task force from 10th Mountain Division to Camp Shorabak in February to provide training for 215 Corps.[142] These days there is far less news from Helmand reaching the outside world: a combination of less demand (with no British and few US troops) and the growing difficulty (given the growing insecurity) of reporting from the province. The news that does get out paints a depressing picture. One report in late July claimed that the Taliban had overrun Kanashin district in southern Helmand, killing at least twenty-four Afghan police officers, and had surrounded government and police compounds in Nad-e Ali district. According to one senior Helmand official, the Taliban were in control of most of the province.[143] There were no reports from Marjah, which fell to the Taliban in late 2015 and was only retaken with assistance from US special forces in January 2016.[144] Notwithstanding the paucity of reporting, the overall trend is unmistakable: the Afghan security forces are losing Helmand.

TALKING TO THE TALIBAN

Karzai made a rhetorical commitment to pursuing an accommodation with the Taliban but he never developed a coherent strategy to achieve this. The Afghan president had been involved in talks with Gulbuddin Hekmatyar's Hizb-i Islami party since 2006; while Hizb-i Islami is aligned to the Taliban, many former Hizb-i Islami members joined the Afghan government and security forces. Karzai's hope, which he never realised, was to get Hekmatyar to break with the Taliban.[145] However, Karzai's engagement with the Quetta Shura was much more haphazard.

In early 2010, Mullah Baradar, the deputy leader of the Taliban and then head of the Quetta Shura, was arrested in Pakistan, reportedly because he was engaged in 'unauthorised' talks with members of the Karzai family. The ISI were sending a very clear message to the Taliban leadership: don't engage in talks without our say-so. In October, there were multiple news reports of talks between senior Taliban figures and the Afghan government taking place in Dubai and Kabul, including 'one or two meetings' with Karzai. The CIA and the ISI were also involved. NATO subsequently confirmed that it had facilitated these talks by providing safe passage for Taliban officials travelling from Pakistan. Afghan and Western officials played down the significance of these talks. Karzai described them as 'rather unofficial personal contacts', while Holbrooke said in late October that 'there's less here than meets the eye'. Indeed this seems true when we take into account that it was subsequently revealed that the highest-ranking contact, thought to be Mullah Mansour, was in fact an imposter.[146]

Alongside this hotchpotch of 'informal contacts' and secret meetings was a more formalised process called the Afghan Peace and Reintegration Programme (APRP).[147] Launched by Karzai in June 2010, the APRP had been developed with the support of the international community and was backed by $140 million pledged by donors at the London conference six months later. The APRP was intended to combine low-level reintegration of 'foot soldiers, small groups and local leaders' with strategic-level talks with the Taliban leadership. In September 2010, Karzai appointed a seventy-member High Peace Council, chaired by former Afghan President Burhanuddin Rabbani, to take these talks forward. The Taliban showed what they thought of that initiative when they blew up Rabbani a year later. Critics also questioned Karzai's commitment to the APRP. The appointment of forty-year-old Salahuddin Rabbani to succeed his father did little to assuage the sceptics; while he impressed in Western circles, in a society where age denotes seniority Salahuddin completely lacked credibility.[148]

In any case, the United States was not fully ready to enter peace talks with the Taliban in 2010. In October, Holbrooke did try to champion the idea of opening negotiations but he was strongly opposed by Petraeus, who was intent on militarily defeating the insurgents, and closed down the discussion with the terse response: 'That is a fifteen-second conversation. No, not now.'[149] The White House was not prepared to side against the general leading America's war effort; as one insider notes, Secretary of State Hillary Clinton was 'a lone voice making the case for diplomacy' on the US National Security Council, 'but without the White House's backing [her] influence was no match for that of the Pentagon and CIA'.[150]

ISAF was prepared to support the low-level reintegration of Taliban fighters, which it saw as a way of 'decomposing the insurgency' and therefore complementary to its military strategy.[151] To this end a special unit was created within ISAF headquarters, named the Force Reintegration Cell, to help the effort. However, the APRP was mainly supposed to be implemented through a network of provincial peace councils, and to combine outreach, confidence-building and demobilisation efforts. Actual implementation was a mess, characterised by poor coordination between the various peace councils, shoddy outreach, little support for former Taliban fighters (including failure to provide immunity from arrest), and cynical exploitation of the demobilisation process by local warlords to disarm rivals or make a profit by giving up useless weapons. According to one council member from Ghazni province, 'The process is fake, people are doing it for money. It's all just for show, it's nothing. These people are told to show up with a few old guns so it looks like a success.' One year after the APRP was launched, nobody knew for sure how many former insurgents had been reintegrated, with different Western and ISAF officials quoting figures ranging from 900 to 1,800. One ISAF officer in the Force Reintegration Cell suggested that over 12,000 Taliban fighters would need to be reintegrated for this aspect of the APRP to have 'strategic effect'. Whatever the actual figure, it was way below this.[152]

In 2011, the United States finally put its weight behind getting talks started with the Taliban. This shift in policy was first indicated in a speech in February by Clinton, in which she declared that the United States no longer required preconditions to be met – including that the Taliban renounce al-Qaeda and accept the Afghan constitution – before entering exploratory talks. Following this statement, it was reported in May that there had been a number of meetings 'in recent months', facilitated by Germany and Qatar, between US officials and Tayeb Agha, the former chief of staff to Mullah Omar. A key issue raised in these talks was the idea of a Taliban diplomatic mission in a neutral state, possibly Qatar or Turkey. Western officials and the Taliban alike could see the benefit of loosening the ISI grip on the Taliban leadership. As one European diplomat put it, 'You cannot do reconciliation without Pakistan, but also they can be a spoiler.'[153] Accordingly, the United States flew eight Taliban diplomats (including Tayeb Agha) to Qatar in mid 2011.[154]

Exploratory talks continued in Doha in 2012. As a confidence-building measure, and to demonstrate to sceptics on both sides that the talks could bear fruit, they focused on a prisoner exchange. The proposed trade was that of the only American soldier in Taliban captivity, Sergeant Bowe Bergdahl, for five high-level Taliban prisoners in Guantánamo Bay; the Taliban were getting the better end of this deal. However, the deal stalled when the Obama administration faced bipartisan opposition in Washington. This demonstrated to critics on the Taliban side – mostly the military commanders – that the foreign invaders could not be trusted.[155]

To get the exploratory talks back on track, the United States put pressure on Qatar to allow the Taliban to open a diplomatic office in Doha, and on Karzai to accept the necessity of such a move.[156] Preliminary talks between US and Taliban officials were scheduled to begin just three days after the formal launch of the diplomatic office, and in Washington all hope was resting on this 'Doha track'. As one senior White House official noted in early 2013, 'It's the only game in town.'[157]

The Taliban opened their diplomatic office to much fanfare on 18 June 2013. In what was hardly a coincidence, this was the very same day that security responsibility for the whole of Afghanistan was formally handed over to the Afghan security forces in a ceremony in Kabul. In opening their office, the Taliban announced that they were seeking 'a political and peaceful solution to the conflict'. They also stated that they 'would not allow anyone to threaten the security of other countries from the soil of Afghanistan', which was as close as they were prepared to come at that stage to renouncing al-Qaeda; this had reportedly been a condition laid down by Qatar for hosting the office. President Obama cautiously hailed the opening of the Doha office as 'an important first step toward reconciliation'.[158] Only two days later, however, the Doha track was dead.

It quickly became clear that the Taliban had broader ambitions for the Doha office than simply facilitating peace talks; they viewed it as an embassy for what they considered to be the rightful government in Afghanistan. The Taliban spokesman referred repeatedly to the 'Islamic Emirate of Afghanistan', and declared that the diplomatic office would enable the Islamic Emirate 'to improve its relations with countries around the world through understandings and talks', as well as establish relations with the United Nations and non-governmental organisations, and to give press briefings. The Taliban statement said that meetings would take place with Afghan government officials 'if needed'.[159] Karzai had not signed up for this. Indeed, he had specifically told the Americans that he did not want the Taliban to use the office to promote their shadow government. He further said that there should be no emblems to suggest that it had any formal diplomatic standing; yet the office was flying the Taliban white flag. Karzai expressed his displeasure to US officials with characteristic forcefulness, and just two days after it was opened, the office was closed down and US–Taliban talks were cancelled.[160] What was plain diplomatic incompetence by US officials (in failing to manage the expectations of all parties) would have been viewed by the Taliban as American duplicity.

In any case, it is doubtful that the Doha track would have got very far. The Taliban had consistently made clear that they would not enter into negotiations with Karzai, who they viewed as a puppet of the Americans. For his part, Karzai consistently insisted that the Taliban recognise the Afghan constitution, something the Taliban refused to do. Moreover, the depth of loathing and distrust between Karzai and the Pakistan Army was simply too great to overcome. This meant that while Karzai was in power, peace was impossible.

It was just as well that on coming into office, Ghani clearly identi-fied achieving peace as his top priority and he brought a fresh stra-tegic approach to that challenge.[161] The motivation for prioritising peace was economic – and it was compelling. Ghani appreciated that there was no plausible scenario in which the Afghan state could attain fiscal sustainability while being locked into the level of security expenditure that he had inherited.[162] Ghani also rethought the mechanism for pursuing peace in what amounted to a strategic gambit.

The president judged that Pakistani support to the Afghan Taliban was critical to the movement's successful insurgency campaign. He thus set himself the challenge of bringing to an end Pakistan's proxy warfare in Afghanistan. He engaged in détente with the Pakistani military, by symbolically visiting their headquarters, promoting frequent top-level meetings between the Afghan and Pakistani military and intelligence chiefs, and offering to conduct security operations against Pakistani Taliban who attacked Pakistan across the frontier from Afghanistan. The quid pro quo Ghani demanded of the Pakistani military was that they use their influence on the Afghan Taliban to bring them to the negotiating table, and thus kick-start a process that might generate a ceasefire and political agreement.[163]

Thus, Ghani tried to orchestrate the talks by resetting Afghanistan–Pakistan relations rather than placating or wooing the Taliban. Soon after the Afghan presidential visit to Pakistan the military leadership gave an undertaking to Ghani that they would indeed prevail upon the Taliban to attend direct talks.[164] Much of the reconciliation-related activity in 2015 revolved around that undertaking. In February, the Taliban leadership apparently received a request from the Pakistan Army to clarify their position on whether they would attend talks. The Taliban convened a shura meeting to discuss the issue but avoided giving a clear response. Instead, the acting leader, Mullah Akhtar Mohammad Mansour, was reported as having referred the matter to the supreme leader, Mullah Omar, and deferred the decision pending receipt of an answer.[165]

While the Taliban delayed their response, they announced their 2015 'spring offensive', in line with the pattern of previous years. In May, Ghani's gambit seemed to generate its first tangible output. Kabul revealed that government representatives had met with Taliban envoys in Urumqi, China, in a meeting hosted by the Chinese authorities and facilitated by the Pakistan Army. The discussions were preliminary and so Afghan officials did not claim any substantive progress. Rather, they emphasised that the significance of Urumqi lay in the fact that the Taliban had agreed to meet face-to-face with government representatives. Moreover the meeting was described as unofficial, and so neither side delivered a formal negotiating position.[166] The Taliban delegation was led by former interior minister Abdul Razaq Achakzai, who was known to be a member of the Taliban Leadership Council. However, the Afghan government was unable to confirm that he had a clear mandate to speak for the Taliban leadership. Indeed, shortly afterwards the Taliban official spokesman issued a statement rejecting that the meeting had even taken place.[167]

In June Kabul and the Pakistani government announced that they had finally succeeded in holding official face-to-face talks between the Taliban and Afghan government representatives at a cantonment in the Pakistani hill resort of Murree. This time official observers from the United States and China were present, signifying high-level international political blessing for the process. The Afghan government delegation was this time led by a deputy foreign minister and senior member of the High Peace Council, and included members deliberately chosen to be representative of the multiple political tendencies present in the National Unity Government. The composition of both delegations indicated a certain seriousness of engagement. As one analyst noted, 'Those Taleban who participated in the four-hour Murree talks included figures of such seniority and authority that no room was left but to conclude the meeting had been endorsed, at least tacitly, by the movement's leadership.'[168] However, after the conclusion of the meeting, participants provided conflicting accounts of the tenor of discussions, ranging from suggestions that the Taliban seemed to be ready to discuss a ceasefire, to claims that the Taliban provocatively said they were only interested in receiving the government's surrender. Communiqués from the Pakistan hosts and the visiting Afghans concurred that the main outcome was an agreement to meet again.[169]

Despite the significant investment of diplomatic capital made at the Murree meeting by all four countries involved, doubts concerning the extent to which the engagement was formally authorised by the Taliban leadership recurred. These doubts were reinforced by the Taliban's official communications, on the website controlled by their Cultural Commission. In the wake of the Murree meeting this website carried ambiguous statements endorsing the principle of political contacts in pursuit of peace but claiming that the authorised body within the movement to conduct such contacts was the Political Commission's office based in Doha, Qatar. These announcements implied that the Taliban delegation in Murree may not have been competent to represent the movement. One interpretation is that, distrustful of Pakistan, the Taliban Political Commission were opposed to the Murree talks. Nonetheless, under pressure from Pakistan, Mansour 'gave a green light' for them to go ahead on condition that they stayed secret. When the talks were made public by the Afghan and Pakistani governments, this strengthened the position of those in the Political Commission who argued that it was they who should manage any future talks, far from Pakistani interference.[170]

Ghani offered the opportunity to reset Afghan relations with Pakistan. Karzai had believed that it was impossible for Afghanistan to have normal relations with Pakistan. However, Ghani's gambit was based on the assumption that Pakistan's calculations had changed regarding their support for the Taliban's military campaign in Afghanistan. Pakistan had its own Taliban problem. The state authority in the Federally Administered Tribal Areas, imperfect in the best of times, was being directly challenged through a terrorist campaign by a coalition of Islamist militant groups called Tehrik-i-Taliban Pakistan (TTP). In response, the Pakistan Army launched a major offensive against the insurgents' strongholds in north Waziristan over the summer of 2014. In retaliation, the TTP attacked a Pakistan army school in Peshawar in December, murdering 145 children.[171] While the Afghan Taliban and TTP are completely different movements, Pashtun militancy in the border areas had grown to such an extent as to present a threat to the Pakistani state and to alarm public opinion. Ghani's view, therefore, was that Pakistani now had good reason to cooperate in ending the conflict in Afghanistan in order to improve security in Pashtun areas on both sides of the border.[172]

Underlying Ghani's new approach was the assumption that the Pakistan Army could force the Taliban to enter peace negotiations. The simple fact is that nobody knows how much influence the Pakistan Army has over the Taliban, let alone how much it is willing to exert at any moment in time. Afghan security officials describe the Taliban as being under the thumb of the Pakistan Army.[173] Some analysts more sympathetic to the Pakistan Army suggest that its interaction with the Taliban is limited and leverage is minimal.[174] The evidence is pretty overwhelming that the Pakistan Army continues to provide extensive support to the Taliban. However, this generates little gratitude from a Taliban leadership which resents the army's attempts to control them.

The formal opening of the office in Qatar in 2013 was an attempt by the Taliban to escape Pakistani control. It was met with displeasure: the brothers of Tayeb Agha were picked up by the ISI and held in jail for a number of months.[175] This episode reveals something of the methods by which Pakistan exerts pressure on the Taliban leadership. In response to this kind of harassment, a number of Taliban leaders have relocated with their families to Iran and the Gulf. This suggests that while Pakistan may be able to exercise some control over the Taliban through such crude means, it cannot get the Taliban to do its bidding. Put another way, as the Murree talks suggest, Pakistan may be able to get the Taliban to come to the negotiating table, but this is not to say that they can get the Taliban to negotiate.

PROSPECTS FOR PEACE

Ultimately, the success of any peace negotiations will depend on the Taliban wanting to make peace. Any effort to influence this process faces the immensely challenging task of understanding Taliban intentions and decision-making. The Taliban movement has organised itself as the 'Islamic Emirate of Afghanistan', constituted of formal structures with functional commissions at national, regional, provincial and district level. Embedded within these formal structures are various informal networks, such as the 'Haqqani Network' led by Sirajuddin Haqqani. Sirajuddin has extended the influence of his network across half of the country, even though the Quetta Shura does not formally acknowledge its existence. Likewise, powerful Mahaz commanders in the south are able to exert more influence than recognised in their formal emirate positions. This complicates any attempt to discern 'what the Taliban want'.[176] Nonetheless, the Taliban has a powerful doctrine of obedience that has imposed hierarchy on the movement and has served to contain the ever-present risk of organisational fragmentation. According to Taliban dogma, it is the existence of a single divinely guided leader, the *amir ul momineen* ('commander of the faithful'), which guarantees that the movement will serve the interest of Islam. This doctrine is inimical to power-sharing, which would necessarily form the heart of any sustainable peace.

In July 2015, it was revealed that Mullah Omar had been dead for
two years. This fact had been kept secret by the deputy head of the
Taliban, Akhtar Mohammad Mansour. The Taliban's top religious
scholars and senior members of the leadership council allowed
Mansour to invoke Omar's authority while running the movement.[177]
The cultural wing was able to produce multiple declarations attributed
to Mullah Omar to justify leadership decisions. The period of the
cover-up coincided with key developments in the putative peace
process, including the attempt to open an office in Qatar in 2013, and
the launch of talks in China and Pakistan in 2015. Mansour's hand was
likely behind these tentative efforts. Taliban adherence to the doctrine
of leadership obedience would have facilitated such a development,
by enabling Mansour to rule for the amir while provoking little debate
or disagreement.[178]

The first serious dissent within the Taliban leadership occurred
in the wake of the revelation of Mullah Omar's death, with a group
of veterans challenging the legitimacy of Mansour's elevation to the
position of amir. The movement was split but unevenly so, with all
the national structures and most of the military commanders
declaring loyalty to Mansour as the new amir. Mansour also had the
active backing of the ISI, which helped him to overcome his chal-
lengers. More importantly, the sense of common purpose within
the movement was sufficient for its cohesiveness to survive and for
loyalty to be transferred to a new leader, despite the record of
deception.

The culture and politics of the Taliban indicate that its military
commanders constitute the most important internal constituency.
The movement has a long tradition of blurring the distinction
between civil and military, as positions such as provincial governor
embrace both military and civilian responsibilities. As we saw, the
insurgency is led by *mahaz* commanders who operate largely independently of the central Taliban leadership. Although the doctrine
of leadership obedience dictates that military commanders submit
to the authority of the Quetta Shura, in reality the leadership feels
compelled to strive constantly to maintain the loyalty of the field
commanders. This was illustrated during the succession struggle,
where Mansour's ability to consolidate his position depended critically on the relations he had developed in the military during his

period as deputy. The fact that the military is powerful within the Taliban does not in itself preclude a settlement; rather it dictates that the leadership patronise the military. Hitherto the simplest way it has found to do this is to sustain the armed campaign, which provides a pretext for channelling resources to the military. The leadership is also aware that it is vulnerable to accusations of 'selling out' and alienating the military if it were to pursue political engagement without taking them into confidence.

It is hard to see a sustainable peace deal that does not involve some kind of power-sharing arrangement with the Taliban. Afghans are well familiar with power-sharing compromises, whether from the coalitions of the differing mujahedin parties in the mid 1990s or the current National Unity Government. However, such arrangements sit uneasily with the Taliban's doctrine of the supreme amir. During the 1990s, in their dealings with armed opposition, the one non-negotiable demand of the Taliban was that the opposition submit to the authority of the amir. Moreover, political coalitions have tended to fracture and fail in Afghanistan. In this sense, the National Unity Government is following a well-worn path. Thus the inherent doctrinal and pragmatic unattractiveness of coalition may make continuing with the military campaign the most attractive strategy.

At the same time, there is a more pragmatic strain in Taliban thinking which understands the need for compromise if they are to return to government. This view recognises that the limitations of Taliban political power, as much as their military might, make a solely Taliban national government unsustainable. The Taliban realise that much has changed in terms of public attitudes towards them. As one Taliban leader noted in October 2014:

> The High Commission [Quetta Shura] doesn't have any strategies or plans in order to take over Kabul once again as they believe that a lot of changes have taken place in the past twelve years which have resulted in people no longer having the same opinion about the Taliban movement and it will make it harder for people to accept the Taliban.[179]

It is further evident from discussions with senior Taliban figures that they have thought about the practicalities of how power-sharing might work, including the division of cabinet posts.[180] This more pragmatic view is to be found, in particular, within the Taliban's Political Commission. Senior leaders within the commission eagerly anticipated the onset of peace talks following Ghani's inauguration.[181] Indeed, it appears that informal talks occurred between Ghani and a representative of the Political Commission in 2014.[182]

It is not clear how much sway these more pragmatic ideas have held with the Taliban's core leadership, especially given that the Quetta Shura must be attentive to the views of the military base. Perhaps not surprisingly, many Taliban field commanders are suspicious of Taliban diplomats in the Political Commission. One senior leader noted that 'a lot of military commanders believe that there is no difference between the Afghan government and members of the Taliban Political Commission'.[183] A different Taliban leader took a more balanced view, acknowledging that there were differences of opinion among military commanders – some think that the Political Commission misrepresent the Taliban and distract it from fighting, while others recognise the virtue of the Political Commission in developing 'very good relations with the international community'.[184]

The Taliban leadership has reason to be concerned about the risks of fragmentation from entering peace talks. An important complicating factor here is the Taliban's ties to various other jihadi groups, and most importantly to al-Qaeda. During the Taliban diplomatic initiative through its Political Commission in Qatar, the movement's representatives have generally stressed that the Taliban's political objectives are restricted to Afghanistan. The Taliban announced in Doha that they would not allow Afghan soil to be used for attacks on other countries.[185] However, at the same time, the Taliban military have developed their cooperation with a range of militant groups, relying upon them for military expertise and claiming responsibility for military operations or terrorist attacks which they have undertaken. The links between the Haqqani family and al-Qaeda are especially deep.[186] The extensive Taliban links with international jihadi allies impinge on strategic decision-making because these groups are inimically opposed to any settlement in Afghanistan short of a Taliban victory. Thus any Taliban move towards substantive talks would risk alienating the movement's allies and potentially push them into open opposition.

A further complicating factor is the emergence of Islamic State (IS) in Afghanistan. The UN mission in Afghanistan reports IS as being present in most provinces in Afghanistan, but it has 'dominant presence' in only one, Nangarhar, and most of its fighters are in fact 'rebranded' TTP from Pakistan.[187] Quite unlike al-Qaeda and its affiliates, IS has directly challenged the Taliban's claim to leadership of the jihad in Afghanistan. The Taliban has responded to that challenge by publicly warning IS that it is undermining jihadi unity and by launching concerted attacks on groups affiliated to the organisation wherever they emerge in Afghanistan.[188] The number of fighters pledged to IS in Afghanistan is a fraction of those affiliated with the Taliban. Nevertheless, the Taliban have started to factor IS into their strategic decision-making. In entering a peace process, the Taliban leadership would be concerned about the risk of fighters who oppose peace defecting to IS.

The power struggle within the Taliban following the announcement of Mullah Omar's death caused the embryonic peace talks to grind to a halt. In January 2016, a Quadrilateral Coordination Group was formed, comprising representatives from Afghanistan, China, Pakistan and the United States, to push forward the stalled peace talks. Following its second meeting, held in Kabul in late February, the Quadrilateral Coordination Group issued an ultimatum for the Taliban to return to the exploratory talks or else face the consequences. The *New York Times* reported that at the meeting 'Pakistan representatives had … given assurances that violence will be noticeably reduced in coming weeks' and that the Taliban might not even launch a spring offensive in 2016.[189] The meeting ended with officials saying that they expected talks between the Afghan government and the Taliban to begin in early March. However, the Taliban issued a statement bluntly rejecting the possibility of talks until 'the occupation of Afghanistan is ended, [UN] blacklists eliminated, and innocent prisoners freed'.[190]

The United States delivered the 'or else' part of the ultimatum on 22 May, when a US drone killed Mansour as he was driving in the Pakistani province of Baluchistan. According to US officials, Obama authorised the strike when it became clear that Mansour was not interested in peace talks.[191] When Mansour's death was announced, Obama said that he hoped the Taliban would 'seize the opportunity … to pursue the only real path for ending this conflict – joining the Afghan government in a reconciliation process that leads to lasting peace and security'. As Barnett Rubin, an expert on Afghanistan and former adviser to Holbrooke, wryly noted, 'So far, the Taliban do not seem to have interpreted the assassination of their leader as an outstretched hand for peace.'[192]

The Taliban wasted no time selecting Mansour's successor. On 25 May 2016, it was announced that Maulavi Haibatullah Akhundzada had been appointed as the new amir. Haibatullah is a former chief justice and head of the Taliban Ulema Council of religious leaders. Unlike Mansour, who was a very prominent Taliban figure, Haibatullah is a behind-the-scenes operator. The little that is known about him is not encouraging, however. Like Omar, Haibatullah is austere in outlook and how he lives (in contrast to Mansour, who had extensive financial interests and enjoyed a lavish lifestyle). Haibatullah is reputed to have been a stern Taliban judge noted for dishing out harsh sentences. 'He is by no means a moderate figure' was how one expert put it. Haibatullah was responsible for issuing the fatwas justifying suicide bombings. It is as yet unknown how much authority he will wield within the Taliban leadership. Another expert suggested that 'Mawlawi Haibatullah's area of influence is with the mullahs and the religious leaders, not the management and the commanders'. Sirajuddin Haqqani was appointed deputy to Haibatullah, further consolidating the influence of the hardline network within the Taliban; the Haqqanis have been responsible for most of the suicide attacks in Kabul. The consensus appears to be that Haibatullah will have neither the inclination nor the influence to restart the peace talks. As Rubin observes, 'The new leader, who is weak and untried, will be totally unable to make the decision to join the process.'[193] Certainly, US officials don't have high hopes. The spokesman for US forces in Afghanistan, Brigadier General Charles Cleveland, told journalists, 'I don't believe that we will see peace talks any time in the short-term with Mullah Haibatullah.'[194]

This pessimistic view of Haibatullah's leadership was echoed in lengthy interviews that Michael Semple and I conducted with seven senior Taliban figures, outside Afghanistan over a week in November 2016. All seven confirmed that the Taliban leadership is in disarray under Haibatullah. One said that 'everybody is saying there are problems'. Another noted how 'the position of the Tehreek [the Taliban movement] right now is very precarious because Haibatullah is not able to run the movement, he is sitting there as a symbol'. The interviews described the rise of factionalism within the Taliban and the breakdown of obedience to the amir. Of particular note is the rise of the Mansour network, based primarily in Helmand and whose members include the new head of the Taliban's National Military Commission, Saddar Ibrahim. Several interviews noted how Haibatullah was effectively controlled by the 'comrades of Mansour'. The Mansour network has little interest in any peace that threatens their extensive drug interests in Helmand.[195]

Predictably, Pakistani assurances that the Taliban would show military restraint in 2016 have rung hollow. Instead the insurgents have pursued their 2016 offensive with vigour and considerable success. At the time of writing, they are on the cusp of seizing the whole of Helmand, and have made significant gains in the east, in districts around Kabul, and in the north. In late April, following a week of deadly terrorist attacks in Kabul which left over sixty dead, the Afghan president denounced continued Pakistani support for the Taliban. Ghani threatened to lodge a complaint with the United Nations Security Council if Pakistan did not take military action against the Afghan Taliban sheltering on its soil. This was an empty threat but it did dramatically signal that Ghani's gambit has failed and the all-too-brief détente with Pakistan is dead.[196] The prospects for peace are now very remote. The new Taliban leadership is not predisposed to entering peace talks, nor does it have any reason to do so given that the insurgency has renewed momentum and is making major gains on the ground. In July 2016, Obama announced that 8,400 US troops would remain in Afghanistan until the end of his term in office. At the NATO Summit in Warsaw a few days later, Britain matched this commitment by increasing the size of its modest training mission from 450 to 500 troops, and confirming that these troops would remain in Afghanistan until 2017.[197] As the New York Times noted, the war that 'Mr. Obama pledged to end on his watch … now seems likely to grind on indefinitely'.[198]

GOOD WAR GONE WRONG

The catastrophic terrorist attacks on 9/11 gave the United States just cause in going to war in October 2001. Britain's support for this US military campaign was necessary and proportionate, in the context of the loss of British lives on 9/11 and the reasonable fear of future such attacks against other Western cities including London. In December 2001, Britain led the international peacekeeping force that went in to secure Kabul and from this humanitarian impulse ISAF was born. Where the United States under George W. Bush refused to get drawn into nation-building and began instead to prepare for war against Iraq, Britain under Tony Blair promised not to abandon Afghanistan. Each leader drew different lessons from the 1990s: Bush thought of Somalia and the ignominy of American failure; Blair thought of Rwanda and the tragedy of failing to act to stop genocide. In Sierra Leone, a country and conflict far smaller in scale than Afghanistan, Blair also saw how force could be used effectively for humanitarian ends.

By degrees Britain became drawn ever deeper into the Afghan conflict. NATO politics and the US desire to offload Afghanistan combined to see ISAF expand beyond Kabul, first to the more peaceful north and west, and then to the Pashtun 'badlands' of the south and the east. Britain led the southern expansion of ISAF. For the British Army, Helmand seemed to offer a way out of Iraq. However, the Ministry of Defence grossly underestimated how fast British forces could draw down from Iraq and how difficult it would be to bring security to Helmand. The British should have expected trouble. One of the first British officers in Helmand predicted that 'with so many problems we are bound to draw fire – it really is like poking a stick in a hornets nest'.[199]

British soldiers and marines fought valiantly in southern Afghanistan. For the first six months, the troops holed up in platoon houses stopped the Taliban from completely overrunning the northern towns of Helmand. In the year that followed, ever larger British task forces tried to hunt down and militarily defeat the Taliban. Time and again, British units resorted to firepower to overwhelm their opponents. The Apache helicopter gunship, originally built to destroy Soviet tanks at distance, proved especially helpful in bailing out troops in trouble. Liberal use of air power and artillery reduced the district centres of northern and southern Helmand to bombed-out and largely deserted shells of what were once thriving market towns. A cack-handed push to eradicate opium poppy resulted in a general uprising against the British in 2007. In a dramatic low point in the campaign, the Taliban almost overran Lashkar Gah in October 2008. Once again, Apache gunships saved the day.

Two years into the Helmand campaign, the British changed tactics towards less use of firepower and more focus on protecting the people and supporting the civilian effort to rebuild Helmand and re-establish governance. The Taliban also shifted tactics, away from frontal assaults by large groups of insurgents towards greater use of 'shoot-and-scoot' ambushes, sniper fire and IEDs. The latter proved especially deadly for British and ISAF troops, but at least it reduced the number of pitched battles in populated areas. An increasing focus on central Helmand from late 2008 on enabled the British to concentrate sufficient forces to push the Taliban out of Nad-e Ali and away from Lashkar Gah. This was made possible by the arrival of large numbers of US Marines, who picked up the load in southern and northern Helmand, including, much to British relief, taking over in Sangin.

As the war ground on, both ISAF and the Taliban strove to improve command and control of field units. For the Taliban, it was essential to find ways to concentrate forces in order to achieve some strategic effect from insurgent operations. For ISAF, the imperative was to impose order on what had hitherto been a large number of national task force campaigns that were waged largely in isolation from one another. Obama came into office in 2009 determined to turn around a war that was floundering, and McChrystal brought the necessary order by producing a coherent war plan and creating ISAF Joint Command to ensure its implementation by the Regional Commands and national task forces. Britain took charge of Regional Command South at this critical juncture. McChrystal decided that Helmand would be the place to inflict 'a strategic defeat' on the Taliban in early 2010. British General Nick Carter, as commander of Regional Command South, produced a plan that focused on governance and minimising loss of civilian life. The ISAF offensive in Helmand in February 2010, and the one that followed in Kandahar in the summer, inflicted many tactical defeats on the Taliban but these did not achieve the strategic effect that McChrystal had hoped for.

Tactically, British forces got ever better at waging counter-insurgency warfare. A revolution in doctrinal thinking has resulted in a British approach to planning and operations that focuses on under-standing the cultural and political environment, and the effects one is trying to achieve. The key insight is that effects may be achieved through means other than use of lethal force – such as shows of force (patrolling or jet fly-bys), information campaigns, low-level diplomacy, and helping to improve local services and infrastructure. A revolution in surveillance capabilities, information networks and precision strike systems, combined with a more aggressive approach to special forces operations, enabled the British and Americans to eviscerate Taliban tactical leadership in Helmand; the ramping up of the US drone campaign in Pakistan under the Obama administration also proved costly for Taliban strategic leadership. Thus, targeting killing was a major enabler of British efforts to bring security to Helmand.[200] Equally important was the hard slog of working with local communities to improve their lives. Given this was often in places where civilians could not reach, this unglamorous work was left to enterprising British Army and Royal Marine officers.

Britain and its allies have achieved much good in Afghanistan. NATO brought democratically elected government, albeit one riven by corruption. Many more Afghans have access to public services than ever before; 5.8 million children were attending school and 85 per cent of people were covered by basic health care in 2013.[201] And yet, NATO has failed to stop the Taliban, and most British gains in Helmand have been lost these past two years. Despite spending many tens of billions of dollars, the Afghan police and army are not able to stand up to the Taliban without Western help.

Improvements in the operational command and tactical conduct of the war, the gathering of ever greater amounts of data, and the tracking of campaign metrics, produced the illusion of progress.[202] In his brilliant polemic *Voltaire's Bastards*, the philosopher John Ralston Saul explores the dark shadow of the Enlightenment, namely the development and empowering in Western society of arcane systems of expert knowledge disconnected from everyday realities. 'In general terms,' Saul writes, 'all this means that management methods are being mistaken for solutions and so, as if in some sophisticated game, the problem is pushed on with a long rational stick from point to point around the field.'[203] The theory and practice of counter-insurgency, which focuses on the human dimension of war but is curiously apolitical, is an excellent example of what Saul is getting at. Thus the US Army and Marine Corps doctrine on counter-insurgency

(FM 3–24), produced primarily to guide the military conduct of America's war in Iraq (and widely adopted in Afghanistan), failed to analyse the underlying political dynamics of the conflict, and the constraints imposed by host nation and regional politics. Equally, during the Afghanistan and Iraq wars, proponents of counter-insurgency failed to address head-on the contradiction between the huge cost of these wars, in terms of blood and treasure for Britain and the United States, and the diminishing appetite for the publics and political classes in both countries to endure such costs. Instead, practitioners and proponents of counter-insurgency have ploughed on as if 'a knowledgeable soldiery [acting] under the guidance of an expert elite' would be able to create the conditions for strategic success.[204]

Thus, it did not matter how good the British military got at waging counter-insurgency, nor ISAF in improving unity of effort across the whole campaign. The Taliban could not be defeated so long as Pakistan continued to provide support. Camps and madrasas in Pakistan have given the Taliban secure areas for fighters to recuperate, train and muster. There is considerable evidence that the Pakistan Army also has continued to provide direct assistance with funding, training, logistics and military advisers. Pakistan provides shelter for the Taliban leadership as well, though sometimes they are successfully targeted by US drone strikes. Just as important, endemic Afghan government corruption has undermined the sustainability of hard-won gains by Western forces. In rural communities where local power-holders and their militias in the guise of officialdom commonly preyed on the people, government corruption proved a major aid for insurgent recruitment. Corruption has also eaten away at the Afghan security forces and undermined the operational effectiveness of the army and the police. In Helmand, the British were able to make significant improvements to district and provincial governance, and some modest progress in cleaning up the police. All of this is now in jeopardy given spectacular Taliban gains in the province. Moreover, corruption remains a profound threat to the functioning and sustainability of Afghan national institutions.

Ultimately, the British campaign in Helmand was characterised by political absenteeism and military hubris. Blair committed the British military to southern Afghanistan when it was still tied down in Iraq. This was in clear breach of defence planning assumptions, which included that Britain could not fight two wars at the same time. Government ministers never properly challenged the military's ability to sustain this level of overstretch. Once committed the British military were left to their own devices. There was no political oversight of military plans that were, even without the benefit of hindsight, unrealistic. There was not even much oversight from the Ministry of Defence and PJHQ, aside from keeping within the troop cap and keeping down costs. London tended to defer to the commander in the field, with the result that the British campaign in Helmand see-sawed as successive commanders arrived with their own ideas about what the campaign should be about. There was no British strategy as such, beyond doing enough to be seen as the senior partner to a US-led war.

In the latter stages of the war, Britain was shackled to American strategy. As early as mid 2008, the British Foreign Secretary, Defence Secretary and Development Secretary had reached a consensus that the war could not be won militarily and that it was necessary to find a political solution.[205] However, Britain followed the US lead for the next two years in doubling down on the military campaign. The simple fact was that as prime minister, Gordon Brown was focused on dealing with the 2007–8 global financial crisis and Afghanistan was not a priority. Equally, the coalition government under Cameron was content to play along with the charade of 'conditions-based' transition to Afghan security forces, as the priority at that stage for Whitehall was simply to walk in step with the Americans – in other words, to leave Afghanistan when they left. Writing in 2009, two academics from the Department of War Studies at King's College London offered a biting critique of British strategy, or lack thereof, in Iraq and Afghanistan. They argued:

> British 'strategy' is motivated simply by the desire to be in the world 'game' and to be partnered with the United States … That is why Whitehall behaves strategically rather in the manner of an inveterate gambler with a small pot of chips. Britain wishes to stay in the strategic 'game,' the rules of which are set in Washington, and it perceives that in order to do so it needs to place a stake on the table. That stake is the Army.[206]

This may have put it crudely but that does not make it any less true.

Missing for Afghanistan was a British strategy that addressed the many great challenges to the campaign and recognition of just how little the UK government could do about them. British and US officials had scant understanding of what was happening inside the Pakistan Army and even less the ISI. Moreover, as most of ISAF's supplies were shipped in through Pakistan, the United States had limited leverage over Pakistan. US and British officials had a better understanding of what was happening inside Afghan government, but here also they were caught in a bind. Building the capacity of Afghan government and the Afghan security forces was NATO's ticket out of an increasingly tiresome war. However, the volume of international aid flowing into Afghanistan was fuelling the corruption that was undermining the very institutions it was intended to build. What was desperately needed was a strategy that enabled capacity-building while also ensuring that Afghan political and security elites undertook necessary reforms. Attaching conditions to aid would have been a good place to start; something the United States failed to do in Afghanistan before 2013, and has struggled to do effectively since then.[207] As it happens, America's record on this score is pretty dismal. Time and again when intervening in counter-insurgency wars, the United States has failed to hold client governments to account for their corruption, fearing they might fall if aid does not continue to flow.[208]

Any British strategy would also have needed to take account of NATO disunity and poor US strategic leadership in the war. The split between the 'peacekeeping' and 'war-fighting' countries in NATO seriously eroded unity of effort in the ISAF campaign, and even more so the civilian effort to reconstruct the country; national PRTs operated largely independently of each other and ISAF. There is nothing new in NATO disunity, and most states within the alliance look to the United States to provide strategic leadership and direction (with the obvious exception of France). This is especially the case in coalition operations. However, the United States was disengaged under a Bush administration that had quickly turned its attention to Iraq. From 2003 to 2007, Iraq was a conflict that dwarfed Afghanistan in scale, in terms of the consumption rate of US dollars and American lives. It took Obama to bring US attention back onto 'the central front' in the global war on terror, and McChrystal to impose unity of command on the military campaign. An independent assessment of the campaign for ISAF in October 2010 concluded that ISAF Joint Command was 'generally effective in providing direction to the Regional Commands. It ensures that security operations are consistent with ISAF strategy and provides continuity of command as subordinate headquarters rotate.' McChrystal was unable, however, to impose order on the international civilian effort that involved a bewildering multitude of actors and agendas. This was reflected in the assessment for ISAF Joint Command which found 'pervasive disunity of direction and effort within ISAF and the international community support to governance and development'.[209] The more closely he looked at Afghanistan, the more Obama had doubts about what was militarily achievable. However, as he had made a commitment in his presidential campaign to win the 'good war' in Afghanistan, he was bound to give his military commanders the chance to succeed. It would be almost two years before he began to provide cautious support for exploratory talks with the Taliban. By this stage, the Taliban had endured the worst that America and Britain could throw at them. Thereafter they would recover ground as Western forces withdrew from Afghanistan and the need for talking would increasingly diminish.

In the spring of 2013, Michael Semple and I convened an 'academic workshop' in a neutral country to explore the potential for local ceasefires in Afghanistan. We brought together three Afghan government officials and two Taliban figures, a field commander and a district governor. We thought it would take us two days to get all five to sit around the same table. They did so from the start, and were soon trading ideas, arguments and stories. Dressed in formal white Afghan attire, the Taliban commander cut a serious figure; he had previously been imprisoned by the Americans in Guantánamo Bay. Dressed in more casual Afghan clothes, the Taliban district governor was talkative, charming and razor-sharp. At the first tea break, he approached me and said, in near-perfect English, 'I learned English many years ago in Pakistan, and you are the first Englishman that I have spoken to.' Michael and I are both Dublin-born and -bred, and we spent some time explaining to the Taliban the difference between Ireland and England. We talked about the shared culture between the two countries, and also about Irish rebels and the fight for independence from Britain.

At the end of three days of hard work, and much tea and talking, our Afghan participants had produced a template, drawn from experience in Musa Qala, Sangin and elsewhere, for de-escalating the conflict at the local level. In a note to senior British and US policymakers, Michael and I advised that 'Early declared ceasefires are possible at the district level in Helmand, Kandahar, Nangarhar and Kapisa', and we explained how these could be designed to be sustainable. This was in 2013 and ISAF still had no guidance on how (or even if) to support local ceasefires. ISAF headquarters worried that ceasefires might be manipulated by the Taliban to resupply and spread their influence safe from attack.

Now the shoe is on the other foot. In many rural areas in the south and east, the Taliban are on the ascendancy. At the same time, many Taliban are tiring of a war that has gone on for too long and cost too many lives. One very senior Taliban veteran we interviewed in November 2016 claimed that 'there are thousands [in the Taliban] who think that the war has nothing to offer but destruction and the slaughter of Afghans'.[210] Many senior Taliban commanders feel that the armed struggle has lost direction and that for all their recent tactical successes, the prospect of victory is nowhere in sight. They point to the fact that while the Taliban may seize provincial capitals, such as Kunduz, they are unable to hold them for long.[211] Thus we may yet see ceasefires, especially outside Helmand and in those areas where commanders at the local level on both sides see virtue in tolerating one another's presence over unnecessary violence. The future for Afghanistan looks uncertain. The country will hold together, but sooner rather than later some political accommodation will need to be made with the Taliban. What is clear is that the West is increasingly irrelevant to this. Afghans will decide their own future, on their own timelines, and according to their own ways and customs.

The Taliban district governor suggested that perhaps he might visit London and stay with me. He was poking fun. He was much amused to see the 'Englishman' struggle to find a polite way to deflect such a proposal. In 2013, such an idea was alarming. In decades to come, it might seem less so.

Acknowledgements

I started research on this book in 2009. Seven years later it was completed. Along the way, I had the good fortune to rub shoulders with many experts on Afghanistan. I have learned an immense amount through my research and writing collaborations with two leading scholars on the Taliban, Antonio Giustozzi and Michael Semple. My understanding of the politics and conduct of the war was greatly enriched by interactions with Nick Abbott, Alex Alderson, David Betz, Bob Cassidy, Rudra Chaudhuri, Ben Connable, Deedee Derkson, Lawrence Freedman, Stuart Gordon, Steve Grenier, Adam Grissom, Peter Viggo Jakobsen, Tony King, Carter Malkasian, Dan Moran, Mike Rainsborough, Mikkel Rasmussen, Sten Rynning, James Russell and Jon Schroden. I am especially grateful to Mark Beautement, Ryan Evans, Chris Kolenda and Mike Martin for providing detailed feedback on specific chapters.

Family and friends also chipped in to help. My thanks to Jaz Azari, John Murnane and Miriam Shtaierman for their feedback on the narrative and writing style. I owe a special note of gratitude to my wife, Helene, and daughter, Eloise, for tolerating my trips to Afghanistan, as well as many years of working on the book over weekends and on holidays.

I greatly appreciate the excellent guidance and support provided by my agent, Bill Hamilton, and the marvellous team at The Bodley Head, Stuart Williams and Jörg Hensgen, as well as Katherine Fry and Alison Rae. My sincere thanks also to Sir Paul Curran, the President of City, University of London, for giving me the time to complete this book before assuming my duties as Dean of Arts and Social Sciences.

The research for this book was funded by two grants provided by the UK Research Councils: 'Organisations, Innovation and

Security in the 21st Century', ESRC/AHRC Research Fellowship RES-071–27–0069; 'The Taliban's War: The Other Side of the Taliban Conflict', ESRC Grant ES/L008041/1. My former PhD students, Martin Bayly and Olivier Schmitt, provided much appreciated research assistance on the book.

Some material in chapter 10 was previously published in Theo Farrell and Antonio Giustozzi, 'The Taliban at war: inside the Helmand insurgency, 2004–2012', *International Affairs*, vol. 89, no. 4 (2013), pp. 845–72 (http://onlinelibrary.wiley.com/). Some material in chapter 11 was previously published in Theo Farrell and Michael Semple, 'Making peace with the Taliban', *Survival*, vol. 57, no. 6 (2015–2016), pp. 79–110 (www.tandfonline.com).

Finally, my sincere thanks to the very large number of participants who kindly agreed to be interviewed – including many British brigade, battlegroup and company commanders, and their civilian counterparts, American allies and Taliban opponents. Without these interviews, it would not have been possible to tell the story of Britain's war in Afghanistan.

Notes

Introduction

1   Directorate Land Warfare, Lessons Exploitation Centre, Operation HERRICK Campaign Study, March 2015 [redacted and publicly released version], p. xxviii; BBC News, 'UK military deaths in Afghanistan: Full list,' http://www.bbc.co.uk/news/uk-10629358.

2   This is argued in Frank Ledwidge, *Investment in Blood: The True Cost of Britain's Afghan War* (New Haven: Yale University Press, 2013).

3   Ian S. Livingston and Michael O'Hanlon, *The Afghanistan Index* (Washginton DC: Brookings Institution, 31 March 2016), p. 9, figure 1.1.2.

4   Amy Belasco, *The Cost of Iraq, Afghanistan, and Other Global War on Terror Operations since 9/11*, Congressional Research Service Report, 7–5700, RL33110, 8 December 2014.

5   This study estimates the total cost to the United States of the wars in Iraq and Afghanistan to be between 4 and 6 trillion dollars. Linda J. Bilmes, 'The Financial Legacy of Iraq and Afghanistan: How Wartime Spending Decisions Will Constrain Future National Security Budgets', *Faculty Research Working Paper Series*, RWP13-006, March 2013.

6   Emma Graham-Harrison and Rob Evans, 'Afghan civilian death toll "much higher than official estimates"', *Observer*, 8 May 2016.

7   In order of brigade tours, these books include: Patrick Bishop, *3 Para* (London: HarperPress, 2007); Doug Beattie, *Ordinary Soldier* (London: Simon & Schuster, 2009); Col. Stuart Tootal, *Danger Close: Commanding 3 Para in Afghanistan* (London: John Murray, 2009); Sean Rayment, *Into the Killing Zone* (London: Constable, 2008); Stephen Grey, *Operation Snakebite* (London: Viking, 2009); Patrick Bishop, *Ground Truth* (London: HarperPress, 2009); Doug Beattie, *Task Force Helmand* (London: Pocket Books, 2009); Ewen Southby-Taylor, *Helmand, Afghanistan: 3 Commando Brigade* (London: Ebury Press, 2008); Sam Kiley, *Desperate Glory* (London: Constable, 2009); Col. Richard Kemp and Chris Hughes, *Attack State Red* (London: Michael Joseph, 2009); Patrick Bury, *Callsign Hades*

(London: Simon & Schuster, 2010); Major Russell Lewis, *Company Commander* (London: Random House, 2012); Chris Terrill, *Commando* (London: Century, 2007); Ewen Southby-Taylor, *3 Commando Brigade: Helmand Assault* (London: Ebury Press, 2010); Toby Harnden, *Dead Men Risen* (London: Quercus, 2012); Max Benitz, *Six Months Without Sundays* (Edinburgh: Birlinn, 2012); Richard Streatfeild, *Honourable Warriors: Fighting the Taliban in Afghanistan* (Barnsley: Pen and Sword, 2014).

8   The same shortcoming applies to an otherwise very informative, self-published history of British operations in Afghanistan, written anonymously by somebody with an insider understanding of British military matters. Sallust, *Operation Herrick: An Unofficial History of British Military Operations in Afghanistan, 2001–2014* (available from Amazon, 2015).

9   Frank Ledwidge, *Losing Small Wars: British Military Failure in Iraq and Afghanistan* (New Haven: Yale University Press, 2011); Ledwidge, *Investment in Blood*; David H. Ucko and Robert Egnell, *Counterinsurgency in Crisis: Britain and the Challenges of Modern Warfare* (New York: Columbia University Press, 2013); Sandy Gall, *War Against the Taliban: Why It All Went Wrong* (London: Bloomsbury, 2012); Sherard Cowper-Coles, *Cables from Kabul: The Inside Story of the West's Afghanistan Campaign* (London: HarperPress, 2011); Tim Bird and Alex Marshall, *Afghanistan: How the West Lost Its Way* (New Haven: Yale University Press, 2011); Seth G. Jones, *In the Graveyard of Empires: America's War on Afghanistan* (New York: W. W. Norton & Co., 2009); Rajiv Chandarsekaran, *Little America: The War within the War for Afghanistan* (London: Bloomsbury, 2012).

10   William Dalrymple, *Return of a King: The Battle for Afghanistan* (London: Bloomsbury, 2013) , pp. 490–1.

11   The 'formula' stated by David Galula in his classic text is that insurgency, and therefore counter-insurgency, is 'twenty percent military action and eighty percent political'. Galula, *Counterinsurgency Warfare: Theory and Practice* (Westpoint, CT: Praeger Security International, 2006 [1964]), p. 63.

12   This is now recognised in British Army doctrine, that 'the population is central to the outcome' of a counter-insurgency campaign and that, accordingly, 'the principal security task is to secure the population'. Army Field Manual Countering Insurgency, vol. 1, Part 10, AC 71876, January 2010, paragraphs 1–22, 1–3.

13   Anthony King, 'Understanding the Helmand campaign: British military operations in Afghanistan', *International Affairs*, vol. 86, no. 2 (2010), pp. 311–32; Warren Chin, 'Colonial warfare in a post-colonial state: British operations in Helmand Province, Afghanistan', *Defence Studies*, vol. 10, nos 1–2 (2010); Robert Egnell, 'Lessons from Helmand: what now for British counterinsurgency?', *International Affairs*, vol. 87, no. 2

(2011), pp. 297–310; Sergio Catignani, '"Getting COIN" at the tactical level in Afghanistan: reassessing counter-insurgency adaptation in the British Army', *Journal of Strategic Studies*, vol. 35, no. 4 (2012), pp. 513–39.

14   Thomas Barfield, *Afghanistan: A Cultural and Political History* (Princeton, NJ: Princeton University Press, 2010), pp. 1–2.

15   Ahmed Rashid, *Taliban: The Story of the Afghan Warlords* (London: Pan, 2000); Rob Johnson, *The Afghan Way of War: Culture and Pragmatism* (London: Hurst, 2011); Antonio Giustozzi, *Koran, Kalashnikov and Laptop: The Neo-Taliban Insurgency in Afghanistan* (London: Hurst, 2007); Antonio Giustozzi, *Empires of Mud: Wars and Warlords in Afghanistan* (London: Hurst, 2009); Antonio Giustozzi, ed., *Decoding the New Taliban: Insights from the Afghan Field* (London: Hurst, 2009); Alex Strick van Linschoten and Felix Kuehn, *An Enemy We Created: The Myth of the Taliban/Al Qaeda Merger in Afghanistan, 1970–2010* (London: Hurst, 2012); Peter Bergen, ed., *Talibanistan* (Oxford: Oxford University Press, 2012); Mike Martin, *An Intimate War: An Oral History of the Helmand Conflict* (London: Hurst, 2014); Carter Malkasian, *War Comes to Garmser: Thirty Years of Conflict on the Afghan Frontier* (London: Hurst, 2013).

16   Theo Farrell and Antonio Giustozzi, 'The Taliban at war: inside the Helmand insurgency, 2004–2012', *International Affairs*, vol. 89, no. 4 (2013), pp. 844–71.

17   Email to author from COIN Education Team, UK Land Warfare Centre, 17 September 2013.

18   Michael Semple, *Reconciliation in Afghanistan* (Washington DC: US Institute of Peace Press, 2009). The findings of our 2012 talks were published as Michael Semple, Theo Farrell, Anatol Lieven and Rudra Chaudhuri, *Taliban Perspectives on Reconciliation* (London: Royal United Services Institute, 2012), http://www.rusi.org/downloads/assets/Taliban_Perspectives_on_Reconciliation.pdf; the findings of our 2016 talks were published as Theo Farrell and Michael Semple, *Ready for Peace? The Afghan Taliban after a Decade of War* (London: Royal United Services Institute, 2016), https://rusi.org/publication/briefing-papers/ready-peace-afghan-taliban-after-decade-war.

19   For a recent invocation of this label, see Jones, *In the Graveyard of Empires*. This reputation is undeserved. The British fought wars in Afghanistan in 1839–42 and 1878–80, and a brief war from May to August 1919. None of them finished off the British Empire, rather it took the world wars of 1914–18 and 1939–45 to do that. The Soviet Union did collapse shortly after the end of its war in Afghanistan in 1979–89. Certainly, the Soviets paid dearly for invading Afghanistan; of the 625,000 Soviet citizens that served in the war, almost 90 per cent fell sick or were injured, 50,000 returned home with more serious injuries, and

over 15,000 did not return home alive. But it was steady economic decline over a twenty-five-year period, and not foreign wars, that finished off the Soviet Union. Rodric Braithwaite, *Afgantsy: The Russians in Afghanistan, 1979–1989* (London: Profile Books, 2011), pp. 329–30. On economic decline and the collapse of the Soviet Union, see William Wohlforth and Stephen G. Brooks, 'Power, globalization, and the end of the Cold War: reevaluating a landmark case for ideas', *International Security*, vol. 53, no. 3 (2000–01), pp. 5–53.

20   Dalrymple, *Return of a King*; see also Martin J. Bayly, *Taming the Imperial Imagination: Colonial Knowledge, International Relations, and the Anglo-Afghan Encounter, 1808–1878* (Cambridge: Cambridge University Press, 2016).

21   Michael Barthorp, *Afghan Wars and the North-West Frontier, 1839–1947*, 2nd edn (London: Cassell, 2002); David Loyn, *Butcher and Bolt: Two Hundred Years of Foreign Engagement in Afghanistan* (London: Windmill Books, 2008).

22   Daniel Moran, 'The Great Game and the Quagmire: Military Adaptation in the British and Soviet Wars in Afghanistan, 1839–1989', in Theo Farrell, Frans Osinga and James A. Russell, eds, *Military Adaptation in Afghanistan* (Stanford, CA: Stanford University Press, 2013), p. 33.

23   Barthorp, *Afghan Wars*, pp. 149–61; Loyn, *Butcher and Bolt*, pp. 168–74.

24   Theo Farrell and Rudra Chaudhuri, 'Campaign disconnect: operational progress and strategic obstacles in Afghanistan, 2009–2011', *International Affairs*, vol. 87, no. 2 (2011), pp. 271–96; Theo Farrell, 'Improving in war: military adaptation and the British in Helmand Province, Afghanistan, 2006–2009', *Journal of Strategic Studies*, vol. 33, no. 4 (2010), pp. 567–94; Theo Farrell, *Appraising Moshtarak: The Campaign in Nad-e-Ali District, Helmand*, Royal United Services Institute, June 2010, at http://www.rusi.org/downloads/assets/Appraising_Moshtarak.pdf.

Chapter 1: Atta in America

1   Peter Finn and Charles Lane, 'Will gives a window into suspect's mind', *Washington Post*, 6 October 2001, A16.

2   Anthony Summers and Robbyn Swan, *The Eleventh Day: The Ultimate Account of 9/11* (London: Doubleday, 2011), pp. 271–2.

3   Elena Lappin, 'Atta in Hamburg', *Prospect*, 20 September 2002.

4   Jason Burke, *Al-Qaeda: The True Story of Radical Islam,* 3rd edn (London: Penguin, 2007), Kindle edn, loc. 4461.

5   Summers and Swan, *Eleventh Day*, pp. 295–7.

6 http://www.youtube.com/watch?v=1TxodXsZW2s.

7 http://www.nytimes.com/interactive/2011/09/08/us/sept-11-reck-oning/cost-graphic.html?_r=0.

8 Eric Nalder, 'Twin Towers engineered to withstand jet collision', *Seattle Times*, 27 February 1993.

9 Summers and Swan, *Eleventh Day*, p. 24.

10 Chris Ayres, 'I watched as people leapt from flames to death', *The Times*, 12 September 2001.

11 Ben Macintyre, 'Thousands dead in triple attack', *The Times*, 12 September 2001. Initially it was feared that many tens of thousands had perished. Analysing data from the turnstiles at the entrances to the Twin Towers, the New York Port Authority later calculated that some 14,000 people were in the buildings that morning. Some weeks later the death toll was estimated downwards at 6,000, twice the final confirmed figure.

12 Donald Rumsfeld, *Known and Unknown: A Memoir* (New York: Sentinel, 2011), p. 341.

13 Esther Schrader, 'Pentagon, a vulnerable building, was hit in the least vulnerable spot', *Los Angeles Times*, 16 September 2001.

14 Summers and Swan, *Eleventh Day*, p. 45.

15 Rumsfeld, *Known and Unknown*, p. 335.

16 Schrader, 'Pentagon'.

17 Richard Clarke, *Against All Enemies: Inside America's War on Terror* (New York: Free Press, 2004), p. 16.

18 Condoleezza Rice, *No Higher Honour: A Memoir of My Years in Washington* (London: Simon & Schuster, 2011), p. 71.

19 George W. Bush, *Decision Points* (Virgin Digital, 2010), Kindle edn, loc. 126.

20 http://www.youtube.com/watch?v=1TxodXsZW2s.

21 Bush, *Decision Points*, loc. 126.

22 *The 9/11 Commission Report: Final Report of the National Commission on Terrorist Attacks Upon the United States* (New York: W. W. Norton & Co., 2011), p. 38.

23 *9/11 Commission Report*, pp. 39–40.

24 Clarke, *Against All Enemies*, p. 18.

25 'That's me in the picture: Andrew Card', *Guardian* magazine, 13 September 2014, p. 110.

26 *9/11 Commission Report*, p. 39.

27 Bush, *Decision Points*, loc. 2299.

28 Summers and Swan, *Eleventh Day*, p. 47.

29 Ibid., p. 52.

30 Clarke, *Against All Enemies*, p. 12.

31 Bush, *Decision Points*, loc. 2369.

32 *9/11 Commission Report*, pp. 40–2.

33 Ibid., pp. 43–4.

34 Steve Hendrix, 'F-16 pilot was ready to give her life on September 11th', *Washington Post*, 8 September 2011.

35 Interview with retired very senior British officer, London, 29 January 2014.

36 http://www.historycommons.org/entity.jsp?entity=robert_natter_1.

37 Alex Strick van Linschoten and Felix Kuehn, *An Enemy We Created: The Myth of the Taliban/Al Qaeda Merger in Afghanistan, 1970–2010* (London: Hurst, 2012), p. 99.

38 Burke, *Al-Qaeda*, loc. 346.

39 Lawrence Wright, *The Looming Tower: Al-Qaeda's Road to 9/11* (London: Penguin, 2006), p. 22.

40 The popular myth of heroic Jewish forces defeating larger Arab armies in the 1948 war has been challenged by revisionist history, which has revealed that in fact, by mid 1948 the total number of Arab troops operating in Palestine was 25,000 whereas the new Israel Defence Forces numbered 35,000. Moreover, Israeli forces grew at a far higher rate during the course of the war than Arab forces. Avi Shlaim, *The Iron Wall: Israel and the Arab World* (London: Penguin, 2000).

41 Syed Qutb Shaheed, *Milestones* (1964), translated version, p. 7. http://www.izharudeen.com/uploads/4/1/2/2/4122615/milestones_www.izharudeen.com.pdf.

42 Strick van Linschoten and Kuehn, *An Enemy We Created*, pp. 28–9, 34.

43 Burke, *Al-Qaeda*, loc. 357.

44 Strick van Linschoten and Kuehn, *An Enemy We Created*, p. 35.

45 Wright, *Looming Tower*, p. 272.

46 The 1995 bombing had targeted the US military mission to the Saudi National Guard in Riyadh, killing five US military personnel. The 1996 bombing targeted a US military housing facility in the city of Khobar, killing nineteen US Air Force personnel. Clarke, *Against All Enemies*, pp. 112–13.

47 George Tenet, *At the Center of the Storm: My Years at the CIA* (New York: HarperCollins, 2007), p. 154.

48 Clarke, *Against All Enemies*, p. 149.

49 *9/11 Commission Report*, p. 118.

50 Tenet, *At the Center of the Storm*, p. 154.

51 *9/11 Commission Report*, pp. 109, 118.

52 Clarke, *Against All Enemies*, p. 184.

53 Steve Coll, *Ghost Wars: The Secret History of the CIA, Afghanistan and Bin Laden, from the Soviet Invasion to September 10, 2001* (London: Penguin, 2004), p. 422.

54 Clarke, *Against All Enemies*, p. 202.

55 Coll, *Ghost Wars*, pp. 421–30.

56 Peter L. Bergen, *The Osama Bin Laden I Know: An Oral History of al-Qaeda's Leader* (New York: Free Press, 2006), Kindle edn, loc. 4366.

57 John Stone, 'Escalation and the war on terror', *Journal of Strategic Studies*, vol. 35, no. 5 (2012), p. 643. See also Tom Parker, 'It's a trap: provoking an overreaction is Terrorism 101', *RUSI Journal*, vol. 160, no. 2 (2015), pp. 38–47. The outcome of the US-led invasion that followed 9/11 would suggest that al-Qaeda overplayed its hand. On this risk in terrorist strategy, see Peter R. Neumann and M. L. R. Smith, *The Strategy of Terrorism: How It Works, and Why It Fails* (London: Routledge, 2008).

58 Jason Burke, *The 9/11 Wars* (London: Allen Lane, 2011), p. 22.

59 Bergen, *Osama*, loc. 4422.

60 Bruce Riedel, *The Search for al-Qaeda: Its Leadership, Ideology and Future* (Washington DC: Brookings Institution, 2008), p. 121.

61 Rodric Braithwaite, *Afgantsy: The Russians in Afghanistan, 1979–89* (Oxford: Oxford University Press, 2011).

62 Summers and Swan, *Eleventh Day*, pp. 220–45; *9/11 Commission Report*, pp. 145–50, 153–4.

63 *9/11 Commission Report*, pp. 153–4; Wright, *Looming Tower*, pp. 307–8.

64 Barnett R. Rubin, *The Fragmentation of Afghanistan*, 2nd edn (New Haven: Yale University Press, 2005).

65 Fiona Terry, *Condemned to Repeat? The Paradox of Humanitarian Action* (Ithaca, NY: Cornell University Press, 2002), p. 58.

66 Rob Johnson, *The Afghan Way of War: Culture and Pragmatism: A Critical History* (London: Hurst, 2011), pp. 217–39.

67 Strick van Linschoten and Kuehn, *An Enemy We Created*, p. 45.

68 Hassan Abbas, *The Taliban Revival: Violence and Extremism on the Pakistan–Afghanistan Frontier* (New Haven: Yale University Press, 2014), pp. 66–7.

69 Antonio Giustozzi, *Empires of Mud: Warlords and Warlordism in Afghanistan* (London: Hurst, 2009).

70 James Fergusson, *Taliban: The True Story of the World's Most Feared Guerrilla Fighters* (London: Bantam Press, 2010), p. 99.

71 Ahmed Rashid, *Taliban: The Story of the Afghan Warlords* (London: Pan Books, 2001), chapters 1–3.

72 Seth G. Jones, *In the Graveyard of Empires: America's War on Afghanistan* (New York: W. W. Norton & Co., 2009), pp. 75, 83; Strick van Linschoten and Kuehn, *An Enemy We Created*, pp. 143–57.

73 The adverse impact of Taliban rule on women's lives in Afghanistan is well recounted in Christina Lamb, *The Sewing Circles of Herat: A Memoir of Afghanistan* (London: HarperCollins, 2004).

74 Coll, *Ghost Wars*, pp. 334–5.

75   Roy Gutman, *How We Missed the Story: Osama Bin Laden, the Taliban, and the Hijacking of Afghanistan* (Washington DC: US Institute of Peace, 2008), p. 99.

76   Rashid, *Taliban*, pp. 113–15.

77   Ibid., pp. 190–1.

78   Coll, *Ghost Wars*, pp. 301–2.

79   Riaz Mohammad Khan, *Afghanistan and Pakistan: Conflict, Extremism, and Resistance to Modernity* (Washington DC: Woodrow Wilson Center Press, 2011), pp. 32–50.

80   Carlotta Gall, *The Wrong Enemy: America in Afghanistan, 2001–2014* (New York: Houghton Mifflin Harcourt, 2014), pp. 43–4.

81   Ibid., p. 45.

82   Rashid, *Taliban*, p. 183.

83   Abbas, *Taliban Revival*, p. 68.

84   Khan, *Afghanistan and Pakistan*, pp. 86–7.

85   Abbas, *Taliban Revival*, p. 69.

86   Khan, *Afghanistan and Pakistan*, p. 80.

87   Gall, *The Wrong Enemy*, p. 51.

88   Burke, *9/11 Wars*, pp. 16–17.

89   According to James Fergusson, 'A class of "career Taliban" grew up in the capital that was far divorced from the lofty idealism of Kandahar. In time, Mullah Omar's edicts began to be taken as standards to aspire to rather than laws to be applied.' Fergusson, *Taliban*, p. 75.

90   Interview with former Taliban deputy minister, Dubai, 18 July 2012.

91   Fergusson, *Taliban*, pp. 76–7.

92   Abdul Salam Zaeef, *My Life with the Taliban* (London: Hurst, 2010), p. 84.

93   Quote from interview with former Taliban deputy minister, Dubai, 18 July 2012.

94   Anand Gopal, *No Good Men Among the Living: America, the Taliban and the War Through Afghan Eyes* (New York: Henry Holt & Co., 2014), p. 59.

95   Interview with Afghan woman activist, Kabul, January 2015.

96   Quote from interview with former Taliban deputy minister, Dubai, 18 July 2012. See also Fergusson, *Taliban*, pp. 67–9.

97   Khan, *Afghanistan and Pakistan*, p. 77; Rashid, *Taliban*, pp. 64–5.

98   Madeleine Albright, *Madam Secretary: A Memoir*, 2nd edn (London: HarperCollins, 2013), p. 364.

99   Zaeef, *My Life with the Taliban*, p. 136–7.

100   Albright, *Madam Secretary*, p. 371.

101   Strick van Linschoten and Felix Kuehn, *An Enemy We Created*, p. 164.

102   Jones, *In the Graveyard of Empires*, p. 84; Coll, *Ghost Wars*, p. 414.

103 *9/11 Commission Report*, pp. 193–5.

104 Bergen, *Osama*, loc. 5530–58.

105 *9/11 Commission Report*, pp. 353–8.

106 Ibid., pp. 1–10.

107 Ibid., p. 201.

Chapter 2: Shoulder to Shoulder

1 Matthew Tempest, 'TUC row over privatisation', *Guardian*, 10 September 2001.

2 Alastair Campbell, *The Alastair Campbell Diaries, Volume 3: Power and Responsibility, 1999–2001* (London: Arrow Books, 2012), p. 690.

3 Tony Blair, *A Journey* (London: Random House, 2010), p. 345.

4 Campbell, *Diaries, Volume 3*, p. 692.

5 Anthony Seldon with Peter Snowdon and Daniel Collings, *Blair Unbound* (London: Pocket Books, 2008), pp. 6, 9.

6 Jonathan Powell, *The New Machiavelli: How to Wield Power in the Modern World* (London: Vintage Books, 2011), p. 49.

7 Interview with Jack Straw, London, 9 April 2014.

8 Seldon et al., *Blair Unbound*, pp. 8–9.

9 Interview with Geoff Hoon, London, 2 May 2014.

10 Interview with David Blunkett, London, 25 February 2014.

11 Seldon et al., *Blair Unbound*, p. 8.

12 Mark Henderson, 'Skyscrapers vulnerable to high-level impact', *The Times*, 12 September 2001.

13 Confidential interview, 22 January 2014.

14 Dearlove was travelling low-key and incognito, and was surprised to see his car and a police escort waiting for him on the airport runway when his plane flew into Heathrow later that afternoon. Confidential source.

15 Seldon et al., *Blair Unbound*, p. 11.

16 Confidential interview, 22 January 2014.

17 Christopher Andrew, *The Defence of the Realm: The Authorized History of MI5* (London: Penguin, 2010), pp. 808–9.

18 Seldon et al., *Blair Unbound*, p. 13.

19 Confidential interview, 22 January 2014.

20 Interview with David Blunkett, London, 25 February 2014.

21 Interview with senior MoD official, London, 30 January 2014.

22 Seldon et al., *Blair Unbound*, pp. 14–15.

23 Interview with David Blunkett, London, 25 February 2014. These shoot-down criteria were never approved by the prime minister; as one senior

Cabinet Office official noted: 'The initial fear of an airborne attack dissipated quickly.' Confidential interview, 22 January 2014.

24   Seldon et al., *Blair Unbound*, p. 15.

25   https://www.youtube.com/watch?v=QGNDZ8HPIGQ.

26   Blair, *A Journey*, p. 252.

27   Jack Straw, *Last Man Standing: Memoirs of a Political Survivor* (London: Macmillan, 2012), Kindle edn, loc. 4775.

28   Interview with David Blunkett, London, 25 February 2014.

29   Alastair Campbell, *The Alastair Campbell Diaries, Volume 4: The Burden of Power: Countdown to Iraq* (London: Hutchinson, 2012), p. 7.

30   https://www.youtube.com/watch?v=XbqCquDl4k4.

31   http://www.telegraph.co.uk/news/worldnews/september-11-attacks/8745304/911-Newspaper-front-pages-the-day-after-September-11.html.

32   'Terror for all', *The Times*, 12 September 2001.

33   Seldon et al., *Blair Unbound*, pp. 48–9.

34   Campbell, *Diaries, Volume 4*, p. 7.

35   Seldon et al., *Blair Unbound*, p. 49.

36   Campbell, *Diaries, Volume 4*, p. 9.

37   http://www.nato.int/docu/update/2001/0910/e0912a.htm.

38   Interview with senior MoD official, London, 30 January 2014.

39   Fred Kaplan, 'Bush's many miscalculations', *Slate*, 9 September 2003.

40   John Kampfner, *Blair's Wars* (London: Free Press, 2003), p. 117.

41   Quote from Douglas J. Feith, *War and Decision: The Pentagon at the Dawn of the War on Terrorism* (New York: HarperCollins, 2008), p. 13.

42   Michael Howard, 'What's in a name?: how to fight terrorism', *Foreign Affairs*, January/February, 2002.

43   Bob Woodward, *Bush at War* (London: Pocket Books, 2003), p. 37.

44   Hew Strachan, *The Director of War: Contemporary Strategy in Historical Perspective* (Oxford: Oxford University Press, 2013), p. 11.

45   Donald Rumsfeld, *Known and Unknown: A Memoir* (London: Penguin 2013), Kindle edn, loc. 6495–510.

46   Douglas Feith presentation at conference, 'Diplomacy, alliances and war: Anglo-American perspectives on history and strategy in the 9/11 era', University of Texas at Austin, 1–2 November 2013.

47   Strachan, *Director of War*, p. 11.

48   Feith, *War and Decision*, p. 8.

49   Stefan Halper and Jonathan Clarke, *America Alone: The Neo-Conservatives and the New Global Order* (Cambridge: Cambridge University Press, 2004).

50   Feith, *War and Decision*, pp. 12–16; Woodward, *Bush at War*, p. 49. On the rise of the 'neocons', see Halper and Clarke, *America Alone*.

51   Kampfner, *Blair's Wars*, pp. 109–10.

52 Confidential interview, 14 February 2014.

53 Confidential interview, 29 January 2014.

54 Seldon et al., *Blair Unbound*, p. 52.

55 Campbell, *Diaries, Volume 4*, p. 12.

56 Ibid., p. 11.

57 Interview with Gisela Stuart MP, Westminster, 23 January 2014.

58 Interview with Sir Gerald Howarth MP, Westminster, 23 January 2014.

59 Interview with Gisela Stuart MP, Westminster, 23 January 2014.

60 House of Commons Hansard Debates, 14 September 2001, column 605.

61 Ibid., column 608.

62 Ibid., column 630.

63 Ibid., column 614.

64 107th Congress, S.J.Res. 23, Public Law 107–40, 18 September 2001.

65 As one senior US official noted, 'There was not much of a role for Blair in helping to shape the American response to the attacks of 9/11, to be honest. By the end of that first weekend at Camp David we knew what we were going to do.' Seldon et al., *Blair Unbound*, p. 53.

66 George Tenet, *At the Centre of the Storm: My Years at the CIA* (New York: HarperCollins, 2007), p. 271.

67 General Tommy Franks with Malcolm McConnell, *American Soldier* (New York: Regan Books, 2004), p. 259.

68 Hugh Shelton with Ronald Levinson and Malcolm McConnell, *Without Hesitation: The Odyssey of an American Warrior* (New York: St. Martin's Press, 2010), p. 445, cited in Yaniv Barzilai, *102 Days of War: How Osama bin Laden, al Qaeda & the Taliban Survived 2001* (London: Potomac Books, 2013), p. 26.

69 Woodward, *Bush at War*, pp. 78–85.

70 Campbell, *Diaries, Volume 4*, p. 13.

71 Ben Macintyre, 'On board the Blair flight of diplomacy', *The Times*, 22 September 2001.

72 Campbell, *Diaries, Volume 4*, p. 15.

73 Macintyre, 'On board the Blair flight of diplomacy'.

74 Campbell, *Diaries, Volume 4*, pp. 22–5.

75 http://edition.cnn.com/2001/US/09/20/gen.bush.transcript/.

76 Blair, *A Journey*, p. 355.

77 Campbell, *Diaries, Volume 4*, p. 25.

78 Christopher Meyer, *DC Confidential: The Controversial Memoirs of Britain's Ambassador to the US at the Time of 9/11 and the Run-up to the Iraq War* (London: Phoenix, 2011), Kindle edn, loc. 3942–56.

79 Peter L. Bergen, *The Osama Bin Laden I Know: An Oral History of al-Qaeda's Leader* (New York: Free Press, 2006), Kindle edn, loc. 5856; Jason Burke, *The 9/11 Wars* (London: Allen Lane, 2011), p. 24.

80   Abdul Salam Zaeef, *My Life with the Taliban* (London: Hurst, 2010), p. 142.

81   Alex Strick van Linschoten and Felix Kuehn, *An Enemy We Created: The Myth of the Taliban/Al Qaeda Merger in Afghanistan, 1970–2010* (London: Hurst, 2012), p. 218.

82   Riaz Mohammad Khan, *Afghanistan and Pakistan: Conflict, Extremism, and Resistance to Modernity* (Washington DC: Woodrow Wilson Center Press, 2011), pp. 90–1.

83   Robert Grenier, *88 Days to Kandahar: A CIA Diary* (New York: Simon & Schuster, 2015), pp. 80–6, 112–22.

84   Barzilai, *102 Days of War*, p. 38.

85   Anand Gopal, *No Good Men Among the Living: America, the Taliban and the War Through Afghan Eyes* (New York: Henry Holt & Co., 2014), p. 12.

86   Bergen, *The Osama Bin Laden I Know*, loc. 6033; Strick van Linschoten and Kuehn, *An Enemy We Created*, pp. 223–5.

87   According to one account, a British company was providing the Internet service to Omar's Special Office, which suggests that MI6 may have been able to monitor the Taliban leader's communications. James Fergusson, *Taliban: The True Story of the World's Most Feared Guerrilla Fighters* (London: Bantam Press, 2010), p. 106.

88   Fergusson, *Taliban*, p. 99; Strick van Linschoten and Kuehn, *An Enemy We Created*, pp. 175, 226, 228.

89   Woodward, *Bush at War*, pp. 121–3, 128.

90   Ibid., p. 127.

91   Seth G. Jones, *In the Graveyard of Empires: America's War in Afghanistan* (New York: W. W. Norton & Co., 2009), pp. 88–9; Dr Donald P. Wright and the Contemporary Operations Study Team, *A Different Kind of War: The United States Army in Operation ENDURING FREEDOM, October 2001–September 2005* (Fort Leavenworth, KS: Contemporary Studies Institute Press, 2010), p. 58.

92   Interview with Jonathan Powell, London, 27 March 2014; Campbell, *Diaries, Volume 4*, pp. 16, 18, 30.

93   Confidential interview, London, 2 April 2014.

94   Donald H. Rumsfeld, 'A new kind of war', *New York Times*, 27 September 2001.

95   Frederick W. Kagan, *Finding the Target: The Transformation of American Military Policy* (New York: Encounter Books, 2006), pp. 272–80.

96   Woodward, *Bush at War*, pp. 51–2.

97   Feith, *War and Decision*, pp. 75–8. For one such argument by a former CIA official, see Milton Bearden, 'Afghanistan, graveyard of empires', *Foreign Affairs*, November/December 2001.

98   Wesley K. Clark, *Waging Modern War: Bosnia, Kosovo, and the Future of Conflict* (New York: Public Affairs, 2001), p. 224.

99   Interview with retired intelligence official, London, 3 March 2012.

100   Barzilai, *102 Days of War*, p. 101.

101   Ibid., p. 41.

102   Ibid., p. 27.

103   Woodward, *Bush at War*, p. 193.

104   Franks, *American Soldier*, p. 280.

105   Franks, *American Soldier*, pp. 265–6; Barzilai, *102 Days of War*, pp. 35–6; Woodward, *Bush at War*, p. 195.

106   Franks, *American Soldier*, p. 256.

107   In the event, the K2 runways were too short for the US Air Force's largest cargo planes (the C-5) and so troops and heavy equipment were flown in C-5 planes from the United States to airbases in Europe, and from there loaded onto smaller C-17 or C-130 transport planes and flown to K2. Wright et al., *Different Kind of War*, p. 60.

108   Woodward, *Bush at War*, p. 164.

109   Interview with Geoff Hoon, London, 2 May 2014.

110   Seldon et al., *Blair Unbound*, p. 59.

111   Confidential interview, London, 4 February 2014.

112   Woodward, *Bush at War*, pp. 199, 203.

113   Seldon et al., *Blair Unbound*, p. 59.

114   'The UK's Bin Laden dossier in full', *BBC News*, 4 October 2001, http://news.bbc.co.uk/1/hi/uk_politics/1579043.stm.

115   Campbell, *Diaries, Volume 4*, pp. 33–4, 36.

116   'Blair statement in full', *BBC News*, 7 October 2001, http://news.bbc.co.uk/1/hi/uk_politics/1585238.stm.

Chapter 3: Original Sin

1   Dr Donald P. Wright and the Contemporary Operations Study Team, *A Different Kind of War: The United States Army in Operation ENDURING FREEDOM, October 2001–September 2005* (Fort Leavenworth, KS: Contemporary Studies Institute Press, 2010), p. 64.

2   Richard Norton-Taylor, 'British cruise missiles fired from Arabian Sea', *Guardian*, 8 October 2001.

3   Alastair Campbell, *The Alastair Campbell Diaries, Volume 4: The Burden of Power: Countdown to Iraq* (London: Hutchinson, 2012), p. 42.

4   Yaniv Barzilai, *102 Days of War: How Osama bin Laden, al Qaeda & the Taliban Survived 2001* (London: Potomac Books, 2013), p. 47.

5   Campbell, *Diaries, Volume 4*, p. 41.

6   http://georgewbush-whitehouse.archives.gov/news/releases/
       2001/10/20011007–8.html;   http://news.bbc.co.uk/1/hi/uk_politics/
       1585238.stm.

7   http://www.operations.mod.uk/veritas/faq/objectives.htm.

8   Barzilai, *102 Days of War*, pp. 43–5.

9   James Fergusson, *Taliban: The Unknown Enemy* (Boston, MA: Da Capo
       Press, 2013), p. 161.

10   Gary C. Schroen, *First In: An Insider's Account of How the CIA Spearheaded
       the War on Terror in Afghanistan* (New York: Presidio Press, 2007); Gary
       Berntsen, *Jawbreaker: The Attack on Bin Laden and Al-Qaeda* (New York:
       Three Rivers Press, 2005).

11   Schroen, *First In*, p. 40.

12   Ibid., p. 119.

13   Wright et al., *Different Kind of War*, pp. 61–2, 67.

14   Schroen, *First In*, pp. 184–7.

15   General Tommy Franks with Malcolm McConnell, *American Soldier*
       (New York: Regan Books, 2004), p. 302.

16   Wright et al., *Different Kind of War*, p. 75.

17   Schroen, *First In*, pp. 129–37, 145–50.

18   Adam Sherwin, 'Taleban seize British journalist', *The Times*, 29
       September 2001.

19   Stephen Farrell, 'Taleban accuse journalist of being SAS', *The Times*, 4
       October 2001.

20   Patrick Wintour, Kamal Ahmed and Ed Vulliamy, 'It's time for war,
       Bush and Blair tell Taliban', *Guardian*, 7 October 2001.

21   Claire Cozens, 'High Commissioner pushes for journalist's release',
       Guardian, 2 October 2001; 'Ridley "deported" to Pakistan', *Guardian*, 8
       October 2001.

22   Stephen Farrell, 'Afghanistan releases journalist', *The Times*, 9 October
       2001.

23   Schroen, *First In*, p. 163.

24   Franks, *American Soldier*, pp. 291–5.

25   Campbell, *Diaries, Volume 4*, p. 58.

26   Michael Evans, 'Two British nuclear submarines join attack', *The Times*,
       8 October 2001; Michael Evans, 'Airstrikes are easiest phase of the war',
       The Times, 9 October 2001; Wright et al., *Different Kind of War*, pp. 64, 84.

27   Wright et al., *Different Kind of War*, p. 96.

28   Schroen, *First In*, p. 245.

29   Bob Woodward, *Bush at War* (New York: Pocket Books, 2002), p. 254.

30   Campbell, *Diaries, Volume 4*, pp. 61–2, 67.

31   Michael Evans, 'Military chief wars of four-year war', *The Times*, 27
       October 2001.

32 Campbell, *Diaries, Volume 4*, p. 69.

33 Berntsen, *Jawbreaker*, pp. 88–91; Franks, *American Soldier*, pp. 309–13.

34 Barzilai, *102 Days of War*, pp. 64–6.

35 Schroen, *First In*, p. 328.

36 Ibid., p. 354.

37 Barzilai, *102 Days of War*, p. 69.

38 Ben Fenton and David Rennie, 'Alliance troops enter key city', *Daily Telegraph*, 10 November 2001.

39 Wright et al., *Different Kind of War*, p. 79.

40 Peter Clark, 'Obituary: Paul Bergne', *Guardian*, 17 April 2007.

41 Confidential interview, London, 3 March 2012.

42 Confidential interview, London, 2 April 2014.

43 Confidential source. Bergne was famously independently minded. Monica Whitlock, 'Paul Bergne: a personal tribute', *BBC News*, 23 April 2007.

44 Michael Evans and Michael Smith, 'British troops played key role in advance', *The Times*, 31 November 2001.

45 Wright et al., *Different Kind of War*, pp. 80–1.

46 Mark Kukis, *My Heart Came Attached: The Strange Journey of Walter Lindh* (Washington DC: Potomac Books, 2005), chapter 6.

47 Carlotta Gall, *The Wrong Enemy: America in Afghanistan, 2001–2014* (New York: Houghton Mifflin Harcourt, 2014), pp. 1–10.

48 Ibid., pp. 15–18.

49 Barzilai, *102 Days of War*, pp. 77–8.

50 Anthony Loyd and Martin Fletcher, 'Taleban in retreat as allies march on Kabul', *The Times*, 12 November 2001.

51 Jessica Hodgson, '"BBC liberated Kabul" says Simpson', *Guardian*, 13 November 2001; Sally Pook, 'Simpson sorry for liberated Kabul claim', *Daily Telegraph*, 19 November 2001.

52 'Eye witness: the liberation of Kabul', *BBC News*, 13 November 2001.

53 UN Security Council meeting record, 13 November 2001, S/PV.4414, pp. 5–6.

54 Woodward, *Bush at War*, p. 308.

55 Confidential interview, 14 February 2014.

56 Anthony Seldon with Peter Snowdon and Daniel Collings, *Blair Unbound* (London: Pocket Books, 2007), p. 67.

57 Michael Evans, '4,000 British troops could fly out by Sunday', *The Times*, 15 November 2001.

58 Philip Webster, Michael Evans and Richard Beeston, 'Paras and Marines put on 48-hour frontline standby', *The Times*, 15 November 2001.

59 Philip Webster and Michael Evans, 'First British troops land outside Kabul', *The Times*, 16 November 2001.

60 Berntsen, *Jawbreaker*, p. 210.

61   Interview with Francesc Vendrell, London, 5 March 2015.

62   Interview with Jack Straw, London, 9 April 2014.

63   Confidential interview, 2 April 2014.

64   Confidential interview, 4 February 2014.

65   Confidential interview, 3 March 2012.

66   Anthony Loyd, 'First British troops touch down', *The Times*, 17 November 2001.

67   Michael Evans and Anthony Loyd, 'Mistrust keeps 6,000 British troops at bay', *The Times*, 19 November 2001.

68   Michael Evans, 'British troops not needed', *The Times*, 23 November 2001.

69   Michael Binyon, 'Envoy says Afghans must run the peace', *The Times*, 26 November 2001.

70   David Wastell, Sean Rayment and David Harrison, 'This is the moment when special forces launched the ground war', *Daily Telegraph*, 21 October 2001.

71   Confidential interview, 4 February 2014.

72   Bette Dam, *A Man and a Motorcycle: How Hamid Karzai Came to Power* (Utrecht, NL: Ipso Facto Publishers, 2014), pp. 49–58.

73   Anand Gopal, *No Good Men Among the Living: America, the Taliban, and the War Through Afghan Eyes* (New York: Henry Holt & Co., 2014), p. 33.

74   Dam, *A Man and a Motorcycle*, pp. 74–5.

75   Wright et al., *Different Kind of War*, p. 101.

76   Lucy Morgan Edwards, 'The lost Lion of Kabul', *New Statesman*, 10 November 2011.

77   Wright et al., *Different Kind of War*, p. 98.

78   Christina Lamb, *Farewell Kabul: From Afghanistan to a More Dangerous World* (London: William Collins, 2015), p. 47; Dam, *A Man and a Motorcycle*, pp. 103–4.

79   Dam, *A Man and a Motorcycle*, pp. 100–4.

80   Wright et al., *Different Kind of War*, pp. 99–100.

81   Interestingly enough, the story does not appear in the US Army's official history of the war, which suggests that US special forces arrived and stayed with Karzai rather than extracting him and returning on 14 November. Wright et al., *Different Kind of War*, p. 100.

82   Dam, *A Man and a Motorcycle*, p. 118.

83   Ibid., pp. 121–2.

84   Wright et al., *Different Kind of War*, pp. 103–4.

85   Gall, *Wrong Enemy*, p. 32.

86   Wright et al., *Different Kind of War*, pp. 106–8.

87   Interview with Sir Robert Cooper, London, 3 April 2014.

88   Lamb, *Farewell Kabul*, p. 52.

89   Dam, *A Man and a Motorcycle*, pp. 159–60.

90   Wright et al., *Different Kind of War*, p. 109.

91   UN Security Council meeting record, 13 November 2001, S/PV.4414, pp. 5–6.

92   James F. Dobbins, *After the Taliban: Nation Building in Afghanistan* (Washington DC: Potomac Books, 2008), pp. 84–7.

93   Gopal, *No Good Men*, p. 47.

94   Wright et al., *Different Kind of War*, pp. 109–10.

95   Ibid.

96   Sarah Chayes, *The Punishment of Virtue* (London: Portobello Books, 2006), pp. 44–5.

97   Alex Strick van Linschoten and Felix Kuehn, *An Enemy We Created: The Myth of the Taliban/Al Qaeda Merger in Afghanistan, 1970–2010* (London: Hurst, 2010), pp. 240–1.

98   Jack Fairweather, *The Good War: The Battle for Afghanistan, 2006–14* (London: Jonathan Cape, 2014), p. 55.

99   Brian Knowlton, 'Rumsfeld rejects plan to allow Mullah Omar to "live in dignity": Taliban fighters agree to surrender Kandahar', *New York Times*, 7 December 2001.

100   Interview with Michael Semple, London, 28 April 2015. See also Fotini Christia and Michael Semple, 'Flipping the Taliban', *Foreign Affairs*, July/August 2009, pp. 34–45.

101   The classic work on this is Russell F. Weigley, *The American Way of War* (Bloomington and Indianapolis: Indiana University Press, 1997 [paperback edition]).

102   Knowlton, 'Rumsfeld rejects plan'.

103   Fairweather, *Good War*, p. 56.

104   Gall, *Wrong Enemy*, pp. 33–5; interview with Michael Semple, Atlanta, Georgia, 17 March 2016.

105   Wright et al., *Different Kind of War*, p. 113.

106   Ibid., pp. 112–13.

107   Peter Beaumont, 'Kandahar on brink of chaos as warlords ready for battle', *Observer*, 9 December 2001.

108   Chayes, *Punishment of Virtue*, p. 77.

109   Some months later, Sherzai would even manage to persuade the US special forces team in Kandahar that the governor of next-door Helmand province was actually working for the Taliban, and responsible for an ambush on a US military convoy in which two American troops had been killed. Chayes, *Punishment of Virtue*, pp. 272–4.

110   Gall, *Wrong Enemy*, p. 34.

111   UN Security Council resolution 1383, 6 December 2001, S/RES/1383 (2001).

112　United Nations, 'Agreement on Provisional Arrangements in Afghanistan Pending the Re-establishment of Permanent Government Institutions, Annex I: International Security Force', 5 December 2001, S/2001/1154.

113　Stephen Farrell, Roland Watson and Michael Evans, 'Britons unlikely to join security force', *The Times*, 6 December 2001.

114　Campbell, *Diaries, Volume 4*, p. 103.

115　Ibid., pp. 106–7.

116　Interview with General Sir John McColl, London, 22 March 2014.

117　Alan Philips, 'Britain reopens its embassy as "commitment to better future"', *Daily Telegraph*, 20 November 2001.

118　Interview with General Barney White-Spunner, London, 2 April 2014.

119　Interview with General Sir John McColl, London, 22 March 2014.

120　Fairweather, *Good War*, p. 69.

121　Berntsen, *Jawbreaker*, p. 302.

122　Peter Baker, 'Quietly, in dark, Karzai arrives in Kabul', *Washington Post*, 14 December 2001.

123　Berntsen, *Jawbreaker*, p. 302.

124　Stephen Farrell, James Bone and Michael Evans, 'Marines fly in to protect new Afghan leaders', *The Times*, 21 December 2001. This Royal Marine detail was replaced in mid 2002 by a fifty-strong US special operations forces team dedicated to protecting the Afghan president. Zalmay Khalilzad, *The Envoy: From Kabul to the White House, My Journey Through a Turbulent World* (New York: St. Martin's Press, 2016), Kindle edn, loc. 2577–604.

125　Michael Evans, 'British troops' duties in Kabul to be restricted', *The Times*, 11 December 2001.

126　Interview with General Sir John McColl, London, 22 March 2014.

127　House of Commons Hansard Debates, 19 December 2001, columns 304, 307.

128　Seldon et al., *Blair Unbound*, p. 67.

129　Campbell, *Diaries, Volume 4*, p. 111.

130　Michael Evans and James Bone, 'Britain sets time limit on peacekeeping', *The Times*, 20 December 2001.

131　House of Commons Hansard Debates, 19 December 2001, column 308.

132　UN Security Council resolution 1386, 20 December 2001, S/RES/1386(2001).

133　Interview with General Sir John McColl, London, 22 March 2014.

134　'Military Technical Agreement Between the International Security Assistance Force and the Interim Administration of Afghanistan', 2002. Signed by the Minister of Interior Qanouni, and COMISAF General McColl.

135　Interview with General Barney White-Spunner, London, 2 April 2014.

136 Interview with General Sir John McColl, London, 22 March 2014.

137 Interview with senior MoD official, London, 30 January 2014.

138 Interview with Geoff Hoon, London, 2 May 2014.

139 Interview with General Barney White-Spunner, London, 2 April 2014.

140 Michael Evans, 'British to be in Kabul by Christmas', *The Times*, 31 December 2001.

141 Interview with General Barney White-Spunner, London, 2 April 2014.

142 Interview with General Barney White-Spunner, London, 2 April 2014; Stephen Farrell and Michael Evans, 'British troops to join Afghan patrols in Kabul', *The Times*, 19 December 2001.

143 Interview with General Barney White-Spunner, London, 2 April 2014.

144 Interview with General Sir John McColl, London, 22 March 2014.

145 Interview with General Barney White-Spunner, London, 2 April 2014.

146 Confidential interview, 21 February 2014.

147 Interview with former senior US national security official, 4 June 2013.

148 Fairweather, *Good War*, p. 71.

149 Interview with General Sir John McColl, London, 22 March 2014; Fairweather, *Good War*, pp. 169–70.

150 Interview with General Sir John McColl, London, 22 March 2014.

151 Statement by Secretary of State for Defence, House of Commons Hansard Debates, 20 June 2002, columns 407–8.

152 Jason Burke, *The 9/11 Wars* (London: Allen Lane, 2011), p. 62.

153 Berntsen, *Jawbreaker*, p. 214.

154 Ibid., p. 266.

155 Benjamin Lambeth, *Air Power Against Terrorism: America's Conduct of Operation Enduring Freedom* (Santa Monica: RAND, 2005), pp. 149–50.

156 Barzilai, *102 Days of War*, p. 98.

157 Burke, *9/11 Wars*, p. 66.

158 *Tora Bora Revisited: How We Failed to Get Bin Laden and Why It Matters Today: A Report to Members of the Committee on Foreign Relations, United States Senate, 111th Congress first session*, 30 November 2009, p. 13.

159 Wright et al., *Different Kind of War*, p. 115.

160 Burke, *9/11 Wars*, pp. 62–3.

161 Strick van Linschoten and Kuehn, *An Enemy We Created*, p. 243.

162 Burke, *9/11 Wars*, p. 68.

163 Wright et al., *Different Kind of War*, p. 117.

164 Richard B. Andres, Craig Wills and Thomas Griffith Jr, 'Winning with allies: the strategic value of the Afghan model', *International Security*, vol. 30, no. 3 (2005/06), p. 148.

165 Dalton Fury, *Kill Bin Laden* (New York: St. Martin's Press, 2008), pp. 227–8.

166 Wright et al., *Different Kind of War*, p. 119.

167 Cited in Peter Bergen, 'The Battle for Tora Bora', *New Republic*, 22 December 2009.

168 *Tora Bora Revisited*, p. 5.

169 Ibid., p. 10.

170 Berntsen, *Jawbreaker*, p. 290.

171 Wright et al., *Different Kind of War*, p. 115–16.

172 *Tora Bora Revisited*, p. 19.

173 Peter John Paul Krause, 'The last good hope: a reassessment of U.S. operations at Tora Bora', *Security Studies*, vol. 17, no. 4 (2008), pp. 656–7.

174 Barzilai, *102 Days of War*, p. 102.

175 Burke, *9/11 Wars*, pp. 63–4, 66.

176 Michael Evans, 'British special forces to join cave assault', *The Times*, 3 December 2001.

177 Bergen, 'The Battle for Tora Bora'.

178 Lamb, *Farewell Kabul*, p. 91.

179 Wright et al., *Different Kind of War*, p. 127; Lester W. Crau and Dodge Billingsley, *Operation Anaconda: America's First Major Battle in Afghanistan* (Lawrence, KS: University of Kansas Press, 2011), p. 121.

180 Michael Evans, 'Six-nation force aids US assault on diehard Taleban', *The Times*, 6 March 2002.

181 For detailed accounts of Operation Anaconda, see Wright et al., *Different Kind of War*, pp. 141–73; and Crau and Billingsley, *Operation Anaconda*.

182 This Amphibious Readiness Force comprised the headquarters element and two companies from 40 Commando on HMS *Fearless*.

183 Interview with very senior MoD planner, 29 January 2014.

184 Interview with Colonel Tim Chicken, Surbiton, 3 March 2014.

185 Confidential source; interview with Geoff Hoon, 2 May 2014.

186 The Secretary of State for Defence's Statement in the Commons, 18 March 2002, http://www.operations.mod.uk/veritas/statements/statement_18mar.htm.

187 George Jones, Andrew Sparrow and Anton La Guardia, 'Britain sends 1,700 troops to war in Afghanistan', *Daily Telegraph*, 19 March 2002; Michael Evans, 'Thousands of fighters await UK troops', *The Times*, 20 March 2002.

188 Anthony Loyd, 'Marines sweep in, a month too late', *The Times*, 7 May 2002.

189 Michael Evans, 'War-bound troops must make detour', *The Times*, 23 March 2002; Michael Evans and Catherine Philip, 'Marines adopt new route to Kabul in face of Pakistan's opposition', *The Times*, 26 March 2002.

190 Interview with Major General Roger Lane, Havant, 30 April 2014.

191 Interview with senior MoD official, London, 30 January 2014.

192 Confidential source.

193 Interview with Major General Roger Lane, Havant, 30 April 2014.

194 Interview with Colonel Tim Chicken, Surbiton, 3 March 2014.

195 Ibid.

196 Julius Strauss and Michael Smith, 'Marines go into action at 10,000 ft', *Daily Telegraph*, 17 April 2002.

197 Interview with Colonel Tim Chicken, Surbiton, 3 March 2014.

198 In a later operation, Royal Marines would play a trick on accompanying journalists, by sneakily putting rocks in their backpacks to give them a taste of what it is like to carry weight where the oxygen is so low.

199 Anthony Loyd, 'Royal Marines go looking for trouble', *The Times*, 3 May 2002.

200 Jason Burke, 'Troops fight boredom in the war on terror', *Observer*, 28 April 2002.

201 Anthony Loyd, 'Marines sweep in, a month too late', *The Times*, 7 May 2002.

202 Interview with Major General Roger Lane, Havant, 30 April 2014.

203 Interview with Lieutenant Colonel Richard King, London, 15 January 2015.

204 Interview with Colonel Tim Chicken, Surbiton, 3 March 2014.

205 Interview with Lieutenant Colonel Richard King, London, 15 January 2015.

206 Carlotta Gall, 'Huge arms cache discovered in caves', *The Times*, 10 May 2002.

207 Anthony Loyd, 'Mystery over discovery of "Taleban" arms dump caves', *The Times*, 11 May 2002.

208 Interview with Colonel Tim Chicken, Surbiton, 3 March 2014.

209 'Marines blitz on bin Laden men', *Sun*, 2 May 2002.

210 'Sham in Bagram', *Mirror*, 16 May 2002.

211 Wright et al., *Different Kind of War*, p. 187.

212 Confidential source.

213 Interview with Colonel Tim Chicken, Surbiton, 3 March 2014.

214 Madeleine Bunting, 'This futile campaign', *Guardian*, 20 May 2002.

215 Interview with Major General Roger Lane, Havant, 30 April 2014.

216 Interview with Colonel Tim Chicken, Surbiton, 3 March 2014.

217 Interview with Lieutenant Colonel Richard King, London, 15 January 2015.

218 Interview with Major General Roger Lane, Havant, 30 April 2014.

219 Interview with Lieutenant Colonel Richard King, London, 15 January 2015.

220   'Marines commander removed', *Guardian*, 20 May 2002.

221   Michael Smith, 'Brigadier put troops before politics', *Daily Telegraph*, 21 May 2002.

222   Matthew Hickley and David Williams, 'Brigadier caught in the crossfire', *Daily Mail*, 21 May 2002.

223   Michael E. O'Hanlon, 'A flawed masterpiece', *Foreign Affairs*, vol. 81, no. 3 (March/April 2002), p. 48.

224   Stephen D. Biddle, 'Allies, airpower and modern warfare: the Afghan model in Afghanistan and Iraq', *International Security*, vol. 30, no. 1 (2005/06), p. 168.

225   Al-Qaeda militants showed more competence when it came to preparing defensive positions. Stephen Biddle notes that in Operation Anaconda, launched in March 2002, 'well-prepared al Qaeda positions survived repeated aerial attack by PGM [precision guided munitions]'. Indeed, Biddle notes that '[o]ne dug-in al Qaeda command post was found surrounded by no fewer than five JDAM [PGM] craters, yet its garrison survived and resisted until they were overrun by U.S. infantry'. Biddle, *Afghanistan and the Future of Warfare: Implications for Army and Defense Policy* (Carlisle, PA: Strategic Studies Institute, November 2002), p. 35.

226   Gopal, *No Good Men*, pp. 17, 19.

227   O'Hanlon, 'A flawed masterpiece', p. 57.

228   Dobbins, *After the Taliban*, chapter 3.

229   Interview with Sir Robert Cooper, London, 3 April 2014.

230   Khalilzad, *The Envoy*, loc. 2298.

231   According to one account based on an interview with a senior Taliban present, 'senior Taliban leaders gathered in Pakistan and considered reaching out to the Afghan government in an attempt to participate in the national political arena through legitimate means. There was, however, no interest from the Afghan interim government.' Alex Strick van Linschoten and Felix Kuehn, *Lessons Learnt: 'Islamic, Independent, Perfect and Strong': Parsing the Taliban's Strategic Intentions, 2001–2011*, AHRC Public Policy Series (Swindon: Arts and Humanities Council, 2012), p. 7.

Chapter 4: Road to Helmand

1   Confidential interview, 14 February 2014.

2   Tony Blair, *A Journey* (London: Hutchinson, 2010), p. 369.

3   Alastair Campbell, *The Alastair Campbell Diaries, Volume 4: The Burden of Power: Countdown to Iraq* (London: Hutchinson, 2012), pp. 133–4.

4   This case was based on five tests outlined by Blair in his famous Chicago speech of 24 April 1999. These five tests were originally formulated in a memorandum from Sir Lawrence Freedman (Professor of War Studies at King's College London) to the prime minister on 16 April 1999. See www.iraqinquiry.org.uk/media/42664/freedman-powell-letter.pdf.

5   On the rise of humanitarian intervention as post-Cold War state practice, see Nicholas J. Wheeler, *Saving Strangers: Humanitarian Intervention in International Society* (Oxford: Oxford University Press, 2000).

6   A right of humanitarian intervention was discussed but not adopted at the San Francisco conference on the drafting of the UN Charter in 1945. Thomas M. Frank, *Recourse to Force: State Action Against Threats and Armed Attacks* (Cambridge: Cambridge University Press, 2002), p. 136.

7   David Armstrong, Theo Farrell and Helene Lambert, *International Law and International Relations*, 2nd edn (Cambridge: Cambridge University Press, 2012), pp. 140–1.

8   Often referred to as a Chapter VI and a half activity, as it lies between peaceful measures (Chapter VI) and forceful measures (Chapter VII) specified in the UN Charter to restore international peace and security, it is in fact nowhere mentioned in the Charter.

9   William J. Durch, ed., *The Evolution of Peacekeeping: Case Studies and Comparative Analysis* (New York: St. Martin's Press, 1993).

10 Sheena Chesnut Greitens and Theo Farrell, 'Humanitarian interventions and peace operations', in John Baylis, James J. Wirtz and Colin S. Gray, eds, *Strategy in the Contemporary World*, 4th edn (Oxford: Oxford University Press, 2013), p. 287.

11 Stephen John Stedman, 'Spoiler problems in peace processes', *International Security*, vol. 22, no. 2 (1997), pp. 5–53; for overview and assessment of post-Cold War peace operations, see Taylor B. Seybolt, *Humanitarian Military Intervention: The Conditions for Success and Failure* (Oxford: SIPRI and Oxford University Press, 2008).

12 Mats Berdal, 'Fateful encounter: the United States and UN peacekeeping', *Survival*, vol. 36, no. 1 (1994), pp. 30–50.

13 One analysis suggests that Bush decided to send a US peace force to Somalia in order to prevent the incoming Clinton administration from deploying US troops to Bosnia. Jon Western, 'Sources of humanitarian intervention: beliefs, information, and advocacy in the U.S. decisions on Somalia and Bosnia', *International Security*, vol. 26, no. 4 (2002), pp. 112–42.

14 Theo Farrell, 'Sliding into war: the Somalia imbroglio and US Army peace operations doctrine', *International Peacekeeping*, vol. 2, no. 2 (1995), pp. 194–214.

15 David Halberstam, *War in a Time of Peace: Bush, Clinton and the Generals* (London: Bloomsbury, 2002).

16   Brendan Simms, *Unfinest Hour: How Britain Helped Destroy Bosnia* (London: Penguin, 2002).

17   Mark Wickham-Jones and Richard Little, eds, *New Labour's Foreign Policy: A New Moral Crusade* (Manchester: Manchester University Press, 2000). For a critical assessment, see Nicholas J. Wheeler and Tim Dunne, *Moral Britannia? Evaluating the Ethical Dimension of Labour's Foreign Policy* (London: Foreign Policy Centre, 2004).

18   Colin McInnes, 'Labour's Strategic Defence Review', *International Affairs*, vol. 74, no. 4 (1998), pp. 823–45.

19   'Introduction by the Secretary of State for Defence, the Rt. Hon. George Robertson, MP', *The Strategic Defence Review*, CM 3999 (London: TSO, 1998), paras 6, 9.

20   Interview with senior MoD official, London, 29 January 2014.

21   The Rt Hon. George Robertson MP, 'The Strategic Defence Review', *RUSI Journal*, vol. 142, no. 5 (1997), p. 3.

22   John Kampfner, *Blair's Wars* (London: The Free Press, 2003).

23   Sir Nigel Sheinwald presentation at conference, 'Diplomacy, alliances and war: Anglo-American perspectives on history and strategy in the 9/11 era', University of Texas at Austin, 1–2 November 2013.

24   Condoleezza Rice, 'Campaign 2000: promoting the national interest', *Foreign Affairs*, January/February 2000.

25   Sten Rynning, *NATO in Afghanistan: The Liberal Disconnect* (Stanford, CA: Stanford University Press, 2012), p. 82.

26   Zalmay Khalilzad, *The Envoy: From Kabul to the White House, My Journey Through a Turbulent World* (New York: St. Martin's Press, 2016), Kindle edn, loc. 2155.

27   Bob Woodward, *Plan of Attack* (New York: Simon & Schuster, 2004), pp. 8, 38. See also General Tommy Franks with Malcolm McConnell, *American Soldier* (New York: Regan Books, 2004), p. 329.

28   Quotes from Lawrence Freedman, *A Choice of Enemies: America Confronts the Middle East* (New York: Public Affairs, 2008), p. 404.

29   Transcript of Admiral the Lord Boyce's testimony to the Iraq Inquiry, 3 December 2009, p. 4.

30   Transcript of Admiral the Lord Boyce's testimony to the Iraq Inquiry, 27 January 2011, p. 4.

31   Transcript of Jonathan Powell's testimony to the Iraq Inquiry, 18 March 2010, p. 17.

32   https://web.archive.org/web/20110129035903/http://georgewbush-whitehouse.archives.gov/news/releases/2002/01/20020129-11.html.

33   Transcript of Rt Hon. Geoffrey Hoon's testimony to the Iraq Inquiry, 19 March 2010, p. 13.

34   Transcript of David Manning's testimony to the Iraq Inquiry, 30 November 2009, pp. 10–11.

35   Quoted in Anthony Seldon with Peter Snowdon and Daniel Collings, *Blair Unbound* (London: Pocket Books, 2008), p. 87.

36   Ibid., p. 88.

37   Ibid., p. 91.

38   Campbell, *Diaries, Volume 4*, p. 198.

39   Report of a Committee of Privy Counsellors, *The Report of the Iraq Inquiry*, HC 264 (London: HMSO, 6 July 2016), section 6.1, p. 190.

40   Memorandum from Secretary of State for Defence, Geoffrey Hoon, to the prime minister, MO 6/17/15K, 22 March 2002.

41   All quotes from Seldon et al., *Blair Unbound*, pp. 92–3.

42   Sumit Ganguly and Michael R. Kraig, 'The 2001–2002 Indo-Pakistani crisis: exposing the limits of coercive diplomacy', *Security Studies*, vol. 14, no. 2 (2005).

43   Campbell, *Diaries, Volume 4*, p. 124.

44   Jack Straw, *Last Man Standing: Memoirs of a Political Survivor* (Basingstoke: Macmillan, 2012), Kindle edn, loc. 4861.

45   James F. Dobbins, *After the Taliban: Nation Building in Afghanistan* (Washington DC: Potomac Books, 2008), pp. 119–20; Peter Marsden, *Afghanistan: Aid, Armies and Empires* (London: I.B. Tauris, 2009), p. 117.

46   Marsden, *Afghanistan*, pp. 138–40.

47   Thomas Barfield, *Afghanistan: A Cultural and Political History* (Princeton, NJ: Princeton University Press, 2010), p. 281.

48   Astri Suhrke, *When More Is Less: The International Project in Afghanistan* (London: Hurst, 2011), pp. 123–4.

49   Suhrke, *When More Is Less*, pp. 130–1; Marsden, *Afghanistan*, p. 139.

50   Suhrke, *When More Is Less*, pp. 134–5; Marsden, *Afghanistan*, p. 140.

51   Adam Grissom, 'Shoulder-to-Shoulder Fighting Different Wars: NATO Advisors and Military Adaptation in the Afghan National Army, 2001–2011', in Theo Farrell, Frans Osinga and James A. Russell, eds, *Military Adaptation in Afghanistan* (Stanford, CA: Stanford University Press, 2013), pp. 264–5; Sgt 1st Class Kathleen T. Rhem, 'American soldiers training Afghan national army', Defence News, 21 May 2002.

52   Grissom, 'Shoulder-to-Shoulder', p. 266.

53   *Securing Afghanistan's Future: Accomplishments and Strategic Path Forward*, A Government/International Agency Report, 17 March 2004, p. 88.

54   Quotes from Seth G. Jones, *In the Graveyard of Empires: America's War in Afghanistan* (New York: W. W. Norton & Co., 2009), pp. 165, 169–71, 174.

55   House of Commons Hansard Debates, 8 October 2001, column 814.

56 New Labour election manifesto 1997, at http://www.politicsresources. net/area/uk/man/lab97.htm.

57 Interview with former senior Foreign Office official, London, 21 April 2015.

58 Dawood Azami, 'The Politics of Drugs and Conflict: The Challenges of Insurgency and State-Building in Afghanistan', PhD thesis, University of Westminster, 2015, chapters 5 and 6.

59 Jack Fairweather, *The Good War: The Battle for Afghanistan, 2006–14* (London: Jonathan Cape, 2014), pp. 95–8.

60 Special Inspector General for Afghanistan Reconstruction, 'Future U.S. Counternarcotics Efforts in Afghanistan', Statement of John F. Sopko, Special Inspector General for Afghanistan, 15 January 2014, p. 4.

61 Interview with Jack Straw, London, 9 April 2014.

62 Interview with former US State Department official, Washington DC, 7 March 2012.

63 Interview with former senior US Department of Defense official, Washington DC, 9 March 2012.

64 Interview with former US senior national security official, London, 4 June 2013.

65 Interview with General Nick Carter, Army Headquarters, Andover, 1 April 2014.

66 Ibid.

67 Interview with Major General Dickie Davis, London, 13 July 2015.

68 Ibid.

69 Ibid.

70 Barbara J. Stapleton, *Disarming the Militias: DDR and DIAG and the implications for Peace Building*, Afghan Analysts Network, April 2013; Tim Bird and Alex Marshall, *Afghanistan: How the West Lost Its Way* (New Haven: Yale University Press, 2011), p. 129.

71 'Afghanistan: A Call for Security (Joint NGO Letter)', 17 June 2003.

72 Save the Children, *Provincial Reconstruction Teams and Military–Humanitarian Relations in Afghanistan* (London: Save the Children, 2004), p. 5.

73 Peter Viggo Jakobsen, *PRTs in Afghanistan: Successful But Not Sufficient*, DIIS Report 2005: 6 (Copenhagen: Danish Institute for International Studies, 2005), pp. 20–2.

74 Philip H. Gordon and Jeremy Shapiro, *Allies at War: America, Europe and the Crisis over Iraq* (New York: McGraw-Hill, 2004), chapter 5.

75 Ivo H. Daadler, 'The end of Atlanticism', *Survival*, vol. 45, no. 2 (2003), p. 147.

76 Rynning, *NATO in Afghanistan*, p. 87.

77 Seldon et al., *Blair Unbound*, pp. 135–71.

78 Campbell, *Diaries, Volume 4*, p. 513.

79 Bird and Marshall, *Afghanistan*, p. 117.

80   Jones, *In the Graveyard of Empires*, pp. 116–17.

81   Khalilzad, *The Envoy*, loc. 3444.

82   Interview with former US senior national security official, London, 4 June 2013.

83   Rynning, *NATO in Afghanistan*, pp. 48–9

84   Rob Johnson, *The Afghan Way of War* (London: Hurst, 2011).

85   General Sir Rob Fry, oral evidence to the House of Commons Defence Committee, 8 February 2011, in House of Commons Defence Committee, *Operations in Afghanistan*, Fourth Report of Session 2010–12, HC 554 (London: TSO, 17 July 2011), Ev 86, Q397.

86   Lord John Reid, oral evidence to the House of Commons Defence Committee, 8 February 2011, in House of Commons Defence Committee, *Operations in Afghanistan*, Fourth Report of Session 2010–12, HC 554 (London: TSO, 17 July 2011), Ev 90, Q409.

87   Interview with very senior British Army general, London, 28 February 2012.

88   Interview with General the Lord Richard Dannatt, London, 16 February 2012.

89   Interview with Desmond Bowen, London, 3 March 2012.

90   Confidential interview.

91   Interview with General Sir Rob Fry, London, 3 March 2012.

92   Interview with Desmond Bowen, London, 3 March 2012.

93   Interview with General the Lord Richard Dannatt, London, 16 February 2012.

94   Reid oral evidence to House of Commons Defence Committee, Ev 88, Q401.

95   Fry oral evidence to House of Commons Defence Committee, Ev 89, Q408.

96   Stephen M. Saideman, 'Canadian Forces in Afghanistan: Minority Government and Generational Change While Under Fire', in Theo Farrell, Frans Osinga and James A. Russell, eds, *Military Adaptation in Afghanistan* (Stanford, CA: Stanford University Press, 2013), p. 221.

97   Nick Beadle, 'Afghanistan and the Context of Iraq', in Michael Clarke, ed., *The Afghan Papers: Committing Britain to War in Helmand, 2005–06*, Whitehall Paper 77 (London: Royal United Services Institute for Defence and Security Studies, 2011), p. 75.

98   James Fergusson, *A Million Bullets: The Real Story of the British Army in Afghanistan* (London: Bantam Press, 2008), p. 172; Fry oral evidence to House of Commons Defence Committee, Ev 89, Q408.

99   Beadle, 'Afghanistan and the Context of Iraq', p. 75.

100 Fairweather, *Good War*, pp. 146–7.

101 Interview with General Sir Rob Fry, London, 3 March 2012.

Chapter 5: Bad Beginning

1   Mike Martin, *An Intimate War: An Oral History of the Helmand Conflict, 1978–2012* (London: Hurst, 2014), p. 113.

2   Interview with local elder no. 3, Nahr-e Seraj district, 2011.

3   Interview with local elder no. 8, Nad-e Ali district, 2011.

4   Interview with local elder no. 7, Nad-e Ali district, 2011.

5   Carter Malkasian, *War Comes to Garmser: Thirty Years of Conflict on the Afghan Frontier* (London: Hurst, 2013), p. 72.

6   Rajiv Chandrasekaran, 'In Afghanistan's Garmsir district, praise for a U.S. official's tireless work', *Washington Post*, 13 August 2011.

7   Malkasian, *War Comes to Garmser*, pp. 75–9.

8   Martin, *Intimate War*, p. 114.

9   Thomas E. Ricks, *Fiasco: The American Military Adventure in Iraq* (London: Allen Lane, 2006); George Packer, *The Assassins' Gate: America in Iraq* (London: Faber and Faber, 2007); Rajiv Chandrasekaran, *Imperial Life in the Emerald City: Inside Baghdad's Green Zone* (London: Bloomsbury, 2008).

10 Jack Fairweather, *A War of Choice: The British in Iraq, 2003–9* (London: Jonathan Cape, 2011), pp. 99–110; Patrick Cockburn, *Muqtada al-Sadr and the Shia Insurgency in Iraq* (London: Faber and Faber, 2008), pp. 172–202; Richard North, *Ministry of Defeat: The British War in Iraq, 2003–2009* (London: Continuum, 2009), p. 49.

11 Fairweather, *War of Choice*, p. 113.

12 Anthony Seldon with Peter Snowdon and Daniel Collings, *Blair Unbound* (London: Pocket Books, 2007), pp. 258–60.

13 Fairweather, *War of Choice*, p. 115.

14 Frank Ledwidge, *Losing Small Wars: British Military Failure in Iraq and Afghanistan* (New Haven: Yale University Press, 2011), p. 37.

15 Confidential interview, 6 April 2014.

16 Interview with General Sir Rob Fry, London, 3 March 2012.

17 Seldon et al., *Blair Unbound*, pp. 283–4.

18 Interview with General the Lord Richard Dannatt, London, 16 February 2012.

19 Jack Fairweather, *The Good War: The Battle for Afghanistan, 2006–14* (London: Jonathan Cape, 2014), pp. 145–6.

20 Confidential interview, February 2012.

21 Christopher Andrew, *The Defence of the Realm: The Authorized History of MI5* (London: Penguin, 2010), pp. 821–2.

22 *Report of the Official Account of the Bombings in London on 7 July 2005*, HC 1087 (London: The Stationery Office, 11 May 2006), p. 20, para. 45.

23 Philip Webster, '"War fuelled terrorism," says Kennedy', *The Times*, 13 July 2005.

24 Peter Bale, 'Blair vows attack on roots of terror', *The Times*, 9 July 2005.

25 BBC interview with Tony Blair on *BBC News*, 7 July 2015, at http://www.bbc.co.uk/news/uk-politics-33415477.

26 Lord John Reid, oral evidence to the House of Commons Defence Committee, 8 February 2011, in House of Commons Defence Committee, *Operations in Afghanistan*, Fourth Report of Session 2010–12, HC 554 (London: TSO, 17 July 2011), Ev 90, Q408–409.

27 David H. Ucko and Robert Egnell, *Counterinsurgency in Crisis: Britain and the Challenges of Modern Warfare* (New York: Columbia University Press, 2013), pp. 57–60.

28 North, *Ministry of Defeat*, p. 82.

29 Tony Blair, *A Journey* (London: Hutchinson, 2010), p. 470.

30 Confidential interview, April 2014.

31 Interview with Mark Etherington, London, 11 May 2012.

32 Rory Stewart, *The Places in Between* (London: Picador, 2004).

33 Interview with Minna Jarvenpaa, London, 16 February 2012.

34 Interview with former PCRU official, 22 February 2012.

35 Interview with Major General Gordon Messenger, MoD London, 11 May 2010.

36 Christina Lamb, 'Focus: Taking the fight to the Taliban', *Sunday Times*, 18 June 2006.

37 'Judges Special Award: Winner/Camp Bastion Military Base, Afghanistan', *Architects Journal*, 25 October 2007.

38 Nick Hopkins, 'Inside Camp Bastion', *Guardian*, 15 August 2011.

39 Interview with Mark Etherington, London, 11 May 2012.

40 Interview with Minna Jarvenpaa, London, 16 February 2012.

41 Interview with Mark Etherington, London, 11 May 2012.

42 Interview with former PCRU official, 22 February 2012.

43 Interview with Minna Jarvenpaa, London, 16 February 2012.

44 Interview with Major General Gordon Messenger, MoD London, 11 May 2010.

45 Joel Hafvenstein, *Opium Season: A Year on the Afghan Frontier* (Guilford, CT: The Lyons Press, 2007), p. 306.

46 Interview with former PCRU official, 22 February 2012.

47 Interview with Mark Etherington, London, 11 May 2012.

48 'Joint UK Plan for Helmand'. Document with author.

49 Theo Farrell and Stuart Gordon, 'COIN machine: the British military in Afghanistan', *Orbis*, vol. 53, no. 4 (2009), p. 667.

50 John Ware, 'UK's original Helmand deployment plan examined', *BBC News*, 22 June 2011, at http://www.bbc.co.uk/news/uk-13855804.

51 Christina Lamb, 'Focus'.

52 Interview with Minna Jarvenpaa, London, 16 February 2012; interview with former PCRU official, 22 February 2012.

53 Interview with former PCRU official, 22 February 2012.

54 Fairweather, *War of Choice*, pp. 233–4.

55 Secretary of State for Defence, Rt Hon. John Reid, Statement to the House of Commons, House of Commons Hansard Debates, 26 January 2006, column 1532; Thomas Harding, 'British troops will take control of lawless province as part of a multi-national Nato brigade', *Daily Telegraph,* 27 January 2006.

56 Cited in House of Commons Defence Committee, *UK Operations in Afghanistan*, Thirteenth Report of Session 2006–07, HC 408 (London: TSO, 18 July 2007), para. 95, p. 29.

57 Sean Rayment, *Into the Killing Zone* (London: Constable and Robinson, 2008), p. 36.

58 Ed Butler, 'Setting ourselves up for a fail in Afghanistan: where does accountability lie for decision-making in Helmand in 2005–06?', *RUSI Journal*, vol. 160, no. 1 (Feb/March 2015), p. 51.

59 Colonel Stuart Tootal, *Danger Close: Commanding 3 Para in Afghanistan* (London: John Murray, 2009), p. 30.

60 Matt Cavanagh, 'Ministerial decision-making in the run-up to the Helmand deployment', *RUSI Journal*, vol. 157, no. 2 (April/May 2012), p. 51.

61 Michael Evans, '3,300 British troops head into Taleban territory for first time', *The Times*, 27 January 2006.

62 Fairweather, *War of Choice*, p. 224.

63 Seldon et al., *Blair Unbound*, p. 392.

64 Ibid., p. 511.

65 Tom Bower, 'Chilcot's smoke screen', *Sunday Times*, 10 July 2016.

66 Cavanagh, 'Ministerial decision-making', p. 51; interview with senior government adviser, London, 4 April 2014.

67 Butler, 'Setting ourselves up for a fail in Afghanistan', p. 47.

68 Interview with senior government adviser, London, 4 April 2014.

69 House of Commons Defence Committee, *The UK Deployment to Afghanistan*, Fifth Report of Session 2005–06, HC 558 (London: TSO, 6 April 2006), Ev 15, Q89, Q92.

70 Ibid., Ev 21, Q129–130.

71 Ibid., para. 49, p. 17.

72 Mike Martin, *A Brief History of Helmand*, British Army Afghan COIN Centre, August 2011, pp. 48–9.

73 Martin, *Intimate War*, p. 119

74 Interview with local elder no. 7, Nad-e Ali district, March 2012.

75 Interviews with local elder no. 1, Nad-e Ali district, April 2012; local elder no. 6, Nad-e Ali district, June 2012.

76 Interviews with local elder no. 2, Garmsir district, June 2012; local elder no. 1, Nahr-e Seraj district, April 2012; local elder no. 2, Nahr-e Seraj district, June 2012; local elder no. 1, Nad-e Ali district, April 2012; local elder no. 6 Nad-e Ali district, June 2012; local elder no. 7, Nad-e Ali district, March 2012; group of local elders no. 9, Nad-e Ali district, March 2012; group of local elders no. 10, Nad-e Ali district, May 2011; group of local elders no. 11, Nad-e Ali district, May 2011; local elder no. 2, Musa Qala district, March 2012; local elder no. 4, Musa Qala district, March 2012.

77 Interview with local elder no. 2, Musa Qala district, March 2012.

78 Interviews with Taliban commander no. 2, Nad-e Ali district, December 2011; Taliban commander no. 3, Sangin district, May 2012; local elder no. 5, Nahr-e Seraj district, June 2012; local elder no. 2, Musa Qala district, March 2012; local elder no. 1, Sangin district, May 2012.

79 Interview with group of elders no. 9, Nad-e Ali district, March 2012.

80 Anand Gopal, 'The Taliban in Kandahar', p. 13, and Martine van Bijlert, 'The Taliban in Zabul and Uruzgan', p. 106, both in Peter Bergen, ed., *Talibanistan* (Oxford: Oxford University Press, 2012).

81 Antonio Giustozzi, presentation at International Studies Association annual convention, Atlanta, Georgia, 17 March 2016.

82 Martin, *Intimate War*, pp. 125–6.

83 Carlotta Gall, *The Wrong Enemy: America in Afghanistan, 2001–2014* (New York: Houghton Mifflin Harcourt, 2014), p. 110.

84 Christina Lamb, *Farewell Kabul: From Afghanistan to a More Dangerous World* (London: William Collins, 2015), p. 247.

85 Martin, *Brief History*, p. 49.

86 Cited in Tom Coghlan, 'The Taliban in Helmand: An Oral History', in Antonio Giustozzi, ed., *Decoding the New Taliban: Insights from the Afghan Field* (London: Hurst, 2009), p. 136.

87 Interview with local elder no. 1, Sangin district, May 2012.

88 Interviews with local elder no. 1, Sangin district, May 2012; local elder no. 2, Musa Qala district, March 2012.

89 Claudio Franco and Antonio Giustozzi, 'Revolution in the counter-revolution: efforts to centralize the Taliban's military leadership', *Central Asian Affairs*, vol. 3 (2016), p. 252.

90 Antonio Giustozzi, *Koran, Kalashnikov and Laptop: The Neo-Taliban Insurgency in Afghanistan* (London: Hurst, 2007), p. 101; see also Rob Johnson, *The Afghan Way of War* (London: Hurst, 2011), p. 272.

91 Interview with local elder no. 3, Musa Qala district, March 2012.

92   Interview with local elder no. 4, Musa Qala district, March 2012.

93   Interview with group of local elders no. 3, Sangin district, March 2012. Likewise, in Nahr-e Seraj, Taliban from outside the district began arriving 'in groups of two or three'. Interview with local elder no. 2, Nahr-e Seraj district, June 2012.

94   Interviews with local elder no. 1, Sangin district, May 2012; local elder no. 2, Musa Qala district, March 2012.

95   Interview with group of local elders no. 9, Nad-e Ali district, March 2012.

96   Interviews with local elder no. 5, Nahr-e Seraj district, June 2012; local elder no. 4, Nahr-e Seraj District, June 2012.

97   Interview with group of local elders no. 9, Nad-e Ali district, March 2012.

98   Malkasian, *War Comes to Garmser*, pp. 82–5.

99   Interview with local elder no. 1, Garmsir district, April 2012.

100 Malkasian, *War Comes to Garmser*, pp. 86–94.

101 Barbara J. Stapleton, 'Disarming the Militias: DDR and DIAG and the Implications for Peace Building', ANN Occasional Paper 02/2013, April 2013 (reprint of paper first published in 2008), p. 6.

102 Martin, *Intimate War*, p. 142.

103 Gall, *Wrong Enemy*, p. 122.

104 Interview with local elder no. 2, Nahr-e Seraj district, April 2012. This view was confirmed by a second local elder in a separate interview: interview with local elder no. 1, Nahr-e Seraj district, April 2012.

105 Fairweather, *Good War*, pp. 154–5.

106 Interview with Minna Jarvenpaa, London, 16 February 2012.

107 Interview with Sher Mohammed Akhundzada, BBC documentary, *Afghanistan: The Lion's Last Roar*, broadcast on BBC2, 26 October 2014.

108 Interview with Minna Jarvenpaa, London, 16 February 2012.

109 House of Commons Defence Committee, *The UK Deployment to Afghanistan*, Fifth Report of Session 2005–06, HC 558 (London: TSO, 6 April 2006), Ev 14, Q88.

110 Martin, *Intimate War*, pp. 153–4.

111 US Embassy cable, Kabul 001285, 23 March 2006, 'PRT/LASHKAR GAH – HELMAND VIOLENCE: CAUSES AND PROSPECTS', para. 1.

112 Tim Bird and Alex Marshall, *Afghanistan: How the West Lost Its Way* (New Haven: Yale University Press, 2011), p. 150.

113 Ronald E. Neumann, *The Other War: Winning and Losing in Afghanistan* (Washington DC: Potomac Books, 2009), pp. 52, 58.

114 Bird and Marshall, *Afghanistan*, p. 150.

115 'UK troops "to target terrorists"', *BBC News*, 24 April 2006, http://news. bbc.co.uk/go/pr/fr/-/1/hi/uk_politics/4935532.stm.

116 On their tour from April to October 2006, 16 Air Assault Brigade fired 480,000 bullets and 31,000 cannon rounds. James Fergusson, *A Million Bullets: The Real Story of the British Army in Afghanistan* (London: Bantam Press, 2008), p. 9.

117 The Parachute Regiment is the only infantry regiment to have its own selection course, called 'P Company', which all ranks and officers must pass before joining the regiment. Over a gruelling twenty-eight weeks in North Yorkshire, recruits are pushed to their very limits, both physically and psychologically. Typically, fewer than 50 per cent pass the course to become Paras. Rayment, *Into the Killing Zone*, pp. 34–5.

118 Interview with Brigadier Ed Butler, London, 16 May 2012.

119 Colonel Stuart Tootal, *Danger Close: Commanding 3 Para in Afghanistan* (London: John Murray, 2009), p. 19.

120 Ibid., p. 39.

121 Patrick Bishop, *3 Para* (London: HarperPress, 2007), pp. 33–4.

122 RC-South covered six provinces – Helmand, Kandahar, Uruzgan, Kabul, Nimroz and Day Kundi – but there was no international presence in the latter two.

123 Tootal, *Danger Close*, p. 29.

124 Marco Giannangeli, 'British soldiers suffer injuries from too-heavy weights', *Daily Express*, 25 July 2010.

125 Bishop, *3 Para*, pp. 39–40.

126 Tootal, *Danger Close*, p. 45.

127 General Sir Rob Fry, oral evidence to the House of Commons Defence Committee, 8 February 2011, in House of Commons Defence Committee, *Operations in Afghanistan*, Fourth Report of Session 2010–12, HC 554 (London: TSO, 17 July 2011), Ev 86, Q415.

128 Michael Clarke, 'The Helmand Decision', in Michael Clarke, ed., *The Afghan Papers: Committing Britain to War in Helmand, 2005–06*, Whitehall Paper 77 (London: RUSI, 2011), p. 22.

129 Ibid., p. 21.

130 Interview with UK official, London, 22 February 2012.

131 Interview with Mark Etherington, London, 11 May 2012.

132 Interview with Minna Jarvenpaa, London, 16 February 2012.

133 Post-Operation Interview, Brigadier E. A. Butler, Comd 16 Air Assault Brigade, Operation HERRICK 4, 21 November 2006, cited in British Army, Directorate Land Warfare, Lessons Exploitation Centre, Operation HERRICK Campaign Study, March 2015 [Redacted and released under FOI, January 2016], p. 1-1-4.

134 Interview with Major General Gordon Messenger, MoD, London, 11 May 2010.

135 Butler, 'Setting ourselves up for a fail in Afghanistan', p. 52; Michael Smith, 'Army pleads for more troops after firefight', *Sunday Times*, 23 April 2006.

136 Butler, 'Setting ourselves up for a fail in Afghanistan', p. 52.

137 US Embassy cable, Kabul 001285, 23 March 2006, 'PRT/LASHKAR GAH – HELMAND VIOLENCE: CAUSES AND PROSPECTS', para. 7.

138 US Embassy cable, Kabul 001353, 28 March 2006, 'PRT/LASHKAR GAH – MOUSA [*sic*] QALA DISTRICT CHIEF AND ELDERS WELCOME UK DEPLOYMENT', para. 3.

139 Interview with Brigadier Ed Butler, London, 16 May 2012.

140 Bishop, *3 Para*, p. 56.

141 Ben Farmer, 'British troops hand over Sangin in Afghanistan to US forces', *Daily Telegraph*, 20 September 2010.

142 Interview with Minna Jarvenpaa, London, 16 February 2012.

143 Tootal, *Danger Close*, p. 86.

144 Quote in Bishop, *3 Para*, p. 108.

145 Bishop, *3 Para*, pp. 118–20; Tootal, *Danger Close*, p. 104.

146 Rayment, *Into the Killing Zone*, p. 117.

147 Tootal, *Danger Close*, p. 111.

148 Major Mark Hammond, *Immediate Response* (London: Michael Joseph, 2009), quotes from pp. 121, 151, 157.

149 Tootal, *Danger Close*, pp. 102–3.

150 Captain Andrew Charchuk, '"Contact C": a forward observation officer with Task Force Orion', *Canadian Army Journal*, vol. 10, no. 2 (Summer 2007), p. 33.

151 Christina Lamb, 'Have you ever used a pistol?', *Sunday Times*, 2 July 2006.

152 Lamb, *Farewell Kabul*, pp. 288, 291.

153 General David Richards, *Taking Command* (London: Headline, 2014), Kindle edn, loc. 3307.

154 Tootal, *Danger Close*, pp. 119–24.

155 Fairweather, *Good War*, p. 198.

156 Interview with General the Lord David Richards, London, 19 November 2015.

157 Richards, *Taking Command*, loc. 2910–33; interview with General the Lord David Richards, London, 19 November 2015.

158 Sandy Gall, *War Against the Taliban: Why It All Went Wrong in Afghanistan* (London: Bloomsbury, 2012), p. 229.

159 Richards, *Taking Command*, loc. 2968–90;

160 Ibid., loc. 3002–14.

161 One RAND study noted of PAG that 'Such a structure is needed for any multinational counterinsurgency operation to be effective in drawing together all efforts by the host nation and outsiders'. Report of the Policy Panel (draft), 'Integrating Instruments of Power and Influence: The Bottom-Up Approach', RAND Corporation & American Academy of Diplomacy, 23 March 2009, p. 14.

162 Neumann, *The Other War*, p. 107.

163 Sherard Cowper-Coles, *Cables from Kabul: The Inside Story of the West's Afghanistan Campaign* (London: HarperPress, 2011), p. 91.

164 Daniel Korski, *Afghanistan: Europe's Forgotten War* (London: European Council on Foreign Relations, 2008), p. 34.

165 International Crisis Group, 'Tackling Afghanistan's Insurgency: No Quick Fixes', Asia Report no. 123 (November 2006), p. 21.

166 Neumann, *The Other War*, pp. 106–7.

167 Bishop, *3 Para*, pp. 199, 211; Tootal, *Danger Close*, p. 170.

168 Tootal, *Danger Close*, p. 173.

169 Bishop, *3 Para*, pp. 224–5.

170 Anthony Loveless, *Blue Sky Warriors: The RAF in Afghanistan in Their Own Words* (Somerset: Hayes Publishing, 2010), pp. 22–3.

171 Tootal, *Danger Close*, pp. 205–6.

172 Bishop, *3 Para*, pp. 227–31.

173 Tootal, *Danger Close*, pp. 188, 192.

174 Tootal, *Danger Close*, pp. 194–5; Bishop, *3 Para*, pp. 251–2.

175 Bishop, *3 Para*, pp. 245–8. The story is recounted in the 2014 movie *Kilo Two Bravo* (originally released under the title *Kajaki*). See http://kajaki-movie.com/.

176 Tootal, *Danger Close*, p. 233.

177 Gall, *War Against the Taliban*, pp. 210–11.

178 Ibid., p. 111.

179 Richard J. Stacpoole-Ryding, *Maiwand: The Last Stand of the 66th (Berkshire) Regiment in Afghanistan, 1880* (Stroud, Glos: The History Press, 2008).

180 Interview with General the Lord David Richards, London, 19 November 2015.

181 Bishop, *3 Para*, pp. 255–6.

182 Richards, *Taking Command*, loc. 3658; Gall, *War Against the Taliban*, p. 239.

183 Gall, *War Against the Taliban*, p. 111.

184 Interview with General the Lord David Richards, London, 19 November 2015.

185   Interview with Taliban leader, Dubai, March 2013.

186   Michael Semple, *Reconciliation in Afghanistan* (Washington DC: United States Institute for Peace, 2009), pp. 79–82; Bishop, *3 Para*, pp. 257–60.

187   'US envoy takes British to task over pullout', *The Times*, 25 October 2006.

188   US Department of State cable, Kabul 005584, 27 November 2006, 'MUSA QALA AGREEMENT: OPPOSING INTERESTS AND OPPOSING VIEWS, BUT ONE WAY FORWARD', para. 19.

189   Richards, *Taking Command*, loc. 3882–94.

190   US Department of State cable, Kabul 005399, 7 November 2006, 'PRT LASHKAR GAH – NORTH QUIET AFTER ISAF WITHDRAWAL', paras 1, 2 and 14.

191   Michael Evans, 'British leave after "tactical defeat" of Taleban', *The Times*, 18 October 2006.

192   US Department of State cable, Kabul 005442, 13 November 2006, 'BOUCHER AND SPANTA ON JIRGAS, MUSA QALA, IRAN AND STRATEGIC PARTNERSHIP', para. 9.

193   Martin, *Intimate War*, p. 166.

194   US Department of State cable, Kabul 005584, 27 November 2006, 'MUSA QALA AGREEMENT: OPPOSING INTERESTS AND OPPOSING VIEWS, BUT ONE WAY FORWARD', para. 7.

195   Martin, *Intimate War*, p. 166; US Department of State, Kabul 005399, 7 November 2006, 'PRT LASHKAR GAH – NORTH QUIET AFTER ISAF WITH-DRAWAL', para. 3.

196   Anthony Loyd, 'Attempts by warlords and criminals to sack the Governor of Helmand would dash peace efforts, writes our correspondent', *The Times*, 9 November 2006.

197   US Department of State cable, Kabul 005584, 27 November 2006, 'MUSA QALA AGREEMENT: OPPOSING INTERESTS AND OPPOSING VIEWS, BUT ONE WAY FORWARD', paras 15–16.

198   Carlotta Gall, 'Taliban truce in district of Afghanistan sets off debate', *New York Times*, 2 December 2006.

199   US Department of State cable, Kabul 005584, 27 November 2006, 'MUSA QALA AGREEMENT: OPPOSING INTERESTS AND OPPOSING VIEWS, BUT ONE WAY FORWARD', para. 19.

200   Martin, *Intimate War*, p. 166.

201   Semple, *Reconciliation*, p. 83.

202   US Department of State cable, Kabul 005698, 1 December 2006, 'MUSA QALA ELDERS RETURN TO EMBASSY TO PROVIDE ASSURANCES AND APPEAL FOR ASSISTANCE', para. 7.

203   Jeremy Page and Tim Albone, 'Blow for Britain as Helmand's "cleanest" governor is sacked', *The Times*, 9 December 2006.

204   Semple, *Reconciliation*, pp. 83–4.

205 Gall, *War Against the Taliban*, p. 242.

206 US Department of State cable, Kabul 005584, 1 December 2006, 'CODEL DREIER AND PRESIDENT KARZAI ON PAKISTAN, MUSA QALA, CORRUPTION AND POLITICAL PARTIES', para. 4.

207 Interview with Taliban leader, Dubai, March 2013.

208 Martin, *Intimate War*, p. 163.

209 US Department of State cable, Kabul 001014, 6 April 2007, 'ONDCP WALTERS' MARCH 17–20 VISIT TO AFGHANISTAN', para. 2.

210 Lamb, *Farewell Kabul*, p. 380.

Chapter 6: Mission Impossible

1 Operation HERRICK 5, Post Operation Report (POR), April 2007.

2 Sean Rayment, *Into the Killing Zone* (London: Constable, 2008), p. 131.

3 Op HERRICK 5, POR.

4 Ewen Southby-Tailyour, *Helmand, Afghanistan: 3 Commando Brigade* (London: Ebury Press, 2008), pp. 34–5.

5 Ibid., p. 60.

6 Op HERRICK 4, POR, October 2006.

7 Tom Coghlan, 'The Taliban in Helmand: An Oral History', in Antonio Giustozzi, ed., *Decoding the New Taliban: Insights from the Afghan Field* (London: Hurst, 2009), p. 130.

8 Foreign and Commonwealth Office, eGram 448542/06 (attached document), 'Musa Qala and Sangin Shura Agreements', 2 November 2006, para. 2.

9 Foreign and Commonwealth Office, eGram 40720/06, 'NOSEC: Afghanistan: The Sangin Shura', 18 September 2006, para. 6.

10 Foreign and Commonwealth Office, eGram 41931/06, 'NOSEC: Afghanistan: Helmand Shuras – How Far Should We Go', 25 September 2006, summary and paras 5–6.

11 Foreign and Commonwealth Office, eGram 448542/06 (attached document), 'Musa Qala and Sangin Shura Agreements', 2 November 2006, paras 10–11.

12 US Department of State cable, Kabul 005399, 7 November 2006, 'PRT LASHKAR GAH – NORTH QUIET AFTER ISAF WITHDRAWAL', para. 13.

13 Foreign and Commonwealth Office, eGram 45506/06, 'NOSEC: Afghanistan: Sangin Update', 23 November 2006, para. 5.

14 Southby-Tailyour, *Helmand*, p. 34.

15 Sean Rayment, 'Commandos kill up to 10 Taliban in gun battle', *Daily Telegraph*, 31 October 2006.

16   Southby-Tailyour, *Helmand*, p. 45.

17   Commander Ade Orchard with James Barrington, *Joint Force Harrier* (London: Penguin, 2009), p. 142.

18   Southby-Tailyour, *Helmand*, p. 123.

19   16 Air Assault Brigade had formed similar units, which they called Manoeuvre Outreach Groups (also abbreviated to MOGs). But the Paras made less use of MOGs and gave them more discrete tasks, such as escorting convoys or resupplying British outstations. Colonel Stuart Tootal, *Danger Close* (London: John Murray, 2009), p. 242; Rayment, *Into the Killing Zone*, p. 120.

20   Op HERRICK 5, POR.

21   Southby-Tailyour, *Helmand*, p. 77.

22   Carter Malkasian, *War Comes to Garmser: Thirty Years of Conflict on the Afghan Frontier* (London: Hurst, 2013), p. 104; for a first-hand account by the commander of the 1 Royal Irish advisory group, see Doug Beattie, *An Ordinary Soldier* (London: Pocket Books, 2008).

23   Southby-Tailyour, *Helmand*, pp. 247–52; Rayment, *Into the Killing Zone*, pp. 156–9.

24   Op HERRICK 5, POR.

25   Op HERRICK 6, POR, October 2007.

26   Interview with Brigadier John Lorimer, PJHQ Northwood, 29 June 2010.

27   Confidential source.

28   Hansard, 24 July 2006, column 758W; Hansard, 12 December 2007, column 332; Hansard, 29 October 2008, columns 28WS–30WS. Similarly, in 2007 the US Defense Secretary launched a 'crash program to buy thousands of these vehicles' as fast as possible. Robert Gates, *Duty: Memoirs of a Secretary at War* (Virgin Digital, 2014), Kindle edn, loc. 2189.

29   Op HERRICK 6, POR.

30   Interview with Brigadier John Lorimer, PJHQ Northwood, 29 June 2010; Headquarters 12 Mechanised Brigade, Ward Barracks, Bulford, Wiltshire, TFH/H6/1513/22/POR, 19 October 2007.

31   Colonel Richard Kemp and Chris Hughes, *Attack State Red* (London: Michael Joseph, 2009), p. 402.

32   John Stone, 'The point of the bayonet', *Technology and Culture*, vol. 53, no. 4 (2012), pp. 885–908.

33   Kemp and Hughes, *Attack State Red*, p. 407.

34   Ibid., p. 303.

35   12 Mechanised Brigade, 'Operation Herrick 6: Afghanistan, 11 April – 10 October 2007', post-operation booklet, 2007, p. 11.

36   Op HERRICK 6, POR.

37   Interview with Brigadier John Lorimer, PJHQ Northwood, 29 June 2010.

38   Jack Fairweather, *A War of Choice: The British in Iraq, 2003–9* (London: Jonathan Cape, 2011), p. 237.

39   US Department of State cable, Kabul 001023, 28 March 2007, 'PRT/ LASHKAR GAH – GOVERNOR: SECURITY LIMITS TRIBAL OUTREACH EFFORTS', para. 7; US Department of State cable, Kabul 001055, 11 April 2007, 'PRT LASHKAR GAH: SEMI-ANNUAL HELMAND REVIEW', para. 9.

40   Stephen Grey, *Operation Snakebite: The Explosive True Story of an Afghan Desert Siege* (London: Viking, 2009), p. 62.

41   Op HERRICK 5, POR, p. 2–0–3; Op HERRICK 6, POR, p. 2.

42   Christina Lamb, *Farewell Kabul: From Afghanistan to a More Dangerous World* (London: William Collins, 2015), p. 292.

43   David Killcullen, *The Accidental Guerilla: Fighting Small Wars in the Midst of a Big One* (London: Hurst, 2011).

44   Grey, *Operation Snakebite*, p. 13.

45   Ian S. Livingston, Heather L. Messera and Michael O'Hanlon, 'Afghanistan Index: Tracking Variables of Reconstruction and Security in Post 9/11 Afghanistan', Brookings Institution, 29 March 2011, figures 1.29 and 1.30, p. 15.

46   Sarah Sewall, 'The civilian in American warfare: normative pathways and institutional imperatives', DPhil thesis, St Antony's College, Oxford, 2010, p. 281.

47   Barry Bearak, 'Karzai calls coalition "careless"', *New York Times*, 24 June 2007.

48   Lamb, *Farewell Kabul*, pp. 384–6.

49   Leigh Neville, *The British Army in Afghanistan, 2006–14* (Oxford: Osprey, 2015), p. 33.

50   Sean Rayment, 'Soldier who shot dead suspected Taliban bomber facing murder charges', *Daily Telegraph*, 31 December 2011.

51   Post Operation Interview (POI) with Brigadier Andrew Mackay, p. 2.

52   Interview with Major General Andrew Mackay, London, 6 February 2013.

53   Ibid.

54   POI, Mackay, p. 18.

55   Grey, *Operation Snakebite*, pp. 130–1.

56   Theo Farrell, Sten Rynning and Terry Terriff, *Transforming Military Power since the Cold War: Britain, France and the United States, 1991–2012* (Cambridge: Cambridge University Press, 2013), pp. 138–40.

57   POI, Mackay, p. 8.

58   Interview with Major General Andrew Mackay, London, 6 February 2013.

59   Ibid.

60   Grey, *Operation Snakebite*, pp. 61, 64–5.

61   Commander British Forces, Op HERRICK 7, 'Counterinsurgency in Helmand: Task Force Operational Design', 30 October 2007, para. 9.

62   'Counterinsurgency in Helmand', p. 6. Mackay's thinking on this was influenced by David Galula's classic short book, *Counterinsurgency Warfare: Theory and Practice* (1964).

63   Mackay found British Army doctrine on COIN to be completely outdated. In fact, the army did have a COIN manual from 1995 called *Countering Insurgent Operations*, that was fit for purpose, and indeed informed the US Army's new FM 3–24. However, it was not mass-produced and promulgated because in the mid 1990s the main focus of the British Army was on peace operations, and so it had been forgotten about a decade later. For discussion, see Col. Alex Alderson, 'The validity of British Army Counterinsurgency Doctrine after the war in Iraq, 2003–2009', PhD thesis, UK Defence Academy College of Management and Technology, Cranfield University, 2009.

64   John A. Nagl, *Learning to Eat Soup with a Knife: Counterinsurgency Lessons from Malaya and Vietnam* (Chicago: Chicago University Press, 2002).

65   This idea has been challenged by revisionist historians. First, new historical scholarship on Britain's 'dirty wars of decolonisation' has revealed that British military campaigns were not as 'population-centric' as previously believed. Second, the British Army had no institutional memory of its various colonial counter-insurgency campaigns from the 1940s to 1960s: learning happened *within* campaigns but not across them. See Benjamin Grob-Fitzgibbon, *Imperial Endgame: Britain's Dirty Wars and the End of Empire* (New York: Palgrave Macmillan, 2011); David French, *The British Way in Counter-Insurgency, 1945–1967* (Oxford: Oxford University Press, 2011); Huw Bennett, *Fighting the Mau Mau: The British Army and Counter-Insurgency in the Kenya Emergency* (Cambridge: Cambridge University Press, 2012); Victoria Nolan, *Military Leadership and Counterinsurgency: The British Army and Small War Strategy since World War II* (New York: I.B. Tauris, 2012).

66   James A. Russell, *Innovation, Transformation and War: Counterinsurgency Operations in Anbar and Ninewa Provinces, Iraq, 2005–2007* (Stanford: Stanford University Press, 2011); Philipp Rotmann, David Tohn and Jaron Wharton, 'Learning under fire: progress and dissent in the US military', *Survival*, vol. 51, no. 4 (2009), pp. 31–48.

67   'Can this man save Iraq?', *Newsweek*, 27 June 2004.

68   Moreover, he persuaded the US Marine Corps to publish it as a joint army–marine field manual. FM 3–24 was subsequently published by a university press. *The U.S. Army and Marine Corps Counterinsurgency Field*

Manual (Chicago: Chicago University Press, 2007). The story is captured in Fred Kaplan, *The Insurgents: David Petraeus and the Plot to Change the American Way of War* (New York: Simon & Schuster, 2013).

69 Interview with Major General Andrew Mackay, London, 6 February 2013.

70 'Counterinsurgency in Helmand', para. 9.

71 Interview with Major Geoff Minton, 52 Brigade headquarters, Redford Barracks, Edinburgh, 29 June 2009.

72 'Counterinsurgency in Helmand', Annex A, para. 7.

73 Interview with Major Geoff Minton, 52 Brigade headquarters, Redford Barracks, Edinburgh, 29 June 2009.

74 Interview with Brigadier Andrew Mackay, 23 April 2008.

75 Ibid., DCDC Shrivenham, 29 January 2009.

76 Telephone interview with Lieutenant Colonel Richard Wardlaw, 9 February 2009.

77 Ibid.

78 Interview with NKETs officer for Operations Company in Lashkar Gar, 2 YORKS BG, 52 Brigade HQ, Redford Cavalry Barracks, Edinburgh, 29 June 2009.

79 Mike Martin, *An Intimate War: An Oral History of the Helmand Conflict* (London: Hurst, 2014), p. 169.

80 Grey, *Operation Snakebite*, pp. 54–7, 69–70.

81 Ibid., pp. 53–4, 128.

82 Ibid., pp. 93–7, 102; POI, Mackay, pp. 11–12.

83 Rory Stewart, 'Ousted, the men who rumbled the Afghan fantasy', *Sunday Times*, 30 December 2007.

84 Michael Semple, *Reconciliation in Afghanistan* (Washington DC: United States Institute for Peace Press, 2009), pp. 54–6.

85 Martin, *Intimate War*, p. 171.

86 Grey, *Operation Snakebite*, pp. 42–3.

87 Interview with Michael Semple, Atlanta, Georgia, 16 March 2016.

88 Grey, *Operation Snakebite*, pp. 124, 152.

89 Sherard Cowper-Coles, *Cables from Kabul: The Inside Story of the West's Afghanistan Campaign* (London: HarperPress, 2011), p. 118.

90 Grey, *Operation Snakebite*, p. 148.

91 Ibid., pp. 188–9.

92 Ibid., p. 200.

93 Michael Evans, 'Brigadier strides into battle against Taleban', *The Times*, 17 December 2007.

94 Grey, *Operation Snakebite*, pp. 230–51.

95 Stephen Grey, 'Inside the Taliban's fallen town of fear', *Sunday Times*, 16 December 2007.

96   Grey, *Operation Snakebite*, pp. 276–7, 280–1.

97   Ibid., pp. 291–2.

98   On the first day of the US air campaign, the entire Taliban air force was destroyed. With no air force to run, the following day Naquib switched sides, much to the delight of his wife, who could see even then that things were not going to end well for the Taliban. Interview with Michael Semple, Atlanta, Georgia, 16 March 2016.

99   Interview with Michael Semple, Atlanta, Georgia, 16 March 2016.

100 Alastair Leithead, '"Great Game" or just misunderstanding', *BBC News*, 5 January 2008.

101 Grey, *Operation Snakebite*, p. 294.

102 Cowper-Coles, *Cables from Kabul*, p. 130.

103 Interview with Michael Semple, Atlanta, Georgia, 16 March 2016.

104 Grey, *Operation Snakebite*, p. 289.

105 POI, Mackay, p. 12.

106 Nick Meo, 'Taleban warlord gets new job as governor', *The Times*, 9 January 2008.

107 Anthony Loyd, 'The mysterious Afghan warlord trusted to spread peace in a divided province', *The Times*, 12 January 2008.

108 Martin, *Intimate War*, p. 170.

109 US Department of State cable, Kabul 001280, 26 May 2008, 'MUSA QALA POLITICAL UPDATE: MULLAH SALAAM'S LEADERSHIP WAVERING', para. 2.

110 Jack Fairweather, *The Good War: The Battle for Afghanistan, 2006–14* (London: Jonathan Cape, 2014), p. 246.

111 Directorate Land Warfare, Lessons Exploitation Centre, Operation HERRICK Campaign Study, March 2015 [redacted and publicly released version], p. 2–1–12.

112 Grey, *Operation Snakebite*, pp. 305–7.

113 Ibid., p. 306.

114 Islamic Republic of Afghanistan, Ministry of Counter-Narcotics, *National Drug Control Strategy: An Updated Five-Year Strategy for Tackling the Illicit Drug Problem* (Kabul, January 2006), p. 10; David Mansfield, *A State Built on Sand: How Opium Undermined Afghanistan* (London: Hurst, 2016), p. 219; Lamb, *Farewell Kabul*, pp. 256, 265.

115 Mansfield, *A State Built on Sand*, pp. 56–7.

116 Lamb, *Farewell Kabul*, pp. 257–8, 265.

117 Ministry of Counter-Narcotics, *National Drug Control Strategy*, p. 21.

118 Mansfield, *A State Built on Sand*, p. 234.

119 David Mansfield and Adam Pain, 'Alternative Livelihoods: Substance or Slogan?', AREU Briefing Paper, Kabul, October 2005.

120 Joel Hafvenstein, *Opium Season: A Year on the Afghan Frontier* (Guilford, CT: The Lyons Press, 2007).

121 Lamb, *Farewell Kabul*, p. 255.

122 US Department of State cable, Kabul 001267, 22 March 2006, 'AMBASSADOR'S VISIT TO HELMAND: POPPY ERADICATION EFFORTS', paras 2 and 3.

123 Antonio Giustozzi, *Koran, Kalashnikov and Laptop: The Neo-Taliban Insurgency in Afghanistan* (London: Hurst, 2007), p. 61.

124 Jon Lee Andersen, 'Letter from Afghanistan: the Taliban's opium war: the difficulties and dangers of the eradication program', *New Yorker*, 9 July 2007.

125 Interview with group of local elders no. 9, Nad-e Ali district, March 2012.

126 Interview with local elder no. 1, Nad-e Ali district, December 2011.

Chapter 7: The Campaign Flounders

1 Interview with Hugh Powell, London, 13 May 2010.

2 UK Regional Coordinator for Afghanistan, 'Review of the UK Joint Plan for Helmand', October 2006.

3 Confidential source.

4 Theo Farrell and Stuart Gordon, 'COIN machine: the British military in Afghanistan', *Orbis* (Autumn 2009), pp. 672–3. Gordon was a member of the team that produced the 2008 Helmand Road Map. See also Peter Dahl Thruelsen, 'Counterinsurgency and the comprehensive approach: Helmand Province, Afghanistan' (2008), www.smallwars-journal.com.

5 This is the key finding from Stuart Gordon, *Winning Hearts and Minds? Examining the Relationship between Aid and Security in Afghanistan's Helmand Province* (Medford, MA: Feinstein International Center, Tufts University, 2011).

6 Interviews on BBC documentary, *Afghanistan: The Lion's Last Roar*, broadcast on BBC2, 26 October 2014.

7 Interview with Hugh Powell, London, 13 May 2010; numbers on growth of PRT staff from FCO conference on 'Capturing Lessons from the Helmand PRT', Wilton Park, 3–4 December 2014.

8 Patrick Bishop, *Ground Truth, 3 Para: Return to Afghanistan* (London: HarperPress, 2009), p. 18.

9 Post-operational interview with Brigadier Mark Carleton-Smith, Colchester, 24 November 2008.

10 Bishop, *Ground Truth*, p. 18.

11   Interview with Brigadier Mark Carleton-Smith, MoD, London, 20 May 2010.

12   Interview with Hugh Powell, London, 13 May 2010.

13   Sherard Cowper-Coles, *Cables from Kabul: The Inside Story of the West's Afghanistan Campaign* (London: HarperPress, 2011), p. 167.

14   Interview with Brigadier Mark Carleton-Smith, MoD, London, 20 May 2010.

15   Frank Ledwidge, *Losing Small Wars: British Military Failure in Iraq and Afghanistan* (New Haven: Yale University Press, 2011), pp. 69–70; Sam Kiley, *Desperate Glory: At War in Helmand with Britain's 16 Air Assault Brigade* (London: Bloomsbury, 2009), pp. 6–7.

16   Interview with Brigadier Mark Carleton-Smith, MoD, London, 20 May 2010.

17   Sallust, *Operation Herrick: An Unofficial History of British Military Operations in Afghanistan, 2001–2014* (self-published book, 2015), chapter 7, no page numbers.

18   Jack Fairweather, *The Good War: The Battle for Afghanistan, 2006–14* (London: Jonathan Cape, 2014), p. 282; interview with senior Foreign Office official, London, 21 April 2015.

19   Kiley, *Desperate Glory*, pp. 13–21, 24–5.

20   Carter Malkasian, *War Comes to Garmser: Thirty Years of Conflict on the Afghan Frontier* (London: Hurst, 2013), pp. 120–1.

21   24th MEU Public Affairs, 'Op Azada Wosa: Recounting the 24th MEU's Progress in Garmsir', 21 July 2008, http://www.24thmeu.marines.mil/News/ArticleDisplayPage/tabid/374/Article/511001/operation-azada-wosa-recounting-the-24th-meus-progress-in-garmsir.aspx.

22   Interview with Taliban commander no. 8, Garmsir district, 2012.

23   Malkasian, *War Comes to Garmser*, pp. 120–4.

24   Kiley, *Desperate Glory*, p. 24.

25   Malkasian, *War Comes to Garmser*, pp. 124–5.

26   Kiley, *Desperate Glory*, p. 37.

27   Terri Judd, 'How British forces took Garmsir from the Taliban', *Independent*, 25 August 2008.

28   Cowper-Coles, *Cables from Kabul*, p. 193.

29   Malkasian, *War Comes to Garmser*, p. 129.

30   Terri Judd, 'A dam shame: what a stalled hydropower project says about failures in Afghanistan', *Time*, 15 December 2011.

31   Interview with former senior Foreign Office official, London, 21 April 2015.

32   Kiley, *Desperate Glory*, pp. 181–2.

33   Interview with Brigadier Mark Carleton-Smith, MoD, London, 20 May 2010.

34 Kiley, *Desperate Glory*, pp. 136–7, 181–2.

35 Bishop, *Ground Truth*, pp. 226–8.

36 Rufus McNeil, 'How we got a 200-tonne turbine past the Taliban', *The Times*, 25 September 2008.

37 Notes from campaign debrief, 16 Air Assault Brigade, Merville Barracks, Essex, 3 December 2008.

38 Kiley, *Desperate Glory*, pp. 200–16; Sallust, *Operation Herrick*, chapter 7 (no page numbers).

39 Jeremy Page, 'Triumph for British forces in Boy's Own-style Kajaki mission', *The Times*, 3 September 2008.

40 Terri Judd, 'Operation Eagle's Summit: the inside story of a daring foray into Taliban territory', *Independent*, 2 September 2008.

41 Noah Arjomand, *Eagle's Summit Revisited: Decision-Making in the Kajaki Dam Project*, Afghan Analysts Network report, 2013.

42 Sune Engel Rasmussen, 'British engineers evacuated from key Afghan dam as Taliban approach', *Guardian*, 18 September 2015.

43 Arjomand, *Eagle's Summit Revisited*, p. 22.

44 Interview with Brigadier Mark Carleton-Smith, MoD, 20 May 2010.

45 Interview with former senior US national security official, Washington DC, 9 March 2010.

46 Caroline Gammel, 'War in Afghanistan cannot be won, British commander Brigadier Mark Carleton-Smith warns', *Daily Telegraph*, 5 October 2008.

47 Richard Norton-Taylor, 'Talks with Taliban the only way forward in Afghanistan, says UK commander', *Guardian*, 6 October 2008.

48 Notes from collective debrief of 3 Commando Brigade at RM Barracks, Stonehouse, Plymouth, 7 July 2009.

49 Interview with 3 Commando Brigade officer (A), MoD, London, 1 July 2010.

50 POR, 3 Commando Brigade, H9, April 2009.

51 Jon Riley, 'NATO Operations in Afghanistan, 2008–2009: A Theatre-Level View', in Jonathan Bailey, Richard Iron and Hew Strachan, eds, *British Generals in Blair's Wars* (Abingdon, Oxon: Routledge, 2016), p. 262.

52 Sallust, *Operation Herrick*, chapter 9 (no page numbers).

53 Ewen Southby-Tailyour, *3 Commando Brigade: Helmand Assault* (London: Ebury Press, 2010), p. 49.

54 Interview with 3 Commando Brigade officer (A), MoD, London, 1 July 2010; Southby-Tailyour, *3 Commando Brigade*, pp. 58–61.

55 Mike Martin further suggests that Abdul Rahman Jan may have been behind the attacks along with Sher Mohammed Akhundzada, in order

to demonstrate that Mangal had lost control of Helmand. Martin, *An Intimate War: An Oral History of the Helmand Conflict* (London: Hurst, 2014), pp. 177–8.

56 Kiley, *Desperate Glory*, p. 229.

57 POR, 3 Commando Brigade, H9, April 2009.

58 Interview with 3 Commando Brigade officer (B), MoD, London, 1 July 2010.

59 Email to author from Major General Gordon Messenger, 5 January 2012.

60 Southby-Tailyour, *3 Commando Brigade*, pp. 61–5.

61 Interview with 3 Commando Brigade officer (A), MoD, London, 1 July 2010.

62 Interview with 3 Commando Brigade officer (B), MoD, London, 1 July 2010.

63 Interview with 3 Commando Brigade officer (A), MoD, London, 1 July 2010.

64 http://helmandblog.blogspot.co.uk/2009/09/one-of-toughest-building-sites-in-world.html.

65 Directorate Land Warfare, Lessons Exploitation Centre, *Operation HERRICK Campaign Study*, March 2015 [redacted and publicly released version], pp. 2–1–12 to 2–1–14.

66 Interview with 3 Commando Brigade officer (B), MoD, London, 1 July 2010.

67 Martin, *Intimate War*, pp. 182–3.

68 Ibid., p. 183.

69 Ibid., pp. 88–9.

70 Interview with senior PRT official, Lashkar Gah, Helmand, 29 May 2010.

71 Notes from collective debrief of 3 Commando Brigade at RM Barracks, Stonehouse, Plymouth, 7 July 2009.

72 Southby-Tailyour, *3 Commando Brigade*, p. 158.

73 POR, 3 Commando Brigade, H9, April 2009.

74 Interview with Brigadier Tim Radford, MoD, London, 17 May 2010.

75 Jack Fairweather, *The Good War: The Battle for Afghanistan, 2006–14* (London: Jonathan Cape, 2014), p. 303.

76 Interview with Hugh Powell, London, 13 May 2010; interview with Brigadier Tim Radford, MoD, London, 17 May 2010.

77 Confidential source.

78 Interview with Brigadier Tim Radford, MoD, London, 17 May 2010.

79 Jon Boone, 'Battle of Babaji: a fight for hearts and minds in Afghanistan, but none are to be found', *Guardian*, 24 June 2009.

80 Sallust, *Operation Herrick*, chapter 10 (no page numbers).

81 Toby Harnden, *Dead Men Risen* (London: Quercus, 2012), p. 296.

82 Ibid., pp. 301–8.

83 Ibid., pp. 327–33.

84 'Prince Charles "mortified" by death of Rupert Thorneloe in Helmand', *The Times*, 3 July 2009.

85 Sean Rayment, 'Helmand surgeon tells of her fight to save lives', *Daily Telegraph*, 25 July 2009.

86 Margaret Evison, *Death of a Soldier: A Mother's Story* (London: Biteback Publishing, 2012), pp. 10–11.

87 Michael Evans, 'US surgeons drafted in as British medics exhausted by casualty surge', *The Times*, 31 July 2009.

88 Sallust, *Operation Herrick*, chapter 10 (no page numbers).

89 Richard Norton-Taylor, 'Deadly, and maybe decisive: officers hail Panther's Claw', *Guardian*, 27 July 2009.

90 Conversations with a number of very senior British military officers, summer 2009; Thomas Harding, 'MoD sends 125 troops to Afghanistan after heavy losses', *Daily Telegraph*, 24 July 2009; Sallust, *Operation Herrick*, chapter 10 (no page numbers).

91 Deborah Haynes, 'Two more British troops killed as Afghan operation hailed a success', *The Times*, 27 July 2009.

92 Harnden, *Dead Men Risen*, pp. 472–3, 492–3.

93 Nick Meo, 'Afghan election dispatch: the perils of voting in Helmand province', *Daily Telegraph*, 15 August 2009.

94 Tom Coghlan, 'President Karzai's supporters "buy" votes for Afghanistan election', *The Times*, 12 August 2009.

95 Jeremy Page, 'Hamid Karzai accused by rival candidate of rigging Afghan election', *The Times*, 24 August 2009.

96 Michael Smith, Sarah Baxter and Jerome Starkey, 'New British and US strategy to break Taliban', *The Times*, 5 July 2009.

97 Rajiv Chandrasekaran, 'U.S. troops move deeper into Afghanistan's Helmand province; one Marine killed', *Washington Post*, 3 July 2009.

98 Author's observations from three-day visit to 2/8 headquarters, FOB Delhi, Garmsir, October 2009.

99 Interview with Lieutenant Colonel Christian Cabaniss, FOB Delhi, Garmsir district, Helmand, 31 October 2009.

100 Interview with Colonel Christian Cabaniss, London, 31 March 2011.

101 Malkasian, *War Comes to Garmser*, pp. 147–8.

102 Rajiv Chandrasekaran, 'In Afghanistan's Garmsir District, praise for a U.S. official's tireless work', *Washington Post*, 13 August 2011.

103 Ipsos MORI, 'Attitudes to Afghanistan campaign', 24 July 2009. Report downloaded from https://www.ipsos-mori.com/researchpublications/researcharchive/2414/Attitudes-to-Afghanistan-campaign.aspx.

104 In Britain, the 'rally round the flag' effect is especially pronounced where the use of force is perceived to be in defence of the national

interest, as opposed to a humanitarian intervention. Brian Lai and Dan Reiter, 'Rally "round the Union Jack?" Public opinion and the use of force in the United Kingdom, 1948–2001', *International Studies Quarterly*, vol. 49, no. 2 (2005), pp. 255–72.

105 For recent reviews of this debate, see Christopher Gelpi, Peter D. Feaver and Jason Reifler, 'Success matters: casualty sensitivity and the war in Iraq', *International Security*, vol. 30, no. 3 (2005/06), pp. 7–46; and Adam J. Berinsky and James N. Druckman, 'Public opinion research and support for the Iraq War', *Public Opinion Quarterly*, vol. 71, no. 1 (2007), pp. 126–41.

106 Margarette Driscoll, 'The British bereaved by the Afghanistan War', *Sunday Times*, 27 September 2009.

107 Nicola Lester, 'When a soldier dies', *Critical Military Studies*, vol. 1, no. 3 (2015), p. 249.

108 Ibid., p. 251. A coroner's inquest is held into the death of every member of the armed forces killed overseas. Usually this is eighteen months to two years after the death has occurred. For some families this offers closure, but for others it deepens their loss or raises new questions.

109 'Bodies of four soldiers killed in Afghanistan return home', *The Times*, 13 May 2009.

110 Will Pavia, 'Wootton Bassett fears being in front line of "grief tourism"', *The Times*, 29 July 2009.

111 Photographic essay, text by Hew Strachan, photos by Susan Schulman, 'The town that weeps: commemorating life and loss in Wootton Bassett, October 2010', *RUSI Journal*, vol. 155, no. 6 (2010), p. 78.

112 *Channel 4 News*, 'Britons believe "Afghan war is failing"', 24 October 2009, at http://www.channel4.com/news/articles/uk/britons+believe +aposafghan+war+is+failingapos/3397902.html.

113 *Channel 4 News*, 'Afghan poll: majority want troops home', 5 November 2009, at http://www.channel4.com/news/articles/uk/afghan+poll+ majority+want+troops+home/3411597.html.

114 Interview with Lord Hutton, House of Lords, 26 November 2014.

115 Sarah Baxter and Nicola Smith, 'US opens fire on Brown's "war fatigue"', *Sunday Times*, 31 December 2008.

116 Anthony Seldon and Guy Lodge, *Brown at 10* (London: Biteback Publishing, 2010), pp. 302–3.

117 General Sir Richard Dannatt, *Leading from the Front* (London: Bantam Press, 2010), p. 346.

118 Max Hastings, *Daily Mail*, 13 July 2009; see also Kim Sengupta, 'Army fury at refusal to bolster Afghan campaign', *Independent*, 1 June 2009.

119 Jon Swaine, Aislinn Simpson and Thomas Harding, 'Afghanistan: Gordon Brown accused of "dereliction of duty"', *Sunday Times*, 12 July 2009.

120 Testimony of Lord Browne (former Secretary of State for Defence) before the House of Commons Defence Committee, House of Commons, *Operations in Afghanistan*, Fourth Report of Session 2010–12, HC 554 (London: TSO, 2011), Ev. 124 at Q587.

121 Michael Evans and Philip Webster, 'British Army chief forced to use US helicopter in Afghanistan', *The Times*, 15 July 2009.

122 Interview with General the Lord Richard Dannatt, London, 16 February 2012.

123 Michael Evans and Nico Hines, 'General Dannatt forces Afghanistan shopping list on Gordon Brown', *The Times*, 17 July 2009.

124 Francis Elliot and Michael Evans, 'General Sir Richard Dannatt told to keep out of helicopter politics', *The Times*, 16 July 2009.

125 House of Commons Defence Committee, *Helicopter Capability*, Eleventh Report of Session 2008–09, HC 434 (London: TSO, 2009).

126 Nick Allen and Rosa Prince, 'Gordon Brown faces grilling over Afghanistan helicopters', *Daily Telegraph*, 16 July 2009.

127 Interview with senior government adviser, London, 4 April 2014.

128 Interview with Lord Hutton, House of Lords, 26 November 2014.

129 Interview with General Sir David Richards, 18 November 2013, cited in Directorate Land Warfare, Lessons Exploitation Centre, *Operation HERRICK Campaign Study*, March 2015 [redacted and publicly released version], p. xxxv.

130 Email correspondence with British Army officer, 4 July 2011.

131 Email correspondence with Chief of the General Staff, General Sir David Richards, 3 July 2011.

132 This is discussed in detail in chapter 10.

133 The classic example much cited by military historians is the partnership between Winston Churchill as prime minister and Field Marshal Alan Brooke as Chief of the Imperial General Staff during World War II. See Andrew Roberts, *Masters and Commanders: The Military Geniuses Who Led the West to Victory in WWII* (London: Allen Lane, 2008).

Chapter 8: American Surge

1 Candidate Barack Obama, speaking at Woodrow Wilson International Center, Washington DC, 15 July 2008, at http://www.youtube.com/watch?v=3vpCBpTbEds.

2 Presidential debate between John McCain and Barack Obama at the University of Mississippi, Oxford, Mississippi, 26 September 2008, at http://www.youtube.com/watch?v=HO2uA2t9e-I.

3 Bob Woodward, *Obama's Wars: The Inside Story* (New York: Simon & Schuster, 2010), pp. 62–72.

4   Dexter Filkins, 'Biden arrives in Afghanistan to discuss the war', *New York Times*, 10 January 2009.

5   Woodward, *Obama's Wars*, pp. 40–3.

6   Peter Baker and Thom Shanker, 'Obama plans to retain Gates at Defense Department', *New York Times*, 25 November 2008.

7   Bruce Riedel, *The Search for Al Qaeda: Its Leadership, Ideology, and Future* (Washington DC: Brookings Institution, 2008), pp. 148–51.

8   Robert Gates, *Duty: Memoirs of a Secretary at War* (Virgin Digital, 2014), Kindle edn, loc. 5998–6010.

9   Woodward, *Obama's Wars*, pp. 97–8.

10 Gates, *Duty*, loc. 6035.

11 Office of the Press Secretary, the White House, 'Remarks by the President on a New Strategy for Afghanistan and Pakistan', room 450, Dwight D. Eisenhower Executive Office Building, 27 March 2009.

12 http://www.fas.org/sgp/crs/row/pakaid.pdf.

13 Peter Baker and Thom Shanker, 'Obama sets new Afghan strategy', *New York Times*, 27 March 2009.

14 Transcript of Michelle Flournoy, Under Secretary of Policy, U.S. Department of Defense, speaking at the Center for International and Strategic Studies, Washington DC, 21 April 2009.

15 Woodward, *Obama's Wars*, p. 103.

16 Ibid.

17 Gates, *Duty*, loc. 6095. At the height of the military surge in 2010 when there were 100,000 US troops in Afghanistan, the State Department had managed to deploy around a thousand civilians, many of whom were rookies with limited field experience hired on one-year contracts. One US general sarcastically commented that he could feel the civilian surge 'lapping at my ankles'. Todd Greentree, 'The Accidental Counterinsurgents: U.S. Performance in Afghanistan', paper for Historical Lessons Learned Workshop, Johns Hopkins Applied Physics Laboratory, July 2015, pp. 12–13.

18 Stephen Biddle, Jeffrey A. Friedman and Jacob N. Shapiro, 'Testing the urge: why did violence decline in Iraq in 2007?', *International Security*, vol. 37, no. 1 (2012), pp. 7–40.

19 James A. Russell, *Innovation, Transformation, and War: Counterinsurgency Operations in Anbar and Ninewa Provinces, Iraq, 2005–2007* (Stanford, CA: Stanford University Press, 2011); Chad C. Serena, *A Revolution in Military Adaptation: The U.S. Army in Iraq* (Washington DC: Georgetown University Press, 2011).

20 Thomas E. Ricks, *The Gamble: General Petraeus and the Untold Story of the American Surge in Iraq, 2006–2008* (London: Allen Lane, 2009); Philip Rothmann, David Tohn and Jaron Wharton, 'Learning under fire:

progress and dissent in the US military', *Survival*, vol. 51, no. 4 (2009), pp. 31–48.

21 Rajiv Chandrasekaran, 'Pentagon worries led to command change', *Washington Post*, 17 August 2009.

22 Woodward, *Obama's Wars*, p. 118.

23 Gates, *Duty*, loc. 6143.

24 http://www.defense.gov/transcripts/transcript.aspx?transcriptid=4424.

25 http://www.c-span.org/video/?286758-1/military-nominations-hearing.

26 General Stanley McChrystal, *My Share of the Task: A Memoir* (New York: Portfolio/Penguin, 2013), p. 289.

27 Ibid., p. 291.

28 Ibid., p. 376.

29 Major General Michael T. Flynn, Captain Matt Pottinger and Paul. D. Batchelor, *Fixing Intel: A Blueprint for Making Intelligence Relevant in Afghanistan* (Washington DC: Center for a New American Security, January 2010).

30 'White House SEAL', *Shipmate*, March–April 2012, pp. 28–9.

31 McChrystal, pp. 295, 300.

32 Ibid., pp. 300–6.

33 'COMISAF Listening Tour Common Themes', undated memorandum, ISAF HQ; and interview with former senior US military officer, Washington DC, 9 March 2012.

34 Interview with former senior ISAF officer, via telephone, 22 March 2014.

35 Interview with former US task force commander in 2007–8, 24 March 2014.

36 Sten Rynning, *NATO in Afghanistan: The Liberal Disconnect* (Stanford, CA: Stanford University Press, 2012), pp. 57–60.

37 Memorandum from US Mission NATO to various US government and military agencies, 'ISAF Comprehensive Strategic Pol-Mil Plan (CSPMP)', 08USNATO212, 18 June 2008.

38 Interview with former senior ISAF officer, via telephone, 11 March 2014.

39 Biddle wrote a widely acclaimed social scientific analysis of success in battle in his book *Military Power: Explaining Victory and Defeat in Modern Battle* (Princeton, NJ: Princeton University Press, 2004).

40 Soldier X, *This Man's Army* (London: Penguin, 2004).

41 Interview with former member of strategic assessment team, via telephone, 23 March 2014.

42 'On Woodward's book: a (very minor) correction', post by Andrew Exum on his blog, Abu Muqawama, 18 October 2010.

43 Stephen Biddle, 'A tale of two convoys', op-ed, *New York Times*, 9 March 2010.

44 Interview with former member of strategic assessment team, via telephone, 23 March 2014.

45 McChrystal, *My Share*, p. 330.

46 Commander NATO International Security Assistance Force, Afghanistan, and US Forces, Afghanistan, 'Commander's Initial Assessment', 30 August 2009, unclassified.

47 COMISAF/CDR USFOR-A, 'Tactical Directive', headquarters ISAF and United States Forces, Afghanistan, Kabul, 6 July 2009. Copy with author.

48 'Commander's Initial Assessment', p. 2–2.

49 Interview with former senior ISAF officer, via telephone, 11 March 2014.

50 'Commander's Initial Assessment', p. 1–2.

51 Interview with former senior ISAF officer, via telephone, 24 March 2014.

52 COMISAF/CDR USFOR-A, 'Partnering Directive', headquarters ISAF and United States Forces, Afghanistan, Kabul, 29 August 2009. Copy with author.

53 Gates, *Duty*, loc. 6264.

54 McChrystal, *My Share*, p. 320.

55 Ibid., p. 326.

56 Interview with former member of strategic assessment team, via telephone, 23 March 2014.

57 Cited in Woodward, *Obama's Wars*, p. 150.

58 Fred Kagan, 'We're not the Soviets in Afghanistan', *Weekly Standard*, 21 August 2009; Gates, *Duty*, loc. 6397, 6408.

59 Gates, *Duty*, loc. 6495.

60 Bob Woodward, 'McChrystal: more forces or "mission failure"', *Washington Post*, 21 September 2009.

61 Gates, *Duty*, loc. 6532–77.

62 Woodward, *Obama's Wars*, p. 192; Gates, *Duty*, loc. 6699.

Chapter 9: Showdown

1 Author observation of visit by British Muslim Delegation to Nad-e Ali district, Helmand province, September 2009.

2 Interview with former senior US military officer, Washington DC, 9 March 2012.

3 COMISAF General Stanley McChrystal, HQ ISAF, 'Tactical Directive', 1 July 2009.

4 Confidential source.

5 CJTF 6, POR, November 2010.

6 Author attendance at 1 Grenadier Guards Battlegroup briefing, Nad-e Ali district, Helmand province, September 2009.

7   Mike Martin, *An Intimate War: An Oral History of the Helmand Conflict* (London: Hurst, 2014), p. 135.

8   Interviews with Colonel Roly Walker and command staff, 1 Grenadier Guards, Wellington Barracks, London, 3 May 2010.

9   Sean Rayment, 'Special forces troops open up new front against the Taliban in Helmand', *Daily Telegraph*, 12 December 2009.

10   Ben Farmer, 'Elite forces in secret raids against Taliban bomb-makers', *Daily Telegraph*, 8 August 2013.

11   Interview with deputy commander, TF Helmand, TFH HQ, Lashkar Gah, 28 May 2010.

12   Interviews with Colonel Roly Walker and command staff, 1 Grenadier Guards, Wellington Barracks, London, 3 May 2010.

13   Interview with Royal Welsh company commander, London, 1 October 2010.

14   Confidential source. RC-S, Op Tor Shpa'h, Key Observations, January 2010.

15   Interview with deputy commander, TF Helmand, TFH HQ, Lashkar Gah, 28 May 2010.

16   Interview with ISAF planners, RC-South HQ, Kandahar airfield, 30 May 2010.

17   Ibid.

18   Interview with General Nick Parker, former deputy commander of ISAF, London, 10 March 2014.

19   ISAF Joint Command, Operational Order, November 2009.

20   Rajiv Chandrasekaran, *Little America: The War Within the War for Afghanistan* (London: Bloomsbury, 2012).

21   Discussions with ISAF planners, ISAF HQ, Kabul, 9–13 January 2010.

22   Max Benitz, *Six Months Without Sundays: The Scots Guards in Afghanistan* (Edinburgh: Birlinn, 2011), p. 27.

23   http://www.whitehouse.gov/the-press-office/remarks-president-address-nation-way-forward-afghanistan-and-pakistan.

24   Sheryl Gay Stolberg and Helene Cooper, 'Obama adds troops, but maps exit plan', *New York Times*, 2 December 2009.

25   Interview with former senior ISAF officer, Washington DC, 11 March 2014.

26   Robert Gates, *Duty: Memoirs of a Secretary at War* (Virgin Digital, 2014), Kindle edn, loc. 6748–803.

27   CNN Opinion Research Corporation, poll 19, 16–20 December 2009; see also CNN.com, 'Afghanistan war still unpopular but troop increase isn't', 23 December 2009. Polling by the *Washington Post* and ABC News showed a similar trend. Jennifer Agiesta and Jon Cohen, 'Poll shows most Americans oppose war in Afghanistan', *Washington Post*, 20 August 2009.

28   Bob Woodward, *Obama's Wars: The Inside Story* (New York: Simon & Schuster, 2010), pp. 324–30.

29   General Stanley McChrystal, *My Share of the Task: A Memoir* (New York: Portfolio/Penguin, 2013), p. 323.

30   Discussions with ISAF staff, ISAF HQ, Kabul, 9–13 January 2010.

31   Eric Schmitt, 'Two top aids show unity on Afghan strategy', *New York Times*, 9 December 2009.

32   Gates, *Duty*, loc. 6762.

33   Robert Burns, 'At least 7,000 fresh NATO troops to bolster war', Associated Press, 5 December 2009.

34   Federal News Service: Transcript of hearing of the Senate Armed Services Committee; chaired by Sentator Carl Levin (D-MI); witnesses Ambassador Karl W. Eikenberry and General Stanley A. McChrystal, 8 December 2009.

35   US Department of State cable, Kabul 002810, 16 September 2009, 'UK PRIME MINISTER VISITS HELMAND; WELCOMES ANSF FOCUS AND SEEKS METRICS TO MEASURE WAR EFFORT'.

36   Lieutenant General Jim Dutton, 'Holding our nerve in Afghanistan', *Guardian*, 29 December 2009.

37   Thomas Harding, 'Taliban have the initiative, British general admits', *Daily Telegraph*, 21 December 2009.

38   '100th British soldier killed in Afghanistan this year named by MoD', *Guardian*, 8 December 2009.

39   Dutton, 'Holding our nerve in Afghanistan'.

40   *BBC News*, 'Taliban defiant over Obama surge', 2 December 2009, at http://news.bbc.co.uk/go/pr/fr/-/1/hi/world/south_asia/8390466.stm.

41   Interviews with ISAF planners, RC-South HQ, Kandahar airfield, 30 May 2010.

42   Ibid.

43   ISAF Joint Command (IJC) understood the imperative to develop governance at the district level and, to this end, to provide support to the under-resourced Independent Directorate of Local Governance. Interview with Brigadier General Kim Field (US Army retired), IJC lead mentor to IDLG, Washington DC, 6 July 2015.

44   Islamic Republic of Afghanistan, Independent Directorate of Local Governance, District Delivery Programme Secretariat, 'Support to the District Delivery Programme', draft version 2.3, 2010.

45   Author observation of final coordination meeting for District Delivery Programme launch, IDLG, Kabul, 9 January 2010.

46   Interviews with intelligence officers, RC-South HQ, Kandahar airfield, 25 May 2010.

47   Interview with deputy commander, Task Force Helmand, Lashkar Gah, 28 May 2010.

48   Commander RC-South, Op Moshtarak, Direction, January 2010.

49   Confidential source.

50   Benitz, *Six Months*, p. 41.

51   Confidential source.

52   Ibid.

53   Interview with Brigadier James Cowan, Commander TFH, 11 Brigade headquarters, Aldershot, 23 April 2010.

54   Confidential source.

55   McChrystal, *My Share*, pp. 364–5. McChrystal's memoir fails to mention that this meeting occurred at D+1. But this was confirmed to me in numerous confidential interviews with senior ISAF officers in RC-South headquarters, May 2010.

56   Interview with Air Commodore Stuart Atta, CO No. 83 Expeditionary Air Group and UK Air Component Commander – Afghanistan, 4 March 2010.

57   TFH POR, 2010.

58   Jeffrey Dressler, 'Operation Moshtarak: preparing for the battle of Marjah', Institute for the Study of War, March 2010, p. 1.

59   Martin, *An Intimate War*, p. 176.

60   Dressler, 'Operation Moshtarak', p. 1.

61   Interview with ISAF intelligence officer, RC-South HQ, Kandahar airfield, 25 May 2010.

62   Dexter Filkins, 'Afghans try to reassure elders on offensive', *New York Times*, 10 February 2010.

63   Interview with stabilisation officer, RC-South headquarters, Kandahar airfield, 30 May 2010.

64   Dressler, 'Operation Moshtarak', p. 3.

65   Dexter Filkins, 'Afghans try to reassure elders'.

66   Dressler, 'Operation Moshtarak', pp. 3–4.

67   C. J. Chivers, 'Afghan attack gives Marines a taste of war', *New York Times*, 14 February 2010.

68   Chandrasekaran, *Little America*, p. 137.

69   Interview with US stabilisation officer for Marjah, 15 April 2010.

70   Rajiv Chandrasekaran, 'US curtails use of airstrikes in assault on Marja', *Washington Post*, 16 February 2010.

71   C. J. Chivers, 'Soldiers keep up push in Taliban stronghold', *New York Times*, 16 February 2010.

72   C. J. Chivers, Dexter Filkins and Rod Nordland, 'Half of town's Taliban flee or are killed, allies say', *New York Times*, 16 February 2010.

73 TFH POR, 2010.

74 The Focused Delivery Program was run by the US Combined Security Transition Command – Afghanistan, which in 2009 came under ISAF Command. Peter Dahl Thruelsen, 'Striking the right balance: how to rebuild the Afghan national police', *International Peacekeeping*, vol. 17, no. 1 (2010), p. 87.

75 Interview with colonel, ANSF, TFH headquarters, Lashkar Gah, 27 May 2010.

76 Confidential source.

77 Interview with Habibullah Khan, district governor of Nad-e Ali, Nad-e Ali district centre, Helmand, 27 May 2010; interview with senior official, provincial governor's office, Lashkar Gah, 29 May 2010.

78 Confidential source.

79 Confidential source.

80 Based on personal visits to Nad-e Ali in late September 2009 and late May 2010.

81 Survey conducted between 7 and 14 May 2010. Of 503 callers to Radio Nad-e Ali, 97 per cent freely agreed to participate in the survey. Capt. Nick Carter, Influence Officer, Combined Force Nad-e Ali, 'Public perception of security in Nad-e Ali, Helmand', PowerPoint slides, 7 June 2010.

82 Interviews with TFH command staff, 11 Brigade headquarters, Aldershot, 23 April 2010.

83 Interview with Lindy Cameron, head of the Helmand Provincial Reconstruction Team, Lashkar Gah, 28 May 2010.

84 Interview with senior Helmand PRT official, London, 17 May 2010.

85 11 Brigade command team, Herrick 11 campaign debrief to Land Warfare Centre, Warminster, 28 April 2010.

86 Interview with Gavin Davis, district political officer, Nad-e Ali district centre, Helmand, 27 May 2010.

87 Interview with Brigadier General Thomas Murray, deputy commander RC-South, RC-South headquarters, Kandahar airfield, 25 May 2010.

88 Carlotta Gall, 'Farmers flee area taken by US, saying Taliban hold sway', *New York Times*, 16 May 2010.

89 Chandrasekaran, *Little America*, p. 144.

90 Interview with senior official, Helmand Provincial Reconstruction Team, Lashkar Gah, 29 May 2010.

91 This was certainly my impression when I visited the 1st Marine Expeditionary Force headquarters, at Camp Leatherneck in Helmand, in October 2010. The 1st MEF took over from the 2nd MEB in Helmand.

92 Joshua Partlow and Jabeen Bhatti, 'New top official in Marja, Afghanistan, was convicted of stabbing stepson', *Washington Post*, 6 March 2010.

93 US Department of State cable, Kabul 000726, 28 February 2010, 'CRIMINAL ALLEGATIONS SURROUNDING MARJAH SUB-DISTRICT GOVERNOR HAJI ZAHIR'.

94 RC-South headquarters, Op Moshtarak POR, April 2010.

95 Interview with senior stabilisation officer, RC-South headquarters, Kandahar airfield, 30 May 2010.

96 Ibid.

97 Jack Fairweather, *The Good War: The Battle for Afghanistan, 2006–2014* (London: Jonathan Cape, 2014), p. 371.

98 Partlow and Bhatti, 'New top official in Marja'.

99 For instance, the British Army's ill-fated Bowman tactical communication network, introduced in 2005, involved acquiring over 90,000 infantry radio sets, 15,000 vehicle radio sets and 20,000 terminals at a cost of £2.5 billion. Theo Farrell, Sten Rynning and Terry Terriff, *Transforming Military Power since the Cold War: Britain, France and the United States, 1991–2012* (Cambridge: Cambridge University Press, 2013), p. 139.

100 Larisa Brown, 'Spies foil Taliban raid on UK base', *Daily Mail*, 31 December 2014.

101 Interviews with Taliban commander no. 5, Sangin, 2011; Taliban commander no. 4, Sangin, 2011; Taliban commander no. 4, Nahr-e Seraj, 2011; and Taliban commander no. 3, Marjah, 2011.

102 Interview with Taliban commander no. 4, Nahr-e Seraj, 2011.

103 Ben Anderson, *No Worse Enemy: The Inside Story of the Chaotic Struggle for Afghanistan* (Oxford: Oneworld, 2011), p. 12.

104 Interviews with Taliban commander no. 6, Nad-e Ali, 2011; Taliban commander no. 3, Sangin, 2011; and Taliban commander no. 5, Musa Qala, 2011.

105 Interviews with Taliban commanders nos 1–3, Kajaki, 2011; and Taliban commanders nos 4 and 5, Marjah, 2011.

106 Interviews with Taliban commander no. 1, Nahr-e Seraj, 2011; Taliban commander no. 3, Sangin, 2011; Taliban commander no. 7, Sangin, 2011; and Taliban commander no. 8, Garmsir, 2011.

107 Interviews with Taliban commander no. 2, Musa Qala, 2011; Taliban commander no. 7, Sangin, 2011; Taliban commander no. 3, Nahr-e Seraj, 2011; Taliban commander no. 6, Nad-e Ali, 2011; and Taliban commanders nos 1 and 5, Marjah, 2011.

108 Interview with Taliban commander no. 7, Garmsir, 2011.

109 Interview with Taliban commander no. 3, Now Zad, 2011.

110 Interview with Taliban commander no. 5, Kajaki, 2011.

111 Confidential source.

112 Interview with Taliban commander no. 1, Now Zad, 2011.

113 Dexter Filkins, 'Afghan offensive is new war model', *New York Times*, 13 February 2010.

114 David E. Singer, 'A test for the meaning of victory in Afghanistan', *New York Times*, 13 February 2010; Filkins, 'Afghan offensive is new war model'.

115 Confidential source.

116 Dion Nissenbaum, 'McChrystal calls Marjah a "bleeding ulcer" in Afghanistan campaign', McClatchy Newspapers, 24 May 2010.

117 Discussions with ISAF officers, RC-South headquarters, Kandahar airfield, May 2010. Others in ISAF headquarters saw nothing wrong with the metaphor; one senior officer thought that McChrystal was simply saying 'let's have something ready to roll in behind the Marines'. But she admitted that the metaphor was open to misinterpretation. Interview with Brigadier General Kim Field (US Army retired), Washington DC, 6 July 2015.

118 Interview with senior official, provincial governor's office, Lashkar Gah, 29 May 2010.

119 Jeffrey Dressler, 'Operation Moshtarak: taking and holding Marjah', Institute for the Study of War, March 2010, p. 7.

120 Medical Branch, RC-South HQ, POR Op Moshtarak, 9 March 2009.

121 Commander's update briefing, RC-South headquarters, Kandahar airfield, 26 May 2010.

122 Julian Borger, 'Afghan conference sets out plan for two-tier peace process', *Guardian*, 28 January 2010.

123 Confidential source.

124 HBO documentary, *The Battle for Marjah*, directed by Ben Anderson, February 2011.

125 Chandrasekaran, *Little America*, p. 141.

126 ANATC/Doctrine Directorate, Afghan Army Lessons Learned Center, 'Helmand Province: Observations from Marjah', April 2010, p. 5.

127 HBO documentary, *The Battle for Marjah*, directed by Ben Anderson, February 2011.

128 Interview with British Army mentors, 205 Corps headquarters, Camp Hero, Kandahar, 26 May 2010.

129 US Department of State cable, Kabul 000582, 16 February 2010, 'OPERATION MOSHTARAK – SITUATIONAL REPORT FOR FEBRUARY 15, 2010'. Patrick Hennessey tells a similar story of how over a two-month period in one area of Sangin, the ANA found thirty-six IEDs as against one by British troops. See Hennessey, *Kandak: Fighting with Afghans* (London: Allen Lane, 2012), p. 117.

130 Benitz, *Six Months*, p. 60.

131 Major E. C. Hill OC B Coy 1R Welsh, 'All together now – observations of embedded partnering with ANA on Op Moshtarak', Bravo Company Group, 1 Royal Welsh Battlegroup (Combined Force 31), 2010, p. 3.

132 Interview with senior British mentor, central Helmand, 28 May 2010.

133 The Rule of Three was specifically intended to compensate for command weaknesses in the Afghan security forces.

134 Interview with senior adviser, COIN Advisory and Assistance Team, RC-South headquarters, Kandahar airfield, 30 May 2010.

Chapter 10: Undefeated

1 Author observations from visits to Nad-e Ali district centre in September 2009 and late May 2010.

2 Interview with Brigadier Richard Felton, Task Force Helmand headquarters, Lashkar Gah, 28 May 2010; interview with Lieutenant Colonel Frazer Lawrence, 1 Lancs Battlegroup headquarters, FOB Shawqat, Nad-e Ali district, Helmand, 27 May 2010.

3 Interview with Lieutenant Colonel Frazer Lawrence, 1 Lancs Battlegroup headquarters, FOB Shawqat, Nad-e Ali district, Helmand, 27 May 2010; Sallust, *Operation Herrick: An Unofficial History of British Military Operations in Afghanistan, 2001–2014* (self-published book, 2015), chapter 11 (no page numbers).

4 Sallust, *Operation Herrick*, chapter 11 (no page numbers).

5 Richard Norton-Taylor, 'Rate of British military deaths in Afghanistan "has nearly doubled"', *Guardian*, 19 July 2010.

6 Michael Hastings, 'The runaway general', *Rolling Stone*, 22 June 2010.

7 Mark Landler, 'Short, tense deliberation, then a general is gone', *New York Times*, 23 June 2010.

8 Alissa J. Rubin and Dexter Filkins, 'Petraeus is now taking control of a "tougher fight"', *New York Times*, 23 June 2010.

9 In military jargon, this was called the F3EA cycle, which stood for 'find, fix, finish, exploit, assess'.

10 For a remarkably frank account, see General Stanley McChrystal, *My Share of the Task: A Memoir* (New York: Portfolio/Penguin, 2013). See also Christopher J. Lamb and Evan Musing, *Secret Weapon: High-Value Target Teams as an Organizational Innovation*, INSS Strategic Perspectives 4 (Washington DC: US National Defense University, 2011).

11 Interview with senior US officer, Washington DC, 3 September 2012.

12 Opening Statement by General David H. Petraeus, Confirmation Hearing: Commander ISAF/US Forces – Afghanistan, 29 June 2010. Copy with author.

13 COMISAF/CDR USFOR-A, 'COMISAF's Counterinsurgency Guidance', Headquarters ISAF and United States Forces – Afghanistan, Kabul, 1 August 2010. Copy with author.

14   The exact numbers are: 2,795 operations conducted, 285 insurgent leaders killed or captured, 2,084 insurgents captured and 889 insurgents killed. 'SOF Summary: (23 Sept 10) 90-Day Accumulated Effects', PowerPoint slide with author.

15   Author notes from briefing by COMISAF General David Petraeus, Headquarters ISAF, Kabul, 9 October 2010.

16   Gregory A. Daddis, *No Sure Victory: Measuring US Army Effectiveness and Progress in the Vietnam War* (Oxford: Oxford University Press, 2011).

17   The Open Societies Foundation and the Liaison Office, *The Cost of Kill/ Capture: Impact of the Night Raid Surge on Afghan Civilians*, 9 September 2011.

18   Thom Shanker, Elizabeth Bumiller and Rod Nordland, 'Despite gains, Afghan night raids split US and Karzai', *New York Times*, 15 November 2010.

19   'A dubious history of targeted killings in Afghanistan', *Spiegel Online*, 28 December 2014.

20   Cyril Dixon, 'Afghanistan: "dead or alive" hunt for 2,000 Taliban warlords', *Daily Express*, 2 August 2010; 'Afghanistan war logs: drones target top Taliban', *Guardian*, 25 July 2010.

21   Mark Urban, *Task Force Black: The Explosive True Story of the SAS and the Secret War in Iraq* (London: Little, Brown, 2010).

22   Kim Sengupta, 'SAS comes out fighting as details of top-secret missions are exposed', *Independent*, 4 May 2010.

23   Thomas Harding, 'Quarter of senior Taliban killed by SAS in "kill or capture" targeting', *Daily Telegraph*, 10 September 2010.

24   Mike Martin, *An Intimate War: An Oral History of the Helmand Insurgency* (London: Hurst, 2014), pp. 145, 173.

25   Carter Malkasian, *War Comes to Garmser: Thirty Years of Conflict on the Afghan Frontier* (London: Hurst, 2013), p. 118.

26   Robert Gates, *Duty: Memoirs of a Secretary at War* (Virgin Digital, 2014), Kindle edn, loc. 9946–55.

27   Off-the-record comment by US Central Command officer at conference attended by author in 2011.

28   There was a clear upward trend in casualties even when the figures were normalised for the increased numbers of ISAF and Afghan troops in the south and higher tempo of counter-insurgency operations. ISAF Regional Command South Casualty Summary 2007–2010. Not classified. PowerPoint slide with author.

29   Antonio Giustozzi, *Koran, Kalashnikov and Laptop: The Neo-Taliban Insurgency in Afghanistan* (London: Hurst, 2007), pp. 123–5; Alex Strick van Linschoten and Felix Kuehn, *An Enemy We Created: The Myth of the Taliban/Al Qaeda Merger in Afghanistan, 1970–2010* (London: Hurst, 2010), pp. 273–5.

30 Interviews with Taliban commander no. 1, Nad-e Ali, 2011; Taliban commander no. 7, Nad-e Ali, 2011; and Taliban commander no. 2, Marjah, 2011.

31 Interview with elder no. 3, Nahr-e Seraj, 2011.

32 Mike Martin reconstructs this story through multiple interviews with Helmandi elders and former officials. Martin, *An Intimate War*, chapter 5.

33 Gretchen S. Peters, 'The Taliban and the Opium Trade', in Antonio Giustozzi, ed., *Decoding the New Taliban: Insights from the Afghan Field* (London: Hurst, 2009), pp. 7–22.

34 Here, too, we see a pattern which is consistent with that identified by Giustozzi in his earlier study. In contrast to the view that most Taliban were mere mercenaries (the so-called 'ten-dollar-a-day Taliban'), or that the Taliban forcibly recruited, Giustozzi argues that most Taliban are volunteers who join for a variety of reasons. Giustozzi, *Koran*, p. 42.

35 Interview with Taliban commander no. 3, Nahr-e Seraj, 2011.

36 Interview with Taliban commander no. 7, Garmsir, 2011.

37 Interviews with Taliban commander no. 5, Marjah, 2011; Taliban commander no. 2, Now Zad, 2011; and Taliban commander no. 7, Sangin, 2011.

38 Malkasian, *War Comes to Garmser*, p. 105.

39 Five elders, from three different districts, stated emphatically that the Taliban did not forcibly recruit locals. Interviews with elder no. 2, Garmsir, 2011; elders nos 2–4, Musa Qala, 2011; elder no. 4, Nahr-e Seraj, 2011.

40 Interview with elder no. 2, Musa Qala, 2011.

41 Interview with Taliban commander no. 6, Musa Qala, 2011.

42 Interview with Taliban commander no. 1, Sangin, 2011.

43 Interview with Taliban commander no. 2, Sangin, 2011; see also Taliban commander no. 5, Sangin, 2011.

44 Interview with Taliban commander no. 1, Sangin, 2011.

45 Interviews with Taliban commander no. 4 and no. 8, Garmsir, 2011; and Taliban commander no. 3, Now Zad, 2011.

46 Interviews with Taliban commander no. 4, Marjah, 2011; and Taliban commander no. 1, Kajaki, 2011.

47 Interviews with Taliban commander no. 2, Kajaki, 2011; Taliban commander no. 4, Musa Qala, 2011; Taliban commander no. 3, Nad-e Ali, 2011; Taliban commander no. 5, Nad-e Ali, 2011; Taliban commander no. 6, Nad-e Ali, 2011; Taliban commander no. 3, Nahr-e Seraj, 2011; Taliban commander no. 1, Sangin, 2011; and Taliban commander no. 5, Kajaki, 2011.

48 Interviews with Taliban commander no. 1, Musa Qala, 2011; and Taliban commander no. 2, Nahr-e Seraj, 2011; see also Alex Strick van Linschoten and Felix Kuehn, *Lessons Learnt: 'Islamic, Independent, Perfect and Strong':*

Parsing the Taliban's Strategic Intentions, 2001–2011, AHRC Public Policy, Series 3, 2012, p. 8.

49 Interviews with Taliban commander no. 3, Sangin, 2011; Taliban commander no. 4, Kajaki, 2011; Taliban commander no. 5, Marjah, 2011; and Taliban commander no. 1, Nahr-e Seraj, 2011.

50 As Lawrence Freedman notes, '[strategic] narratives go beyond rhetoric scripted for manipulative ends', but instead 'provide a grounded expression of people's experiences, interests and values'. Freedman, *The Transformation of Strategic Affairs*, Adelphi Paper 379 (Abingdon, Oxon: Routledge for IISS, 2006), p. 22.

51 Interview with elder no. 4, Musa Qala, 2011.

52 Carter Malkasian, Jerry Meyerle and Megan Katt, *The War in Southern Afghanistan, 2001–2008* (Washington DC: Center for Naval Analysis, 2009), pp. 11, 14.

53 Malkasian, *War Comes to Garmser*, p. 86.

54 Interview with elder no. 8, Nad-e Ali, 2011; also field team interviews with elders nos 1–2, Musa Qala, 2011. It would appear that Taliban pay is irregular. According to one Taliban commander, 'We don't have a fixed salary. When we have money, we give out 20,000 or 10,000 afghani at times.' This is between £250 and £125. Interview with Taliban commander no. 1, Marjah, 2011.

55 Interview with Taliban commander no. 1, Nad-e Ali, 2011.

56 Interview with Taliban commander no. 2, Nad-e Ali, 2011. This interviewee does not appear to have been tied to either Baradar or Dadullah.

57 Interview with Taliban commander no. 2, Nad-e Ali, 2011.

58 For critical views on the Taliban spring offensives in the early years of the insurgency, see Christopher N. Koontz, ed., *Enduring Voices: Oral Histories of the US Army Experience in Afghanistan 2003–5*, US Army Center of Military History, 2009, p. 417; 'Afghanistan: hearing before the Committee on Armed Services, United States Senate, 110th Congress, first session', Washington DC: US Congress, 1 March 2007, p. 10.

59 Interview with elder no. 2, Now Zad, 2011.

60 Ibid.

61 Interview with elder no. 1, Garmsir, 2011.

62 Interview with elder no. 1, Now Zad, 2011.

63 This commander goes on to note that 'there are some foreigners' in his district, 'but not in the frontline fighting'. Interview with Taliban commander no. 2, Nad-e Ali, 2011.

64 Interview with Taliban commander no. 3, Sangin, 2011, reports having Pakistani Taliban in this role. Taliban commander nos 1 and 2, Sangin, 2011, report the presence of Pakistanis in Sangin, but say that there are no foreign Taliban in their respective delgai.

65   Interviews with Taliban commander no. 1, Musa Qala, 2011; Taliban commander no. 2, Musa Qala, 2011; Taliban commander no. 3, Musa Qala, 2011; Taliban commander no. 1, Nahr-e Seraj, 2011; Taliban commander no. 2, Nahr-e Seraj, 2011; Taliban commander no. 1, Now Zad, 2011; Taliban commander no. 2, Now Zad, 2011; Taliban commander no. 4, Now Zad, 2011; Taliban commander no. 5, Now Zad, 2011; Taliban no. 4, Garmsir, 2011; Taliban commander no. 7, Garmsir, 2011; Taliban commander no. 8, Garmsir, 2011.

66   From 2006, for example, Baradar was actively involved with his network in fostering the expansion of the Taliban to northern Afghanistan. Interviews with Taliban cadres in Pakistan, 2010.

67   Interview with elders nos 1–2, Now Zad, 2011; Taliban commander no. 1, Nad-e Ali, 2011.

68   Claudio Franco and Antonio Giustozzi, 'Revolution in the counter-revolution: efforts to centralize the Taliban's military leadership', *Central Asian Affairs*, vol. 3 (2016), p. 255.

69   Tom Coghlan, 'The Taliban in Helmand: An Oral History', in Giustozzi, ed., *Decoding*, p. 145.

70   Vahid Brown and Don Rassler, *Fountainhead of Jihad: The Haqqani Nexus, 1973–2012* (London: Hurst, 2013).

71   Franco and Giustozzi, 'Revolution in the counter-revolution', based on communication with Taliban high-level cadres in Peshawar, 2011–12.

72   Interview with Taliban commander no. 2, Nad-e Ali, 2011.

73   Interview with Taliban commander no. 2, Nad-e Ali, 2011.

74   Interviews with Taliban commander no. 1, Now Zad, 2011; also confirmed by Taliban commander no. 4, Garmsir, 2011; Taliban commander no. 4, Marjah, 2011; Taliban commander no. 1, Now Zad, 2011; Taliban commander no. 2, Now Zad, 2011; Taliban commander no. 4, Kajaki, 2011.

75   Interview with Taliban commander no. 5, Sangin, 2011.

76   Antonio Giustozzi, Adam Baczko and Claudio Franco, *The Politics of Justice: The Taliban's Shadow Judiciary* (Berlin: Afghan Analysts Network, 2013).

77   Thomas H. Johnson and Matthew C. DuPee, 'Analysing the new Taliban Code of Conduct (Layeha): an assessment of changing perspectives and strategies of the Afghan Taliban', *Central Asian Survey*, vol. 31, no. 1 (2012), pp. 77–91.

78   Interview with Taliban commander no. 2, Nad-e Ali, 2011.

79   Interview with Taliban commander no. 7, Sangin, 2011.

80   Interviews with Taliban commander no. 4, Garmsir, 2011; Taliban commander no. 5, Nad-e Ali, 2011; Taliban commander no. 4, Now Zad, 2011; Taliban commander no. 3, Nahr-e Seraj, 2011; Taliban commander no. 5, Nahr-e Seraj, 2011; Taliban commander no. 1, Musa Qala, 2011; Taliban commander no. 6, Musa Qala, 2011.

81   Interview with Taliban commander no. 4, Garmsir, 2011.

82   Interview with Taliban commander no. 1, Nahr-e Seraj, 2011.

83   Interview with Taliban commander no. 3, Marjah, 2011.

84   Interview with staff officer, Defence Intelligence, MoD, London, November 2008. Tom Coghlan reports that 'British commanders estimated that approximately 1,000 Taliban died during 2006'. He places less credence in newspaper reports of many thousands of Taliban dead. Coghlan, 'Taliban in Helmand', p. 130.

85   Interview with Taliban commander no. 3, Sangin, 2011. This is confirmed by twelve interviewees, with a number referring specifically to a 'general order' from the Quetta Shura. This order probably originated from the Military Commission in Peshawar and was signed off and transmitted through the Quetta Shura.

86   Interview with Taliban commander no. 3, Sangin, 2011.

87   Ibid.

88   Interview with Taliban commander no. 3, Marjah, 2011.

89   Ian S. Livingston and Michael O'Hanlon, *Afghan Index*, 28 February 2013, Brookings Institution, figure 1.19, p. 12.

90   Directorate Land Warfare, Lessons Exploitation Centre, *Operation HERRICK Campaign Study*, March 2015 [redacted and publicly released version], Annex A and Annex E to chapters 3–6; also Olivier Grouille, 'Bird and Fairweather in context: assessing the IED threat', *RUSI Journal*, vol. 154, no. 4 (2009), p. 40.

91   Sean Rayment, *Bomb Hunters: In Afghanistan with Britain's Elite Bomb Disposal Unit* (London: HarperCollins, 2011), p. 67.

92   Karen McVeigh, 'Royal Marines speak of "horrible" reality of life on patrol in Afghanistan', *Guardian*, 17 November 2010.

93   Rayment, *Bomb Hunters*, pp. 69–70.

94   Directorate Land Warfare, *Operation HERRICK*, pp. 3–6–2 and 3–6–3.

95   McVeigh, 'Royal Marines speak'.

96   Ibid.

97   The Burley Review: PJHQ C-IED Study Team Report, LWC/DSG/Comd 101/08, 14 November 2008. Summary of recommendations reproduced in Directorate Land Warfare, *Operation HERRICK*, Annex A to chapters 3–6.

98   Sallust, *Operation Herrick*, chapter 12 (no page numbers).

99   Rayment, *Bomb Hunters*, p. 65.

100   Livingston and O'Hanlon, *Afghan Index*, figure 1.19, p. 12.

101   Jasper Copping, '"Bomb magnet" soldier survives 17 explosions', *Sunday Telegraph*, 23 March 2014; Ben Farmer, '"Bomb magnet" soldier says blasts "occupational hazard"', *Daily Telegraph*, 11 July 2014.

102   Ahmed Rashid, *Taliban* (London: Pan Books, 2001), pp. 203–4.

103 Confidential source.

104 Jack Fairweather, *The Good War: The Battle for Afghanistan, 2006–2014* (London: Jonathan Cape, 2014), p. 109.

105 Ibid., p. 111.

106 Cited in Christina Lamb, *Farewell Kabul: From Afghanistan to a More Dangerous World* (London: William Collins, 2015), p. 341.

107 Riaz Mohammad Khan, *Afghanistan and Pakistan: Conflict, Extremism, and Resistance to Modernity* (Washington DC: Woodrow Wilson Center Press, 2011), p. 128.

108 Hassan Abbas, *The Taliban Revival: Violence and Extremism on the Pakistan–Afghanistan Frontier* (New Haven: Yale University Press, 2014), chapters 6 and 7.

109 For a critical account suggesting as much and more, see Carlotta Gall, *The Wrong Enemy: America in Afghanistan, 2001–2014* (New York: Houghton Mifflin Harcourt, 2014).

110 Anatol Lieven, *Pakistan: A Hard Country* (London: Allen Lane, 2011), p. 9.

111 Ahmed Rashid, 'Trotsky in Baluchistan', *The National Interest*, no. 104 (Nov–Dec 2009), pp. 61–71

112 He undertook his postgraduate studies in the Indian city of Shimla. His masters dissertation was published as Hamid Karzai, 'Attitudes of the leadership of Afghan tribes toward the regime from 1953 to 1979', *Central Asian Survey*, vol. 7 (1998), pp. 33–9.

113 Sherard Cowper-Coles, *Cables from Kabul: The Inside Story of the West's Afghanistan Campaign* (London: HarperPress, 2011), p. 73.

114 Khan, *Afghanistan and Pakistan*, pp. 131.

115 It was also claimed that Afghanistan offered Pakistan 'strategic depth'; that if Pakistan ever suffered wholesale invasion by India, Pakistani forces could pull back to Afghanistan in order to regroup. This is less plausible as a strategic rationale as it ignores Pakistan's nuclear arsenal as a credible deterrent to any Indian invasion and, in any case, it is not clear how supporting the Afghan Taliban is necessary to realise this option. See Vipin Narang, 'Posturing for peace? Pakistan's nuclear postures and South Asian stability', *International Security*, vol. 34, no. 3 (2009/10), pp. 38–78.

116 Brown and Rassler, *Fountainhead of Jihad*, p. 151.

117 Lamb, *Farewell Kabul*, p. 371.

118 Lieven, *Pakistan*, p. 8.

119 'Pakistan rally against US strike', *BBC News*, 16 January 2006; Khan, *Afghanistan and Pakistan*, p. 139.

120 David Ignatius, 'How to aggravate Pakistan', *Washington Post*, 11 October 2009; Khan, *Afghanistan and Pakistan*, pp. 158–9.

121 Eric Schmitt and David Sanger, 'US offers Pakistan army $2 billion aid package', *New York Times*, 22 October 2010.

122 In 2010 over eight hundred people were killed by American drones; according to the CIA, 95 per cent of these were militants. Peter Bergen and Jennifer Rowland, 'CIA Drone Strikes and the Taliban', in Peter Bergen with Katherine Tiedemann, eds, *Talibanistan: Negotiating Borders Between Terror, Politics and Religion* (New York: Oxford University Press, 2013), pp. 231, 233.

123 Jason Burke, *The 9/11 Wars* (London: Allen Lane, 2011), p. 462.

124 Gall, *Wrong Enemy*, pp. 246–8. As it transpired, from the reaction of senior Pakistani officials and generals, picked up by US signals intelligence, it was clear that a number were completely surprised and had no idea where bin Laden had been hiding. Peter Bergen, *Manhunt: From 9/11 to Abbottabad – the Ten-Year Search for Osama Bin Laden* (London: The Bodley Head, 2012), p. 236.

125 David E. Sanger, *Confront and Conceal: Obama's Secret Wars and Surprising Use of American Power* (New York: Crown, 2012), pp. 107–8.

126 Vanda Felbab-Brown, *Aspiration and Ambivalence: Strategies and Realities of Counterinsurgency and State Building in Afghanistan* (Washington DC: Brookings Institution Press, 2013), p. 195.

127 Vali Nasr, *The Dispensable Nation: American Foreign Policy in Retreat* (Scribe, 2013), Kindle edn, loc. 1439–528; Gall, *Wrong Enemy*, pp. 259–61.

128 Brown and Rassler, *Fountainhead of Jihad*, p. 153.

129 Lamb, *Farewell Kabul*, pp. 403–4.

130 Under the revised ISAF campaign plan (OMID 1390), Operation Hamkari was designated ISAF main effort, with Regional Command South-West formally acting in support.

131 Interview with Major General James Chiswell, London, 6 July 2016.

132 Lieutenant Colonel Colin Weir, 'Using air power in a small war – a battlegroup commander's reflections on operations in Afghanistan, winter 2010/11', *Air Power Review*, vol. 16, no. 1 (2013), p. 112.

133 Lt Col. C. R. J. Weir, 'CO – End of Tour Report', in *Op Herrick 13: Securing the Canal Zone: 1 Battalion the Royal Irish Regiment, Combined Force (Nad-e Ali South) 2010–2011* (end-of-tour book produced by 1 Royal Irish, n.d.), p. 186.

134 Combined Force Nad-e Ali South, Weekly SIGACTS, 2010–2011. Not classified. PowerPoint slide with author.

135 Weir, 'Using air power', p. 111.

136 Interview with Major General James Chiswell, London, 6 July 2016.

137 Weir, 'Using air power', p. 113.

138 Interview with Colonel Colin Weir, London, 12 June 2014.

139   Weir, 'Using air power,' p. 117.

140   Christopher Leake, '2,000ft up, the new "barrage balloon" spying on the Taliban', *Daily Mail*, 26 September 2010; Graham Bowley, 'Spy balloons become part of the Afghanistan landscape, stirring unease', *New York Times*, 12 May 2012.

141   Sallust, *Operation Herrick*, chapter 12 (no page numbers).

142   Ibid.

143   Interview with Major General James Chiswell, London, 6 July 2016.

144   Weir, 'Using air power', p. 118.

145   Interview with Colonel Colin Weir, London, 12 June 2014.

146   Weir, 'CO – End of Tour Report', p. 190.

147   Sallust, *Operation Herrick*, chapter 12 (no page numbers); Weir, 'Using air power', p. 118.

148   Fairweather, *Good War*, p. 355.

149   Anthony Seldon and Peter Snowdon, *Cameron at 10: The Inside Story, 2010–2015* (London: William Collins, 2015), pp. 63–4.

150   Jon Boone and Richard Norton-Taylor, 'Sangin – town that became a death trap for UK soldiers – passed to US', *Guardian*, 20 September 2010.

151   Max Hastings, 'Blame our generals and politicians for this mess. But our soldiers can hold their heads up high', *Daily Mail*, 21 September 2010.

152   Bill Ardolino, 'US Marines battle the Taliban for control of Musa Qala', *Long War Journal*, 15 July 2010.

153   When Cowan first suggested to Brigadier General Larry Nicholson that 2nd Marine Expeditionary Brigade take over in Sangin, Nicholson retorted that the British 'should stick it out in Sangin' and 'get off their bases'. Fairweather, *Good War*, p. 356.

154   Hastings, 'Blame our generals'.

155   Tom Allan, 'From Sangin to Redford – 3 Rifles', *Guardian*, 5 April 2010.

156   'Interview: Lt Col Nick Kitson – 3 Rifles commanding officer', *Scotsman*, 7 May 2010.

157   3 Rifles Battlegroup POR, April 2010.

158   Mark Urban, 'Ingredients making Sangin so lethal', BBC *Newsnight* website, 8 March 2010.

159   3 Rifles Battlegroup POR, April 2010.

160   Thomas Harding, 'US forces "ignore British advice" in Sangin handover', *Daily Telegraph*, 20 September 2010.

161   Mark Moyar, 'The Third Way of COIN: Defeating the Taliban in Sangin', *Orbis Operations* (July 2011), pp. 35–6. Moyar interviewed members of the 3/5 during and after their tour.

162   Thomas Harding, 'Sangin handover: Taliban "will always have stranglehold on Afghanistan's Fallujah"', *Daily Telegraph*, 21 September 2010.

163　Mark Beautement, 'Peace in whose time? Ripeness and local negotiated agreements: the Sangin Accord, Helmand Province, Afghanistan, 2006–2011', PhD thesis, King's College London, 2016, pp. 229–30, fn. 844.

164　Julius Cavendish, 'US troops take hard line to tame rebels in Sangin', *Independent*, 3 December 2010.

165　Interview with elder no. 12, Sangin, 2011.

166　Interview with elder no. 10, Sangin, 2011.

167　Bing West, *One Million Steps: A Marine Platoon at War* (New York: Random House, 2014), p. 115.

168　Interviews with Taliban commander no. 1, Sangin, 2011.

169　Interviews with Taliban commander no. 7, undisclosed location, 2012; Taliban commander no. 2, undisclosed location, and Taliban commander no. 3, undisclosed location, May 2012.

170　Foreign and Commonwealth Office, eGram 9758/10, 'Sangin update: CIVCAS allegations', 3 August 2010.

171　Tony Perry, 'Marines pay a price trying to secure an Afghan hot spot', *Los Angeles Times*, 22 January 2011; West, *One Million Steps*, p. 129.

172　Ben Anderson, *No Worse Enemy: The Inside Story of the Chaotic Struggle for Afghanistan* (Oxford: Oneworld, 2011), p. 202.

173　Ibid., p. 201.

174　West, *One Million Steps*, p. 193.

175　Moyar, 'The Third Way', p. 40.

176　Anderson, *No Worse Enemy*, p. 217.

177　Ibid., p. 210.

178　Phil Weatherill, 'Targeting the Centre of Gravity: Adapting Stabilisation in Sangin', *RUSI Journal*, vol. 156, no. 4 (2011), p. 98, fn. 23.

179　This question is considered in detail in Beautement, 'Peace in whose time?' Beautement was the district political officer in Sangin from late 2009 to late 2010.

180　The Ishaqzai insurgency was also financed by Ishaqzai narcotic traffickers based in Lashkar Gah and Kandahar. Foreign and Commonwealth Office, eGram 4173536, 'Afghanistan/Helmand: Making Progress in Sangin', 22 March 2010, para. 11.

181　Tom Coghlan, 'The Taliban in Helmand: An Oral History', in Giustozzi, ed., *Decoding*, pp. 119–53, p. 120 for quote on madrasa.

182　Michael Smith, 'Taliban leader killed after RAF tracks phone', *Sunday Times*, 27 December 2006.

183　Interviews with Taliban commander nos 10–12, Sangin, 2011.

184　Interview with elder no. 13, Sangin, 2011.

185　For a detailed review of this incident, see Mark Beautement, 'Negotiated Agreements in Tactical Transitions: The Sangin Accord 2011', in Timothy Clack and Robert Johnson, eds, *At the End of Military Intervention:*

Historical, Theoretical and Applied Approaches to Transition, Handover and Withdrawal (Oxford: Oxford University Press, 2014), pp. 323–59, 329–30.

186 Confidential source who had met Haq on numerous occasions.

187 Mark Beautement, 'Peace in whose time?', pp. 185, 197.

188 Foreign and Commonwealth Office, eGram 4173536, 'Afghanistan/ Helmand: Making Progress in Sangin', 22 March 2010, para. 6.

189 Beautement, 'Peace in whose time?', pp. 197–8.

190 Foreign and Commonwealth Office, eGram 4173536, 'Afghanistan/ Helmand: Making Progress in Sangin', 22 March 2010, para. 10.

191 Foreign and Commonwealth Office, eGram 17084/10, 'Afghanistan/ Reintegration: Is the Ball Now Rolling in Helmand?', 9 December 2010.

192 Interview with Mohammad Sharif, Helmand, July 2013.

193 Interview with elder no. 13, Sangin, 2011.

194 Beautement, 'Peace in whose time?', pp. 183–4.

195 Interview with elder no. 10, Sangin, 2011.

196 Interviews with elders nos 11–14, Sangin, 2011.

197 Interview with Mohammad Sharif, Helmand, July 2013.

198 Foreign and Commonwealth Office, eGram 648/11, 'Sangin – Latest Developments', 12 January 2011, para. 5.

199 Interviews with Taliban commander nos 11–12, Sangin, 2011.

200 Interview with Taliban commander no. 4, Sangin, 2011.

201 Author's interviews with personnel in Regional Command South-West (1st Marine Expeditionary Force) and Helmand PRT, October 2010.

202 Field interview with journalist, Lashkar Gah, Helmand, July 2013.

203 Commander NATO International Security Assistance Force, Afghanistan, and US Forces, Afghanistan, 'Commander's Initial Assessment', 30 August 2009, unclassified, pp. 2–5.

204 For example, Thomas H. Johnson and Matthew C. DuPee argue that 'The Taliban shadow justice system is easily one of the most popular and respected elements of the Taliban insurgency by local communities especially in southern Afghanistan'. Johnson and DuPee, 'Analysing the new Taliban Code', p. 84. See also Coghlan, 'Taliban in Helmand', pp. 148–9.

205 Beautement, 'Peace in whose time?', pp. 108–11. For discussion on how the Helmand and Arghandab Valley Authority intensified the competition over land and access to water in Helmand, see Martin, *Intimate War*, pp. 27–36.

206 Interview with elder no. 7, Nad-e Ali, 2011; similar view offered by elder no. 3, Nahr-e Seraj, 2011.

207 Interview with elder no. 5, Nahr-e Seraj, 2011. Also confirmed by elder no. 1, Now Zad, 2011; elder no. 6, Nad-e Ali, 2011; elder no. 2, Garmsir, 2011.

208 Giustozzi, Baczko and Franco, *Politics of Justice.*

209 Johnson and DuPee, 'Analysing the new Taliban Code', pp. 85–6. See Niaz Shah, 'The Islamic Emirate of Afghanistan: a *layeha* [rules and regulations] for mujahidin', *Studies in Conflict & Terrorism*, vol. 35, no. 6 (2012), pp. 456–70, for a translation.

210 Interview with elder no. 3, Musa Qala, 2011.

211 Interviews with elder no. 4, Nahr-e Seraj, 2011; and elder no. 3, Musa Qala, 2011.

212 Interview with elder no. 4, Nahr-e Seraj, 2011.

213 See Antonio Giustozzi and Claudio Franco, *The Battle for the Schools: The Taleban and State Education* (Berlin: Afghan Analysts Network, 2011); 'Afghanistan: protection of civilians in armed conflict', Kabul: UNAMA, half-yearly reports.

214 Weatherill, 'Targeting the centre of gravity', p. 98, fn. 22.

215 Weir, 'CO – End of Tour Report', p. 189.

216 Brigadier James Chiswell, presentation to the International Institute for Strategic Studies, 16 June 2011.

217 Sergio Catignani, '"Getting COIN" at the tactical level: reassessing counterinsurgency adaptation in the British Army', *Journal of Strategic Studies*, vol. 35, no. 4 (2012), pp. 1–27, 3, 22–23.

Chapter 11: Time Runs Out

1 My account of this policy summit is taken from Anthony Seldon and Peter Snowdon, *Cameron at 10: The Inside Story, 2010–2015* (London: William Collins, 2015), pp. 55–69.

2 James Fergusson, *Taliban: The True Story of the World's Most Feared Guerrilla Fighters* (London: Bantam Press, 2010), p. 257.

3 It would be three more years before Zaeef visited the United Kingdom for the first time, to attend a workshop on regional security convened at King's College London.

4 Rory Stewart, *The Places in Between* (London: Picador, 2004).

5 Rory Stewart and Gerald Knaus, *Can Intervention Work?* (New York: W. W. Norton & Co., 2014), p. 13.

6 Rory Stewart, 'The irresistible illusion', *London Review of Books*, vol. 31, no. 13 (2009), pp. 3–6.

7 Ipsos MORI, 'Attitudes to the Afghanistan Campaign', 24 July 2009; YouGov/*The Sun* Survey, 4–5 July 2010.

8 Rudra Chaudhuri and Theo Farrell, 'Campaign disconnect: operational progress and strategic obstacles in Afghanistan, 2009–2011', *International Affairs*, vol. 87, no. 2 (2011), p. 289, table 2; Stephen M. Saideman, *Adapting*

in the Dust: Lessons Learned from Canada's War in Afghanistan (Toronto: University of Toronto Press, 2016), p. 104, figure 8.2.

9   Nicholas Watt, 'David Cameron sets stage for eventual UK withdrawal from Afghanistan as he visits Kabul', *Guardian*, 10 June 2010.

10   Richards was especially forthright in pushing for more time and resources. On becoming Chief of the Army Staff in August 2009, he controversially declared that the British Army could be in Afghanistan for up to forty years. 'New Army Chief under fire over "40 years" claim', *The Times*, 9 August 2009.

11   Seldon and Snowden, *Cameron at 10*, pp. 63–4.

12   'David Cameron outlines Afghanistan exit strategy', *Daily Telegraph*, 4 July 2010.

13   Sten Rynning, *NATO in Afghanistan: The Liberal Disconnect* (Stanford, CA: Stanford University Press, 2012), p. 63.

14   COMISAF communication to ISAF Command, 20 August 2012. Copy with author.

15   Dr Stephen Downes-Martin, 'Assessment Process of RC(SW)', 24 May 2010. Copy with author.

16   Alejandro S. Hernandez, Julian Ouellet and Christopher J. Nannini, 'Circular Logic and Constant Progress: IW Assessments in Afghanistan', in Leo J. Blanken, Hy Rothstein and Jason J. Lepore, eds, *Assessing War: The Challenge of Measuring Success and Failure* (Washington DC: Georgetown University Press, 2015), p. 222.

17   Ben Connable, *Embracing the Fog of War: Assessment and Metrics in Counterinsurgency* (Santa Monica, CA: The RAND Corporation, 2012).

18   International Crisis Group, *A Force in Fragments: Reconstituting the Afghan National Army*, Asia Report No. 190, 12 May 2010, pp. 16–17.

19   C. J. Chivers, 'Gains in Afghan training but struggles in war', *New York Times*, 12 October 2010.

20   Antonio Giustozzi, *The Army of Afghanistan: A Political History of a Fragile Institution* (London: Hurst, 2015), pp. 166, 180, 193, 197.

21   United States Special Inspector General for Afghanistan Reconstruction (SIGAR), *Actions Needed to Improve the Reliability of Afghan Security Force Assessments*, SIGAR Audit-10–11 Security/ANSF Capability Ratings, 29 June 2010.

22   US Department of Defense, *Report on Progress Toward Security and Stability in Afghanistan*, October 2011, pp. 43–4.

23   Giustozzi, *Army of Afghanistan*, p. 217.

24   International Crisis Group, *The Future of the Afghan Local Police*, Asia Report No. 268, 4 June 2015, p. 7, fn. 39.

25   Interviews with command staff at Regional Command North (Mazar-e-Sharif) and Regional Command East (Bagram airfield), October 2010.

26   Austin Long, 'The Anbar Awakening', *Survival*, vol. 50, no. 2 (2008), pp. 67–94.

27   Seth G. Jones and Arturo Munoz, *Afghanistan's Local War: Building Local Defense Forces* (Santa Monica, CA: The RAND Corporation, 2010), p. 32.

28   International Crisis Group, *Future of the Afghan Local Police*, p. 6.

29   Ministry of Interior statement on Afghan Local Police, current as of 28 December 2011. Copy with author.

30   Human Rights Watch, *Just Don't Call It a Militia: Impunity, Militias, and the 'Afghan Local Police'* (New York: Human Rights Watch, 2011), p. 5.

31   International Crisis Group, *Future of the Afghan Local Police*, p. 3. The US team of experts included Carter Malkasian and the former US ambassador to Afghanistan, Ronald Neumann.

32   Howard Gambrill Clark, 'Lions of Marjah: Why Marjah's Militia Combats Violent Extremists', PhD thesis, King's College London, 2014. This thesis is based on extensive field research in Marjah.

33   Interview with Major General James Chiswell, London, 6 July 2016.

34   Confidential source.

35   Interview with Brigadier Doug Chalmers, 12 Mechanised Brigade headquarters, Budford, 11 December 2012.

36   Michael Stevens, 'Afghan Local Police in Helmand: calculated risk or last gamble?', *RUSI Journal*, vol. 158, no. 1 (2013), pp. 46–70.

37   International Crisis Group, *Future of the Afghan Local Police*, pp. 10–13; Human Rights Watch, *Just Don't Call It a Militia*, pp. 60–6; Special Inspector General for Afghanistan Reconstruction, *Afghan Local Police: A Critical Rural Security Initiative Lacks Adequate Logistics Support, Oversight, and Direction*, SIGAR 16–2 Audit Report, October 2015, pp. 3–4.

38   https://www.theguardian.com/news/datablog/2012/sep/18/nato-afghanistan-insider-attacks-soldiers.

39   Ray Rivera and Eric Schmitt, 'U.S. sending training agents to Afghanistan to stem infiltration of local forces', *New York Times*, 10 June 2011.

40   Rod Nordland, 'Afghan army's turnover threatens US strategy', *New York Times*, 15 October 2012.

41   Matthew Rosenberg, 'Insider attacks in Afghanistan shape late stages of a war', *New York Times*, 3 January 2013.

42   '"Guardian angels" assigned to watch over US troops in Afghanistan', *Guardian*, 29 March 2012.

43   Chris McGreal, Emma Graham-Harrison and Haroon Siddique, 'Nato Afghan strategy in disarray after joint ground operations suspended', *Guardian*, 18 September 2012.

44   Patrick Wintour, 'No change in UK-Afghan patrols after latest "insider attacks", says Hammond', *Guardian*, 18 September 2012.

45 US Department of the Army Report, *Army Regulation (AR) 15–6 Investigation of the 14–15 September 2012 Attack on the Camp Bastion, Leatherneck, and Shorabak (BLS) Complex, Helmand Province, Afghanistan* [redacted version], 19 August 2013.

46 House of Commons Defence Committee, *Afghanistan – Camp Bastion Attack*, Thirteenth Report of Session 2013–14, HC 830 (London: The Stationery Office, 16 April 2014); Rajiv Chandrasekaran, 'Two Marine generals fired for security lapses in Afghanistan', *Washington Post*, 30 September 2013.

47 House of Commons Defence Committee, *Afghanistan*, Fifteenth Report of Session 2013–14, paras 62 and 64.

48 This discussion draws on the author's experience when he spent a month in ISAF headquarters as the British member of a Red Team assembled to conduct a strategic review of the ISAF campaign for Dunford in March 2013.

49 Confidential source.

50 Author was present in ISAF headquarters when this crisis broke.

51 Frud Bezhan and Mustafa Sarwar, 'Afghans failing security test in Badakhshan', Radio Free Europe, 28 March 2013.

52 Emma Graham-Harrison, 'Afghanistan security forces' readiness for NATO withdrawal still a hard sell', *Guardian*, 4 September 2013.

53 Discussions with ISAF planners, HQ ISAF, Kabul, March 2013.

54 Rod Nordland and Azam Ahmed, 'Taliban attack highly regarded Afghan army unit', *New York Times*, 12 April 2013.

55 Discussions with ISAF intelligence officers, HQ ISAF, Kabul, March 2013.

56 Jonathan Schroden, Patricio Asfura-Heim, Catherine Norman and Jerry Meyerle, *Were the Afghan National Security Forces Successful in 2013?*, DOP-2014-U-006817-Final, Center for Naval Analysis, January 2014, pp. 2–5.

57 Schroden et al., *Were the Afghan National Security Forces Successful in 2013?*, p. 11.

58 Nordland and Ahmed, 'Taliban attack'.

59 Emma Graham-Harrison, 'Afghanistan's forces losing more than a few good men. And women', *Guardian*, 3 September 2013.

60 Emma Graham-Harrison, 'Afghan forces suffering too many casualties, says top Nato commander', *Guardian*, 2 September 2013.

61 House of Commons Defence Committee, *Securing the Future of Afghanistan*, Tenth Report of Session 2012–13, HC 413 (London: The Stationery Office, 10 April 2013), pp. 17, 19–27.

62 Ben Farmer, 'Milestone in Afghan withdrawal as British HQ leaves Lashkar Gah', *Daily Telegraph*, 19 August 2013.

63 Emma Graham-Harrison, 'UK leaves its Helmand project – like its roads, clinics and bridges – unfinished', *Guardian*, 27 February 2014.

64   Heather Saul, 'British troops leave Helmand in further move towards total Afghanistan withdrawal', *Independent*, 2 April 2014.

65   Staff reporters, 'Relief and optimism as British troops hand Camp Bastion to Afghan forces', *Guardian*, 28 October 2014.

66   Jonathan Foreman, 'The one good thing we're leaving in Afghanistan', *Spectator*, 2 November 2013.

67   Vali Nasr, *The Dispensable Nation: American Foreign Policy in Retreat* (New York: Doubleday, 2013), Kindle edn, loc. 318.

68   Ian Pannell, 'Afghan fraud is unearthed', *BBC News*, 18 August 2009.

69   Kim Sengupta, 'A dubious litmus test for the poll', *Independent*, 20 August 2009.

70   Ben Farmer, Leonard Doyle and Nick Meo, 'US tries to force Afghanistan election deal', *Telegraph*, 12 September 2009.

71   Sabrina Tavernise and Helene Cooper, 'Afghan leader said to accept runoff after election audit', *New York Times*, 19 October 2009.

72   US Department of State cable, Kabul 003378, 20 October 2009, 'KARZAI AND IEC ANNOUNCE SECOND ROUND.'

73   Helene Cooper and Jeff Zeleny, 'Obama warns Karzai to focus on tackling corruption', *New York Times*, 2 November 2009.

74   US Department of State cable, Kabul 001767, 7 July 2009, 'KARZAI ON THE STATE OF US-AFGHAN RELATIONS', paras 6 and 7.

75   Richard A. Oppel Jr. and Neil MacFarquhar, 'After clash over Afghan election, UN fires a diplomat', *New York Times*, 30 September 2009.

76   Kai Eide, *Power Struggle Over Afghanistan* (Skyhouse Publishing, 2011), Kindle edn., loc. 2521.

77   US Department of State cable, Kabul 003587, 9 November 2009, 'AFGHAN MFA REBUKES UN SRSG ON ANTI-CORRUPTION COMMENTS', para 1.

78   US Department of State cable, Kabul 000572, 6 November 2009, 'COIN STRATEGY: CIVILIAN CONCERNS'.

79   Eric Schmitt, 'U.S. envoy's cables show worries on Afghan plans', *New York Times*, 26 January 2010.

80   General Stanley McChrystal, *My Share of the Task: A Memoir* (New York: Portfolio/Penguin, 2013), pp. 297–9.

81   General Stanley McChrystal, Commander, International Security Assistance Force, Afghanistan/US Forces – Afghanistan, and Ambassador Mark Sedwell, NATO Senior Civilian Representative, Afghanistan, 'ISAF Anti-Corruption Guidance', 10 February 2010.

82   Adam Entous, Julian E. Barnes and Siobhan Gorman, 'US shifts Afghan graft plan', *Wall Street Journal*, 20 September 2010.

83   Sarah Chayes, *Thieves of State: Why Corruption Threatens Global Security* (New York: W. W. Norton & Co., 2015), pp. 52–7.

84 Astri Suhrke, *When More Is Less: The International Project in Afghanistan* (London: Hurst, 2011), p. 124.

85 Rod Nordland and Dexter Filkins, 'Anti graft units, backed by US, draw Karzai's fire', *New York Times*, 6 August 2010; Rajiv Chandrasekaran, 'Karzai rift prompts US to reevaluate anti-corruption strategy in Afghanistan', *Washington Post*, 13 September 2010; Chayes, *Thieves of State*, p. 154.

86 Anne Gearan, 'Petraeus calls relationship with Karzai sound', *Washington Times*, 2 September 2010.

87 General Stanley McChrystal, Commander, International Security Assistance Force, Afghanistan/US Forces – Afghanistan, 'COMISAF's Counterinsurgency (COIN) Contracting Guidance', 8 September 2010.

88 Chayes, *Thieves of State*, pp. 138–9.

89 Transparency International, 'Corruption perception index 2010', http://www.transparency.org/policy_research/surveys_indices/cpi/2010/results.

90 United Nations Office on Drugs and Crime, *Corruption in Afghanistan: Bribery as Reported by the Victims* (New York: UNODC, January 2010).

91 Suhrke, *When More Is Less*, p. 133.

92 Special Inspector General for Afghanistan Reconstruction (SIGAR), *Quarterly Report to the United States Congress*, 30 July 2015, p. 72.

93 Mike Martin, 'Thoughts from Kabul', June 2012. Note with author. Martin discusses this myth in *An Intimate War*, pp. 229–30.

94 Chayes, *Thieves of State*, p. 59.

95 Adam Grissom, 'Should-to-Shoulder Fighting Different Wars: NATO Advisors and Military Adaptation in the Afghan National Army', in Theo Farrell, Frans Osinga and James Russell, eds, *Military Adaptation in Afghanistan* (Stanford, CA: Stanford University Press, 2013), p. 274.

96 The Asia Foundation, *Afghanistan in 2013: A Survey of the Afghan People* (2013), figure 3.8, p. 37.

97 David Zucchino, 'Report cites extensive corruption involving Afghan bank', *Los Angeles Times*, 28 November 2011.

98 Jon Boone, 'Afghan finance minister admits doubts over Kabul Bank's missing $1bn', *Guardian*, 15 November 2011.

99 Shashank Bengali, 'Critics say Afghan court was lenient in bank corruption case', *Los Angeles Times*, 5 March 2013.

100 Ben Farmer, 'Karzai cancels press conference after anti-American rant', *Daily Telegraph*, 10 March 2013.

101 Jawad Sukhanyar and Rod Nordland, 'Afghanistan release prisoners over U.S. objections', *New York Times*, 13 February 2014.

102 Alissa J. Rubin and Rod Nordland, 'U.S. general puts troops on security alert after Karzai remarks', *New York Times*, 13 March 2013.

103 Confidential source.

104 Alissa J. Rubin, 'Karzai bets on vilifying U.S. to shed his image as a lackey', *New York Times*, 12 March 2013.

105 Interviews with senior officers in Ministry of Defence and Ministry of Interior, Kabul, March 2013.

106 The author was a member of the strategic assessment team.

107 Kate Clark, 'Not Signed and Sealed Just Yet: Kerry and Karzai's Deal on the Bilateral Security Agreement', Afghan Analysts Network, 14 October 2013.

108 House of Commons Defence Committee, *Afghanistan*, Fifteenth Report of Session 2013–14, HC 994 (London: The Stationery Office, 13 May 2014), para. 47.

109 Emma Graham-Harrison, 'Hamid Karzai refuses to sign US–Afghan security pact', *Guardian*, 24 November 2013; Rod Nordland, 'Afghan council approves security pact, but Karzai withholds his signature', *New York Times*, 24 November 2013.

110 Dan Roberts and Spencer Ackerman, 'White House threatens to pull all US troops out of Afghanistan', *Guardian*, 26 November 2013.

111 Azam Ahmed, 'Abdullah Abdullah moves toward centre of Afghan power', *New York Times*, 13 June 2014.

112 Confidential source.

113 Emma Graham-Harrison, 'Ashraf Ghani claims Afghan presidential election victory', *Guardian*, 27 June 2014.

114 May Jeong, 'Afghanistan's presidential rivals reach agreement after Kerry flies into Kabul', *Guardian*, 8 August 2014.

115 Rod Nordland, 'Ashraf Ghani is named President of Afghanistan by elections panel', *New York Times*, 21 September 2014. For the terms of the power-sharing deal, see https://www.afghanistan-analysts.org/miscellaneous/aan-resources/the-government-of-national-unity-deal-full-text/.

116 'Cabinet joiners: fingers crossed, a government at last', *The Economist*, 17 January 2015.

117 Timor Sharan and Srinjoy Rose, 'NUG one year on: struggling to govern', *Foreign Policy*, 25 September 2015.

118 'New Afghanistan pact means America's longest war will last until at least 2024', *Guardian*, 30 September 2014.

119 Joseph Goldstein, 'A Taliban prize, won in a few hours after years of strategy', *New York Times*, 30 September 2015.

120 Alissa J. Rubin, 'Afghan forces rally in Kunduz, but fight is far from decided', *New York Times*, 1 October 2015; Rod Nordland and Jawad Sukhanyar, 'Taliban and Afghan government dispute status of Kunduz', *New York Times*, 21 June 2015.

121 Margherita Stancati and Habib Khan Totakhil, 'Afghan forces recapture central Kunduz from Taliban', *Wall Street Journal*, 1 October 2015.

122 Sayed Salahuddin, 'Taliban annouce pullout from Kunduz', *Washington Post*, 13 October 2015.

123 General John Campbell, Commander of US Forces – Afghanistan, testimony on US Military Operations in Afghanistan before the Senate Armed Services Committee, 6 October 2015.

124 See Ian S. Livingston and Michael O'Hanlon, *Brookings: Afghanistan Index*, 31 July 2015, figure 1.26, p. 15, http://www.brookings.edu/~/media/Programs/foreign-policy/afghanistan-index/index20150731.pdf.

125 Ibid., figure 1.21, p. 13.

126 Lauren McNally and Paul Bucala, *The Taliban Resurgent: Threats to Afghanistan's Security*, Afghanistan Report 11, Institute for the Study of War (March 2015), pp. 13–17, 19–20.

127 SIGAR, *Quarterly Report*, 30 July 2015, pp. 93, 96.

128 'Season of bloodshed: the Taliban are waging a fierce new offensive in the north', *The Economist*, 30 May 2015.

129 Martine van Bijlert, 'Trouble in Khas Uruzgan: Insults, Assaults, a Siege and an Airlift', Afghan Analysts Network, 2 September 2015.

130 Correspondence with Carter Malkasian, 26 October 2015.

131 Thomas Ruttig, 'The Second Fall of Musa Qala: How the Taleban Are Expanding Territorial Control', Afghan Analysts Network, 3 September 2015, p. 3; see also Sune Engel Rasmussen, 'Afghan forces retake Musa Qala from Taliban', *Guardian*, 30 August 2015.

132 Robin Pagnamenta, Tom Coghlan and Eltaf Asefy, 'Taliban takes terror into Afghanistan parliament', *The Times*, 23 June 2015.

133 Sune Engel Rasmussen, 'Afghanistan's warlord vice-president spoiling for a fight with the Taliban', *Guardian*, 4 August 2015.

134 Borhan Osman, 'The Fall of Kunduz: What Does It Tell Us About the Strength of the Post-Omar Taliban?', Afghan Analysts Network, 30 September 2014.

135 Lola Cecchinel, 'The End of a Police Chief: Factional Rivalries and Pre-election Power Struggles in Kunduz', Afghan Analysts Network, 31 January 2014.

136 Alissa J. Rubin, 'For Afghans in Kunduz, Taliban assault is just the latest affront', *New York Times*, 7 October 2015.

137 Agence France-Presse, 'Afghan forces repel Taliban attack on Ghazni as offensive spreads', *Guardian*, 13 October 2015.

138 Special Inspector General for Afghanistan Reconstruction, *Quarterly Report to the United States Congress*, 30 July 2016, p. 86.

139 Mohammad Stanekzai, 'Taliban attacks end lull in combat in Afghan province of Helmand', Reuters, 8 May 2016.

140 Taimoor Shah and Mujib Mashal, 'Taliban overrun police checkpoints in Helmand province', *New York Times*, 30 May 2016; 'Afghanistan: more

than 50 police killed in Helmand', Al Jazeera, 30 May 2016. According to a wholly reliable confidential source, these news reports failed to accurately capture how close the Taliban came to breaching the inner defences of Lashkar Gah.

141 Mujib Mashal and Taimoor Shah, 'Airstrikes barely holding off Taliban in Helmand, Afghan officials say', *New York Times*, 8 August 2016.

142 Tim Craig, 'U.S. troops are back in restive Afghan province, a year after withdrawal', *Washington Post*, 8 April 2016.

143 'Taliban attacks over two days in Helmand province kill 24 police officers', *Japan Times*, 31 July 2016.

144 Heath Druzin, 'A look at how the US-led coalition lost Afghanistan's Marjah district to the Taliban', *Stars and Stripes*, 16 January 2016.

145 Thomas Ruttig, *The Battle for Afghanistan. Negotiations with the Taliban: History and Prospects for the Future*, National Security Studies Program Policy Paper, New America Foundation, May 2011, p. 2.

146 Ibid., pp. 2, 12–14.

147 On the reintegration side of things, APRP was a successor to the 'Strengthening for Peace Programme' launched in 2005.

148 Discussions with members of the APRP and with senior Taliban figures, Dubai, March 2013.

149 Nasr, *The Dispensable Nation*, loc. 592

150 Ibid., loc. 619.

151 John Alexander, '"Decomposing" an insurgency: reintegration in Afghanistan', *RUSI Journal*, vol. 157, no. 4 (2012), pp. 48–54.

152 Deedee Derksen, *Peace from Bottom-Up? The Afghan Peace and Reintegration Program* (Oslo: Peace Research Institute Oslo, 2011); Ghazni quote from Ben Farmer, 'The truth about "Taliban reintegration"', *Daily Telegraph*, 11 February 2012.

153 Carlotta Gall and Ruhullah Khapalwak, 'U.S. has held meetings with aide to Taliban leader, officials say', *New York Times*, 26 May 2011.

154 Rod Nordland, 'Peace envoys from Taliban at loose ends in Qatar', *New York Times*, 9 April 2013.

155 Matthew Rosenberg and Rod Nordland, 'U.S. abandoning hopes for Taliban peace deal', *New York Times*, 1 October 2012.

156 Julian Borger, 'Taliban told to distance itself from al-Qaida before it opens Qatar office', *Guardian*, 2 May 2013.

157 Confidential interview, Washington DC, March 2013.

158 Matthew Rosenberg and Alissa J. Rubin, 'Taliban step toward Afghan peace talks is hailed by U.S.', *New York Times*, 18 June 2013.

159 Ibid.

160 Dan Roberts and Emma Graham-Harrison, 'US–Taliban Afghanistan peace talks in Qatar cancelled', *Guardian*, 20 June 2013.

161 Inaugural speech by Dr Ashraf Ghani Ahmadzai as president of Afghanistan, 29 September 2014, http://president.gov.af/en/news/36954.

162 William Byrd, 'Afghanistan's Continuing Fiscal Crisis: No End in Sight', Peace Brief 185, United States Institute of Peace, 15 May 2015.

163 Jon Boone, 'Ashraf Ghani visit may mark new chapter in Afghan–Pakistan relations', *Guardian*, 14 November 2014; Barnett Rubin, 'Ghani's gambit – can Afghanistan and Pakistan ever get along?', *New York Times*, 19 March 2015.

164 Jon Boone and Sune Engel Rasmussen, 'Talks could begin between Taliban and Afghan government after 13 years of war', *Guardian*, 19 February 2015.

165 Ankit Panda, 'Who's negotiating with the Taliban anyway?', *The Diplomat*, 20 February 2015.

166 Edward Wong and Mujib Mashal, 'Taliban and Afghan peace officials have secret talks in China', *New York Times*, 25 May 2015.

167 Statement by Zabihullah Mujahid, Spokesman of Islamic Emirate of Afghanistan, 24 May 2015, http://shahamat-english.com/we-strongly-reject-propaganda-of-meeting-with-representatives-of-kabul-administration-in-china/.

168 Borhan Osman, 'The Murree Process: Divisive Peace Talks Further Complicated by Mullah Omar's Death', Afghan Analysts Network, 5 August 2015.

169 Mateen Haider, 'First round of Afghan govt, Taliban dialogue concludes in Murree', *Dawn*, 8 July 2015.

170 Osman, 'The Murree Process'.

171 Declan Walsh, 'Taliban besiege Pakistan school, leaving 145 dead', *New York Times*, 16 December 2014.

172 United States Institute of Peace, 'A Conversation with H. E. Mohammad Ashraf Ghani, President of the Islamic Republic of Afghanistan', 25 March 2015.

173 Sanjay Kumar, 'Afghanistan's ex-intelligence chief reflects on Mullah Omar's death', *The Diplomat*, 30 July 2015.

174 Lisa Curtis, 'How Pakistan is tightening its grip on the Taliban', *National Interest*, 15 August 2015.

175 Interview with Taliban political leader no. 1, undisclosed location, 2014.

176 Alex Strick van Linschoten and Felix Kuehn, *Lessons Learnt: 'Islamic, Independent, Perfect and Strong': Parsing the Taliban's Strategic Intentions, 2001–2011*, AHRC Public Policy Series No. 3 (Swindon: Arts and Humanities Research Council, 2012).

177 Interview with Taliban political leader no. 3, undisclosed location, 2014.

178 Thus in his 2015 Eid message, Mullah Omar supposedly endorsed the possibility of peace talks. Sune Engel Rasmussen, 'Taliban peace talks

with Afghan government "endorsed" by Mullah Omar', *Guardian*, 15 July 2015.

179 Interview with Taliban military leader no. 10, undisclosed location, 2014. The interviewee went on to disagree with the Quetta Shura's view on this.

180 Discussions with former Taliban minister and former Taliban deputy minister, Gulf, July 2012.

181 Interview with Taliban commander no. 2, undisclosed location, 2014.

182 Interview with Taliban commander no. 1, undisclosed location, 2014.

183 Interview with Taliban commander no. 17, undisclosed location, 2014.

184 Interview with Taliban commander no. 12, undisclosed location, 2014.

185 In private discussions with us, senior Taliban leaders stated that the movement would be prepared to renounce al-Qaeda as part of a future peace deal. See Michael Semple, Theo Farrell, Anatol Lieven and Rudra Chaudhuri, *Taliban Perspectives on Reconciliation*, Royal United Services Institute, September 2012, p. 3.

186 Vahid Brown and Don Rassler, *Fountainhead of Jihad: The Haqqani Nexus, 1973–2012* (London: Hurst, 2013).

187 Statement of General John F. Campbell, Commander of US Forces in Afghanistan, Before the Senate Armed Services Committee on The Situation in Afghanistan, 6 October 2015, Version 1.9_FINAL, p. 14; Joseph Goldstein, 'US steps up airstrikes in Afghanistan, even targeting ISIS', *New York Times*, 15 July 2015.

188 Mujib Mashal and Taimoor Shah, 'Taliban's new leader in Afghanistan moves to quash dissent', *New York Times*, 6 September 2015.

189 Thomas Ruttig, *In Search of a Peace Process: A 'New' HPC and an Ultimatum for the Taleban*, Afghanistan Analysts Network, 26 February 2016.

190 Reuters, 'Taliban refuse to take part in Afghanistan peace talks', *Guardian*, 5 March 2016.

191 Mujib Mashal, 'Taliban chief targeted by drone strike in Pakistan, signaling a U.S. shift', *New York Times*, 22 May 2016.

192 Barnett Rubin, 'An assassination that could bring war or peace', *The New Yorker*, 4 June 2016.

193 Sune Engel Rasmussen and Jon Boone, 'Afghan Taliban appoint Mullah Haibatullah Akhundzada as new leader', *Guardian*, 25 May 2016; Jessica Donati and Habib Khan Totakhil, 'Taliban names Maulavi Haibatullah as new leader', *Wall Street Journal*, 25 May 2016; Mujib Mashal and Taimoor Shah, 'Taliban's new leader, more scholar than fighter, is slow to impose himself', *New York Times*, 11 July 2016.

194 Idress Ali, 'Afghan peace talks with new hardline Taliban leader unlikely: US military', *The Wire*, 1 June 2016.

195 Interviews with Taliban, undisclosed location, November 2016.

196 Jessica Donati and Habib Khan Totakhil, 'Ashraf Ghani attacks Pakistan for sheltering terrorist groups', *Wall Street Journal*, 25 April 2016; Mujib Mashal, 'Afghan president demands Pakistan take military action against Taliban', *New York Times*, 25 April 2016.

197 Rowena Mason, 'UK to increase troops in Afghanistan from 450 to 500', *Guardian*, 9 July 2016.

198 Mark Landler, 'Obama says he will keep more troops in Afghanistan than planned', *New York Times*, 6 July 2016.

199 Christina Lamb, *Farewell Kabul: From Afghanistan to a More Dangerous Place* (London: William Collins, 2015), p. 263.

200 The scholarly view of counter-leadership targeting is divided. Some argue that killing insurgent leaders often stiffens the resolve of followers and makes it easier to recruit more insurgents. Recent scholarship argues that while not 'a silver bullet', taking out 'insurgent leaders significantly increases governments' chances of reducing violence, terminating wars, and defeating insurgents'. See Jenna Jordan, 'When heads roll: assessing the effectiveness of leadership decapitation', *Security Studies*, vol. 18, no. 4 (2009), pp. 719–55; Stephen T. Hosmer, *Operations Against Enemy Leaders* (Santa Monica, CA: The RAND Corporation, 2001); Patrick B. Johnston, 'Does decapitation work? Assessing the effectiveness of targeting in counterinsurgency campaigns', *International Security*, vol. 36, no. 4 (2012), p. 77.

201 Data provided by the UK Ministry of Defence, reported in House of Commons Defence Committee, *Securing the Future of Afghanistan*, Tenth Report of Session 2012–13, HC 413 (London: The Stationery Office, 10 April 2013), p. 14.

202 This is well explored in Christian Tripoli, 'The British Army, "understanding", and the illusion of control', *Journal of Strategic Studies*, published online 15 July 2016.

203 John Ralston Saul, *Voltaire's Bastards: The Dictatorship of Reason in the West* (New York: Vintage, 1992), p. 11.

204 M. L. R. Smith and David Martin Jones, *The Political Impossibility of Modern Counterinsurgency: Strategy Problems, Puzzles and Paradoxes* (New York: Columbia University Press, 2015), p. xv. This may also be applied to all forms of war and the false promise of the 'science of strategy'. Lawrence Freedman writes: 'Wars are not won through applying some formula that only seasoned military professionals could grasp.' Rather he highlights the importance of 'political skill' and the ability to forge and manage coalitions as key to success in war. Freedman, *Strategy: A History* (Oxford: Oxford University Press, 2013), p. 242.

205 Anthony Seldon and Guy Lodge, *Brown at 10* (London: Biteback Publishing, 2010), p. 207.

206 David Betz and Anthony Cormack, 'Iraq, Afghanistan and British strategy', *Orbis* (Spring 2009), p. 336.

207 SIGAR, *Quarterly Report*, 30 July 2015, pp. 3–15.

208 Walter C. Ladwig III, *The Forgotten Front: Patron–Client Relationships in Counterinsurgency* (Cambridge: Cambridge University Press, 2017).

209 ISAF Joint Command study, October 2010. Copy with author.

210 Interview with very senior Taliban commander, undisclosed location, November 2016.

211 For discussion, see Theo Farrell and Michael Semple, *Ready for Peace? The Afghan Taliban after a Decade of War* (London: Royal United Services Institute, 2016), https://rusi.org/publication/briefing-papers/ready-peace-afghan-taliban-after-decade-war.

Select Bibliography

Albright, Madeleine. *Madam Secretary: A Memoir*, 2nd edn (London: HarperCollins, 2013).

Andersen, Ben. *No Worse Enemy: The Inside Story of the Chaotic Struggle for Afghanistan* (Oxford: Oneworld, 2011).

Andres, Richard B., Craig Wills and Thomas Griffith Jr. 'Winning with allies: the strategic value of the Afghan model', *International Security*, vol. 30, no. 3 (2005/06), pp. 124–60.

Andrew, Christopher. *The Defence of the Realm: The Authorized History of MI5* (London: Penguin Books, 2010).

Armstrong, David, Theo Farrell and Helene Lambert. *International Law and International Relations*, 2nd edn (Cambridge: Cambridge University Press, 2012).

Barfield, Thomas. *Afghanistan: A Cultural and Political History* (Princeton, NJ: Princeton University Press, 2010).

—— *Afghan Wars and the North-West Frontier, 1839–1947*, 2nd edn (London: Cassell, 2002).

Barzilai, Yaniv. *102 Days of War: How Osama Bin Laden, Al Qaeda and the Taliban Survived 2001* (London: Potomac Books, 2013).

Bayly, Martin J. *Taming the Imperial Imagination: Colonial Knowledge, International Relations, and the Anglo–Afghan Encounter, 1808–1878* (Cambridge: Cambridge University Press, 2016).

Beattie, Doug. *Ordinary Soldier* (London: Simon and Schuster, 2009).

—— *Task Force Helmand* (London: Pocket Books, 2009).

Benitz, Max. *Six Months Without Sundays: The Scots Guards in Afghanistan* (Edinburgh: Birlinn, 2011).

Bennett, Huw. *Fighting the Mau Mau: The British Army and Counter-Insurgency in the Kenya Emergency* (Cambridge: Cambridge University Press, 2012).

Bergen, Peter L. *The Osama Bin Laden I Know: An Oral History of al-Qaeda's Leader* (New York: Free Press, 2006).

—— *Manhunt: From 9/11 to Abbottabad – The Ten-Year Search for Osama Bin Laden* (London: The Bodley Head, 2012).

—— (ed.) *Talibanistan* (Oxford: Oxford University Press, 2012).

Berinsky, Adam J., and James N. Druckman. 'Public opinion research and support for the Iraq War', *Public Opinion Quarterly*, vol. 71, no. 1 (2007), pp. 126–41.

Bernsten, Gary. *Jawbreaker: The Attack on Bin Ladin and Al-Qaeda* (New York: Three Rivers Press, 2005).

Betz, David, and Anthony Cormack. 'Iraq, Afghanistan and British strategy', *Orbis*, vol. 53, no. 2 (2009), pp. 319–36.

Biddle, Stephen D. *Afghanistan and the Future of Warfare: Implications for Army and Defense Policy* (Carlisle, PA: Strategic Studies Institute, November 2002).

—— *Military Power: Explaining Victory and Defeat in Modern Battle* (Princeton, NJ: Princeton University Press, 2004).

—— 'Allies, airpower and modern warfare: the Afghan model in Afghanistan and Iraq', *International Security*, vol. 30, no. 1 (2005/06), pp. 161–76.

Bird, Tim, and Alex Marshall. *Afghanistan: How the West Lost Its Way* (New Haven: Yale University Press, 2011).

Bishop, Patrick. *3 Para* (London: HarperPress, 2007).

—— *Ground Truth* (London: HarperPress, 2009).

Blair, Tony. *A Journey* (London: Random House, 2010).

Blanken, Leo J., Hy Rothstein and Jason J. Lepore (eds). *Assessing War: The Challenge of Measuring Success and Failure* (Washington, DC: Georgetown University Press, 2015).

Braithwaite, Rodric. *Afgantsy: The Russians in Afghanistan, 1979–1989* (London: Profile Books, 2011).

Brown, Vahid, and Don Rassler. *Fountainhead of Jihad: The Haqqani Nexus, 1973–2012* (London: Hurst, 2013).

Burke, Jason. *Al-Qaeda: The True Story of Radical Islam*, 3rd edn (London: Penguin Books, 2007).

—— *The 9/11 Wars* (London: Allen Lane, 2011).

Bury, Patrick. *Callsign Hades* (London: Simon and Schuster, 2010).

Bush, George W. *Decision Points* (Virgin Digital, 2010).

Campbell, Alastair. *The Alastair Campbell Diaries. Volume 3: Power and Responsibility, 1999–2001* (London: Arrow Books, 2012).

Campbell, Alastair. *The Alastair Campbell Diaries. Volume 4: The Burden of Power: Countdown to Iraq* (London: Hutchinson, 2012).

Catignani, Sergio. "Getting COIN' at the tactical level in Afghanistan: reassessing counter-insurgency adaptation in the British Army', *Journal of Strategic Studies*, vol. 35, no. 4 (2012), pp. 513–39.

Chandrasekaran, Rajiv. *Imperial Life in the Emerald City: Inside Baghdad's Green Zone* (London: Bloomsbury, 2008).

—— *Little America: The War within the War for Afghanistan* (London: Bloomsbury, 2012).

Chayes, Sarah. *The Punishment of Virtue* (London: Portobello Books, 2006).

—— *Thieves of State: Why Corruption Threatens Global Security* (New York: W. W. Norton, 2015).

Chin, Warren. 'Colonial warfare in a post-colonial state: British operations in Helmand Province, Afghanistan', *Defence Studies*, vol. 10, nos 1–2 (2010), pp. 215–47.

Christia, Fotini, and Michael Semple. 'Flipping the Taliban,' *Foreign Affairs*, July/August 2009, pp. 34–45.

Clack, Timothy, and Robert Johnson (eds). *At the End of Military Intervention: Historical, Theoretical and Applied Approaches to Transition, Handover and Withdrawal* (Oxford: Oxford University Press, 2014).

Clarke, Michael (ed.) *The Afghan Papers: Committing Britain to War in Helmand, 2005–06, Whitehall Paper 77* (London: Royal United Services Institute, 2011).

Clarke, Richard. *Against All Enemies: Inside America's War on Terror* (New York: Free Press, 2004).

Cockburn, Patrick. *Muqtada al-Sadr and the Shia Insurgency in Iraq* (London: Faber and Faber, 2008).

Coll, Steve. *Ghost Wars: The Secret History of the CIA, Afghanistan and Bin Laden, from the Soviet Invasion to September 10, 2001* (London: Penguin Books, 2004).

Connable, Ben. *Embracing the Fog of War: Assessment and Metrics in Counterinsurgency* (Santa Monica, CA: The RAND Corporation, 2012).

Cowper–Coles, Sherard. *Cables from Kabul: The Inside Story of the West's Afghanistan Campaign* (London: HarperPress, 2011).

Crau, Lester W., and Dodge Billingsley. *Operation Anaconda: America's First Major Battle in Afghanistan* (Lawrence, KS: University of Kansas Press, 2011).

Daddis, Gregory A. *No Sure Victory: Measuring US Army Effectiveness and Progress in the Vietnam War* (Oxford: Oxford University Press, 2011).

Dam, Bette. *A Man and a Motorcycle: How Hamid Karzai Came to Power* (Utrecht, NL: Ipso Facto Publishers, 2014).

Derksen, Deedee. *Peace from Bottom Up? The Afghan Peace and Reintegration Program* (Oslo: Peace Research Institute Oslo, 2011).

Directorate Land Warfare, Lessons Exploitation Centre, *Operation HERRICK Campaign Study*, March 2015 (redacted and publicly released version).

Dobbins, James F. *After the Taliban: Nation Building in Afghanistan* (Washington, DC: Potomac Books, 2008).

Egnell, Robert. 'Lessons from Helmand: what now for British counter-insurgency?', *International Affairs*, vol. 87, no. 2 (2011), pp. 297–310.

Evison, Margaret. *Death of a Soldier: A Mother's Story* (London: Biteback Publishing, 2012).

Fairweather, Jack. *The Good War: The Battle for Afghanistan, 2006–14* (London: Jonathan Cape, 2014).

Farrell, Theo. *Appraising Moshtarak: The Campaign in Nad-e-Ali District, Helmand* (London: Royal United Services Institute, 2010).

Farrell, Theo. 'Improving in war: military adaptation and the British in Helmand Province, Afghanistan, 2006–2009', *Journal of Strategic Studies*, vol. 33, no. 4 (2010), pp. 567–94.

Farrell, Theo, and Antonio Giustozzi. 'The Taliban at war: inside the Helmand insurgency, 2004–2012', *International Affairs* vol. 89, no. 4 (2013), pp. 844–71.

Farrell, Theo, Frans Osinga and James A. Russell (eds). *Military Adaptation in Afghanistan* (Stanford, CA: Stanford University Press, 2013).

Farrell, Theo, and Michael Semple. *Ready for Peace? The Taliban After a Decade of War* (London: Royal United Services Institute, 2017).

Farrell, Theo, and Rudra Chaudhuri. 'Campaign disconnect: operational progress and strategic obstacles in Afghanistan, 2009–2011', *International Affairs*, vol. 87, no. 2 (2011), pp. 271–96.

Farrell, Theo, Sten Rynning and Terry Terriff. *Transforming Military Power Since the Cold War: Britain, France and the United States, 1991–2012* (Cambridge: Cambridge University Press, 2013).

Farrell, Theo, and Stuart Gordon. 'COIN machine: the British military in Afghanistan', *Orbis* vol. 53, no. 4 (2009), pp. 665–83.

Feith, Douglas J. *War and Decision: The Pentagon at the Dawn of the War on Terrorism* (New York: HarperCollins, 2008).

Fergusson, James. *Taliban: The True Story of the World's Most Feared Fighters* (London: Bantam Press, 2010).

Flynn, Major General Michael T., Captain Matt Pottinger and Paul. D. Batchelor, *Fixing Intel: A Blueprint for Making Intelligence Relevant in Afghanistan* (Washington, DC: Center for a New American Security, January 2010).

Franco, Claudio, and Antonio Giustozzi. 'Revolution in the Counter-Revolution: efforts to centralize the Taliban's military leadership', *Central Asian Affairs*, vol. 3, no. 3 (2016), pp. 249–86.

Franks, Tommy (with Malcolm McConnell). *American Soldier* (New York: Regan Books, 2004).

Freedman, Lawrence. *A Choice of Enemies: America Confronts the Middle East* (New York: Public Affairs, 2008).

——— *Strategic: A History* (Oxford: Oxford University Press, 2013).

French, David. *The British Way in Counter-Insurgency, 1945–1967* (Oxford: Oxford University Press, 2011).

Fury, Dalton. *Kill Bin Laden* (New York: St. Martin's Press, 2008).

Gall, Carlotta. *The Wrong Enemy: America in Afghanistan, 2001–2014* (New York: Houghton Mifflin Harcourt, 2014).

Gall, Sandy. *War Against the Taliban: Why It All Went Wrong in Afghanistan* (London: Bloomsbury, 2012).

Galula, David. *Counterinsurgency Warfare: Theory and Practice* (Westpoint, CT: Praeger Security International, 2006 [1964]).

Gates, Robert. *Duty: Memoir of a Secretary at War* (Virgin Digital, 2014).

Gelpi, Christopher, Peter D. Feaver and Jason Reifler. 'Success matters: casualty sensitivity and the war in Iraq', *International Security*, vol. 30, no. 3 (2005/06), pp. 7–46.

Giustozzi, Antonio. *Koran, Kalashnikov and Laptop: The Neo-Taliban Insurgency in Afghanistan* (London: Hurst, 2007).

—— (ed.) *Decoding the New Taliban: Insights from the Afghan Field* (London: Hurst, 2009).

—— *Empires of Mud: Wars and Warlords in Afghanistan* (London: Hurst, 2009).

Giustozzi, Antonio, and Claudio Franco. *The Battle for the Schools: The Taleban and State Education* (Berlin: Afghan Analysts Network, 2011).

Giustozzi, Antonio, Adam Baczko and Claudio Franco. *The Politics of Justice: The Taliban's Shadow Judiciary* (Berlin: Afghan Analysts Network, 2013).

Giustozzi, Antonio. *The Army of Afghanistan: A Political History of a Fragile Institution* (London: Hurst, 2015).

Gopal, Anand. *No Good Men Among the Living: America, the Taliban and the War Through Afghan Eyes* (New York: Henry Holt, 2014).

Gordon, Philip H., and Jeremy Shapiro. *Allies at War: America, Europe and the Crisis over Iraq* (New York: McGraw-Hill, 2004).

Gordon, Stuart. *Winning Hearts and Minds? Examining the Relationship between Aid and Security in Afghanistan's Helmand Province* (Feinstein International Center, Tufts University, 2011).

Grenier, Robert. *88 Days to Kandahar: A CIA Diary* (New York: Simon and Schuster, 2015).

Grey, Stephen. *Operation Snakebite* (London: Viking, 2009).

Grob-Fitzgibbon, Benjamin. *Imperial Endgame: Britain's Dirty Wars and the End of Empire* (New York: Palgrave Macmillan, 2011).

Gutman, Roy. *How We Missed the Story: Osama Bin Laden, the Taliban, and the Hijacking of Afghanistan* (Washington, DC: US Institute of Peace, 2008).

Hafvenstein, Joel. *Opium Season: A Year on the Afghan Frontier* (Guilford, CT: The Lyons Press, 2007).

Halberstam, David. *War in a Time of Peace: Bush, Clinton and the Generals* (London: Bloomsbury, 2002).

Halper, Stefan and Jonathan Clarke. *America Alone: The Neo-Conservatives and the New Global Order* (Cambridge: Cambridge University Press, 2004).

Hammond, Mark. *Immediate Response* (London: Michael Joseph, 2009).

Harden, Tody. *Dead Men Risen* (London: Quercus, 2012).

Hastings, Michael. 'The Runaway General', *Rolling Stone,* 22 June 2010.

Hennessey, Patrick. *Kandak: Fighting with Afghans* (London: Allen Lane, 2012).

Hosmer, Stephen T. *Operations Against Enemy Leaders* (Santa Monica, CA: The RAND Corporation, 2001).

Human Rights Watch, *Just Don't Call It a Militia: Impunity, Militias, and the 'Afghan Local Police'* (New York: Human Rights Watch, 2011).

Johnson, Rob. *The Afghan Way of War: Culture and Pragmatism* (London: Hurst, 2011).

Johnson, Thomas H., and Matthew C. DuPee. 'Analysing the new Taliban code of conduct (layeha): an assessment of changing perspectives and strategies of the Afghan Taliban', *Central Asian Survey*, vol. 31, no. 1 (2012), pp. 77–91.

Johnston, Patrick B. 'Does decapitation work? Assessing the effectiveness of targeting in counterinsurgency campaigns', *International Security*, vol. 36, no. 4 (2012), pp. 47–79.

Jones, Seth G. *In the Graveyard of Empires: America's War in Afghanistan* (New York: W. W. Norton, 2009).

Jones, Seth G. and Arturo Munoz. *Afghanistan's Local War: Building Local Defense Forces* (Santa Monica, CA: The RAND Corporation, 2010).

Jordan, Jenna. 'When heads roll: assessing the effectiveness of leadership decapitation', *Security Studies*, vol. 18, no. 4 (2009), pp. 719–55.

Kagan, Frederick W. *Finding the Target: The Transformation of American Military Policy* (New York: Encounter Books, 2006).

Kampfner, John. *Blair's Wars* (London: Free Press, 2003).

Kaplan, Fred. *The Insurgents: David Petraeus and the Plot to Change the American Way of War* (New York: Simon and Schuster, 2013).

Kemp, Richard, and Chris Hughes. *Attack State Red* (London: Michael Joseph, 2009).

Khalilzad, Zalmay. *The Envoy: From Kabul to the White House – My Journey Through a Turbulent World*, Kindle edn (New York: St. Martin's Press, 2016).

Khan, Riaz Mohammad. *Afghanistan and Pakistan: Conflict, Extremism, and Resistance to Modernity* (Washington, DC: Woodrow Wilson Center Press, 2011).

Kiley, Sam. *Desperate Glory* (London: Constable, 2009).

Killcullen, David. *The Accidental Guerilla: Fighting Small Wars in the Midst of a Big One* (London: Hurst, 2011).

King, Anthony. 'Understanding the Helmand campaign: British military operations in Afghanistan', *International Affairs*, vol. 86, no. 2 (2010), pp. 311–32.

Koontz, Christopher N. (ed.). *Enduring Voices: Oral Histories of the US Army Experience in Afghanistan 2003–5* (US Army Center of Military History, 2009).

Korski, Daniel. *Afghanistan: Europe's Forgotten War* (London: European Council on Foreign Relations, 2008).

Krause, Peter John Paul. 'The last good hope: a reassessment of U.S. operations at Tora Bora', *Security Studies*, vol. 17, no. 4 (2008), pp. 644–86.

Kukis, Mark. *My Heart Came Attached: The Strange Journey of Walter Lindh* (Washington, DC: Potomac Books, 2005).

Ladwig III, Walter C. *The Forgotten Front: Patron–Client Relationships in Counterinsurgency* (Cambridge: Cambridge University Press, 2017).

Lai, Brian and Dan Reiter. 'Rally "round the Union Jack?" Public opinion and the use of force in the United Kingdom, 1948–2001', *International Studies Quarterly*, vol. 49, no. 2 (2005), pp. 255–72.

Lamb, Christina. *The Sewing Circles of Herat: A Memoir of Afghanistan* (London: HarperCollins, 2004).

—— *Farewell Kabul: From Afghanistan to a More Dangerous World* (London: William Collins, 2015).

Lamb, Christopher J., and Evan Musing, *Secret Weapon: High-Value Target Teams as an Organizational Innovation*, INSS Strategic Perspectives 4 (Washington, DC: US National Defense University, 2011).

Lambeth, Benjamin. *Air Power against Terrorism: American's Conduct of Operation Enduring Freedom* (Santa Monica, CA: The RAND Corporation, 2005).

Ledwidge, Frank. *Losing Small Wars: British Military Failure in Iraq and Afghanistan* (New Haven: Yale University Press, 2011).

Ledwidge, Frank. *Investment in Blood: The True Cost of Britain's Afghan War* (New Haven: Yale University Press, 2013).

Lester, Nicola. 'When a soldier dies', *Critical Military Studies*, vol. 1, no. 3 (2015), pp. 249–53.

Lewis, Russell. *Company Commander* (London: Random House, 2012).

Lieven, Anatol. *Pakistan: A Hard Country* (London: Allen Lane, 2011).

Long, Austin. 'The Anbar Awakening', *Survival*, vol. 50, no. 2 (2008), pp. 67–94.

Loyn, David. *Butcher and Bolt: Two Hundred Years of Foreign Engagement in Afghanistan* (London: Windmill Books, 2008).

Malkasian, Carter. *War Comes to Garmser: Thirty Years of Conflict on the Afghan Frontier* (London: Hurst, 2013).

Malkasian, Carter, Jerry Meyerle and Megan Katt. *The War in Southern Afghanistan, 2001–2008* (Washington, DC: Center for Naval Analysis, 2009).

Mansfield, David. *A State Built on Sand: How Opium Undermined Afghanistan* (London: Hurst, 2016).

Marsden, Peter. *Afghanistan: Aid, Armies and Empires* (London: I. B. Tauris, 2009).

Martin, Mike. *An Intimate War: An Oral History of the Helmand Conflict* (London: Hurst, 2014).

McChrystal, General Stanley. *My Share of the Task: A Memoir* (New York: Portfolio/Penguin, 2013).

McInnes, Colin. 'Labour's Strategic Defence Review', *International Affairs*, vol. 74, no. 4 (1998), pp. 823–45.

Meyer, Christopher. *DC Confidential: The Controversial Memoirs of Britain's Ambassador to the US at the Time of 9/11 and the Run-up to the Iraq War* (London: Phoenix, 2011).

Nagl, John A. *Learning to Eat Soup with a Knife: Counterinsurgency Lessons from Malaya and Vietnam* (Chicago: Chicago University Press, 2002).

Nasr, Vali. *The Dispensable Nation: American Foreign Policy in Retreat* (Scribe, 2013).

Neumann, Peter R., and M. L. R. Smith. *The Strategy of Terrorism: How It Works, and Why It Fails* (London: Routledge, 2008).

Nolan, Victoria. *Military Leadership and Counterinsurgency: The British Army and Small War Strategy since World War II* (New York: I. B. Tauris, 2012).

North, Richard. *Ministry of Defeat: The British War in Iraq, 2003–2009* (London: Continuum, 2009), pp. 47–63.

O'Hanlon, Michael E. 'A flawed masterpiece', *Foreign Affairs*, vol. 81, no. 3 (March/April 2002).

Packer, George. *The Assassins' Gate: America in Iraq* (London: Faber and Faber, 2007).

Parker, Tom. 'It's a trap: provoking an overreaction is Terrorism 101', *RUSI Journal*, vol. 160, no. 2 (2015), pp. 38–47.

Powell, Jonathan. *The New Machiavelli: How to Wield Power in the Modern World* (London: Vintage Books, 2011).

Rashid, Ahmed. *Taliban: The Story of the Afghan Warlords* (London: Pan, 2000).

Rayment, Sean. *Into the Killing Zone* (London: Constable, 2008).

—— *Bomb Hunters: In Afghanistan with Britain's Elite Bomb Disposal Unit* (London: HarperCollins, 2011).

Reidel, Bruce. *The Search for al-Qaeda: Its Leadership, Ideology and Future* (Washington, DC: The Brookings Institution, 2008).

Rice, Condoleezza. *No Higher Honour: A Memoir of My Years in Washington* (London: Simon and Schuster, 2011).

Richards, General David. *Taking Command* (London: Headline, 2014).

Ricks, Thomas E. *Fiasco: The American Military Adventure in Iraq* (London: Allen Lane, 2006).

Rotmann, Philipp, David Tohn and Jaron Wharton. 'Learning under fire: progress and dissent in the US military', *Survival*, vol. 51, no. 4 (2009), pp. 31–48.

Rubin, Barnett R. *The Fragmentation of Afghanistan*, 2nd edn (New Haven: Yale University Press, 2005).

Rumsfeld, Donald. *Known and Unknown: A Memoir* (New York: Sentinel, 2011).

Russell, James A. *Innovation, Transformation and War: Counterinsurgency Operations in Anbar and Ninewa Provinces, Iraq, 2005–2007* (Stanford: Stanford University Press, 2011).

Ruttig, Thomas. *The Battle for Afghanistan. Negotiations with the Taliban: History and Prospects for the Future* (New America Foundation, May 2011).

Rynning, Sten. *NATO in Afghanistan: The Liberal Disconnect* (Stanford, CA: Stanford University Press, 2012).

Saideman, Stephen M. *Adapting in the Dust: Lessons Learned from Canada's War in Afghanistan* (Toronto: University of Toronto Press, 2016).

Sallust, *Operation Herrick: An Unofficial History of British Military Operations in Afghanistan, 2001–2014* (available from Amazon, 2015).

Seldon, Anthony, and Guy Lodge. *Brown at 10* (London: Biteback Publishing, 2010).

Seldon, Anthony, and Peter Snowdon. *Cameron at 10: The Inside Story, 2010–2015* (London: William Collins, 2015).

Seldon, Anthony (with Peter Snowdon and Daniel Collings). *Blair Unbound* (London: Pocket Books, 2008).

Semple, Michael. *Reconciliation in Afghanistan* (Washington DC: US Institute of Peace Press, 2009).

Semple, Michael, Theo Farrell, Anatol Lieven and Rudra Chaudhuri. *Taliban Perspectives on Reconciliation* (London: Royal United Services Institute, 2012).

Shroen, Gary C. *First In: An Insider's Account of How the CIA Spearheaded the War on Terror in Afghanistan* (New York: Presidio Press, 2007).

Simms, Brendan. *Unfinest Hour: How Britain Helped Destroy Bosnia* (London: Penguin, 2002).

Smith, M. L. R., and David Martin Jones. *The Political Impossibility of Modern Counterinsurgency: Strategic Problems, Puzzles and Paradoxes* (New York: Columbia University Press, 2015).

Southby-Taylor, Ewen. *Helmand, Afghanistan: 3 Commando Brigade* (London: Ebury Press, 2008).

—— *3 Commando Brigade: Helmand Assault* (London: Ebury Press, 2010).

Stacpoole-Ryding, Richard J. *Maiwand: The Last Stand of the 66th (Berkshire) Regiment in Afghanistan, 1880* (Stroud: The History Press, 2008).

Stevens, Michael. 'Afghan local police in Helmand: calculated risk or last gamble?', *RUSI Journal*, vol. 158, no. 1 (2013), pp. 46–70.

Stewart, Rory. *The Places in Between* (Basingstoke: Pan Macmillan, 2004).

—— 'The irresistible illusion', *London Review of Books*, vol. 31, no. 13 (2009), pp. 3–6.

Stewart, Rory, and Gerald Knaus. *Can Intervention Work?* (New York: W. W. Norton, 2014).

Stone, John. 'Escalation and the War on Terror', *Journal of Strategic Studies*, vol. 35, no. 5 (2012), pp. 639–61.

Strachan, Hew. *The Direction of War: Contemporary Strategy in Historical Perspective* (Oxford: Oxford University Press, 2013).

Straw, Jack. *Last Man Standing: Memoirs of a Political Survivor* (London: Macmillan, 2012).

Streatfeild, Richard. *Honourable Warriors: Fighting the Taliban in Afghanistan* (Barnsley: Pen and Sword, 2014).

Strick van Linschoten, Alex, and Felix Kuehn. *Lessons Learned: 'Islamic, Independent, Perfect and Strong': Parsing the Taliban's Strategic Intentions,*

2001–2011, AHRC Public Policy Series, no. 3 (Swindon: Arts and Humanities Research Council, 2012).

—— *An Enemy We Created: The Myth of the Taliban/Al Qaeda Merger in Afghanistan, 1970–2010* (London: Hurst, 2012).

Suhrke, Astri. *When More Is Less: The International Project in Afghanistan* (London: Hurst, 2011).

Summers, Anthony, and Robbyn Swan. *The Eleventh Day: The Ultimate Account of 9/11* (London: Doubleday, 2011).

Tenet, George. *At the Center of the Storm: My Years at the CIA* (New York: HarperCollins, 2007).

Terrill, Chris. *Commando* (London: Century, 2007).

Thruelsen, Peter Dahl. 'Striking the right balance: how to rebuild the Afghan national police', *International Peacekeeping*, vol. 17, no. 1 (2010), pp. 80–92.

Tootal, Stuart. *Danger Close: Commanding 3 Para in Afghansitan* (London: John Murray, 2009).

Tripoli, Christian. 'The British Army, "understanding", and the illusion of control', *Journal of Strategic Studies,* published online 15 July 2016.

Ucko, David H., and Robert Egnell. *Counterinsurgency in Crisis: Britain and the Challenges of Modern Warfare* (New York: Columbia University Press, 2013).

Urban, Mark. *Task Force Black: The Explosive True Story of the SAS and the Secret War in Iraq* (London: Little, Brown, 2010).

Weigley, Russell F. *The American Way of War* (Bloomington and Indianapolis: Indiana University Press, 1997).

West, Bing. *One Million Steps: A Marine Platoon at War* (New York: Random House, 2014).

Wheeler, Nicholas J. *Saving Strangers: Humanitarian Intervention in International Society* (Oxford: Oxford University Press, 2000).

Wheeler, Nicholas J., and Tim Dunne. *Moral Britannia? Evaluating the Ethical Dimension of Labour's Foreign Policy* (London: Foreign Policy Centre, 2004).

Wickham-Jones, Mark, and Richard Little (eds). *New Labour's Foreign Policy: A New Moral Crusade* (Manchester: Manchester University Press, 2000).

Woodward, Bob. *Bush at War* (London: Pocket Books, 2003).

—— *Obama's Wars: The Inside Story* (New York: Simon and Schuster, 2010).

Wright, Donald P., and the Contemporary Operations Study Team. *A Different Kind of War: The United States Army in Operation ENDURING FREEDOM, October 2001– September 2005* (Fort Leavenworth, KS: Contemporary Studies Institute Press, 2010).

Wright, Lawrence. *The Looming Tower: Al-Qaeda's Road to 9/11* (London: Penguin, 2006).

Zaeef, Abdeul Salam. *My Life with the Taliban* (London: Hurst, 2010).

Index

A-10 Warthogs, 175, 176, 183, 185
A-teams, 69, 74, 75, 85–6, 89, 101, 161
Abdul Haq, 84, 85
Abdul Khaleq, 367
Abdul Majan, 143
Abdullah Abdullah
    2001 British troops deployed to Bagram, 81–2; recommends Karzai for leadership, 87; appointed minister for foreign affairs, 88; deployment of ISAF, 95
    2009 presidential election, 263, 388–9
    2014 presidential election, 397–9
    2015 fall of Kunduz, 401
Abu Ghraib prison abuse scandal (2003–4), 147
AC-130 gunships, 72, 101, 103, 111, 175, 185, 219, 220
'Accelerating Success in Afghanistan' (2003), 138
Achakzai, Abdul Razaq, 409
Aden, Yemen, 36
Adi Wal, Hussein, 223
aerial surveillance, 342, 354
aerostats, 354
Afghan Analysts Network, 401
Afghan Civil Order Police, 401
Afghan Development Zones (ADZs), 170, 172, 180–81, 194, 202
Afghan Election Authority, 263
Afghan Eradication Force, 227–8
Afghan Local Police (ALP), 377–80, 400
Afghan National Army (ANA), 113, 132, 374–5
    2003 formation of, 128–9
    2005 CSTC-A takes over training, 375
    2006 British forces deployed to Helmand, 172; IED attack in Gereshk, 170; Royal Marines deployed to Helmand, 193; battle for Garmsir, 199
    2007 capture of Sangin, 200; Mechanised Brigade deployed to Helmand, 193, 203–4

2008 Operation Oqab Tsuka, 242; Taliban attack on Lashkar Gah, 248–9
2009 Obama announces new strategy, 278; McChrystal takes command of ISAF, 281, 283, 287, 288, 295, 302; Operation Panchai Palang, 254, 256, 257, 262, 308; Operation Tor Shpa'h, 298; Obama announces surge and drawdown, 302–3
2010 NATO agrees new growth target, 374; Operation Moshtarak, 307–12, 322–4; holding of Nad-e Ali, 314, 315
2011 Sangin peace accord, 364
2012 Allen orders protective measures against insider attacks, 381; Allen halts joint operations, 381; casualties mount, 385–6; responsibility for Lashkar Gah and Nahr-e Seraj taken, 386
2013 Karzai bans requests for ISAF air support, 383–5; battle of Badakhshan, 384; Taliban attack in Kunar, 385; inteqal process reaches 'Milestone 13', 384
2014 Karzai proposes seizure of Parwan Detention Facility, 395; British withdrawal from Helmand, 387
2015 Taliban offensive, 399–402
2016 Taliban offensive, 402–3
Afghan National Guard (ANG), 99, 128, 132
Afghan National Police (ANP), 251, 255, 256, 273, 374–7, 393–4
    2002 formation of, 99, 128–9, 145, 161, 165
    2003 US State Department takes over training, 129
    2005 insurgent attacks increase, 154, 155; Strengthening Peace Programme launched, 217; CSTC-A takes over training, 129, 375
    2006 CSTC-A report, 129; British forces deployed to Helmand, 173, 174; conflict in Sangin, 174; Royal Marines deployed to Helmand, 193; conflict in Musa Qala, 184, 188, 189, 190, 191; battle for Garmsir, 199

2007 capture of Sangin, 200; Mechanised Brigade deployed to Helmand, 193, 204; reintegration of Gereshk Taliban, 217; Adi Wadl appointed Helmand chief, 223

2008 Kaduz expelled from Babaji area, 255; EU opposition to ISAF training, 284–5; conflict with Mullah Salaam in Musa Qala, 225; Operation Azada Wosa, 238; Taliban attack on Lashkar Gah, 246–8; Operation Sond Chara, 250, 251, 252;

2009 Obama announces new strategy, 278; McChrystal takes command of ISAF, 281, 283, 287, 289, 302; Operation Panchai Palang, 256, 308; 'consent-based clear' operation in Nad-e Ali, 297; insider attack in Nad-e Ali, 380; Obama announces surge and drawdown, 302; Helmand training academy established, 314, 376

2010 NATO agrees new growth target, 374; Operation Moshtarak, 307, 314; holding of Nad-e Ali, 314; Taliban attacks in Marjah, 316

2012 Allen orders protective measures against insider attacks, 381; Allen halts joint operations, 381; casualties mount, 385–6

2015 Taliban offensive, 400–401

2016 Taliban offensive, 403

Afghan Peace and Reintegration Programme (APRP), 404

Agha, Haji Shah, 187–8, 190

Aghezai clan, 251, 257

AGM-142 Have Nap missiles, 101

Ahmed Shah, 296, 309

Ahmed, Mahmud, 54

aid, 1, 5, 95, 119, 125–7, 132, 135–6, 138, 181
  aid workers, 68, 70–71, 119, 154
  and Atmar, 391
  Berlin conference (2004), 126–7
  and corruption, 127, 391, 393, 423
  and counter-narcotics, 227
  and Helmand Road Map (2007), 230
  and ISAF, 135–6, 230, 287, 316, 325
  to Pakistan, 278, 347–9
  to Taliban, 32, 34
  Tokyo conference (2002), 125

Ainsworth, Robert 'Bob', 270

Air Assault Brigade
  2001 deployment to Bagram, 81; deployment to Kabul with ISAF, 94, 98, 107, 169; battle of Tora Bora, 105
  2006 deployment to Helmand, 156, 168–70, 179–80, 233; IED attack in Gereshk, 170; Platoon House strategy adopted, 171; IED attacks in Lashkar Gah, 172;

deployment to Sangin cancelled, 173–4; platoon houses established in Now Zad and Musa Qala, 173, 174; Gul Mohammad Khan killed by Taliban, 174; fighting with Taliban in Sangin, 174–5, 177; Lamb's report on Gereshk ambush, 177–8; fighting in Sangin, 182–3; fighting in Musa Qala, 184–7; ceasefire in Musa Qala, 187–91

2008 redeployed to Helmand, 231–4, 352; Operation Oqab Tsuka, 239–43

2010 redeployed to Helmand, 367–8; operations in Chah-e Anjir Triangle, 355; ALP established in Saidabad, 378

Air Force One, 17–18, 39

Airborne Division, 105, 132, 199

AK-47 assault rifles, 377, 380

Akhundzada, Amir Mohammed, 167, 187

Akhundzada, Haibatullah, 416

Akhundzada, Nasim, 144

Akhundzada, Sher Mohammed, 214, 233
  2001 return to Lashkar Gah, 144, 163
  2002 opium eradication programme launched, 226, 228; conflict with Jan and Mir Wali, 160
  2004 Jan removed from Garmsir governorship, 165
  2005 removed from Helmand governorship, 166–8
  2006 conflict in Musa Qala, 187, 189, 190
  2009 Mangal seeks Sangin peace deal, 362

Albright, Madeleine, 34–6, 119

Aldred, Margaret, 156, 179

Alec Station, 23

Alexander, Douglas, 269

Ali, Hazarat, 102–3, 106

Alikozai tribe, 89, 91, 144, 163–4, 173–4, 360–64

Alikozai, Naqibullah, 89–91

Alizai tribe, 144, 163, 165, 187, 214, 225, 226

Alizai, Abdul Qayyam, 214

Allen, John, 373–4, 381–3

Allied Rapid Reaction Corps (ARRC), 140–41, 148, 178–9, 191

Alternative Livelihoods Programme, 293, 367

American Civil War (1861–65), 90

American Enterprise Institute, 285

Amir Agha, Garmsir, 235, 236–7, 264

amir ul momineen, 28, 411

Amir, Sultan, 32

Amos, James, 383

Amphibious Readiness Group, 107

Amritsar Massacre (1919), 8

Amrullah Saleh, 346

Anbar Awakening (2006–7), 279, 377

Anderson, Ben, 319, 323

Anderson, Donald, 49

Anglo-Afghan Wars
  First (1839–42), 4, 7, 49, 97, 335
  Second (1879–82), 7–8, 49, 186, 335, 392
  Third (1919), 8, 335
Angola, 118
Antonov AN-224 transport planes, 240
Apache helicopters, 418–19
  2006 deployment to Helmand, 156, 179;
    fighting in Sangin and Musa Qala, 175,
    176, 183, 184, 185; fighting in Now Zad,
    198
  2007 support for Mechanised Brigade, 203;
    battle for Musa Qala, 219
  2008 Taliban attack on Lashkar Gah, 246,
    247–8, 419; Operation Sond Chara, 251
  2009 Operation Panchai Palang, 258; British
    Muslim leaders visit Nad-e Ali, 292
  2011 killing of Niaz Mohammed, 330
Arab-Israeli War (1948), 21
arbakai, 377
Arghendab Bridge, Kandahar, 86
Armitage, Richard, 122
Armoured Brigade, 378
Army War College, US, 285
Asia Foundation, 394
Asian Development Bank, 125
Assault Breacher Vehicles, 360
Atlantic Fleet, 19
Atmar, Hanif, 312, 391
Atta, Mohamed, 11–12, 27, 37
Atta, Mohammad Noor, 74, 75, 134–5, 330
Australia, 106, 111, 112
Authorization for Use of Military Force (2001),
  50
'axis of evil', 123
Azzam, Adballah, 22

B-1B supersonic bombers, 65, 101, 197, 199, 219,
  247, 312, 357
B-2 stealth bombers, 50, 65
B-52 strategic bombers, 65, 75, 101
Ba'ath Party, 146
Babaji, Helmand, 308, 326, 355, 402
  2008 Taliban attack on Lashkar Gah, 248
  2009 Operation Panchai Palang, 253, 255–7,
    261–2; presidential elections, 263; 'consent-
    based clear' operation, 297
  2010 Operation Moshtarak, 308, 310; Scots
    Guards deployed, 326; Parachute Regi-
    ment deployed, 355
  2016 Taliban offensive, 402
Badakhshan, Afghanistan, 384, 400
Badr Brigade, 150
Baghlan, Afghanistan, 139, 380
Baghran, Helmand, 162–3, 337, 402
Baghrani, Mullah, 162–3

Bagram airfield, Parwan, 163
  2001 British troops deployed, 81; ISAF
    deployed to Kabul, 93; Karzai meets with
    Fahim, 94; battle of Tora Bora, 104;
    Operation Anaconda, 107; Operation
    Jacana, 108–12
  2002 Blair makes visit, 117; abuse and death
    of Dilawar in custody, 163
  2009 McChrystal makes visit, 283
  2014 Karzai proposes seizure of Parwan
    Detention Facility, 395
al-Bahlul, Ali, 53
Baily, Peter, 380
Baldwin, Gil, 155
Balkh, Afghanistan, 65, 70, 73, 74–6, 77, 330
Balochistan, Pakistan, 32, 165, 235, 346, 348, 415
Baluchan, Nad-e Ali, 249, 297, 299
Bamiyan, Bamiyan Province, 76, 134
  Buddhas, destruction of (2001), 32–3
banditry, 28
Baradar, Abdul Ghani, 336–7, 404
Barakzai tribe, 144, 217, 379
Barech, Naim, 143
Barfield, Thomas, 6, 126
Bariullah Khan, 77
Bashir, Mullah, 217, 222
Basic Warrior Training, 375
Basra, Iraq, 145, 146–7, 151, 248–9, 345
Battle Damage Assessment, 212
Battle for Marjah, The, 323
Battle of Badakhshan (2013), 384
Battle of Fallujah (2004), 146, 236, 312, 360
Battle of Kabul (2001), 79–82
Battle of Kandahar (1880), 8
Battle of Kandahar (2001), 86, 89–92
Battle of Kunduz (2001), 77
Battle of Lashkar Gah (2008), 244–8, 340, 419
Battle of Maiwand (1880), 7, 186, 335, 392
Battle of Mazar-e-Sharif (2001), 74–6
Battle of Mogadishu (1993), 119
Battle of Panjwai (2006), 186
Battle of Pashmul (2006), 337
Battle of Tarin Kot (2001), 85–6
Battle of Tora Bora (2001), 101–6, 115
Battlegroup Centre, 208, 234, 245
Battlegroup Centre-South, 252, 254, 292, 296
Battlegroup North, 207, 234, 295, 357
Battlegroup North-West, 234, 245–6
Battlegroup South, 207–8, 234, 246
Bayazo, Helmand, 379
Beadle, Nick, 141–2
beards, 30, 33
Belgium, 137, 290
Bergdahl, Bowe, 406
Bergen, Peter, 6
Bergne, Paul, 76, 82

Berkeley, University of California, 126
Berlin donor conference (2004), 126–7
Berntsen, Gary, 67, 79, 94, 101, 104
Bhutto, Benazir, 31
Biddle, Stephen, 114, 285
Biden, Joseph, 274–7, 278, 289, 291, 327
Bilateral Security Agreement (BSA), 396
bin Laden, Osama
  1987 fights Soviets in Afghanistan, 26
  1988 formation of al-Qaeda, 20, 22
  1996 CIA investigation begins, 23; MI6
    investigation begins, 41–2; arrives in
    Afghanistan, 29; joined by Khalid Sheikh
    Mohammed, 26
  1998 East African US embassy bombings,
    23–5, 41; US Operation Infinite Reach, 25,
    35, 37, 53; sheltered by Taliban, 35–7
  1999 preparation for September 11 attacks,
    27–8
  2001 September 11 attacks, 12, 26, 37, 41–2,
    44, 53–4; sheltered by Taliban, 54–7;
    Jalalabad speech, 100–101; sets up base at
    Tora Bora, 101; battle of Tora Bora, 104,
    115
  2010 located by CIA, 349
  2011 killed by US SEALs, 349–50
biometric profiles, 344
Bismullah Khan, 70, 79, 98, 99
Black, Cofer, 59, 67, 68
Blackhawk helicopters, 68, 185
Blair, Tony
  1997 becomes prime minister, 119
  2001 September 11 attacks; COBRA
    meeting, 38–45; call from Bush, 48;
    Parliament debates response to attacks,
    48–50; diplomatic visits in support of
    war, 51; meets with Boyce, 57; visits US,
    51–3, 63; meets with defence and intel-
    ligence chiefs, 58; Brighton Conference;
    dossier on 9/11 released, 63–4; visits
    Russia, Pakistan and India, 64; airstrikes
    in Afghanistan begin, 64, 65–6, 71;
    speech on Afghan drug trade, 129–30;
    Marines and paratroops deployed, 81,
    121, 418; ISAF deployed to Kabul, 92–3,
    95–6, 117
  2002 visits Afghanistan, 117; warns of
    danger from Iraq, 123; meets with Bush
    in Crawford, 123–4; meets with military
    chiefs at Chequers, 123–4
  2003 invasion of Iraq, 159
  2004 announces ARRC takeover of ISAF,
    140–41, 148–9, 158
  2005 July 7 attacks, 149–50
  2006 forces deployed to Helmand, 158, 159,
    421; retreat of forces in Basra, 151

BLU-82 'Daisy Cutter' bombs, 75, 101
Blunkett, David, 40, 42
Bofors cannons, 72
Bolan Bridge, Helmand, 247–8
Bolan, Helmand, 143
Bonino, Emma, 34
Bonn Agreement (2001), 67, 87–8, 90, 92, 95,
  99, 116, 125, 133
Bosnian War (1992–95), 80, 81, 96, 119, 132, 169
Bostanzai clan, 164
Bowman radio system, 208–9
Boyce, Michael, 57–8, 61, 63, 71, 73, 92–3, 107
Brahimi, Lakhdar, 67, 80, 87, 88, 92, 99, 116
Bremer, Paul, 146–7
Brigade 055, 29, 56
Brighton, East Sussex, 38, 39, 43, 63
British Army
  2001 deployment to Bagram, 81, 121, 418;
    deployment to Kabul with ISAF, 94, 97–9,
    107, 169, 418; battle of Tora Bora, 105
  2003 invasion of Iraq, 137, 140, 145; Mazar-
    e-Sharif PRT established, 134; disarma-
    ment of Atta and Dostum, 134–5
  2004 conflict with Mahdi Army in Basra,
    146–7; Maymaneh PRT established, 134;
    Blair announces ARRC takeover of ISAF,
    140–41, 148–9, 158, 179
  2005 agreement on ISAF expansion to
    Helmand, 141–2, 150; ground lost to Shia
    militias in Iraq, 150–51
  2006 construction of Camp Bastion, 152,
    169; deployment to Helmand, 145,
    156–60, 168–70, 179–80, 233, 333, 421; IED
    attack in Gereshk, 170; Platoon House
    strategy adopted in Helmand, 171; IED
    attacks in Lashkar Gah, 172; deployment
    to Sangin cancelled, 173–4; platoon
    houses established in Now Zad and Musa
    Qala, 173, 174; Gul Mohammad Khan
    killed by Taliban, 174; fighting with
    Taliban in Sangin, 174–5, 177; Lamb's
    report on Gereshk ambush, 177–8; rein-
    forcements sent to Helmand, 178;
    Pathfinders sent to Musa Qala, 178, 183;
    Danes sent to relieve Pathfinders, 178,
    183–4; Somme Battalion relieves Danes,
    183–4; fighting in Sangin, 182–3; fighting
    in Musa Qala, 184–7; Operation Medusa
    launched, 186; capture of Garmsir, 199;
    ceasefire in Musa Qala, 187–91; Royal
    Marines take command of Task Force
    Helmand, 192–3; ceasefire in Sangin, 189,
    191, 195–7; withdrawal from Musa Qala,
    194; ceasefire in Now Zad, 189, 197;
    resumption of fighting in Now Zad, 189,
    197–8; retreat of forces in Basra, 151

2007 fighting in Garmsir, 199; Operation Silver in Sangin, 199–200; Mechanised Brigade takes command of Task Force Helmand, 200–205; introduction of Guidance Card Alpha, 206; reintegration of Gereshk Taliban, 217, 222; withdrawal from Basra Palace, 248; 52nd Infantry Brigade takes command of Task Force Helmand, 207–12; launch of TCAF, 212–14; defection of Mullah Salaam, 215; Taliban attacks in Garmsir and Sangin, 216; capture of Musa Qala, 215–21; conflict over reintegration of Musa Qala Taliban, 221–3

2008 Parachute Regiment deployed to Helmand, 231–4, 352; Powell takes command of Helmand campaign, 229–33; Operation Azada Wosa, 237–8; Operation Oqab Tsuka, 239–43; Royal Marines take command of Task Force Helmand, 244; Taliban attack on Lashkar Gah, 244–8, 340, 419; Brown agrees to send reinforcements, 269; Operation Sond Chara, 249–53

2009 Richards launches Operation Entirety, 273; Light Brigade takes command of Task Force Helmand, 253; Dannatt pressures Brown on reinforcements, 271; McChrystal takes command of ISAF, 294–5; Dannatt visits troops, 271–2; Operation Panchai Palang, 254–63, 271, 272, 294, 304, 307, 308; Brown visits Camp Leatherneck, 304; British Muslim leaders visit Helmand, 292–4; 11th Infantry Brigade deployed to Helmand, 295, 357, 367; command of RC-South taken, 296, 419; 'consent-based clear' operation in Nad-e Ali, 296–7; insider attack in Nad-e Ali, 380; Operation Tor Shpa'h, 297–300, 355; death of Drane in Nad-e Ali, 305; loss of three bomb disposal officers, 342

2010 introduction of 'ground sign awareness', 342; Operation Moshtarak, 296, 297, 305–11, 341, 355, 358; withdrawal from Musa Qala, 356; holding of Nad-e Ali, 313–16, 325; 4th Infantry Brigade deployed to Helmand, 325, 344; Felton takes command of Task Force Helmand, 325; Operation Hamkari, 352; Cameron visits Camp Bastion, 356, 372; Alikozai peace offer in Sangin, 360; operations in Saidabad and Babaji, 326; Royal Irish Regiment deployed; fighting in Nad-e Ali, 352–4; Chiswell takes command of Task Force Helmand, 352; Parachute Regiment deployed, 355, 367–8; ALP established in Saidabad, 378; launch of Persistent Threat Detection System, 354; battle for Red Wedge, 355; withdrawal from Sangin, 173, 356, 372

2011 Sangin peace accord, 363–4; killing of Niaz Mohammed, 330; Armoured Brigade deployed to Helmand, 378

2012 Taliban attack on Camp Bastion, 381–3; Allen halts joint operations with ANSF, 381; shipping back of material begins, 383

2013 withdrawal from Helmand begins, 386–7

2014 PRT and Task Force Helmand dissolved, 387

British Broadcasting Corporation (BBC), 53, 80, 205, 388

British India (1757–1947), 8, 28, 97

Brize Norton, Oxfordshire, 268

Brookings Institution, 276

Brown, Gordon
  2001 September 11 attacks, 40–41
  2003 invasion of Iraq, 159
  2004 Blair announces ARRC takeover of ISAF, 159
  2007 visits Afghanistan, 218
  2008 bank bailout package, 269, 422; agreement of troop increase, 269
  2009 Obama presses for troop increase, 270; conflict over troop increase, 270–71; Operation Panchai Palang, 262, 272–3, 304; death of Thorneloe, 272; visits Camp Leatherneck, 304; announces transition, 322; rules out withdrawal from Sangin, 356
  2010 general election, 356

Browne, Desmond, 159, 201–2, 269

Bucharest, Romania, 284

Buddhas of Bamiyan, 32–3

Buffalo armoured vehicles, 344

burkas, 30

Burley review (2008), 343

Bush, Barbara, 52

Bush, George Herbert Walker, 24, 119

Bush, George Walker
  2001 takes office as president, 36; Clarke's memorandum on Bin Laden, 37; September 11 attacks 15, 17–18, 39, 43; Pentagon war cabinet, 45–7; calls Blair, 48; Authorization for Use of Military Force, 50; CIA launch Afghanistan operation, 61; Camp David war cabinet, 50–51; Blair's visit, addresses Congress, 52–3, 57; CIA assessment on Mullah Omar, 56; war cabinet, 61; K2 airbase negotiations, 63; airstrikes in Afghanistan begin, 64, 65–6, 71; Pakistan launches

Kunduz airlift, 78–9; rules out occupation force for Kabul, 81, 121, 418; ISAF deployed to Kabul, 95–6; battle of Tora Bora, 115
2002 State of the Union speech, 122–3; launch of aid package to Pakistan, 347; meets with Blair in Crawford, 123–4; Virginia Military Institute speech, 138; CJTF takes over Operation Enduring Freedom, 133
2003 invasion of Iraq, 146; Khalilzad plan drawn up, 138
2005 reduction of forces in southern Afghanistan, 168
2007 NSC meeting on war strategy, 275
Butler, Edward, 157, 159, 168–70, 171–4, 178, 184, 186–8, 195
Butler Review (2004), 147

C-130 transport planes, 75, 81, 83, 94, 98, 108
C-17 Globemaster cargo planes, 73
Cabaniss, Christian, 264–6
Cabinet Office
    Infantry Brigade (52nd), deployment of (2007), 209
    Helmand, forces deployed to (2006), 140, 152, 154–6, 158, 167, 171
    September 11 attacks (2001), 42–5
Cable, Mullah, 114
Callwell, Charles Edward, 264
Cambodia, 118
Cameron, David, 356, 370–73, 422
Cameron, Lindy, 315–16
Camp Bastion, Helmand
    2006 establishment of, 152, 169; Parachute Regiment deployed, 169, 170; battle for Sangin, 175, 177; evacuation of wounded from Sangin and Musa Qala, 185
    2008 Taliban attack on Lashkar Gah; proposed relocation, 248; C-IED Task Force established, 344
    2009 escalation of IED injuries, 259–60; Operation Minimise instituted, 267; 'consent-based clear' operation in Nad-e Ali, 296; RC-South switches focus to Kandahar, 301; arrival of ANA troops, 308
    2010 Operation Moshtarak, 310, 324; Cameron makes visit, 356, 372
    2012 insider attacks, 381–3
    2013 British withdrawal, 386
    2014 handed over to ANA, 387
Camp David, Maryland, 50–51
Camp Dwyer, Helmand, 310, 317, 323
Camp Leatherneck, Helmand, 304, 381, 382
Camp Price, Helmand, 161

Camp Rhino, Kandahar, 104
Camp Shorabak, Helmand, 307–8, 381, 382, 403
Campbell, Alastair
    2001 September 11 attacks, 38–9, 43; debate on war, 48, 51; Bush's address to Congress, 53; preparations for war, 57, 58; airstrikes in Afghanistan begin, 65; meetings on progress of war, 73; ISAF deployed, 96; India–Pakistan standoff, 125
    2002 Blair visits Afghanistan, 117; Blair meets with military chiefs at Chequers, 123
Canada
    2002 Operation Anaconda, 106, 108; Operation Jacana, 109
    2005 agreement on ISAF deployment to Kandahar, 141–2, 149, 150
    2006 Fraser appointed commander of RC-South, 169, 296; fighting in Sangin, 177; PAG established, 180–81
    2008 Operation Oqab Tsuka, 241
    2011 withdrawal from ISAF, 372
canals, 155, 177, 228, 237, 249, 341, 363
    Nahr-e Bughra Canal, 249, 251, 256, 294, 297
    Shamalan Canal, 249, 251, 256, 257–9, 261, 262, 308
    Trikh Zabur Canal, 249
Canary Wharf, London, 40
Canberra PR9 reconnaissance planes, 72
Capability Milestones, 375
capacity building, 98, 230, 392, 423
Capewell, David, 383
Capitol, Washington DC, 13, 17, 18, 19, 52
Card, Andrew, 16
cards, banning of, 29
Carl Vinson, USS, 65
Carleton-Smith, Mark, 231–44
Carter, Nicholas 'Nick'
    2002 posted to Afghanistan; development of PRT system, 132–3
    2004 posted to Iraq, 147
    2009 takes command of RC-South, 296, 300, 419
    2010 Operation Moshtarak, 305, 308, 321; Operation Hamkari, 352
    2013 Dunford takes command of ISAF, 383
Casey, George, 147
casualties, 1–2, 216, 259–62, 271, 305, 307, 321–2, 327, 332
    Afghan forces, 323, 332, 385–6, 400
    civilian, *see* civilian casualties
    evacuation of, 175–6, 184–6, 321
    IEDs, 170, 215, 253, 259–60, 323, 342
    and public support, 267–9, 272
    replacement systems, 253, 261
    Taliban, 115, 205, 248, 251, 340

Catignani, Sergio, 368
Cavanagh, Matthew, 158, 159
CB (citizens band) radios, 318
Center for a New American Security, 285
Central African Republic, 118
Central Command (CENTCOM)
  2001 planning of Afghanistan campaign, 59, 61–2, 66; airstrikes on Afghanistan begin, 71; A-teams deployed to assist Northern Alliance, 69; bombing of Taliban forces, 72, 75; battle of Tarin Kot, 86; revision of Iraq war plan, 121–2; Pakistan launches Kunduz airlift, 79; discussions on Karzai for Afghan president, 87; Taliban surrender at Kandahar, 90, 115; battle of Tora Bora, 104, 105, 115; command of ISAF proposed, 96
  2002 Operation Anaconda, 107; plans for Iraq War, 123–4
  2003 invasion of Iraq, 146
  2008 Operation Azada Wosa, 238; Petraeus takes command, 327
  2009 RC-South requests deployment of Marines to Kandahar, 300–301
Central Intelligence Agency (CIA)
  1996 Alec Station established, 23
  1998 East African embassy bombings, 24–5
  2000 plans for rendition of Bin Laden, 36; USS Cole bombing, 36
  2001 increase in funding; rivalry with FBI festers, 37; Massoud assassination, 60; September 11 attacks, 47, 48; planning of Afghanistan campaign, 50, 59, 61, 63; Mullah Omar assessment, 56; Grenier meets with Osmani, 54–5; capture of Wasiq, 55; Jawbreaker team arrives in Afghanistan, 67–8, 70, 114; meeting with Franks, 61; evacuation of Karzai to Pakistan, 85; battle of Tarin Kot, 85; fall of Kabul, 80; British forces deployed, 81; attack on Tora Bora, 101; Qala-i-Jangh Taliban surrender, 78; Pakistan's Kunduz airlift, 79; ground assault on Tora Bora, 102, 103, 104, 105; Karzai meets with Fahim, 94
  2006 drone strikes in Pakistan begin, 348, 351
  2007 review of war strategy, 275
  2010 arrest of Saleh in Afghanistan, 391; spike in Pakistan drone strikes, 349, 420; talks with Taliban in Dubai begin, 404; Bin Laden located, 349
  2011 Petraeus beomes director, 373
Centre for Naval Analysis, 266
Chah-e Anjir, Nad-e Ali, 249
  2008 Operation Sond Chara, 249, 251
  2009 Operation Panchai Palang, 257, 262
  2010 Operation Moshtarak, 297, 305, 309–11, 326
Chah-e Anjir Triangle (CAT), 262, 297–8, 308–9, 312, 322, 355
Chah-e Mirza, Nad-e Ali, 249, 251, 297, 299
Challenger 2 tanks, 250
Chalmers, Douglas, 378, 386
Chandrasekaran, Rajiv, 323
Channel 4 News, 269
Charles, Prince of Wales, 157–8, 259
Chayes, Sarah, 393
Chechnya, 77, 165, 236
Cheltenham, Gloucestershire, 319
chemical weapons, 137
Cheney, Richard 'Dick', 16, 17–18, 19, 39, 47, 56
Chequers, Buckinghamshire, 123, 370–72
Chicken, Tim, 108–9, 110, 112
childbirth, 99
China, 36, 51, 240, 242, 408–9, 412, 415
'Chinese Restaurant', 183
Chinook helicopters, 209, 271
  2001 invasion of Aghanistan, 68
  2002 Operation Jacana, 108, 109, 110, 111
  2006 deployment to Helmand, 156, 157; fighting in Sangin and Musa Qala, 174–7, 185, 186
  2007 battle for Musa Qala, 219
  2009 Operation Panchai Palang, 256; British Muslim leaders visit Nad-e Ali, 292; Operation Tor Shpa'h, 298
  2010 Operation Moshtarak, 307
Chirac, Jacques, 96
Chiswell, James, 352–3, 355, 356, 368, 378
Christianity, 71
Churchill, Winston, 123, 238
City of London, 40
Civil Contingencies Unit, 40
civil service, 127
civilian casualties, 2, 71, 251, 273, 294
  and Afghan forces, 324
  and counterinsurgency, 280, 286–7, 294, 321, 353
  and targeted killings, 330
  and Karzai, 205, 218, 275, 328
Clark, Vern, 19
Clarke, Richard, 16, 24, 36–7
Claymore mines, 177
'clear–hold–build', 211, 283
Cleveland, Charles, 416
Clinton, Hillary, 277, 278, 349, 405
Clinton, Bill, 24, 35, 52, 119, 121, 276
Cloak of the Prophet Muhammad shrine, Kandahar, 28
CNN (Cable News Network), 12, 15–16, 105, 302

Coalition Provisional Authority (CPA), 146, 152

Coates, James, 355

COBRA (Cabinet Office Briefing Room), 42–5

Colchester, Essex, 157

Cold War, 14, 17, 118

Coldstream Guards, 208, 217, 219, 222

Cole, John, 153

Cole, USS, 36, 41

Combat Air Patrol, 17–19

Combined Joint Special Operations Task Force (CJSOTF), 188

Combined Joint Task Force (CJTF), 132–3

combined search and rescue (CSAR), 63

Combined Security Transition Command-Afghanistan (CSTC-A), 129, 375

Commander of the Faithful, 28, 411

Commander's Emergency Response Program, 392

'Commander's Initial Assessment' (2009), 365

Community Defence Initiative, 377

Comprehensive Strategic Political-Military Plan (2008), 284–5, 290

Congressional Research Service, 285

'consent-based clear', 296

Conservative Party, 38, 49, 95, 119, 120

Continuity of Government programme, 17

Conway, James, 277

Cook, Robin, 119, 137

Cooper, Robert, 87, 116

Cordesman, Anthony, 285

corruption, 387–97, 420, 421
  and aid, 127, 391, 393, 423
  and Afghan government, 3, 5, 127, 217, 223–4, 233, 278, 283, 286, 303, 420
  and Afghan police, 129, 191, 204, 251, 273, 278, 297, 314–15, 376, 393–4, 400–401
  and counterinsurgency, 278, 283, 286, 288, 295, 297, 303, 393–4, 421
  and elections, 213, 387–9, 398
  and Karzai, 387–97
  and Taliban, 3, 33, 333, 365, 367
  and warlords, 144–5, 161, 166, 333, 380

Cougar MRAPs, 201

Council on Foreign Relations, 285

counter-insurgency, 4, 180, 210, 419–21, 423
  assessment of, 373–4
  and Cabaniss, 264–6
  and Cameron, 372
  and Chiswell, 352–3, 368
  and civilian casualties, 280, 286–7, 294, 321, 353
  'clear–hold–build', 211, 283
  and corruption, 278, 283, 286, 288, 295, 297, 303, 393–4, 421
  and Dunford, 384

'find, feel, understand, influence', 353

FM 3–24 *Counterinsurgency Field Manual*, 211, 233, 253, 264, 283, 421

hold phase, 315–18

holistic, 281

and local governance, 230, 288, 306, 316, 361, 368

and McChrystal, 279–91, 295, 320, 327

and Petraeus, 210–11, 279, 327

population-centric approach, 206–14, 231, 279–91, 320, 327, 368

and Riedel review (2009), 278

'shape–clear–hold–build', 283, 296, 308

and surveillance, 367

counter-narcotics, 129–32, 142, 224, 226–8, 273, 418
  Afghan Eradication Force, 227–8
  Akhundzada, 226
  Alternative Livelihood Programme, 293, 367
  Daoud, 228
  DFID, 228
  Foreign Office, 130, 131, 253
  and Jan, Abdul Rahman, 311, 333
  Jan, Abdullah, 165
  Joint Helmand Plan (2005), 154–5
  Major Crimes Task Force, 390–91
  Mangal, 311
  in Marjah, 311, 333
  MI6, 131
  in Musa Qala, 220–21
  in Nad-e Ali, 293, 333
  Operation Sond Chara (2008), 252–3
  Operation Tolo (2008), 245
  Taliban, 130
  UN, 130–31, 227
  USAID, 227–8
  Wood, William, 227

'counter-terrorism plus', 278, 291

Counterterrorism Security Group (CSG), 16, 17, 23, 36

'courageous restraint', 324, 326, 328, 352, 353, 357

Coventry, West Midlands, 208

Cowan, James, 295, 314, 376

Cowper-Coles, Sherard
  2002 Karzai becomes Afghan president, 347
  2007 becomes ambassador to Kabul, 181; defection of Mullah Salaam, 215; battle for Musa Qala, 217–18; Brown visits Afghanistan, 218; conflict over reintegration of Taliban, 221–3; civilian surge planned, 231
  2008 Mangal appointed Helmand governor, 233; US Marines capture Garmsir, 238; Operation Oqab Tsuka, 239
  2011 Haqqani network attacks, 351

Craddock, John, 269
Crawford, Texas, 123
cruise missiles, 25, 36
    Afghanistan, US-led invasion (2001), 65
    Iraq, bombing of (1993), 24
    Operation Infinite Reach (1998), 25, 35, 37, 53
    September 11 attacks (2001), 19, 50
Crumpton, Hank, 105
CRV-7 rockets, 183
'Cyprus group' 87
Czech Republic, 225

Dad Mohammad Khan, 144, 163, 174–5
Dadullah Lang, 331, 333, 336
Daily Express, 123
Daily Mail, 44
Daily Mirror, 147
Daily Post, 349
Daily Telegraph, 44, 83, 219, 304, 331
'Daisy Cutter' bombs, 75, 101
Dale, Catherine, 285
Dalrymple, William, 4, 7
dancing, banning of, 30
Dannatt, Richard, 140, 142, 149, 179, 186, 205, 270–73
Daoud Khan, 77
Daoud, Mohammad
    2005 appointed governor of Helmand, 167
    2006 opium eradication campaign launched, 228; British troops deployed, 169, 172–4; Musa Qala ceasefire, 187, 189, 195; Sangin ceasefire, 196; sacked by Karzai, 190
Dar es Salaam, Tanzania, 23, 25, 41, 42, 46
Dari language, 76, 216, 308, 371, 373
Darveshan, Garmsir, 235, 237
Davis, Dickie, 134
Dearlove, Richard, 41
'death ray', 72
Defense Condition (DEFCON), 14
Deh Adan Khan, Helmand, 205
DeLong, Michael, 66, 104
Delta force, 72
demobilisation, disarmament and reintegration (DDR), 128, 135, 166
Denmark
    2002 Operation Anaconda, 106
    2005 agreement on ISAF deployment to south, 149
    2006 battle for Musa Qala, 178, 183–4; Musa Qala ceasefire, 190
    2007 reconnaissance squadron deployed, 201; command of Battlegroup Centre taken, 208, 250
    2008 suicide bombing in Gereshk, 225; arrival of Royal Irish support, 234;

Operation Oqab Tsuka, 241; Royal Marines take command of Task Force Helmand, 245; Operation Sond Chara, 250
    2009 Operation Panchai Palang, 256, 260–61; UK purchases Merlin helicopters, 271
Deobandism, 28
Department for International Development (DFID), 98, 150, 153, 209
    counter-narcotics, 228
    and District Delivery Programme, 306
    and Kabul Bank collapse (2010), 394
    and PCRU, 151
    and Reid group, 158
Department of Agriculture, US, 279
Department of Defense, US
    and ANSF, 129, 376
    battle of Tora Bora (2001), 115
    CIA, relations with, 59
    and development contracts, 392
    and Iraq, 47
    Lute review (2007), 275
    and al-Qaeda, 37
    Rumsfeld's reforms, 58
    September 11 attacks (2001), 14, 17
    and Taliban offensive (2016), 402
    and 'war on terror', 46
Deployment Readiness Brigade, 104–5
Derleth, James, 213
Development and Influence Teams, 212
Diego Garcia, 65
Disbandment of Illegal Armed Groups, 135
District Delivery Programme, 306–7, 314, 316
District Stabilisation Teams, 316, 362
Dobbins, James, 87, 88, 99, 100, 116, 121, 125
Donilon, Tom, 276, 350
'Doody', 330
Dost Mohammad Khan, Emir of Afghanistan, 7
Dostum, Abdul Rashid, 28
    1996 battle for Herat, 29; Taliban takeover, 29, 30, 33
    1997 flees to Turkey, 29
    2001 US-led invasion, 69; fighting on northern front, 70; battle of Mazar-e-Sharif, 74–5; battle of Kunduz, 77; surrender of Taliban fighters at Qala-i-Jangh, 77, 78
    2003 disarmament negotiations with British PRT, 134–5
    2014 presidential election, 398
    2015 Taliban offensive, 401
Downing Street, London, 41
Drane, Adam, 305
drones

British withdrawal (2014), 387
improvised explosive devices (IEDs), 344
and Joint Prioritized Effects List (JPEL), 330
Lashkar Gah, battle of (2008), 246, 247, 248
Mansour, killing of (2016), 415
and Mobile Operations Groups (MOGs), 198
Musa Qala, battle for (2006), 219
Operation Khanjar (2009), 264
Operation Moshtarak (2010), 311, 318
Operation Oqab Tsuka (2008), 241–2
Operation Panchai Palang (2009), 259
Operation Snipe (2002), 110
Pakistan, strikes in, 348, 349, 351, 415, 420
surveillance, 330, 354
targeted killings, 339, 348, 349, 351, 415, 420, 421
drugs, see narcotics
Dubai, UAE, 6, 393
Duke of Lancaster Regiment, 326
Duke of Wellington's Regiment, 261
Duncan Smith, Iain, 49
Dunford, Joseph, 383–4, 395, 396
Durand Line, 8, 346
Dushanbe, Tajikistan, 73
Dutton, James 'Jim', 304–5
DynCorp International, 129

East India Company, 7, 97
East Pakistan (1955–71), 118
East Timor, 120
Eastern Alliance, 102, 104, 106, 143
Economist, The, 180
Edinburgh, Scotland, 207
education, 102, 126, 144, 278, 293, 304, 306, 368, 371, 420
    girls', 30, 34, 75, 144, 189
    literacy, 106, 129, 155, 262, 311, 323, 375, 376
    madrasas, 28, 334, 351
    at refugee camps, 126
    schools, 126, 144, 188–9, 212, 224, 255, 293, 315, 364, 420
    and Taliban, 30, 34, 127, 144, 189, 366
Eggers, Jeff, 282, 286
Egypt, 11, 20–22
Ehsanullah Ehsan, 162
Eide, Kai, 389–90
Eikenberry, Karl, 180, 303, 389, 390
elections
    2009 presidential election, 255, 262–3, 277, 387–9
    2014 presidential election, 395, 396, 397–9
electricity, 126, 127, 174, 196, 234, 239–43, 363
Elizabeth II, Queen of the United Kingdom, 52
Elysée Treaty (1963), 137

Emanuel, Rahm, 276
'embedded partnering', 289, 376
Emma E. Booker Elementary School, Sarasota, 15, 17
Empire State Building, New York, 13
Engineering Regiment, 152
enhanced interrogation techniques, 26
Enlightenment, 155, 420
Enterprise, USS, 65
Estonia, 201, 249, 251, 257, 310
ETA (Euskadi Ta Askatasuna), 20
Etherington, Mark, 152–6, 171
Eton College, Berkshire, 232, 371
European Union (EU), 34, 216, 217, 222
    EUPOL (European Union Police), 285, 289, 314, 376
Evison, Mark, 260
Exum, Andrew, 285, 286

F-14 fighter-bombers, 65
F-16 fighter-bombers, 219
F/A-18 fighter-bombers, 65, 219, 358
F15E Strike Eagles, 357
Fahim, Mohammed, 60, 68, 69, 73–4, 88, 94, 95, 98, 128
Fairweather, Jack, 204
Falklands War (1982), 169, 183
Fallujah, Iraq, 146, 236, 312, 360
Faraj, Mohammad Abd al-Salam, 20–22
FARC (Fuerzas Armadas Revolucionarias de Colombia), 20
Farnood, Sherkhan, 394
Farouk, King of Egypt, 21
Faryab, Afghanistan, 134, 380, 400, 401, 402
Fawlty Towers, 264
Fearless, HMS, 98
fedayi, 340
Federal Aviation Administration (FAA), 16, 17–18
Federal Bureau of Investigation (FBI), 24, 36, 37
Federally Administered Tribal Areas (FATA), Pakistan, 346–7, 410
Feith, Douglas, 46–7
Felton, Richard, 176, 325–6
Fergusson, James, 370
Ferozi, Khalilullah, 394
Feyzabad, Badakhshan, 139
fighting birds, 30
Fiji, 203
'find, feel, understand, influence', 353
Fisher, Joschka, 122
'flawed masterpiece', 114
floods, 363, 364
Flynn, Michael, 281, 289
FM 3–24 Counterinsurgency Field Manual, 211, 233, 253, 264, 283, 421

FOB Delhi, Garmsir, 199, 235, 237, 264, 266
FOB Inkerman, Sangin, 216
FOB Price, Gereshk, 170, 198
FOB Rhino, Garmsir, 235
FOB Robinson, Sangin, 175, 177, 196, 197
FOB Shawqat, Nad-e Ali, 249, 258, 292, 296
FOB Wishtan, Sangin, 357
FOB Zeebrugge, Kajaki, 242
Focused District Delivery Program, 314
football, 32
Force Reintegration Cell, 405
foreign fighters, 73, 77–8, 105, 165, 236, 336–7, 345
Foreign Office
    and British Muslim delegation (2009), 292
    and counter-narcotics, 130, 131, 253
    and Garmsir, battle for (2008), 235, 238
    and Helmand campaign, 209
    and Iraq invasion (2003), 51
    and ISAF, 97
    and Musa Qala, battle for (2006), 218
    and PCRU, 151
    and Reid group, 158
    and September 11 attacks (2001), 45
    and Soviet-Afghan War (1979–89), 58
    'four fundamental pillars', 287
Fox, David, 90, 91
Fox, Liam, 271
France
    1979 intervention in Central African Republic, 118
    1992 intervention in Bosnia begins, 119
    2001 September 11 attacks, 45, 48, 51; Bonn Conference, 87; ISAF deployed to Kabul, 96, 98; Operation Anaconda, 106; G8 meeting in Geneva, 128
    2003 opposition to Iraq War announced, 136–7
    2004 takeover of ISAF command, 148
    2005 NATO meeting in Nice, 141
    2008 opposition to counterinsurgency and ISAF training of Afghan police, 284–5
    2010 withdrawal from ISAF announced, 371
Franks, Tommy
    2001 planning of Afghanistan campaign, 59, 61, 62, 63; A-teams deployed to assist Northern Alliance, 69; meets with Fahim, 73–4; revises Iraq war plan, 121–2; battle of Tora Bora, 104–5
    2003 invasion of Iraq, 146
Fraser, David, 169, 170, 187
Freakley, Ben, 178–9
'frogs', 354
'front-footed precision', 353, 355
Fry, Robert, 141, 148, 158, 179

G20 states, 270
G8 states, 128, 272
Galbraith, Peter, 389
Gall, Carlotta, 77, 78, 86, 163, 166, 349
Galloway, George, 150
Gardez, Afghanistan, 110, 129, 133, 134
Garmsir, Helmand, 202, 208
    2001 expulsion of Taliban, 143
    2004 Jan removed as governor, 165
    2005 Taliban begin to return, 166
    2006 Taliban takeover, 166; capture by British, 199, 333; ceasefire deal sought, 196
    2007 Royal Marines deployed, 199, 200; Mechanised Brigade deployed, 202; Battlegroup Centre established, 208; deployment of 52nd Infantry Brigade, 212; Helmand Road Map created, 230; Taliban attacks, 216
    2008 Operation Azada Wosa, 234–8; Queen's Dragoon Guards deployed, 245
    2009 US Marines deployed, 254, 264; Operation Khanjar, 264–6
Gates, Robert, 275–80, 285, 289, 290, 302, 350, 365
Gatling guns, 72, 176
George Washington, USS, 19
Georgetown University, 168
Gereshk, Helmand
    2001 US airstrikes, 143
    2002 return of warlords, 144; Camp Price established, 161
    2004 return of Taliban, 164
    2006 British forces deployed, 155–6, 170, 195; IED attack on ANA, 170; British patrol ambushed, 177–8; Royal Marines deployed, 198
    2007 Mechanised Brigade deployed, 202; Royal Anglians deployed, 203; reintegration of Taliban group, 217, 222; Battlegroup Centre established, 208; Helmand Road Map created, 230; deployment of 52nd Infantry Brigade, 215; ex-Taliban group disbanded, 222
    2008 suicide attack, 225; Royal Marines deployed, 245
    2012 security operations transferred to ANSF, 386
Germany
    1998 formation of al-Qaeda Hamburg cell, 11, 26
    2001 September 11 attacks, 51; Bonn Conference, 67, 87–8, 90, 92, 95, 99, 116, 125; ISAF deployed to Kabul, 96, 98
    2002 formation of Afghan National Police, 99, 128, 129; Operation Anaconda, 106; G8 meeting in Geneva, 128

2003 opposition to Iraq War announced,
136–7; joint command of ISAF begins,
136, 140; Kunduz PRT established, 139
2004 Berlin donors' conference, 126–7;
Feyzabad PRT established, 139
2006 British takeover of ISAF, 180
2008 McKiernan takes command of ISAF,
284; opposition to ISAF training of
Afghan police, 284–5
2009 Exum visits Mazar-e-Sharif, 286
2011 facilitation of US-Taliban talks in
Qatar, 406
Ghani, Ashraf, 126, 153, 401, 407–8, 410, 414
Abdullah, relations with, 401
presidential election (2009), 389
presidential election (2014), 397–9
'Securing Afghanistan's Future' (2004),
126–7
Pakistan, relations with, 408, 410, 417
Taliban, relations with, 401, 408, 410, 414,
417
Ghaus, Mohammed, 30
Ghazni, Afghanistan, 400, 402
Ghorak Pass, Helmand, 240, 241
'ghost soldiers', 166
Giuliani, Rudolph 'Rudy', 13
Giustozzi, Antonio, 6, 164, 228
global financial crisis (2007–8), 269, 422
global war on terror, 46–7, 139, 244
GMLRS (Guided Multiple Launch Rocket
System), 201, 354
'golden hour', 317–18
Government Communications Headquarters
(GCHQ), 48, 318–19, 330
'government in the box', 321
'graveyard of empires', 7, 26
'Green Knock', 295, 299
Green Zone, Helmand, 155, 198, 202, 203, 209,
256
'green-on-blue attacks', 380–83
Grenadier Guards, 201, 203–4, 296, 298, 309
Grenier, Robert, 54–5
Grey, Stephen, 220, 221
Grossman, Marc, 45
'ground sign awareness', 342
Guantánamo Bay, 53, 102, 145, 162–3, 214, 345,
370, 406, 424
Guardian, 44, 304
'guardian angels', 381
guerrilla warfare, 335–7, 340
Guidance Card Alpha, 206
Gul Mohammad Khan, 174
Gulf War (1990–91), 47, 59, 169, 282
Gunningham, Adam, 343
Gur, Afghanistan, 70
Gurganus, Charles, 381–3

Habibullah Khan, 252, 293, 297, 299, 305, 308,
311
Hadley, Stephen, 189
Hagel, Charles 'Chuck', 395
Hagenbeck, Franklin, 106–9
Haiti, 119
hajj, 98
Hamburg, Germany, 11, 26–7
Hamdard, Abdul Aziz, 262
Hammond, Mark, 176, 185
Hammond, Philip, 381, 386
Haq, Faisal, 361
Haqqani Network, 338, 348, 350, 411, 414
Haqqani, Jalauddin, 29
Haqqani, Sirajuddin, 411
Harakat-e Inqilab-e Islami, 144
Harding, Toby, 262
Harrier jets, 183, 197, 198, 219, 251, 382
Harvard University, 371
Hassanzai clan, 187–9
Hastings, Max, 271
Haston, Nick, 208
Hazar Joft, Garmsir, 235, 237
Hazaras, 28, 60, 84, 326, 378
Hazrat, Qari, 166
'hearts and minds', 5, 211, 223–4, 256, 333
Hekmatyar, Gulbuddin, 28, 29, 32, 403–4
Hellfire missiles, 176, 330, 354
Helmand, Afghanistan
2001 US-led invasion; fall of Taliban, 143
2002 return of warlords, 144, 160; Camp Price
established, 161; Akhundzada launches
opium eradication programme, 226
2004 Taliban begin to return, 145, 334;
Taliban return to Sangin, 164, 165, 334;
Abdullah Jan removed as Garmsir
governor, 165
2005 agreement on ISAF deployment,
141–2; PCRU team visits Lashkar Gah,
153–4, 167 Taliban return to Musa Qala,
164; Akhundzada removed from governorship, 166–7
2006 construction of Camp Bastion, 152,
169; deployment of British forces, 145,
156–60, 168–70, 179–80, 233, 333; IED
attacks in Lashkar Gah, 172; IED attack
in Gereshk, 170; British forces adopt
Platoon House strategy, 171; Gul
Mohammad Khan killed by Taliban, 174;
fighting in Sangin, 174–5, 177; Taliban
capture Garmsir, 166; arrival of British
reinforcements, 178; fighting in Sangin
and Musa Qala, 178, 182–7; British capture
Garmsir, 199; ceasefire in Musa Qala,
187–91; Royal Marines deployed, 192–3;
ceasefire in Sangin, 189, 191, 195–7; British

withdrawal from Musa Qala, 194; cease-fire in Now Zad, 189, 197; resumption of fighting in Now Zad, 189, 197–8, 218

2007 US airstrikes in Musa Qala, 190; fighting in Garmsir, 199; resumption of fighting in Musa Qala, 200; Operation Silver in Sangin, 199–200; Mechanised Brigade deployed, 200–205; civilian casualties in Deh Adan Khan and Heyderbad, 206; reintegration of Gereshk Taliban, 217, 222; 52nd Infantry Brigade deployed, 207–12; construction of Park for Women in Lashkar Gah, 230–31; launch of TCAF, 212–14; Britain captures Musa Qala, 215–21; conflict over reintegration of Musa Qala Taliban, 221–3

2008 Mullah Salaam appointed Musa Qala governor, 224–5; suicide attack in Gereshk, 225; IED attack in Kajaki, 225; Parachute Regiment deployed, 231, 352; Powell takes command of British campaign, 229–33; Mangal appointed governor, 233; Operation Azada Wosa, 234–8; Operation Oqab Tsuka, 239–43; Royal Marines deployed, 244; Taliban attack on Lashkar Gah, 244–8, 340, 419; Operation Sond Chara, 249–53

2009 Light Brigade deployed, 253; US Marines deployed, 254, 263, 277; McChrystal takes command of ISAF, 294–5; Dannatt makes visit, 271–2; Operation Panchai Palang, 254–63, 271, 272, 294, 304, 307, 308, 343; presidential elections, 255, 263; Operation Khanjar, 264–6; 11th Infantry Brigade deployed, 295, 357, 367; 'consent-based clear' operation in Nad-e Ali, 296–7; USAID suspends Kajaki project, 243; British Muslim leaders make visit, 292–3; Operation Tor Shpa'h, 297–300, 355; Obama announces surge and drawdown, 303

2010 Operation Moshtarak, 296, 297, 305–24, 341, 355, 358; US Marines move into Musa Qala, 356, 357; ISAF holds Nad-e Ali, 313–16, 321; 4th Infantry Brigade deployed, 325, 344; Taliban attacks in Marjah, 316–18; Alikozai peace offer in Sangin, 360; Petraeus takes command of ISAF, 327–32; ISAF operations in Saidabad and Babaji, 326; Royal Irish Regiment deployed; fighting in Nad-e Ali, 352–4; Parachute Regiment deployed, 355, 367–8; ALP established in Saidabad, 378; US Marines move into Sangin, 356–60, 372, 419; launch of Persistent Threat Detection System, 354

2011 Sangin peace accord, 363–4; Niaz Mohammed killed in British strike, 330; Taliban return to Nad-e Ali, 332; Allen takes command of ISAF, 373; Armoured Brigade deployed to Helmand, 378

2012 insider attack at Camp Bastion, 382; Taliban attack on Camp Bastion, 381–3; security in Lashkar Gah transferred to ANSF, 386

2013 Dunford takes command of ISAF, 383; British withdrawal begins, 386–7

2014 British PRT and Task Force Helmand dissolved, 387

2015 Taliban offensive, 243, 400–402

2016 Taliban offensive, 402–3

Helmand and Arghandab Valley Authority, 249, 257

Helmand Provincial Reconstruction Team (UK), 317, 361

2006 IED attacks in Lashkar Gah, 172; Knaggs takes command, 187; review of Joint Helmand Plan, 229; Musa Qala ceasefire, 188; Sangin ceasefire, 195–6

2007 Slinn takes command, 230; expansion of team, 204; Park for Women commissioned, 230; TCAF launched, 213; civilian surge announced, 231

2008 Ryder takes civilian command, 231; Powell takes command, 229, 232; US Marines move into Garmsir, 235–6; Operation Oqab Tsuka, 243; Taliban attack on Lashkar Gah, 246, 247; Operation Sond Chara, 252

2009 McChrystal makes visit, 294; British Muslim leaders make visit, 292–3

2010 development with District Delivery Programme, 316, 317; preparations for Operation Moshtarak, 317; Chiswell takes command of Task Force Helmand, 352, 368; Sharif appointed Sangin governor, 361–2

2011 Sangin peace accord, 363–4

2014 withdrawal from Afghanistan, 386

Helmand River, 154, 155, 183, 237, 247, 249

Helmand Road Map (2007), 230, 239

Herat, Afghanistan, 29, 32, 65, 70, 283

Hercules transport aircraft, 177, 216

heroin, 58, 130–31, 220; *see also* narcotics; opium

HESCO defensive barriers, 182

Heyderbad, Helmand, 206

High Peace Council, 362, 404, 409

Highway 1, Afghanistan, 156, 170, 202, 240

Highway 4, Afghanistan, 89

Hizb-i Islami, 28, 144, 217, 255, 379, 392, 403–4

Holbrooke, Richard, 389, 404–5, 416

holistic counterinsurgency, 281

Holmes, Matt, 195
Hong Kong, 207
Hoon, Geoffrey
  2001 September 11 attacks, 40; planning of
    Afghanistan campaign, 63; ISAF deployed
    to Kabul, 95–8
  2002 Bush's State of the Union speech, 123;
    Operation Jacana, 107, 113
  2004 Blair announces ARRC takeover of
    ISAF, 149
  2005 agreement on ISAF expansion to
    south, 141; replaced by Reid, 140, 149
Hopwood, Dan, 220
Horse Guards Parade, London, 271
hostage taking, 68, 70–71
Houghton, Nick, 186–7, 234
House of Commons Defence Committee, 386
Household Cavalry Regiment, 156, 188, 208,
  219
Howard, Martin, 160, 167
Howard, Michael, 46
Howes, Francis 'Buster', 244–5
howitzers, 72
Human Rights Watch, 380
humanitarian assistance, 80, 81
humanitarian intervention, 117–21
Hussein, Saddam, 146
Hutton, John, 269, 270, 272
Hyde, Patrick, 344–5
Hyderabad village, Sangin, 165
hydro-electricity, 174, 196, 234, 239–43, 363

'i-comm chatter', 318
improvised explosive devices (IEDs), 194,
  201–2, 259–60, 271–2, 337, 340–45, 385, 419
  2006 attacks in Lashkar Gah, 172; attack in
    Gereshk, 170
  2007 battle for Musa Qala, 215, 220
  2008 attack in Kajaki, 225; Operation Azada
    Wosa, 237; Operation Oqab Tsuka, 240,
    241; Operation Sond Chara, 252; attacks
    in Sangin, 253; Burley review, 343
  2009 Operation Panchai Palang, 256–61,
    272, 343; Operation Khanjar, 265; Taliban
    operations in Nad-e Ali, 294; fighting in
    Sangin, 357, 358; loss of three British
    bomb disposal officers, 342
  2010 Taliban adopt guerrilla warfare
    strategy, 340; ISAF introduces 'ground
    sign awareness', 342; Operation
    Moshtarak, 313, 323–4, 341; operations in
    Saidabad, 326; fighting in Sangin, 359–60
  2011 Sangin peace accord, 363
Independent, 388
Independent Elections Commission, 263,
  388–9, 397

Independent National Commission for Peace,
  216–17
India
  Afghanistan, relations with, 31, 60, 64, 84,
    87, 347–8
  Bonn Conference (2001), 87
  British India (1757–1947), 8, 28, 97
  East Pakistan, invasion of (1971), 118
  Pakistan, relations with, 31, 64, 118, 124–5,
    347–8
Indian Ocean, 65, 80, 107
Infantry Brigade
  4th, 325–6, 344–5
  11th, 295, 307–10, 313–17, 357, 367
  52nd, 207–24, 230, 233, 235, 273
Inge, Peter, 96
Ingram, Adam, 160
'insider attacks', 380–83
intelligence, surveillance, targeting and recon-
  naissance (ISTAR), 354–5
inteqal process, 373, 384
Inter-Continental Hotel, Kabul, 350
Inter-Services Intelligence (ISI), 423
  Baradar, arrest of (2010), 336, 404
  and Bin Laden, 54, 349–50
  and Karzai, 87, 346–7, 404
  and Haqqani Network, 338, 348, 351
  and India, 346–7
  and Taliban, 31–2, 54, 346–8, 351, 382, 404,
    406, 411–12
International Conference on Afghanistan
  2006, 158, 181
  2010, 324, 374
International Crisis Group, 181
International Monetary Fund (IMF), 347
International Security Assistance Force (ISAF),
  2–6, 9, 133
  2001 deployed to Kabul, 82, 92–9, 117, 169,
    282, 418; proposals for expansion, 99
  2002 proposals for expansion, 100; forma-
    tion of Afghan National Guard, 99, 128;
    Turkey takes command, 100, 136
  2003 aid agencies call for expansion, 135–6;
    NATO takes control, 138–9; German PRT
    established in Kunduz, 139
  2004 Blair announces ARRC takeover,
    140–41, 148, 158, 179
  2005 agreement for expansion to south,
    141–2
  2006 forces deployed to Helmand, 145,
    156–60, 168–70, 179–80, 233, 333, 335, 421;
    Britain takes command, 178, 187; Canada
    takes command of RC-South, 169, 296;
    fighting in Sangin, 174–5, 177; Taliban
    capture Garmsir, 166; fighting in Sangin
    and Musa Qala, 178, 182–7; Operation

Medusa launched, 186; recapture of Garmsir, 199; ceasefire in Musa Qala, 187–91; ceasefires in Sangin and Now Zad, 189, 191, 195–7; battle of Pashmul, 337; fighting resumes in Now Zad, 189, 197–8, 218

2007 US takes command, 191; Operation Silver, 199–200; reintegration of Gereshk Taliban, 217, 222; launch of TCAF, 212–14; Musa Qala offensive, 215–21; conflict over reintegration of Musa Qala Taliban, 221–3

2008 Operation Azada Wosa, 234–8; McKiernan takes command, 239–40, 283–4; Operation Oqab Tsuka, 239–43; Operation Tolo, 245; Taliban attack on Lashkar Gah, 244–8, 340; Operation Sond Chara, 249–53

2009 Biden visits HQ, 275; McChrystal takes command, 280–89, 294, 365, 419, 423–4; Operation Panchai Palang, 254–63, 271, 272, 294, 304, 307, 308, 343; McChrystal issues restraint of force measures, 294–5; British Muslim leaders make visit, 292; Britain takes command of RC-South, 296, 300, 419; 'consent-based clear' operation in Nad-e Ali, 296–7; insider attack in Nad-e Ali, 380; RC-South shifts focus to Kandahar, 300–301; Operation Tor Shpa'h, 297–300, 355; Obama announces surge and drawdown, 301–5

2010 France announces withdrawal, 371; Netherlands announces withdrawal, 372; Operation Moshtarak, 296, 297, 305–24, 341, 355, 358; 'anti-corruption guidance' issued, 390; US Marines move into Musa Qala, 356, 357; holding of Nad-e Ali, 313–16; Taliban attacks in Marjah, 316–18; Alikozai peace offer in Sangin, 360; Petraeus takes command, 327–32; division of RC-South, 352; Operation Hamkari, 352; operations in Saidabad and Babaji, 326; fighting in Nad-e Ali, 352–4; US Marines move into Sangin, 356–60, 372, 419; ALP established in Saidabad, 378; launch of Persistent Threat Detection System, 354

2011 Sangin peace accord, 363–4; killing of Niaz Mohammed, 330; Allen takes command, 373; Pakistan closes supply routes, 351

2012 insider attack at Camp Bastion, 382; Allen orders protective measures against insider attacks, 381; Taliban attack on Camp Bastion, 381–3; Allen halts joint operations with ANSF, 381; shipping back of material from Afghanistan begins, 383

2013 Dunford takes command, 383; Hagel visits Afghanistan, 395; Karzai bans ANSF from requesting air support, 385–5; *inteqal* process reaches 'Milestone 13', 384; British withdrawal from Helmand begins, 386–7

2014 Karzai proposes seizure of Parwan Detention Facility, 395; Task Force Helmand dissolved, 387

Iran
and 'axis of evil', 47, 123
Bonn Conference (2001), 87, 88
Iraq, relations with, 150, 345
Karzai, relations with, 389
narcotics trade, 58, 130
Northern Alliance, relations with, 73
refugees, 126
Taliban, relations with, 57, 320, 336, 345, 411
trade routes, 31, 141
United States, relations with, 47, 51, 57, 123, 389

Iraq, 121–4, 145–51, 184, 206, 207, 285, 423
1991 Operation Desert Storm, 47, 59, 169, 282
1993 US cruise missile strikes, 24
2001 September 11 attacks, 47, 48, 50, 51; US revises plans for war, 121–2
2002 US plans for war, 122–4
2003 US-led invasion, 4, 137, 140, 145, 159, 274; CPA established, 146; Saddam captured by US forces, 146
2004 development of Persistent Threat Detection System, 354; first battle of Fallujah, 146; Mahdi Army insurgency begins, 146, 345; Abu Ghraib prison scandal breaks, 147; CPA hands authority to interim government, 148; counter-insurgency launched in Mosul, 210–11; second battle of Fallujah, 236, 360
2005 Britain cedes ground to Shia militias, 150
2006 fighting in Ramadi, 236; retreat of British forces in Basra, 151; Anbar Awakening begins, 279, 377
2007 US troop surge, 279; fighting in Ramadi, 236; British withdrawal from Basra Palace, 248; US review of war strategy, 275
2008 Operation Saulat al-Fursan, 248–9; Obama's Woodrow Wilson Center speech, 274
2009 Obama plans drawdown, 276

Irish Guards, 270
Irish Republican Army (IRA), 20, 38, 39, 41, 342
irrigation, 78, 155, 228, 249, 341, 363; *see also* canals

Ishaqzai tribe, 163, 164, 173, 359, 36
Islamabad, Pakistan, 54, 347
Islamic State (IS), 415
Ismail Khan, 28, 29, 32, 33, 69, 70, 144
Israel, 11, 14, 21, 22, 26
Istanbul, Turkey, 140, 148
Italy, 51, 87, 128, 140, 272, 284
ITN, 80

Jackal armoured vehicles, 241, 299
Jackson, Michael, 158
jahiliyyah, 21
Jalalabad, Nangarhar, 29, 100, 129
Jalali, Ali Ahmad, 129
Jama't-e Islam, 128
Jan Mohammed, 379
Jan, Abdul Rahman, 145, 160, 247, 250, 311, 333
Jan, Abdullah, 144, 165
Jan, Umer, 362
Japan, 46, 62, 125, 128, 135
Jarrah, Ziad 11, 15, 27
Jarvenpaa, Minna, 152–6, 167, 171, 173
Javelin anti-tank missiles, 175
Jawbreaker, 67
al-Jazeera, 205
Jenkin, Bernard, 95, 96
Jermy, Steven, 147
jihad, 21
    Bin Laden, 22
    Taliban, 28, 334–5, 375
al-Jihad, 21–2
John F. Kennedy, USS, 19
John Paul II, Pope, 26
John Radcliffe Hospital, Oxford, 259
Johns Hopkins University, 126
Johnson, Robert, 6
Joint Chiefs of Staff, 47, 59, 61–2, 66, 72, 121–2, 276, 301, 350
Joint Co-ordination and Monitoring Board, 181
Joint Command, ISAF (IJC), 280, 287, 300, 306, 374–6, 385, 419, 424
Joint Force Harrier, 183
Joint Helicopter Force, 175–6
Joint Helmand Plan (2005), 154–6, 159, 170–72, 180, 194, 229–30, 245
Joint Intelligence Committee, 41
Joint Prioritized Effects List (JPEL), 330, 355
Joint Regional Teams, 133
Jones, James, 276
Judaism, Jews, 55
Jugroom Fort, Garmsir, 199, 237–8
July 7 attacks (2005), 149
Jushaley, Sangin, 361
Jutland Dragoons Regiment, 250

Kabul, Afghanistan, 33, 36
    1839 outbreak of Anglo-Afghan War, 7
    1919 Anglo-Afghan War, 8
    1978 Saur Revolution, 27
    1992 fall of Najibullah government, 31
    1996 Taliban takeover, 29–30
    1997 international condemnation of public executions, 31; Bonino detained, 34
    2001 September 11 attacks, 54–5; CIA capture Wasiq, 55; US airstrikes, 65; battle of Kabul, 79–82; deployment of ISAF, 92–3, 95–6, 117
    2002 formation of ANP, 129
    2003 State Department takes over ANP, 129; arrival of CSTC-A, 129
    2005 PCRU team makes visit, 152–3
    2006 Musa Qala Jirga makes visit, 189
    2007 Brown makes visit, 218; conflict over reintegration of Musa Qala Taliban, 222–3
    2008 Biden makes visit, 274–5; Haqqani network bombs Indian embassy, 348
    2009 McChrystal makes visit, 283
    2010 Cameron makes visit, 356, 372; International Conference, 373; collapse of Kabul Bank, 394
    2011 Haqqani network attacks, 350
    2013 security handed over to Afghan forces, 384, 406; Loya Jirga on BSA, 396–7
    2014 British withdrawal, 406
    2015 Taliban offensive, 400, 401, 402
    2016 Taliban offensive, 417
Kabul Bank, 394
Kabul University, 153
Kaduz, Haji, 255
Kagan, Fred, 285, 286, 290
Kagan, Kimberley, 285, 286
Kajaki, Helmand
    2004 return of Taliban, 164
    2006 British forces deployed, 171, 174, 175; Taliban attacks, 185, 186; Sangin ceasefire, 196–7
    2007 Royal Marines deployed, 200, 202; Mechanised Brigade deployed, 203; Battlegroup North established, 207
    2008 IED attack, 225; Royal Irish Regiment deployed, 234; Operation Oqab Tsuka, 239–43
    2009 USAID suspends Turbine Two project, 243
    2015 Taliban offensive, 243, 401, 402
Kajaki Dam, 174, 196–7, 234, 239–43, 363
Kakul Military Academy, Pakistan, 349
Kalashnikovs, 85
kalays, 249
Kanashin, Helmand, 403

Kandahar, Afghanistan, 27, 28, 33, 36
  1880 battle of Kandahar, 8
  1996 Taliban takeover, 28–9, 32
  1998 sheltering of Bin Laden, 24; Omar's compound reinforced, 56
  2000 Pakistani football team deported, 32; Turki al-Faisal's visit, 36
  2001 sheltering of Bin Laden, 54–5; US airstrikes, 65; Operation Rhino, 72; battle of Kandahar, 86, 88–92, 115
  2002 Mansour flees to Pakistan, 162
  2003 ANP training centre opened, 129
  2005 agreement on ISAF deployment, 141–2, 150; PCRU team deployed, 152–3; Canadian troops deployed, 150
  2006 Butler and Tootal visit PCRU, 171; Taliban assault, 333; battle of Panjwai, 186; battle of Pashmul, 337
  2009 escalation of insurgency, 289; McChrystal makes visit, 283; RC-South shifts focus, 300–301; Obama announces surge and drawdown, 303; High Peace Council conference, 362
  2010 Operation Hamkari, 352, 419
  2015 Taliban offensive, 400
  2016 Taliban offensive, 403
kandaks, 128, 203–4
Kapisa, Afghanistan, 400
Karachi, Pakistan, 108, 347
Karamat, Jehangir, 32
Kargil War (1999), 124–5
Karimi, Sher Mohammad, 132–3, 282, 284
Karimov, Islam, 63
Karimullah Agha, 363
Karshi Khanabad (K2) airfield, Uzbekistan, 62–3, 68, 69, 72, 80, 104
Karzai, Abdul Ahad, 30, 84
Karzai, Ahmed Wali, 84
Karzai, Hamid, 347, 387–97
  1996 meetings on UN membership, 30–31
  1999 assassination of father, 30, 84
  2001 evacuated to Pakistan by US forces, 85; battle of Tarin Kot, 85–6; battle of Kandahar, 86, 88–9; meeting with Omar on Taliban surrender, 89–91; meetings with Northern Alliance leaders, 94–5; ISAF deployed to Kabul, 98; proposal for expansion of ISAF, 99
  2002 Blair makes visit, 117; Bush's State of the Union speech, 122–3 Loya Jirga; becomes interim president, 60, 84, 100, 162; establishment of PRTs, 133
  2005 Independent National Commission for Peace launched, 216; sacking of Akhundzada, 167

  2006 talks with Hekmatyar begin, 403; Gul Mohammad Khan killed by Taliban, 174; PAG established, 180; Musa Qala ceasefire, 189, 190; Sangin ceasefire, 196; sacking of Daoud, 190
  2007 public denouncement of civilian casualties, 205–6; meets with Taliban group in Lashkar Gah, 217; defection of Mullah Salaam, 214–15; meets with Brown, 218; conflict over reintegration of Musa Qala Taliban, 222–3
  2008 meets with Biden, 274–5; Mullah Salaam appointed Musa Qala governor, 224; Mangal appointed Helmand governor, 233
  2009 presidential election, 263, 387–9; meets with McChrystal, 283; meets with Eide, 389–90; High Peace Council conference, 362
  2010 Eikenberry cable leaked, 390; Operation Moshtarak, 307, 309–10, 313; meetings with Cameron, 356, 370, 372; closure of Major Crimes Task Force, 391; Kabul International Conference, 373; anger over civilian casualties in Sangin, 359; APRP launched, 404; talks with Taliban begin, 404
  2012 US-Taliban talks in Qatar, 406
  2013 Hagel makes visit, 395; bans ANSF from requesting ISAF air support, 383–5; battle of Badakhshan, 384; Taliban open diplomatic office in Qatar, 407; Loya Jirga on BSA, 396–7
  2014 proposes seizure of Parwan Detention Facility, 395; presidential election, 397
Karzai, Mahmood, 394
Kay, Nicholas, 188
Kayani, Ashfaq Parvez, 350
Kazemi, Sayed Mustafa, 189–90
Kennedy, Charles, 150
Kennedy, John Fitzgerald, 123
Kennedy Space Center, Florida, 243
Kenya, 22, 25, 41, 42, 46
Kerry, John, 389, 396, 398
Khalid, Hamid, 217, 221
Khalid, Sheikh Mohammed, 26
Khalilzad, Zalmay, 116, 138, 389
Khaneshin, Garmsir, 264
Khanon, Agha Mohammed, 367
Kharoti tribe, 251, 297
Khel, Nabi Jan Mullah, 217, 223
Khmer Rouge, 118
Khost, Afghanistan, 110, 111, 112, 398
Khotezai clan, 164
Khushhal Kalay, Nad-e Ali, 249, 250, 252, 309

kidnappings, 28, 242, 379, 380
King, Richard, 111–13
King's College London, 285, 422
King's Royal Hussars, 215, 219
Kissinger, Henry, 137
kite-flying, banning of, 30
Kitson, Nick, 357
Kitty Hawk, USS, 62, 80
Knaggs, Charlie, 170, 172, 173, 187
Koka, Abdul Wali, 225
Kolenda, Christopher, 282, 286, 393
Korean War (1950–53), 157
Kosovo War (1998–99), 24, 60, 80, 81, 119, 120
de Kruif, Mart, 255
Kuchinay Darveshan, Garmsir, 265
Kuehn, Felix, 6
Kunar, Afghanistan, 282, 385
Kunduz, Afghanistan, 75, 76–7, 133–4, 139, 380
  Kunduz airlift (2001), 78–9
  Taliban offensive (2015), 399–402
Kurds, 136
Kut, Iraq, 146, 152

Labour Party, 38, 48–9, 63, 120, 124, 272
Laghman, Afghanistan, 233
Laity, Mark, 178
Lakari, Garmsir, 265
Lal Mohammed, 379
Lamb, Christina, 163, 177–8
Lamb, Graeme, 63, 82, 83, 133, 282, 371
Land Command, 142, 148, 158, 208
land disputes, 144, 173, 225, 332
Land Rovers, 78, 112, 133, 151, 154, 198, 247
Lander, Stephen, 41
Lane, Roger, 108–13
Langley, Virginia, 17, 26, 48, 63
Lashkar Gah, Helmand
  2001 US airstrikes, 143; return of Akhundzada, 144
  2005 Marsden meets with Akhundzada, 166–7; PCRU make visit, 153–4, 155–6
  2006 ADZ established, 170; Messenger meets with shura on opium, 227; Taliban IED attacks, 172; Butler and Knaggs make visit, 173; Freakley makes visit, 178–9; Britain takes command of ISAF, 178–9, 186; Royal Marines deployed, 193; suicide attack on British patrol, 193
  2007 Helmand Road Map created, 230; construction of Park for Women, 230–31; launch of TCAF, 213–14; Karzai meets with Taliban group, 217; conflict over reintegration of Musa Qala Taliban, 221–2
  2008 Powell takes command of Helmand campaign, 232; planning of Operation

Azada Wosa, 236; Royal Gurkha Rifles deployed, 246; Taliban attack, 244–8, 340, 419
  2009 Taliban encirclement, 289; British Muslim leaders make visit, 292; Obama announces surge and drawdown, 303
  2010 Atmar meets with Marjah elders, 312; Operation Moshtarak, 322
  2011 Petraeus makes visit, 364
  2012 security operations transferred to ANSF, 386
  2015 Taliban offensive, 400
  2016 Taliban offensive, 402, 403
Lashkah Kalay, Helmand, 256
layeha, 339, 365–7
'lead nation' approach, 128
Lebanon, 11, 207
Leopard 2 tanks, 260
Levin, Carl, 303
Liberal Democrats, 150
Lieberman, Joseph, 122
Lieven, Anatol, 347
Light Armored Reconnaissance Battalion, 265
Light Brigade, 253–63, 267, 295
Light Dragoons, 254, 256, 260–61, 262, 264
'Lion of Kabul' 84
'Lions of Marjah', 378
Lisbon, Portugal, 373
literacy, 106, 129, 155, 262, 311, 323, 375, 376
'loan brides', 226–7
Local Governance Directorate, 306
Logar, Afghanistan, 53, 380, 400
London
  G20 Summit (2009), 270
  International Conferences on Afghanistan (2006, 2010), 158, 181, 324, 374
  July 7 attacks (2005), 149–50
  London Underground, 112, 149
  Scotland Yard, 390
  and September 11 attacks (2001), 39, 40, 43, 44
Lorimer, John, 200–205
Loy Mandah Wadi, Helmand, 256, 257
Loya Jirga
  2002 Kabul, 88, 99, 100
  2006 Musa Qala, 188
  2013 Kabul, 396–7
Loyd, Anthony, 110
Lunt, Nicholas, 205–6
Lute, Douglas, 275
Lyneham, Wiltshire, 268
Lynx helicopters, 156, 175

M1A Abrams tanks, 250
M60 machine guns, 176
Mackay, Andrew, 207–24

Macmillan, Harold, 123
madrasas, 28, 334, 351
mahaz, 336, 338, 411, 412
Mahdi Army, 146–7, 150, 248–9, 345
Maiwand, Kandahar, 92, 162
    battle of Maiwand (1880), 7, 186, 335, 392
Major Crimes Task Force, 390–91
Major, John, 48, 119
Malayan Emergency (1948–60), 180, 210
Malgir, Helmand, 255–7, 260, 261
al-Maliki, Nouri, 248–9
Malkasian, Carter, 6, 144, 165–6, 236, 238, 266, 331
Mangal, Gulab
    2008 appointed Helmand governor, 233; opium eradication programme launched, 311; Operation Azada Wosa, 236; Taliban attack on Lashkar Gah, 246, 247; Operation Sond Chara, 250, 252
    2009 British Muslim leaders visit Nad-e Ali, 293–4; High Peace Council convenes, 362
    2010 peace negotiations in Sangin, 362–3
    2010 Haji Zahir appointed Marjah governor, 317; Operation Moshtarak, 305, 317, 321, 322
    2014 presidential election, 398
Mangal, Munir, 221
Manning, David, 40, 48, 81, 123
Mansour, Akhtar Mohammad, 162, 408, 410, 412–13, 415
marijuana, 323
Marjah, Helmand
    2008 opium eradication programme launched, 311, 333; Taliban attack on Lashkar Gah, 247, 248; Operation Sond Chara, 250
    2009 US Marines deployed, 254, 264, 296, 300; McChrystal takes command of ISAF, 303, 321
    2010 Haji Zahir appointed governor, 317; Operation Moshtarak, 305, 307, 310, 311–13, 316–24, 325; US Marines support *arbakai*, 378
    2015 Taliban offensive, 403
Marsden, Rosalind, 153
Marsden, William, 166
Marshall, George, 138
Marshall Plan, 138, 155
Martin, Michael, 6, 161, 162, 225, 392
Massoud, Ahmad Shah, 28–30, 33, 58, 60, 67, 69, 82, 144
Mastiff MRAPs, 201, 208, 246, 271, 344
    Musa Qala, battle for (2006), 215, 219
    Operation Oqab Tsuka (2008), 241
    Operation Panchai Palang (2009), 258, 260
    Operation Tor Shpa'h (2009), 298

Matthews, Dai, 259
Mattis, James 'Mad Dog', 104
Maymaneh, Faryab province, 134, 140
Mazar-e-Sharif, Balkh
    1998 Taliban kill Iranian diplomats, 345
    2001 US airstrikes, 65; fighting on northern front, 70, 73, 74; captured by Northern Alliance, 74–6; surrender of Taliban fighters at Qala-i-Jangh, 77
    2003 ANP training centre set up, 129; CJTF takes over Operation Enduring Freedom, 133; British PRT established, 134, 140; disarmament of Atta and Dostum, 134–5
    2009 Exum makes visit, 286; McChrystal makes visit, 283
Mazloom, Fazel, 77
McCain, John, 122, 274, 281
McChrystal, Stanley
    2009 takes command of ISAF, 279–91, 304, 328, 332, 357, 365, 419, 423–4; builds relations with Karzai, 390; sets growth target for ANA, 377; Operation Panchai Palang, 294; introduces restraint of force measures, 294–5; operations in Marjah, 300; Obama announces surge and drawdown, 302–3
    2010 Operation Moshtarak, 307, 309–10, 313, 320–21, 323; fired by Obama, 327
McCleod, Carl, 236
McColl, John, 93, 94, 95, 97–100
McKiernan, David
    2008 takes command of ISAF, 239–40, 283–4; persuaded by Nicholson to concentrate on south, 255; Operation Oqab Tsuka, 239–40, 243; requests additional troops, 276, 281
    2009 Biden visits Afghanistan, 275; replaced by McChrystal, 275, 279–80
McMaster, Herbert Raymond, 390
McNeil, Rufus, 241, 242
McNeill, Dan
    2002 takes command of Operation Enduring Freedom, 132
    2003 development of PRTs, 133–4
    2007 takes command of ISAF, 191, 283; Karzai condemns civilian casualties, 205–6; defection of Mullah Salaam, 215; battle for Musa Qala, 218
    2008 Operation Azada Wosa, 235–6
Mecca, Saudi Arabia, 98
Mechanised Brigade, 200–205, 211, 212, 378
medical emergency response teams (MERTs), 185
Mercian Regiment, 201, 254, 261
Mercy Corps, 228
Merlin helicopters, 271

Messenger, Gordon, 142, 152–4, 156, 194, 227, 245–6, 248–9
Metropolitan Police, 40, 42, 44
Meyer, Christopher, 52
Meyers, Richard, 66
Mezai Mountains, Gardez Province, 110
MH-53 Pave Lows, 62
MH-60 Direct Action Penetrators, 62
Mi-17 transport helicopters, 375
MI5, 41, 42, 48
MI6, 41, 42, 48, 58, 61, 67, 76, 131, 159
Mian Poshtay, Garmsir, 144, 265
Mianroady, Sangin, 361
micro-drones, 344
Milam, William, 35
Milawa Valley, 101, 102
'Milestone 13', 384
Milestones (Qutb), 21
Miliband, David, 269
Military Cross, 344
Military Technical Agreement (2001), 97
militias (arbakai), 377
'milky fish', 354
mines, 100, 108, 110, 117, 177, 185
Ministry of Defence, Afghanistan, 128, 133, 135, 207, 284, 381, 384, 395
Ministry of Defence UK
    2001 September 11 attacks, 40, 45, 63; troops deployed to Bagram, 82; deployment of ISAF to Kabul, 97
    2002 Bush's State of the Union speech, 123; Operation Jacana, 108, 110, 113; planning for Iraq War, 124
    2004 ARRC takeover of ISAF announced, 140, 141
    2005 adoption of pivot strategy, 148; Hoon replaced by Reid, 149; PCRU established, 151, 155, 158, 160
    2006 forces deployed to Helmand, 170, 172, 418, 422; takeover of ISAF command, 179; Lamb's report on Gereshk ambush, 177–8; complaint about Harriers goes viral, 183
    2007 acquisition of MRAPs, 201–2; 52nd Infantry Brigade takes command of Task Force Helmand, 209
    2009 Operation Minimise instituted, 267; Richards launches Operation Entirety, 273; Dannatt pressures Brown on reinforcements, 271; death of Thorneloe during Operation Panchai Palang, 259
    2010 refocus of ISTAR programme, 354
Ministry of Interior, Afghanistan, 135, 167, 184, 217, 307, 377–9, 384, 395
Mir Azar, Mullah, 312
Mir Wali, Malem, 144, 160–61, 166, 379

'mission creep', 96
Mission Rehearsal Exercises, 213
Mobile Operations Groups (MOGs), 198, 200
Mohaydin, Brigadier, 221
Mojadedi, Sebghatullah, 216, 397
Monde, Le, 45
money laundering, 58
Monty Python, 264
Mountain Division, 80, 104, 106, 108–9, 132
'mowing the lawn', 205
MRAPs (Mine Resistant Ambush Protected) vehicles, 201–2; see also Mastiffs
MREs (meal ready to eat), 204
Muhammad, Prophet of Islam, 363
mujahedin, 20, 25–9, 31–2, 34, 60, 101, 112, 120, 130, 348
Mulholland, John, 68, 69, 101, 103
Mullen, Michael, 276, 279, 282, 290, 291, 350
Murree, Pakistan, 409–10
Musa Qala, Helmand
    2005 return of Taliban, 164
    2006 Taliban attacks, 168; British platoon houses established, 171, 173, 174, 333; Taliban attacks, 175, 176, 178, 183–7; ceasefire agreement, 187–91; British withdrawal, 194
    2007 resumption of fighting, 200; deployment of 52nd Infantry Brigade, 212; Helmand Road Map created, 230; launch of TCAF, 214; defection of Mullah Salaam, 214–15; captured by ISAF, 215–21; conflict over reintegration of Taliban, 221–3; arrival of British Support and Stabilisation Team, 224
    2008 Mullah Salaam appointed governor, 224–5; Royal Gurkha Rifles deployed, 245
    2010 British withdrawal; US Marines move in, 356, 357
    2015 Taliban offensive, 401, 402
Musa, Saeed, 362
Musharraf, Pervez, 32, 54, 57, 64, 78, 347
mushrooms, 228
music, banning of, 29
Mutawakil, Wakil Ahmed, 54
Myers, Richard, 62, 72

Nad-e Ali, Helmand
Nagl, John, 210
Nahr-e Bughra Canal, 249, 251, 256, 294, 297
Nahr-e Seraj, Helmand, 143, 164, 166, 255, 337, 366, 379, 386
Naim, Mullah, 165, 166, 199, 238
Nairobi, Kenya, 22, 25, 41, 42, 46
Najibullah, Mohammed, 34
Namibia, 118
nanawatai, 35
Nangarhar, Afghanistan, 29, 415

Naqibullah, *see* Alikozai, Naqibullah
Naqilabad Qalay, Helmand, 310
narcotics, 30, 58, 102, 160, 168, 175, 244, 273,
   332, 418
  and Afghan security forces, 129, 154, 314, 323,
    375, 376
  and Akhundzada, 166–7, 226, 233
  and Alikozai-Ishaqzai dispute, 173
  in Babaji, 255
  and Daoud, 228
  in Garmsir, 165
  and Jan, Abdul Rahman, 311, 333
  and Jan, Abdullah, 165
  in Lashkar Kalay, 256
  and Major Crimes Task Force, 390–91
  in Malgir, 255
  and Mangal, 311
  in Marjah, 311, 333
  and Mir Wali, 161
  in Musa Qala, 189, 191, 220–21
  in Nad-e Ali, 228, 252–3, 293, 315, 333
  in Sangin, 191, 196
  in Spin Masjid, 255
  and Taliban, 130–31, 144, 175, 226, 311, 333
  taxation of, 131, 144, 226, 311, 333
  see also counter-narcotics; opium
Nasiriyah, Iraq, 146
nation-building, 117, 121, 123, 138, 418
National Auxiliary Police, 377
National Directorate of Security
  and Afghan Local Police, 377
  and Alikozai tribe, 361–2
  creation of (2002), 128
  and Dad Mohammad Khan, 145, 174
  and Lashkar Gah, battle of (2008), 246, 248
  and Musa Qala, battle for (2007), 215, 221
  and Pakistan, 346
  and US airstrikes (2010), 359
National Guard, US, 17
National Military Command Center (NMCC),
  16, 18
National Recruiting Centre, 380
National Security Agency (NSA), 318
National Security Council, US
  Afghanistan, invasion of (2001), 81
  and Iraq, 122
  and ISAF expansion, 100
  and Lute review (2007), 275
  and Operation Oqab Tsuka (2008), 243
  and Riedel review (2009), 278
  and Taliban talks, 405
  and troop increases, 270, 276
  and withdrawal from Afghanistan, 331
National Security, International Relations and
    Development Subcommittee (NSID),
    270, 272

National Unity Government, 398–9, 401, 409, 413
Natter, Robert, 19
Naval Squadron, 183
Nawa, Helmand, 154, 264, 300, 306, 326
Netherlands, 136, 139, 141, 149, 150, 181, 284,
  296, 372
Neumann, Ronald, 168, 181, 188
New York Post, 349
New York Times, 403, 415, 417
  Bin Laden, killing of (2011), 349
  Eikenberry's cable on Karzai (2010), 390
  Kunduz, fall of (2015), 402
  Obama's drawdown announcement (2009),
    301
  Operation Moshtarak (2010), 312, 316
  Quadrilateral Coordination Group formed
    (2016), 415
  Qala-i-Jangh surrender (2001), 77
  Rumsfeld on 'new kind of war' (2001), 58
  September 11 attacks (2001), 13
  Taliban offensive (2016), 403, 417
  Taliban surrender (2001), 90
  Tarin Kot, battle of (2001), 86
  Tora Bora, battle of (2001), 104
Newsweek, 211
Niaz Mohammed, 330
Nice, France, 141
Nicholson, John 'Mick', 255, 351
Nicholson, Larry, 254, 263, 266, 322
Nimrod reconnaissance aircraft, 186
nizami masoul, 338–9
'NOFORN' (No Foreigners), 108
Non-Kinetic Effects Teams (N-KETs), 212
Noori, Norrullah, 77
Noorzai tribe, 145, 251, 297, 361, 379
Noorzoy Kalay, Nad-e Ali, 297–9
North American Aerospace Defense
  Command (NORAD), 16, 18
North Atlantic Treaty Organisation (NATO),
  2, 3, 19, 423
  2001 September 11 attacks; Washington
    Treaty invoked, 45; US rejects assistance
    in Afghanistan, 60
  2003 crisis over proposed Iraq War, 136–7;
    takeover of ISAF, 138–9
  2004 Istanbul summit; Blair announces
    ARRC takeover of ISAF, 140–41, 148, 158,
    179
  2005 agreement for British expansion of
    ISAF to south, 140
  2006 British takeover of ISAF command,
    179, 180, 181, 186; Musa Qala ceasefire, 190
  2007 airstrikes in Helmand; Karzai
    denounces civilian casualties, 205–6, 209
  2008 Comprehensive Strategic Political-
    Military Plan approved, 284–5, 290

2009 announcement of additional troops for Afghanistan, 303
2010 Lisbon Summit; withdrawal from Afghanistan approved, 373
2011 Pakistan closes Afghan supply routes, 351
2014 Operation Resolute Support approved, 383
2015 Taliban offensive, 400
2016 Taliban offensive, 402–3; Warsaw Summit, 417
see also International Security Assistance Force
North Korea, 47, 123
North-West Frontier Province, Pakistan, 32
Northeast Air Defense Sector (NEADS), 18
Northern Alliance, 50, 58–61, 334
assassination of Massoud, 60
arrival of CIA Jawbreaker team, 67–8
US airstrikes begin, 71
arrival of US Special Operations teams, 68–9
fighting on Northern front, 70
frustration over US support, 73
Fahim meets with Franks, 73–4
capture of Mazar-e-Sharif, 74–6
capture of Taloqan, 77
capture of Kabul, 79–80
deployment of British Marines, 81–2
battle of Kunduz, 77
Taliban surrender at Qala-i-Jangh, 77–8
Pakistan launches Kunduz airlift, 79
Bonn Conference, 87–8
meetings with Karzai, 94–5
ISAF deployed to Kabul, 93, 94, 95, 98
Northern Ireland, 30, 38, 39, 41, 99, 112, 170, 342
Northwood, Hertfordshire, 93
Norway, 106
Notification Officers, 267
Now Zad, Helmand
2006 Taliban attacks, 168; British troops deployed, 171, 333; British platoon houses established, 173, 174; Taliban attacks, 175, 187, 191; ceasefire agreement, 189, 195, 196; fighting resumes, 189, 197–8, 218
2007 US airstrikes, 190; Royal Anglians deployed, 203; Battlegroup North established, 207; deployment of 52nd Infantry Brigade, 209, 210
2008 Royal Gurkha Rifles deployed, 245; British bombing, 257
2015 Taliban offensive, 401, 402
nuclear weapons, 14, 83, 124–5, 347–9
Nuristan, Afghanistan, 282

O'Hanlon, Michael, 114–15
Obaid Rahman, 238
Obaidullah Akhund, 89–90
Obama, Barack, 390
2008 presidential election campaign, 274, 424; visits Afghanistan, 274
2009 Biden visits Afghanistan, 275; takes office as president, 4, 419; Gates kept on as Defense Secretary, 275; meetings on troop increases, 276–7, 290; presses Brown on troop increases, 270; announces new Af-Pak strategy, 277, 290, 423; aid package to Pakistan, 278, 348; McChrystal's assessment on Afghanistan, 290, 304; Afghan presidential election, 389; announces surge and drawdown in Afghanistan, 301–5, 356
2010 increase in Pakistan drone strikes, 420; sets timeline for transition, 331–2, 373; sacking of McChrystal, 327; Karzai demands end to night raids, 329–30
2011 killing of Bin Laden, 349
2012 Taliban talks in Qatar, 406
2013 Taliban open diplomatic office in Qatar, 407
2014 BSA negotiations with Afghanistan, 397
2016 killing of Mansour, 415; announces troops to remain in Afghanistan, 417
Observer, 110
Ocean, HMS, 108
oil, 31
Oklahoma City bombing (1995), 14, 41
Oman, 65, 72, 104, 108
Omar, Mohammed, 28–9, 33, 84, 254, 366
1994 return of Taliban to Afghanistan, 28, 89; capture of Kandahar, 28–9
1998 US Operation Infinite Reach, 35, 56
2000 meets with Turki al-Faisal, 36
2001 destruction of Bamiyan Buddhas, 32–3; September 11 attacks, 54–6; US invasion, 67; US Operation Rhino, 72; surrender at Kandahar, 89–92, 115
2015 Pakistani request for talks, 408; death revealed, 412
Omar, Ramzi, 11, 27
Operating, Mentoring and Liaison Team (OMLT), 203–4, 208, 222, 245, 254
Operation Anaconda (2002), 106–8
Operation Azada Wosa (2008), 234–8
Operation Barma (2009–), 342
Operation Buzzard (2002), 109, 112–13
'Operation Certain Death' (2008), 240
Operation Condor (2002), 109, 111–12, 113
Operation Desert Storm (1991), 47, 59, 169, 282
Operation Enduring Freedom (2001–14), 65, 96, 114, 132, 139, 150, 206, 276
Operation Entirety (2009), 273

'Operation Evil Airlift' (2001), 78–9
Operation Hamkari (2010), 352, 419
Operation Herrick (2007–8), 207, 234
Operation Infinite Reach (1998), 25, 35, 37, 53, 56
Operation Jacana (2002), 1, 107–14
Operation Khanjar (2009), 264–6, 300
Operation Medusa (2006), 186
Operation Minimise (2009–), 267
Operation Moshtarak (2010), 296, 297, 305–24, 341, 355, 358
Operation Oqab Tsuka (2008), 239–43
Operation Panchai Palang (2009), 254–63, 271, 272, 294, 304, 307, 308, 343
Operation Ptarmigan (2002), 109–10
Operation Resolute Support (2015–), 383
Operation Rhino (2001), 72
Operation Saulat al-Fursan (2008), 248–9
Operation Silver (2007), 199–200
Operation Snipe (2002), 109, 110–11, 113
Operation Sond Chara (2008), 249–52
Operation Tolo (2008), 245
Operation Tor Shpa'h (2009), 297–300, 308, 355
Operation Veritas (2001–5), 66
opium, 244
    and Akhundzada, 166–7, 226, 233
    in Babaji, 255
    and Daoud, 228
    eradication, see under counter-narcotics
    in Garmsir, 165
    and Jan, Abdul Rahman, 311, 333
    and Jan, Abdullah, 165
    in Lashkar Kalay, 256
    in Malgir, 255
    in Marjah, 311, 333
    in Musa Qala, 189, 191, 220–21
    in Nad-e Ali, 228, 252–3, 293, 315, 333
    in Sangin, 191, 196
    in Spin Masjid, 255
    and Taliban, 130–31, 144, 175, 226, 311, 333
    taxation of, 131, 144, 226, 311, 333
Osborne, George, 371
Osmani, Akhtar Mohammad, 54–5, 361
Osprey body armour, 342
Oxford University, 46, 371

Page, Jonathan 'Jacko', 216
Pakistan, 1, 3, 27–8, 29, 31–2, 57, 235, 320, 345–51, 421, 423
    1979 outbreak of Soviet–Afghan War, 27
    1988 formation of al-Qaeda, 20
    1994 Taliban return to Afghanistan, 28
    1995 support for Taliban begins, 31
    1996 Simons meets with Ghaus, 30
    1997 recognition of Taliban Emirate, 32
    1998 nuclear tests, 124, 347; Zaeef meets with Milam on Bin Laden, 35
    1999 Kargil War, 124–5; UN imposes sanctions on Taliban, 32
    2000 football team deported from Afghanistan, 32
    2001 Taliban destroy Bamiyan Buddhas, 32–3; September 11 attacks, 54, 55, 57, 345, 348; Ridley kidnapped by Taliban, 71; Blair makes visit, 64; arrival of USS Kitty Hawk, 62; US airstrikes on Afghanistan; return of insurgents, 67, 143; Taliban release Ridley, 71; jihadis flock to Afghanistan, 73; evacuation of Karzai, 85; Kunduz airlift, 78–9; Bonn Conference, 87; Taliban surrender at Kandahar, 90; battle of Tora Bora, 105; standoff with India begins, 124; ISI meetings with Taliban, 346
    2002 US aid package launched, 347; UK refused use of Karachi airfield, 108; Operation Buzzard on border, 112–13; repatriation of Afghan refugees, 126
    2003 formation of Quetta Shura, 164
    2004 July 7 bombers visit, 149
    2006 construction of Camp Bastion in Helmand, 152; CIA drone strikes begin, 348, 351
    2007 offensive against tribes in FATA, 347
    2008 Riedel calls for pressure for terror crackdown, 276
    2009 Biden makes visit, 274; Obama announces new counter-terror strategy, 277–9; US military aid package launched, 348–9; Peshawar Military Commission negotiates deals with Taliban leaders, 338
    2010 Quetta Military Commission adopts guerrilla warfare strategy, 340; ISI arrests Baradar, 336, 404; spike in CIA drone strikes, 349, 420; talks with Taliban in Dubai begin, 404; CIA locates Bin Laden, 349
    2011 Bin Laden killed by US SEALs, 349–50; US-Taliban talks in Qatar, 406; Haqqani network attacks in Afghanistan, 350; closure of supply routes to NATO, 351
    2012 Taliban attack on Camp Bastion, 382
    2013 Taliban open diplomatic office in Qatar, 407, 411
    2014 Ghani takes office in Afghanistan, 408, 410; TTP attack in Peshawar, 410
    2015 request made to Taliban for talks, 408; talks with Taliban in Urumqi, 408–9; talks with Taliban in Murree, 409–10; death of Omar revealed, 412
    2016 establishment of Quadrilateral Coordination Group, 415; Mansour killed in US drone strike, 415; Ghani denounces support for Taliban, 417

Pakistan–Afghanistan Coordination Cell, 279, 351
Paktia, Afghanistan, 106, 109, 398
Paktika, Afghanistan, 233, 398
'pals platoons', 334
Panjshir Valley, 29, 60, 68, 69, 75
Panjwai, Kandahar, 186
Parachute Regiment
  2001 deployment to Bagram, 81; deployment to Kabul with ISAF, 94, 98, 107, 169; battle of Tora Bora, 105
  2006 deployment to Helmand, 156, 168–70, 179–80, 233; IED attack in Gereshk, 170; Platoon House strategy adopted, 171; IED attacks in Lashkar Gah, 172; deployment to Sangin cancelled, 173–4; platoon houses established in Now Zad and Musa Qala, 173, 174; Gul Mohammad Khan killed by Taliban, 174; fighting with Taliban in Sangin, 174–5, 177; Lamb's report on Gereshk ambush, 177–8; fighting in Sangin, 182–3; fighting in Musa Qala, 184–7; ceasefire in Musa Qala, 187–91
  2008 redeployed to Helmand, 231–4, 352; Operation Oqab Tsuka, 239–43
  2010 redeployed to Helmand, 367–8; operations in Chah-e Anjir Triangle, 355; ALP established in Saidabad, 378
Park for Women, Lashkar Gah, 230–31
Parker, Nicholas, 300, 304–5, 356, 372
Parwan Detention Facility, Bagram, 395
Pashto, 216, 239, 249, 254, 266, 318, 336, 371, 373
Pashtuns, 28
  atrocities against, 73
  and CIA, 60, 61
  and nanawatai, 35
  and police force, 376
  and presidential election (2014), 398
  and Taliban, 50, 60, 83, 401–2
  tribal feuds, 34
  women, segregation of, 34
Pathfinders Platoon, 178, 183–4, 240–41
Patrols Platoon, 188
Patterson, Mervyn, 221–3
Paveway II bombs, 183
PB Argyll, Nad-e Ali, 293
PB Pimon, Nad-e Ali, 294, 297
PB Shahzad, Chah-e Anjir, 257, 259
PB Silab, Nad-e Ali, 294, 296
PB Wahid, Loy Mandah, 257, 258, 294
peacekeeping, 117–21
Peach, Stuart, 272
Pearl Harbor attack (1941), 46
Pentagon, Virginia, 14, 16, 53, 63, 275, 351
Permanent Joint Headquarters (PJHQ), 83
  2001 forces deployed to Kabul, 93

2002 Operation Jacana, 108
2005 adoption of pivot strategy, 148
2006 forces deployed to Helmand, 152, 153, 158, 169, 170, 172, 233, 422
2007 introduction of Guidance Card Alpha, 206; 52nd Infantry Brigade takes command of Task Force Helmand, 209
2008 Parachute Regiment redeployed to Helmand, 234; Burley review, 343
2009 Brown briefed on Operation Panchai Palang, 272; Operation Tor Shpa'h, 300
Persistent Threat Detection System, 354
Peshawar, Pakistan, 7, 20, 31, 165, 228, 335, 338, 410
Peshawar Accord (1992), 31
'Peshawar group', 87
Peshawar Military Commission, 338–9
Petraeus, David
  2003 takes command of Joint Special Operations, 327
  2004 counterinsurgency in Mosul, 210–11
  2006 publication of FM 3–24 Counterinsurgency Field Manual, 211
  2007 takes command of forces in Iraq, 285, 327, 377
  2008 takes command of CENTCOM, 279; McKiernan replaced with McChrystal, 279
  2009 meetings on troop increases, 276, 290, 291
  2010 Obama sets timeline for transition, 331–2; takes command of ISAF, 327–32, 359; prioritizes corruption, 390, 393; persuades Karzai on irregular forces, 377; Saleh's CIA links revealed, 391; fighting in Nad-e Ali, 353; proposals for talks with Taliban, 405
  2011 Sangin peace accord, 364; reports on progress of ALP, 377–8; takes command of CIA, 373
Petronzio, Peter, 236
Pew Research, 349
Pharmacy Road, Sangin, 357, 360
Philippines, 26
Pinzgauer ATVs, 112
Pirzai tribe, 187–9
'Platoon House' strategy, 171
Poland, 417
Policy Action Group (PAG), 180–81, 190
Popalzai tribe, 84, 85
Pope, see John Paul II
population-centric counterinsurgency, 206–14, 231, 279–91, 320, 327, 368
Portugal, 179, 373
Post-Conflict Reconstruction Unit (PCRU), 151, 152–6, 167, 171, 230
Powell, Charles, 229

Powell, Colin, 48, 51, 56, 93, 100
  'Powell Doctrine', 59
Powell, Hugh, 229–33, 239, 255
Powell, Jonathan, 39–41, 122, 229
PowerPoint, 293
precision strikes, 330, 355
Predator drones, 110, 219, 247, 330, 348
Presidential Decision Directive 622 (1998), 24
Presidential Emergency Operations Center (PEOC), 17, 18
Princess of Wales Royal Regiment, 246
Principals meeting on al-Qaeda (2001), 37
prisoners of war, 69
'protecting the people', 280
Provincial Reconstruction Teams (PRTs), 133–6, 423
  Baghlan (Netherlands), 139
  Bamyan (US), 134
  Feyzabad (Germany), 139
  Gardez (US), 134
  Kunduz (Germany), 139
  Kunduz (US), 134
  Lashkar Gah (UK), see Helmand Provincial Reconstruction Team
  Lashkar Gah (US), 153–4, 156, 172
  Maymaneh (UK), 134, 140
  Mazar-e-Sharif (UK), 134–5, 140
public executions, 31
Public Protection Programme, 377
public support, 267, 273, 302, 304, 371
Punjab, Pakistan, 336
purdah, 34
Putin, Vladimir, 64

al-Qaeda, 20–27, 414
  1988 formation, 20
  1996 CIA opens Alec Station, 23; Bin Laden arrives in Afghanistan, 29, 120; joined by Khalid Sheikh Mohammed, 26
  1998 East African US embassy bombings, 22–5, 41, 42, 46; Operation Infinite Reach, 25, 35, 37, 53, 56; Bin Laden sheltered by Taliban, 35–7; formation of Hamburg cell, 11, 26
  1999 preparation for September 11 attacks, 27–8
  2000 Hamburg cell arrives in US, 28; USS *Cole* bombing, 36, 41
  2001 assassination of Massoud, 60; September 11 attacks, 1, 2, 4, 11–20, 26, 37, 38–57, 63–4; Afghanistan War begins; leaders escape to Pakistan, 66–7, 114, 143, 267; Bin Laden's Jalalabad speech, 100–101; Taliban surrender at Qala-i-Jangh, 77–8; Kunduz airlift, 78–9; battle of Tora Bora, 101–6, 115

  2002 Operation Anaconda, 106–8; Operation Jacana, 110–11, 112–13
  2006 Anbar Awakening begins in Iraq, 279, 377
  2009 Obama announces new Af-Pak strategy, 277, 278, 290
  2010 CIA locates Bin Laden, 349
  2011 Bin Laden killed by US SEALs, 349–50
  2012 US-Taliban talks in Qatar, 405, 406
Qala-i-Jangh, Mazar-e-Sharif, 77
Qanouni, Mohammed Yunus, 88, 95
Qassim, Mullah, 217, 222
Qatar, 77, 406–7, 409, 411, 412
quad bikes, 112
Quadrilateral Coordination Group, 415
al-Quds al-Arabi, 25
al-Quds Mosque, Hamburg, 11
Queen's Dragoon Guards, 238, 245–6
Queen's Royal Lancers, 241
Quetta, Pakistan, 54–5, 84, 165, 335
Quetta Military Commission, 311, 338–9, 340
Quetta Shura, 413, 414
  creation of (2003), 164
  Dadullah's offensive (2006), 333
  Haqqani Network, relations with, 411
  and Inter-Services Intelligence (ISI), 351
  Karzai, relations with, 404
  layeha, 339
  and leadership obedience, 412
  and *mahaz*, 336, 337
  and *nizami masoul*, 339
  and Sangin peace accord (2011), 364
  shadow government, 365–6
Qutb, Sayyed, 20–21, 22

Rabbani, Burhanuddin, 94, 404
Radford, Tim, 253–6, 261, 262
Rahbari Shura, 164
Rahmatullah, 379
'rally round the flag', 267
Ramadan, 103
Ramadi, Iraq, 236
RAND Corporation, 374, 377
Ranger pickup trucks, 385
Ranger Regiment, 104
rape, 28, 174, 315, 380, 393, 400
Rashid, Ahmed, 6
Rassoul, Zalmai, 180
Rayment, Sean, 193
Reagan, Ronald, 123
Red Crescent Society, 317
Red Wedge, 355
refugee camps, 27, 126
Regional Command Centre, 283, 286, 300, 424
Regional Command East, 275, 283, 284, 286, 300, 376, 424

Regional Command North, 283, 286, 300, 376, 424

Regional Command South
2006 Fraser takes command, 169, 187; Joint Helicopter Force deployed, 176; Danish reconnaissance deployed to Musa Qala, 178
2007 launch of TCAF, 213; battle for Musa Qala, 216, 218
2008 deployment of 3 Para, 234; deployment of 42 Commando, 245
2009 Biden visits Afghanistan, 275; Royal Regiment of Scotland deployed, 254; McChrystal takes command of ISAF, 283, 286; Operation Panchai Palang, 255; Carter takes command, 296, 300, 419; attempt to divert forces to Kandahar, 300
2010 Operation Moshtarak, 305, 307, 308, 311, 313, 316–18, 321; creation of RC-South-West, 352

Regional Command South-West, 352, 363–4, 374, 381, 386–7

Regional Command West, 284, 286, 300, 424

Reid, John, 140, 149, 151, 156–9, 168, 179–80

reintegration, 128, 135, 216–17, 221–3, 282, 362, 404–5

Reith, John, 113

'relentless pursuit', 353

'Responsibility for the Terrorist Atrocities in the United States', 63–4

'retrograde', 383

Reuters, 402

Riaz Mohammad Khan, 54

Rice, Condoleezza, 15, 40, 46, 57, 66, 121, 123, 138

Rice, Susan, 397

Richards, David, 142, 157, 178–81, 184, 186, 191, 194, 272–3, 381
2005 agreement on ISAF deployment to south, 142
2006 takes command of ISAF, 157, 178–81, 184, 187, 194; battle for Musa Qala, 186–7; Musa Qala ceasefire, 187–8, 191
2009 takes command of Land Forces, 272–3; launch of Operation Entirety, 273
2012 Allen suspends joint operations with Afghan forces, 381

Ridgeback MRAPs, 202, 271, 355

Ridley, Yvonne, 70–71

Riedel, Bruce, 276, 277, 278, 282, 284

Riga, Sangin, 359

rocket-propelled grenades (RPGs), 110, 174, 175, 176, 199, 237, 246

Rodriguez, David, 280, 287, 290, 307

Rolling Stone, 327

Romania, 284

'Rome group', 87, 88

Roosevelt, Franklin, 123

Roshan Hill, Musa Qala, 219–20

'Route Cornwall', 257–8

'Route Harriet', 241, 242

Royal Air Force (RAF)
2001 September 11 attacks, 40, 42, 63; airstrikes in Afghanistan, 72; troops deployed to Bagram, 82; ISAF deployed to Kabul, 98, 108
2006 deployment to Helmand, 156, 175, 183; complaint about Harriers goes viral at MoD, 183; fighting in Musa Qala, 186; fighting in Now Zad, 197, 198
2007 capture of Musa Qala, 219
2008 Operation Sond Chara, 251
2009 Operation Tor Shpa'h, 298
2012 insider attack at Camp Bastion, 382

Royal Anglian Regiment, 100, 134, 201–3

Royal Artillery, 195, 215, 354

Royal Engineers, 108, 182, 220, 241, 242, 257, 260

Royal Green Jackets Regiment, 132

Royal Gurkha Rifles, 208, 216, 245–6

Royal Horse Artillery, 156, 175

Royal Irish Regiment, 184–5, 188, 199, 234, 245, 252–4

Royal Marines
2001 planning of Afghanistan campaign, 57; deployment to Bagram, 81; deployed to assist Karzai, 94; deployment to Kabul with ISAF, 98; battle of Tora Bora, 105
2002 Operation Jacana, 1, 107–13
2006 construction of Camp Bastion, 152; deployment in Helmand, 175; takeover of Task Force Helmand, 192–3, 202; covering of Musa Qala withdrawal, 195; ceasefire in Sangin, 197; fighting in Now Zad, 197
2007 operations in Garmsir, 199, 237; Operation Silver in Sangin, 199–200; support for Mechanised Brigade, 201; Taliban attacks in Sangin, 216; battle for Musa Qala, 219
2008 IED attack in Kajaki, 225; Operation Azada Wosa, 237–8; takeover of Task Force Helmand, 244, 267; Taliban attack on Lashkar Gah, 244–8; Operation Sond Chara, 249–53

Royal Military Police, 380

Royal Navy, 65, 107

Royal Regiment of Fusiliers, 178, 199, 254

Royal Regiment of Scotland, 234, 237, 245, 254, 255–7, 261, 265

Royal Tank Regiment, 258

Royal United Services Institute (RUSI), 92–3

Rubin, Barnett, 416
rule of law, 133, 154, 224
'Rule of Three', 314, 324
rules of engagement (ROE), 42, 71, 172, 206, 258, 313
Rumsfeld, Donald
 2001 September 11 attacks, 14; comments on 'war on terror', 46; proposals for war in Iraq, 47, 51; meets with Franks, 61; meeting on Mullah Omar, 56; announces 'new kind of war', 58; negotiates use of K2 with Karimov, 63; airstrikes in Afghanistan begin, 66, 71; evacuation of Karzai, 85; revision of Iraq war plan, 121–2; Taliban surrender at Kandahar, 90, 115; battle of Tora Bora, 104, 115; ISAF deployed to Kabul, 92, 95
 2002 proposal for expansion of ISAF, 100, 121; Operation Jacana, 113; CJTF takes over Operation Enduring Freedom, 133; establishment of PRTs, 134
 2003 Germany and France oppose Iraq War, 136–7; invasion of Iraq, 146; NATO takes control of ISAF, 138
Russian Federation, 36, 48, 51, 63, 64, 87, 98
Rwanda, 23, 418
Ryder, Michael, 131, 231, 235, 236

Sadat, Anwar, 22
Saddar Ibrahim, 417
al-Sadr, Muqtada, 146
saffron, 131
Saidabad, Nad-e Ali, 296, 309, 326, 355–6, 378
Salaam, Mullah, 214–15, 224–5
Saleh, Mohammad Zia, 391
Sanchez, Ricardo, 147
'Sandhurst in the Sands', 387
Sangin, Helmand, 163
 2002 return of warlords, 144
 2004 return of Taliban, 164, 165, 334
 2006 Taliban attacks, 168; deployment of British troops, 171–4, 333; assassination of Gul Mohammad Khan, 174; Taliban attacks, 174–5, 177, 182–3, 185, 186; ceasefire agreement, 189, 191, 195–7
 2007 Operation Silver, 199–200; Mechanised Brigade deployed, 202; Royal Anglians deployed, 203; Battlegroup North established, 207; deployment of 52nd Infantry Brigade, 209; Helmand Road Map created, 230; launch of TCAF, 214; Taliban attacks, 216
 2008 Royal Marines deployed, 245; IED attacks, 253
 2009 3rdr Rifles deployed, 357

 2010 4th Infantry Brigade deployed, 325; Alikozai peace offer, 360; British withdrawal; US Marines move in, 173, 356–60, 372
 2011 Alikozai peace accord, 363–4; Taliban attacks, 332
 2015 Taliban offensive, 400, 402
Saudi Arabia
 Deobandi madrasas, 28
 jihadis in Afghanistan, 77
 Khobar Towers bombing (1996), 23
 Riyadh car bombing (1995), 23
 and Soviet–Afghan War (1979–89), 27
 and Taliban Emirate (1996–2001), 32, 36
 Wahhabi Islam, 11
Saul, John Ralston, 420
Saunders, Patrick, 378
Save the Children, 34, 136
Sayyaf, Abdul Rasoul 29
Sayyid tribe, 363
Scarlett, John, 41
Schroen, Gary, 67–8, 71, 72–3
Scimitar tanks, 156, 217, 250, 258, 260
Scotland Yard, London, 390
Scots Guards, 215, 216, 219, 301, 309, 326
Scud missiles, 282
Sea King helicopters, 271
SEALs (Sea, Air, and Land Teams), 241, 312, 349
'second civil service', 127
Secret Intelligence Service (SIS), 75–6, 82
'Securing Afghanistan's Future', 126
Sedwell, Mark, 390
Semple, Michael, 6, 90, 216–17, 221–4, 362, 416, 424
Senate Armed Services Committee, 328, 377
Senate Foreign Relations Committee, 102
September 11 attacks (2001), 1, 2, 4, 11–20, 26, 37, 38–57, 63–4, 345, 348, 370, 417–18
9/11 Commission, 16, 18, 23
Serbia, 24, 60
shadow government, 365–6
Shah Kariz, Helmand, 225
Shah-i Kowt Valley, Paktia Province, 106, 109
Shamalan Canal, 249, 251, 256, 257–9, 261, 262, 308
Shamsi, Abdul Ali, 362–3
'shape–clear–hold–build', 283, 296, 308, 315
shari'a law, 29–30, 31, 32, 33, 35, 161
Sharif, Mohammad, 361–3
Sharif, Nawaz, 31
al-Shehhi, Marwan, 11, 27
Sheinwald, Nigel, 120, 187, 372
Shelton, Hugh, 47, 50, 51, 56
Sherin Shah, 307–8, 344, 383
Sherzai, Gul Agha, 86, 89, 91

al-Shifa plant, Sudan, 25
Shin Kalay, Nad-e Ali, 249, 250–51, 252, 297–9,
    380
Shomali Plain, 70, 79
'shoot-and-scoot', 419
Short, Clare, 137
'shoulder to shoulder', 43
Showal, Helmand, 296, 310, 324
Shuja Pasha, Ahmed, 350
Shuja ul-Mulk Durrani, Emir of Afghanistan, 7
Sierra Leone, 42, 96, 120, 418
signals intelligence, 318–19
significant activities (SIGACTS), 315, 353,
    364
Simon, Jamey, 97
Simons, Tom, 30
Simpson, John, 80
singing, banning of, 30
'six day week', 231
Skinner, Dennis, 49
Slack, Richard, 208
Slim, David, 204
Small Wars: Their Principles and Practice
    (Callwell), 264
'Snake's Head', 235, 237, 238, 264, 266
Somalia, 23, 119, 418
'Somme' Platoon, 184
Sopranos, The, 154
Soviet Union (1922–91), 14, 25, 31, 62, 67, 68,
    201, 233, 341, 418
Soviet–Afghan War (1979–89), 336, 347, 360
    and Abdul Haq, 84
    and Bin Laden, 26, 29, 36
    and CIA, 60
    economy, effects on, 120, 130, 347
    and 'graveyard of empires', 25, 49, 290
    and Haqqani Network, 351
    and irregular forces, 59
    and MI6, 58
    mujahedin, 20, 25–9, 31–2, 34, 60, 101, 112,
        120, 130, 348
    and Naqibullah, 89
    and al-Qaeda, 20, 25, 26, 29, 36
    and Taliban, 27–9, 336
    and Tora Bora, 101
soya beans, 228
Spain, 148, 284
Spartan tanks, 156
Special Activities Division (SAD), 67
Special Air Service (SAS), 61, 67, 169, 233, 355
    2001 deployed to Afghanistan, 82–3; forma-
        tion of ISAF, 93; battle of Tora Bora, 103
    2002 Blair visits Afghanistan, 117
    2003 Mazar-e-Sharif PRT established, 134
    2005 recce of Helmand, 233

2006 Taliban attack on Lashkar Gah, 246,
    247
2010 press reports on JPEL, 330–31
Special Air Service (SAS), Australia, 111–12
Special Boat Service (SBS), 61, 67, 81, 82, 298,
    331
Special Forces Support Group, 298
Special Inspector General for Afghanistan
    Reconstruction, 402
Special Operations Aviation Regiment, 62, 68
Spiegel, Der, 330
Spin Masjid, Helmand, 255–7
'spray and pray', 323
St Antony's College, Oxford, 76
St Thomas's Church, New York, 52
Stanekzai, Mohammed Masoom, 401
Stanikzai, Naquib, 221–2
State Department, US, 14, 30, 35, 129, 239, 275,
    288, 350
Status of Forces Agreement, 396
Stavridis, James, 290
'steal, the', 296, 305
Stewart, Andrew, 146–7
Stewart, Rory, 151, 216, 371
Stirrup, Graham 'Jock' 105, 186, 187, 270
Strachan, Hew, 46–7, 269
Strategic Defence Review (1998), 119–20, 148
Straw, Jack, 39, 125, 132
Strengthening Peace Programme, 216–17, 255
Strick van Linschoten, Alex, 6
Struck, Peter, 139
Stuart, Gisela, 49
Sturdevant, Gregg, 383
Sudan, 25, 29
Sugden, Robert, 222
suicide attacks, 78, 193, 225, 294, 340, 361, 395,
    400
Sun, 111, 326
Sunday Express, 71
Sunday Times, 151, 177–8, 220, 269, 312
Sunni Awakening (2006–7), 279, 377

T-55 tanks, 76
T-62 tanks, 76
Tactical Conflict Assessment Framework
    (TCAF), 212–14
'Tajaki Three', 95
Tajikistan, 57, 63, 70, 73, 76
Tajiks, 28, 29, 60, 70, 73, 87, 347, 398
takfir, 21
Takhar front, 70, 71, 73, 77
Talbott, Strobe, 24
Taliban, 27–36, 335–9, 365–7, 421, 424–5
    1994 return to Afghanistan from Pakistan,
        28

1995 Pakistani support begins, 31–2; capture of Herat, 32

1996 capture of Kandahar, 28; Bin Laden arrives in Afghanistan, 29; capture of Kabul, 29–30; Ghaus meets with Simons, 30; Hamid Karzai proposed as UN representative, 30

1997 international condemnation of human rights abuses, 31; Saudi Arabia and UAE recognise government, 32; Bonino arrested in Kabul, 34

1998 al-Qaeda bombs US embassies in East Africa, 24–5; killing of Iranian diplomats in Mazar-e-Sharif, 345; Operation Infinite Reach, 35, 56; sheltering of Bin Laden, 35–7

1999 assassination of Abdul Ahad Karzai, 30, 84; UN imposes sanctions, 32

2000 opium cultivation banned, 130; Pakistani football team beaten and deported, 32; Omar meets with Turki al-Faisal, 36

2001 destruction of Bamiyan Buddhas, 32–3; aid workers detained, 68; September 11 attacks, 43–4, 52–7, 370; US airstrikes begin, 66–7, 72, 114, 143; release of Ridley, 70–71; fighting on Northern front, 68, 69, 70; Operation Rhino, 72; foreign fighters swell ranks, 73; battle of Mazar-e-Sharif, 74–6; execution of Abdul Haq, 84; Bin Laden's Jalalabad speech, 100–101; withdrawal from Taloqan, 76–7; battle of Tarin Kot, 85–6; Northern Alliance capture Kabul, 79–80; battle of Kunduz, 77; surrender of forces at Qala-i-Jangh, 77–8; Kunduz airlift, 78–9; exclusion from Bonn Conference, 67, 116; surrender at Kandahar, 89–92, 162; battle of Tora Bora, 102–6, 115; expulsion from Garmsir, 143; meetings with ISI, 346

2002 Operation Anaconda, 106–8; Operation Jacana, 110–11, 112–13

2003 formation of Quetta Shura, 164

2004 return to Helmand begins, 145, 334; return to Sangin, 164, 165, 334

2005 return to Musa Qala, 164

2006 CIA drone strikes in Pakistan begin, 348; ISAF forces deployed to Helmand, 145, 157, 160, 333, 335–6; IED attacks in Lashkar Gah, 172; IED attack in Gereshk, 170; killing of Gul Mohammad Khan, 174; fighting in Sangin, 174–5, 177, 333; capture of Garmsir, 166, 333; fighting in Sangin and Musa Qala, 178, 182–7, 333; Operation Medusa launched, 186; ISAF capture Garmsir, 199; ceasefire in Musa Qala, 187–91; ceasefires in Sangin and Now Zad, 189, 191, 195–7; battle of Pashmul, 337; fighting resumes in Now Zad, 189, 197–8, 218

2007 US airstrikes in Musa Qala, 190; fighting in Garmsir, 199; fighting in Sangin, 199–200; Mechanised Brigade deployed, 202–5; SAS kill Dadullah Lang, 331, 336; reintegration of Gereshk group, 217; defection of Mullah Salaam, 214–15; attacks in Garmsir and Sangin, 216; ISAF capture Musa Qala, 215–21; conflict over reintegration in Musa Qala, 221–3

2008 Mullah Salaam appointed Musa Qala governor, 224–5; IED attack in Kajaki, 225; return of Parachute Regiment, 232, 352; Operation Azada Wosa, 234–8; Operation Oqab Tsuka, 239–43; attack on Lashkar Gah, 244–8, 340, 418; Operation Sond Chara, 249–53

2009 Obama announces new strategy, 277; Operation Panchai Palang, 254–63, 271, 272, 294, 304, 307, 308, 343; encirclement of Lashkar Gah, 289; escalation of insurgency in Kandahar, 289; Operation Khanjar, 264–6; operations in Nad-e Ali, 294, 295; 'consent-based clear' operation in Nad-e Ali, 296–7; insider attack in Nad-e Ali, 380; Operation Tor Shpa'h, 297–300, 355; shooting of Drane in Nad-e Ali, 305

2010 adoption of guerrilla warfare strategy, 340; SEAL raids in Marjah, 312; Operation Moshtarak, 305–24, 341, 355, 358; US Marines move into Musa Qala, 356, 357; Nad-e Ali held by ISAF forces, 313–16; attacks in Marjah, 316–18; Alikozai peace offer in Sangin, 360; ISAF operations in Saidabad and Babaji, 326; Royal Irish Regiment deployed; fighting in Nad-e Ali, 352–4; US Marines move into Sangin, 356–60, 419; fighting in Chah-e Anjir Triangle, 355; battle for Red Wedge, 355; Kabul–Dubai talks begin, 404

2011 Sangin peace accord, 363–4; Niaz Mohammed killed in British strike, 330; meetings with US in Qatar, 406

2012 insider attack at Camp Bastion, 382; negotiations with US in Qatar, 406; attack on Camp Bastion, 381–3

2013 battle of Badakhshan, 384; attack in Kunar, 385; opening of diplomatic office in Qatar, 406–7, 411, 412

2014 meetings with Ghani, 414

2015 Pakistani request for talks, 408; offensive launched; territory recaptured, 243, 399–402; talks in Urumqi, 408–9, 412; talks in Murree, 409–10; death of Omar revealed, 412, 415; Mansour declared amir, 412

2016 establishment of Quadrilateral Coordination Group, 415; offensive launched, 402–3, 417; Mansour killed in US drone strike, 415–16; Haibatullah declared amir, 416

Talisman Programme, 344

Talon remote-controlled robots, 344

Taloqan, Takhar, 74, 76–7

Tangi Gap, Balkh, 75

tanker aircraft, 63, 72

Tanzania, 23, 25, 41, 42, 46, 118

'targeting cycle', 328

Tarin Kot, Uruzgan, 84, 85

Tashkent, Uzbekistan, 63

Task Force Leatherneck, 296

Tatters, Simon, 219

taxation, 126, 144, 163, 188, 196, 225, 296, 380, 393
  of opium, 131, 144, 226, 311, 333

Tayeb Agha, 406, 411

Tehrik-i-Taliban Pakistan (TTP), 410, 415

telephone system, 126

television, banning of, 30

Tenet, George, 23, 24, 47, 56, 59, 61

Territorial Army, 71, 260

Thatcher, Margaret, 38, 123, 229

Thomas, Jerry, 192, 194, 195, 198, 199, 200

Thomson, Adam, 231

Thorneloe, Rupert, 259, 262, 272

Thuraya satellite phones, 319

Times, The, 44, 81, 110, 123, 158, 220, 224, 263

'tipping point', 290

Tokyo donors' conference (2002), 125, 131

Tomahawk cruise missiles, 65

Tootal, Stuart
  deployment to Helmand, 157–8, 169–71, 174, 180
  fighting in Sangin and Musa Qala, 174, 176, 178, 183–6

toothpaste, banning of, 30

Tora Bora, 101–6, 115

Torchlight, 344

Tornado GR4 fighter-bombers, 72

'Touring Afghanistan by Submarine' (Exum), 286

Trades Union Congress, 38, 39, 43

Trafalgar, HMS, 65

Trafalgar-class submarines, 63

'train, advise, assist', 384

Treasury, 150, 158

tribal feuds, 34, 163–4, 173, 332, 360

Trikh Zabur Canal, 249

TriStars, 72

Triumph, HMS, 65

Turkey, 58, 98, 99, 136, 137, 148, 406

Turki al-Faisal, Prince of Saudi Arabia, 36

Turkmenistan, 31, 57

twenty-foot equivalent units (TEUs), 383

Uganda, 118

ulema, 55

unemployment, 335, 392

United Airlines flight 93, 15, 17

United Arab Emirates (UAE), 6, 32, 220, 393

United Kingdom
  1982 Falklands War, 169, 183
  1984 Brighton bombing, 38
  1989 evacuation of Kabul embassy, 93
  1991 Operation Desert Storm, 169, 282; Downing Street mortar attack, 41
  1992 intervention in Bosnia begins, 81, 96, 119, 169
  1996 MI6 begins investigating Bin Laden, 41–2
  1997 Blair takes office, 119
  1998 MI5 meetings on terror financing begin, 42; Strategic Defence Review, 119–20, 148
  1999 intervention in Kosovo War, 81, 120; intervention in East Timor, 120
  2000 intervention in Sierra Leone begins, 42, 96, 120, 169, 418
  2001 September 11 attacks; COBRA meeting, 38–45; NATO invokes Washington Treaty, 45; intelligence chiefs visit Washington, 48; Parliament debates response to September 11 attacks, 48–50; meetings on Afghanistan campaign, 57–8, 60–61; Blair's diplomacy in support of war, 51; Blair visits US, 51–3; Blair meets with defence and intelligence chiefs, 58; Ridley detained by Taliban, 71; preparations for offensive, 63; Labour Party conference, 63–4; 'Responsibility for the Terrorist Atrocities in the United States' dossier released, 63; Blair visits Russia, Pakistan and India, 64; airstrikes on Afghanistan begin, 64, 65–7, 71–2, 266; Blair's speech on Afghan drug trade, 129–30; Ridley released by Taliban, 71; Boyce's assessment on progress of war, 73; SAS deployed to Afghanistan, 82–3; SIS arrive in Panjshir Valley, 75–6; Northern Alliance capture Kabul, 79–81; Marines and paratroops deployed to Bagram, 81–2, 121, 418; Taliban surrender

at Qala-i-Jangh, 78; Bonn Conference, 67, 87, 92, 116; battle of Tora Bora, 103, 105–6; Royal Marines deployed to assist Karzai, 94; ISAF deployed to Kabul, 82, 92–9, 107, 169, 418; proposals for expansion of ISAF, 99

2002 Blair visits Afghanistan, 117; formation of ANG, 99, 128; Afghan counter-narcotics programme funded, 131; proposals for expansion of ISAF, 100; Operation Jacana, 1, 107–13; Blair meets with military chiefs at Chequers, 123; Bush–Blair meeting in Crawford, 123–4; G8 meeting in Geneva, 128; ISAF command handed over to Turkey, 100; MI6 launch counter-narcotics programme, 131; CJTF takes over Operation Enduring Freedom, 132–3

2003 invasion of Iraq, 137, 140, 145, 159; Mazar-e-Sharif PRT established, 134; disarmament of Atta and Dostum, 134–5

2004 launch of Butler Review, 147; conflict with Mahdi Army in Basra, 146–7; Maymaneh PRT established, 134; *Daily Mirror* Iraq torture hoax, 147; Blair announces ARRC takeover of ISAF, 140–41, 148–9, 158, 179

2005 agreement for ISAF expansion to south, 141–2, 150; July 7 attacks, 149–50; ground lost to Shia militias in Iraq, 150–51; foundation of PCRU, 151; PCRU team deployed to Afghanistan, 152–6, 167, 171; Joint Helmand Plan created, 154–6; Akhundzada removed from Helmand governorship, 166–7

2006 London conference on Afghanistan, 158, 181; Joint Co-ordination and Monitoring Board established, 181; construction of Camp Bastion, 152, 169; Prince Charles visits Air Assault HQ, 157–8; forces deployed to Helmand, 145, 156–60, 168–70, 179–80, 233, 333, 421; Platoon House strategy adopted in Helmand, 171; takeover of ISAF command, 178, 187; Lamb's report on Gereshk ambush, 177–8; reinforcements sent to Helmand, 178; PAG established, 180; ceasefires in Musa Qala and Sangin, 187–91, 195–7; review of Joint Helmand Plan, 229; Royal Marines take command of Task Force Helmand, 192–3; retreat of forces in Basra, 151

2007 Mechanised Brigade takes command of Task Force Helmand, 200–205; SAS kill Dadullah Lang, 331, 336; Browne announces acquisition of MRAPs, 201–2;

Karzai denounces civilian casualties, 205–6; introduction of Guidance Card Alpha, 206; reintegration of Gereshk Taliban, 217, 222; withdrawal from Basra Palace, 248; 52nd Infantry Brigade takes command of Task Force Helmand, 207–12, 230; Helmand Road Map created, 230; launch of TCAF in Helmand, 212–14; defection of Mullah Salaam, 215; Brown visits Afghanistan, 218; capture of Musa Qala, 215–21; conflict over reintegration of Musa Qala Taliban, 221–3

2008 Parachute Regiment deployed to Helmand, 231–4, 352; Powell takes command of Helmand campaign, 229–33; Operation Azada Wosa, 238; Operation Oqab Tsuka, 239–43; Royal Marines take command of Task Force Helmand, 244; bank bailout package, 269, 422; Brown agrees to reinforcements for Helmand, 269; Operation Sond Chara, 249–53

2009 London G20 Summit, 270; Richards launches Operation Entirety, 273; Infantry Brigade takes command of Task Force Helmand, 253; Dannatt pressures Brown on reinforcements, 271; McChrystal takes command of ISAF, 294–5; Dannatt visits troops, 271–2; Operation Panchai Palang, 254–63, 271, 272, 294, 304, 307, 308, 343; Brown visits Camp Leatherneck, 304; British Muslim leaders visit Afghanistan, 292–4; takeover of RC-South command, 296, 300; Brown announces drawdown, 322; insider attack in Nad-e Ali, 380; formation of Afghan Major Crimes Task Force, 390; Operation Tor Shpa'h, 297–300, 355; death of Drane in Nad-e Ali, 305

2010 International Conference on Afghanistan, 324, 374; Operation Moshtarak, 296, 297, 305–24, 341, 355, 358; withdrawal from Musa Qala, 356; Felton takes command of Task Force Helmand, 325; general election, 356; Alikozai peace offer in Sangin, 360; Karzai makes visit, 370; Chequers summit on Afghanistan, 370–72; Cameron visits Afghanistan, 356, 372; Operation Hamkari, 352; closure of Afghan Major Crimes Task Force, 391; Chiswell takes command of Task Force Helmand, 352; launch of Persistent Threat Detection System, 354; withdrawal from Sangin, 173, 356, 372, 419

2011 Sangin peace accord, 363–4; killing of Niaz Mohammed, 330

2012 Taliban attack on Camp Bastion, 381–3; Allen halts joint operations with ANSF, 381; shipping back of material from Afghanistan begins, 383

2013 Commons Defence Committee assessment of Afghan forces, 386

2016 additional troops for Afghanistan announced, 417

United Nations, 2, 118, 130, 131

1996 Taliban propose Karzai as representative, 30

1997 High Commissioner for Refugees suspends operations in Afghanistan, 34

1999 sanctions imposed on Taliban, 32

2001 verification of Taliban opium ban, 131; meeting on fall of Kabul, 80, 120; Britain deploys forces to Afghanistan, 81–2; Bonn Conference, 67, 87–8; ISAF deployed to Kabul, 82, 92–9; proposals for expansion of ISAF, 99

2002 proposals for expansion of ISAF, 100; Tokyo donors' conference, 125; repatriation of Afghan refugees, 126

2003 DDR campaign in Afghanistan, 166; NATO takes control of ISAF, 138–9

2004 Berlin donors' conference, 126; Resolution 1546 on Iraq, 148

2005 counter-narcotics programme in Afghanistan, 227

2008 UNAMA collaborates on McKiernan plan, 284

2009 McChrystal takes command of ISAF, 287; Afghan presidential election, 388, 389

2010 Operation Moshtarak, 322; report on corruption in Afghanistan, 391–2

2013 Taliban open diplomatic office in Qatar, 407

2016 establishment of Quadrilateral Coordination Group, 415; Ghani threatens complaint against Pakistan, 417

United States

1991 Operation Desert Storm, 47, 59, 282

1992 intervention in Somalia, 23, 119, 418

1993 Clinton takes office, 119; World Trade Center bombing, 26; cruise missile strikes in Iraq, 24; battle of Mogadishu, 119, 418

1995 peacekeepers withdrawn from Haiti, 119; Oklahoma City bombing, 14, 41

1996 CIA opens Alec Station, 23; Simons meets with Ghaus, 30

1997 Albright indicates shift on Taliban policy, 34–5

1998 Presidential Decision Directive 622 signed, 24; East African embassy bombings, 22–3, 25, 41, 42, 46; Operation Infinite Reach, 25, 35, 37, 53, 56

1999 intervention in Kosovo War, 119

2000 CIA plan to capture Bin Laden, 36; USS *Cole* bombing, 36, 41

2001 Bush takes office, 36; Hainan Island incident, 36; Clarke's memorandum on Bin Laden, 37; Principals meeting on al-Qaeda, 37; September 11 attacks, 1, 2, 4, 11–20, 26, 37, 38–45, 417–18; Pentagon war cabinet, 45–7; NATO invokes Washington Treaty, 45; Pakistan offers support, 57, 345, 348; war cabinet meeting, 59; Authorization for Use of Military Force, 50; CIA operations in Afghanistan approved, 61; Camp David war cabinet, 50–51; Grenier meets with Osmani, 54; Joint Chiefs of Staff meeting, 61; New York memorial service, 51; Bush addresses Congress, 51–2, 57; war cabinet meeting, 61; meeting on CIA Mullah Omar assessment, 56; Rumsfeld announces 'new kind of war', 58–9; CIA Jawbreaker team arrives in Afghanistan, 67–8; Grenier meets with Osmani, 54–5; Franks meets with CIA, 61; Uzbeks give permission to use K2 airbase, 63, 68; airstrikes on Afghanistan begin, 64, 65–7, 71–2, 114, 143; Special Operations Group arrives in Afghanistan, 68–9; USS *Kitty Hawk* arrives in Pakistan, 62; Operation Rhino, 72; Franks meets with Fahim, 73–4; capture of Mazar-e-Sharif, 74–6; evacuation of Karzai to Pakistan, 85; capture of Taloqan, 77; Bush rules out occupation of Kabul, 81; battle of Tarin Kot, 85–6; Northern Alliance capture Kabul, 79–80; UNSC meeting in New York, 80; CIA begins attack on Tora Bora, 101; Franks revises Iraq war plans, 121–2; battle of Kunduz, 77; Taliban surrender at Qala-i-Jangh, 77–8; Pakistan launches Kunduz airlift, 78–9; battle of Kandahar begins, 86; Bonn Conference, 67, 87, 92, 116, 125; friendly fire bombing outside Kandahar, 88–9; fall of Kandahar, 89–92; ground assault on Tora Bora, 102–6, 115; al-Bahlul captured, 53; ISAF deployed to Kabul, 92, 95; proposals for expansion of ISAF, 99

2002 proposals for expansion of ISAF, 100; Tokyo donors' conference, 125; Bush's State of the Union speech, 122–3; launch of aid package to Pakistan, 347; Operation Anaconda, 106–8; Operation Jacana, 107–13; Bush–Blair meeting in

Crawford, 123–4; Bush's Virginia Military Institute speech, 138; G8 meeting in Geneva, 128; training of ANG, 128; CJTF takes over Operation Enduring Freedom, 132–3; establishment of Camp Price in Helmand, 161; establishment of PRTs, 134

2003 Germany and France oppose Iraq War, 136–7; troops ambushed in Baghran, 162–3; Khalid Sheikh Mohammed captured, 26; invasion of Iraq, 4, 137, 145, 274; CPA established in Iraq, 146; State Department takes over ANP, 129; Khalilzad plan drawn up, 138; NATO takes control of ISAF, 138–9; formation of ANA, 128–9; capture of Saddam Hussein, 146

2004 first battle of Fallujah, 146; Mahdi Army insurgency, 146–7; Abu Ghraib prison scandal breaks, 147; Blair announces ARRC takeover of ISAF, 140; CPA hands authority to interim government, 148; counter-insurgency launched in Mosul, 210–11; 9/11 Commission report, 16, 18, 23; second battle of Fallujah, 236, 360

2005 CSTC-A takes over ANSF training, 129, 375; nuclear deal with India, 348; reduction of forces in southern Afghanistan, 168

2006 drone strikes in Pakistan begin, 348, 351; Neumann's talk at Georgetown University, 168; ceasefire in Musa Qala, 188–90; ceasefire in Sangin, 196–7

2007 troop surge in Iraq, 279; FM 3–24 *Counterinsurgency Field Manual* published, 211; airstrikes on Musa Qala, 190; takeover of ISAF command, 191; Operation Silver in Garmsir, 199; Karzai denounces civilian casualties, 205–6; defection of Mullah Salaam, 215; battle for Musa Qala, 218, 219; NSC meeting on war strategy, 275

2008 Mullah Salaam appointed Musa Qala governor, 225; Operation Azada Wosa, 234–8; McKiernan takes command of ISAF, 239–40, 283–4; Obama's Woodrow Wilson Center speech, 274; Obama visits Afghanistan, 274; Operation Oqab Tsuka, 241

2009 Biden visits Afghanistan, 274–5, 289; Obama takes office, 274–6, 419; Riedel review launched, 275–6, 282, 284; London G20 Summit, 270; additional troops approved for Afghanistan, 276–7, 290; Obama announces new Af-Pak strategy, 277, 290; McChrystal takes command of ISAF, 280–90, 294–5, 365, 419, 423–4; Marine Expeditionary Brigade deployed to Helmand, 254, 263, 277, 300, 302; Operation Panchai Palang, 256, 264; Operation Khanjar, 264–6, 300; Afghan presidential election, 389; McChrystal's assessment delivered, 290–91; launch of military aid package to Pakistan, 348–9; USAID suspends Kajaki project, 243; Obama announces surge and drawdown in Afghanistan, 301–5

2010 Eikenberry cable on Karzai leaked, 390; SEAL raids in Marjah, 312; Operation Moshtarak, 305–24, 341, 358; Marines move into Musa Qala, 356, 357; Obama sets date for Afghan transition, 331; McChrystal replaced by Petraeus, 327–32; Marines move into Sangin, 356–60, 372, 419; spike in Pakistan drone strikes, 349, 420; Taliban Dubai talks begin, 404–5; Bin Laden located, 349

2011 Sangin peace accord, 363–4; Clinton indicates shift on Taliban policy, 405; killing of Bin Laden, 349–50; meetings with Taliban in Qatar, 406; Allen takes command of ISAF, 373; counter-intelligence agents dispatched to Afghanistan, 380; Haqqani network attacks in Afghanistan, 350; Pakistan closes NATO supply routes, 351

2012 insider attack at Camp Bastion, 382; Allen orders protective measures against insider attacks, 381; negotiations with Taliban in Qatar, 406; Taliban attack on Camp Bastion, 381–3; Allen halts joint operations with ANSF, 381

2013 Dunford takes command of ISAF, 383; Hagel visits Afghanistan, 395; Kerry meets with Karzai on BSA, 396

2014 Karzai proposes seizure of Parwan Detention Facility, 395; BSA with Afghanistan signed, 399

2015 Taliban offensive in Afghanistan, 400; talks with Taliban in Murree, 409–10

2016 establishment of Quadrilateral Coordination Group, 415; Taliban offensive in Afghanistan, 403; killing of Mansour, 415–16; Obama announces continued deployment in Afghanistan, 417

United States Agency for International Development (USAID), 99, 279
counter-narcotics, 227–8
District Delivery Programme, 306
Kajaki Dam project, 239–40, 243
TCAF, 213

United States Air Force
  2001 September 11 attacks, 17–19, 50; invasion of Afghanistan, 61, 62–3, 65, 71, 114; Operation Rhino, 72; battle of Mazar-e-Sharif, 74; battle of Tarin Kot, 85–6; battle of Kunduz, 77; battle of Kandahar, 88–9; battle of Tora Bora, 101–2
  2006 support for British forces in Helmand, 175, 176, 183
United States Marine Corps
  2001 fall of Kabul, 80
  2004 development of Persistent Threat Detection System, 354
  2008 Powell takes command of ISAF Helmand campaign, 233; Operation Azada Wosa, 234–8
  2009 1st Expeditionary Brigade deployed to Helmand, 254, 263, 277; Operation Panchai Palang, 256, 264; Operation Khanjar, 264–6, 300, 307; Task Force Leatherneck formed, 296; RC-South requests deployment to Kandahar, 300–301; Obama announces surge in Afghanistan, 303
  2010 Operation Moshtarak, 305, 310, 311–13, 322–3; Taliban attacks in Marjah, 316–18; command of Musa Qala operations taken, 356, 357; support for *arbakai* in Marjah, 378; operations in Saidabad, 326; command of Sangin operations taken, 356, 357–60, 372, 419; 2nd Expeditionary Brigade deployed to Helmand, 351
  2011 Sangin peace accord, 364; Allen takes command of ISAF, 373; command of RC-South-West taken, 374
  2012 insider attack at Camp Bastion, 382; Taliban attack on Camp Bastion, 383
  2013 Dunford takes command of ISAF, 383
United States Navy, 36
  Afghanistan, invasion of (2001), 62, 65, 114
  Bin Laden, killing of (2011), 349
  Operation Infinite Reach (1998), 25, 35, 37, 53, 56
  Operation Oqab Tsuka (2008), 241
  September 11 attacks (2001), 19, 50
  USS *Cole* bombing (2000), 36, 41
  see also United States Marine Corps
United States Special Forces
  Afghanistan, invasion of (2001), 68–9
  Bin Laden, killing of (2011), 349–50
  Camp Price, 161
  Kandahar, battle of (2001), 86, 89
  Karzai, evacuation of (2001), 83–5
  Kunduz, battle of (2001), 77
  Operation Rhino (2001), 72

Mazar-e-Sharif, battle of (2001), 74, 75
Mir Wali, raids on (2004), 166
Musa Qala, battle of (2007), 218
Taliban offensive (2016), 403
Tarin Kot, battle of (2001), 85–6
Tora Bora, battle of (2001), 103
uranium, 392
Urgent Operational Requirement programme, 202
Urumqi, China, 408–9, 412
Uruzgan, Afghanistan, 84–5, 87, 141, 150, 380, 400, 401
Uzbekistan, 57, 76, 236
  jihadis in Afghanistan, 77–8
  Karshi Khanabad (K2) airfield, 62–3, 68, 69, 72, 80
Uzbeks, 28, 29, 32, 60, 70, 87, 398

Vallon metal detectors, 342–3
Varsity, 344
VC10s, 63, 72
Vector armoured vehicles, 241, 257
Vendrell, Francesc, 81–2, 222
Vietnam, 118, 210
Viking armoured vehicles, 194, 198, 201, 241, 257–9, 298
Vines, John, 134
Virginia Military Institute, 138
Voltaire's Bastards (Saul), 420

Wafa, Asadullah, 190, 204, 222, 228, 233, 361
Wahhabi Islam, 11
Walker, Michael, 149, 179
Walker, Roland 'Roly', 296–7, 300
Wall Street Journal, 137
Wall, Peter, 93, 95, 97, 231
'war on terror', 46–7, 139, 244
Wardak, Afghanistan, 350, 377, 400
Wardlaw, Richard, 213
warlords
  Afghan Civil War (1992–96), 28–33
  and Afghan Local Police, 379, 380
  demobilisation, disarmament and reintegration (DDR), 135
  Helmand, return to (2002), 144–5, 160–62, 333
  National Guard, formation of (2002–3), 128
  opium production, 131, 132
  PRTs established, 133, 134–5
  rents, 392
  US-led invasion (2001), 86, 91, 95, 126, 144
Warrior armoured vehicles, 151, 207, 215, 219, 246
Warsaw, Poland, 417
Washington Post, 137, 266, 291, 323, 349
Washington Times, 45

Washington, Rudy, 19
Washington Treaty (1949), 45
Wasiq, Abdul Haq, 55
Watchkeeper drones, 246
water, access to, 213, 332, 365; *see also* irrigation
Waterloo Station, London, 76
Waters, George, 222
Watt, Redmond, 208
'Way Forward in Afghanistan' (2009), 301
Waziristan, Pakistan, 410
Weapon Mounted Installation Kit (WMIK), 198, 216, 241
'weapons of mass destruction', 122, 140
Weir, Colin, 352–4, 367
Welsh Guards, 254, 256, 257, 259, 260, 262, 296, 298–9, 308
Westmoreland, William, 329
wheat, 131, 132, 144, 293, 367
Wherley, David, 19
White House, Washington DC, 13, 16, 18, 19
White Mountains, 101–6
White-Spunner, Barney, 93, 95, 97, 98
Whiteman Air Force Base, Missouri, 65
Wikileaks, 330
'wild men', 370–71
Williams, Huw, 232
Williams, Richard, 331
Wilson, Richard, 40
Wolf hound MRAPs, 202, 271
Wolfowitz, Paul, 47, 51
women's rights, 11, 30, 31, 33, 34–5, 130, 226–7
  education, 30, 34, 75, 144, 189
  'loan brides', 226–7

Wood, William, 227
Woodward, Bob, 121, 277
Wootton Bassett, Wiltshire, 268–9
Worcestershire and Sherwood Foresters Regiment, 201
World Bank, 125, 394
World Trade Center, New York
  September 11 attacks (2001), 12–13, 15, 39–40, 44, 53
  truck bombing (1993), 26
World War II (1939–45), 46, 90, 138
'worm's-eye view', 4
Wright, Gareth, 193

Yemen, 36, 77
Yes Minister, 264
Yom Kippur War (1973), 14, 22
Yorkshire Regiment, 208, 381
YouGov, 269
Yousef, Ramzi, 26

Zaborabad, Nad-e Ali, 355–6
Zaeef, Abdul Salam, 35, 54, 55, 90, 370
Zahir Shah, King of Afghanistan, 88
Zahir, Haji, 317–18
Zakir, Mullah, *see* Alizai, Abdul Qayyam
Zaman Ghamsharik, 102–3
Zardari, Asif Ali, 349
Zarghun Kalay, Nad-e Ali, 249, 251, 355
al-Zawahiri, Ayman, 22
'zero-risk approach', 353
Zorlu, Hilmi Akin, 100
Zorobad, Nad-e Ali, 297, 299